Great

American

Drives *of the East*

37 Tours, 26 States, and More Than 1,800 Listings

Fodor's Travel Publications
New York Toronto London Sydney Auckland
www.fodors.com

Fodor's Road Guide USA: Great American Drives of the East

Contributors
Editor: Shannon Kelly
Editorial Contributors: Andrew Collins (AL, MS, NH, VT), Kristi Delovitch (DE, MD, VA, WV), Amy Eckert (MI), Joe Frey (OH), Hollis Gillespie (GA), Laura Knowles Callanan (PA), Diana Lambdin Meyer (IL), Mary Sue Lawrence (NC, SC), Diane Marshall (FL), Elise Meyer (CT, MA, RI), John Motoviloff (WI), Hilary Nangle (ME), Jeremy Olshan (NJ), Susan Reigler (IN, KY, TN), Karyn Siobhan Robinson (VA), Karen Schlesinger (FL), Patti Singer (NY)
Editorial Production: Tom Holton
Maps: Rebecca Baer, Robert Blake, David Lindroth, Todd Pasini
Design: Siobhan O'Hare
Cover Photograph: Ron Watts/Corbis
Production/Manufacturing: Angela L. McLean

Second Edition
ISBN 1–4000–1373–9

ISSN 1538–7607

Special Sales
This book is available for special discounts for bulk purchases for sales promotions or premiums. Special editions, including personalized covers, excerpts of existing books, and corporate imprints, can be created in large quantities for special needs. For more information, write to Special Markets/Premium Sales, 1745 Broadway, MD 6-2, New York, New York 10019, or e-mail specialmarkets@randomhouse.com. Inquiries from Canada should be directed to your local Canadian bookseller or sent to Random House of Canada, Ltd., Marketing Department, 2775 Matheson Boulevard East, Mississauga, Ontario L4W 4P7. Inquiries from the United Kingdom should be sent to Fodor's Travel Publications, 20 Vauxhall Bridge Road, London SW1V 2SA, England.

PRINTED IN THE UNITED STATES OF AMERICA
10 9 8 7 6 5 4 3 2 1

CONTENTS

Great American Drives

For some vacationers, driving is a means to get from one destination to the next as fast as Mother Nature, the roads, and the law will permit. If this is how you drive, you've picked up the wrong book.

If, for you, driving is the destination, and you pull over for reasons that don't necessarily involve food, fuel, or driving faster than the law permits, congratulate yourself on finding this guide. Inside are all the tools you'll need to plan perfect road trips in the 26 glorious states east of the Mississippi River.

Every chapter includes one or two easy-to-follow, point-by-point driving tours, corresponding maps, and specific rules of the road. And since this wouldn't be a Fodor's guide without reviews, we harvested our multivolume Road Guide series to give you more than 1,800 listings for attractions, restaurants, and hotels along the way. With all the specific and practical information we provide, you can easily call to confirm the details that matter and study up on what you'll want to see and do before you leave home.

These drives set you on specific paths, but by all means allow yourself a few detours. Because as wonderful as it is to know the correct exit, it can be serendipitous to turn off elsewhere to discover that hole-in-the-wall diner with transcendent tomato soup, or a gallery crammed with dusty local curiosities. After all, it's this sense of adventure that helped shape the Great American Drives you have in your hands.

How to Use This Book

Alphabetical organization should make it a snap to navigate these pages. Still, in putting them together, we've made certain decisions and used certain terms you need to know about.

ORGANIZATION

Following each tour are alphabetical, town-by-town listings with additional information about many of the sights mentioned in the tours, as well as listings for other attractions in those towns. We've also included information on nearby restaurants and hotels.

Attractions, restaurants, and hotels are listed under the nearest town covered in the tour.

Parks and forests are sometimes listed under the main access point.

Exact street addresses are provided whenever possible; when they are not available or applicable, directions and/or cross-streets are indicated.

FODOR'S CHOICE

Stars denote sights, restaurants, and hotels that are Fodor's Choices—our editors' picks of the best in a given region or price category.

SIGHTS

Sights and attractions that are especially appealing to children are indicated by a rubber-duckie icon (🦆) in the margin.

RESTAURANTS

We have provided restaurant listings for almost every town mentioned in these drives. Restaurants are grouped by price category, from most to least expensive, and arranged alphabetically within each category.

CATEGORY	COST*
$$$$	OVER $25
$$$	$20–$25
$$	$12–$20
$	$7–$12
¢	UNDER $7

per person for a dinner entrée (or a lunch entrée if no dinner is served)

Some restaurants are marked with a price range ($$–$$$, for example). This indicates one of two things: either that the average cost straddles two categories, or that if you order strategically you can get out for less than most diners. All restaurants are air-conditioned unless otherwise noted.

Dress: Assume that no jackets or ties are required for men unless otherwise specified.

Meals and hours: Assume that restaurants are open for lunch and dinner unless otherwise noted. We always indicate days closed.

Reservations: They are always a good idea. We don't mention them unless they're essential or are not accepted.

HOTELS

Hotels are listed only for towns we suggest as overnight stops. Properties are grouped by price category, from most to least expensive, then arranged alphabetically within each category.

CATEGORY	COST*
$$$$	OVER $200
$$$	$150–$200
$$	$100–$150
$	$50–$100
¢	UNDER $50

cost of a double room for two during peak season, excluding tax and service charges.

Some hotels are marked with a price range ($$–$$$, for example). This indicates that the average cost straddles two categories.

Bear in mind that the prices gathered for this book are for standard double hotel or motel rooms, and you may pay more for suites or cabins. If a property we recommend is comprised only of suites, cabins, and other atypical lodgings, assume that the given price category applies. Assume that hotels operate on the European Plan (EP, with no meals) unless we specify otherwise.

Baths: You'll find private bathrooms with bathtubs unless otherwise noted.

BP: Breakfast Plan. The rate includes breakfast only.

Business services: We note these only for properties with significant business amenities.

CP: Continental Plan. The rate includes continental breakfast only.

Facilities: We list what's available but don't note charges for use. When pricing accommodations, always ask what's included.

FAP: Full American Plan. The rate includes all meals.

Hot tub: This term denotes hot tubs, Jacuzzis, and whirlpools.

MAP: Modified American Plan. The rate incudes two meals.

Opening and closing: Assume that properties are open year-round unless otherwise indicated.

Pets: We note whether or not they're welcome and whether there's a charge.

Pools: Assume they're outdoors; indoor pools are noted.

Telephone and TV: Assume that you'll find them unless otherwise noted.

NATIONAL PARKS

National parks protect and preserve the treasures of America's heritage, and they're always worth visiting. Many warrant a long detour. If your drive brings you to many national parks, consider purchasing the National Parks Pass ($50), which gets you and your companions free admission to all parks for one year. (Camping and parking are extra.) A percentage of the proceeds from sales of the pass helps fund park projects. Both the Golden Age Passport ($10), for those 62 and older, and the Golden Access Passport (free), for travelers with disabilities, entitle holders to free entry to all national parks, plus 50% off fees for the use of the many park facilities and services. You must show proof of age and of U.S. citizenship or permanent residency (such as a U.S. passport, driver's license, or birth certificate) and, if requesting Golden Access, proof of your disability. You must get your Golden Access or Golden Age passport in person; the former is available at all federal recreation areas, the latter at federal recreation areas that charge fees.

You may purchase the National Parks Pass by mail or through the Internet. For information, contact the National Park Service (Department of the Interior, 1849 C St. NW, Washington, DC 20240-0001, 202/208–4747, www.nps.gov): To buy the National Parks Pass, write to 27540 Ave. Mentry, Valencia, CA 91355, call 888/GO–PARKS, or visit www.nationalparks.org.

IMPORTANT TIP

Although all prices, opening times, and other details in this book are based on information supplied to us at press time, changes occur all the time in the travel world, and Fodor's cannot accept responsibility for facts that become outdated or for inadvertent errors or omissions. So always confirm information when it matters, especially if you're making a detour to visit a specific place.

LET US HEAR FROM YOU

Keeping a travel guide fresh and up-to-date is a big job, and we welcome any and all comments. We'd love to have your thoughts on places we've listed, and we're interested in hearing about your own special finds, even the ones in your own backyard. Our guides are thoroughly updated for each new edition, and we're always adding new information, so your feedback is vital. Contact us via e-mail at editors@fodors.com (specifying the name of the book on the subject line) or via snail mail care of Fodor's Travel Publications, 1745 Broadway, New York, NY 10019. We look forward to hearing from you.

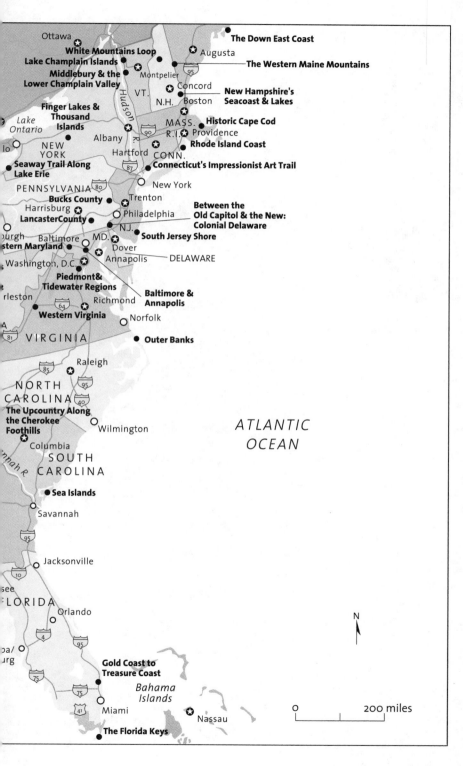

Ottawa

White Mountains Loop

The Down East Coast

Augusta

Lake Champlain Islands

Middlebury & the Lower Champlain Valley

The Western Maine Mountains

Montpelier

VT.

Concord

Finger Lakes & Thousand Islands

N.H.

Boston

New Hampshire's Seacoast & Lakes

Lake Ontario

MASS.

Historic Cape Cod

Albany

R.I.

Providence

NEW YORK

Hartford

Rhode Island Coast

CONN.

Seaway Trail Along Lake Erie

Connecticut's Impressionist Art Trail

New York

PENNSYLVANIA

Bucks County

Trenton

Harrisburg

Philadelphia

Between the Old Capitol & the New: Colonial Delaware

LancasterCounty

N.J.

ourgh

Baltimore

MD.

South Jersey Shore

stern Maryland

Dover

Washington, D.C.

Annapolis

DELAWARE

Piedmont & Tidewater Regions

rleston

Richmond

Baltimore & Annapolis

Western Virginia

Norfolk

VIRGINIA

Outer Banks

Raleigh

NORTH CAROLINA

The Upcountry Along the Cherokee Foothills

Wilmington

ATLANTIC OCEAN

Columbia

SOUTH CAROLINA

Sea Islands

Savannah

Jacksonville

see

FLORIDA

Orlando

pa/

urg

Gold Coast to Treasure Coast

Bahama Islands

Miami

Nassau

The Florida Keys

N

0   200 miles

ALABAMA GULF COAST
FROM DAUPHIN ISLAND TO GULF SHORES

Distance: 105 mi   Time: 3 days
Overnight Breaks: Fairhope, Mobile

Centered on historic Mobile Bay, the charming cities along Alabama's Gulf Coast—from European-influenced Mobile to tourist-friendly Gulf Shores—are easily accessible. Explore at a leisurely pace or do a quick tour, but do take note of hurricane season, which is from June through November: the entire region can suddenly go on alert as tropical storms develop in the warm Gulf of Mexico.

❶ Sleepy **Dauphin Island,** the barrier island flanking Mississippi Sound and Mobile Bay, is a good place to begin your Gulf Coast visit. There's a dramatic view from the Route 193 bridge over Mobile Bay, the only route onto the island. The western end of Dauphin Island is mostly residential, but the eastern end has such interesting areas to explore as **Fort Gaines,** the site of the Civil War's Battle of Mobile Bay (in which Admiral David Farragut issued his famous command, "Damn the torpedoes, full speed ahead!"). Check out Dauphin Island Sea Lab's **Estuarium,** which has a boardwalk along the dunes where you can see native birds like brown pelicans and great blue herons. Inside the Estuarium are aquariums and exhibits where you can learn about the four habitats of coastal Alabama: the delta, Mobile Bay, the barrier islands, and the northern Gulf of Mexico.

The **Mobile Bay Ferry** departs from a dock near the Estuarium and leaves you off on the other side of Mobile Bay in Fort Morgan. Use the ferry for a day trip to Fort Morgan and then return.

❷ If you're continuing by car from Dauphin Island toward Mobile, take a popular and worthy detour to **Theodore** and **Bellingrath Gardens and Home.** Follow the signs from Route 193 North, left onto Route 188, then right on Bellingrath Road (Rte. 59). The riverfront property, on 65 sprawling acres, was developed by Coca-Cola Bottling Company owner Walter Bellingrath and his flower-loving wife, Bessie. Their 15-room home, now a museum, was completed in 1935. Bellingrath is open year-round and has beautiful gardens, walking paths, and plenty of blooms. Tour the museum home to see family antiques, and the world's largest public collection of Boehm porcelain. During the

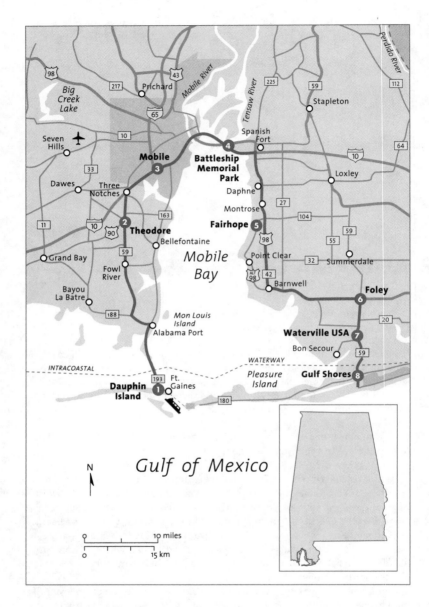

warmer months, a sightseeing cruise along the Fowl River aboard the **Southern Belle** is a wonderful way to appreciate the area's beauty from the water.

From the gardens, follow Bellingrath Road north, turning east onto U.S. 90 toward Mobile, the state's second-largest and oldest city. With its location on the Mobile River and Mobile Bay, the nickname "Port City" is apt; it's also known as "the Azalea City" for its gorgeous display of the flowers in early spring.

❸ Travel along U.S. 90—which eventually becomes oak-canopied **Government Street,** one of Mobile's most beautiful thoroughfares—until you reach downtown **Mobile.** Visit the **Fort Condé Mobile Visitor Welcome Center.** Volunteers can answer questions about the area and provide you with brochures. While there, tour the re-created Fort

Condé, a partially restored 18th-century fort. Tours are led by guides in French period uniforms.

Drive west from Fort Condé on Church Street back to Government Street to the **Museum of Mobile,** which showcases the city's more-than-300-year history under French, British, Spanish, and eventually U.S. rule. Mobilians love telling visitors that the U.S. version of Mardi Gras, the annual pre-Lenten celebration, actually originated in Mobile and then caught on in New Orleans. Mardi Gras still plays a major role in Mobile culture, as evidenced by the museum's Queens' Gallery, which displays the elaborate gowns worn by each queen of Mobile's Mardi Gras, including the gown that belonged to young Alexis Herman, a Mobile native and past queen who went on to become the U.S. Secretary of Labor. Nearby is the **Phoenix Fire Museum.** Built in 1859 to house the Phoenix Volunteer Fire Company, the museum traces the history of the city's volunteer firefighters from 1819.

Continue west on Government Street past Broad Street to the Oakleigh Historic Garden District, a neighborhood of restored historic homes. Turn left onto George Street and follow the signs to the **Oakleigh Period House Museum,** one of Mobile's best examples of Greek Revival architecture. Take a guided tour of the 1833 mansion, which is rumored to have a playful ghost who turns lights on and off.

Go back to Broad Street and turn north, and then go two blocks to **Dauphin Street,** which stretches east toward the Mobile River. During the day, you can visit an art gallery or relax in Cathedral Square Park, opposite the stately Cathedral of the Immaculate Conception, or Bienville Square, a live-oak–shaded oasis in the heart of downtown.

The **Gulf Coast Exploreum Museum of Science** is at Government and Water streets. The kid-friendly children's museum houses traveling exhibits as well as Hands-on Hall, a permanent exhibit that explains many scientific theories in simple terms. Directly across Water Street from the Exploreum is **Cooper Riverside Park,** where you can learn about Mobile's waterfront. The *Cotton Blossom* riverboat is docked at the adjacent Mobile Convention Center and has daily one-hour excursions along the river.

❹ Leaving downtown Mobile via Government Street, you enter the Bankhead Tunnel, which takes you under the Mobile River and onto the Battleship Parkway, also known as the Causeway, which crosses Mobile Bay. (If you take the Wallace Tunnel from I–10, you emerge on the bridge known to locals as the Bayway, which also crosses the bay. Take Exit 27 onto Battleship Pkwy.) Follow the signs to **Battleship Memorial Park,** where you can tour the World War II battleship USS *Alabama* and the submarine USS *Drum*.

❺ Continue on I–10 east to the Daphne exit and follow U.S. 98 south to U.S. 98 Scenic to **Fairhope,** whose streets overflow with flowers year-round. Take a right off Section Street (U.S. 98 Scenic) onto Fairhope Avenue, park the car, and check out Fairhope's many shops and restaurants. At the foot of the hill, the **Fairhope Municipal Pier** and adjacent bay-front park are perfect for sunsets. For children, the nearby park area has swings and seesaws on a sand beach and a duck pond. The sidewalk that extends along the bluff overlooks the bay and is a good place to stroll among oak trees laden with Spanish moss.

❻ The next morning, return to U.S. 98 and follow the signs past Magnolia Springs (mail is still delivered by boat to residents who live along the Fish River) to **Foley,** and turn south on Route 59.

❼ Also on the way to the beach are several places enticing to children, including the **Waterville USA** water park, the **Track Family Recreation Center,** and **Alabama Gulf Coast Zoo.**

8 After you cross the intercoastal canal, you reach Pleasure Island. Route 59 ends at **Gulf Shores,** where the main drag along the beach is Route 182. Drive east along here; in addition to countless hotels and condominiums, there are several well-marked public beaches where families can spend a day sunbathing on sugar-white sand and swimming in the gulf. Beware of occasionally strong currents, stinging nettles, and jellyfish. Driving east on Route 182 through **Orange Beach,** you eventually cross the Alabama Point Bridge, where there is a wonderful panoramic view, and reach the Florida border at the **Flora-Bama Lounge,** which straddles the state line and is famous for its annual Interstate Mullet Toss. It's easy to spend a day or many more relaxing on the beaches in Gulf Shores and Orange Beach. There are several championship golf courses nearby, deep-sea fishing charters, wave-runner rentals, and other diversions. From Gulf Shores follow Route 59 North through the towns of Foley, Robertsdale, and Loxley to I–10 West, which leads back across Mobile Bay to Mobile, where I–10 and I–65 converge.

Dauphin Island

Estuarium. At the Dauphin Island Sea Lab, the Estuarium spotlights the unique local ecosystems of the Mobile Bay estuary. A Living Marsh Boardwalk includes interpretive signs explaining the natural history of the state's marshes, geography, and evolution of the barrier islands. There are displays, interactive exhibits, a 9,000-gallon aquarium simulating the brackish underwater environment of Mobile Bay, and a 16,000-gallon tank with sea life from the Gulf of Mexico. Smaller aquariums focus on

ALABAMA RULES OF THE ROAD

License Requirements: The legal driving age in Alabama is 17.

Right Turn on Red: Alabama allows a right turn on red *after* making a full stop, unless otherwise posted.

Seat-Belt & Helmet Laws: Alabama law requires all front-seat occupants to buckle up. In front and back seats, children under 6 must use federally approved safety restraints. Four- and five-year-olds can use safety belts or the child safety seats, which are required for children under 5. Bicycle helmets are required for cyclists under age 16. Motorcyclists must wear helmets and shoes.

Speed Limits: Alabama's maximum speed limit is 70 mph on specified rural interstates, 65 mph on other highways with four or more lanes, 55 mph on most other highways, and 45 mph on county roads. Speed limits often drop in congested areas.

Other Regulations: It is illegal for passengers to possess open alcoholic containers. The legal blood-alcohol concentration in Alabama is under .08%.

For More Information: Alabama Department of Public Safety | 334/242–4371, *47 cell phone emergency hot line | www.dps.state.al.us. Alabama Department of Transportation | 334/242–6358 | www.dot.state.al.us.

individual species. | 101 Bienville Blvd. | 251/861–7500 | www.disl.org | $6 | Mar.–Aug., Mon.–Sat. 9–6, Sun. noon–6; Sept.–Feb., Mon.–Sat. 9–5, Sun. 1–5.

Fort Gaines. The pre–Civil War fort was the setting for the famous Battle of Mobile Bay. You can touch cannons used in battle, explore tunnels and bastions, and visit a blacksmith shop, kitchen, and bakery. Living-history events are staged on selected weekends. | 51 Bienville Blvd. | 251/861–6992 | www.dauphinisland.org/fort.htm | Free | Daily 9–6.

Mobile Bay Ferry. The ferry, which accommodates cars, RVs, and sightseers, shuttles daily between Fort Morgan and Dauphin Island. | 251/540–7787 | Passengers $4, cars $10, RVs $25 (all one-way) | Daily 8–5; departs Dauphin Island every 90 mins.

Dining

Pelican Pub & Faux Pas Cafe. Seafood. In Aloe Bay, this restaurant and bar was built and raised on pilings. The original building is the Pelican Pub, and below it, in the space among the pilings, is the Faux Pas. Dine outdoors either up or downstairs: both locations look out onto the bay. The restaurant serves mainly seafood and steaks, including a first-rate grilled grouper topped with crabmeat and a tangy mustard-cream sauce. | 1102 Desoto Ave. | 334/861–7180 | Closed Sun. Memorial Day–Labor Day | MC, V | $$–$$$

Fairhope

Riviera Centre. This sprawling shopping paradise has more than 120 factory mid-range to upscale outlet stores. Favorite stops include Banana Republic, Bose, J. Crew, Polo Ralph Lauren, Rockport, Tommy Hilfiger and Tommy Hilfiger/Kids, Waterford Wedgwood, and Zales. | 2601 Rte. 59, Foley, 22 mi south of Fairhope and 9 mi north of Gulf Shores | 251/943–8888 | www.shoprivieracentre.com | Mar.–Dec., Mon.–Sat. 10–9, Sun. 11–6; Jan. and Feb., Mon.–Sat. 10–7, Sun. 11–6.

Dining

Guy's Gumbo Shack. Cajun/Creole. There's more than hearty gumbo at this Louisiana-style bar and grill with a lushly landscaped patio. Fried oyster po'boys, smoked-tuna wraps, and red beans and rice round out the offerings. Weekends bring live blues and zydeco. | 2 S. Church St. | 251/928–4100 | Closed Sun. | AE, D, MC, V | ¢–$

Restaurant Varnedoe. Contemporary. Come to this intimate downtown spot with exposed-brick walls and high ceilings for creative creole-Mediterranean dishes like shrimp-and-crawfish spring rolls with wasabi-curry aioli, and broiled redfish over smoked-Gouda grits with sautéed crabmeat and a roasted red pepper beurre blanc. | 14 S. Church St. | 251/928–0029 | No lunch Sun.–Wed. | AE, MC, V | $$–$$$$

Lodging

Church Street Inn. In the center of town, this early 1920s white-stucco home sits three blocks from Mobile Bay and several miles of public beaches, rose gardens, and parks. Restored throughout, the home contains five generations of family antiques and heirlooms. There's a large living room, a porch with high-back wicker chairs, and a garden courtyard. The three guest rooms each have period antiques. Bicycles; no room phones, no TV in some rooms, no kids under 16, no smoking. | 51 S. Church St., 36533 | 251/928–8976 or 866/928–8976 | www.bbonline.com/al/churchstreet | 3 rooms | CP | AE, MC, V | $$

Holiday Inn Express. The strengths of this cookie-cutter hotel are leafy grounds and proximity to Fairhope shops, restaurants, and golfing—as well as to downtown Mobile. In-room data ports, refrigerators, cable TV, pool, laundry facilities, laundry service, business services. | 19751 Greeno Rd., 36532 | 251/928–9191 or 800/465–4329 | fax 334/990–7874 | www.holiday-inn.com | 58 rooms, 7 suites | CP | AE, D, DC, MC, V | $–$$

Key West Inn. One of only two full-scale hotels in Fairhope (Holiday Inn Express is the other), the Key West Inn is just minutes from downtown Fairhope on U.S. 98 on a busy commercial strip near several fast-food restaurants. The clean rooms are decorated with watercolors by a local artist. In-room data ports, some microwaves, some refrigerators, cable TV, pool, laundry facilities, some pets allowed. | 231 S. Greeno Rd., 36532 | 251/990–7373 or 800/833–0555 | fax 334/990–9671 | www.keywestinn.net | 46 rooms, 9 suites | CP | AE, D, DC, MC, V | $

Magnolia Springs Bed & Breakfast. Halfway between Fairhope and Gulf Shores, this 1897 gabled wood-frame house is less than two blocks from the Magnolia River, one of the few remaining places in the country where mail is delivered by boat. The restored home has a wide front porch overlooking the property, which is dotted with regal live oaks. Inside, the heart-pine floors, walls, and ceilings are original. Breakfast is a lavish three-course affair. In-room data ports, cable TV; no kids under 7, no smoking. | 14469 Oak St., Magnolia Springs 36555, 15 mi southeast of Fairhope | 251/965–7321 or 800/965–7321 | www.magnoliasprings.com | 4 rooms, 1 suite | BP | AE, D, MC, V | $$

Gulf Shores

Alabama Gulf Coast Zoo. Alabama's coastal zoo is the place to explore the natural habitats of more than 250 animals. Elevated decks facilitate close-up views of everything from alligators to giraffes and lions. | 1204 Gulf Shores Pkwy. | 251/968–5731 | www.alabamagulfcoastzoo.com | $8.80 | Daily 9–4.

Bon Secour National Wildlife Refuge. If nature is your passion, there's plenty to do at this 6,200-acre preserve: hike among numerous nature trails (some lead to the beach and bird-watching areas); fish in fresh- and salt water or paddle a small two-person boat into an alligator-inhabited lake. The area is known for its changing beach dunes, oak forests, and wildlife—look for bobcats, squirrels, rabbits, opossum, raccoons, and armadillos. | 12295 Rte. 180 | 251/540–7720 | bonsecour.fws.gov | Free | Daily dawn–dusk.

Fort Morgan Historic Site. Built in the early 1800s to guard the entrance to Mobile Bay, Fort Morgan was the scene of fiery action during the Battle of Mobile Bay in 1864, when Confederate torpedoes sank the ironclad *Tecumseh.* The fort's original outer walls still stand. | 51 Rte. 180 | 251/540–7125 | $3 | Daily 8–6.

    Fort Morgan Museum. The fort's history is chronicled at this museum that displays artifacts from pre-colonial days through World War II. The emphasis is on the Civil War. | 51 Rte. 180 | 251/540–7125 | Free with admission to Fort Morgan Historic Site | Daily 9–5.

Gulf State Park. Covering more than 6,100 acres of Pleasure Island, the park stretches along 2½ mi of pure-white beaches and glimmering dunes. It has two freshwater lakes where you can canoe and fish, and trails through pine forests for biking, hiking, and jogging. Near a large beach pavilion, a concrete fishing pier juts some 800 feet into the gulf. The park also has a gulf-front resort lodge and convention center, campsites, cottages, tennis, and an 18-hole golf course. | 20115 Rte. 135 | 251/948–7275 | Free | Daily dawn–dusk.

Track Family Recreation Center. The popular amusement complex has go-carts, bumper boats, bungee jumping, and video arcades to keep your teens amused while the wee ones enjoy trains, swings, and a Ferris wheel. | 3200 Gulf Shores Pkwy. | 251/968–8111 | www.gulfcoastrooms.com/thetrack | Admission varies per activity | Call for hrs.

Waterville USA. On 17 acres, the park has a wave pool that creates 3-foot waves, seven water slides, and a lazy river ride that goes around the circumference. For younger children there are gentler rides in a play area. Adding to the fun are the 36-hole miniature golf course and the video-game arcade. | 906 Gulf Shores Pkwy. | 251/948–2106 | fax 334/948–7918 | www.watervilleusa.com | Water park $21, amusement park admission varies per activity | Water park Memorial Day–Labor Day, daily 10–6. Amusement park Mar.–Sept., daily 10–midnight.

Dining

Gulf Bay Seafood Grill. Seafood. For a contemporary take on the usual over-fried seafood doled out at many restaurants in these parts, head to this open and airy space. Start with oyster Rockefeller or a crab-and-shrimp quesadilla before moving on to seared ahi tuna with a mango-peanut dressing, or sweet potato–encrusted grouper topped with crawfish and a pecan-cream sauce. | 24705 Canal Rd., Orange Beach, 8 mi northeast of Gulf Shores | 251/974–5090 | AE, D, DC, MC, V | $–$$

Mango's on the Island. Caribbean. An elegant but informal spot with an expansive deck overlooking the exclusive Orange Beach Marina, Mango's turns out nouvelle Caribbean fare, such as crawfish-smoked Gouda cheesecake, and tamarind-grilled rib eye with roasted garlic–mashed potatoes. There's a hearty Cuban-style paella, too. | 27075 Marina Rd., Orange Beach, 9 mi east of Gulf Shores | 251/981–1416 | AE, D, DC, MC, V | $$–$$$

Mikee's. Seafood. The food at this popular restaurant in the heart of Gulf Shores is worth the inevitable wait. Meanwhile, enjoy looking at the mounted fish and photos of the owners' biggest catches, among the other local memorabilia. Top picks from the seafood-intensive menu include the barbecue shrimp, and shellfish sautéed over linguine with a garlic-butter sauce. Walk off the big portions at the nearby beach. Kids' menu. | E. 2nd Ave. at 1st St. | 251/948–6452 | AE, D, DC, MC, V | $–$$

Mobile

★**Battleship Memorial Park, USS *Alabama*.** Public subscription saved the mighty gray USS *Alabama* from being scrapped after her heroic World War II service. A tour of the ship gives a fascinating look into the life of a 2,500-member crew. Anchored next to the battleship is the World War II submarine USS *Drum*. Other exhibits in the 100-acre Battleship Park include dozens of war planes, among them a B-52 bomber called *Calamity Jane* and a P-51 Mustang fighter plane. | 2703 Battleship Pkwy. (U.S. 90/98) | 251/433–2703 | www.ussalabama.com | $10 | Apr.–Sept., daily 8–6; Oct.–Mar., daily 8–4.

Fort Condé Mobile Visitor Welcome Center. The original Fort Condé has survived, thanks to an ambitious reconstruction in the late 1990s. Inside are the city's visitor center, a museum, and several re-created rooms. Costumed guides interpret and enlighten. | 150 S. Royal St. | 251/208–7304 | Free | Daily 8–5.

Gulf Coast Exploreum Museum of Science. Across from the Mobile Convention Center, this touch-friendly science center allows a sensory immersion, hands-on experience. It's a place to touch, smell, magnify, build, and explore. There also is an OmniMax theater. Parking is limited; call ahead for advice on where to park. | 65 Government St. | 334/208–6883 | fax 334/208–6889 | www.exploreum.net | Museum $8, theater $8, combo ticket $12 | Jan.–Aug., weekdays 9–5, Sat. 10–5, Sun. noon–5; Sept.–Dec., Tues.–Fri. 9–5, Sat. 10–5, Sun. noon–5.

Museum of Mobile. In the city's 1857 Old City Hall, this exhaustive collection of documents, photos, and creatively mounted exhibits traces the city's and the region's history, from colonization, the Civil War, and the 19th century to the present. | 111 S. Royal St. | 251/208–7569 | $5 | Mon.–Sat. 9–5, Sun. 1–5.

Oakleigh Historic Complex. This Greek Revival mansion has a stairway circling under ancient live oaks to a small portico. The high-ceilinged, half-timber house was built in 1833 and is typical of the most expensive dwellings of its day. Fine period furniture, portraits, silver, jewelry, kitchen implements, toys, and more are displayed. Costumed guides lead tours. You can also tour the Mardi Gras Cottage—a tribute to the city's history of celebrating Carnival—and another of the city's fine old museum homes, the 1850 Cox-Deasy Cottage. | 350 Oakleigh Pl. | 251/432–1281 | www.historicmobile.org | Oakleigh $5, Cox-Deasy Cottage $3, Mardi Gras Cottage $3, combo ticket $10 | Mon.– Sat. 9–3, guided tours every ½ hr, last tour 2:30.

Phoenix Fire Museum. Once home to the Phoenix Fire Company, this restored 1855 firehouse holds steamers and fire engines that date back to the 19th century. Exhibits showcase the men who fought the city's early fires. | 203 S. Claiborne St. | 251/208–7554 | fax 334/208–7686 | $3 | Tues.–Sat. 10–5, Sun. 1–5.

Dining

Brick Pit. Barbecue. It's "the best damn barbecue in the state of Alabama," owner Bill Armbrecht boasts of this Mobile favorite. Chicken, ribs, and pork are smoked for hours over a blend of hickory and pecan to achieve a distinct flavor. Barbecue sauce comes spicy or sweet, with soft white bread for dipping. Add your name to the graffiti scrawled in red marker all over the walls and ceiling. Try the smoked pulled-pork plate. | 5456 Old Shell Rd. | 251/343–0001 | Closed Sun. and Mon. | MC, V | ¢–$

Drayton Place. Contemporary. Head to this sophisticated restaurant on the ground floor of the Southeast's oldest skyscraper to enjoy live jazz, shoot a game of billiards, or try rare single-malt whiskies and small-batch bourbons. The food has plenty going for it: consider crab cakes with a piquant *rémoulade* or traditional shrimp-and-grits with andouille sausage. | 1757 Government St. | 251/471–3411 | AE, D, DC, MC, V | $$–$$$

★**Justine's at the Pillars.** Contemporary. Fans of creative Southern cuisine rave about this upscale restaurant in a grand Italianate mansion with fireplaces, ornate columns, and soft lighting. Sample innovate creations like filet mignon stuffed with Stilton cheese and crabmeat with a bacon-brandy butter, or snapper with lobster meat, mangoes, and a port-Mornay sauce. Sunday champagne brunch. | 1757 Government St. | 251/471–3411 | No lunch Mon.–Sat. | AE, D, DC, MC, V | $$–$$$$

Roussos Seafood Restaurant. Seafood. The same Greek family has been serving terrific seafood at several restaurants around Mobile since the 1950s. The current incarnation, in a renovated warehouse near historic Fort Condé, is filled with memorabilia and old photos of the city. Baked oysters, stuffed flounder, and sautéed crabmeat are among the favorite Greek-style dishes. Kids' menu. | 166 S. Royal St. | 251/433–3322 | Reservations not accepted | Closed Sun. | AE, D, MC, V | $–$$

Lodging

Lafayette Plaza. In the heart of downtown Mobile's business and historic districts, this reasonably priced hotel is within walking distance of the Museum of Mobile, Phoenix Fire Museum, and Gulf Coast Exploreum. The rooftop lounge has breathtaking views of the city and the waterfront. Restaurant, room service, in-room data ports, cable TV, pool, gym, hair salon, bar, laundry facilities, concierge floor, business services, meeting rooms, some pets allowed, parking (fee). | 301 Government St., 36602 | 334/694–0100 or 800/692–6662 | fax 334/694–0160 | 171 rooms, 39 suites | AE, D, DC, MC, V | $

Malaga Inn. In the Church Street East historic district, this inn consists of two 1862 town houses that wrap around a gaslit courtyard centered with a fountain. The rooms are furnished with antiques, have high ceilings and hardwood floors, and each is individually decorated. The inn is within walking distance of Mobile Civic Center and downtown attractions. In-room data ports, cable TV, pool, business services, parking (fee). | 359 Church St., 36602 | 251/438–4701 or 800/235–1586 | 35 rooms, 3 suites | BP | AE, D, MC, V | $–$$

Radisson Admiral Semmes. It's managed by a chain, but this 1940 downtown high-rise feels like a grande dame of yesteryear. Rooms have reproduction Queen Anne and Chippendale furnishings, and tile-and-marble baths with full-length dressing mirrors. The hotel is in the heart of the downtown historic area, a short walk from attractions. Restaurant, room service, in-room data ports, cable TV, pool, hot tub, pub, business services, meeting rooms, parking (fee). | 251 Government St., 36602 | 251/432–8000 or 800/333–3333 | fax 251/405–5942 | 148 rooms, 22 suites | AE, D, DC, MC, V | $$–$$$

Towle House. The oldest B&B in Mobile was built in 1874 as a boy's school. The Italianate mansion, surrounded by dogwoods, azaleas, and gardens, retains its original heart-pine and cypress floors and paneling. The color schemes of the four Victoriana-filled guest rooms are each inspired by a different flower: rose, azalea, magnolia, and lilac. The house is a mile west of downtown, in a gracious historic neighborhood. In-room data ports, some in-room hot tubs, cable TV. | 1104 Montauk Blvd., 36604 | 251/432–6440 or 800/938–6953 | fax 251/433–4381 | www.towle-house.com | 4 rooms | BP | AE, D, MC, V | $$

Theodore

★**Bellingrath Gardens and Home.** One of the South's most popular gardens is some 20 mi south of Mobile in Theodore. The gardens, which bloom year-round, are a sanctuary to more than 200 species of birds. You can also visit the brick home of the gardens' creators, which has one of the finest collections of antiques in the Southeast. | 12401 Bellingrath Rd. | 251/973–2217 or 800/247–8420 | www.bellingrath.org | Gardens $9, gardens and home $16.50 | Jan.–Nov., daily 8–5; Dec., daily 8 AM–9 PM.

Southern Belle. Sightseeing cruises (45 minutes) along the Fowl River take place aboard the *Southern Belle,* which departs from the grounds of Bellingrath Gardens. Dinner cruises (2 hours) are offered April–December. | 251/973–1244 | www.bellingrath.org/Rcruise/boat.htm | $17–$35 (includes admission to gardens) | Tours Feb.–Nov.; call for schedule.

CONNECTICUT

CONNECTICUT'S IMPRESSIONIST ART TRAIL
FROM GREENWICH TO NEW LONDON

Distance: Approximately 115 mi   Time: 2 days
Overnight Breaks: New London, Old Lyme

This tour, following the coastline of Connecticut, provides a rich historical exploration of the artists known as the American impressionists, who, like their counterparts in France, sought to capture in paint the beauty of the changing conditions of the natural landscape in which they lived.

❶ **Greenwich** (I–95, Exit 3 or 4) is the starting point for this tour. The **Bush-Holley Historic Site,** run by the Historical Society of the Town of Greenwich, is the site of the earliest Connecticut art colony. The **Bruce Museum** has a small but worthwhile collection of local impressionist art.

❷ If you are not limited by time and would like to add a leisurely trail walk in pristine New England woodlands consider a stop at the **Weir Farm National Historic Site** in Wilton (I–95, Exit 15 to U.S. 7 N). Weir Farm was once the summer home of artist J. Alden Weir (1852–1919), whose rural hospitality enabled the development of the coastal art community. Childe Hassam, John Twachtman, Albert Pinkham Ryder, and John Singer Sargent all spent time here. The 53 acres, the only National Park in the state, has lovely walking paths and a visitor center that introduces the art and the artists, but the house and studios are open only by appointment. The Historic Painting Sites Trail allows you to actually stand where the artists did and compare paintings with the scenes that inspired them. Take the Merritt Parkway or I–95 to Route 7 North in Norwalk. Follow Route 7 to the Branchville section of Ridgefield. Turn onto Route 102 West at the light. Take the second left onto Old Branchville Road. Turn left at the first stop sign onto Nod Hill Road. Follow Nod Hill Road ³⁄₄ mi to the top of the hill. The parking lot is on the left and the visitor center is on the right at 735 Nod Hill Road.

❸ If you're returning from Weir Farm, take the **Merritt Parkway** (U.S. 7 to Rte. 33 to Rte. 15 [Merritt Pkwy.]) en route to New Haven, and transfer to I–95 North at Exit 53 in

Milford. One of the first parkways in the country, it was opened in 1940, having employed over 2,000 workers for two years during the Depression. Designed in an informal garden-landscape style, the lovely roadway offers vistas of the rolling farmland adjacent. Along the road are 38 unique bridges in Gothic, classical, art deco, and art moderne styles.

❹ If you're not detouring to Weir Farm, remain on I–95 North from Greenwich and continue on to **New Haven** (I–95, Exit 47 "Downtown New Haven"; stay on the connector to the third and final exit, turn right on York St. at the first intersection. The art gallery is on the right after the 3rd stoplight). The **Yale University Art Gallery,** founded in 1832, is on the Yale campus.

❺ In **Old Lyme** (I–95 N from New Haven; come over the bridge at the mouth of the Connecticut River. Stay in the right lane. Take Exit 70; at the bottom of the exit ramp, turn left at light onto Rte. 156. Turn right at the second traffic light onto Halls Rd. Take Halls Rd. to the end. At the end, take a left at the light onto Lyme St. The museum is the 2nd building on the left.), the **Florence Griswold Museum** was once a boardinghouse that served as the center of the impressionist movement in Connecticut in the early 20th century. Prominent members of the Old Lyme Art Colony included Willard Metcalf, Clark Voorhees, Childe Hassam, and Henry Ward Ranger. The artists painted for their hostess the row of panels in the dining room that now serve as the museum's centerpiece.

❻ In **New London** (I–95 N to Exit 83. Left at light onto Williams St. Go through next light and across overpass. Museum entrance is 2nd driveway on right), the **Lyman Allyn Art Museum at Connecticut College** has a noteworthy gallery devoted to the American impressionists, including works by William Chadwick, Willard Metcalf, and other members of the nearby Mystic and Lyme art colonies. Galleries show important works from the tonalist and Hudson River schools that inspired the Connecticut impressionist artists. Spend the night in Old Lyme at a quaint country B&B or at a more traditional hotel in New London.

Greenwich

Bruce Museum. In a Victorian stone mansion, this museum has a section devoted to environmental history, with a wigwam, a spectacular mineral collection, a marine touch tank, and a 16th-century-era woodland diorama. There's also a small but worthwhile collection of American impressionist paintings, including works by Childe Hassam, Emil Carlsen, and Leonard and Mina Fonda Ochtman. Also of interest are historical documents such as sketchbooks, letters, and photographs. | 1 Museum Dr. | 203/869–0376 | www.brucemuseum.com | $5 | Tues.–Sat. 10–5, Sun. 1–5.

Bush-Holley Historic Site. Over 200 artists lived and worked here around the turn of the 20th century, at Connecticut's earliest art colony. The original saltbox dwelling (circa 1732) has been restored to reflect life in the early 1900s and houses a wide-ranging collection of artworks by sculptor John Rogers, potter Leon Volkmar, and painters Childe Hassam, Elmer Livingstone MacRae, and John Twachtman. See excellent period Connecticut furniture on the guided tours, visit the exhibition galleries and gift shop at the 1805 storehouse, and tour the old post office and renovated barn. There's also a research library. Workshops and lectures are given throughout the year. | 39 Strickland Rd. | 203/869–6899 | hstg.org | Visitor center free, guided tours $6 | Jan.–Mar., Sat. 11–4, Sun. 1–4; Apr.–Dec., Wed.–Fri. noon–4, Sat. 11–4, Sun. 1–4.

Greenwich Avenue. A stroll down Greenwich Avenue exploring the dozens of elegant specialty shops and attractive watering holes can have you longing for the Main

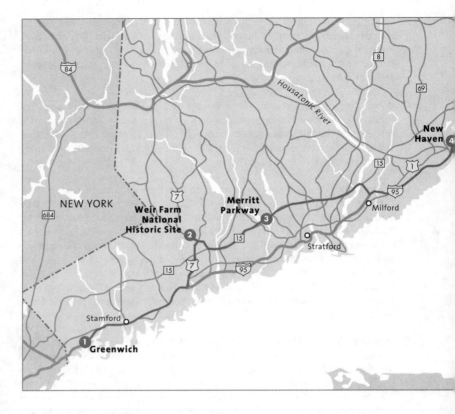

Streets of gentler eras. Be sure to obey the white-gloved crossing guards while walking and driving or you could get an old-fashioned scolding.

Putnam Cottage Museum. The small, barn-red cottage was built in 1690 and served as Knapp's Tavern during the Revolutionary War. As such, it was a frequent meeting place of Revolutionary War hero General Israel Putnam. Today you can stroll through the herb garden and examine the cottage's colonial furnishings and prominent field-stone fireplaces. | 243 E. Putnam Ave. | 203/869–9697 | Free | Sun. 1–3 or by appointment.

Dining

Le Figaro Bistro de Paris. French. An elegant French bistro on Greenwich Avenue, Le Figaro serves such tasty entrées as free-range chicken, veal paillard, lamb shank, and steak. Save room for the chef's special apple tart. | 372 Greenwich Ave. | 203/622–0018 | AE, DC, MC, V | $$–$$$$

Manero's. American. A huge, bustling, family-style restaurant, Manero's has three dining rooms that can seat a total of 600. A wide range of choices (and prices), from hamburgers to steak, lobster, and lamb chops, is available. | 559 Steamboat Rd. | 203/869–0049 | AE, DC, MC, V | $–$$$$

New Haven

Peabody Museum of Natural History. The largest natural-history museum in Connecticut, Peabody has more than 9 million specimens. In addition to exhibits on Andean, Mesoamerican, and Pacific cultures, the museum has an excellent collection of birds, including a stuffed dodo and passenger pigeon. The main attractions for children

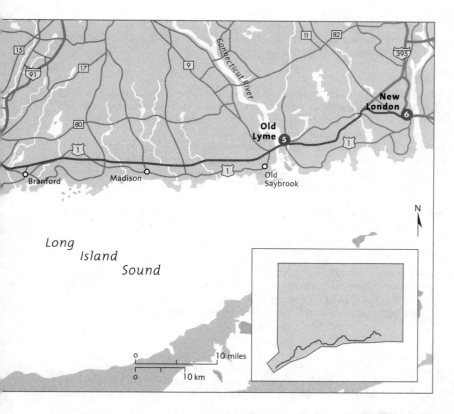

and amateur paleontologists alike are some of the world's earliest reconstructions of dinosaur skeletons. | 170 Whitney Ave. | 203/432–5050 recording of current information | www.peabody.yale.edu | $5 | Mon.–Sat. 10–5, Sun. noon–5.

★ **Yale University.** New Haven may be a manufacturing center dating from the 19th century, but the city owes its fame to Elihu Yale. In 1718 Yale's contributions enabled the Collegiate School, founded in 1701, to settle in New Haven, where it changed its name to Yale University. This is one of the nation's great universities and its fourth oldest. The campus has some handsome neo-Gothic buildings and a number of noteworthy museums, including the Beineke Rare Book and Manuscript Library and a collection of musical instruments. | 149 Elm St. | 203/432–2300 | www.yale.edu | Free | Tours weekdays at 10:30 and 2, weekends at 1:30.

★ **Yale Center for British Art.** Dating from the Elizabethan period onwards, this collection of British art is the most comprehensive outside Britain. The center's pleasant skylighted galleries include works by Constable, Hogarth, Gainsborough, Reynolds, and Turner. Extensive research materials and many free programs are open to the public. | 1080 Chapel St. | 203/432–2800 | fax 203/432–9628 | www.yale.edu/ycba | Free | Tues.–Sat. 10–5, Sun. noon–5.

Yale University Art Gallery. Since its founding in 1832, this gallery has amassed more than 85,000 objects from around the world, dating from prehistory to the present day. Highlights include a fine collection of French impressionist paintings, Etruscan and Greek antiquities, Asian decorative arts, and some of the most important American paintings, sculpture, and decorative arts to be found anywhere. The beautiful galleries exhibit a meticulous collection that includes works of Winslow Homer, Thomas Eakins, and Edward Hopper, as well as American impressionists Childe

Hassam, William Merritt Chase, John Twachtman, and many others. Tours of the permanent collection are given by Yale student docents. | 1111 Chapel St. | 203/432–0600 | fax 203/432–7159 | Free | Tues.–Sat. 10–5, Sun. 1–6.

Dining

Caffé Adulis. Ethiopian. The attractive loftlike brick dining room with high ceilings and friendly service is popular with Yale students. Vegetarian dishes, stews, and shellfish dominate the menu. Try the shrimp in tomato-basil sauce with unsweetened coconut. | 228 College St. | 203/777–5081 | No lunch | AE, MC, V | $–$$

★**Frank Pepe's Pizzeria.** Pizza. Plenty of people believe that the best pizza in the world is here at Pepe's (or next door at rival Sally's), so expect to wait for a table. Wood-burning ovens produce crisp-crust pizza (be sure to ask for cheese—it's often optional). Pepe's opened in 1925. | 157 Wooster St. | 203/865–5762 | Closed Tues. No lunch Mon., Wed., Thurs. | No credit cards | $–$$

★**Ibiza.** Spanish. Excellent and authentic Spanish cuisine is the hallmark of this chic, colorful, and cosmopolitan restaurant. A wonderful wine list completes the fine dining experience. The tapas are extraordinary. | 39 High St. | 203/865–1933 | Closed Mon. No lunch Sun. | AE, MC, V | $$–$$$$

Louis' Lunch. American. Legend has it that this luncheonette is the birthplace of the hamburger in America. The first-rate burgers are cooked in an old-fashioned upright broiler. Steak sandwiches are served at dinner. | 261–263 Crown St. | 203/562–5507 | Closed Aug. and Sun. and Mon. No dinner Sun.–Wed. | No credit cards | ¢

CONNECTICUT RULES OF THE ROAD

License Requirements: To drive in Connecticut you must be at least 16 years old and have a valid driver's license.

Right Turn on Red: You can make a right turn at a red light after coming to a full stop unless a posted sign indicates otherwise.

Seat-Belt & Helmet Laws: All drivers and front-seat passengers must wear seat belts. Children under the age of 4 must ride in a federally approved child-restraint system. Connecticut state law requires that anyone under the age of 12 wear a helmet while riding a bike.

Speed Limits: Connecticut's speed limit ranges from 55 mph to 65 mph depending on traffic density and specific road conditions. Check posted speed limits carefully as they change frequently.

For More Information: Connecticut Department of Transportation | 800/842–8222 | www.dot.state.ct.us. Connecticut State Police | 860/685–8441 | www.state.ct.us/dps.

New London

Connecticut College. Founded in 1911, Connecticut College is one of the Seven Sisters and was formerly a women's college. Today it is a private, coed, liberal-arts university with 1,600 students. | 270 Mohegan Ave. | 860/447-1911 | www.conncoll.edu | Daily dawn–dusk.

Connecticut College Arboretum. The expansive arboretum has 750 acres of natural ecosystems, native trees and shrubs, ponds, walkways, and hiking trails. | 270 Mohegan Ave. | 860/439-5020 | fax 860/439-5482 | www.conncoll.edu/ccrec/greennet/arbo/welcome.html | Free | Daily dawn–dusk; tours May–Oct., weekends at 2.

Lyman Allyn Art Museum. At the southern end of the campus, this museum was named by its founder Harriet U. Allyn after her father, a whaling merchant. In a neoclassical building designed by Charles Platt are collections of American fine arts from the country's earliest years through present day. The galleries of Connecticut's decorative arts and American impressionist paintings are also noteworthy. | 625 Williams St. | 860/443-2545 | $3 | Tues.–Sat. 10–5, Sun. 1–5.

Eugene O'Neill Theater Center. Catch special readings, panels, or performances by residents from mid-June to mid-August at the small indoor and outdoor stages that overlook Long Island Sound. Throughout the year, the theater runs conferences for critics, playwrights, puppeteers, and students. | 305 Great Neck Rd., Waterford, just south of New London | 860/443-5378 | www.oneilltheatercenter.org | $10–$12 | Call for performance schedules.

Monte Cristo Cottage. The Registered National Landmark was the childhood home of Pulitzer and Nobel Prize–winning playwright Eugene O'Neill. Fans of *Long Day's Journey into Night* should check out the re-creation of the room that O'Neill describes in the play. His only comedy, *Ah, Wilderness*, was also set in this cottage. | 325 Pequot Ave. | 860/443-0051 or 860/443-5378 | $5 | Memorial Day–Labor Day, Tues.–Sat. 10–5, Sun. 1–5.

Dining

Captain Scott's Lobster Dock. Seafood. A New England treasure, Captain Scott's has the freshest fish and seafood from Connecticut's waters. Locals adore the lobster rolls. Dine outside and watch the boats. | 80 Hamilton St. | 860/438-1741 | Closed Dec.–Mar. | AE, D, V | $–$$

Timothy's. Contemporary. Excellent updated Continental cuisine is served in the lovely Victorian Lighthouse Inn overlooking Long Island Sound. Don't miss the seafood bisque or chowder, duck specialties, lobster dinners, and the white-chocolate hazelnut mousse. Sunday brunch. | 6 Guthrie Pl. | 860/437-0526 | AE, D, DC, MC, V | $$–$$$

Lodging

Howard Johnson. This two-story hotel is 5 mi from the beach and Mystic. Some rooms have king-size beds, some just queens, but a roll-away bed fits in all of them. In-room data ports, microwaves, refrigerators, cable TV, no-smoking rooms. | 580 Poquonnock Rd., Groton 06340, 2 mi north of New London | 860/445-0220 or 800/406-1411 | fax 860/445-6184 | www.hojo.com | 48 rooms | CP | AE, D, DC, MC, V | $–$$

Mystic Marriott Hotel and Spa. The old-world touches accent the modern rooms of this six-story Georgian-style hotel with rich fabrics, gleaming wood furnishings, and elegant detailing. An Elizabeth Arden Red Door Spa is attached. Restaurant, coffee shop, in-room data ports, some in-room hot tubs, pool, health club, spa, lounge, shop, business services, meeting rooms. | 625 North Rd. (Rte. 117), Groton 06340, 7 mi north of New London | 860/446-2600 or 800/228-9290 | fax 860/446-2696 | www.marriott.com | 285 rooms, 6 suites | AE, D, DC, MC, V | $$$–$$$$

Quality Inn. This pleasant budget alternative is near the U.S. Submarine Base, golf course, and beach. Restaurant, in-room data ports, cable TV, pool, wading pool, gym, bar, laundry facilities, business services. | 404 Bridge St., Groton 06340, 4 mi east of New London | 860/445–8141 | www.choicehotels.com | 110 rooms | CP | AE, D, DC, MC, V | $–$$$

Old Lyme

★**Florence Griswold Museum.** Central to Old Lyme's artistic reputation is this museum that hosted members of the Old Lyme art colony. "Miss Florence" Griswold, the descendant of a well-known family, opened her home to artists in 1899. Works by America's finest artist are on display in the restored late-Georgian mansion. Don't miss the 30 painted wood panels in the dining room. Beyond the house is a lovely gallery housing changing exhibits of related American art, and an extensive permanent collection of American paintings that were formerly property of the Hartford Steam Boiler Company. Guided tours begin about every 45 minutes. | 96 Lyme St. | 860/434–5542 | fax 860/434–9778 | www.flogris.org | $7 | Tues.–Sat. 10–5, Sun. 1–5.

Lyme Academy of Fine Arts. In an 1817 federal home, this academy has a popular gallery with works by contemporary artists, including the academy's students and faculty. | 84 Lyme St. | 860/434–5232 | Free | Tues.–Sat. 10–4, Sun. 1–4.

Dining

Anne's Bistro. Contemporary. Tasty and sophisticated Italian bistro fare including grilled duck and excellent pasta dishes. Salads and interesting appetizers are deservedly popular for breakfast, lunch, and dinner. | 9 Halls Rd. | 860/434–9837 | Closed Sun. | MC, V | $–$$

★**Bee and Thistle Inn.** American. Firelight, candlelight, and floral prints augment the romance of this 1756 colonial inn. The small dining room is surrounded by bay windows overlooking the property. Try the breast of duck with duck ravioli, roulade of chicken breast filled with duxelles of mushroom and Parmesan, crab ravioli, or Thai green curry shrimp. Sunday brunch. Breakfast served. | 100 Lyme St. | 860/434–1667 | www.beeandthistleinn.com | Closed Tues. and 1st 3 wks in Jan. | AE, D, DC, MC, V | $$$–$$$$

The Hideaway. American. Sit by a window and for a view of the Lieutenant River from this two-story eatery in the Old Lyme Shopping Center. The menu includes salads, burgers, sandwiches, seafoods, burritos, and steaks. Try the daily fish specials. | 19 Halls Rd. | 860/434–3335 | fax 860/434–0702 | AE, MC, V | $$

Old Lyme Inn. American. The inn's open and spacious dining room has chandeliers and white linen tablecloths. A hand-painted mural of a ship on the sea graces one wall. Steak is a favorite, or try the crab cakes or rack of lamb, which is slow-roasted and has an herb-and-citrus crust. Sunday brunch. | 85 Lyme St. | 860/434–2600 | AE, D, DC, MC, V | $$–$$$$

Pat's Kountry Kitchen. American/Casual. Maple chairs, blue calico curtains, and friendly waitstaff that serve homey classics any time of the day equals real, old-fashioned family dining at Pat's. The restaurant is known for its more than 20 homemade pies, including chicken potpie. A specialty is clam hash, made from the large local quahogs, minced with potato, fried in a patty, and served with eggs. | 70 Mill Rock Rd., at Rte. 154, Old Saybrook | 860/388–4784 | Closed Wed. | MC, V | $$

Lodging

★**Bee and Thistle Inn.** After exploring the perennial and herb gardens and walking the lawns of this 1756 inn, rest in a lounge chair by the Lieutenant River. Some of the antiques-filled rooms have four-poster beds or canopy beds. All have wing-back chairs, hardwood floors, Oriental rugs, Victorian-style wallpaper, and are adorned with plants and flowers from the garden. Restaurant; no TV in some rooms, no smoking. | 100 Lyme St., 06371 | 860/434-1667 or 800/622-4946 | fax 860/434-3402 | www.beeandthistleinn.com | 11 rooms, 1 cottage | Closed 3 wks in Jan. | AE, MC, V | $$$–$$$$

Old Lyme Inn. The two-story, white clapboard 1850s inn is on 2 acres in Old Lyme's historic district. It's filled with Empire and Victorian furnishings and a maple spiral staircase leads to the smallish but romantic rooms. Play chess on the table drawn up to the hearth. Restaurant, cable TV, bar, business services. | 85 Lyme St., 06371 | 860/434-2600 or 800/434-5352 | fax 860/434-5352 | www.oldlymeinn.com | 13 rooms | CP | AE, D, DC, MC, V | $$$

DELAWARE

BETWEEN THE OLD CAPITAL & THE NEW: COLONIAL DELAWARE
FROM WILMINGTON TO DOVER

Distance: 50 mi   Time: 1–2 days
Overnight Breaks: Dover, Wilmington

Between the old state capital of Wilmington and the new one at Dover lies the bulk of Delaware's colonial history. Most of the trip is on Route 9, which follows the Delaware River down to the great bay. It was this waterway that allowed the early adventurers—including William Penn—to navigate the region and found their settlements.

❶ Begin in the medium-size city of **Wilmington,** which is almost exactly halfway between New York and Washington. This advantageous location has led many of America's major corporations to set up offices here. But commerce has not robbed the town of its soul, and many attractions draw colonial buffs. The **Delaware History Museum** is an ever-changing venue for exhibits on Delaware history, crafts, and culture in the "First State."

  The city was founded as Fort Christina in 1638 by Swedes who named the region after the then Queen of Sweden. **Fort Christina Monument** marks their settlement. Two 17th-century structures worth a visit are the **Holy Trinity (Old Swedes) Church and the Hendrickson House Museum.** The church, built in 1698, is still used for services and is a National Historic Landmark. Hendrickson House was built in Pennsylvania in 1690 but was moved to the church site in 1959. **Willingtown Square** is a handsome cluster of 18th-century houses now used as offices. **Winterthur Museum, Garden, and Library** has one of the world's foremost collections of American furniture and antiques.

❷ Five miles south of Wilmington on Route 9 lies **New Castle,** at the heart of colonial Delaware, with restored colonial houses, cobblestone streets, and historic sites along the Delaware River. William Penn first landed here, and the occasion is noted in **Battery Park.** Two blocks west, on the waterfront, the **Old New Castle Courthouse,** once the seat of government, is now a museum of state history. The **George Read II House** and

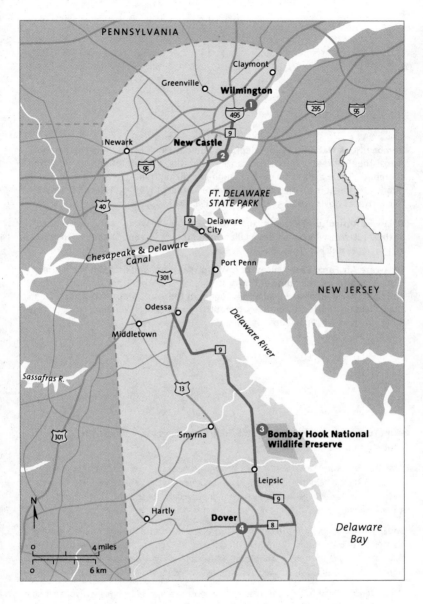

formal gardens were built in 1801 in federal style by the son of a signer of the Declaration of Independence. The **Amstel House Museum** is in the restored brick mansion of a former governor, with colonial furnishings and art.

❸ About 35 mi southeast of New Castle you spot the towering marsh grasses of **Bombay Hook National Wildlife Preserve,** some 15,000 acres of marshlands favored by hundreds of species of waterfowl.

❹ End your trip in **Dover** (from Bombay Hook, south on Rte. 9 to Rte. 8 W for 6 mi), the capital of Delaware since 1777, laid out by William Penn himself. The **John Dickinson Plantation** is the former home of one of Delaware's most distinguished sons of the colonial era. The **Old State House Museum,** built in 1802, is the second-oldest seat of government in continuous use in the nation.

Delaware's agricultural history is explored at the **Delaware Agricultural Museum and Village.** You can't pass through Dover without stopping off at the **Delaware State Museum.** The focus here is on Delaware's role as the first state to ratify the U.S. Constitution.

Dover

Bombay Hook National Wildlife Refuge. Bombay Hook is a bird-lover's paradise. Across the 16,000-acre refuge you can see migrating and wintering waterfowl and shorebirds. There are a 12-mi car loop and five walking trails that access marshland, ponds, and forest in an inlet of the Delaware Bay. | 2591 Whitehall Neck Rd., Smyrna, 9 mi south of Dover | 302/653–6872 | $4 per car | Daily 5–5.

Delaware Agricultural Museum and Village. Explore Delaware's agricultural history at this museum, which includes a village and farmstead. | 866 N. DuPont Hwy. (U.S. 13) | 302/734–1618 | $5 | Tues.–Sat. 10–4, Sun. 1–4.

Delaware Air Force Base Museum. A World War II hangar, listed in the National Historic Register, is the home of this museum. Special exhibitions, demonstrations, and military weapons are displayed throughout the year. Community Appreciation Day is held the third Saturday of each month from April to November. | 1301 Heritage Rd. | 302/677–5938 | Free | Tues.–Sat. 9–4.

DELAWARE RULES OF THE ROAD

License Requirements: The minimum driving age in Delaware is 16.

Right Turn on Red: Drivers are permitted to make a right turn on red after coming to a full stop, unless otherwise posted.

Seat-Belt & Helmet Laws: Seat belts are mandatory for all front-seat passengers in any vehicle and for all children under 16 years anywhere in the vehicle. Children under 40 pounds or 4 years of age must travel in an approved safety seat. Motorcycle operators and passengers under 18 are required to wear helmets.

Speed Limits: Speed limits in Delaware are 55 mph on four-lane and major highways; 50 mph on two-lane roads; 25 mph in specially zoned areas such as business or residential districts; and 20 mph in school zones. Speed limits can vary based on road conditions and/or specific areas, so always refer to posted signs.

Other Regulations: It is illegal to operate a motor vehicle in Delaware if your blood-alcohol concentration is more than .10%. Using a handheld phone is prohibited while operating a vehicle, except in an emergency.

For More Information: Delaware Department of Transportation | 302/760–2080, 800/ 652–5600 in DE | www.deldot.net. Delaware State Police | 302/739–5901 | www.state.de.us/dsp.

Delaware Archeology Museum. There are three small museums in one at this site: the Delaware Archeology Museum, Small Town Life, and the John Dickinson Victrola Museum. Make a stop at Small Town Life and learn how the state shaped the U.S. Constitution and browse the 1880 Gallery, a reconstruction of a 19th-century street, complete with a general store. | 316 S. Governors Ave. | 302/739–4266 | Free | Tues.–Sat. 10–3:30.

Delaware State Museums Visitors Center. This visitor center dispenses information on 11 museums of greater Dover, including the John Dickinson Plantation, the Delaware Agricultural Museum, and the Johnson Victrola Museum, a museum dedicated to old-time records. Most museums are closed Monday. | 406 Federal St. | 302/739–4266 | Free | Mon.–Sat. 8:30–4:30, Sun. 1:30–4:30.

Dover Downs International Speedway. One of the most popular race destinations in the Northeast, this track claims to draw the biggest crowds to a sporting event between New York and North Carolina. Seating capacity is about 107,000. Built in 1969, the track started hosting NASCAR Winston Cup Series races that year and expanded to two races a year in 1971. Drivers such as Richard Petty, David Pearson, Cale Yarborough, and Bobby Allison drove to victory here. Harness races take place periodically. Call or check the Web site for race schedules and prices. | 131 N. DuPont Hwy., 1 mi north of downtown, across from Delaware State University campus | 302/674–4600 schedules, 302/734–7223 or 800/441–7223 tickets | www.doverspeedway.com.

John Dickinson Plantation. Tour this restored farm complex, home to Delaware's delegate to the 1787 Constitutional Convention. | Kitts Hummock Rd. at Rte. 9 | 302/739–3277 | www.destatemuseums.org/jdp | Free | Mar.–Dec., Tues.–Sat. 10–3:30, Sun. 1:30–4:30; Jan. and Feb., Tues.–Sat. 10–3:30.

The Old State House. Built in 1792, the heart of Delaware's central county and state capital sits on the historic Green, surrounded by the halls of government. | Federal St. between Loockerman and Water Sts. | 302/739–4266 | Free | Tues.–Sat. 10–4:30, Sun. 1:30–4:30.

Prime Hook Wildlife Refuge. A smaller rendition of Bombay Hook, this refuge attracts some different migrating waterfowl and shorebirds. Fishing and hunting are allowed in season, and there are four walking trails and a 7-mi canoe trail. | 11978 Turtle Pond Rd., Milton, 33 mi south of Dover | 302/684–8419 | Free | Daily dawn–dusk.

Sewell C. Biggs Museum of the Decorative Arts. This 10-year-old museum in downtown Dover has an American fine art collection of paintings, furniture, and ceramics. The Delaware State Museums Visitors Center is in the same building. | 406 Federal St. | 302/674–2111 | Free | Wed.–Sat. 10–4, Sun. 1:30–4:30.

Spence's Auction and Flea Market. Every Tuesday and Friday an indoor and outdoor farmers' market complete with antiques, local Amish products, baked goods, and produce is held in two warehouses in the center of Dover. The first building is mostly food vendors, and the second a flea market. Outside the buildings a live auction is held, where you can find everything from antiques to cars. | 550 S. New St., at Queen St. | Free | Tues. and Fri. 8–dusk.

Dining

Village Inn. Seafood. Chef Bob Thomas, a former New York City restaurateur, is making the most of Delaware Bay seafood. At least one local catch is included in almost every dish. Try the clams on the half shell or the famous clam chowder. The chef and his wife also own the Inn at Little Creek, just up the road. | S. Little Creek Rd. at Rte. 9 | 302/734–3245 | AE, MC, V | $–$$$

Where Pigs Fly. American. Pigs *do* fly at this family restaurant. Off the spit, that is—in the form of hickory-smoked baby back ribs and "pulled pig" sandwiches.

Chicken and trimmings are also served. | 617 Loockerman St. | 302/678–0586 | AE, D, DC, MC, V | ¢–$

Lodging

Fairfield Inn Dover. In the heart of this small city, this chain hotel is the newest property in the area. Expect tasteful and spacious rooms with thoughtful amenities like a well-lighted work desk and a complimentary newspaper. The hotel is convenient to Dover Air Force base and Dover Downs. In-room data ports, cable TV with movies, indoor pool, gym, laundry service, free parking. | 665 N. DuPont Hwy., 19901 | 302/677–0900 | fax 302/677–0907 | www.marriott.com | 58 rooms, 19 suites | CP | AE, D, MC, V | $$–$$$

Little Creek Inn. This three-story Italianate farmhouse is surrounded by miles of working farmland. The home sits in the migratory path of many birds, especially migrating waterfowl. You can bird-watch on the property or take a 10-minute drive to Bombay Hook Nature Refuge, a national treasure for bird-watchers and nature-seekers alike. The rooms are each tastefully decorated with original antiques and collectibles hand-picked by the owner, a former New York antiques shopkeeper and interior designer. The house is filled with fine linens and textured fabrics on the walls, the beds, and each piece of furniture in the common areas. The chef and owner of a nearby seafood restaurant often prepares lavish breakfasts. In-room data ports, some in-room hot tubs, cable TV, pool, gym, fishing, bicycles, hiking, laundry facilities, some pets allowed, no-smoking rooms; no kids under 12. | 2623 N. Little Creek Rd. (Rte. 8), 19901, 2 mi east of Dover; from Rte. 1 S take Exit 98, turn left and inn is 1 mi on the left | 302/730–1300 or 888/804–1300 | fax 301/730–4070 | www.littlecreekinn.com | 4 rooms, 1 suite | BP | AE, MC, V | $$–$$$

Rose Tower Bed & Breakfast. In historic Camden, this 1807 federal-style home was built in an interesting "two over two," meaning the parlor and dining room are on the first floor and the bedrooms are upstairs. The inn is surrounded by gardens. Each room has a king-size bed. Rooms are decorated in three different styles: French Provincial, early American, and Asian. In-room data ports, some pets allowed; no room TVs, no smoking. | 228 E. Camden–Wyoming Ave., Camden 19934, 5 mi south of Dover | 302/698–9033 or 877/893–3031 | fax 302/698–9033 | www.rosetower.com | 3 rooms | BP | AE, D, MC, V | $

New Castle

Amstel House Museum. A bit of 18th-century life is preserved in this colonial house where George Washington is said to have attended a wedding. | 2 E. 4th St. | 302/322–2794 | $4, with Old Dutch house $6 | Mar.–Dec., Tues.–Sat. 11–3:30, Sun. 1–3:30; Jan. and Feb., weekends 11–3:30 or by appointment.

The Green. Old New Castle's historic center is bordered by cobblestone pathways and colonial buildings. | 3rd St. | Free | Daily dawn–dusk.

Immanuel Episcopal Church. Built in 1703, the original church was destroyed by a fire in the 1980s. It was carefully and lovingly restored by local experts, who were able to use the original walls and foundation. Tombstones in the adjoining graveyard date from 1707. | 100 Harmony St. | 302/328–2413 | Free | Daily 9–dusk.

New Castle–Frenchtown Railroad Ticket Office. Trains pulled by the Delaware steam locomotive operated in the pre–Civil War period. The ticket office was built in 1832 and occupied a number of locations before finding its current site in the 1950s. | Battery Park, Delaware St. | No phone | Free | Daily dawn–dusk.

New Castle Presbyterian Church. The first congregation of Dutch settlers built this now-restored church in 1707. | 25 E. 2nd St. | 302/328–3279 | Free | Weekdays 9–noon or by appointment. Services July and Aug., Sun. at 10 AM; Sept.–May, Sun. at 11 AM.

Old Dutch House. Delaware's oldest dwelling, this tiny house reflects the 1651 founding of New Castle by the Dutch, who called the area Fort Casimir. Period furnishings and art are the main attractions. | 32 E. 3rd St. | 302/322–2794 | $4, with Amstel House Museum $6 | Mar.–Dec., Tues.–Sat. 11–3:30, Sun. 1–3:30; Jan. and Feb., weekends 11–3:30 or by appointment.

Old New Castle Court House Museum. The history and government of the colonial capital are the focus of this museum with exhibits on William Penn and the Delaware abolitionists. The Flight to Freedom exhibit tells the story of the Underground Railroad in Delaware, focusing on Thomas Garrett, who was hailed a "stationmaster" in the railroad, helping more than 2,700 escaped slaves cross the border to the North. | 211 Delaware St. | 302/323–4453 | Free | Tues.–Sat. 10–3:30, Sun. 1:30–4:30.

Read House & Gardens. George Read, whose father signed both the Declaration of Independence and the U.S. Constitution, built this federal-style house in 1801. Formal gardens, designed in 1847, surround the house. Ten rooms are open to the public. Forty-minute tours are available most of the year. | 42 The Strand | 302/322–8411 | $5 | Mar.–Dec., Tues.–Thurs. and Sun. 11–4, Fri. and Sat. 10–4; Jan. and Feb., Sat. 10–4, Sun. 11–4.

Dining
Salty Sam's Pier 13. Seafood. Flounder is the pride of this casual spot. Also try the seafood-stuffed Atlantic salmon or the Steamed Seafood Mix Combo, a plate of crab legs, shrimp, and clams. Kids' menu. | 130 S. DuPont Hwy. | 302/323–1408 | AE, D, DC, MC, V | $$–$$$$

Wilmington
Bellevue State Park. The former estate of William DuPont, this sprawling complex includes stables, tennis courts, a fitness track, a fishing pond, a lawn popular for summer concerts or year-round picnicking, and a band shell for summer concerts. | 800 Carr Rd. | 302/761–6963 | May–Oct. residents $2.50, nonresidents $5; Nov.–Apr. free | Daily 8 AM–dusk.

Delaware Art Museum. The museum houses a well-organized and highly respected collection of late-19th-century English Pre-Raphaelite art. The American section includes works by Homer and Hopper. Take the children to the participatory gallery. At this writing, the museum is undergoing renovations due for completion in fall 2004. Until that time, the museum's temporary quarters are at 800 South Madison Street. | 2301 Kentmere Pkwy. | 302/571–9590 | $7 | Tues.–Fri. 10–4, Sat. 10–5, Sun. 1–5.

Delaware History Museum. Paintings, costumes, and regional crafts give you a taste of what "the First State" was like during colonial times. | 504 Market St. | 302/656–0637 | Free | Weekdays noon–4, Sat. 10–4.

Delaware Toy and Miniature Museum. Exhibits include antique and contemporary dollhouses, miniatures, and sample furniture, as well as dolls, toys, trains, boats, and planes from Europe and America, dating from the 18th century to the present. The museum has a collection of Noah's Ark figurines dating from 1840 that were extremely popular during Victorian times. | 6 Old Barley Mill Rd. | 302/427–8697 | $6 | Mar.–Jan., Tues.–Sat. 10–4, Sun. noon–4.

Fort Christina Monument. The monument, marking the settling of Wilmington by Swedes, sits in a picturesque park. | Foot of 7th St. | No phone | Free | Daily dawn–dusk.

Hagley Museum. The original site of the giant DuPont company, the museum displays industrial advances of the past two centuries. The site includes a working water mill and steam engine and a 19th-century schoolhouse. | Rte. 141, 3 mi north of town | 302/658–2400 | www.hagley.org | $11 | Mar. 15–Jan. 1, daily 9:30–4:30; Jan. 2–Mar. 14 weekends 9:30–4:30; tour weekdays at 1:30.

Holy Trinity (Old Swedes) Church and Hendrickson House Museum. Built in 1698, the church retains its original hipped roof and high wooden pulpit and is used regularly for religious services. Hendrickson House contains furniture and art from later periods. | 606 Church St. | 302/652–5629 | Free | Wed.–Sat. 10–4.

Longwood Gardens. Eleven thousand species of plants, along with awe-inspiring fountains, are on 1,050 acres of gardens, meadows, and woodlands. Wandering through the 20 indoor and 20 outdoor gardens can take a day. Make sure to check out the 4 acres of heated greenhouses that hold a multitude of exotic flowers, including an impressive collection of orchids. | Rte. 1, Kennett Square, PA, 8 mi north of Wilmington | 610/388–1000 | www.longwoodgardens.com | Wed.–Mon. $14, Tues. $10 | Jan.–Mar., daily 9–5; Apr. and May, daily 9–6; June–Aug., Mon., Wed., Fri., Sun. 9–6, Tues., Thurs., Sat. 9–10; Sept. and Oct., daily 9–6; Nov. 1–Nov. 26, daily 9–5; Dec., daily 9–9.

Nemours Mansion and Gardens. The former home of philanthropist Alfred I. DuPont, this mansion sits next to the world-renowned children's hospital that bears his name. The large formal gardens are perfect for a stroll. | Rockland Rd. | 302/651–6912 or 800/651–6912 | www.nemoursmansion.org | $12 | May–Dec., Tues.–Sun. by appointment.

Riverfront Market. In the riverfront area of the city, revamped in 2001, this popular market draws a huge lunch and weekend crowd. The bright, cheerful indoor market on the side of the Christina River is packed with vendors selling fresh produce, flowers, meats, breads, and more. | 1 S. Orange St. | 302/425–4890 | www.riverfrontwilmington.com | Free | Tues.–Fri. 9–7, Sat. 9–6.

Willingtown Square. Now used as office space, these four 18th-century houses escaped demolition in 1976 when they were moved here from various sites around Wilmington. | 500 Market St. | 302/655–7161 | Free | Daily 9–5.

Winterthur Museum, Garden, and Library. The museum and its splendid gardens were once the home of Henry Francis DuPont. Each year the museum's Point-to-Point Race is the city's premier social and sporting event, attracting more than 10,000 visitors. | Rte. 52, 6 mi northwest of town | 302/888–4600 or 800/448–3883 | $15 | Tues.–Sat. 10–5.

Dining

Buckley's Tavern. American. In the historic town of Centerville this old-time tavern from the early 1800s has a seasonal menu with an emphasis on local, organic herbs and vegetables. A favorite is the mushroom soup made with more than five varieties of local fungi. Expect to find anything from shrimp and grits to crab cakes and a daily fish special on the eclectic menu. Dine in a semiformal dining room; in the dark, casual, historic tavern; or on the rooftop deck. On Sunday you can don your favorite pj's for a pajama brunch. | 5812 Kennett Pike, Centerville, 8 mi north of Wilmington | 302/656–9776 | AE, DC, MC, V | $–$$$

Harry's Savoy Grill and Ballroom. Continental. The staple entrée at this local institution is the prime rib. Not surprisingly then, the favorite sandwich is the huge prime rib sandwich. Besides steak you can also get seafood, pasta, and sandwiches. | 2020 Naamans Rd. | 302/475–3000 | No lunch Sat. | AE, D, DC, MC, V | $$–$$$$

La Tolteca. Mexican. Besides the great Mexican fare, this Delaware chain is also known for its 13 types of margaritas in myriad flavors, from peach and raspberry to the more traditional lime and strawberry. The most popular dish is the sizzling Texas Fajita, an abundance of beef, chicken, large shrimp, and onions. Enchiladas *poblanas* are a sure thing, considering the authentic poblano sauce made with spices and chocolate. | 2209 Concord Pike | 302/778–4646 | AE, D, DC, MC, V | ¢–$$

Pizza by Elizabeths. Italian. Two Elizabeths own the restaurant, in turn playfully naming each pizza after a famous Elizabeth. The Elizabeth Taylor is a creative symphony of goat cheese, rosemary, sun-dried tomatoes, and black olives. The Bette Davis, on the other hand, gives a bit more of a kick, with flavorful blackened chicken, bacon, fire-roasted peppers, and a splash of honey mustard. Everything, including the pizza, is made on the premises, including salad dressings, soups, and desserts. | 4019 Kennett Pike, Greenville, 4 mi northwest of Wilmington | 302/654–4478 | AE, D, MC, V | $–$$

Lodging

Best Western Brandywine Valley Inn. All rooms in this upscale Best Western were refurbished in 2003. Most are equipped with high-speed Internet access, cordless phones, and DVD players. Many of the suites are decorated with reproduction antiques, the originals found in nearby Winterthur. The Einstein Brothers Bagel Cafe is in the lobby. The hotel is a few miles from historic downtown and just off I–95. In-room data ports, some kitchenettes, cable TV, pool, wading pool, gym, hot tub, business services, free parking, some pets allowed. | 1807 Concord Pike (U.S. 202), 19803 | 302/656–9436 | fax 302/656–8564 | www.brandywineinn.com | 98 rooms, 12 suites | CP | AE, D, DC, MC, V | $$

Inn at Montchanin Village. In the beautiful and remote Brandywine River valley, this inn is actually a village and one of the country's last intact examples of a 19th-century workers' hamlet. A stay in one of the 11 historic buildings on the 2½-acre triangular plot is filled with quirky surprises like unique furniture, colorful original artwork, and etched cows hidden on the marble tiles in each bathroom. It is said that no two pieces of furniture on the property are alike. Restaurant, room service, in-room data ports, in-room safes, microwaves, refrigerators, in-room VCRs, gym, massage, laundry service, dry cleaning, meeting rooms, free parking; no smoking. | Rte. 100 and Kirk Rd., Montchanin 19710, 6 mi north of Wilmington | 302/888–2133 | fax 302/691–0198 | www.montchanin.com | 28 rooms | AE, D, DC, MC, V | $$$

Wyndham Hotel Wilmington. In the heart of downtown, this hotel is convenient to many restaurants and the business district. Rooms are spacious and well appointed with dark-wood furniture. Many amenities, such as high-speed Internet access, cater to business travelers. Restaurant, café, room service, in-room data ports, cable TV, indoor pool, gym, bar, laundry service, dry cleaning, business services, meeting rooms, parking (fee), no-smoking rooms, no-smoking floors. | 700 King St., 19801 | 302/655–0400 | fax 302/429–5979 | www.wyndham.com | 213 rooms, 6 suites | CP | AE, D, DC, MC, V | $$

FLORIDA

GOLD COAST TO TREASURE COAST
FROM BOCA RATON TO VERO BEACH

Distance: 130 mi   Time: 5 days
Overnight Breaks: Boca Raton, Jensen Beach, Palm Beach, Fort Pierce

Drive north from Boca Raton to Palm Beach and continue along the Treasure Coast, to experience one of the wealthiest places in the world. Consider staying an extra night or more in any of the coastal towns to enjoy the year-round beaches and outdoor dining. The weather is optimum from November to May, but the trade-off is that facilities are more crowded and prices somewhat higher. In summer you'll need a tolerance for heat and humidity; also watch for frequent afternoon downpours. No matter when you visit, bring insect repellent.

❶ Begin your tour in **Boca Raton,** on A1A, 45 minutes south of Palm Beach. This upscale town at the south end of Palm Beach County reflects the unmistakable architectural presence of Addison Mizner, the principal developer of Boca in the mid-1920s. Visit the **Town Hall Museum,** to learn how key players from an oil tycoon to a barefoot mailman helped shape the community. The permanent collection at the **Boca Raton Museum of Art** includes works by Picasso, Degas, and Matisse. The **Children's Science Explorium** is a pleaser for kids with inquisitive minds. Another big draw for children is the **Gumbo Limbo Nature Center.**

❷ From Boca Raton, drive 30 mi north on Highway A1A to **Palm Beach,** whose Gatsby-era architecture, stunning mansions, and highbrow shopping make it unlike any other place in Florida. It is the indisputable focus of the region, and Mizner's Moorish-Gothic style is also prevalent. The **Henry Morrison Flagler Museum,** the palatial mansion commissioned by the cofounder of Standard Oil, is a must-see. Stop in at **The Breakers** for a peek at the enormous lobby and dining room or for a relaxing afternoon tea.

Break for lunch and then head to **Worth Avenue** (between Cocoanut Row and S. Ocean Blvd.) for some posh, pricey shopping. Spend the next two nights in Palm Beach.

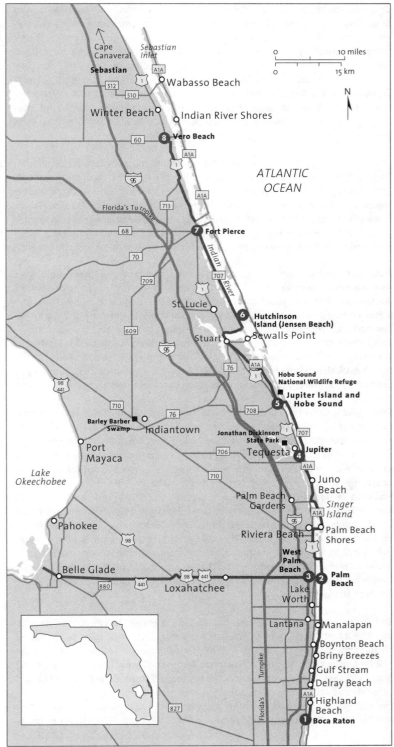

❸ On the fourth day, proceed west for about 2 mi on Royal Poinciana Way to **West Palm Beach.** Far larger than its wealthy neighbor to the east, West Palm has become the cultural, entertainment, and business center of the county and of the region to its north. There's a small but attractive downtown area, which has been spurred on by an active historic preservation movement. Along beautifully landscaped **Clematis Street** are boutiques, restaurants, and exuberant nightlife: live music venues, bars, and dance clubs. The 3-acre **Ann Norton Sculpture Gardens** honor the late American sculptor Ann Weaver Norton. Don't miss the **Norton Museum of Art** with its extensive collection of 19th- and 20th-century American and European paintings. When you're finished exploring West Palm Beach, return to Palm Beach and spend a second night.

❹ From Palm Beach, head north on Highway A1A to **Jupiter** (19 mi north of Palm Beach). There are no barrier islands east of Jupiter; the beaches are part of the mainland, and Highway A1A runs for almost 4 mi along the beachfront dunes. Visit the **DuBois House,** a modest pioneer home dating from 1898. Permanent exhibits at the **Florida History Center and Museum** review modern-day development along the Loxahatchee River. The **Jupiter Inlet Lighthouse,** a redbrick Coast Guard navigational beacon designed by Civil War hero General George Meade, has operated here since 1860.

❺ Five miles north of Jupiter off Route 707 are **Jupiter Island** and **Hobe Sound.** Visit **Blowing Rocks Preserve,** a 73-acre Nature Conservancy holding. The **Hobe Sound National Wildlife Refuge** actually consists of two tracts: 232 acres of sand pine and scrub oak forest in Hobe Sound; and 735 acres of coastal sand dune and mangrove swamp on Jupiter Island. Trails are open to the public in both places. Ogle baby alligators, baby crocodiles, and scary-looking tarantulas at **Hobe Sound Nature Center** (on the grounds of the Hobe Sound National Wildlife Refuge). Once you've gotten to the **Jonathan Dickinson State Park,** follow signs to Hobe Mountain. An ancient dune topped with a tower, it yields a panoramic view of the park and the Intracoastal Waterway.

❻ From Hobe Sound, drive north on Highway A1A for about 15 mi to **Hutchinson Island.** Environmental conservation limits development here and prevents the commercial crowding found to the north and south, although there are some high-rises here and there along the shore. Part of the small town of **Jensen Beach** is on the central part of the island. Sea turtles dominate here; between late April and August more than 600 turtles come to nest along the town's Atlantic beach. Built in 1875, the **Gilbert's House of Refuge Museum** is the only remaining building of nine such structures erected by the U.S. Life Saving Service (a predecessor of the Coast Guard) to aid stranded sailors. The **Florida Oceanographic Coastal Center** includes a mangrove forest, visitor center, and science center. The pastel-pink **Elliott Museum** was built in 1961 in honor of Sterling Elliott, inventor of an early automated addressing machine and a four-wheeled cycle. **Bathtub Reef Beach** (MacArthur Blvd. off Rte. A1A) is a draw for families with young children: the waters are shallow and unusually calm for about 300 feet offshore.

❼ Six miles north of Hutchinson Island on Route 707, you arrive in **Fort Pierce.** This community, about an hour north of Palm Beach, has a rural feel, focusing on ranching and citrus farming rather than tourism. While following Route 707, have a look at the five biological communities at **Savannas Recreation Area,** from flat woods and prairies to lakes, marshes, and scrub. At the **Heathcote Botanical Gardens** a self-guided tour takes you through a palm walk, Japanese garden, and subtropical foliage. As the home of the Treasure Coast Art Association the **A. E. "Bean" Backus Gallery** displays the works of one of Florida's foremost landscape artists. The **St. Lucie County**

Historical Museum includes early-20th-century memorabilia and vintage farm tools, while the **UDT-SEAL Museum** commemorates the site where more than 3,000 navy frogmen trained during World War II. Spend a night in Fort Pierce or Jensen Beach.

❽ Continue north along Route 707 for about 12 mi to **Vero Beach.** There's a tranquillity to this Indian River county seat, an affluent town with a strong commitment to the environment and the arts. At the **Indian River Citrus Museum,** exhibits explore a time when oxen hauled the citrus crop to the railroads and family fruit stands dotted the roadsides. The outstanding 51-acre **Environmental Learning Center** has a 600-foot boardwalk through mangrove shoreline and a 1-mi canoe trail. The center is on the north edge of Vero Beach, on Wabasso Island, but it's a pretty drive and worth the trip.

To return to Boca Raton, turn around and drive south on U.S. 1, Route 707, and Highway A1A for approximately 90 mi.

Boca Raton
★**Boca Raton Museum of Art.** In Mizner Park, the museum has works by Picasso, Klee, Degas, Matisse, and Modigliani. Also on the property are an outdoor sculpture garden and an interactive education gallery for kids. | 501 Plaza Real | 561/392–2500 | www.bocamuseum.org | $8 | Tues., Thurs., Sat. 10–5; Wed. and Fri. 10–9; Sun. noon–5.

Children's Museum. History, science, and humanities are explored through hands-on exhibits such as Dr. Dig's Back Porch, where kids uncover fossils and win prizes.

FLORIDA RULES OF THE ROAD

License Requirements: Drivers in Florida must be 16 years of age.

Right Turn on Red: Unless posted otherwise, it is legal to take a right turn at a red light in clear traffic *after* a full stop.

Seat-Belt & Helmet Laws: All automobile passengers must wear seat belts, and motorcycle riders are encouraged to wear helmets.

Speed Limits: Speed limits are 55 mph on state highways, 30 mph within city limits and residential areas, and 55 mph–70 mph on interstates and Florida's Turnpike, unless otherwise posted. Be alert for signs announcing exceptions.

Other Regulations: Passengers cannot possess open containers of alcohol in a vehicle. The legal blood-alcohol concentration limit in Florida is .08%.

For More Information: Florida Department of Transportation | 850/414–4100, 866/374–3368 toll free | www.dot.state.fl.us.

The Faces, an exhibit with crafts, costumes, and storytelling, celebrates Florida's cultural history. | 498 Crawford Blvd. | 561/368–6875 | $3 | Tues.–Sat. noon–4.

Children's Science Explorium. In this Sugar Sand Park interactive attraction, kids can create their own laser light shows, explore a 3-D kiosk that illustrates wave motion, and enjoy wind tunnels, microscopes, and microwave and radiation experiment stations. | 300 S. Military Trail | 561/347–3913 | Free | Weekdays 9–6, weekends 10–5.

Gumbo Limbo Nature Center. Huge saltwater tanks house sea turtles, mangroves, and coral in this environmental education center. Habitats include a coastal dune, a tropical hardwood *hammock* (a fertile, elevated area), and a sabal palm hammock. From mid-May to mid-July join a nighttime walk to see nesting sea turtles come ashore and lay their eggs. In August witness hatchlings being released. The center is on an island off A1A, 10 minutes from downtown Boca. | 1801 N. Ocean Blvd. | 561/338–1473 | www.gumbolimbo.org | Nature center free, turtle tours $4 | Center: Mon.–Sat. 9–4, Sun. noon–4. Turtle tours: May–Aug., Mon.–Thurs. 9 PM–midnight.

Mizner Park. The 30-acre, open-air shopping village has apartments and town houses among its gardenlike spaces. Upscale specialty shops and national retailers mingle with fine restaurants, outdoor cafés, galleries, a museum, and eight movie screens. An 1,800-seat outdoor amphitheater hosts acts from Norah Jones and the White Stripes to ballet and the Florida Philharmonic. | 433 Plaza Real, at Federal Hwy. | 561/362–0606 | www.miznerpark.org | Free | Mon.–Sat. 10–midnight, Sun. noon–10.

Town Hall Museum. This building with its shimmering golden dome houses a vital repository of archival material and special exhibits on the area's development. Tours and the gift shop are hosted by the Boca Raton Historical Society. | 71 N. Federal Hwy. | 561/395–6766 | www.bocahistory.org | Museum free, tours $7 | Tues.–Fri. 10–4; tour dates and times vary.

Dining

La Tre. Vietnamese. An adventuresome menu distinguishes this simple, stylish eatery. Try the crispy eggplant and the Happy Pancake, a Vietnamese crepe stuffed with pork, shrimp, and vegetables. The tamarind squid is another winner. | 249 E. Palmetto Park Rd. | 561/392–4568 | No lunch Sun. | AE, DC, MC, V | $$

Mario's of Boca. Italian. Hearty portions of pasta, chicken, and fish are the hallmarks here, although there is a strong stable of vegetarian appetizers. The dining room of this popular bistro in the Holiday Inn is laid-back and noisy, while the outdoor patio offers a refuge. | 1901 N. Military Trail | 561/392–5595 | AE, MC, V | $–$$$

Tom's Place. Barbecue. A heavenly experience is on hand when you sample Tom Wright's dripping ribs, pork-chop sandwiches, or chicken grilled over hickory and oak in a pepper-and-mustard sauce. Southern sweetness seeps into everything from tea and coleslaw to sweet-potato pie. | 7251 N. Federal Hwy. | 561/997–0920 | Closed Sun., also Mon. May–mid-Nov. | AE, MC, V | $–$$

Uncle Tai's. Chinese. House specialties include sliced duck with snow peas and water chestnuts in a tangy plum sauce, and sliced fillet of snapper. | 5250 Town Center Circle | 561/368–8806 | No lunch weekends | AE, MC, V | $$–$$$$

Lodging

Boca Raton Marriott. The Boca Center's numerous shops and restaurants are connected to this elegant 11-story hotel. The beach is 2½ mi away. Restaurant, in-room data ports, refrigerators, cable TV, pool, gym, hot tub, sauna, bar, laundry facilities, business services, airport shuttle. | 5150 Town Center Circle, 33486 | 561/392–4600 or 800/228–9290 | fax 561/368–9223 | www.marriott.com | 256 rooms | AE, D, DC, MC, V | $$$–$$$$

Doubletree Guest Suites. All units are suites in this appealing hotel with a lovely courtyard. The hotel is 2 mi from the beach and in the heart of the business district. Rooms have two TVs and views of either the courtyard or the pool. Restaurant, room service, in-room data ports, microwaves, refrigerators, cable TV, pool, hot tub, laundry facilities, business services, some pets allowed (fee). | 701 N.W. 53rd St., 33487 | 561/997–9500 | fax 561/994–3565 | www.doubletree.com | 182 suites | AE, D, DC, MC, V | $–$$

Hampton Inn Boca Raton. Breakfast, beverages, and a daily newspaper are complimentary at this hotel adjacent to the Athletic Club of Boca Raton. Mizner Park and the beach are both within 4 mi. Some microwaves, refrigerators, cable TV, pool, laundry service, business services. | 1455 Yamato Rd., 33431 | 561/988–0200 or 800/426–7866 | fax 561/988–0203 | www.hampton-inn.com | 94 rooms | BP | AE, D, DC, MC, V | $–$$$

Ocean Breeze Inn. As a guest of the inn, you can play the outstanding course at the adjoining Ocean Breeze Golf & Country Club, otherwise available only to club members. The comfortable and contemporary small rooms are in a three-story building, and most have a patio or balcony. Restaurant, cable TV, 27-hole golf course, 6 tennis courts, pool, recreation room, laundry facilities. | 5800 N.W. 2nd Ave., 33487 | 561/994–0400 or 800/344–6995 | fax 561/998–8279 | www.oceanbreezegolf.com | 46 rooms | AE, DC, MC, V | $–$$

Fort Pierce

A. E. "Bean" Backus Gallery. The home of the Treasure Coast Art Association, this gallery displays the works of Florida landscape artist A. E. Backus and has changing exhibits of regional artists. | 500 N. Indian River Dr. | 772/465–0630 | www.backusgallery.org | Free | Tues.–Sat. 10–4, Sun. noon–4; summer hrs by appointment.

Fort Pierce Inlet State Recreation Area. Surfers and boaters flock to the 340 acres of beach, dunes, and coastal hammock on the north shore of Fort Pierce Inlet on North Hutchinson Island. Landlubbers can picnic or go biking and hiking. | 905 Shorewinds Dr. | 772/468–3985 | $3.25 per vehicle with up to 8 people | Daily 8–sunset.

Jack Island Wildlife Refuge. Accessible only by a footbridge north of Fort Pierce Inlet State Recreational Area, this nature preserve is a hit with bird-watchers. You can spot roseate spoonbills, ibis, eagles, and many other species along the 4 mi of trails. You can also picnic, or fish in the River Lagoon. | Rte. A1A | 772/468–3985 | Free | Daily 8–sunset.

Heathcote Botanical Gardens. The 3½-acre gardens include a Japanese garden and a palm walk. | 210 Savannah Rd. | 772/464–4672 | www.heathcotebotanicalgardens.org | $4 | Year-round Tues.–Sat. 9–5, Nov.–Apr., Sun. 1–5.

St. Lucie County Historical Museum. A Seminole encampment, a reconstructed portion of a Spanish galleon, and mock-ups of the 1715 Spanish treasure fleet are among the exhibits. A replica of a turn-of-the-20th-century train station includes a model of Henry Flagler's Florida East Coast Railway. | 414 Seaway Dr. | 772/462–1795 | $3 | Tues.–Sat. 10–4, Sun. noon–4.

Savannas Recreation Area. This 550-acre semiwilderness park, with its unique biological and geographical features, is a state reserve and recreation area. There are campsites and picnic facilities, boat ramps and fishing, and interpretive trails on both land and water. | 1400 E. Midway Rd. | 772/464–7855 | $1 per vehicle | Daily 8–6.

★**UDT-SEAL Museum.** Commemorated here are the more than 3,000 Navy frogmen trained during World War II. Learn about the development of the elite Navy SEALs (Sea, Air, Land teams) and their forerunners. Displays include boats, weapons, and artifacts from World War II, Korea, and Vietnam. | 3300 N. Rte. A1A | 772/595–5845 | www.udt-sealmuseum.org | $4 | Tues.–Sat. 10–4, Sun. noon–4.

Dining

Kristi's. American. Lovely beach and ocean views enhance this casual eatery, whose menu might include lamb and prime rib. There's a wide selection of seafood dishes. | 2400 S. Ocean Dr. | 772/465–4200 | Reservations essential | Closed Mon. and Tues. | AE, MC, V | $$–$$$$

Mangrove Mattie's. Seafood. Fresh fish dishes are the pride of this Fort Pierce Inlet establishment. Try the nut-crusted flounder or coconut-fried shrimp. Outdoor dining on a small uncovered patio provides a dazzling waterfront view. | 1640 Seaway Dr. | 772/466–1044 | AE, D, DC, MC, V | $$–$$$

Theo Thudpucker's Raw Bar. Seafood. People dressed for work mingle here with shorts-clad folks fresh from the beach. Specialties include oyster stew, smoked fish spread, conch salad and conch fritters, fresh catfish, and alligator tail. | 2025 Seaway Dr., at South Jetty | 772/465–1078 | MC, V | $–$$

Lodging

Days Inn at Fort Pierce Beach. Some of the rooms in this hotel in south Hutchinson Island have wonderful views of the Intracoastal Waterway. Two restaurants and a few bars are a short walk away. Picnic area, microwaves, refrigerators, cable TV, pool, fishing, laundry facilities, business services. | 1920 Seaway Dr., 34949 | 772/461–8737 or 800/544–8313 | fax 772/460–2218 | 36 rooms | AE, D, DC, MC, V | $

★**Dockside Harbor Light Resort.** This motel-style resort is the pick of the pack of lodgings lining the Fort Pierce Inlet along Seaway Drive. Some units have a wet bar and a waterfront porch or balcony. Some kitchens, 2 pools, spa, boating, fishing, laundry facilities. | 1160 Seaway Dr., 34949 | 772/468–3555 or 800/286–1745 | fax 772/489–9848 | www.docksideinn.com | 64 rooms | CP | AE, D, DC, MC, V | ¢–$

Econo Lodge. All rooms overlook the pool at this two-story motel on the outskirts of downtown Fort Pierce. The location, along the U.S. 1 thoroughfare, makes it a convenient place to stop after seeing the sights and before heading back south. In-room data ports, some kitchenettes, cable TV, pool, outdoor hot tub, laundry facilities, business services, some pets allowed (fee). | 3236 S. U.S. 1, 34982 | 772/461–2323 or 800/228–5150 | fax 772/464–5151 | www.econolodge.com | 60 rooms | CP | AE, D, DC, MC, V | $

Jensen Beach

Bathtub Reef Beach. At the north end of Hutchinson Island, this beach has an intriguing name that describes its allure: a reef in waters so shallow and quiet that it forms a "bathtub" safe enough for children to explore. At low tide, you can walk out to the reef and see jellyfish, blue crabs, and wildly colorful parrot fish. There are rest rooms and showers here, too. | MacArthur Blvd. off Rte. A1A | 772/225–0505 | Free | Daily dawn–dusk.

Elliott Museum. Sterling Elliott was an inventor of note at the turn of the 20th century who created an addressing machine, among other useful items. This museum salutes him and displays an array of antiques from automobiles to dolls and toys. You can also visit an old-time blacksmith shop and an apothecary. | 825 N.E. Ocean Blvd. | 772/225–1961 | fax 772/225–2333 | $6 | Daily 10–4.

Florida Oceanographic Coastal Center. Run by the Florida Oceanographic Society, this science center includes a coastal hardwood hammock and mangrove forest, a visitor and science center with interpretive exhibits on coastal science and environmental issues, and a ½-mi interpretive boardwalk. | 890 N.E. Ocean Blvd. | 772/225–0505 | www.fosusa.org | $6 | Mon.–Sat. 10–5, Sun. noon–4; nature walks Mon.–Sat. 10:30–4, Sun. noon–3.

Gilbert's House of Refuge Museum. The U.S. Life Saving Service built this structure to aid stranded sailors. Today it houses a model ship collection, aquariums of tropical and native fish, and changing exhibits related to the history of the Florida coast. On the grounds is a lookout tower built during World War II, as well as a handcrafted replica of an 1840s surfboat, once used to rescue shipwreck victims. The boathouse displays early lifesaving equipment and maritime artifacts. | 301 S.E. MacArthur Blvd. | 772/225–1875 | $4 | Daily 10–4.

Maritime & Yachting Museum of the Treasure Coast. Historic boats, maritime artifacts, ship models, and nautical paintings are part of the extensive collection at this museum. | 3250 S. Kanner Hwy., Stuart, 5 mi southwest of Jensen Beach | 772/692–1234 | Free | Mon.–Sat. noon–4, Sun. 1–5.

Dining

Conchy Joe's. Seafood. The layout is half the fun at this ultracasual spot filled with stuffed fishing trophies, gator hides, and mounted snakeskins. The whole joint is on stilts, and a large palm tree grows straight through the roof. The menu changes nightly, but you might find grouper marsala or fried, cracked conch. Joe's also serves fruity rum drinks with exotic names. There's live music Thursday–Saturday nights. | 3945 N. Indian River Dr. | 772/334–1130 | AE, D, MC, V | $–$$

★ **11 Maple Street.** Continental. The menu at this restaurant changes nightly, but the portions are consistently large. Salmon with leeks, porcini mushroom risotto, and blue-crab cakes are a few of the entrées. For dessert, there is usually white-chocolate custard with blackberry sauce. Jazz plays softly in the background. | 3224 Maple Ave. | 772/334–7714 | Reservations essential | Closed Mon. and Tues. No lunch | MC, V | $$–$$$

New England Fish Market. Seafood. What began as a take-out place is now a 65-seat operation with a large selection of seafood from both northern and southern waters. Try the "clambake for two," which includes two lobsters, a dozen littleneck clams, a pound of mussels, two ears of corn, potatoes, and andouille sausage. | 1419 N.E. Jensen Beach Blvd. | 772/334–7328 | D, MC, V | $$–$$$$

Peter's Steakhouse. Steak. Before opening his own restaurant, chef Peter Buchner spent 20 years working at New York's Peter Luger's Steak House. His menu is built around five cuts of steak, lamb chops, chicken, and a fresh fish of the day. Selections include onion-laced, crisply sautéed German potatoes and creamed spinach. | 3200 N.E. Maple Ave. | 772/225–2516 | Closed Sun. | AE, D, DC, MC, V | $$–$$$$

Lodging

Hutchinson Inn. Sandwiched among Hutchinson Island's high-rises, this modest mid-1970s two-story motel feels like a B&B thanks to the friendly management. Continental breakfast is served in the lobby or on tables outside, and you can borrow books or magazines to take to your room, where homemade cookies are delivered nightly. Pool, beach. | 9750 S. Ocean Dr., 34957 | 772/229–2000 | fax 772/229–8875 | www.hutchinsoninn.com | 21 rooms, 2 suites | CP | MC, V | $–$$$

Jupiter/Jupiter Island

Blowing Rocks Preserve. Within this 73-acre nature conservancy thrive plant communities native to beachfront dune, coastal strand (that's the landward side of the dunes), mangrove, and hardwood hammock environments. | 574 S. Beach Rd. (Rte. 707), Jupiter Island | 561/744–6668 | www.tncflorida.org | $3 | Daily 9–4:30.

DuBois Pioneer Home. Built in 1898 by pioneer Henry DuBois, who chose this spot atop a prehistoric Jeaga Indian shell mound, this historic house presents a look at early pioneer life in Florida and houses a collection of antique furnishings and memorabilia. | DuBois Park, Rte. A1A, Jupiter | 561/747–6639 | Free | Wed. and Sun. 1–4 or by appointment.

Florida History Center and Museum. Permanent exhibits at this Burt Reynolds Park complex include 18th- and 19th-century photographs and artifacts that show how nature coexists with development along the Loxahatchee River. On the grounds is a Seminole Living History Village and the Tindall House, built in 1892. | 805 N. U.S. 1, Jupiter | 561/747–6639 | $5 | Tues.–Fri. 10–5, weekends 1–5.

Hobe Sound National Wildlife Refuge. These 967 acres include three distinct plant communities: coastal dune, mangrove swamps, and sand pine scrub forest. Among the numerous wildlife species you might spot here are brown pelicans, bald eagles, and American crocodiles. Sea turtle nesting beaches are a lure when the turtles swim in here each summer, and the carefully preserved ecosystem along these 3 mi of Jupiter Island offers a glimpse of old Florida. | 13640 S.E. Federal Hwy., Hobe Sound, 10 mi north of Jupiter | 772/546–6141 | $5 per vehicle | Daily dawn–dusk.

Hobe Sound Nature Center. Baby reptiles and a tarantula prowl the beach section of this nature center that also has interpretive exhibits detailing the area's ecosystem. You can trek a short trail that winds through the sandhills. The center is north of Jupiter and west of Jupiter Island. | 13640 S.E. Federal Hwy., Hobe Sound, 2 mi north of Jupiter and just west of Jupiter Island | 772/546–2067 | Free | Trail daily dawn–dusk; nature center weekdays 9–3, call for Sat. hrs.

Jonathan Dickinson State Park. About 20% of this 11,500-acre wildlife-rich park is covered in sand pine scrub, a biological community so rare that it has been designated as globally imperiled. Much of the rest is pine flat woods and wetlands. A favorite camping and canoeing spot, the park also offers bicycling and picnicking along the banks of the Loxahatchee River. Freshwater and saltwater fishing can yield mullet and snook. Two-hour boat tours aboard the 44-passenger *Loxahatchee Queen II* make the trip upriver to the pioneer homesite of Trapper Nelson, who came to the area in the 1930s. | 16450 S.E. Federal Hwy., Hobe Sound, 5 mi north of Jupiter | 772/546–2771 | Park $3.25 per vehicle, boat tours $12 | Daily 8–sundown.

Jupiter Inlet Lighthouse. Overlooking Jupiter Inlet since 1860, the 105-foot lighthouse was built on a mound of shells that turned out to be an ancient Indian burial ground. A museum at the base of the lighthouse tells the history of the structure, which includes attacks and severe damaged by Seminole Indians during its construction. Tours of the lighthouse are given every half hour. | Captain Armour's Way, U.S. 1 and Beach Rd., Jupiter | 561/747–8380 | www.jupiterlighthouse.com | $6 | Sun.–Wed. 10–4, tours 10–3:15; start times vary.

Dining

Charley's Crab. Seafood. Distinguished by a glass, three-tier atrium overlooking the Intracoastal Waterway and Jupiter Inlet, this chic dining spot specializes in seafood but has some selections for landlubbers as well. Grouper and yellowfin tuna are popular. You can also dine outside on a covered patio. Kids' menu. | 1000 N. U.S. 1, Jupiter | 561/744–4710 | Reservations essential | AE, D, DC, MC, V | $$$–$$$$

Lighthouse Restaurant. American. Chicken breast stuffed with sausage and fresh vegetables, burgundy beef stew, and king crab cakes are some of the dishes at this coffee shop–style restaurant with a menu that changes daily. | 1510 N. U.S. 1, Jupiter | 561/746–4811 | D, DC, MC, V | $–$$

Sinclair's Ocean Grill & Rotisserie. Seafood. Tall French doors look out on a pool and tropical greenery at this restaurant, which is part of the Jupiter Beach Resort. Cashew-encrusted Florida grouper, Cajun-spiced tuna, mahimahi with pistachio sauce, and filet mignon are some popular choices, as is the Sunday brunch. | 5 N. Rte. A1A, Jupiter | 561/745–7120 | AE, MC, V | $$–$$$

Palm Beach

The Breakers. Built by Standard Oil founder Henry Flagler in 1895, this luxury hotel resembles an ornate Italian Renaissance palace. Painted arched ceilings are hung with crystal chandeliers and 15th-century Flemish tapestries fill the Florentine dining room. There is limited free parking in front of the hotel and valet under the porte cochere. | 1 S. County Rd. | 561/655–6611 | www.thebreakers.com | Free | Daily 7 AM–1 AM.

★ **Henry Morrison Flagler Museum (Whitehall).** Flagler helped establish agriculture and tourism as the state's leading industries. In 1902, he built this museum for his third wife, Mary Lily Kenan. The building looks like an elegant wedding cake with soaring columns fronting a two-story veranda. Many of the original furnishings of the 1901 home are on display, and Flagler's personal railroad car, the *Rambler*, is parked behind the building. The museum is on the National Register of Historic Places. | 1 Whitehall Way | 561/655–2833 | www.flagler.org | $8 | Tues.–Sat. 10–5, Sun. noon–5.

Worth Avenue. A stroll down this ¼-mi-long street of grand Moorish architecture takes in some of the most exclusive shops, boutiques, and ateliers in the world. | Between Cocoanut Row and S. Ocean Blvd. | 561/659–6909 | www.worth-avenue.com | Free | Shops Mon.–Sat. 10–5.

Dining

Amici. Italian. Crowded, trendy, and visually exciting, Amici serves northern Italian fare. Entrées include gourmet pizzas and homemade pastas such as tagliolini with shrimp, asparagus, sun-dried tomatoes, and crushed red pepper; and white or red linguine with fresh clams, garlic, olive oil, crushed red pepper, and parsley in white wine. | 288 S. County Rd. | 561/832–0201 | Reservations essential | No lunch Sun. | AE, D, DC, MC, V | $$–$$$$

★ **Café Boulud.** French. Celebrity chef Daniel Boulud opened this restaurant in the historic Brazilian Court hotel. Boulud's signature four-muse menu pairs appetizers with entrées within four classifications: classic French, seasonal, vegetarian, and international. This is the place to splurge on a meal and dine among Palm Beach glitterati. Equally exciting for people-watching is the casual lounge, which serves an abbreviated menu and does not require jackets. Breakfast served. | 301 Australian Ave. | 561/655–6060 | Reservations essential | Jacket required | AE, D, DC, MC, V | $$$–$$$$

Chuck and Harold's. Continental. Some of the country's biggest celebrities power-lunch at this palm-lined sidewalk café. Specialties include Bahamian conch chowder, terrific hamburgers, gazpacho topped with crunchy onions, grilled steaks, and tangy key lime pie. Breakfast served. | 207 Royal Poinciana Way | 561/659–1440 | www.muer.com | AE, D, DC, MC, V | $$–$$$

Testa's. Steak. Family-operated since 1921, the year Flagler's railroad opened Palm Beach to the world, Testa's has a popular, family-friendly sidewalk café and a tropical garden dining room with a sliding roof. Specialties include the double center-cut sirloin steak (for two), mahimahi, tuna, and snapper. Sunday brunch. Kids' menu. Breakfast served. | 221 Royal Poinciana Way | 561/832–0992 | www.testasrestaurants.com | Reservations essential | AE, D, DC, MC, V | $$–$$$

Lodging

The Chesterfield. Two blocks north of Worth Avenue, this elegant four-story, white stucco, European-style hotel has inviting rooms ranging from small to spacious. All are richly decorated with plush upholstered chairs, antique desks, paintings, and marble baths. A quiet courtyard surrounds a large pool and the happening Leopard Lounge is known for its lively cocktail hour. Restaurant, room service, some refrigerators, some in-room VCRs, pool, bar, library, concierge, Internet, business services, meeting rooms.

| 363 Cocoanut Row, 33480 | 561/659–5800 or 800/243–7871 | fax 561/659–6707 | www.chesterfieldpb.com | 55 rooms | AE, D, DC, MC, V | $$$–$$$$

Heart of Palm Beach Hotel. Three blocks north of Worth Avenue and a three-minute walk from the beach, the two low, pink buildings of this hotel date from 1960 and 1975. Rooms are spacious and sunny, with private balconies and terraces. Restaurant, refrigerators, in-room data ports, cable TV, pool, bicycles, 2 bars, laundry facilities, business services, some pets allowed. | 160 Royal Palm Way, 33480 | 561/655–5600 or 800/523–5377 | fax 561/832–1201 | 88 rooms | AE, D, MC, V | $$–$$$$

Palm Beach Historic Inn. Downtown, tucked between Town Hall and a seaside residential block, this inn has a Continental breakfast served in bed or in the courtyard, and tea and cookies delivered to your room upon your arrival. Guest rooms tend toward the frilly with Victorian antiques and reproductions. Refrigerators, some in-room VCRs, library. | 365 S. County Rd., 33480 | 561/832–4009 | fax 561/832–6255 | www.palmbeachhistoricinn.com | 13 rooms | CP | AE, D, DC, MC, V | $–$$$

Palm Beach Oceanfront Inn. Families are attracted to this hotel's reasonable prices and beachfront location. The staff is laid-back and knowledgeable. A wide wooden sundeck surrounds the free-form pool and looks out to the sand, where you can rent umbrellas and rafts. An adjoining restaurant has a bar and patio. Restaurant, room service, in-room data ports, in-room safes, some kitchenettes, some microwaves, refrigerators, cable TV, some in-room VCRs, pool, beach, fishing, bar, laundry facilities, laundry service, some pets allowed. | 3550 S. Ocean Blvd., 33480 | 561/582–5631 or 800/457–5631 | fax 561/588–4563 | www.palmbeachoceanfrontinn.com | 58 rooms | AE, D, DC, MC, V | $–$$$

Plaza Inn. The three-story 1939 art deco building that houses this B&B-style hotel is fronted in pale pink stucco with light green trim. It is a block from the beach, and four blocks north of Worth Avenue. The French- and Italian-style rooms come with antique and high-quality reproduction furniture. Tucked in the back is a secluded garden, tropical plants set around a fountain, and the outdoor pool and hot tub with waterfalls and plenty of room for sunbathing. In-room data ports, refrigerators, cable TV, some in-room VCRs, pool, hot tub, bar, laundry service, business services, free parking, some pets allowed. | 215 Brazilian Ave., 33480 | 561/832–8666 or 800/233–2632 | fax 561/835–8776 | www.plazainnpalmbeach.com | 53 rooms | BP | AE, MC, V | $$–$$$$

Vero Beach

Environmental Learning Center. Aquariums filled with Indian River lagoon life dot this 51-acre preserve on Wabasso Island. A 600-foot boardwalk takes you through the mangrove area along the shore. You can also canoe through mangroves along a 1-mi trail. | 255 Live Oak Dr. | 772/589–5050 | www.elcweb.org | Free | Tues.–Fri. 10–4, Sat. 9–noon, Sun. 1–4.

Humiston Park. You can access the beach from this park, which has a large children's play area and picnic tables; shops are across the street. | Ocean Dr. below Beachland Blvd. | 772/231–5790 | Free | Daily 7 AM–10 PM.

Indian River Citrus Museum. The museum re-creates a time when the Florida roadsides were lined with family fruit stands. A video, photos, and tool displays take visitors back in time to the preindustrial farming era. You can also book tours of nearby citrus groves. | 2140 14th Ave. | 772/770–2263 | Free | Tues.–Fri. 10–4.

Riverside Children's Theatre. Local and professional touring productions are hosted here; acting workshops also are held at the Agnes Wahlstrom Youth Playhouse. | 3280 Riverside Park Dr. | 772/234–8052 | www.indianrivertheatre.com | Call for ticket prices | Shows usually weekends at 1:30, but call for exact times.

Vero Beach Museum of Art. In Riverside Park's Civic Arts Center, this site hosts a full schedule of exhibitions, art movies, lectures, workshops, and other events, with a focus on Florida artists. | 3001 Riverside Park Dr. | 772/231–0707 | www.vbmuseum.org | Free | Mon.–Wed. 10–4:30, Thurs. 10–8, Fri. and Sat. 10–4:30.

Dining

Black Pearl Riverfront. Contemporary. Although there are many "Pearl" eateries in Vero, this is the trendiest option, with a stunning riverfront location and a martini bar. Choose from appetizers like fish chowder or chilled leek and asparagus soup and from entrées like onion-crusted grouper and beef Wellington. Reservations are essential October through April. | 4455 N. Rte. A1A | 772/234–4426 | No lunch weekends | AE, MC, V | $$$–$$$$

Ocean Grill. Seafood. Driftwood paneling, Tiffany lamps, and chandeliers fill this rustic and elegant restaurant on the ocean. Popular dishes include crab au gratin and seafood casserole. | Sexton Plaza shopping center, 1050 Ocean Dr. | 772/231–5409 | Closed for 10 days after Labor Day. No lunch weekends | AE, D, DC, MC, V | $$–$$$$

Pearl's Bistro. Caribbean. At the Black Pearl's more laid-back and less expensive sister restaurant, try Bahamian conch fritters, seafood chowder, or Jamaican jerk shrimp for starters. Move on to grilled Yucatan-spiced local fish, barbecued ribs, and blackened New York strip with peppery rum sauce. | 56 Royal Palm Blvd. | 772/778–2950 | No lunch weekends | AE, MC, V | $–$$

Tangos. American. Upbeat and casual, this steak-and-seafood restaurant across from Humiston Beach has outside dining. If you have eclectic taste buds, try the lobster quesadillas with pineapple and papaya salad or the roasted barbecue pork tenderloin with country-style grits and Jack Daniels sauce. | Park Place shopping center, 3001 Ocean Dr. | 772/231–1550 | www.tangosrestaurant.com | Closed Sun. and Mon. | AE, D, DC, MC, V | $$–$$$$

West Palm Beach

Ann Norton Sculpture Gardens. Seven English-style granite figures and six brick megaliths are displayed over the 3-acre grounds. The gardens are a monument to the late American sculptor and environmentalist Ann Weaver Norton, the second wife of steel magnate Ralph H. Norton. | 253 Barcelona Rd., 33401 | 561/832–5328 | $5 | Wed.–Sun. 11–4 or by appointment.

Clematis Street. A mix of food, art, performance, landscaping, and retailing has renewed downtown West Palm around Clematis Street. Water-view parks, outdoor performing areas, and attractive plantings and lighting add to the pleasure of browsing, window-shopping, and resting at an outdoor café. | Between Dixie Hwy. and Flagler Dr.

Lion Country Safari. More than 1,300 wild animals roam free in this 500-acre wildlife preserve that is 15 mi west of downtown West Palm Beach. View zebras, ostriches, and rhinoceroses from your car along 8 mi of paved roads. Make time for the aviary, alligator moat, petting zoo, and Pelican Island, a refuge for injured pelicans. | 2003 Lion Country Safari Rd., at Southern Blvd., Loxahatchee, 15 mi west of I-95 | 561/793–1084 | www.lioncountrysafari.com | Park $16.95, van rental $8 per 1½ hrs | Daily 9:30–5:30; last vehicle in by 4:30.

Mounts Botanical Gardens. More than 14 acres of rare trees, serene gardens, native plants, and butterfly and rain-forest gardens thrive at this little-known horticultural center across from Palm Beach International Airport. | 531 N. Military Trail | 561/233–1749 | www.mounts.org | Gardens free, tours $2 | Mon.–Sat. 8:30–4:30, Sun. 1–5; tours Sat. at 11, Sun at 2.

★**Norton Museum of Art.** Steel magnate Ralph H. Norton built this museum in 1941 to showcase his extensive collection of 19th- and 20th-century American and European paintings and sculpture. The nine galleries display traveling exhibits and the permanent collections of Chinese art, Renaissance through baroque art, photographs, and contemporary pieces. Don't miss the manicured gardens and the sublime glass ceiling by Dale Chihuly. | 1451 S. Olive Ave., 33401 | 561/832–5196 | www.norton.org | $8 | Tues.–Sat. 10–5, Sun. 1–5.

Okeeheelee Nature Center. Explore 5 mi of paved and shallow rock trails amid 100 acres of native pine flat woods and wetlands. The visitor center and gift shop has hands-on exhibits and offers guided walks given by Okeeheelee Nature Center volunteers. Okeeheelee is in western Palm Beach County near the Florida Turnpike. | 7715 Forest Hill Blvd., 5 mi west of I–95 | 561/233–1400 | Free | Center Tues.–Fri. 1–4:45, Sat. 8:15–4:45; trails daily dawn–dusk.

Palm Beach Zoo at Dreher Park. See 500 animals representing 100 species at this 22-acre zoo, including the endangered Florida panther, two Bengal tigers, and red kangaroos. Tour the reptile house, walk through a tropical rain forest, and visit a children's zoo. | 1301 Summit Blvd. | 561/533–0887 | www.palmbeachzoo.org | $7.50 | Daily 9–5.

Dining

Angelo & Maxie's. Steak. A cool crowd packs into this noisy steak house and clublike bar. Come with an appetite, the portions of grilled veal chop and teriyaki filet mignon are large enough to share with the table. | CityPlace shopping center, 651 Okeechobee Blvd. | 561/833–6550 | www.angelo-maxies.com | AE, D, DC, MC, V | $$–$$$$

Café Protégé. Contemporary. At this Florida Culinary Institute restaurant, watch chefs chopping, dicing, and slicing in the observation kitchen. Try the rack of lamb served with cabernet mashed potatoes, sautéed mushrooms, and bok choy ragout in a balsamic reduction. Another superb dish is the Floridian bouillabaisse, with shrimp, scallops, clams, mussels, and whitefish. | 2400 Metrocentre Blvd. | 561/687–2433 | Reservations essential | Closed Sun. No lunch weekends | AE, MC, V | $$–$$$

Pescatore Seafood and Oyster Bar. Seafood. There's a sophisticated bustle beyond the handsome French doors of this trendy spot across from the fountain in Centennial Square in downtown West Palm Beach. The *pescatore* for two is shrimp, scallops, clams, mussels, calamari, and lobster on a bed of linguine in a light marinara sauce. | 200 Clematis St. | 561/837–6633 | AE, DC, MC, V | $–$$

★**Tsunami.** Pan-Asian. This is where the hip crowd hangs out to nibble on Asian fusion fare and sushi and wash it down with exotic fruit martinis. Packed into this dramatically lighted multilevel restaurant are two bars, a late-night lounge, a sushi bar, and an enormous Buddha statue. | CityPlace shopping center, 651 Okeechobee Blvd. | 561/835–9696 | www.tsunamirestaurant.com | Reservations essential | No lunch | AE, D, DC, MC, V | $$$–$$$$

Lodging

Hibiscus House. Built in 1922 by Mayor David Dunkle during the Florida land boom, this Cape Cod–style bed-and-breakfast began the beautification trend that landed the neighborhood on the National Register of Historic Places. Rooms are individually decorated with antiques the owner collected during his career as an interior designer. Each room has a terrace view of the attractive poolside covered in tropical Florida foliage. In-room data ports, microwaves, cable TV, pool, airport shuttle, some pets allowed. | 501 30th St., 33407 | 561/863–5633 or 800/203–4927 | fax 561/863–5633 | www.hibiscushouse.com | 8 rooms | BP | AE, D, MC, V | $–$$

★**Hotel Biba.** In the El Cid historic district, this 1940s motel is fun and stylish. Each guest room has a vibrant mélange of colors, plus handcrafted mirrors, mosaic bathroom floors, and custom mahogany furnishings. Luxury touches include Egyptian cotton sheets, down pillows and duvets, and lavender-scented closets. Clematis Street nightlife is about a mile away. In-room data ports, pool, bar. | 320 Belvedere Rd., 33405 | 561/832–0094 | fax 561/833–7848 | www.hotelbiba.com | 43 rooms | AE, DC, MC, V | $–$$

Parkview Motor Lodge. Only 1½ mi from the beach, this six-story budget option is beautifully landscaped. The carpeted rooms, some with private balconies, are well kept. It's a simple but comfortable place. In-room data ports, refrigerators, cable TV. | 4710 S. Dixie Hwy., 33405 | 561/833–4644 or 800/523–8978 | fax 561/833–4644 | 28 rooms | CP | AE, DC, MC, V | $

Tropical Gardens Bed & Breakfast. French doors lead from rooms out to the pool at this cottage house painted in a sunny yellow with white trim in the historic Old Northwood area. Tropical colors and a relaxed style makes you feel like you're in Key West. Delicious homemade bread and scones are included in the Continental breakfast. Pool, bicycles; no smoking. | 419 32nd St., 33407 | 561/848–4064 or 800/736–4064 | fax 561/848–2422 | www.tropicalgardensbandb.com | 4 rooms | CP | AE, D, MC, V | $

FLORIDA KEYS
FROM KEY LARGO TO KEY WEST

Distance: 106 mi   Time: 5 days
Overnight Breaks: Big Pine Key, Islamorada, Key Largo, Key West

High season in the Keys, a chain islands connected by 43 bridges, is mid-December through March. Traffic on the mostly two-lane Overseas Highway (U.S. 1), which stretches for 127 mi from the mainland to Key West, is inevitably heavy. From November to the middle of December and April through May, crowds are thinner, the weather is superlative, and hotels and shops drastically reduce their prices. Summer, which is hot and humid, is becoming a second high season, especially among families and Europeans. Key West's annual Fantasy Fest is the last week in October; if you plan to attend, reserve at least six months in advance. Rooms are also scarce the first few weekends of lobster season, which starts in August.

Navigate the Overseas Highway by the green-and-white milepost signs, to which locals often refer when giving an address. For example, an address might be John Pennekamp Park at mile marker (MM) 102.5, OS, the OS being an abbreviation for ocean side versus the bay (BS) or gulf side (GS) of the islands.

❶ Begin the tour by leaving U.S. 1 just south of Florida City and taking Highway 905A. This scenic route rejoins U.S. 1 on **Key Largo** (56 mi south of Miami International Airport on the Florida Tpke.), the first key reachable by car. The island runs roughly from MM 106 to MM 91, and has a 15-mi landmass that juts north of U.S. 1. Thirty-mile-long Key Largo—named *Cayo Largo* (long key) by the Spanish—is the largest island in the chain. Most businesses are on the four-lane divided highway (U.S. 1) that runs down the middle. But away from the overdevelopment and suburban landscape you can find many areas of pristine wilderness. The 2,005-acre **Dagny Johnson Key Largo Hammocks Botanical State Park** is the largest remaining stand of the vast West Indian tropical hardwood hammock and mangrove wetland that once covered most of the Keys' upland areas. The site is home to 84 species of protected plants and animals. **John Pennekamp Coral Reef State Park** encompasses 78 square mi of coral reefs, sea-grass beds, and mangrove swamps. The diving and snorkeling here are famous.

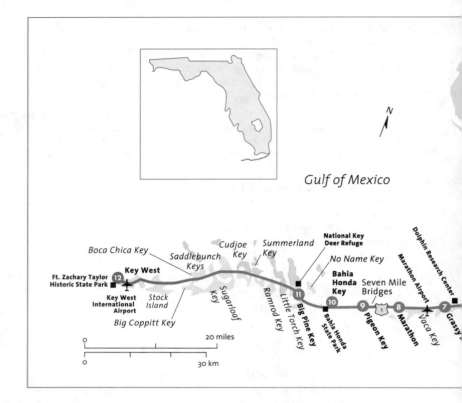

Gulf of Mexico

2 Worth a stop in the southernmost part of Key Largo, in the town of Tavernier, is the waterfront **Florida Keys Wild Bird Rehabilitation Center.** Many birds are kept here for life because of permanent injuries, while others are rehabilitated and set free.

3 Next along the chain is **Islamorada,** a group of islands that runs from MM 86 to MM 70 and includes Plantation Key, Windley Key, Upper Matecumbe Key, Lower Matecumbe Key, Craig Key, and Fiesta Key. Day and night, Islamorada buzzes with activity at shops, galleries, parks, restaurants, and nightclubs. Indian Key, in the Atlantic Ocean, and Lignumvitae Key, in Florida Bay, which are both state parks, also belong to the Islamorada group but are not on U.S. 1.

When the Florida East Coast Railway drilled, dynamited, and carved Windley Key's limestone bed, it exposed the once-living fossilized coral reef that was laid down about 125,000 years ago, now visible in quarries and exhibits at the **Windley Key Fossil Reef Geological State Park.** At **Theater of the Sea,** dolphins, sea lions, stingrays, and tropical fish swim in the 1907 Windley Key railroad quarry, whose huge blasted holes are now filled with seawater. If you can't find lodging in Islamorada for your second night, consider staying in Long Key.

4 **Lignumvitae Key Botanical State Park,** a 280-acre bay-side island, punctuated by the home and gardens that chemical magnate William Matheson built as a private retreat in 1919, is still cloaked by a virgin hardwood forest. Access is only by boat—either your own, a rental, or a ferry operated by the official concessionaire, Robbie's Marina, which also rents kayaks and boats.

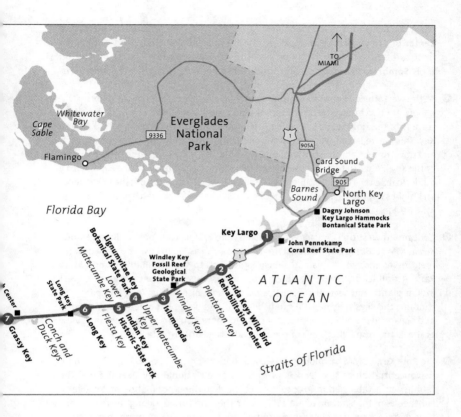

⑤ On the ocean side of the Matecumbe islands, 10½-acre **Indian Key Historic State Park** was inhabited by Native Americans for several thousand years before Europeans arrived. The islet was a county seat and base for early-19th-century shipwreck salvagers until an Indian attack wiped out the settlement in 1840. The island is reachable only by boat—either your own, a rental, or Robbie's ferry. It's a popular kayak trip that takes about 30 minutes to paddle.

⑥ **Long Key** is about 8 mi west of Lignumvitae on U.S. 1 and runs from MM 70 to MM 65. The most popular site on this island is **Long Key State Park,** which has a canoe trail through a tidal lagoon and a not-very-sandy beach fronting a broad expanse of shallow grass flats. Bring a mask and snorkel to observe the marine life in this rich nursery area.

⑦ Continue west from the park along U.S. 1 for approximately 7 mi to **Grassy Key.** It's the easternmost island in the city of Marathon, which encompasses 13 keys between MM 60 and MM 47. The island is primarily inhabited by a few families that operate small fishing camps and motels. The former home of Milton Santini, creator of the original *Flipper* (the movie, which predates the television series) is now a **Dolphin Research Center** and home to a colony of about 15 dolphins. The not-for-profit organization has dolphin swims and interaction programs.

⑧ Continue west on U.S. 1 for about 6 mi to Vaca Key, the heart of the city of **Marathon.** This community is the commercial hub of the Middle Keys. Commercial fishing—

still a big local industry—began here in the early 1800s. The **Museums and Nature Center of Crown Point Hammock**—a 63-acre tract that includes the last-known undisturbed thatch-palm hammock as well as several museums—has several hiking trails. **Sombrero Beach** has separate areas for swimmers, jet boats, and windsurfers.

❾ At the western edge of Marathon, about 3 mi west of the museum complex on U.S. 1, there are two bridges. U.S. 1 continues along the (new) Seven Mile Bridge. A slight turnoff to the right leads to the Old Seven Mile Bridge, which takes you to **Pigeon Key.** This 5-acre island was once a railroad work camp and, later, a fish camp, park, and government administration building. Today it's a park focusing on the history of the Keys. You can tour the museum and historic buildings on your own or with a guide. To reach the island, either take the shuttle, which departs from the ticket depot on Knight's Key (MM 47), or walk, bike, or skate across a 2¼-mi stretch of the Old Seven Mile Bridge.

❿ Continuing west on U.S. 1 across the Seven Mile Bridge, you come to **Bahia Honda Key** at MM 38. *Bahia Honda* translates from Spanish as "deep bay." The state government owns most of the island, which is devoted to 524-acre **Bahia Honda State Park.** A trail leads through a dense tropical forest where you can see rare West Indian plants and several species found nowhere else in the Keys. The park also contains the Keys' only natural sandy beach of notable size; it extends on both gulf and ocean sides and has deep water close to shore. You can get a panoramic view of the island from what's left of the railroad—the Bahia Honda Bridge.

⓫ **Big Pine Key,** at MM 33, about 5 mi west of Bahia Honda Key on U.S. 1, is known for its concentration of Key deer and the 2,300-acre **National Key Deer Refuge.** The refuge was established in 1954 to protect the dwindling population of Key deer, a subspecies of the Virginia white-tailed deer. They can turn up along the road at any time of day—especially in early morning and late afternoon. Admire their beauty, but feeding them is against the law. The **Blue Hole,** a quarry left over from railroad days, is the largest body of freshwater in the Keys. From the observation platform and walking trail, you might see alligators, birds, turtles, Key deer, and other wildlife. There are two well-marked trails for exploring the area.

⓬ **Key West,** last stop on this tour and in the Keys, is about 23 mi south of Big Pine Key on U.S. 1. While bustling restaurants, shops, and galleries give Key West more of a city feel than the other keys, the pace is tempered by quaint 19th-century architecture and a laid-back lifestyle. Park the car and walk, bike, or scooter around the island.

Volunteers give walking tours of the 20-acre **City Cemetery.** Among its plots are a bronze statue resembling a ship's mast and the graves of more than two dozen sailors killed in the sinking of the battleship USS *Maine.* The **Fort Zachary Taylor Historic State Park** (at the end of Southard St., through the Truman Annex) was built between 1845 and 1866 as a base for the Union blockade of Confederate shipping during the Civil War. The park has great snorkeling, an uncrowded beach, and a picnic area. While in Key West, don't miss the **Ernest Hemingway Home and Museum,** which Hemingway bought in 1931. Hundreds of brightly colored tropical fish and other fascinating sea creatures from Key West waters make their home at the **Key West Aquarium.** A touch tank enables you to handle creatures of the sea. If you're into butterflies and birds, check out the **Key West Butterfly Nature Conservatory.**

To return to Key Largo, head north on U.S. 1 for approximately 90 mi.

Big Pine Key

Bahia Honda State Park. Bahia Honda is unique among the Keys because of its extensive sandy beaches—probably the best in the Keys—and deep waters close to shore that are good for swimming and snorkeling. The 524-acre sun-soaked park with a nature center sprawls on both sides of the highway, between the Seven Mile Bridge and Big Pine Key. Camping, boating, and fishing are among the activities. | MM 37, OS | 305/872–2353 | www.floridastateparks.org | $5 per vehicle, plus 50¢ per person | Daily 8–sunset.

Blue Hole. Inside the National Key Deer Refuge is this freshwater lake, the biggest in the Keys. A walkway leads to an observation deck, where you can see alligators and turtles in their naturally crystalline habitat. | Big Pine Key Shopping Plaza, Key Deer Blvd. | 305/872–0774 | Free | Daily dawn–dusk.

National Key Deer Refuge. Key deer, an endangered species, are protected in this 8,500-acre refuge. To spot the creatures, which stand only 24 inches–32 inches at the shoulder, about the height of a golden retriever, follow the self-guided nature trail off Key Deer Boulevard. Your chances of seeing them are best at dawn and dusk. | Key Deer Blvd. | 305/872–0774 | Free | Daily dawn–dusk.

Dining

No Name Pub. American. The only thing fancy about this casual, old-time standard is getting there—turn north at Big Pine Key traffic light, right at the fork, left at the four-way stop, and go over No Name Bridge. The restaurant, known for its fried shrimp, fresh grouper, and pizza, has been open since 1936. The ramshackle walls are covered with dollar bills, and the bar is made from a part of the Old Seven Mile Bridge. | N. Watson Blvd., 33042 | 305/872–9115 | D, MC, V | $

Lodging

Casa Grande. Right on the Atlantic, the rooms of this B&B open onto the patio or the private beach, where a hammock is strung between two palms and you have complimentary use of kayaks and Windsurfers. Each room has tile floors, a queen-size bed, and a couch. Breakfast is served in the garden patio. Fans, refrigerators, outdoor hot tub, beach, dock, bicycles; no room TVs, no kids under 18. | 1619 Long Beach Dr., OS, 33043 | 305/872–2878 | www.floridakeys.net/casagrande | 3 rooms | BP | No credit cards | $$

Deer Run Bed & Breakfast. Three rooms make up this guest house that has an acre on the beach all to itself. Some of the rooms have great ocean views, French doors, and Bahama fans. Verandas, some off the rooms, others off common areas, look out over the water. There are also outdoor grills and beachfront chairs. Microwaves, refrigerators, cable TV, outdoor hot tub, beach, boating, bicycles; no room phones, no kids under 18, no smoking. | 1997 Long Beach Dr., OS, 33043 | 305/872–2015 | fax 305/872–2842 | www.floridakeys.net/deer | 3 rooms | BP | No credit cards | $$–$$$

Looe Key Reef Resort. The operators of this resort know nearly everything about diving and have a boat to take you out into the wild blue. The two-story hotel, with two double beds in each room, has gardens in the front and balconies looking over a canal. More pluses are the open-air tiki bar, which rocks on weekend nights with live music. Restaurant, fans, cable TV, pool, dive shop. | MM 27.5, OS, Ramrod Key 33042, 2 mi west of Big Pine Key | 305/872–2215 | fax 305/872–3786 | www.diveflakeys.com | 20 rooms | MC, V | $

Grassy Key/Crawl Key

Curry Hammock State Park. A birding paradise, this nearly 1,000-acre oceanfront park is also one of the Keys' top kayaking spots. Construction is almost complete on new trails, a ranger station, dumpstation, canoe launch, and 28 campsites to complement the park's beach, bathhouse, trails, and picnic areas. | MM 57, OS Crawl Key | 305/664–4815 Long Key State Park | www.floridastateparks.org | $4 per vehicle plus 50¢ per person | Daily 8–sunset.

Dolphin Research Center. The creator of the movie *Flipper* opened a home for dolphins and sea lions here in the late 1950s. Learn about dolphins and watch them demonstrate their skills at different narrated 30-minute sessions that run throughout the day. You can swim with dolphins (Dolphin Encounter, $155; requires at least a month's advance booking), interact with the dolphins from a submerged platform (Dolphin Splash, $80), or participate in dolphin-training programs. The popular Paint with a Dolphin ($55, plus admission) lets you attend a training session and then hold your souvenir T-shirt while a dolphin paints it. | MM 59, BS | 305/289–1121 | www.dolphins.org | $17.50 | Daily 9–4, narrated sessions every 30 mins.

Dining

The Wreck. Seafood. Steaks, burgers, and seafood are the fare in this relaxed, non–air-conditioned local hangout right off the highway. There's a tiki hut patio outside, and wreckage from old ships that sank in the area hangs inside. A popular dish is the fried, coconut-dipped jumbo shrimp. | MM 59, BS | 305/743–8282 | MC, V | $$

Islamorada

Hurricane Monument. The roadside marker with a platform, obelisk, and crypt memorializes the 423 persons who perished in a 1935 hurricane. Many were World War I veterans who had been working on the Overseas Highway. An art deco–style monument, built by the WPA of Keys coral limestone, depicts wind-driven waves and palms bending in the storm's fury. | MM 81.6, Overseas Hwy.

Indian Key Historic State Park. Indian Key's colorful past is very much a part of early Florida history. In the 1830s, this island 3/4-mi offshore, accessible only by ferry service from Robbie's Marina (MM 77.5, BS) or private boat, was the seat of then-new Dade County. An observation tower, dock, and 1-mi hiking trail are highlights. You can rent boats at Robbie's Marina or kayaks and sailboats at Florida Keys Kayak and Sail (MM 78.5, OS). | MM 78.5, Overseas Hwy. | 305/664–2540 park, 305/664–9814 ferry | www.floridastateparks.org | Park free, ferry $15 | Park daily 8 AM–dusk; ferry departs Thurs.–Mon. at 9 and 1, and returns about 2½ hrs later; arrive at least 30 mins in advance for ferry.

Lignumvitae Key Botanical State Park. To step ashore here is to take a step into the past, when the land and surrounding sea fulfilled most of the residents' needs. In 1919, William Matheson, a wealthy landowner from Long Island, New York, purchased the island and established a caretaker's house and lime and coconut palm groves. The house remains, but the groves were overgrown by the surrounding virgin tropical forest typical of those that once covered most of Florida's Upper Keys. This key is accessible only by ferry service from Robbie's Marina (MM 77.5, BS) or private boat or kayak, which can be rented at Robbie's Marina and Florida Keys Kayak and Sail (MM 78.5, OS). | MM 78.5, Overseas Hwy. | 305/664–2540 park, 305/664–9814 ferry | www.florida-stateparks.org | Donations accepted, ferry $15, tours without ferry $1 | Daily 8–5, ferry Thurs.–Mon. 9:30 and 1:30, tours Thurs.–Mon. 10 and 2.

Long Key State Park. There are three nature trails, two foot and one canoe, at this 966-acre park 12 mi southwest of downtown Islamorada. There are also picnic areas, campsites, and some of the best sportfishing in the Keys. Rangers run programs on birding, sea turtles, plants, history, and local marine ecology. | MM 67.5 Overseas Hwy. | 305/664–4815 | www.floridastateparks.org | $4 per vehicle plus 50¢ per person | Daily 8 AM–dusk.

Theater of the Sea. At this marine park, you can pet a shark, kiss a sea lion, or enjoy a bottomless boat ride in the lagoon. You can also swim with the dolphins and take a snorkel cruise. | MM 84.7, OS | 305/664–2431 | fax 305/664–8162 | www.theaterofthesea.com | $18.50 | Daily 9:30–4.

Dining

Lazy Days Oceanfront Bar and Seafood Grill. Seafood. The lively crowd digs into jumbo portions of steamed clams at this local favorite. Specialties include fish or chicken sautéed in bread crumbs and topped with tomatoes, Parmesan cheese, scallions, and key lime butter. Outdoor dining is on the veranda with a spectacular ocean view. Reservations are essential on weekends. | MM 80, Overseas Hwy. | 305/664–5256 | AE, D, MC, V | $–$$$

Lorelei Restaurant. Seafood. Home of the renowned outdoor Cabana Bar, this lively fish eatery is the place to go for live evening entertainment. Dine on seafood and conch specialties indoors or on the patio and watch the sun set over the water. Kids' menu. Breakfast served. | 96 Madeira Rd., MM 82, Overseas Hwy. | 305/664–4656 | AE, D, DC, MC, V | $$–$$$

Manny & Isa's. Cuban. The namesake owners have been preparing Cuban and Spanish dishes like roasted pork and paella for Keys diners since 1965. Locals and visitors come from miles away for Manny's key lime pie. | MM 81.6, OS | 305/664–5019 | Reservations not accepted | Closed Tues. and mid-Oct.–mid-Nov. | AE, D, MC, V | $–$$$

Lodging

Islander. Spacious studios and suites are being redecorated and the entire 20-acre oceanfront property renovated at this writing. All rooms have large patios, some also have a screened porch. Renovations completed in late 2003 include a new restaurant, pool bar, and outdoor spa. Picnic area, fans, in-room data ports, some kitchens, some kitchenettes, cable TV with movies, pool, saltwater pool, gym, outdoor hot tub, beach, dock, fishing, basketball, shuffleboard, volleyball, dry cleaning, laundry facilities, business services, meeting rooms, no-smoking rooms. | MM 82.1, OS, 33036 | 305/664–2031 | fax 305/664–5503 | www.islanderfloridakeys.com | 113 rooms, 1 suite | AE, D, DC, MC, V | $$$

Kon-Tiki Resort. Pack up the kids, pack up the boat, and check into this laid-back family-friendly resort with motel rooms, apartments, and cottages on Florida Bay. The private pond is stocked with tarpon and tropical fish. The deep-water boat ramp is suited for large boats. Some rooms have porches or sundecks. Some fans, some kitchenettes, some microwaves, refrigerators, cable TV, pool, pond, beach, dock, fishing, bicycles, laundry facilities. | 81200 Overseas Hwy., 33036 | 305/664–4702 | fax 305/664–5305 | www.thefloridakeys.com/kontiki | 25 rooms | AE, D, MC, V | $$

Sands of Islamorada. Spectacular sunrises, an extremely friendly staff, and macaws await you at this oceanfront resort that has a private boat ramp. Some of the rooms have wraparound porches. Picnic area, fans, in-room data ports, some kitchenettes, microwaves, refrigerators, cable TV, pool, outdoor hot tub, beach, dock, boating, fishing, some pets allowed (fee). | MM 80, OS, 33036 | 305/664–2791 | fax 305/664–2886 | www.sandsofislamorada.com | 5 rooms, 1 suite, 3 apartments | MC, V | $$

Key Largo

Dagny Johnson Key Largo Hammocks Botanical State Park. On the northern end of Key Largo, this 2,005-acre site is the largest remaining stand of what was once a vast West Indian tropical hardwood hammock (forest) and mangrove wetland covering most of the Keys. Here you can roam among 84 species of protected plants and animals, including the endangered Schaus butterfly and the American crocodile. Self-guided tour information is available at the gate; guided tours are offered biweekly. | County Rd. 905, North Key Largo | 305/451–1202 | $1 | Daily 8–sunset, tours Thurs. and Sun. at 10.

Dolphins Plus. Swim with trained dolphins who perform stunts, tag along with untrained dolphins as they swim around a saltwater basin, or get in the water with sea lions as they jump through hoops and give out kisses. If you can't get a reservation here, ask about Dolphin Cove, a sister business 2 mi up the road, which also has dolphin swim programs as well as kayaking and eco-tours. The $10 entrance fee is waived for participants in the dolphin swims and sea lion encounters. | 31 Corrine Pl., off MM 99, OS | 305/451–1993 | www.dolphinsplus.com | General admission $10, sea lion encounter $75, dolphin swim $125–$160 | Daily 8–5, sea lion encounters at 9:15 and 1:15, dolphin swims at 8:30, 9:30, 12:45, 1:30, 3.

Florida Keys Wild Bird Rehabilitation Center. This facility is dedicated to the care and repair of hawks, ospreys, pelicans, and cormorants who get fishhooks caught in their bills or are otherwise injured. Many of the recuperating birds have permanent injuries that keep them grounded here for life; others recover and are set free. A short trail takes you into a mangrove forest similar to many of these birds' natural habitat. Bring insect repellent, particularly between May and October. | MM 93.6, BS, Tavernier, south end of Key Largo | 305/852–4486 | Donations accepted | Daily dawn–dusk.

John Pennekamp Coral Reef State Park. The nation's first underwater preserve, this park, together with the adjacent Florida Keys National Marine Sanctuary, encompasses 178 nautical square mi of coral reefs, sea-grass beds, and mangrove swamps, and also has beaches and walking and canoe trails. You can get a video introduction to the fragile underwater ecosystem at the visitor center, but to better see the land down under, take one of the park's snorkeling, diving, or glass-bottom boat trips. | MM 102.5 | 305/451–1202 | www.floridastateparks.org | $5 per vehicle, plus 50¢ per person in the vehicle. | Daily 8 AM–dusk; guided walks Dec.–Mar., Thurs. 10 AM or by request.

Spirit of Pennekamp. See a bevy of playful, colorful fish from this high-speed, 149-passenger glass-bottom boat. | MM 102.5 on U.S. 1, 33037 | 305/451–6300 | www.pennekamppark.com | $20 | Tours daily at 9:15, 12:15, and 3.

Dining

Alabama Jack's. Seafood. Conch fritters and crab cakes are two popular choices at this weathered, open-air seafood restaurant, which floats on two roadside barges in an old fishing community. Locals, including the occasional alligator in the canal, seem to love the place. | 58000 Card Sound Rd. (Rte. 905A), Card Sound, just north of Key Largo | 305/248–8741 | MC, V | $–$$

Bayside Grill. American. A local gathering spot, this grill and lounge is proud of the sunset it orchestrates—well, salutes—each evening, providing a moment of tranquillity for the lively crowds that gather to watch it happen. The grill has chicken, steak, and lots of seafood, ranging from enchiladas to pastas. Watch carefully and you might spot the famous "green flash," said to occur in the split second when the sun disappears below the horizon. | MM 99.5, BS | 305/451–3380 | AE, MC, V | $–$$$

Chad's Deli & Bakery. American/Casual. Originally opened in 1996 as a deli, but made popular—and profitable—by its huge sandwiches served on pita or one of eight kinds of fresh-baked bread, Chad's is now a full-service restaurant with a lunch and dinner menu of sandwiches, pizzas (the barbecue chicken is a favorite), pastas, burgers, and salads. You can order anything to go or eat at the bar or one of about a dozen wooden booths. The dinner menu is Italian-American with pizzas, pastas, burgers, and salads. | MM 92.3, BS | 305/853–5566 | No credit cards | ¢–$$

Mrs. Mac's Kitchen. American. Screened jalousie windows let in breezes at this place that oozes laid-back charm with its wood floors, old license plates on the walls, dusty beer bottles in the rafters, and a large bar surrounded by booths and tables. There's always a crowd for lunch and dinner, so come early or late. Choose from burgers, barbecue, chili, traditional American sandwiches, and seafood dishes like the popular T. J. Dolphin, a mahimahi fillet topped with spicy tomato sauce and served with black beans and rice. | MM 99.4, BS | 305/451–3722 | Closed Sun. | No credit cards | $–$$$

Lodging

Coconut Palm Inn. A residential neighborhood is home to this small waterfront lodge surrounded by towering gumbo-limbo trees. The interior is reminiscent of a British East Indies plantation house. Outside it's tropical, with palm trees, wooden decks, hibiscus flowers, and turquoise waters as far as the eye can see. The units range from standard rooms, some with patios, to one- and two-bedroom suites. Fans, some kitchens, some kitchenettes, refrigerators, cable TV, pool, beach, dock, boating, laundry facilities; no smoking. | MM 92, BS, 198 Harborview Dr., Tavernier 33070, south end of Key Largo | 305/852–3017 or 800/765–5397 | fax 305/852–3880 | www.coconutpalminn.com | 11 rooms, 7 suites | AE, MC, V | $$

Largo Lodge. A tropical garden of palms, sea grapes, and orchids hides this 1950s-style lodge with 200 feet of bay frontage. In the late afternoon, wild birds, including pelicans and herons, come to owner Harriet "Hat" Stokes for a snack. All units are spacious one-bedroom cottages with rattan furnishings and screened porches. Fans, kitchenettes, cable TV, beach, dock; no room phones, no kids under 16. | MM 101.7, BS, 33037 | 305/451–0424 or 800/468–4378 | www.largolodge.com | 7 cottages | MC, V | $$

Popp's Motel. The swings and sandy beach outside this 50-year-old motel attract families, who stay in apartments and one-bedroom cottages with cool tile and terrazzo floors. The motel has everything you need to barbecue your catch, swing in a hammock under 2 acres of palms, and kayak or sail into Florida Bay. Picnic area, fans, kitchenettes, cable TV, beach, dock, boating, fishing, shuffleboard, playground. | MM 95.5, BS, 33037 | 305/852–5201 | fax 305/852–5200 | www.popps.com | 7 apartments, 3 cottages | AE, MC, V | $

Rock Reef Resort. Palm trees, tropical foliage, and plenty of places to watch sunsets on Florida Bay create a relaxing, casual getaway at this resort. A wide range of room configurations in 10 cottages makes it ideal for family gatherings, yet with nearly 4 acres there's lots of privacy. The rooms are rather plain, with wicker furnishings and white tile floors. Some kitchens, cable TV, outdoor hot tub, beach, dock, boating, shuffleboard, volleyball. | MM 98, BS, 33037 | 305/852–2401 or 800/477–2343 | fax 305/852–5355 | www.rockreefresort.com | 9 rooms, 3 suites, 7 apartments, 2 cottages | AE, D, MC, V | $$

Tarpon Flats Inn & Marina. Apartments in this former residential building, which overlook a marina, are furnished with custom mahogany and wicker furniture, wood floors, Oriental carpets, and sliding glass doors with wood shutters that let in the breezes but give privacy. You can cook in your room or outside on the grill. The Continental breakfast is made-to-order fruits and cereal, plus pastries from a local bakery. Room service is for breakfast only. Picnic area, fans, in-room data ports, some kitchens, some kitchenettes, cable TV with movies, in-room VCRs, beach, dock, snorkeling, boating, marina, fishing, bicycles, shop; no smoking. | 29 Shoreland Dr., off MM 103.5, OS, 33037 | 305/453–1313 or 866/546–0000 | fax 305/453–1305 | www.tarponflats.com | 6 apartments | CP | AE, D, DC, MC, V | $$$

Key West

City Cemetery. In this 20-acre graveyard, a bronze statue resembling a ship's mast marks the graves of more than two dozen sailors who lost their lives on the battleship USS *Maine*, which sank in Havana Harbor in 1898. Volunteers of the Historic Florida Keys

Foundation conduct 60-minute walking tours from the sexton's house (reservations required). | Margaret and Angela Sts. | 305/292–6718 | $10 | Daily dawn–dusk; tours Tues. and Thurs. 9:30.

Dog Beach. The only dogs-allowed beach in Key West is small and has a landscape of rocks and sand. It's next to Louie's Backyard (restaurant). | N. Vernon and Waddell Sts. | Free | Daily sunrise–sunset.

Dry Tortugas National Park. Access to this national park made up of coral reefs and seven small islands is only possible via seaplane or boat. Garden Key is home to long-deactivated Fort Jefferson, the largest brick-and-masonry structure in the Western hemisphere. The pre–Civil War fort is most famous for the 1865 incarceration of Dr. Samuel Mudd, who set the broken leg of Lincoln assassin John Wilkes Booth. You can tour the fort and picnic on the beach. More than 250 craft—from Spanish galleons to clipper ships—have been wrecked on the reefs here, a boon for snorkelers and divers today. Exploring the waters requires some skill, as there are powerful currents, fire coral, barracuda, and scorpion fish. Ferries depart around 8 AM and return around 5:30 PM. Food and beverages are not sold in the park, but ferries have breakfast and lunch and sell snacks and beverages, including wine and cocktails. Your transportation options to the island are seaplane, catamaran, or via the *Yankee Freedom II* ferry. | Garden Key, 70 mi west of Key West | 305/242–7700 | www.nps.gov/drto | $5 | Daily dawn–dusk.

Seaplanes of Key West. On the 45-minute ride to Dry Tortugas, you fly at a low-altitude heading to Dry Tortugas National Park, where you can explore Fort Jefferson on your own and still have time for bird-watching, snorkeling, or spotting sea turtles. The entire excursion is about 4 hours, and you have about $2\frac{1}{2}$ hours to explore the island. | Key West Airport, 3471 S. Roosevelt Blvd., 33040 | 305/294–0709 or 800/950–2359 | fax 305/296–5691 | www.seaplanesofkeywest.com | $179, plus $5 park fee | Daily 8 AM–9 PM; call for schedules.

Sunny Days Catamarans. After a two-hour trip to Garden Key at Dry Tortugas National Park, you are treated to a tour of Fort Jefferson and then are free for some snorkeling. The trip includes a Continental breakfast, lunch, soft drinks during the day, and snorkeling gear. Make advance reservations. | Greene and Elizabeth Sts. | 305/292–6100 or 800/236–7937 | www.sunnydayskeywest.com | $95, plus $5 park fee | Tours daily at 8 AM.

Yankee Fleet. *Yankee Freedom II*, a catamaran ferry, takes you to Dry Tortugas National Park in about two hours. Included in the deal are breakfast, lunch, snorkel gear, an onboard naturalist, and a 40-minute tour of Fort Jefferson. | 240 Margaret St. | 305/294–7009 or 800/926–5332 | www.yankeefreedom.com | $119, plus $5 park fee | Tours daily at 8 AM.

Ernest Hemingway Home and Museum. Hemingway was the first well-known writer to discover Key West and make it his home. The Nobel Prize–winning author penned about 70% of his work in Key West. He moved into this house in 1931. His two-story, 1851 Spanish-colonial home was made of native rock hewn from the grounds. | 907 Whitehead St. | 305/294–1575 | www.hemingwayhome.com | $10 | Daily 9–5.

Fort Zachary Taylor Historic State Park. From this fort, built between 1845 and 1866, Union forces mounted their blockade of Confederate shipping during the Civil War; more than 1,500 Confederate vessels were detained in the harbor. Today you can take a 30-minute tour and snorkel around an artificial reef. The beach is uncrowded and has showers and a bathhouse. There's a shady picnic area with grills. | Southard St. on Truman Annex | 305/292–6713 | www.floridastateparks.org | $5 per vehicle, plus 50¢ per person | Daily 8–sundown; tours at noon and 2.

Key West Aquarium. Exhibits offer close-up views of area marine life. You can get a peek inside a conch shell, pet sharks, and feed turtles. | 1 Whitehead St. | 305/296–2051 | www.keywestaquarium.com | $9 | Daily 9–6; tours at 11, 1, 3, and 4:30.

Key West Butterfly & Nature Conservatory. Between 700 and 1,200 butterflies from 30 to 60 species are housed in a humid, 85°, glass-enclosed environment of tropical plants. By summer, seed-eating birds—canaries, finches, and quails—join the population of flyers. There are also a gallery, gift shop, and learning center. | 1316 Duval St. | 305/296–2988 | www.keywestbutterfly.com | $10 | Daily 9–5.

Dining

Alice's at La Te Da. Contemporary. Named one of South Florida's top 10 chefs by *South Florida Gourmet*, chef-owner Alice and her team have created a unique bi-level tropical poolside environment adjoining the small La Te Da guest house. Expect a hearty wine list and a stunning array of new-world fusion specials. A good house standard is Key West yellowtail served with brown butter and capers or the coconut-and-macadamia-crusted shrimp topped with a variety of sauces. | 1125 Duval St. | 305/296–6706 | fax 305/296–3981 | AE, D, MC, V | $$–$$$$

Banana Café. French. The crepes are flying from breakfast through lunch at this favorite on the main drag. Order a dessert crepe such as *Le Mont Blanc,* stuffed with chestnut puree and whipped cream, or a meal crepe like *La Mer,* filled with scallops, white wine, and cream. Salads and sandwiches complete the menu. | 1211 Duval St., 33040 | 305/294–7227 | No dinner | AE, D, MC, V | ¢–$

Finnegan's Wake Irish Pub and Eatery. Irish. You can dine on thick, expensive cuts of Angus beef or inexpensive traditional Irish fare such as *colcannon,* rich mashed potatoes with scallions, sauerkraut, and melted aged white cheddar cheese. The walls are covered with portraits of famous countrymen, the waitresses are heavily accented, and the bar, which has a great selection of beers on tap, is rarely empty. | 320 Grinnell St. | 305/293–0222 | MC, V | $–$$$$

Mangia Mangia Pasta Market & Café. Italian. Dining here is all about making delicious choices. Pick your pasta, which is made on premises fresh daily. Then match it with your favorite sauce, maybe Alfredo or pesto or marinara. Or try simple grilled fish or chicken or a house specialty such as *pollo con funghi e piselli,* chicken breast with mushrooms, green peas, shallots, garlic, and marinara sauce over pasta. The wine list is fabulous. | 900 Southard St. | 305/294–2469 | No lunch | AE, MC, V | $–$$

Lodging

Best Western Key Ambassador Resort Inn. The large rooms at this inn have Caribbean-style furniture and private balconies, which overlook the ocean or have pool and garden views. The 7-acre oceanfront grounds are surrounded by native trees, and the outdoor bar and picnic area are conducive to socializing. Café, picnic area, fans, in-room data ports, refrigerators, cable TV with movies, pool, gym, bar, lounge, laundry facilities, concierge, airport shuttle, no-smoking rooms. | 3755 S. Roosevelt Blvd., 33040 | 305/296–3500 or 800/432–4315 | fax 305/296–9961 | www.keyambassador.com | 100 rooms | AE, D, DC, MC, V | $$$–$$$$

Courtney's Place. This "village" of gardens and cottages is a microcosm of Key West architecture with building styles similar to those common all over the island, including traditional southern shotgun houses and Caribbean styles with wide verandas and ornate trim. The interior is equally varied in coloring and furnishings, but all the rooms have at least a refrigerator, microwave, and coffee pot, if not a full kitchen. It's a family-owned and family-friendly inn. Picnic area, fans, in-room data ports, some kitchens, some kitchenettes, refrigerators, cable TV, pool, bicycles, laundry service, concierge, pets (fee); no smoking. | 720 Whitmarsh La., 33040 | 305/294–3480 or 800/869–4639 | www.courtneysplacekeywest.com | 6 rooms, 3 suites, 8 cottages | AE, MC, V | $$

Eden House. A Hemingway retreat, this '20s-era deco property is the oldest hotel in Key West. Accommodations range from rooms with a shared bath to suites in cottages. It has waterfalls, a hammock area, porch swings, and an elevated sundeck. Happy-hour drinks are complimentary. Restaurant, fans, some kitchens, some microwaves, some refrigerators, pool, outdoor hot tub, bicycles, shop, laundry facilities, concierge; no TV in some rooms, no smoking. | 1015 Fleming St., 33040 | 305/296–6868 or 800/533–5397 | www.edenhouse.com | 40 rooms, 34 with bath | MC, V | $$

Southernmost on the Beach. The Atlantic is at your doorstep at this hotel, and rooms—some with balconies—have great views of the water and the beach. The swimming pool is Olympic size. Restaurant, fans, in-room data ports, in-room safes, some in-room hot tubs, refrigerators, cable TV, pool, beach, dive shop, bicycles, concierge, business services, meeting rooms. | 508 South St., 33040 | 305/296–6577 or 800/354–4455 | fax 305/294–8272 | www.oldtownresorts.com | 47 rooms | AE, MC, V | $$$$

Speakeasy Inn. With a rich history of rum-running and cigars, this inn has some of the most spacious and relaxing rooms in town. The Saltillo-tile rooms and oak floors provide a cool refuge from the heat, but the bright artwork and throw rugs spice it up. The house was formerly owned by Raul Vasquez, who smuggled liquor in from Cuba during Prohibition. Fans, kitchenettes, cable TV with movies, shop, concierge, some pets allowed; no room phones, no smoking. | 1117 Duval St., 33040 | 305/296–2680 or 800/217–4884 | fax 305/296–2608 | www.keywestcigar.com | 10 rooms | D, MC, V | $–$$

Long Key

Long Key State Park. You can fish, rent canoes, picnic, snorkel, and camp at this ecologically rich park that has waterfront on both sides of U.S. 1. Golden Orb Trail leads to a boardwalk through a mangrove swamp alongside a waterbird-filled lagoon. Fishing for bonefish and tarpon is good in the near-shore flats. A park highlight is the Layton Nature Trail (free) on the bay side of U.S. 1. It winds through a tropical hardwood forest to the rocky Florida Bay shoreline overlooking shallow grass flats. | MM 67.6, OS | 305/664–4815 | www.floridastateparks.org | $3.25 per vehicle plus 50¢ per person, $1.50 walk-ins and bicycles | Daily 8–sunset.

Dining

Little Italy. Italian. A traditional family-style Italian restaurant, this island favorite serves up chicken, seafood, salads, snapper, steak, veal, and stone crabs in season. For dessert, ask for the rich chocolate-pecan pie. | MM 68.5, BS | 305/664–4472 | AE, MC, V | $–$$

Lodging

Lime Tree Bay Resort. Sophisticated rooms, suites, studios and cottages are bright with tropical colors and bamboo and wood furniture. Views are of Florida Bay or the 2½-acre landscaped grounds. With a water-sports outfitter next door, there's always plenty to do. Picnic area, fans, in-room data ports, some kitchenettes, some microwaves, some refrigerators, cable TV with movies, tennis court, pool, outdoor hot tub, beach, snorkeling, fishing, bicycles, no-smoking rooms. | MM 68.5, BS, 33001 | 305/664–4740 or 800/723–4519 | fax 305/664–0750 | www.limetreebayresort.com | 34 rooms | AE, D, DC, MC, V | $$

Marathon

Crane Point Hammock. The Museum of Natural History, the Florida Keys Children's Museum, and the Adderley Village Historic Site are on these 63 acres of virtually untouched hardwood hammock in the heart of Marathon. You can hike the 1½ mi of trails that lead to a bay. | MM 50, BS, Marathon | 305/743–9100 | fax 305/743–0429 | www.cranepoint.org | $7.50 | Mon.–Sat. 9–5, Sun. noon–5.

Museum of Natural History of the Florida Keys. Cultural and natural history are central to this museum's exhibits, which cover a little bit of everything, from Keys geography to sea turtles and southeastern Native American culture. The museum grounds are home to 160 native plants, 50 exotic plants, and 10 endangered plant and animal species. Check out the re-created coral reef as well. | MM 50, BS | 305/743–9100 | fax 305/743–0429 | Free with admission to Crane Point Hammock | Mon.–Sat. 9–5, Sun. noon–5.

Pigeon Key. Walk or ride a tram across a 2¼-mi section of the old bridge to this 5-acre island. On the island, you can tour on your own or with a guide. Once a work camp and village for the workers that operated and maintained the Old Bridge, it is now an educational and research center on the culture and natural resources of the Florida Keys. It's a popular spot for snorkeling and picnics. | MM 47, OS, west end of Marathon | 305/289–0025 | fax 305/289–1065 | www.pigeonkey.org | $8.50 | Daily 10–4.

Sombrero Beach. It's easy to spend the entire day at this beach that has good swimming waters, shaded picnic kiosks with barbecue grills, grassy and sandy expanses for stretching out on a blanket, volleyball courts, a large playground, and a bathhouse. It's accessible for people with disabilities and allows leashed pets. | MM 50, OS, Sombrero Beach Rd. | 305/743–0033 | Free | Daily 8–sunset.

Dining

Barracuda Grill. Eclectic. The copper votive candles on the tables at this casual but elegant restaurant resemble the open mouth and sharp teeth of a barracuda. Menu favorites include Thai Money Bags, which are pastry pouches filled with shrimp, veggies, and Thai seasonings. Grilled wahoo is sautéed with lobster, wine, and scallions. Or try the tortilla in lobster sauce or lobster enchilada. The key lime pie is good, as is the wine list. | MM 49.5, BS | 305/743–3314 | Closed Sun. No lunch | AE, MC, V | $$–$$$$

Hurricane Grille. Seafood. When there's not a band playing (Wednesday through Sunday nights), the restaurant is abuzz with TVs broadcasting sporting events. The chicken, steak, and seafood dishes satisfy, but shellfish rules: lobster, shrimp, crab, oysters—steamed or in other forms. | MM 49.8, GS | 305/743–2220 | MC, V | $$–$$$$

Keys Fisheries Market and Marina. Seafood. You would have to cook your catch on the boat to get seafood any fresher than the fish, lobster, shrimp, and scallops served here. It's a casual place with outdoor and screened seating right on the docks. It has a wine and beer bar as well as an ice-cream station. The lobster Reuben is big, juicy, and full of flavor. | MM 49, BS, end of 35th St. | 305/743–4353 | AE, D, MC, V | $–$$

GEORGIA

APPLE ORCHARDS & COTTON PATCHES

*FROM THE BLUE RIDGE MOUNTAINS OF APPALACHIA TO PLANTATION
AND QUAIL COUNTRY*

Distance: 360 mi   Time: 3–4 days
Overnight Breaks: Columbus, Rome

U.S. 27 South from the Appalachian Mountains in western Georgia links historic sites, busy cities, and quaint towns. The road courses through the state's rolling, hilly apple country to southwest Georgia, where cotton fields spread to the horizon and where quail-hunting plantations have provided leisure for the rich and famous since the early 20th century.

❶ Begin the tour in the town of **Rossville,** near Chattanooga, Tennessee, with a visit to the **John Ross House,** named for the Cherokee leader who struggled valiantly against the removal of the Cherokee people to Oklahoma. When he failed, the Cherokee were rounded up and moved west under military escort in 1838. Thousands, including Ross's first wife, succumbed to the harsh rigors of the march. The house, which is the oldest structure in northwest Georgia, is open June through August.

❷ From the Ross House, continue south about 3 mi on U.S. 27 to Fort Oglethorpe and the **Chickamauga & Chattanooga National Military Park,** the nation's oldest military park.

❸ Continue south on U.S. 27 to Summerville, where you find **Paradise Gardens,** former home of the late Howard Finster, famous for his folk-art paintings, many of which are displayed here.

❹ Farther south toward Rome, U.S. 27 passes through the exquisite **Chattahoochee National Forest,** an enormous (almost 750,000 acres) expanse of nationally preserved forest that takes in two substantial, but not contiguous, pieces of the north Georgia mountains. This segment runs north–south along Taylor Ridge.

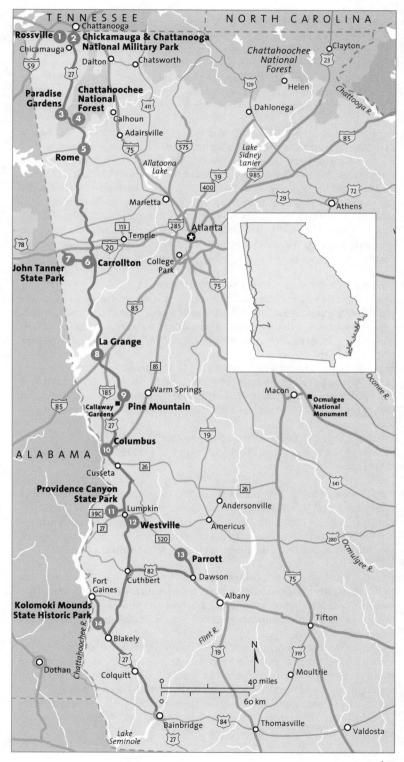

⑤ About 10 mi south of the forest on U.S. 27, you come to **Rome,** named because, like its namesake in Italy, it was built on seven hills. The downtown section of Rome is charming, and there is an extensive rails-to-trails system for hiking and bicycling through the downtown area. In Rome, the **Chieftains Trail** begins, its first site being the **Chieftains Museum and the home of Major Ridge.** The Cherokee were known as excellent carpenters and builders, and the Ridge home typifies the plantation-plain style they preferred. Also significant in Rome is **Berry College.**

⑥ From Rome, U.S. 27 continues south and crosses I–20, soon entering the town of **Carrollton,** named for John Carroll, a signer of the Declaration of Independence. It is also home to the State University of West Georgia. If you're a film buff, you might want to visit Susan Hayward's grave at **Our Lady of Perpetual Help Catholic Church.** Hayward and her husband Eton Chalkey, a Carrollton businessman who is also buried here, lived on a farm across the road from the church. To get there turn east onto U.S. 78 where U.S. 27 crosses it to reach Temple, then turn south (right) and drive 5 mi on Route 113 to just before Abilene, which is barely a blip in the road now marked by a church. The church is just off Route 113; a sign points the way. To reconnect to U.S. 27, go south on Route 113, which leads straight into U.S. 27.

⑦ Six miles west of Carrollton, **John Tanner State Park** has two lakes for swimming, boating, and fishing, plus camping and motor-lodge rooms. There's a 1-mi nature trail for hiking around the upper lake. The park is about 5 mi south of U.S. 27. Turn right on Bowdoin Junction Road, go 3 mi until it dead-ends at Route 16, turn left, and go 1³/₄ mi to Tanner Beach Road and turn right and go ³/₄ mi and through the gate.

⑧ From Carrollton, continue south on U.S. 27 to **La Grange,** named, so the story goes, by the Marquis de Lafayette himself, who bestowed upon it the French term for farm and the name of his own country abode because the area so reminded him of that part of France. His likeness graces a fountain in Lafayette Square, at the center of town.

In La Grange, visit **Bellevue,** the exquisite antebellum Greek Revival home of U.S. Senator and acclaimed orator Benjamin Harvey Hill, and the **Chattahoochee Valley Art Museum.**

⑨ Plan to spend a day or two in **Pine Mountain,** approximately 20 mi south of La Grange on U.S. 27. There is much to see in this area, beginning with a visit to **Callaway Gardens** on Route 18/354. The 14,000-acre gardens provide an amazing array of flower-filled vistas, especially in spring and summer. Here you find hiking trails and bicycle paths. Also within the gardens, is the **Cecil B. Day Butterfly Center.**

⑩ Continue south on U.S. 27 to **Columbus,** which is rich in military history. Here the **National Infantry Museum** as well as the **Port Columbus Civil War Naval Center** will take up the better part of a day. To get a handle on the area and what made it important, start at the **Columbus Museum.** Don't miss a glimpse of the **Springer Opera House.**

During the day, weather permitting, Columbus begs to be explored on foot. The terrain is level, and it's an easy walk around the historic center. Columbus's restored riverfront district—which contains 20 blocks worth of the most historic residential and industrial buildings in the city—hosts the annual Riverfest Weekend every April, with hot-air balloons, folk music, and the celebrated "pig jig" (a barbecue). For guided tours and maps to the historic district, stop in at the Convention and Visitors Bureau. Consider spending the night in Columbus.

⑪ Continue on U.S. 27 South to Lumpkin, just west of which on Route 39C is **Providence Canyon State Park.** This Grand Canyon of Georgia is the result of erosion, but the site is a unique day-use park for hiking and picnicking.

⑫ Follow the signs southeast of Lumpkin to **Westville,** a reconstructed village where costumed docents explain the realities of rural life in western Georgia during the 19th century.

⑬ Back on U.S. 27 South through Cuthbert, take U.S. 82 East to Dawson, then Route 520 North to **Parrott,** whose restored storefronts capture the essence of 19th- and early-20th-century Georgia towns.

⑭ Retracing your steps to return to U.S. 27, you pass near the **Kolomoki Mounds State Historic Park** and then through Blakely, Colquitt, and finally Bainbridge, all historic towns, before exiting the state just north of Tallahassee, Florida. The most interesting of these sites is Colquitt, hometown of one of Georgia's official plays, *Swamp Gravy,* a folk opera presenting the lives and experiences of the local people, and performed by a cast of locals.

Carrollton

John Tanner State Park. In addition to the largest swimming beach of any Georgia state park, the two lakes also provide boating and fishing. Camping, a group lodge,

GEORGIA RULES OF THE ROAD

License Requirements: You must have a valid driver's license and be at least 16 years of age to drive in Georgia.

Right Turn on Red: In Georgia, drivers can turn right on a red light *after* coming to a full stop, unless otherwise posted.

Seat-Belt & Helmet Laws: A state law requires safety belts to be used by all persons riding in the front seat of a vehicle and all minors riding anywhere in the vehicle. Children ages three and four can use a regulation safety belt or be in a safety seat; children ages two and under must be restrained in an approved safety seat.

Speed Limits: Individual speed limits are posted in all municipalities. Most interstates maintain a 50 mph speed limit in metropolitan areas and a 70 mph limit in rural areas.

Other Regulations: The use of handheld phones is prohibited while driving. The legal blood-alcohol concentration limit in Georgia is .08%. Passengers in a vehicle cannot possess open containers of alcohol.

For More Information: Georgia State Government | www.georgia.gov. Georgia Department of Transportation | 404/656–5267 | www.dot.state.ga.us.

motor-lodge rooms (motel efficiency units without phone or TV), a nature trail, and picnicking are among the draws. | 354 Tanner Beach Rd., 30117 | 770/830–2222, 770/389–7275, or 800/864–7275 | www.gastateparks.org | $2, free Weds. | Daily 7–10.

McIntosh Reserve Mansion. As you approach this plantation house of Creek Indian Chief William McIntosh, note the perfectly trimmed hedges and the way the beautiful sweeping staircase meets the drive. Inside, exhibits are devoted to McIntosh's life and ancestry. | Off GA Hwy. 5, 11 mi south of Carrollton | 800/292–0871 | Free | Tues.–Sat. 9–5.

State University of West Georgia. Founded in 1906 as the Fourth District Agricultural and Mechanical School, the school was renamed when it was later designated a university. Antebellum structures still stand on campus. Michael Greene, president of the National Academy of Recording Arts and Sciences, is an alumnus, as is Georgia Terry Kay, author of *To Dance with the White Dog.* | 1600 Maple St. | 770/836–6500 | www.westga.edu | Daily 9–5.

   Thomas Bonner House. This mansion was built in 1845 for Thomas Bonner, an early sheriff of Carroll County. The house was the focal point of Bonner's 700-acre planation and now serves the office of tourism development. The house was moved to its present location in 1917. | 1600 Maple St. | 770/838–3221 | www.westga.edu | Tours by appointment.

Dining

Lazy Donkey. Mexican. Not your basic beans-and-rice joint, this may well be Carrollton's most popular restaurant. Specials include garlic shrimp and *lomitos tropicales* (pork loin medallions with papaya-mango salsa). Kids' menu. | 334 Bankhead Hwy. | 770/834–6002 | Reservations not accepted | Closed Sun. and Mon. | AE, D, DC, MC, V | $–$$

Columbus

Columbus Museum. Georgia's second-largest art museum exhibits regional history and a permanent collection focusing on American art. Visiting exhibitions draw from collections worldwide. | 1251 Wynnton Rd. | 706/649–0713 | www.columbusmuseum.com | $6 | Tues. and Wed. 10–5, Thurs. 10–8:30, Fri.–Sun. 10–5:30.

Fort Benning. Named for Georgian Henry Lewis Benning, a soldier, attorney, politician, and justice of the Georgia Supreme Court, the fort, now on 182,000 acres, grew to become one of the largest military installations in the state and in the nation. Inside the stone gate on Benning Road is a welcome center where you can pick up brochures for self-guided tours. If you're lucky you might arrive to witness parachute training jumps. Be aware that the posted speed limits are fiercely enforced. | 4 Karker St. | 706/545–2238 | www.benning.army.mil/fbhome | Free | Daily 8 AM–dusk.

   National Infantry Museum. Exhibits trace the history of the U.S. Infantry from June 14, 1775, when the U.S. Infantry was established around Boston, Massachusetts, to the present. | Bldg. 396, Baltzell Ave., Fort Benning | 706/545–2958 | www.benningmwr.com/museum.cfm | Free | Weekdays 10–4:30, weekends 12:30–4:30.

Port Columbus Civil War Naval Center. Displays tell the story of the Civil War navies, both Confederate and Union. The hulls of two of the only three surviving Confederate gunboats, rare naval cannon, swords, mines, ship models, and period uniforms are among the displays. | 202 4th St. | 706/327–9798 | www.portcolumbus.org | $4.50 | Daily 9–5.

Springer Opera House. Built in 1871, the stage here has hosted such notables as Edwin Booth and Oscar Wilde. Now lavishly restored, the 130-year-old Victorian theater houses the State Theatre of Georgia. A regional theater, it produces five main-stage shows per year, among other events. | 103 10th St. | 706/324–5714 | www.springeroperahouse.org | Free | Weekdays 10–5.

Dining

Garlic Clove. Contemporary. Specialties include shrimp brûlée in Parmesan phyllo dough and roast duck with potato puree, bacon-braised red cabbage, and port-shallot sauce. The dining room is comfortable, with white tablecloths and candles. Beer and wine only. | 6060 Veterans Pkwy. | 706/321–0882 | Closed Sun. and Mon. No lunch | AE, D, DC, MC, V | $$–$$$

Olive Branch Cafe. Mediterranean. Come to this contemporary bistro for escargots or for regional dishes like Louisiana barbecued shrimp and gumbo. | 1032 Broadway | 706/322–7410 | Closed Sun. No lunch Sat. | D, DC, MC, V | $$–$$$$

Lodging

Rothschild-Pound House Inn. Built in 1870, this B&B is on the National Historic Register and is complete with Victorian carved-wood furniture, wraparound porch, and parlor. The Rothschild-Pound House also has quite an understanding and history-savvy staff. Dining room, in-room data ports, in-room hot tubs, microwaves, refrigerators. | 201 7th St., 31901 | 706/322–4075 or 800/585–4075 | www.thepoundhouseinn.com | 10 suites, 4 cottages | MC, V | $$–$$$$

La Grange

Bellevue. Designed and built over a two-year period in the early 1850s, this Greek Revival mansion, listed on the National Register of Historic Places, was home to Benjamin Harvey Hill, a U.S. congressman. Its facade is formed by Ionic columns, creating wide verandas. Take note of the massive carved-wood cornices over doors and windows, the black Italian marble mantels, and plaster ceiling medallions. Original furnishings include the family rosewood piano. | 204 Ben Hill St. | 706/884–1832 | $4 | Tues.–Sat. 10–noon and 2–5.

Chattahoochee Valley Art Museum. Actually the county jail, this refurbished 1892 commercial building exhibits 20th-century American art. Lamar Dodd, a native of La Grange, is a featured artist in the collection. Exhibits throughout the year focus on work by contemporary regional artists. | 112 Lafayette Pkwy. | 706/882–3267 | Free | Tues.–Fri. 9–5, Sat. 11–5.

Lumpkin

Providence Canyon State Park. Eroded canyons make up this park; some are 150 feet deep and 300 feet across. Take a picnic or hike the miles of trails. | S.R. 39C, off Rte. 27, via I–185, 7 mi west of town | 912/838–6202 | Park free, parking $2 | Apr. 15–Sept. 14, daily 7 AM–9 PM; Sept. 15–Apr. 14 7 AM–6 PM.

Westville. Less than a minute from the highway, Westville nevertheless takes you back 145 years in time as a living-history museum depicting, with amazing detail, an 1850s village steeped in pre-industrial culture. Blacksmiths, potters, weavers, cobblers, syrup makers, even the operators of a mule-powered cotton gin toil away in an effort to chronicle a time before specialized machines took over the work formerly accomplished by hand.

Westville's triple-gated entry is a replica of the gates that led to the state Capitol when it was was located in Milledgeville, but most of the buildings at Westville are the real thing, donated to the village, moved there and restored as necessary. Only a few are replicas. There are 30 buildings in all, indicative of the 1850s and earlier. The Wells house, the oldest in the village, was built by a Yuchi Indian family. | Rte. 27 at I–27, 1 mi south of town | 888/733–1850 or 229/838–6310 | www.westville.org | $10 | Tues.–Sat. 10–5, Sun. 1–5.

Pine Mountain

Callaway Gardens. The sweeping gardens developed in the 1930s to reinvigorate a languishing cotton economy bestow unparalleled spring splendor on this 14,000-acre family-style golf and tennis resort. Each season offers its unique natural display. Bicycle paths, most of them well protected from automobiles, wind throughout the gardens. Four nationally recognized golf courses, 10 tennis courts, and a lakefront beach are on the property. | Rte. 18/354 | 706/663–2281 or 800/285–5292 | www.callawaygardens.com | $10 | Mar.–Aug., daily 9–6; Sept.–Feb., daily 9–5.

    Cecil B. Day Butterfly Center. More than 1,000 butterflies from more than 75 species fly freely in this glass-enclosed space. | Rte. 18/354 | 706/663–2281 or 800/285–5292 | www.callawaygardens.com | Free with admission to Callaway Gardens | Mar.–Aug., daily 9–6; Sept.–Feb., daily 9–5.

Franklin D. Roosevelt State Park. Features of this 10,000-acre park, a national park until 1942, include about 40 mi of hiking trails, 20 mi of horseback-riding trails, and a 500-gallon pool shaped like the Liberty Bell. | Rte. 190 | 706/663–4858 | www.gastateparks.org | $2 | Daily 7–10.

Little White House State Historic Site. Built in 1932 while Franklin D. Roosevelt was governor of New York, and just before his 1933 inauguration as president, the simple Greek Revival cottage became his favorite getaway. He had originally come to Warm Springs in 1924; after suffering polio in 1921, he found swimming in the warm spring waters improved his condition. It was here on April 12, 1945, that he had a stroke while posing for a portrait and died shortly after. The unfinished painting is displayed in the room where he was sitting. You can tour the grounds and wander through the rooms of the house. Among the more touching items are the president's wheelchair, various leg braces, and canes whittled by supporters. Also on view are the guest house and Roosevelt's 1938 Ford roadster. | 401 Little White House Rd., Warm Springs, 15 mi east of Pine Mountain | 706/655–5870 | www.gastateparks.org | $5 | Daily 9–4:45.

Dining

Cricket's. Cajun/Creole. The menu at this fun, elegant restaurant is a compendium of simmered dishes that range from shrimp *rémoulade* to crawfish *étouffée* (in a spicy stew over rice), and jambalaya to fried catfish. At dusk the surrounding population of crickets serenade without fail; pictures of crickets and snakes adorn the walls of this alpine house. Tables are set with paisley and white linen. Kids receive Mardi Gras beads. Sunday brunch. | Hwy. 18 | 706/663–8136 | Closed Mon. and Tues. | D, DC, MC, V | $–$$

Georgia Room. Contemporary. Southern touches on the seasonally changing menu include very fine crab cakes, game (quail, rabbit, wild boar, wood grouse, duck), and heavenly muscadine ice cream. If you're feeling adventurous, there's also Georgia-raised ostrich. Kids' menu. | U.S. 27 | 706/663–2281 or 800/225–5292 | Jacket required | Closed Sun. No lunch | AE, D, DC, MC, V | $$–$$$$

Oak Tree Victorian Dinner Restaurant. Eclectic. An 1871 Victorian mansion is home to a casual restaurant serving dishes ranging from Italian to Southern country. Seafood bisque, stuffed lobster tail, and grilled steak with bordelaise sauce are some of the menu options. Full bar. | U.S. 27, Hamilton, 8 mi south of Pine Mountain | 706/628–4218 | Closed Sun. No lunch | AE, D, DC, MC, V | $–$$$

Rome

Berry College. Berry's 28,000 acres make up the largest college campus in the world. It is certainly among the most beautiful, with towering oaks, rolling fields, stone buildings, and simple cabins. Founded in 1902 by Martha Berry, the school's original mission was the education of mountain children. The extensive grounds include a gristmill, barns, an equine center, hiking and bicycling trails, and a reservoir for fishing. A map is available at the gatehouse. | 2277 Martha Berry Hwy., Mount Berry, 2 mi northwest of Rome | 706/232–5374 | fax 706/290–2658 | www.berry.edu | Free | Daily 7 AM–8 PM.

Oak Hill and the Martha Berry Museum. The magnificent Georgian mansion, on the college campus, was the family home of Martha Berry. The mansion is filled with family mementos and ringed by boxwood gardens. | 2277 Martha Berry Hwy., Mount Berry, 2 mi northwest of Rome | 706/291–1883 or 800/220–5504 | www.berry.edu/oakhill | $5 | Mon.–Sat. 10–5, Sun. 1–5.

Capitoline Wolf Statue. On the Capitoline hill in the Italian city of Rome is a statue of Romulus and Remus, the mythical founders of the city, being suckled by a she-wolf. An identical statue stands in front of the Rome, Georgia, city hall. If you look closely you can see an interesting inscription: "From Ancient Rome to New Rome during the consulship of Benito Mussolini in the year 1928." | Broad St., in front of City Hall, downtown.

Chieftains Museum. The home of former Cherokee chief Major Ridge, this plantation-plain house was built in the 1790s. This is the first site on the Chieftains Trail, a succession of sites throughout Georgia dedicated to the preservation of the state's native-American history. | 501 Riverside Pkwy. | 706/291–9494 | chieftainstrail.com | $3 | Tues.–Sat. 10–4.

Paradise Gardens. This is the former home of the late, colorful, self-anointed minister Howard Finster. Famous for painting religious themes, Finster hewed to a strictly fundamentalist (from his perspective) interpretation of scripture. Today his paintings are more popular than ever, especially among collectors of American folk art, for whom a stop at Paradise Gardens is almost a pilgrimage. | 42 Knox St., Summerville | 706/857–2926 | $5 | Sat. 10–5, or by appointment.

Lodging

Chandler Arms B&B. Listed on the National Register of Historic Places, this 1902 Victorian has rich woodwork, gaslight fixtures, and a wraparound porch. If you like, you can sit by the fireplace in your room with the wine and cheese that the owners provide. All rooms have fireplaces. No room phones, no room TVs, no kids under 18. | 2 Coral Ave., 30161 | 706/235–9883 | 4 rooms | BP | AE, MC | $–$$

Woodbridge Inn. From its beginnings in the mid-19th century through the early 20th century, the lodge was a railroad hotel. Now the original hotel is a restaurant, but there's a lodge out back with modern rooms, including the Eagle's Nest, a second-story loft that you reach by way of a spiral staircase. Restaurant, fishing, bicycles, hiking. | 44 Chambers St., 30143 | 706/692–6072 | fax 706/692–9061 | www.woodbridgeinn.net | 12 rooms | AE, D, MC, V | $

Rossville

Chickamauga & Chattanooga National Military Park. One of America's bloodiest battles was fought here September 19–20, 1863. More than 34,000 men died as General William T. Sherman marched from Chattanooga to Atlanta. U.S. 27 travels right through the military park—the nation's oldest—but this visitor center merits a stop, and it would be a shame not to take some time to walk the grounds, which are loaded with historical markers and monuments. | U.S. 27 at Rte. 2, Fort Oglethorpe, just east of Rossville | 706/866–9241 | www.nps.gov/chch | $3 | Mid-Aug.–mid-June, daily 8–4:45; mid-June–mid-Aug., daily 8–5:45.

Craven House. In 1863, as the Union and Confederate troops pressed nearer, the Craven family evacuated their home. Little did they know their home would end up near the center of the Battle Above the Clouds (as the battle of Lookout Mountain, part of the Chattanooga campaign, came to be known). The original residence was destroyed during the battle as it rapidly changed hands back and forth, but the Cravens later returned and rebuilt it, and today it stands as a museum honoring both the conflict and the tenacity of the family. | U.S. 27 at Rte. 2, Fort Oglethorpe | 706/866–9241 | www.nps.gov/chch | $3 | Memorial Day–Labor Day, daily 9–5.

John Ross House. The oldest structure in northwest Georgia, this house was named for the Cherokee leader who struggled valiantly against the removal of the Cherokee people to Oklahoma. When he failed, the Cherokee were rounded up and moved west under military escort in 1838. Thousands, including Ross's first wife, succumbed to the harsh rigors of the march. | Spring St., off U.S. 27 | 706/375–7702 | Free | June–Aug., daily 1–5.

Dining

Canyon Grill. American. The restaurant takes its name from nearby Cloudland Canyon. Certified Black Angus beef, grilled shrimp, and vegetables are the mainstays. There's an extensive selection of fresh fish. The pasta dishes are good. BYOB. | 28 Scenic Hwy., Rising Fawn, 32 mi southeast of Rossville | 706/398–9510 | Closed Sun.–Tues. No lunch | No credit cards | $–$$

ILLINOIS'S NORTHWEST CORNER
FROM THE ROCK RIVER VALLEY TO THE MISSISSIPPI

Distance: 110 mi Time: 2 days
Overnight Break: Dixon

Dazzling sights highlight this drive through the northwest corner of the state. The trip is particularly lovely in autumn; both the Rock River and Mississippi River valleys captivate with their fine fall colors. But late spring and summer work fine, too. Winter could be trickier; parts of Mississippi Palisades Park can get treacherous in the snow and might be closed.

❶ Start your tour at Route 2 in **Byron.** The road south from here is tree lined and occasionally runs alongside the river. The Rock River has retained much of its natural beauty because it was never deep enough for commercial navigation and so avoided the type of development that sprang up along larger waterways.

❷ The road into Oregon provides a stunning view of the 50-foot Loredo Taft sculpture of a Native American chief that's in **Lowden State Park** on a bluff across the river. To get an up-close look, go through town and across the river to the park itself. The park provides some great views of the river; it also has a camping area and hiking trails.

❸ **Oregon** is a pleasant river town with several local scenic state parks, some interesting old houses, and a small downtown area.

❹ Just south of town is **Castle Rock State Park,** which also skirts the river. There are some hiking trails and a boat ramp in the park, but the prime feature is Castle Rock itself—a tall sandstone overlook that affords a panoramic view of the river. Wooden stairs lead to the top, where on a clear fall day you can watch hawks circling overhead.

❺ Still another state park, **White Pines Forest State Park,** is about 5 mi west of Oregon. It has woods and trails to explore, and there's a dinner theater series in the park's lodge from May through December.

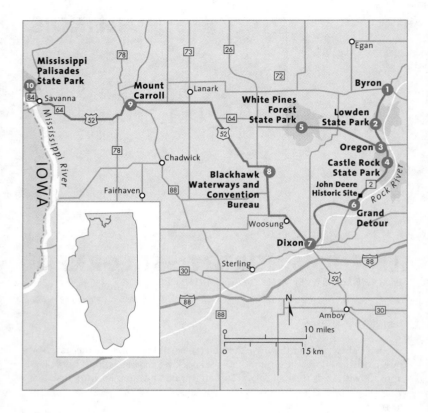

6 Route 2 leads farther south into the tiny hamlet of **Grand Detour.** It was here that blacksmith John Deere forged the first steel plow that allowed farmers to more easily till the rich prairie soil. Today the **John Deere Historic Site** traces the story of Deere's work as well as how it affected the future of farming. On the site is a working blacksmith's shop as well as Deere's refurbished home.

7 A few miles south of Grand Detour, Route 2 heads into **Dixon,** where historical sites honor two presidents. Ronald Reagan lived on Hennepin Avenue for three years as a child, and you can visit the **Ronald Reagan Boyhood Home.** The house has 1920s-era furnishings and guided tours are available. Abraham Lincoln is memorialized by a statue in a riverside park downtown; the statue commemorates Lincoln's service at Fort Dixon during the Black Hawk War.

8 At Dixon, the tour leaves the river, cuts north on U.S. 52, and heads into Polo. The little town (whose football team is the Marcos, making them the Polo Marcos) has some nice turn-of-the-20th-century storefront buildings; it's also the home of the **Blackhawk Waterways and Convention Bureau.** The bureau has put together the Blackhawk Chocolate Trail, which leads chocolate lovers through a four-county area. In autumn ask for their brochures listing haunted sites and pumpkin patches in an eight-county area.

9 U.S. 52 continues northwest through farmland that starts to become hillier. The little town of **Mount Carroll,** about 20 mi from Polo, is a fine place to stop for a look around. The town has a historic district, lined with homes from the 19th and early 20th centuries, and significant houses are marked with plaques. The downtown area is set around the Carroll County courthouse and is a good stroll as well.

⑩ Ten more miles takes you to Savanna, a long, narrow town that sits on the Mississippi. Just north of town along Route 84 is **Mississippi Palisades State Park,** whose steep cliffs rise abruptly from the road. Once you drive into the park, you can get an eye-popping view of the Mississippi from a platform perched at the top of one bluff. The park has many hiking trails, some of them quite rugged and not for the faint of foot.

To return to Oregon, pick up Route 64 in Savanna and drive east for approximately 45 mi.

Dixon

Blackhawk Chocolate Trail. A self-guided tour leads you to the best fudge, sundaes, and other chocolate treats at restaurants and stores throughout the four-county region of Carroll, Ogle, Lee, and White Side counties.

Blackhawk Waterways Convention and Visitors Bureau. Pick up free maps and other information for the Blackhawk Chocolate Trail here. | 201 N. Franklin St., Polo, off Rte. 26, 10 mi northwest of Dixon | 800/678–2108 | www.blackhawkwaterwayscvb.org | Weekdays 8:30–4:30.

ILLINOIS RULES OF THE ROAD

License Requirements: Drivers must be at least 16 years old in Illinois.

Right Turn on Red: Right turn on red is permitted everywhere in the state except where posted.

Seat-Belt & Helmet Laws: Seat belts must be worn by all drivers and front-seat passengers six years of age and over, even if the vehicle has air bags. Children four years old or less must be in a child safety seat. Children between four and six years old must either wear a seat belt or be in a child safety seat. Illinois does not have motorcycle-helmet laws, although riders are required to wear protective eyewear.

Speed Limits: The maximum speed limit in Illinois is 65 mph on rural interstate highways where posted. The maximum speed limit on most other highways is 55 mph. Speed limits in cities and towns are 30 mph unless otherwise posted.

Other Regulations: Vehicle passengers cannot possess open alcoholic containers. A driver's blood-alcohol concentration must not exceed .08%.

For More Information: Illinois Department of Transportation | 217/782–7820 | www.dot.state.il.us. Illinois State Police | 800/865–5394 road conditions | www.isp.state.il.us.

Lincoln Memorial Park. A statue of Abraham Lincoln, who served in the 1832 Black Hawk War, is the focal point of this park, which is also the site of the Old Settlers' Memorial Log Cabin, built in 1894 by Dixon residents as a tribute to those settlers who founded the town. | 100 Lincoln Statue Dr. | 815/284–3306 | Daily 24 hrs.

Ronald Reagan's Boyhood Home. The 40th president of the United States spent three years of his childhood here during the 1920s. | 816 S. Hennepin St. | 815/288–3404 | Donations accepted | Mid-Mar.–Nov., Mon.–Sat. 10–4, Sun. 1–4; Feb.–mid-Mar., Sat. 10–4, Sun. 1–4.

Dining

Rivers Edge Inn. American. Chicken strips and ribs are the favorites in this dining room surrounded by large windows. You have a smashing view of the Rock River. | 2303 W. 1st St. | 815/288–7396 | No lunch | AE, MC, V | ¢–$$

Lodging

Best Western Reagan Hotel. Five state parks, including White Pines Forest, Castle Rock, and Lowden, are within 30 mi of this stucco lodge in the rural Rock River valley. President Reagan stayed in this hotel while visiting the area. His photos and other memorabilia dominate the public areas. Restaurant, room service, in-room data ports, cable TV, some in-room VCRs, pool, gym, hot tub, bar, business services, some pets allowed (fee). | 443 Rte. 2, 61021 | 815/284–1890 or 800/528–1234 | fax 815/284–1174 | www.bestwestern.com | 82 rooms, 9 suites | AE, D, DC, MC, V | $

Comfort Inn. Though surrounded by cornfields, this motel and its rooms are thoroughly modern, and, for Ronald Reagan fans, a suite bearing his name is available here. The suite has a king-size four-poster, step-up bed. Although the former president never stayed here, several murals and displays detail his life and accomplishments. In-room data ports, some in-room hot tubs, some microwaves, some refrigerators, cable TV, indoor pool, gym, business services. | 136 Plaza Dr., 61021 | 815/284–0500 or 800/228–5150 | fax 815/284–0509 | www.choicehotels.com | 41 rooms, 7 suites | CP | AE, D, DC, MC, V | $

Hillendale Bed and Breakfast. The Aloha and the Australian Outback are two of the theme rooms in this 1890s Tudor mansion. Play pool in a cozy billiards room. Some rooms have fireplaces. Some in-room hot tubs, cable TV, some in-room VCRs, gym, cross-country skiing; no smoking. | 600 W. Lincolnway, Morrison 61270, 25 mi west of Dixon | 815/772–3454 | fax 815/772–7023 | www.hillend.com | 10 rooms | BP | AE, D, DC, MC, V | $–$$$

Grand Detour

John Deere Historic Site. In addition to the restored blacksmith shop where Deere developed the self-scouring steel plow, there is an 1830s homestead and archaeological exhibits for you to explore. | 8393 S. Main St., 61021 | 815/652–4551 | www.deere.com | $3 | Apr.–Oct., daily 9–5; Nov.–Mar., by appointment.

Dining

Colonial Rose Inn Restaurant. American. In an 1850s inn, this restaurant is known for its filet mignon, fresh fish, and hickory-smoked pork chops. | 8230 S. Green St. | 815/652–4422 | Closed Sun.–Tues. No lunch | MC, V | $$–$$$$

Oregon

Castle Rock State Park. Sandstone rock formations allow stunning views of the Rock River. There are places to hike, picnic, and fish, and there's a nature preserve in the park. | 1365 W. Castle Rd. | 815/732–7329 | dnr.state.il.us | Daily sunrise–sunset.

Lowden State Park. There's a 48-foot-tall Loredo Taft sculpture of a Native American at this park on the east side of Rock River. Taft, the renowned Illinois sculptor, was inspired to create the statue when he was a guest at Eagle's Nest, an artists' colony that had been on the site. The statue is made of reinforced concrete with a surface of cement and pink granite chips, and weighs about 100 tons. Come to the park for the views, hiking, fishing, and camping. | 1411 N. River Rd., off Rte. 64, 2 mi north of town | 815/732–6828 | dnr.state.il.us | Daily dawn–dusk.

Pride of Oregon Paddle Wheel Boat. This boat takes daily cruises that can include sightseeing activities, lunch, dinner, or Sunday champagne brunch. | 1469 Rte. 2 N | 815/732–6761 or 800/468–4222 | www.maxsonrestaurant.com | $12–$30 | Apr.–Nov., cruise times vary.

White Pines Forest State Park. This is the nation's southernmost stand of white pine. The lovely conifers, which have long silky needles, were once common in the area, but they have mostly disappeared. | 6712 W. Pines Rd., Mount Morris, 5 mi south of town and 8 mi west of Oregon | 815/946–3717 park, 815/946–3817 cabins | dnr.state.il.us | Daily 8–sunset; restaurant hrs vary.

Dining

La Vigna. Italian. Seafood, steaks, pasta, and veal dishes are the specialties in this fine northern Italian spot. | 2190 S. Daysville Rd. | 815/732–4413 or 800/806–4982 | Closed Mon. No lunch | AE, D, DC, MC, V | $–$$

Maxson Riverside Restaurant. Italian. Gaze at the Rock River as you dine on veal marsala, chicken piccata, pasta, or prime rib. This is also the departure point for the *Pride of Oregon* paddle-wheel tours. | 1469 Rte. 2 N, 61061 | 815/732–6761 or 800/468–4222 | AE, D, DC, MC, V | $–$$

Savanna

Mississippi Palisades State Park Near the confluence of the Mississippi and Apple rivers, this 2,500-acre park has steep cliffs and bluffs that provide panoramic views of the river valley. Caves and ravines are filled with wildflowers and wildlife. | 16327A Rte. 84, 61074 | 815/273–2731 | dnr.state.il.us | Daily sunrise–sunset.

A TOUR OF SOUTHERN ILLINOIS HISTORY
FROM COLLINSVILLE TO CARBONDALE

Distance: 100–150 mi   Time: 2 days
Overnight Breaks: Chester, Carbondale

Southern Illinois's heritage and the era spanning early Indian settlers and early-19th-century Americans are the focus of this drive. Southern Illinois, particularly along the Mississippi, is noted for its fall color. Be forewarned—the area's summers can be hot and sticky.

❶ The tour starts outside of Collinsville, at **Cahokia Mounds State Historic Site.** Native Americans who lived here between AD 900 and 1350 built an enormous city covering 6 square mi, with a population of more than 20,000; it was the largest city north of Mexico at the time. Monks Mound, one of the more than 60 ceremonial mounds that remain, is the largest prehistoric earthwork in North America.

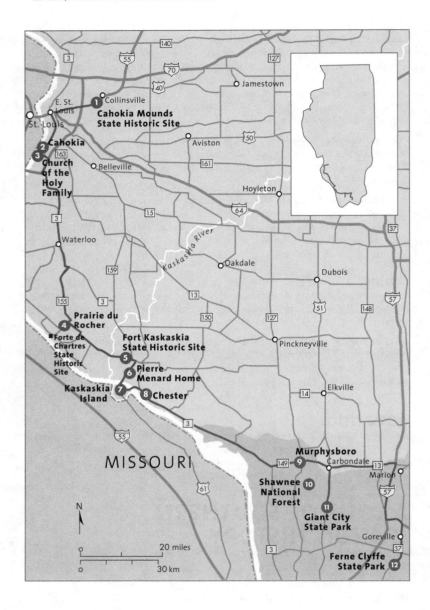

❷ To get to the town of **Cahokia,** take I–55 south through East St. Louis and switch to Route 3. The town is the oldest community in Illinois, founded in 1699 by French-Canadian missionaries. The courthouse at the **Cahokia Courthouse State Historic Site** was originally used as a residence by French colonists. Built in 1737, it's the oldest building in Illinois. You can visit both the courthouse and its visitor center.

❸ Also in Cahokia is the stone-and-wood **Church of the Holy Family,** the oldest church in Illinois, built in 1799. Off-season visits are by appointment only.

❹ Forty miles south of Cahokia is the small town of **Prairie du Rocher,** site of **Fort de Chartres State Historic Site.** The French built the fort in the 1750s and surrendered to the British in 1765. Only one original structure—the powder magazine—still stands; the rest of the garrison has been reconstructed.

❺ Your next stop is the fort and park at **Fort Kaskaskia State Historic Site.** Built by the French on a bluff overlooking the Mississippi during the French and Indian War, it burned in 1766. Also on the site is **Garrison Hill Cemetery,** which contains the graves of some 3,000 early settlers. The graves were moved from their original location to protect them from Mississippi flood waters.

❻ At the foot of the hill where the fort stood, the first lieutenant governor of Illinois built "the Mount Vernon of the West." The French-colonial **Pierre Menard Home** overlooks the river and was built in 1802. Here you can see the mansion's original furnishings and artifacts.

❼ Just south of the home is the broad, flat **Kaskaskia Island**—the only part of Illinois that lies west of the Mississippi. The original Kaskaskia settlement was the first capital of Illinois, but the capital moved to Vandalia not long after statehood was granted. The town struggled continuously against Mississippi flooding, but was eventually washed away during an 1881 flood; during this flood, the river cut a new channel to the east of the town, creating the island. In the middle of the island, in a little pavilion, is the **Kaskaskia Bell State Memorial.** Although it was a gift to French settlers by Louis XV of France, American residents rechristened it "the Liberty Bell of the West." It was fished from the river after the 1881 flood and set in its current location.

❽ Take a break from the historic and venture into a more fanciful realm in **Chester,** just east of Kaskaskia on Route 3. The statue that overlooks the mighty Mississippi in Chester's downtown Segar Park is *Popeye.* The Sailor Man's creator, Elzie Segar, was born in Chester.

❾ Route 3 intersects with Route 149, which will take you into **Murphysboro.** From here you can pick up Route 13, which leads to **Carbondale,** a good base for exploring the next two points on the tour.

❿ The **Shawnee National Forest** sprawls across the southern tip of the state from the Mississippi to the Ohio River. It contains numerous state parks, lakes, and natural areas. Driving through it can take hours or days, depending on your stamina and curiosity. The Little Grand Canyon, off Route 149 near Murphysboro, has stunningly steep canyon walls and a 3½-mi hiking trail that cuts through them.

⓫ **Giant City State Park** is 12 mi south of Carbondale. The park's unusual and imposing blocky stone formations inspired its name.

⓬ To venture farther into the Shawnee National Forest, go east from Carbondale on Route 13, get onto I–57, and travel south to I–24. Take I–24 south to I–57 and pass through Goreville; beyond that lies **Ferne Clyffe State Park.** This park, too, has trails that lead through beautiful rock formations. Ferne Clyffe's proximity to the interstate allows you once again to pick up I–57, which cuts back up through the middle of the state and connects with other main arteries.

For a quick—although less scenic—route back to the tour's starting point, take I–57 North to Mount Vernon; there you can pick up I–64 and take that west to the Cahokia Mounds area. This route takes less than 90 minutes.

Cahokia

Cahokia Courthouse State Historic Site. Learn about the state's history through interactive exhibits at this courthouse, the oldest building in Illinois. | 107 Elm St. | 618/332–1782 | state.il.us/hpa/hs/courthouse.htm | Donations accepted | Wed.–Sun. 9–5.

Church of the Holy Family. Built in 1799, this is the state's oldest continually operating church. Traditional Latin masses are held here at 9 AM each Sunday. | 116 Church St. | 618/337–4548 | Donations accepted | June–Aug., daily 10–4; Sept.–May, by appointment only.

Carbondale

Bald Knob Cross of Peace. At 111 feet, this is the world's largest man-made cross and is visible for more than 50 mi. The view of the Mississippi River and Ozarks of Missouri is more than worth the drive up the winding, narrow road, but you might also find inspiration in the story of how the cross was built, which is told in the visitor center. Easter Sunrise services draw thousands of visitors. | Rte. 127, 6 mi south of Carbondale; watch for signs | 618/833–8672 | www.shawneeheartland.com/baldknob.html | Free | Daily 24 hrs.

Giant City State Park. More than a million visitors a year enjoy the unique geological formations of sandstone that appear as though giants laid out streets and paths here, thus the name Giant City. The 4,000-acre park has 23 mi of nature trails and 12 mi of equestrian trails to enjoy the ferns, flowering trees, and bubbling streams that crisscross the paths of stone. | 235 Giant City Rd., Makanda, 12 mi south of Carbondale | 618/457–4836 | dnr.state.il.us | Free | Daily 24 hrs.

Lodging

Best Inn. Near Giant City State Park and Crab Orchard National Wildlife Refuge, this motel is only 3 mi from Southern Illinois University. The large spacious lobby is filled with wildlife motifs from nearby Crab orchard. Cable TV, pool. | 1345 E. Main St., 62901 | 618/529–4801 | fax 618/529–7212 | www.bestinn.com | 82 rooms | CP | AE, D, DC, MC, V | $

Giant City Lodge. Part of Shawnee National Forest, the one- and two-room sandstone-and-white timber cabins that comprise this lodge sit on the highest point in the park and are surrounded by lush forests. The lodge is on the National Register of Historic Places. Restaurant, some refrigerators, cable TV, pool, hiking, horseback riding, bar, piano, shop, meeting rooms. | 460 Giant City Lodge Rd., Makanda, 12 mi south of Carbondale off U.S. 51, 62958 | 618/457–4921 | fax 618/457–4921 | dnr.state.il.us | 34 cabins | Closed mid-Dec.–Jan. | AE, DC, MC, V | $–$$

Chester

Fort Kaskaskia State Historic Site. Explore the remains of Fort Kaskaskia, built by the French in 1733, as you walk in this 275-acre park, which also has excellent views of the Mississippi River. | 4372 Park Rd., Ellis Grove | 618/859–3741 | Donations accepted | Wed.–Sun. 8–4.

Pierre Menard Home State Historic Site. Built around 1802, this French-colonial house overlooking the Mississippi River was the home of the first lieutenant governor of Illinois. | 4230 Kaskaskia Rd., Ellis Grove | 618/859–3031 | Donations accepted | Wed.–Sun. 8–4.

Popeye Statue. Looking out over the Mississippi River in Segar Memorial Park, this statue of Popeye is a monument to Chester native Elzie Segar, who created the famous cartoon character. The park is the site of the annual Popeye Picnic held each September, which includes parades, spinach-eating contests, and look-like contests for Popeye, Olive Oyle, and Sweet Pea. | Rte. 150 at the river bridge | 618/826–4567 | Daily 24 hrs.

Lodging

Best Western Reids Inn. On partially wooded grounds, this standard motel is 2 mi from the Popeye Statue, 2½ mi from the Mississippi River, and 10 mi from Fort Kaskaskia. In-room data ports, cable TV, some in-room VCRs, pool, hot tub, gym, laundry facilities, business services. | 2150 State St. (Rte. 150), 62233, 1 mi east of downtown | 618/826–3034 or 877/826–4701 | fax 618/826–3034 | www.bestwestern.com | 46 rooms | CP | AE, D, DC, MC, V | $

Goreville

Ferne Clyffe State Park. The abundance of ferns and rare geological features at this park are best seen on the many hiking trails around the cliffs. The park has 18 trails, including an equestrian trail, that range in length from ¼ mi to 8 mi. | 4372 Park Rd. | 618/995–2411 | dnr.state.il.us | Free | Daily 24 hrs.

Prairie du Rocher

Fort de Chartres. Named in honor of Louis duc de Chartres, son of the regent of France, this 1720 stone fort was the seat of the French-colonial government. | 1340 Rte. 155, 4 mi west of town | 618/284–7230 | state.il.us/hpa/hs/dechartres.htm | Donations accepted | Wed.–Sun. 9–5.

Dining

La Maison du Rocher Country Inn. French. In a limestone, tile-floor dining room with wrought-iron chandeliers, you can satisfy your appetite for hearty fare from the Alsatian countryside with sausage dishes, roast pork with an herb dressing, and highly seasoned bouillons. Breakfast served Friday–Sunday. | 2 Duclos St. | 618/284–3463 | Closed Mon. | AE, MC, V | $$–$$$$

INDIANA

UPLANDS & DOWN UNDER
EXPLORING INDIANA'S SOUTHERN HIGHLANDS AND CAVES

Distance: 135 mi   Time: 4 days
Overnight Breaks: Bloomington, French Lick, Nashville

Unlike northern Indiana, which was flattened by prehistoric glaciers, the landscape dips and swells south of Indianapolis. Here century-old small towns nestle in narrow valleys amid dense forests and limestone cave systems. These hills and hollows saw a constant flow of settlers headed for the western frontier during the first half of the 19th century. Traveling on the Ohio River and following animals' trails, some settlers pressed west, while others—including many European immigrants—settled down and established towns that today reflect their ethnic roots. State parks and forests protect much of the hilly terrain. The Hoosier National Forest covers a wide corridor stretching south from Lake Monroe to the Ohio River.

❶ The history of **Jeffersonville,** one of the state's oldest cities, is inextricably linked with that of the Ohio River. Stop at the **Howard Steamboat Museum** to study the history of the Howard Shipyards, Jeffersonville's premier boatbuilder from 1834 to 1941. The museum is housed in the 1890 mansion of the company's owner, Edmonds J. Howard.

❷ Leaving the museum, follow Market Street 1³/₄ mi west until it becomes East Riverside Avenue, and continue ³/₄ mi to the entrance of **Falls of the Ohio State Park and Interpretive Center,** 220 acres of shoreline fossil beds.

❸ Four miles west of Falls of the Ohio on I–64, you come to **New Albany,** which grew to become the state's largest city by 1850 on the strength of Ohio River traffic. Along Mansion Row downtown are gracious homes from the town's golden era. The 20,000-square-foot Second Empire **Culbertson Mansion State Historic Site** has a rosewood staircase, marble fireplaces, and crystal chandeliers.

❹ At the **Forest Discovery Center,** 6 mi northwest of New Albany, a walk-through exhibit and displays explore the topics of wood and wood processing.

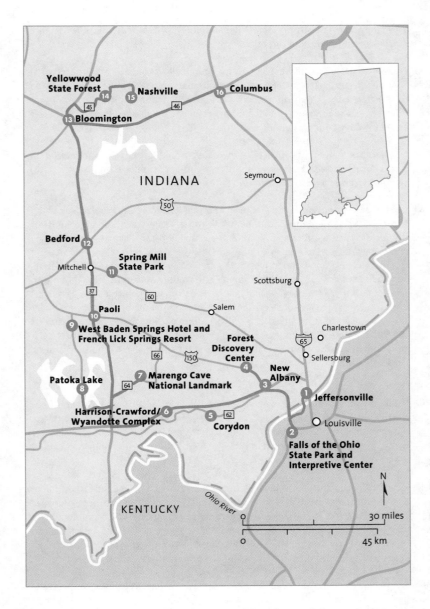

⑤ Continue south along I–64 for about 3 mi to **Corydon,** the state's first capital between 1816 and 1825. Several sites here evoke the state's early days, including the modest blue limestone state capitol building, **Governor Hendricks's Headquarters** with the **Constitution Elm** on its grounds, the **Posey House Museum,** and the **Battle of Corydon Memorial Park.**

⑥ The **Harrison-Crawford/Wyandotte Complex** is composed of three adjacent proper-ties: the **Wyandotte Caves State Recreation Area,** the **Wyandotte Woods State Recre-ation Area,** and the 24,000-acre **Harrison-Crawford State Forest,** one of the state's largest forests. Its hills permit fine views of the Ohio River valley. Tours of the

Wyandotte caves last between 45 minutes and all day; some are easy and others require crawling, scrambling, and climbing.

7 From Wyandotte go 4 mi west on I–64 to Exit 92. Follow Route 66 North about 9 mi to Marengo, site of 122-acre **Marengo Cave National Landmark,** a wide trunk-passage cave that reaches through limestone hills. Two guided tours explore the formation-filled caverns. You can rent canoes and kayaks for paddles down the scenic Blue River at nearby **Cave Country Canoes.**

8 Northwest of Marengo is **Patoka Lake,** the state's second-largest reservoir. Seven state recreation areas with campgrounds, hiking and bridle trails, paved bicycle trails, swimming, and picnic areas surround the sprawling lake.

9 **West Baden Springs Hotel** and **French Lick Springs Resort** were once rivals, spawning towns of the same names. Long before the first settlers arrived, great herds of buffalo stopped at the natural mineral springs and salt licks at what is today known as the town of **French Lick.** As early as the 1840s, tourists started making the trek to the grand hotel at French Lick to partake of the mineral waters there. Soon a huge bottling plant was capping Pluto Water, a sulfurous brew thought to possess curative powers. In the early 1900s, the town was known as the "Las Vegas of the Midwest" because of its elegant casinos. Though the hotel has changed over the years, it is still in business as a golf and tennis resort and spa. The luxurious West Baden Hotel, built in 1902 less than 1 mi away, is topped by a magnificent six-story dome; you can't stay there, but you can tour the structure and its formal gardens. Until 1966, when the Houston Astrodome was erected, the hotel's free-span dome was the largest in the world.

10 **Paoli** is a county seat with a majestic towered courthouse atop a hill. Quakers from North Carolina settled Paoli and named the town for the 12-year-old son of the governor of North Carolina, who had died shortly before. The courthouse was built in 1850 and the clock was added in 1856. The town calls itself the "Dogwood Capital of Indiana."

11 From Paoli, head north for 12 mi on Route 37, then 3 mi east on Route 60 to 1,319-acre **Spring Mill State Park,** where rocky creeks wind through an 80-acre area known as Donaldson's Woods Nature Preserve. Underground, you can float down a subterranean river in one of the park's two cave systems. A reconstructed village dating back to 1814 has a gristmill and a half dozen buildings. The park also pays homage to a local space-age hero with the Virgil I. Grissom State Memorial.

12 Sited roughly in the center of a wide band of limestone that stretches across the state, **Bedford** is known as the "Limestone Capital of the World." Housed in the 1926 offices of Bedford's Indiana Limestone Company, the **Land of Limestone** exhibit documents quarrying and stonecutting in Lawrence County since the 1850s with photographs, tools, and artifacts. Indiana limestone was used when Chicago was rebuilt after the Great Fire of 1871, in 35 state capitol buildings, and in many buildings in Washington, D.C. Lawrence County driving and walking tours take you to residential neighborhoods, city parks, and cemeteries full of richly detailed stone carvings; the Empire Hole here was where the stone used in the Empire State Building was quarried. In **Green Hill Cemetery** don't miss the 1917 limestone monument of stone carver Louis Baker, with a stonecutter's workbench complete with tools. At **Bluespring Caverns** a 1-mi boat tour takes you down the 20-mi-long Myst'ry River, one of the world's longest subterranean streams.

13 The lush green countryside continues to **Bloomington.** The handsome beaux-arts-style **Monroe County Courthouse,** built in 1902, towers over the low-slung downtown. The center city encompasses 11 blocks and a variety of boutiques, galleries, specialty shops, restaurants, and live music clubs. **Fountain Square,** a small shopping mall, hides behind period storefronts with a view of the courthouse square.

Indiana University was established three blocks from the square in 1820. The world's largest student union, the **Indiana Memorial Union** sits in the middle of campus, housing a 190-room hotel, seven dining areas, a bookstore, bowling lanes, a billiards room, a hair salon, and the IMU Gallery. Among the landmarks on the wooded campus are the glass-and-stone I. M. Pei–designed **Indiana University Art Museum,** which has more than 33,000 artworks from the Byzantine era to the times of Claude Monet and Pablo Picasso. **Lilly Library** is known internationally for its rare-books collection. The **Monroe County Historical Society** is in an old Carnegie library building. The **Wylie House** was built in 1835 as the home of the university's first president, Andrew Wylie. On the far north edge of campus, the **Hilltop Garden and Nature Center** is home to one of America's oldest youth gardening programs, established in 1948, as well as display flower gardens.

14 **Yellowwood State Forest,** 13 mi east of Bloomington via Route 46, is a patch of pine, oak, and tulip poplars on the Brown County hills. A quiet lake invites boaters.

15 Leave Yellowwood on Route 46 and proceed about 5 mi east to **Nashville.** This rural village has retained its rustic airs since it caught the eyes of artists nearly a century ago. Today,

INDIANA RULES OF THE ROAD

License Requirements: To drive in Indiana you must be at least 16 years old and have a valid driver's license.

Right Turn on Red: Throughout the state, a right turn on red is permitted after a full stop, unless otherwise indicated by a no-turn-on-red sign.

Speed Limits: The speed limit on most interstate highways is 65 mph, except for portions of road that travel through urban or congested areas. Watch for road signs as the speed limit can change often and quickly.

Seat-Belt & Helmet Laws: Drivers and front-seat passengers must wear seat belts. Children under the age of 5 must use a federally approved child safety seat. Only motorcyclists under the age of 18 are required to wear helmets.

Other Regulations: The legal blood-alcohol concentration limit in Indiana is .08%. Passengers in a vehicle cannot have an open container of alcohol in their possession.

For More Information: Indiana Department of Transportation | www.in.gov/dot. Indiana State Police | 317/232–8248 | ww.in.gov/isp.

artists rub elbows with mobs of tourists in the tiny four-block center of town. Along nearby country roads, log cabins peek through the woods—Brown County claims some 500 of them. Hand-painted signs point down shady lanes to artists' studios. It was a scene like this that attracted Adolph Shulz, an artist searching for the "authentic American landscape," to Brown County at the turn of the 20th century. In 1907, the most prominent figure of the Brown County art colony, Theodore Clement Steele, built a studio and home, the House of the Singing Winds, which is now part of the **T. C. Steele State Historic Site.** On the south edge of town is 15,400-acre **Brown County State Park** with horseback riding, two lakes, trails, and many miles of scenic road.

16 Fifteen miles east of Nashville via Route 46 is **Columbus,** known as the "Athens of the Midwest." Notable contemporary architects have designed more than 50 buildings here, and historic buildings along the brick streets sparkle as if they were new. One- and two-hour guided tours and self-guided tour maps are available at the **Columbus Area Visitor Center,** where displays give an overview of the community and its architectural development. The **Bartholomew County Historical Museum,** in the brick McEwen-Samuels-Marr Home, traces the town's early history in two galleries with permanent and rotating exhibits.

Bedford

Bluespring Caverns. High vaulted passageways is one of the trademarks of this network of caverns, as is one of the world's longest underground streams, the Myst'ry River, which flows for some 20 mi through the main cavern. The main cavern can be viewed on foot from a paved walkway and viewing platform or by boat on a one-hour guided tour of the underground river. | Rte. 11 (Bluespring Caverns Rd.), 4 mi south of Bedford | 812/279–9471 | www.bluespringcaverns.com | $12 | Memorial Day–Oct., daily 9–5; Apr. and May, weekends 9–5.

Green Hill Cemetery. The cemetery on the southwest edge of town has some of the finest examples of limestone carving in the county, with ornate and personalized monuments such as the Lewis Baker monument, which depicts the stone carver's workbench and tools. | 1202 18th St. | 812/275–7637 | www.limestonecountry.com/GreenHillMap.html | Free | Daily dawn–dusk.

Hoosier National Forest. The state's only national forest covers 196,000 acres, with two huge parcels near Bloomington and Columbus and the other stretching south from Bedford to the Ohio River. Some 230 mi of hiking, mountain biking, and equestrian trails crisscross hills that range in height from 400 feet to more than 930 feet. The terrain is surprisingly diverse, from high ridges and hills along the Ohio River to underground cave and karst systems, open meadows, and old-growth forests. | 811 Constitution Ave. | 812/275–5987 | www.fs.fed.us/r9/hoosier/ | $4 | Daily 24 hrs.

Jackson-Washington State Forest. About 17,000 acres of forest are spread across an area known as the "Knobs," sugarloaf hills that poke up above the flat farm fields. They are considered miniature mountains in the Hoosier state, and they afford panoramic, 300-foot vistas. The rugged 1-mi hike to Pinnacle Peak is well worth the effort. Another 20 mi of trails, from moderate to rugged, lace the Knobs area. There's a beach and boating at Starve Hollow State Recreation Area, next to the forest. | 1278 E. Rte. 250, Brownstown, 23 mi east of Bedford | 812/358–2160 | www.in.gov/dnr/forestry | Free | Daily 24 hrs.

Land of Limestone Exhibit. Vintage black-and-white photographs, stonecutters' tools, architectural drawings, and other artifacts trace Lawrence County's limestone industry. In the 1850s, as quarries were opened in the countryside around Bedford and Oolitic, Lawrence County began supplying the nation with building material for its monuments;

the National Cathedral, the Empire State Building, and many of the country's state capitols are built of Indiana limestone. The exhibit is on the north side of Bedford. | Bedford College Center, 405 I St. | 812/275–7637 or 800/798–0769 | Free | Weekdays 9–4:30, Sat. 9–11:30.

★**Spring Mill State Park.** In a 1,319-acre wooded preserve next to a trickling creek is a re-created 1814 pioneer village and gristmill built of limestone and timbers. You can explore Twin Cave by boat and Donaldson's Cave on foot. The park also includes 80 acres of virgin forest and woodsy Spring Mill Inn. Leap ahead to the space age at the park's Grissom Memorial, which displays astronaut Virgil "Gus" Grissom's space suit and the Gemini III space capsule. | Hwy. 60, Mitchell, 13 mi south of Bedford | 812/849–4129 | www.in.gov/dnr/parklake | Park free, cave tours $3 | Daily 7–11.

Dining
Mamma's Mexican and Italian Restaurant. American. Mexican, Italian, and American food are on the menu of this small restaurant, which began as a burger joint. Menu items include sandwiches and steak, chimichangas and burritos, and pasta. | 1701 M St. | 812/275–0684 | Reservations not accepted | D, MC, V | ¢–$

Stoll's Restaurant. American. Fried chicken is always on the menu at this Amish buffet. Meat entrées might be roast beef, meat loaf, barbecued pork, barbecued beef, barbecued ribs, beef stew, or ham and beans. Friday's buffet includes seafood. Everything is made from scratch, including the corn bread. You can also order from a menu of sandwiches, burgers, steaks, pork chops, catfish, shrimp, and baked fish. Most of the restaurant has good views; there's a main dining room with tables and booths, and a loft upstairs. Breakfast served. | 1801 Plaza Dr. | 812/279–8150 | Closed Sun. | MC, V | ¢

Bloomington
Fountain Square Mall. Behind nearly a block of historic storefronts facing the courthouse downtown, Fountain Square is a multilevel mall of small, individually owned specialty shops, galleries, delis, and cafés. | Fountain Sq. | 812/336–7100 | Free | Mon.–Sat. 10–8, Sun. 1–5.

Indiana University. The university has a wooded 1,860-acre campus in the center of town; many Tudor-style brick buildings here date back to 1820. The student union and many of the newer buildings are built of Indiana limestone. | 107 S. Indiana Ave. | 812/855–4848 | www.indiana.edu | Free | Daily 7 AM–midnight.

Hilltop Garden and Nature Center. This peaceful, 5-acre area near the Indiana University campus has community gardens, a greenhouse, ponds, and flower beds. | 2301 E. 10th St. | 812/855–2799 | Free | Weekdays 1–5.

Indiana Memorial Union. The university's student and faculty center, this is the largest student union building in the United States. It includes a hotel, restaurants, recreational facilities, a bookstore, and plenty of lounge areas. The massive limestone building overlooks an area known as Dunn Meadow in the center of campus. | 900 E. 7th St. | 812/856–6381 or 800/209–8145 | www.indiana.edu | Free | Daily 6:30–10.

Indiana University Art Museum. The world-renowned firm of I. M. Pei and Partners designed the soaring angular building that houses a museum with temporary exhibits and a 33,000-piece permanent collection of fine art and artifacts. | Fine Arts Plaza, 1133 E. 7th St. | 812/855–5445 | www.indiana.edu/~iuam | Free | Tues.–Sat. 10–5, Sun. noon–5.

Lilly Library. This seven-story building contains 400,000 books, many of them rare, more than 7 million rare or historical manuscripts, and 100,000 pieces of sheet music. Among the library's holdings on display is a copy of the Gutenberg Bible printed before 1456. The collection also includes the Coverdale Bible of 1535 (the first English printed bible), and original prints from John James Audubon's *Birds of America*. | Fine

Arts Plaza, 1200 E. 7th St. | 812/855–2452 | www.indiana.edu/~liblilly | Free | Weekdays 9–6, Sat. 9–1.

Monroe County Courthouse. A distinctive fish weather vane tops this beaux-arts-style limestone courthouse on a knoll in the center of downtown. Inside, a stained-glass window pierces the domed rotunda ceiling. | Courthouse Sq. | 800/800–0037 | www.cfcincorporated.com | Free | Weekdays 8–4.

Monroe County Historical Society. A Carnegie Library dating from 1918 houses this museum near downtown. Permanent exhibits trace the area's natural development and the growth of limestone quarrying, as well as its history from early settlement through the industrial era and up to the present. Temporary exhibits focus on cultural subjects, including fashion and farming. | 202 E. 6th St. | 812/332–2517 | www.kiva.net/~mchm/museum.htm | Free | Tues.–Sat. 10–4, Sun. 1–4.

Wylie House Museum. The stately 1835 brick Georgian home of the university's first president, Andrew Wylie, is filled with period furnishings, described on guided tours. The garden dates from the period the house was built. Special Christmas programs are presented. It's near downtown. | 317 E. 2nd St. | 812/855–6224 | www.indiana. edu/~libwylie | Free | Mar.–Nov., Tues.–Sat. 10–2.

Dining

Irish Lion. Irish. Behind an old storefront a block from the courthouse square near the center of town, this lively eatery serves American and Irish fare. Dark hardwood floors and old mirrors furnish the interior. Entrées include fresh oysters, mussels, clams, salmon, lamb, beef, poultry, and Irish pub–inspired stews. Beer and ale is served by the pint— or you might try a "yard" of beer. There's live Irish music at night. | 212 W. Kirkwood Ave. | 812/336–9076 | AE, D, MC, V | $$

Le Petit Café. Continental. Bistro cuisine fills the menu of this casual intimate place downtown, which has French posters on the walls. Try the steak Diane or the homemade pasta. Beer and wine only. | 308 W. 6th St. | 812/334–9747 | Closed Mon. | MC, V | $$

Limestone Grille. Continental. A hand-carved limestone bas-relief covers an entire wall of this corner storefront restaurant whose menu might include rainbow trout, New York strip steak, pork chops, filet mignon, prime-cut rib eye, or chicken française. For dessert try the bittersweet chocolate almond torte with raspberry sauce. Beer and wine only. | 2920 E. Covenanter Dr. | 812/335–8110 | www.limestonegrille.com | Closed Sun. and Mon. | AE, D, MC, V | $$–$$$$

Michael's Uptown Café. Eclectic. Near the center of Bloomington, this popular breakfast spot resembles a bustling big-city deli and draws crowds for lunch and dinner. The cooking is inventive, influenced by French, Cajun, and Mediterranean cuisines; the soups are noteworthy, as are the interesting omelets. | 102 E. Kirkwood Ave. | 812/ 339–0900 | AE, D, DC, MC, V | $–$$$

Nick's English Hut. American. Open since 1927, this tavern a couple of blocks from the Indiana University campus is a favorite hangout among locals and students. Booths line the perimeter of the room and framed news clippings and photos hang on the walls. There are several dining rooms and bars, many televisions, pool tables, and seating for up to 500. The fare includes burgers, pizza, and buffalo wings, or entrées like New York strip steak, grilled yellowfin tuna, and jambalaya. Nick's is open until 2 AM Monday through Saturday; until midnight on Sunday. | 423 E. Kirkwood Ave. | 812/332–4040 | www.nicksenglishhut.com | Reservations not accepted | AE, D, DC, MC, V | $–$$

Lodging

Best Western Fireside Inn. On the east side of town and convenient to most area attractions is this comfortable, modern two-story hotel. Indiana University is 2 mi away and

Lake Monroe is 5 mi away. Cable TV, pool, laundry facilities, some pets allowed. | 4501 E. 3rd St., 47401 | 812/332–2141 or 800/528–1234 | www.bestwestern.com | 96 rooms | CP | AE, D, DC, MC, V | ¢–$$

Canyon Inn. The three-story Canyon Inn, part of McCormick's Creek State Park, was originally the Denkewalter Sanitarium. In the 1920s the building was remodeled and given an exterior veneer of brick. Since then, additional wings, a swimming pool, and a recreation center have been added. Restaurant, pool. | State Rd. 46, Spencer 47460 | 812/829–4881 | fax 812/829–1467 | 72 rooms | AE, D, MC, V | ¢–$

Courtyard by Marriott. Across from the Convention Center and two blocks south of the courthouse square shops and restaurants is this five-story hotel. The guest rooms include dark-wood furniture and walls are paneled. Dining room, in-room data ports, some microwaves, some refrigerators, cable TV, indoor pool, gym, hot tub, laundry facilities, business services. | 310 S. College Ave., 47403 | 812/335–8000 or 800/321–2211 | fax 812/336–9997 | www.courtyard.com/bmgcy | 112 rooms, 5 suites | AE, D, DC, MC, V | $

Grant Street Inn. Five blocks from Monroe Country Courthouse, this two-story yellow clapboard home dating from the late 1800s is now a modern lodging. Guest rooms are traditional and include antique furnishings. Some have fireplaces. Some in-room hot tubs. | 310 N. Grant St., 47408 | 812/334–2353 or 800/328–4350 | fax 812/331–8673 | www.grantstinn.com | 24 rooms | AE, D, MC, V | $$–$$$

Hampton Inn. On the outskirts of town, in a row of newer motels, this four-story hotel has bright airy rooms with dark-wood furniture. Some rooms have exercise equipment. There are 25-inch TVs and voice mail in all rooms. In-room data ports, some in-room hot tubs, cable TV, indoor pool, gym, business services, some pets allowed. | 2100 N. Walnut St., 47401 | 812/334–2100 | fax 812/334–8433 | www.hamptoninn.com | 131 rooms | CP | AE, D, DC, MC, V | $–$$

Columbus

Bartholomew County Historical Society. A restored 19th-century brick house mounts exhibitions in two galleries and documents the county's history from pioneer times to the 20th century via artifacts, art, and a Victorian parlor. | 524 3rd St. | 812/372–3541 | barthist.com | Free | Tues.–Fri. 9–4.

Columbus Area Visitor Center. *Yellow Neon Chandelier* and *Persian Window,* works by internationally recognized glass artist Dale Chihuly, are the highlights of this two-story house. There's also a gift shop that carries souvenirs, handmade pottery, architectural and children's books, jewelry, glass, and clothing. | 506 5th St. | 812/372–1954 | www.columbus.in.us | Dec.–Feb., Mon.–Sat. 9–5; Mar.–Nov., also Sun. 10–4.

Architectural Tours. Take in the city's architectural landmarks on a tour or pick up maps to use for self-guided tours. | 812/378–2622 or 800/468–6564 | Mar.–Nov., weekdays at 10, Sat. at 10 and 2, Sun. at 11.

The Commons. Architect Cesar Pelli designed this small one-of-a-kind mall in the center of downtown Columbus in 1973. A kinetic sculpture by Jean Tinguely dominates the huge open space at the center. Off to one side is a carpeted play area where kids can climb and slide to their hearts' content. Upstairs are a movie theater and a branch of the Indianapolis Museum of Art. Innovative though it may be, it continues to lose business to large glitzier malls on the outskirts of town. | 4th and Washington Sts. | 812/372–4541 | Mon.–Sat. 9:30–7, Sun. noon–5.

Muscatatuck National Wildlife Refuge. The state's only federally designated wildlife refuge covers 7,802 acres of wetlands, woodlands, and open fields that were once primarily farmland. Otters were introduced in the mid-1990s and trumpeter swans in the late 1990s. The refuge is known for attracting waterfowl year-round and for migrating bald eagles, ospreys, white pelicans, white-faced ibis, American bitterns, and blue herons. There are eight short wildlife viewing trails and a small information center. | 12985 E. U.S. 50, Seymour, 20 mi northeast of Columbus | 812/522–4352 | www.fws.gov/r3pao/muscatuk | Free | Daily dawn–dusk.

Dining

Zaharako's. American. A huge old-fashioned soda fountain with its original pressed-tin ceiling welcomes you to this vintage building. Along with basic cold sandwiches, burgers, dogs, and fries, the kitchen does a great grilled cheese sandwich with chili. For dessert, fountain treats are the order of the day. You eat at 1950s Formica-and-chrome tables and chairs; there are a few tiny antique tables for little kids. Ask a staffer to crank up the antique orchestra music box in back. | 329 Washington St. | 812/379–9329 | Closed Sun. No dinner | No credit cards | ¢

Corydon

Battle of Corydon Memorial Park. On July 9, 1863, General John Hunt Morgan's Confederate troops met the Harrison County Home Guard in Corydon for the only actual Civil War battle on Hoosier soil. The Home Guard troops surrendered. | Rte. 337, 1 mi south of Corydon | 812/738–8236 or 812/738–2137 | Free | Daily 8–5.

Corydon Capitol State Historic Site. Only 40 square feet, the restored 1816 capitol building in downtown Corydon is built of hand-hewn timbers and blue limestone quarried locally. Plaques inside trace the drafting of the state's first constitution and Corydon's early years as state capital. A block from away is the preserved federal-style home of the state's second governor, William Hendricks. Also at the site is the trunk of the Constitution Elm, a tree that provided shade for the delegates as they labored to draft statehood papers in 1816. | 202 E. Walnut St. | 812/738–4890 | www.ai.org/dnr | Free | Mid-Mar.–mid-Dec., Tues.–Sat. 9–5, Sun. 1–5; mid-Dec.–mid-Mar., call for hrs.

Harrison-Crawford/Wyandotte Complex. The Wyandotte Caves, Wyandotte Woods state recreation areas, and the Harrison-Crawford State Forest comprise this large preserve of 24,000 acres. The complex includes southern Indiana's most impressive limestone cave system in rugged, densely forested hill country. Wyandotte Woods has an Olympic-size swimming pool, a nature center, and over a dozen trails suitable for day hikes. There are also 100 mi of designated bridle trails and two fishing lakes. | 7240 Old Forest Rd. | 812/738–8232 | www.state.in.us/dnr/forestry/htmldocs/harcraw.htm | $5 | Daily 7–11.

Marengo Cave National Landmark. View the cave's stunning formations on one of two tours: the Dripstone Tour views soda-straw formations and totem-pole stalagmites; huge flowstone formations are highlights of the Crystal Palace Tour. | I–64, Exit 118 (Georgetown), Marengo, 20 mi west of Corydon; turn right at the end of the exit ramp and go 25 mi on Rte. 64 | 812/365–2705 | www.marengocave.com | $12 | Late May–early Sept., daily 9–6; early Sept.–late May, daily 9:30–5; tours every 30 mins.

Squire Boone Caverns and Village. Rare rim-stone dams and twisted helictite formations dominate this system of caverns, discovered in 1790 by brothers Daniel and Squire Boone. A log-cabin village includes a gristmill, crafts demonstrations, and a display of Native American artifacts. | Rte. 135, 12 mi south of Corydon | 812/732–4381 | www.squireboonecaverns.com | $11 | Tours daily at 10, 12, 2, 4.

Wyandotte Caves. Guided tours of Big Wyandotte Cave vary in length. The spelunking tour, available by reservation only, entails long crawls and climbing; children must be at least 12 years old or in the sixth grade for these tours. If its larger counterpart is too daunting, the smaller, more manageable Little Wyandotte Cave offers a comprehensive view of flowstone and dripstone formations on ½-mi trips that last 30 to 45 minutes.

| 7315 S. Wyandotte Cave Rd., Leavenworth | 812/738–2782 | www.wyandottecaves.com | Tours $11–$48 | May–Sept., daily 9–5.

Dining

Magdalena's. American. Soups made from recipes provided by the owner's Polish grandmother, plus sandwiches, salads, and hot apple dumplings are served in this casual downtown eatery, brightly styled in mauve and green with floral prints on the walls. There's also an ice-cream parlor. Wine only. | 103 Chestnut St. | 812/738–8075 | AE, D, DC, MC, V | $–$$

French Lick

★ **French Lick Springs Resort.** Tourists started coming to the French Lick area in the middle of the 19th century when mineral springs were first tapped on the property and dubbed Pluto Water. A three-story wood-frame hotel was built by 1840. The heyday was in the Roaring Twenties, when Hollywood celebs frequented the resort and its black-tie casinos. The last of the casinos closed in 1949. The surviving multistory buff-color brick hotel dates from 1902. Many of the original fixtures remain, and the 2,600-acre, 475-room resort now offers year-round lodging, recreational activities, and a spa. | 8670 W. Rte. 56 | 812/936–9300 or 800/457–4042 | www.frenchlick.com | Free.

Indiana Railway Museum. A two-hour train ride aboard the old cars of the French Lick West Baden and Southern line takes you to the Hoosier National Forest through deep cuts in the limestone bedrock and the 2,200-foot Burton Tunnel. The museum at the train station displays railroad memorabilia, railroad cars, and engines. | 1 Monon St. | 812/936–2405 or 800/748–7246 | Museum free, train rides $9 | Museum daily 10–4; train departs Apr.–Oct., weekends at 10, 1, and 4, Tues. at 1.

Patoka Lake. A popular spot for fishing, boating, and swimming, the 8,800-acre Patoka is surrounded by seven state recreation areas with 25,800 acres of wooded land. Among the facilities are an archery range, boat ramps, and more than 500 campsites. A nature center has cultural and naturalist programs in summer. Exhibits at the visitor center explore the local wildlife, including bald eagles. | 3084 N. Dillard Rd., Birdseye, 13 mi south of French Lick | 812/685–2464 | www.state.in.us/dnr | Free | Daily dawn–dusk.

Ski Paoli Peaks. One of three downhill ski areas in the state, Paoli Peaks covers 65 acres and a 300-foot vertical drop ribboned by 15 trails. There's snowmaking, plus one quad, three triple, and one double lift. There's night skiing on weekends. | 2798 W. County Rd. 25 S, Paoli, 15 mi east of French Lick | 812/723–4696, 812/723–4698 snow conditions | www.paolipeaks.com | $40 lift ticket | Dec.–mid-Mar., Mon.–Thurs. 10–9:30, Fri. 10–10 and midnight–6 AM, Sat. 9 AM–10 PM and midnight–6 AM, Sun. 9–8.

★ **West Baden Springs Hotel.** At the turn of the 20th century, French Lick Springs Resort and nearby West Baden Springs drew high-rolling movie stars and the well-to-do. In its time, West Baden was the epitome of elegance and it thrived as a resort hotel until the stock market crash of 1929. It fell into disrepair in the years that followed but is undergoing restoration under the supervision of the Historic Landmarks Foundation of Indiana. You can see the magnificent structure and formal gardens on guided one-hour tours. | Rte. 56, West Baden, 2 mi east of French Lick | 317/639–4534 or 800/450–4534 | www.historiclandmarks.org | $10 | Tours on the hr Apr.–Dec., Mon.–Sat. 10–3, Sun. noon–4.

Dining

Beechwood Country Inn. Continental. The main dining room at this inn built in the early 1900s resembles a train club car. There is a fireplace in the main dining room. A seven-course tea or cream tea is served at 2:30 PM in the Tea Room. There's always fresh seafood, along with veal, rack of lamb, French-cut lamb chops, tenderloin fillet, New York strip, and pasta. French onion gratinée and crab bisque are served daily. | 8313 W. State Rd. 56 | 812/936–9012 | Reservations essential | Closed Sun. and Mon. | AE, D, MC, V | $$–$$$

The Villager. American. Home cooking is available in three dining areas here. Five or six daily vegetables go with such main-plate meals as fried chicken, baked steak, chicken and dumplings, and barbecued ribs. Breakfast served. | Hwy. 56, West Baden Springs, 2 mi east of French Lick | 812/936–4926 | No credit cards | ¢–$

Lodging

Beechwood Country Inn. Four striking white columns line the front veranda of this three-story brick home, built in the early 1900s. The Ballard room has a 300-year-old carved bed from an Irish castle, an Italian marble fireplace, a two-person hot tub, a sitting room, and a private balcony. The Club room is accented with rich, dark colors. Ask to see the headboard with elaborately carved cherubs in one of the bedroom suites. Restaurant, cable TV, bar; no kids under 11, no smoking. | 8313 W. State Rd. 56, 47432 | 812/936–9012 | www.beechwoodin.com | 6 rooms | BP | AE, D, MC, V | $$–$$$$

Big Locust Farm Bed and Breakfast. On 60 acres with flower beds and a fishpond, this two-story Victorian-style home with a large front porch is in the Hoosier National Forest. The inn's name comes from a nearby 250-year-old big locust tree, the largest in the state. Hiking; no smoking. | 3295 W. County Rd. 255, Paoli 47454, ¼ mi from Paoli Peaks, 15 mi east of French Lick | 812/723–4856 | 3 rooms | BP | MC, V | $

Braxtan House Inn. Near the courthouse square in Paoli, this huge three-story Queen Anne Victorian structure is actually two houses (1830 and 1893) joined together with bay windows and a wide front porch. Only one room has a claw-footed bathtub; others have showers. Spacious, high-ceilinged rooms are furnished with 19th-century antiques and hand-hooked rugs. No room phones. | 210 N. Gospel St., Paoli 47454, 15 mi east of French Lick | 812/723–4677 or 800/627–2982 | fax 812/723–2112 | www.kiva. net/~braxtan | 6 rooms | BP | AE, D, MC, V | ¢–$

★**French Lick Springs.** Built in 1902, this six-story resort hotel is in downtown French Lick. The guest rooms have retained their early-1900s furnishings. Suites, which have a parlor room, are available. Dining room, room service, in-room data ports, cable TV, driving range, two 18-hole golf courses, miniature golf, 18 tennis courts, 2 pools (1 indoor), gym, hair salon, hot tub, massage, bowling, horseback riding, bar, baby-sitting, children's programs (ages 5–12), business services. | 8670 W. Rte. 56, 47432 | 812/936–9300 or 800/457–4042 | fax 812/936–2100 | www.frenchlick.com | 471 rooms, 27 suites | AE, D, DC, MC, V | $$–$$$

White Oaks Cabins. Six cabins ranging from small cozy retreats for 2 to larger spaces designed for families of 10 are set on 45 acres near Patoka Lake. Cabins are fully furnished with heat and central air-conditioning and fully equipped kitchens. Screened porches, a children's fishing pond, and a screened fish-cleaning station are also included. Picnic area, kitchens, pond, boating, fishing, hiking. | 2140 N. Morgan Rd., Taswell 47175, 16 mi south of French Lick | 812/338–3120 | fax 812/338–3120 | www.patokalake.com | 6 cabins | AE, MC, V | $–$$

Jeffersonville

Howard Steamboat Museum. Models of steamboats and displays of artifacts and tools used to build the craft tell the history of Jeffersonville boatbuilder Howard Shipyards. The museum is in the 1890 mansion of the company's owner, Edmonds J. Howard. Guided tours are available. | 1101 E. Market St. | 812/283–3728 | $5 | Tues.– Sat. 10–4, Sun. 1–4.

Schimpff's Confectionery. Since the 1880s, Schimpff's has been churning out candy. The shop is known for horehound drops, cinnamon Red Hots, and Modjeskas, a caramel-dipped marshmallow confection named for the famous Polish-born actress, Madame Helen Modjeska, who performed in the area in 1883. | 347 Spring St. | 812/283–8367 | Weekdays 10–5, Sat. 10–3.

Dining

Rocky's Italian Grill. Italian. There's a good view of downtown Louisville and the 2nd Street Bridge from this brightly colored restaurant decked with Italian flags. The chicken with pesto dressing, tomatoes, and artichoke hearts is a house special, as is the whole-wheat pizza. Also consider the seafood pasta, lasagna, or spinach manicotti. Kids' menu. | 715 W. Riverside Dr. | 812/282–3844 | AE, D, DC, MC, V | $–$$

Nashville

Bill Monroe Bluegrass Hall of Fame. Memorabilia honoring the late father of bluegrass is displayed here. The Bluegrass Hall of Fame room showcases artists Lester Flatt and Earl Scruggs. Bluegrass mania peaks in May during a weeklong festival. | 5163 Rte. 135 N, Bean Blossom, 5 mi north of Nashville | 812/988–6422 | www.beanblossom.com | $4 | Dec.–Apr., Mon.–Sat. 10–4; May–Nov., Mon.–Sat. 9–5, Sun. 1–5.

Brown County Art Guild. Guild artist-members show their work—primarily landscapes of the surrounding countryside—in the guild's gallery. | 48 S. Van Buren St. | 812/988–6185 | Free | Mar.–Dec., Mon.–Sat. 10–5, Sun. 11–5; Jan. and Feb. by appointment.

Brown County Historical Museum. A pioneer cabin, log jail, and doctor's office from the mid-1800s are among the displays here; catch spinning and weaving demonstrations in the loom room. | Museum La. | 812/988–6089 | $1.50 | May–Oct., weekends 1–5.

Brown County State Park. With 15,500 acres, this rolling woodland preserve is Indiana's largest state park. A covered bridge marks one entrance, and there are six scenic overlooks along the park's ridgetop roads and a fire tower you can climb for even more amazing hill-behind-hill vistas. Weed Patch Hill is among the tallest summits in Indiana at 1,058 feet. Ten miles of trails skirt two lakes, and a special campground is reserved for equestrians. | Rte. 46 | 812/988–6406 | www.browncountystatepark.com | $5 | Daily 7–11.

Little Nashville Opry. Boot-stomping fun awaits at this northern relative of the real McCoy. Though the show itself is dubbed "little," the headliners here are anything but—unless you'd call Loretta Lynn and the Statler Brothers minor. | 703 State Rd. 46 | 812/988–2235 | Call for ticket prices | Mar.–Nov., Fri. and Sat.

Nashville Express Train Tours. The narrated 20-minute, 2½-mi tour on a simulated steam train is a fine introduction to the historic sites and local businesses in Nashville. You can watch a video while you're on board. Tours depart from most major hotels in town. | Franklin St. at Van Buren St. | 812/988–2355 or 812/988–2308 | $4 | Apr.–Nov., daily every ½ hr 9–5.

T. C. Steele State Historic Site. In 1907, impressionist painter T. C. Steele moved to Brown County with his second wife, Selma Neubacher Steele, and built a home called the House of the Singing Winds. Steele was inspired by Brown County's tranquil woodsy landscape and spent summers here, becoming one of the leading members of the Brown County Art Colony. The hilltop home and studio are filled with paintings and personal mementos. Four trails, the Dewar Log Cabin, and the 92-acre Selma Steele Nature Preserve are also part of the 211-acre property. | 4220 T. C. Steele Rd. | 812/988–2785 | www.browncountystatepark.com | Free | Tues.–Sat. 9–5, Sun. 1–5.

Yellowwood State Forest. At 22,000 acres Yellowwood is one of the larger state forests. Boat rentals on the quiet lake are available. | Yellow and Lake Drs. on State Hwy. 46 | 812/988–7945 | www.browncountystatepark.com | Free | Daily 24 hrs.

Dining

Hobnob Restaurant. American. In Nashville's oldest commercial building, a big white storefront on a downtown corner, Hobnob is a favorite breakfast spot that also serves country-style lunches and dinners, including salads, chicken, and steak. Wine only. | 17 W. Main St. | 812/988–4114 | AE, D, MC, V | $–$$

Nashville House. American. Paintings by Brown County artists line the walls and red-checked tablecloths grace the tables of this rustic family restaurant in the heart of downtown Nashville. Specialties include fried chicken and roast turkey dinners with fried biscuits and apple butter. Kids' menu. | 87 N. Van Buren St. | 812/988–4554 | Closed late Dec.–early Jan. and Tues. Nov.–Sept. | D, MC, V | $$

The Ordinary. Contemporary. Nestled among 350 quaint shops, galleries, and studios, the restaurant serves sandwiches, ribs, and chops. Entertainment Friday and Saturday. Kids' menu. | N. Van Buren St. | 812/988–6166 | Closed Mon. Nov.–Sept. | D, MC, V | $$–$$$

Story Inn. American. Once an 1850s general store, this old-world enclave is known for fine candlelight dining. Try the filet mignon or bourbon strip steak. Seafood and vegetarian dishes are available. | 6404 S. Rte. 135, Story | 812/988–2273 | www.storyinn.com | Reservations essential | Closed Mon. No lunch | $$$–$$$$

Lodging

Abe Martin Lodge. Built of native stone and hand-hewn oak timbers in 1932, the lodge has two spacious lobbies with rustic stone fireplaces. On the south side of town, the main lodge contains 30 rooms; a newer addition has 54. There are 20 newer housekeeping cabins open year-round, and remodeled 1932 cabins open from April until November. Dining room. | Rte. 46, 47448 | 812/988–4418 | fax 812/988–7334 | 84 rooms, 76 cabins | AE, D, MC, V | $–$$

Artists Colony Inn. The three-story wood-frame building, surrounded by gardens and towering trees, sits back off Nashville's busy main street. Reproduction cherry-wood and painted furniture, cupboards, Windsor chairs, and woven coverlets furnish the spare yet comfortable rooms in a palette of deep blue, green, burgundy, and cream. Restaurant, cable TV, hot tub. | 105 S. Van Buren St., 47448 | 812/988–0600 | fax 812/988–9023 | www.artistscolonyinn.com | 20 rooms, 3 suites | AE, MC, V | $–$$$

Brown County Inn. Built in the 1970s, this established motel on the edge of downtown is furnished with antiques, collectibles, and country decor. Restaurant, cable TV, miniature golf, tennis court, indoor-outdoor pool, bar, playground. | 51 State Rd. 46 E, 47448 | 812/988–2291 or 800/772–5249 | fax 812/988–8312 | www.browncountyinn.com | 99 rooms | AE, D, DC, MC, V | $$

Olde Magnolia House. In the heart of Nashville, just one block from most of the shops, is this white Victorian mansion. The homey rooms have queen-size beds, antique furnishings, and in some rooms, gas fireplaces. If you're an early riser, you can enjoy a pre-breakfast coffee and tea service on the porch. All bathrooms are private, though some are across the hall from their respective guest rooms. | 213 S. Jefferson St., 47448 | 812/988–2434 or 877/477–5144 | fax 812/988–2434 | www.theoldemagnoliahouse.com | 4 rooms | D, MC, V | $–$$

Seasons Lodge. On a hillside off the highway, 1½ mi from downtown and across from Brown County State Park, this full-service hotel is nestled among the trees, giving you the feeling of camping out—but in the comfort of a real bed. Rooms are constructed from native stone and painted timbers. Restaurant, room service, cable

TV, indoor-outdoor pool, bar, playground, business services. | 560 Rte. 46 E, 47448 | 812/988–2284 or 800/365–7327 | fax 812/988–7510 | www.seasonslodge.com | 80 rooms | AE, D, DC, MC, V | $–$$

New Albany

Cave Country Canoes. The Blue River is a spring-fed stream that takes on an aqua hue as it runs through limestone bluffs. It was the first river selected for Indiana's Natural and Scenic Rivers System. Canoe and kayak trips here range from half-day, 7-mi trips to two-day and longer excursions. | Milltown | 812/365–2705 | www.cavecountrycanoes.com | $18–$43 | Daily dawn–dusk.

Culbertson Mansion State Historic Site. The 1867 three-story French Second Empire mansion has hand-painted ceilings, a carved rosewood staircase, marble fireplaces, and crystal chandeliers in its 25 rooms. William S. Culbertson was one of Indiana's wealthiest merchants and philanthropists. | 914 E. Main St. | 812/944–9600 | Free | Mar.–Dec., Tues.–Sun. 9–5.

Floyd County Museum. The beaux-arts museum building was the New Albany Public Library from 1904 to 1969. It reopened in 1971 as an art and history museum. Permanent collections depict the pioneer, steamboat, and Civil War eras along the Ohio River. | 201 E. Spring St. | 812/944–7336 | Free | Tues.–Sat. 1–4.

Forest Discovery Center. Visitors can stroll among trees in a glass-enclosed skyway that connects the forest to Koetter Woodworking's state-of-the-art lumber mill and see logs transformed into finished trim products. | 533 Louis Smith Rd., Starlight, 6 mi northwest of New Albany | 812/923–1590 | www.forestcenter.com | $5.50 | Tues.–Sat. 9–5, Sun. 1–5.

Scribner House. Framed in wood, the federal-style two-story home was built in 1814 by Joel and Mary Scribner. Now owned by the local chapter of the Daughters of the American Revolution, the three-bedroom, two-parlor house overlooks the Ohio River. | 201 E. Spring St. | 812/944–7336 or 812/948–2921 | Free | Sept.–July, Tues.–Sat. 10–4; tours by appointment.

Dining

Joe Huber's Family Farm, Orchard and Restaurant. American. What started as a roadside stand in the "Knobs" above New Albany is now a spacious country-style restaurant with specialties like chicken and dumplings with fresh vegetables and fried biscuits. The honeyed ham is also a favorite, as are the desserts, which might include coconut cream pie or peach cobbler. Open-air dining on the patio overlooks a flower and vegetable garden. | 2421 Scottsville Rd., Starlight, 17 mi west of New Albany | 812/923–5255 | www.joehubers.com | MC, V | $–$$

KENTUCKY

FROM LEXINGTON TO DANIEL BOONE COUNTRY
PIONEERS AND MOUNTAIN FOLKWAYS

Distance: 120 mi   Time: 1–2 days
Overnight Break: Middlesboro

Most of this drive is along divided highways, I–75 and Route 25 East. It is a good introduction to mountain culture and to the history of the pioneer settlement of America west of the Appalachians. Boonesborough, surviving portions of the Wilderness Road, and the Cumberland Gap are included. Spring and fall are recommended times to explore this region of Kentucky. The flowering trees and shrubs on the mountainsides are lovely in spring. Fall colors, at their peak in early to mid-October, can rival New England's if the summer hasn't been too dry. You can go in summer, but it will probably be very hot and humid; even at night the mountains can be muggy. Winter travel is not recommended because snow and ice can make the roads hazardous, if not downright impassable.

❶ Start your tour about 20 mi southeast of Lexington at **Fort Boonesborough State Park.** To get there, take I–75 to Exit 95 and follow the signs. The fort, Kentucky's second permanent settlement, has been fully and faithfully reconstructed on a bank of the Kentucky River. It has log cabins, blockhouses, and is outfitted with period furnishings. Resident artisans and actors in pioneer costume reenact life as it would have been at Boonesborough when Boone and his party arrived in 1775.

❷ Consider making a brief stop at **Boone Station State Historic Site** (Rte. 418), a few minutes from Boonesborough. When Daniel Boone left Boonesborough he established this pioneer station. Many Boone family deaths occurred nearby in the Battle of Blue Licks, and Daniel's brothers Samuel and Edward are buried here.

❸ Leaving Boonesborough, take Exit 76 off I–75 to the college town of **Berea,** which is 25 mi south of the Boone settlements. Known as the "Folk Arts and Crafts Capital" of Kentucky, the town could probably contend for this title nationally. More than 50 dulcimer and fiddle makers, jewelers, weavers, quilters, and furniture and cabinet

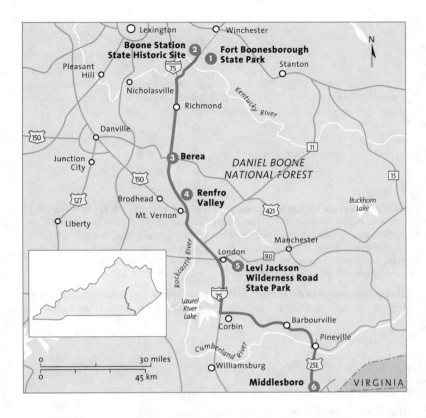

makers have shops lining the streets of the **Old Town.** Drive along Chestnut Street past the campus of **Berea College,** established in 1855 to educate the youth of Appalachia. This private college still provides full-tuition scholarships and only admits low-income students. All students are required to work 10–15 hours per week to help pay their expenses. Some are servers and cooks at **Boone Tavern,** where you should stop for a traditional Southern lunch. Before leaving Berea, stop at **Churchill Weavers,** America's largest and foremost hand-weaving studio. The building, containing a loom room and gift shop, is surrounded by a remarkable rose garden.

❹ As you drive down I–75 you pass **Renfro Valley,** the "Country Music Capital of Kentucky." You can get tickets for a concert on your way back to Lexington. Headliners have included Loretta Lynn, Charley Pride, the Oak Ridge Boys, and Billy Ray Cyrus.

❺ A half hour south of Renfro Valley, east of where the highway crosses through a portion of the Daniel Boone National Forest, is Exit 38 to London. Follow the signs to **Levi Jackson Wilderness Road State Park.** Among the attractions in the park is the **Mountain Life Museum,** open April 1 through October 31. It's a reproduction of a pioneer settlement. Hiking trails include 8½ mi of the original **Wilderness Road,** constructed by Daniel Boone and his party and traveled by more than 200,000 settlers between 1774 and 1776. Also in the 800-acre park is **McHarges's Mill,** built on the banks of the Little Laurel River. The working mill is surrounded by the country's largest collection of millstones.

6 Go back to I–75 and drive 9 mi to Exit 29 at Corbin. This puts you on Route 25 East, from which it's 47 mi to **Middlesboro.** This town near the Cumberland Gap is built in a bowl-shape depression, possibly a meteor crater. The view from the **overlook** at nearby **Cumberland Gap National Historic Park** dramatically shows the tiny break in the mountains where Boone led settlers through to Kentucky. Just outside the entrance to the park is the **Cumberland Gap Tunnel** running under the Cumberland Mountains. Among the longest of its kind in the world, the tunnel takes advantage of state-of-the-art climate control and lighting technology.

Return to Lexington by going northwest on U.S. 25 East from Middlesboro to I–75 North. The drive takes about 2¹/₂ hours.

Berea

Churchill Weavers. You can see all aspects of the hand-weaving process, from warping and weaving to finishing at this loom house. Handwoven goods have been made here since the early 1920s. Self-guided tours are available. Take U.S. 25 and bear off onto Highway 1016; the loom house is ¹/₂ mi from downtown. | 100 Churchill Dr. | 859/986–3127 | www.churchillweavers.com | Free | Loom house Mon.–Thurs. 9–4, Fri. hrs vary. Gift shop Mon.–Sat. 9–6, Sun. noon–6.

Studio Craftspeople of Berea. Many of the craftspeople with shops and studios in the town center formed this organization to provide information about their work.

KENTUCKY RULES OF THE ROAD

License Requirements: The minimum age for drivers in Kentucky is 16.

Right Turn on Red: Throughout the state, it's legal to turn right on red *after* a full stop, unless otherwise posted.

Seat-Belt & Helmet Laws: Seat belts are required by law, as are federally approved restraint seats for all kids under 40 inches tall. Helmets for motorcyclists are also required.

Speed Limits: On interstates and parkways, the speed limit is 65 mph. In metropolitan areas this decreases to 55 mph. If you are traveling on state roads, be aware that the limit through most towns is 35 mph.

Other Regulations: Drivers in Kentucky must have a blood-alcohol concentration of less than .08%. Passengers in a vehicle cannot possess open containers of alcohol.

For More Information: Kentucky State Police | 800/222–5555 emergency hot line, 800/459–7623 road conditions | www.kentuckystatepolice.org. Kentucky Transportation Cabinet | 502/564–4890 | www.kytc.state.ky.us.

Berea Tourism Center. Check with the tourist and convention commission for a list of studios where you can watch crafts being made. | 201 N. Broadway 40403 | 859/986–2540 or 800/598–5263 | www.berea.com | Mon.–Sat. 9–5, Sun. noon–5.

Dining

★**Boone Tavern.** Southern. The white brick Victorian building on the Berea College campus was built in 1909 and is very formal. The dining room has warm wood trim and antiques. Some of the Southern traditional and regional dishes are bourbon flank steak and chicken flakes in a "bird's nest" of shredded potato. Side dishes are served family-style. | 100 Main St. | 859/985–3700 or 800/366–9358 | Reservations essential | AE, DC, MC, V | $$–$$$

Dinner Bell. Southern. Pork tenderloin, pinto beans, and corn bread are some of the regional specialties here. The restaurant displays antiques and has a shop selling local crafts. Breakfast is served all day. | I–75 Plaza Dr. | 859/986–2777 | AE, D, MC, V | ¢–$

Papaleno's. Italian. On the edge of the Berea College campus, this inviting and cozy establishment is known for pizza, pasta, lasagna, and Italian sandwiches. Soup and salad are also available. Kids' menu. | 108 Center St., 40403 | 859/986–4497 | AE, D, MC, V | ¢–$

Middlesboro

Cumberland Gap National Historical Park. Popular with hikers, the park includes many miles of hiking trails, bordered by wildflowers in spring and splashed by a fine display of color in fall. | U.S. 25 E (Cumberland Gap Pkwy.), $\frac{1}{4}$ mi south of town, off I–75 Exit at Corbin | 606/248–2817 | www.nps.gov/cuga | Free | Late May–Oct., daily 8–6; Nov.–late May, daily 8–5.

Pinnacle Overlook. After winding up the 2,400-foot-high mountainside to a parking area, you can take a short walk along a wooded trail to this overlook, which has panoramic views of the Cumberland Mountains, including glimpses of Kentucky, Virginia, and Tennessee. A map at the overlook identifies landmarks. Miles of peaks in all directions are broken only by the Cumberland Gap—through which Daniel Boone led settlers of the region—and by the Cumberland Gap Tunnel. The tunnel's 4,600-foot twin paths connect Kentucky and Tennessee via U.S. 25 East. Air, temperature, and traffic in the passageways are monitored by a computer-controlled system, making this the most technologically advanced tunnel in the world.

Fort McCook. Several Civil War forts are scattered throughout the park. The most notable, Fort McCook, near the Pinnacle Overlook, was built by Confederate troops to guard the passageway through the mountains.

Hensley Settlement. A reconstruction of the mountain community that occupied the site from 1903 to 1951, this settlement includes log cabins and barns, has 70 acres under cultivation, and is accessible only on foot ($3\frac{1}{2}$-mi trail) or in a four-wheel drive vehicle. Call the park office for tour reservations.

Visitor Center. The center has a museum with exhibitions about the history of the region and an orientation film. | Park entrance.

Dining

J. Milton's Steak House. Steak. Middlesboro residents have been flocking to this family spot for over 20 years. Steaks are the main event, and the chicken, seafood, catfish, and hush puppies are also popular. A full buffet is available. Memorabilia and photos help impart the history of the Cumberland Gap and the settling of Middlesboro. | 910 N. 12th St. (U.S. 25 E), 2 mi north of the Cumberland Gap National Park | 606/248–0458 | AE, D, MC, V | ¢–$$

Lodging

Best Western Inn. Just five blocks from the entrance to Cumberland Gap National Historical Park, the motor hotel is 3 mi from Lincoln Museum and Cudjo Caverns. Cafeteria, refrigerators, cable TV, pool, business services, no-smoking rooms. | 1623 E. Cumberland Ave., 40965 | 606/248–5630 | fax 606/248–0875 | 100 rooms | AE, D, DC, MC, V | ¢

Holiday Inn Express. Room are spacious in this three-story hotel with interior corridors. Some rooms have a view of the mountains. Some in-room data ports, some in-room hot tubs, cable TV, golf privileges, pool. | 1252 N. 12th St. (U.S. 25 E), 40965 | 606/248–6860 or 800/544–8313 | fax 606/248–6978 | 60 rooms | CP | AE, D, DC, MC, V | $

Ridgerunner Bed and Breakfast. Built in the 1890s, this Victorian mansion overlooks Middlesboro and the mountains. Intricate woodwork and period furnishings distinguish the interior; outside there are landscaped gardens. No kids under 16, no smoking, no room phones, no room TVs. | 208 Arthur Heights, 40965 | 606/248–4299 | 4 rooms, 2 with bath | Closed Jan. | BP | AE, D, MC, V | $

THE DOWN EAST COAST

ALONG U.S. 1, FROM ELLSWORTH TO CAMPOBELLO ISLAND

Distance: 100 mi, detours excluded   Time: 2 days
Overnight Breaks: Lubec, Machias

The towns and villages that fill this stretch of coast smack of authenticity. Antiques and artisans' shops dot the region. Natural and historic sites are less crowded, roads less congested. Time seems to move a bit more slowly. Fall is an especially good time for this tour, as the hundreds of acres of blueberry barrens that parallel the road blaze red. Build in time for plenty of detours down the peninsulas to get a full glimpse of a rapidly vanishing Maine.

❶ Begin on U.S. 1 in **West Gouldsboro,** the western gateway to the **Schoodic Peninsula.** Take Route 186 South, through Winter Harbor, until you see the entrance sign for the only mainland parcel of **Acadia National Park.** The 2,000 acres are traversed by a 6-mi, one-way loop road that winds along the oceanfront, through towering spruce, and by granite ledges. Picnic spots, hiking trails, and scenic lookouts invite stops. For the most dramatic views and pounding surf (tides willing), stop at **Schoodic Point.**

❷ From the loop road, return to Route 186; follow it through the town of Prospect Harbor to Gouldsboro and proceed north on U.S. 1. You might detour to the **Petit Manan National Wildlife Refuge** (6 mi off U.S. 1 on Pigeon Hill Rd., Steuben), and take a hike through the forests, raised heath wetlands, blueberry barrens, and fresh- and saltwater marshes. More than 300 bird species have been sighted here. Otherwise, take U.S. 1A out of Milbridge (it rejoins U.S. 1 in Harrington) to **Columbia Falls.**

❸ Just off U.S. 1 is the historic **Ruggles House,** a wee manse and an impressive example of federal-Adamesque style, complete with flying staircase, carvings, and period pieces.

❹ Follow Route 187 to **Jonesport.** If you plan ahead, you can take a **puffin-watching cruise.** Since 1940, Captain Barna B. Norton has been guiding naturalists to Machias Seal Island for an up-close-and-personal look at these comical and adorable birds. For more natural pleasures, visit **Great Wass Island** (take the bridge to Beals Island to the Great

Wass causeway, turn right on Duck Cove Rd., then go 3 mi to the parking area on the left), which has excellent hiking, sublime ocean views, abundant wildlife, and spruce- and fir-studded paths. This 1,579-acre preserve is owned and maintained by the Nature Conservancy. From Jonesport, return to U.S. 1 via Route 187 and continue north to Machias. If you're a rail or miniature fan, stop by the **Maine Central Model Railroad** (4 mi east of town center on Rte. 187, look for the railroad crossing sign).

⑤ In **Machias,** depart U.S. 1 and head south for another quick detour: **Roque Bluffs State Park,** a great family park for sunning, picnicking, and an icy dip in the Atlantic. (There is also a freshwater pond for the more faint of heart.) Or just take in the island views from the sandy (albeit windy) mile-long beach. From Roque Bluffs State Park, take Roque Bluffs Road and reconnect with U.S. 1 north. You will soon arrive in Machias. Revolutionary War history comes alive at **Burnham Tavern** in Machias. Built in 1770, it is the oldest building east of the Penobscot. Job and Mary Burnham raised their 11 children here, but it also served as an infirmary and a gathering place for local patriots, who hatched schemes against the British. Period furnishings, documents, clothing, and weapons are on display.

⑥ In East Machias, just north of Machias on U.S. 1, head south on Route 191, better known as the **Cutler Road.** This beautiful coastal drive takes you past fishing shanties, island vistas, and through rolling wooded hills into the picturesque and tiny town of Cutler. There's good hiking along the way: **Western Head** (Destiny Bay Rd., Cutler) has an easy 3- to 4-mi loop trail that emerges through dense woods onto an ocean panorama. The 5.8- and 9-mi loops of the Bold Coast trails on the **Cutler Coast Public**

Reserved Land (4½ mi northeast of Cutler to your right on Rte. 191) require more effort, but the rugged cliffs and ocean views are worth it. Approximately 3 mi south of where Route 191 rejoins U.S. 1, visit **Bailey's Mistake,** where one Captain Bailey purportedly wrecked his schooner and decided to stay. Was it laziness or the black-sand beach? You decide.

❼ When you reach the junction with Route 189, take a slight detour to **Cobscook Bay State Park** (east on Rte. 189, then north on U.S. 1). Here nature has carved out inlets and coves in the seclusion of dense stands of trees, where the 24-foot tides surge and drop. The adjacent Moosehorn National Wildlife Refuge is renowned by bird-watchers. You might want to continue north on U.S. 1 to view **Reversing Falls Park** at Mahar Point, in Pembroke. (To get here from U.S. 1, go to Leighton Rd.; turn right at the SHORE ACCESS, 5.5 MILES sign, go 3¾ mi, and turn right again at the not highly visible REVERSING FALLS sign and then left onto a gravel road.) If you catch these falls a couple of hours before high tide, the twists and turns of the trip will have been worth your trouble.

❽ Retrace your path on U.S. 1 to Whiting, then head northeast on Route 189 to **Lubec,** an economically depressed but resource-rich town surrounded by water on three sides. Take the South Lubec Road, watching for signs to **Quoddy Head State Park,** the easternmost point in the country. The 480-acre park is punctuated by a red-and-white candy-striped lighthouse and has breathtaking hiking trails and great ocean views.

MAINE RULES OF THE ROAD

License Requirements: Any person with a valid driver's license can drive in Maine. The minimum driving age is 16.

Right Turn on Red: Right turns on red are permitted throughout the state, unless otherwise posted.

Seat-Belt & Helmet Laws: Seat belts are mandatory. While you cannot be stopped for not wearing one, you can be cited if stopped for another reason. Motorcycle helmets are required for drivers under 18 years of age and for those holding a license for under one year.

Speed Limits: The speed limit on I-95 (Maine Turnpike) is 65 mph, although it occasionally drops to 50 mph or 55 mph in more congested areas. Speed limits on U.S. 1 and state roads top out at 55 mph, but can quickly change as you approach settled areas. The best bet is to keep alert. If not posted, the speed limit on back roads is 45 mph.

Other Regulations: Some Maine municipalities require cars to have snow tires in season. (All-season tires do not qualify.) It is illegal to drive in Maine if your blood-alcohol concentration is more than .08%. No one in a vehicle can possess an open container of alcohol.

For More Information: Maine Department of Transportation | 207/624–3000 | www.state.me.us/mdot. State Department of Highway Safety | 800/452–4664.

⑨ Cross over the FDR International Bridge at Lubec to New Brunswick, Canada (Rte. 189 becomes Rte. 774), and the **Roosevelt Campobello International Park Natural Area.** Remember to set your clock ahead one hour; you're now on Atlantic time. These 2,800 acres of land are under joint U.S. and Canadian jurisdiction. Stop first at the visitor center, where you can obtain maps and other information. Perhaps best known as the summer retreat of Franklin D. Roosevelt, this island has as much in the way of natural beauty as history. A must-see on the island is the shingle-style **Roosevelt Cottage,** not so much a cottage as a coastal mansion, with manicured grounds and gardens. This is where Roosevelt was stricken with polio. Guides in the 34-room house explain the family artifacts. Make time to explore the island's beaches and rocky cliffs and to view **East Quoddy Head Light,** at the end of the island, accessible only at low tide.

Lubec

Quoddy Head State Park. With dramatic views from 90-foot cliffs overlooking the Bay of Fundy, this 532-acre park is the easternmost point in the nation. A visitor center with exhibits is in the former keeper's house. The park also has a picnic area and hiking trails. | S. Lubec Rd. | 207/733–0911 | Donations accepted | Mid-May–mid-Oct., daily 9 AM–dusk.

Roosevelt Campobello International Park. Connected to Lubec by the Franklin Roosevelt Memorial Bridge, this 2,800-acre preserve 1½ mi east of the border crossing is where FDR spent his summers until 1921. It is the only international park in the world, administered jointly by Canada and the United States. As it is located within the province of New Brunswick, the park is within the Atlantic Time Zone, and is one hour ahead of Eastern Time. | Off Rte. 189, Campobello Island, New Brunswick, Canada, 1 mi northeast of International Bridge | 506/752–2922 | www.fdr.net | Free | Mid-May–late Oct., daily 10–6.

   Roosevelt Cottage. Roosevelt's summer home is open for guided tours; the beautifully landscaped grounds surrounding it are also worth strolling. | Welshpool St. (Rte. 774), Campobello Island, New Brunswick, Canada | 506/752–2922 | Free | Mid-May–mid-Oct., daily 10–6.

Dining

Home Port Inn. Seafood. A cozy nine-table dining room in a Victorian country inn with garden views, the Hope Port is known for local fish dishes. Beer and wine only. No smoking. | 45 Main St. | 207/733–2077 | Closed Nov. 1–May 1. No lunch | D, MC, V | $–$$$

Murphy's Village Restaurant. American/Casual. Home-style cooking is the order at this cheerful restaurant. Stick to the basics and you won't be disappointed. Breakfast is served all day. Live music on Sunday nights. No smoking. | 122 Main St. | 207/733–4400 | MC, V | ¢–$

Phinney's Seaview. Seafood. Perched on a hill with expansive views over Johnson Bay is this bright, casual dining room and lounge. The outdoor lobster cookers illustrate that lobster is a popular choice here. Open-air dining on the deck. Live music on weekends. Kids' menu. No smoking. | Rte. 189 | 207/733–0941 | Closed Nov.–Mar. | MC, V | ¢–$$

Lodging

Eastland Motel. Just minutes from Quoddy Head State Park, this unadorned, family-oriented motel provides good value but no frills. Rooms in the newer wing are more spacious and have full baths. A meager Continental breakfast is served. Cable TV, some pets allowed (fee), no-smoking rooms. | Rte. 189, 04652 | 207/733–5501 | fax 207/733–2932 | www.eastlandmotel.com | 20 rooms | CP | AE, D, MC, V | $

Home Port Inn. Period furnishings enhance the coziness of this stately late-19th-century inn. Tea is served in the spacious living room every afternoon. Restaurant, picnic area, library, piano; no a/c, no room phones, no room TVs, no smoking. | 45 Main St., 04652 | 207/733–2077 or 800/457–2077 | www.homeportinn.com | 7 rooms | Closed Nov.–Apr. | CP | AE, D, MC, V | $

Peacock House. Modern and antique touches are evident in this 1860 Victorian home. Several rooms have good views of Fundy Bay. Relax in the living room, library, or gathering room. Cable TV, some in-room VCRs, piano; no a/c, no room phones, no smoking. | 27 Summer St., 04652 | 207/733–2403 or 888/305–0036 | www.peacockhouse.com | 5 rooms, 2 suites | Closed Nov.–Apr. | BP | MC, V | $

Machias

Burnham Tavern Museum. The oldest building in eastern Maine and the only one with a Revolutionary War history, this tavern served as a meeting place for planning the first naval battle of the Revolution. The gambrel-roof tavern was built in 1770 by Mary and Joe Burnham. The museum contains authentic furnishings from the period, many of them donated by Burnham descendants, as well as artifacts related to the capture of the *Margaretta* during the first naval battle of the American Revolution. | Main St. | 207/255–4432 | $2.50 | June–Sept., weekdays 9–5; tours by appointment.

Great Wass Island. At the tip of Beals Island, this 1,579-acre nature preserve has excellent hiking and bird-watching. Trails lead through the woods, past peat bogs, and open onto the rocky coast and magnificent ocean views. | 207/729–5181 | Free | Daily dawn–dusk.

Maine Central Model Railroad. Helen and Buz Beal have created a 900-square-foot display in a separate building in the front yard of their home. More than 400 freight cars and 20 diesel engines clackety clack along 3,000 feet of track that wind through detailed renditions of the Maine countryside. | Rte. 187 | 207/497–2255 | Donations accepted | Daily dawn–dusk.

Petit Manan National Wildlife Refuge. Easy hiking and renowned bird-watching are the calling cards at this remote refuge. | Pigeon Hill Rd. | 207/546–2124 | petit-manan.fws.gov | Free | Daily sunrise–sunset.

Norton of Jonesport Puffin Watch. Join Captain Barna Norton and his son John for a puffin-watching cruise to Machias Seal Island. The boat (the *Chief*) leaves from Jonesport Marina. Call ahead; reservations are required. | 207/497–5933 or 888/889–3222 | $60 | Cruises depart Memorial Day–Sept. 1, daily at 7 AM.

Roque Bluffs State Park. With a pebble beach on the ocean and a freshwater pond, this unique day-use park has both saltwater and freshwater swimming. There are picnic areas, changing areas with toilets, and playgrounds. | U.S. 1, 7 mi south of town | 207/255–3475 | $1 | May 15–Sept. 30, daily sunrise–sunset.

Ruggles House. This restored federal-style house, with intricately carved interiors, a magnificent flying staircase, and Palladian window, has been furnished with period pieces. | Main St., Columbia Falls, 20 mi south of Machias | 207/483–4637 or 207/546–7903 | $5 | June–mid-Oct., Mon.–Sat. 9–4:30, Sun. 11–4:30.

Dining

Bluebird Ranch Restaurant. American/Casual. Ample portions of down-home cooking with a Down East accent are served at this family-stye restaurant. Lobster and fried seafood are popular choices. No smoking. | 3 E. Main St. (U.S. 1) | 207/255–3351 | AE, D, MC, V | $–$$

Riverside Inn. Seafood. The owners are culinary school graduates who wanted to operate a small inn with emphasis on dining. The small and large dining rooms in this carefully restored 1805 inn have Victorian furnishings and river views. The menu changes seasonally. BYOB. No smoking. | U.S. 1, East Machias, 3½ mi north of town | 207/255–4134 | Reservations essential | Closed Mon. No lunch | AE, MC, V | $$–$$$

Lodging

Bluebird Motel. The pine-paneled rooms give this motel a 1950s feel, but the rooms are pleasant and the staff is friendly and helpful. If you're bothered by road noise, ask for a room in the rear building (there are two buildings). Cable TV, some pets allowed (fee). | U.S. 1, 04654, 1 mi southwest of town | 207/255–3332 | fax 207/255–3662 | 40 rooms | AE, MC, V | $

Machias Motor Inn. Each room in this well-tended, two-story motel on the edge of town has a sundeck overlooking the tidal Machias River. The motel is within walking distance of downtown shops and attractions. Restaurant, some kitchenettes, cable TV, no-smoking rooms. | 26 E. Main St. (U.S. 1), 04654 | 207/255–4861 | fax 207/255–4861 | 29 rooms, 6 suites | AE, MC, V | $

Riverside Inn. Frequent sightings of eagles, seals, and other wildlife are possible from this 1805 inn on the East Machias tidal river. The grounds have splendid vegetable and flower gardens, as well as a pond and waterfall. Rooms are furnished with Victorian-era antiques. Restaurant, some kitchenettes, cable TV; no room phones, no smoking. | U.S. 1, 04630 | 207/255–4134 or 888/255–4344 | fax 207/255–3580 | www.riversideinn-maine.com | 2 rooms, 2 suites | BP | AE, MC, V | $–$$

WESTERN MAINE LAKES & MOUNTAINS

ALONG ROUTE 113, U.S. 2, ROUTE 17, AND ROUTES 16 AND 4.

Distance: 100 mi, detours excluded   Time: 2 days
Overnight Breaks: Bethel, Rangeley

The drive from Fryeburg to Rangeley winds through mountain passes, by rippling streams and massive lakes, through small towns, and past working farms. Foliage season is the best time for the tour, but you'll have to share these often-winding roads with fellow leaf-peepers. Avoid this drive in winter and early spring: Route 113 closes in winter; in spring, you encounter a number of frost heaves, making the going even slower. This is a great tour if you want to get out of your car and do some hiking and exploring.

❶ Begin your tour with a detour. Just outside of Fryeburg is the **Hemlock Covered Bridge** (off U.S. 302, 3 mi northwest of East Fryeburg), a 116-foot-long bridge constructed in 1857.

❷ Return to Fryeburg and take Route 113 North. (You weave in and out of New Hampshire, but you are still mostly in Maine.) The winding road leads you over steep twists and turns in the **White Mountain National Forest** and through **Evans Notch**. The route also travels alongside **Evans Brook,** a good swimming spot in summer. Lounge on the large boulders that dot the brook. Trailheads along the route include the **Roost Loop, Basin Trail,** and **East Royce Trail.**

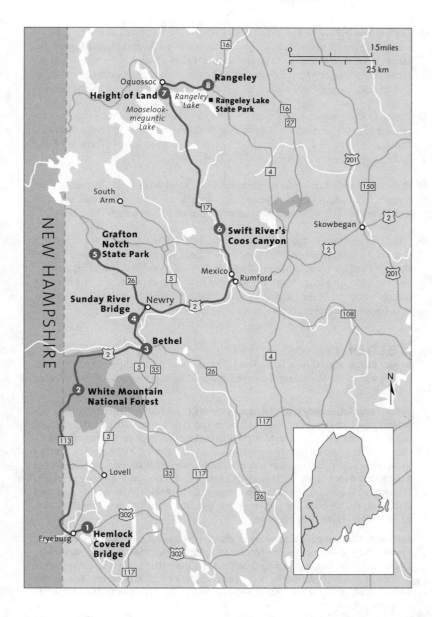

3 At the terminus of Route 113, head east on U.S. 2 to the town of **Bethel.** The **Dr. Moses Mason House Museum** is a restored federal-era home of one of Bethel's most prominent 19th-century citizens. Period furnishings and interesting murals can be seen within.

4 In **Newry,** just outside Bethel on U.S. 2 and Routes 5 and 26, the **Sunday River Ski Resort** offers chairlift rides to take in the full panorama of fall foliage. Visit another covered bridge, the **Sunday River Bridge,** better known as the Artist's Bridge (on U.S. 2 [Rte. 26], 4 mi northwest of North Bethel).

⑤ **Grafton Notch State Park,** 14 mi north of Bethel on Route 26, is a unique geological area, where the ice age made a big impression. Take short jaunts to **Screw Auger Falls, Moose Cave, Mother Walker Falls,** and **Natural Falls**—all within the park. There are also trailheads for the Appalachian Trail and other major mountain hikes, including Old Speck, Table Rock, Eyebrow Loop, and Baldpate. Return on Route 26 South to Newry.

⑥ Return to U.S. 2 and travel east until you come to Rumford and Mexico. In Mexico, pick up Route 17 North. Near the towns of Roxbury and Byron, at the **Swift River's Coos Canyon,** there's a scenic gorge, where you can also pan for gold if you're feeling lucky.

⑦ From Coos Canyon, continue north on Route 17 to **Height of Land,** just outside the town of Oquossoc. An aptly named scenic overlook, it is rimmed by mountains that stretch to the horizon. Mooselookmeguntic Lake sprawls in a deep dish below.

⑧ From Height of Land, Route 17 will take you into the town of Oquossoc. There, a sharp right will put you on Routes 4 and 16 and lead you to **Rangeley.** Covering more than a mile of lakefront, **Rangeley Lake State Park** has swimming, picnicking, fishing, and camping. Also plan to visit the **Wilhelm Reich Museum,** the onetime home of the controversial Viennese psychoanalyst, who believed he could trap airborne sexual energy and use it to treat disease.

Bethel

Artist's Bridge. Also known as the Sunday River Bridge, this is the most painted and photographed of Maine's eight covered bridges. | Sunday River Rd., off Rte. 26, 4 mi northwest of Bethel.

Bethel Historical Society Regional History Center. In the National Historic District, the federal-style Dr. Moses Mason House, built in 1913, is furnished with period pieces and has murals painted by itinerant artist Rufus Porter or his nephew. Changing exhibits pertaining to regional history are on view at the adjacent O'Neil Robinson House. | 10–14 Broad St. | 207/824–2908 or 800/824–2910 | www.bethelhistorical.org | Free, Moses Mason House tour $3 | Moses Mason House June–Oct., Tues.–Fri. 1–4; house tours July 1–Labor Day, Tues.–Sun. 1–4, or by appointment. O'Neil Robinson House July, Aug., and Dec., Tues.–Fri. 10–noon and 1–4, weekends 1–4; Sept.–Nov. and Jan.–June, Tues.–Fri. 10–noon and 1–4, or by appointment.

Grafton Notch State Park. Screw Auger Falls is the high point of this wonderfully scenic area, but also investigate Mother Walker Falls, Spruce Meadow, Old Speck Mountain, and Moose Cave. The Appalachian Trail traverses the park, but there are many other hiking options. A snowmobile trail, maintained by a local club, passes through the park. | Rte. 26, Newry, 14 mi north of Bethel | 207/824–2912 | Free | Mid-May–mid-Oct., daily 9–dusk.

Sunday River Ski Resort. One of Maine's premier ski resorts, Sunday River has high-speed lifts serving 128 trails on eight different peaks. There's plenty of nightlife after the ski lifts close. In summer, the slopes are turned over to mountain bikers. At this writing, an 18-hole golf course is set to open in summer 2004. | Off U.S. Rte. 2, 6 mi northeast of Bethel | 207/824–3000 or 800/543–2754 | www.sundayriver.com | Lift tickets $56, mountain biking $32 | Skiing and snowboarding mid-Nov.–Apr., weekdays 9–4, weekends 8–4; lift-assisted mountain biking June–mid-Sept., Thurs.–Sun. 10–3.

White Mountain National Forest. Although the White Mountains and most of this national forest are in New Hampshire, a portion of it juts into Maine. There are dozens of hiking trails and the views on the Evans Notch Road (Route 113 beginning in Gilead) are among the best in the state. Parking permits are required and available at self-service kiosks at some trailheads and day-use areas. | U.S. Rte. 2, 10 mi west of Bethel | 207/824–2134 or 603/528–8721 | Free, parking $3 | Daily dawn–dusk.

Dining

Bethel Inn and Country Club. Continental. Dine by candlelight, serenaded by piano, on entrées such as hazelnut-crusted duck and pastry-wrapped shrimp or lobster and roasted rack of lamb. The in-house tavern serves more casual, less-expensive fare (¢–$$) and is open for lunch. Kids' menu. | Village Common | 207/824–2175 or 800/654–0125 | Closed mid-Oct.–Dec. and Mar.–May. No lunch | AE, D, DC, MC, V | $$–$$$

Good Food Store. Eclectic. Pick up sandwiches, salads, cheese, wine, cookies, and other goodies to enjoy as a picnic. | 212 Mayville Rd. (Rte. 2) | 207/824–3754 or 800/879–8926 | MC, V | ¢

L'Auberge. French. The menu changes seasonally, but the accent is always French, with a country flair. You might begin with a mushroom ragout in puff pastry or a roasted lobster bisque, then move on to bouillabaisse or roasted garlic–coated rack of lamb. Save room for the homemade desserts. | 24 Mill Hill Rd. | 207/824–2774 or 800/760–2774 | Closed Tues. and Wed. | AE, D, MC, V | $$–$$$$

Sudbury Inn. Continental. The formal dining room serves entrées such as grilled Atlantic salmon, roasted Long Island duckling, and roasted rack of lamb. Much less formal is the Suds Pub, where the options include traditional fish-and-chips, steak, and lasagna as well as pizza, burgers, and sandwiches. Accompany your pub meal with one of 29 beers on tap. | 151 Main St. | 207/824–2174 dining room, 207/824–6558 pub | Dining room closed Mon., and Sun.–Thurs. in Apr. No lunch | AE, D, MC, V | $–$$$

Lodging

Briar Lea Inn and Restaurant. Antiques and country pieces decorate the rooms in this 1850s, Georgian-style farmhouse, where you can snuggle under a down comforter on cool nights. Some rooms can be connected as family suites. Restaurant, hiking, cross-country skiing, some pets allowed; no smoking. | 150 Mayville Rd., 04217, 1 mi north of town | 207/824–4717 or 888/479–5735 | fax 207/824–7121 | www.briarleainn.com | 6 rooms | BP | AE, D, MC, V | $–$$

Inn at the Rostay. Quilts on the beds and a different decorating theme in each room make this quiet motel seem more like an inn. A full country breakfast is available for $5. In-room data ports, some microwaves, some refrigerators, cable TV, in-room VCRs, pool, hot tub, laundry facilities, some pets allowed (fee); no smoking. | 186 Mayville Rd. (Rte. 2), 04217 | 207/824–3111 or 888/754–0072 | fax 207/824–0482 | www.rostay.com | 18 rooms | MC, V | $–$$

Sudbury Inn. You can walk to all in-town Bethel attractions from this sprawling late-19th-century inn. Country-style comfort is augmented by good service and an excellent dining room. 2 restaurants, cable TV, some pets allowed (fee); no room phones, no smoking. | 151 Main St., 04217 | 207/824–2174 or 800/395–7837 | fax 207/824–2329 | www.thesudburyinn.com | 10 rooms, 7 suites | BP | AE, D, MC, V | $–$$$

Rangeley

Height of Land. Right next to the Appalachian Trail, this scenic overlook provides majestic views of Mooselookmeguntic and Richardson lakes, backed by the White Mountains. | Rte. 17 between Rumford and Oquossoc.

★ **Rangeley Lake State Park.** In an area famous for trout and landlocked salmon fishing, this park has some of the most beautiful scenery in the state. Amenities include a boat ramp with floats, swimming, snowmobile, and hiking trails, and well-spaced campsites. | South Shore Dr., 9 mi southwest of town | 207/864–3858 | $2.50 | May–Sept., daily 7 AM–8 PM.

Wilhelm Reich Museum. On a 175-acre historic site called Orgonon, this museum represents and interprets the work of Viennese scientist and psychoanalyst Wilhelm Reich, who believed he could treat diseases by trapping airborne sexual energy. Nature trails lace the property. Don't miss the view over the Rangeley Lakes from the rooftop observatory. | Dodge Pond Rd. | 207/864–3443 | $4 | July and Aug., Wed.–Sun. 1–5; Sept., Sun. 1–5.

Dining

Gingerbread House. American. An antique marble soda fountain, a big fieldstone fireplace, and tables with views to the woods beyond make for a pleasant evening at this gingerbread-trim house. Choices can include hickory-planked salmon and roasted half duckling as well as lighter dishes like quesadillas or Caesar salad with grilled chicken or shrimp. Reservations are essential on summer weekends. Breakfast served. | Rtes. 17 and 4 | 207/864–3602 | Closed Apr. Hrs vary mid-Oct.–mid-May; call ahead | AE, MC, V | $–$$$$

Loon Lodge. Continental. Savor big views down Rangeley Lake and spectacular sunsets along with entrées such as cedar-shingled salmon, pork saltimbocca, and hand-cut grilled steak. | Pickford Rd. | 207/864–5666 | Closed Mon. | MC, V | $$–$$$

Rangeley Inn Tavern. Contemporary. A big stone fireplace adds a cozy touch to the upper level, while the lower level has big windows fronting Rangeley's main street. The menu ranges from bistro meat loaf to filet mignon, chicken potpie to porterhouse pork chop. Soups, salads, sandwiches, and burgers round out the menu. Breakfast served. | Rangeley Inn, 51 Main St. (Rte. 4) | 207/864–3341 or 800/666–3687 | No lunch | AE, D, MC, V | $–$$$$

Lodging

Rangeley Inn. Victorian antiques highlight the decor at this three-story, 1907 inn. Guest rooms in the main inn have a Victorian flair, although many have whirlpool tubs and fireplaces. Rooms in the motel behind the inn are more modern in decor and overlook a bird sanctuary. Restaurant, some in-room hot tubs, some microwaves, some refrigerators, cable TV, bar, Internet, meeting rooms, some pets allowed (fee); no a/c, no phones in some rooms, no smoking. | 51 Main St. (Rte. 4), 04970 | 207/864–3341 or 800/666–3687 | fax 207/864–3634 | www.rangeleyinn.com | 35 inn rooms, 15 motel rooms, 2 cabins | AE, D, MC, V | $–$$

BALTIMORE & ANNAPOLIS
MARYLAND'S MAJOR CITIES

Distance: 73 mi   Time: 3 days
Overnight Breaks: Annapolis, Baltimore

Explore Baltimore and historic Annapolis and take a quick trip over the Chesapeake Bay to the Eastern Shore. The landscape south of Baltimore is largely flat, while the Annapolis area is a maze of creeks and tributaries flowing into the Chesapeake Bay. Your best bet is to visit in spring and fall when the temperatures are cooler and humidity is low.

❶ Begin the tour in **Baltimore** at the **Inner Harbor.** The city's bustling waterfront is an urban Disneyland, with museums, water taxis and boat cruises, famous restaurants, and shops, all within walking distance of one another and rarely out of sight of the water. For a shopper's paradise be sure to visit **Harborplace** and its sister complex across the street, the multilevel Gallery. The **National Aquarium in Baltimore** and National Science Center are must-see attractions for first-time visitors. And don't miss the opportunity to ride in a water taxi, which permits a spectacular view of the city.

❷ When you're ready to leave the Inner Harbor area, head up to the **Baltimore Museum of Art** to see works by Rodin, Matisse, Picasso, Cézanne, Renoir, and Gauguin.

❸ On your way out of the city, stop at the **American Visionary Art Museum** in the southwestern corner of the Inner Harbor. It showcases the eclectic and innovative art of everyday Americans in seven galleries.

❹ **Annapolis** has historic homes and mansions, colonial streets, boat rides, and the United States Naval Academy. Start at the visitor bureau and join a guided walking tour of the city. Visit the historic **Maryland State House** and one of the many restored mansions of the colonial era. The **Hammond-Harwood House,** the only verified full-scale example of the work of William Buckland, colonial America's most prominent architect, is a sure winner. Tours of the **United States Naval Academy** give you a glimpse of the daily life of midshipmen.

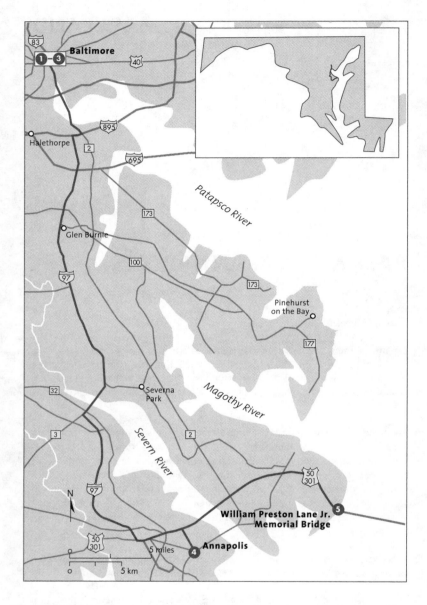

⑤ The **William Preston Lane Jr. Memorial Bridge,** better known as the Bay Bridge, connects Maryland's mainland with the Eastern Shore. Shoppers will enjoy the many outlet stores along U.S. 50, and seafood lovers will find a good selection of restaurants in Grasonville. St. Michaels is a popular sailing and tourist town with museums, boutiques, and restaurants.

To return to Baltimore backtrack west on U.S. 50/301 to Route 2 and head north into the city limits.

Annapolis

★ **Hammond-Harwood House.** Ninety percent of this 1774 home is original. One of the States' finest examples of colonial five-part Georgian architecture, the Hammond-Harwood House is the only verifiable full-scale example of William Buckland's work. Exquisite moldings, cornices, and other carvings appear throughout. It's furnished with 18th- and early-19th-century furniture and paintings. The garden is tended with regard to period authenticity. | 19 Maryland Ave. | 410/269–1714 | www.hammondharwood.org | $6; $10 combination ticket with William Paca House | Apr. 15–Oct., daily noon–5; Nov., Dec., and Mar.–Apr. 14, Mon.–Sat. 10–4, Sun. noon–4; Jan. and Feb., weekends noon–4.

London Town House and Gardens. Maryland's largest archaeological site, this National Historic Landmark is on the South River, 8 mi from Annapolis. The 17th-century tobacco port of London, made up of 40 dwellings, shops, and taverns, disappeared in the 18th century, when its buildings were abandoned and left to decay. The excavation of the town is ongoing. From April to September, you can join the dig one Saturday each month (call for schedule). Docents conduct 30- to 45-minute tours of the 1760 three-story waterfront brick house; allow more time to wander the grounds. | 839 Londontown Rd., Edgewater | 410/222–1919 | www.historiclondontown.com | $6 | Grounds Mar. 15–Dec., Mon.–Sat. 10–4, Sun. noon–4; Jan.–Mar. 14, Tues.–Sat. 10–3. House tours Mar. 15–Dec., daily on the hour (last tour at 3).

★ **Maryland State House.** Completed in 1780, the State House is the oldest state capitol in continuous legislative use; it's also the only one in which the U.S. Congress has sat

MARYLAND RULES OF THE ROAD

License Requirements: To drive in Maryland you must be at least 16 years old and have a valid driver's license. Residents of Canada and most other countries can drive as long as they have valid licenses from their home countries.

Right Turn on Red: Everywhere in Maryland you can make a right turn on red after a full stop, unless otherwise indicated.

Seat-Belt & Helmet Laws: All drivers and front-seat passengers must wear seat belts. Children under four must only ride in a federally approved child safety seat. Bicyclists and motorcyclists—of all ages—must wear helmets when riding on Maryland roads.

Speed Limits: In urban areas, particularly around Baltimore and heavily traveled I–95, the speed limit is 55 mph. On the interstates away from metropolitan area, the speed limit is 60 mph or 65 mph.

Other Regulations: Headlights are required after dusk and before dawn and when weather conditions necessitate them. The legal blood-alcohol concentration in Maryland is below .08%. Handheld-phone use is prohibited while operating a vehicle.

For More Information: Coordinated Highways Action Response Team (CHART) | 410/582–5607 | www.chart.state.md.us. Maryland Department of Transportation | 410/865–1142 or 888/713–1414 in MD | www.mdot.state.md.us.

(1783–84). It was here that General George Washington resigned as commander in chief of the Continental Army and where the Treaty of Paris was ratified, ending the Revolutionary War. Also on the grounds is the oldest public building in Maryland, the tiny redbrick Treasury, built in 1735. | State Circle | 410/974–3400 | Free | Weekdays 8:30–5; weekends 10–4; ½-hr tour daily at 11 and 3.

★ **United States Naval Academy.** Probably the most interesting and important site in Annapolis, the Naval Academy runs along the Severn River and abuts downtown Annapolis. Midshipmen enter from every part of the United States and many foreign countries to undergo rigorous study. The academy, established in 1845 on the site of a U.S. Army fort, occupies 329 waterfront acres. On the grounds midshipmen go to classes and conduct military drills. The Statue of Tecumseh, in front of Bancroft Hall, is a bronze replica of the USS *Delaware*'s wooden figurehead, "Tamanend." The centerpiece of the campus is the bright copper-clad dome of the interdenominational U.S. Naval Academy Chapel. You must have a photo ID to be admitted on the grounds. | www.navyonline.com | Grounds tour $6.50 | USNA Armel-Leftwich Visitor Center: Mar.–Dec., daily 9–5; Jan. and Feb., daily 9–4. Guided walking tours generally leave Mon.–Sat. 10–3 and Sun. 12:30–2:30; call ahead to confirm.

U.S. Naval Academy Museum & Gallery of Ships. Near the chapel in Preble Hall is this museum, which tells the story of the U.S. Navy through displays of model ships and memorabilia from naval heroes and fighting vessels. The U.S. Naval Institute and Bookstore is also in this building. | 118 Maryland Ave. | 410/293–2108 | Free | Mon.–Sat. 9–5, Sun. 11–5.

USNA Armel-Leftwich Visitor Center. Adjoining Halsey Field House, the visitor center has exhibits of midshipman life—including a mockup of a midshipman's room—and the *Freedom 7* space capsule flown by astronaut Alan Shepard, who was a graduate of USNA. Walking tours of the Naval Academy led by licensed guides leave from here. | 52 King George St. | 410/263–6933.

★ **William Paca House and Garden.** Paca (pronounced "PAY-cuh") was a signer of the Declaration of Independence and a Maryland governor from 1782 to 1785. His house was built in 1765, and its original garden was finished in 1772. Inside, the home is furnished with 18th- and 19th-century antiques. The adjacent 2-acre gentlemen's pleasure garden provides a longer perspective on the back of the house, plus worthwhile sights of its own: parterres (upper terraces), a Chinese Chippendale bridge, a pond, a wilderness area, and formal arrangements. | 186 Prince George St. | 410/263–5553 | www.annapolis.org | House and garden $8; combination ticket with Hammond-Harwood House $10 | House and garden mid-Mar.–Dec., Mon.–Sat. 10–5, Sun. noon–5; Jan.–mid-Mar., Fri. and Sat. 10–4, Sun. noon–4.

William Preston Lane Jr. Memorial Bridge. The twin spans of this bridge—also known as the Bay Bridge—cross the bay at its narrowest point, with 4 mi between shores. The bridge connects mainland Maryland with the Eastern Shore and provides a sweeping view of the beautiful Chesapeake Bay.

Dining

aqua terra. Contemporary. This funky restaurant gives history-minded Annapolis an alternative to the colonial-style establishments that predominate. Inside are bare floors, blond-wood furniture, an open kitchen, and a handsome granite counter under a row of blue teardrop-shape lamps. The menu changes with each season, but always includes seafood, beef, and pasta. On a summer menu was Cajun New York strip—a handsome cut of beef topped with pink curls of shrimp, butter, and chopped garlic—and linguine tossed with lumps of crab, fresh tomatoes, and shallots. | 164 Main St. | 410/263–1985 | AE, MC, V | $$–$$$

Cantler's Riverside Inn. Seafood. Opened in 1974, this local institution has a no-nonsense interior with wooden blinds and floors, nautical items laminated beneath tabletops, and metal chairs. Food is served with disposable dinnerware; if you order steamed crabs, your "tablecloth" is brown paper. Outdoor dining is available seasonally. Boat owners tie up at the dock; drivers must fight for parking during the summer season. Specialties are steamed mussels, clams, and shrimp as well as Maryland vegetable crab soup, seafood sandwiches, oysters, crab cakes, and numerous finfish. To get here from Route 50, take Exit 29A onto Busch's Frontage Road. At the flashing light, turn right onto St. Margaret's Road and follow for 2.3 mi. Turn left onto Brown's Woods Road; then take the first right onto Forest Beach Road and follow it to the end. | 458 Forest Beach Rd., St. Margaret's | 410/757–1311 | www.cantlers.com | AE, D, DC, MC, V | $–$$$

★ **McGarvey's Saloon and Oyster Bar.** American/Casual. Since 1975, this dockside eatery and watering hole has been full of good cheer and excellent food and drink. A heritage of seasonal shell- and finfish dishes, the finest burgers and steaks, as well as unstinting appetizers, make the McGarvey's menu one of the most popular in the area. The full menu is available daily until 11 PM. | 8 Market Space | 410/263–5700 | AE, DC, MC, V | ¢–$$$

Rams Head Tavern. American/Casual. A traditional English-style pub also houses the Fordham Brewing Company, which you can tour. The Rams Head serves better-than-average tavern fare, including spicy shrimp salad, crab cakes, beer-battered shrimp, and more than 170 beers—26 on tap—from around the world. The nightclub-like Rams Head Tavern On Stage brings in nationally known folk, rock, jazz, country, and bluegrass artists. Dinner-show combos. Sun. brunch. | 33 West St. | 410/268–4545 | www.ramsheadtavern.com | AE, D, MC, V | $–$$$$

Lodging

Best Western Annapolis. This well-maintained two-story motel is a good value. Although it's set away from traffic intersections, it's just 3 mi from the U.S. Naval Academy. Guest rooms, entered from the parking lot, are decorated in forest green with quilted floral bedspreads. There's an outdoor covered deck for enjoying breakfast or your own picnic. From U.S. 50, take Exit 22 and follow the signs to Riva Road North. The motel is in a business park on your left. In-room data ports, pool, gym, laundry service, meeting rooms, free parking. | 2520 Riva Rd., 21401 | 410/224–2800 or 800/638–5179 | fax 410/266–5539 | www.bestwestern.com | 142 rooms | AE, D, DC, MC, V | CP | $–$$

Gibson's Lodgings. Three detached houses from three decades—1780, 1890, and 1980—are operated together as a single inn. One of the house's hallways is strikingly lined with mirrors. Guest rooms are furnished with pre-1900 antiques. One first-floor room, which has a private bath and porch, is designed for disabled access. Free parking in the courtyards is a big advantage in the heart of this small colonial-era city (the houses are opposite the U.S. Naval Academy). Continental breakfast is served in the formal dining room of the 18th-century Patterson House. Meeting rooms, free parking. | 110–114 Prince George St., 21401 | 410/268–5555 or 877/330–0057 | fax 410/268–2775 | www.avmcyber.com/gibson | 21 rooms, 4 with shared bath | AE, MC, V | CP | $$–$$$

Scotlaur Inn. This family-owned bed-and-breakfast takes up the two floors above Chick and Ruth's Delly. Rooms are papered in pastel colonial prints, and hobnail bedspreads cover the beds. All rooms have private baths, irons, ironing boards, and hair dryers. Breakfast is downstairs. | 165 Main St., 21401 | 410/268–5665 | fax 410/269–6738 | www.scotlaurinn.com | 10 rooms | MC, V | CP | ¢–$

William Page Inn. Built in 1908, this dark-brown, cedar-shingle, wood-frame structure was the local Democratic party clubhouse for 50 years. Today its wraparound porch is furnished with Adirondack chairs. The slope-ceiling third-floor suite with dormer windows includes an Italian-marble bathroom with whirlpool. Breakfast is served in the common room. There's a 2-night minimum for weekend stays. Free parking, no-smoking rooms. | 8 Martin St., 21401 | 410/626–1506 or 800/364–4160 | www.williampageinn.com | 4 rooms, 2 with shared bath, 1 suite | MC, V | BP | $$–$$$$

Baltimore

★ **American Visionary Art Museum.** The nation's museum and education center for self-taught or "outsider" art has won great expert and popular acclaim. Seven galleries exhibit the unusual creations—paintings, sculptures, relief works, and pieces that defy easy classification—of untrained "visionary" artists working outside art's mainstream. The museum's restaurant, the Joy America Cafe, has a view of the Baltimore Harbor and an exuberant menu to match its playful name. | 800 Key Hwy., Federal Hill | 410/244–1900 | www.avam.org | $8 | Tues.–Sun. 10–6.

Baltimore Museum of Art. Roughly 100,000 paintings, sculptures, and decorative arts are on exhibit at this impressive museum, where the holdings include works by Matisse, Picasso, Cézanne, Gauguin, van Gogh, and Monet. The museum also owns the world's second-largest collection of Andy Warhol works. The neoclassical main building was designed by John Russell Pope, the architect of Washington's National Gallery. | 10 Art Museum Dr., Charles Village | 410/396–7100 | www.artbma.org | $7, free 1st Thurs. of month | Wed.–Fri. 11–5, weekends 11–6, 1st Thurs. of month 11–8.

★ **Fells Point Maritime Museum.** This former trolley-car barn is now a museum that focuses on the port's golden age, from the mid-1700s to the 1830s, when Fells Point's ship industry was very important. Among the many seafaring exhibits are 23 models of Baltimore clipper ships. The Maryland Historical Society's collection of artifacts is also on display. | 1724 Thames St., Fells Point | 410/732–0278 or 410/685–3750 | www.mdhs.org | $4 | Thurs.–Mon. 10–5.

Fort McHenry. Francis Scott Key wrote the words for "The Star-Spangled Banner" as he watched the redcoats bombard Fort McHenry during the War of 1812. A visit to the fort includes a 16-minute history film, guided tour, and frequent living history displays (including battle reenactments) on weekends. To see how the formidable fortifications might have appeared to the British, catch a water taxi from the Inner Harbor to the fort instead of driving. | E. Fort Ave., Locust Point, from Light St., take Key Hwy. for 1½ mi and follow signs | 410/962–4290 | www.nps.gov/fomc | $5 | Late May–early Sept., daily 8–8; early Sept.–late May, daily 8–5.

Harborplace and The Gallery. Part of Baltimore's move toward urban renewal, this development built in 1980 has two airy, glass-enclosed structures: the Light Street Pavilion, with two stories of food courts and restaurants, and the Pratt Street Pavilion, dedicated mainly to retail stores. Jugglers, bands, and other buskers entertain crowds at an outdoor amphitheater, and paddleboats can be rented south of the Pratt Street building. A skywalk from the Pratt Street Pavilion leads to The Gallery, a four-story shopping mall with 70 shops. | 100 Pratt St., Inner Harbor | 410/332–4191 | www.harborplace.com | Mon.–Sat. 10–9, Sun. 10–6 (Harborplace and the Gallery have extended summer hrs).

Maryland Science Center. Known as the Maryland Academy of Sciences when it began in 1797, this is one of the oldest scientific institutions in the United States. The three floors of interactive exhibits cover the Chesapeake Bay, applied science, natural history, and outer space and serve as an invitation to engage, experiment, and explore. There's a planetarium, a simulated archaeological dinosaur dig, and an IMAX movie theater with a screen five stories high. | 601 Light St., Inner Harbor | 410/685–5225 | www.mdsci.org | Museum $12, IMAX tickets $7.50, combination $15.50 | Sept.–June, weekdays 10–5, Sat. 10–6, Sun. noon–5; July and Aug., weekdays 10–5, weekends 10–6.

National Aquarium in Baltimore. The most-visited attraction in Maryland has more than 10,000 fish, sharks, dolphins, and amphibians dwelling in 2 million gallons of water. They're joined by the reptiles, birds, plants, and mammals inside the center's rain-forest environment. In the Marine Mammal Pavilion seven Atlantic bottlenose dolphins give several entertaining shows a day. The famed shark tank and Atlantic coral reef exhibits are spectacular. Timed tickets may be required on weekends and holidays; purchase these early in the day. | Pier 3, Inner Harbor | 410/576–3800 | www.aqua.org | $17.50 | Mar.–June, Sept., and Oct., Sat.–Thurs. 9–5, Fri. 9–8; July and Aug., Mon.–Thurs. 9–6, Fri.–Sun. 9–8; Nov.–Feb., Sat.–Thurs. 10–5, Fri. 10–8; visitors can tour for up to 2 hrs after closing.

Walters Art Museum. The 30,000 works of art at the Walters provide an organized overview of human history from the 3rd millennium BC to the early 20th century. The original museum (1904) houses Renaissance and baroque paintings as well as a sculpture court. In two other buildings are Egyptian, Greco-Roman, Byzantine, and Ethiopian art collections, among the best in the nation, along with many 19th-century paintings. | 600 N. Charles St., Mount Vernon | 410/547–9000 | www.thewalters.org | $8, free Sat. 11–1 | Tues.–Sun. 10–5.

Dining

Babalu Grill. Cuban. From the prominent portrait of Desi Arnaz to the conga-drum bar stools to the live salsa music on weekends, this place is about fun. The house cocktail, the *mojito,* is a Cuban drink of rum, sugar, and mint. Many of the classic Cuban dishes on the menu come from the owner's family recipes, including the savory *ropa vieja* (a stew of shredded beef) and seafood paella, brimming with shrimp, shellfish, and chorizo. The bar serves an impressive selection of obscure rums and tequilas. | 32 Market Pl., Inner Harbor | 410/234–9898 | Closed Mon. No lunch Sat.–Wed. | AE, D, DC, MC, V | $$–$$$$

★**Blue Agave Restaurante y Tequileria.** Mexican. To create the authentic regional Mexican and American Southwest dishes, chilies are flown in from New Mexico and spices and chocolate are shipped from Oaxaca. Every sauce and salsa is made daily to create pure, concentrated flavors—the traditional mole sauces are delicious. Grilled quail is served with both green and spicy yellow moles; the more familiar chicken enchiladas are topped with with mole poblano. There are more than 80 kinds of tequila, and you won't find a finer margarita anywhere. | 1032 Light St., Federal Hill | 410/576–3938 | Closed Tues. and Wed. No lunch | AE, D, MC, V | $–$$

★**Helmand.** Afghan. Baltimore's first Afghan restaurant is a great option for vegetarians. Lively crowds pack into the small, no-frills space. Interesting items such as panfried baby pumpkin and leek-filled ravioli share the menu with the very tasty kebabs. Instead of ordering one entrée, get three or four appetizers, exposing yourself to the eclectic choices. The owner, a local celebrity, is a brother of the temporary ruler of postwar Afghanistan. | 806 N. Charles St., Mount Vernon | 410/752–0311 | Reservations essential | AE, DC, MC, V | $–$$

Nacho Mama's. Tex-Mex. A wooden statue of Elvis marks the entrance to this extremely popular bar and restaurant. Inside, a funky mixture of sports and Elvis memorabilia hangs from the ceiling and walls. Try a National Bohemian, a native Baltimore brew ("Natty Bo" to regulars), as you wait for a table. In addition to the south-of-the-border fare, burgers and salads are also served. The spinach salad with feta, roasted red peppers, and avocado dressing is especially good. During the annual Night of 100 Elvises, impersonators convene here. | 2907 O'Donnell St., Canton | 410/675–0898 | AE, MC, V | ¢–$$

Obrycki's Crab House. Seafood. It's Baltimore's crab house of choice—and tasting the steamed crabs yourself helps you understand why. Beyond that, the seafood menu is standard and the food just fair. Talk-show host Oprah Winfrey, once a Baltimore television personality, still has Obrycki's crab cakes mailed to her. | 1727 E. Pratt St., Fells Point | 410/732–6399 | Closed mid-Dec.–early Mar. | AE, D, DC, MC, V | $$–$$$$

Lodging

Abacrombie. Rooms in this 1890 five-story, gray, stone row house are basic compared to the more royal furnishings in the sitting parlor, which has high ceilings and original planked wood floors. The rooms are Victorian in style, though each room is distinctive. Some have four-poster beds and many, especially those on top floors, have striking city views. The Abacrombie is across the street from Symphony Hall and two blocks from the Lyric Opera House. Restaurant, bar, cable TV, business services. | 58 W. Biddle St., Mt. Vernon 21201 | 410/244–7227 | fax 410/244–8415 | www.badger-inn.com | 12 rooms | CP | AE, D, DC, MC, V | $$–$$$

Admiral Fell Inn. This elegant inn is at the center of action in funky Fells Point. By joining together buildings constructed between the late 1770s and the 1920s, the owners created a structure that resembles one small hotel. The rooms, which vary in shape, all have four-poster canopy beds. Suites and eight rooms have whirlpool baths. Some hallways have a few stairs, and some rooms face a quiet interior courtyard: if steps or street noise are a hindrance to your comfort, let the reservation agent know. 3 restaurants, in-room data ports, some in-room hot tubs, cable TV, 3 bars, business services, free parking, some pets allowed. | 888 S. Broadway, 21231 | 410/522–7377, 800/292–4667 outside MD | fax 410/522–0707 | www.admiralfell.com | 77 rooms, 3 suites | CP | AE, DC, MC, V | $$–$$$$

Inn at 2920. An upscale row house that was once a brothel and tavern, the Inn at 2920 is a smooth marriage of old and new. The 1880 brick building has exposed brick walls, copper ceilings, and stark, modern furnishings. The Bordello Room has a king-size canopy bed with rich, red linens and a two-person whirlpool bath lined with limestone tile. Business travelers receive complimentary cell phones and wireless Internet access. Breakfast options change depending on what's available at the local farmer's market, but interesting offerings have included sweet potato home fries and sage sausage. The inn is a quick walk from O'Donnell Square, which has many bars and restaurants. Cable TV, in-room VCRs, hot tub, Internet; no kids under 12, no smoking. | 2920 Elliott St., Canton, 21224 | 410/342–4450 | fax 410/342–6436 | www.theinnat2920.com | 4 rooms | BP | AE, MC, V | $$$

Scarborough Fair. Two blocks from Inner Harbor, this Georgian brick house from 1801 is one of the oldest in the area. On the exterior are gabled roofs and Flemish-bonded brickwork, a traditional style characteristic of the neighborhood. Rooms are done with a blend of contemporary and colonial-era furnishings. The 2nd-floor Round Hill room includes Victorian-era reproductions as well as a gas fireplace and double whirlpool tub. Cable TV, free parking; no room phones, no kids. | 1 E. Montgomery St., Federal Hill, 21202 | 410/837–0010 | fax 410/783–4635 | www.scarborough-fair.com | 6 rooms | BP | AE, D, MC, V | $$–$$$

Tremont Plaza Hotel. Built in the 1960s as an apartment house, the 13-story Tremont in downtown Baltimore is now an elegant and comfortable all-suites hotel. The lobby and hotel restaurant, 8 East, are intimate and private—qualities attracting some guests who might be easily recognized. The suites come in two sizes: both have a toaster oven and a coffeemaker complete with freshly ground beans. The Tremont is near Mount Vernon's cultural attractions and restaurants, and the concierge can help you arrange local transportation, often free of charge. Restaurant, bar, cable TV, business services, parking (fee), some pets allowed. | 222 St. Paul Pl., 21202 | 410/727–2222 or 800/873–6668 | fax 410/244–1154 | www.tremontsuitehotels.com | 60 suites | CP | AE, D, DC, MC, V | $$–$$$

WESTERN MARYLAND
ALONG INTERSTATES 70 AND 68

Distance: 160 mi   Time: 3 days
Overnight Breaks: Cumberland, Deep Creek Lake, Frederick

Discover the state's mountainous region, home to historic Frederick, Civil War battle-fields, and countless small towns. From Frederick the rolling hills evolve into rugged mountains. The colors are breathtaking in fall. In winter the westernmost county, Garrett, becomes a winter playground with downhill and cross-country skiing, ice fishing, and sledding. Summer temperatures are much cooler in Garrett County than in the rest of the state.

❶ Begin in **Frederick.** The city's lovely 50-block historic district has 18th- and 19th-century buildings, many still in use as homes, stores, and restaurants. Start a self-guided walking tour at the **Frederick Visitor Center.** The **Barbara Fritchie House and Museum** recounts the legend of Dame Fritchie, who reportedly waved a Union flag at passing Confederates during the Civil War. For a different kind of history, check out the **National Museum of the Civil War Medicine.** If time permits, visit **Mount Olivet Cemetery,** the resting place of Fritchie, Francis Scott Key, and Union and Confederate soldiers.

❷ **Antietam National Battlefield** is one of the nation's best-preserved battlefields. Antietam (in Sharpsburg) was the site of the bloodiest day of the Civil War.

❸ In **Hagerstown,** the **Washington County Museum of Fine Arts** has an impressive collection of 18th- and 19th-century American art. The museum is within the boundaries of the **City Park,** a 27-acre wooded and landscaped haven.

❹ In **Cumberland** take a ride on the **Western Maryland Scenic Railroad.** Passengers enjoy a 16-mi mostly uphill trek to Frostburg where a 90-minute layover leaves just enough time for shopping and dining along the town's old-fashioned Main Street. Cumberland also was the western terminus of the C&O (Chesapeake&Ohio) Canal. The remnants of **George Washington's Headquarters** during the French and Indian War are in Riverside Park.

❺ **Deep Creek Lake,** Maryland's largest man-made lake, is a boater's paradise. Marinas rent boats and Jet Skis. **Deep Creek Lake State Park** has a boat ramp, beach, hiking trails, and camping facilities. To the southwest of the lake **Swallow Falls State Park** has a spectacular view of Muddy Creek Falls, Maryland's highest waterfall, and a stand of 300-year-old hemlocks.
     To return to Frederick backtrack east on I–68/70.

Cumberland
George Washington's Headquarters. A small portion of the original log structure of Washington's headquarters during the French and Indian War and Whiskey Rebellion remains standing. The cabin is on the walking tour of Fort Cumberland, downtown. This structure is operated by the Daughters of the American Revolution. When the one-room cabin is not open, you can view its interior from behind a glass barrier and press a button to listen to a narrative detailing the cabin's history. | Riverside Park | 301/777–8678 | Free | Site daily 24 hrs. Cabin Presidents' Day, 2nd weekend in June, or by appointment.

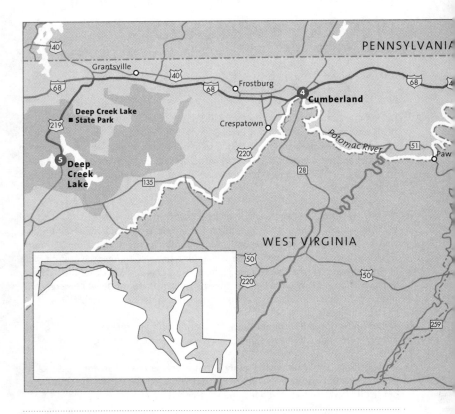

Green Ridge State Forest. Wildlife is plentiful in this 43,000-acre forest with a stunning view of the Potomac and mountain valleys. Camping, hiking, bicycling, and hunting (in season) are favored activities. | I–68, Exit 64 | 301/478–3124 | Free | Sat.–Thurs. 8–4, Fri. 8–8.

Rocky Gap State Park. Nestled between Evitts and Martin mountains is this lovely natural haven popular with hikers, campers, boaters, and swimmers. | 12500 Pleasant Valley Rd., I–68, Exit 50 | 301/777–2139 or 301/777–2138 | www.dnr.state.md.us | Free | Daily dawn–dusk.

Western Maryland Scenic Railroad. Traverse rugged mountains with panoramic vistas on this three-hour round-trip ride to Frostburg. A 1916 Baldwin locomotive, once used in Michigan's Upper Peninsula, does the heavy work. | 13 Canal St. | 301/759–4400 or 800/872–4650 | www.wmsr.com | $19 | Trains depart May–Sept., Thurs.–Sun. at 11:30; Oct. 2–26, Mon.–Thurs. at 11:30, and some Sat. at 4; Nov.–Dec. 7, Sat. and Sun. at 11:30.

Dining

D'Atri's. American/Casual. Locals flock to this sit-down sandwich shop for the freshly baked bread. The cheesesteak and the Italian hoagie are, by far, the best sellers. | 118 National Hwy., La Vale, 3 mi northwest of Cumberland | 301/729–2774 | AE, D, DC, MC, V | $

Hen House West. Seafood. On a winding country road in the mountains on the way to Deep Creek Lake, this casual restaurant serves up an abundance of seafood. In season, expect steamed blue crabs, crab cakes, and fish platters. Barbecued ribs are another popular choice. | 1872 National Pike, off Exit 29, Frostburg, 12 mi west of Cumberland | 301/689–5001 | No lunch | No credit cards | $–$$$$

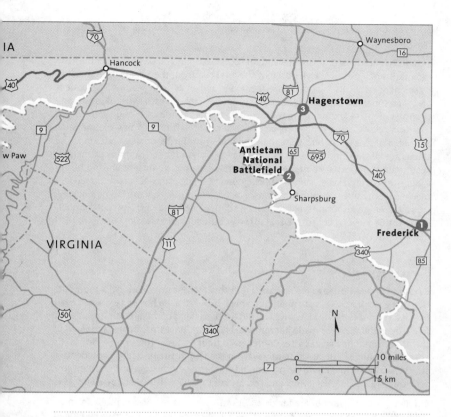

Marshall's. American/Casual. Just past Dan's Mountain State Park on the main street of Lonaconing, a once-hopping mining town, is this old-time diner with well-worn booths. Notice the working soda fountain on the left when you walk in. You can still get an ice-cream soda for 95¢. A "chocolate rickie," chocolate milk with crushed ice, is the local special. Twenty-one sandwiches are on the menu. Breakfast served. | 44 Main St., Lonaconing, 19 mi west of Cumberland | 301/463–6338 | Closed Sun. No dinner | No credit cards | ¢

Savage River Lodge. American. At this remote lodge, the menu is heavy on game, such as venison, bison, and wild boar. Local trout and catfish are staples. Try the savory meat loaf if it's available. The chef tries to use mainly local produce and has been known to use morel mushrooms and ramps, a local onion, from the forest surrounding the lodge. | 1600 Mt. Aetna Rd., Grantsville, 5 mi south of I–8 and 18 mi west of Cumberland | 301/689–3200 | AE, D, DC, MC, V | $$–$$$

When Pigs Fly. American. Six blocks west of Baltimore Street, this restaurant and lounge is chock full of pig paraphernalia. It's famous for its barbecued ribs. | 18 Valley St., 21502 | 301/722–7447 | AE, D, MC, V | ¢–$

Lodging

Rocky Gap Lodge & Golf Resort. Tucked inside one of Maryland's most spectacular state parks, this lakeside resort sits on 243 acres. Wood paneling and rustic furniture give the rooms a country cabin appeal. 2 restaurants, in-room data ports, cable TV, 18-hole golf course, tennis courts, indoor pool, gym, hot tub, beach, boating, fishing, bicycles, volleyball, bar, business services. | 16701 Lakeview Rd. NE, 21539 | 301/784–8400 or

800/724–0828 | fax 301/784–8408 | www.rockygapresort.com | 218 rooms, 4 suites | AE, D, DC, MC, V | $$–$$$

Savage River Lodge. For unspoiled and undiscovered beauty, look no further than the mountains of western Maryland. Enjoy the feral beauty of the Savage River forest in its splendor from this 10,000-square-foot lodge and its 18 luxury cabins. The lodge is on 45 acres, in the middle of 750 acres of Savage River State Forest. Fly-fishing and cross-country skiing are among the many favorite pastimes of guests, though you can opt to simply relax in front of the fireplace in each cabin. Nature activities abound, such as guided nature walks, bird-watching, and spying on the deer that wander near the cabins at night. Biking, horseback riding, canoeing, kayaking, and skiing are all nearby. Restaurant, in-room data ports, refrigerators, massage, mountain bikes, hiking, horseshoes, cross-country skiing, ski shop, bar, lobby lounge, library, piano, shop, business services, meeting room, airport shuttle, some pets allowed (fee); no a/c, no room TVs, no smoking. | 1600 Mt. Aetna Rd., Grantsville 21536, 5 mi south of I–68 and 18 mi west of Cumberland | 301/689–3200 | fax 301/689–2746 | www.savageriverlodge.com | 18 cabins | CP | AE, D, DC, MC, V | $$$

Frederick

Barbara Fritchie House and Museum. From this modest brick cottage, a reproduction of the original, it's easy to imagine Dame Fritchie sticking her white-capped head out of a second-floor window and waving a Union flag at Confederate troops. Poet John Greenleaf Whittier made her famous; his poem "Barbara Fritchie" appeared in the *Atlantic Monthly* a year after Confederate troops passed through Frederick. His stirring account of Fritchie defiantly waving the flag at the invading Confederates stirred patriotism and made the 95-year-old woman a heroine. | 154 W. Patrick St. | 301/698–0630 | $2 | Apr.–Sept., Mon. and Thurs.–Sat. 10–4; Oct.–Nov., Sat. 10–4, Sun. 1–4.

Candlelight Ghost Tour of Frederick. Most of this company's walking tours include stops at "haunted" locations such as the Civil War Medical Museum, where dead soldiers were embalmed during the Civil War. Additional tours are available in October, in time for Halloween. | Brewer's Alley Restaurant and Brewery, 124 N. Market St., Frederick | 301/845–7001 or 301/668–8922 | www.frederickcarriage.com | $8 | June–mid-Oct., Sat. 9 PM; mid-Oct.–mid-Nov., Fri. 8 PM and Sat. 7 and 9 PM, or by reservation.

Mount Olivet Cemetery. Some of Frederick's most famous sons and daughters, including Francis Scott Key and Barbara Fritchie, rest in this 1854 cemetery. Also here are the remains of more than 800 of the Confederate soldiers killed during the battles of Antietam and Monocacy. | 515 S. Market St. | 301/662–1164 | Free | Daily sunrise–sunset.

National Museum of Civil War Medicine. The Civil War, in which two-thirds of its 620,000 fatalities resulted from disease, led to advances in the transportation of the wounded, hospital care, surgery, and prostheses. The more than 3,000 medical artifacts on display in this museum include the only known surviving Civil War surgeon's tent and a horse-drawn Civil War ambulance. The building housing the museum was where the dead were embalmed after the Battle of Antietam; today, it's a popular stop for city ghost tours. | 48 E. Patrick St. | 301/695–1864 | www.civilwarmed.org | $6.50 | Mon.–Sat. 10–5, Sun. 11–5.

Rose Hill Manor Park/The Children's and Farm Museum. Although this lovely Georgian manor is intended as a place for elementary-school kids to study local and regional history, it's more than just that. Maryland's first governor, Thomas Johnson, lived here from 1798 to 1819, and guided tours of his gracious home cover its owners and lifestyles. During the tour, children can card wool, weave on a table loom, play with reproductions of old toys, and dress in period costumes. Also open are several outbuildings, including a log cabin, ice house, smokehouse, blacksmith shop, and large shed housing a carriage collection. | 1611 N. Market St. | 301/694–1648 | www.co.frederick.md.us/parks/rosehill.html | $4 | Apr.–Oct., Mon.–Sat. 10–4, Sun. 1–4; Nov., Sat. 10–4, Sun. 1–4.

Dining

Isabella's. Spanish. This Spanish eatery added some flair to downtown Frederick's predominantly American restaurant scene. Most people head here for the tapas, which include lamb, beef, chicken, and seafood served with spices, herbs, and some wonderful sauces. Try the littleneck clams steamed in beer, garlic, cilantro, pepper, and tomato; the grilled lamb chops, served with a black currant sauce; or the chili shrimp, sautéed in hot oil, garlic, peppers, and caramelized onions. Three or four tapas makes a meal. | 44 N. Market St. | 301/698–8922 | AE, D, MC, V | Closed Mon. | $$–$$$$

The Tasting Room. Contemporary. Huge glass windows showcase the modern interior of this restaurant that began as a wine bar. Of the roughly 150 wines available, 40 are offered by the glass ($5–$17). Dishes change each season; most are a fusion of American, Asian, and French cuisine. Asian chicken salad, coq au vin, and lobster whipped potatoes, made with fresh Maine lobster and chive butter, are popular items. Over 45 specialty martinis are available. | 101 N. Market St. | 240/379–7772 | AE, DC, MC, V | Closed Sun. | $$–$$$$

Tauraso's Restaurant. Italian. In the summer, this popular Italian restaurant draws a big crowd that overflows into the massive outdoor dining area. The standard Italian menu includes a different fish special each night. The brick oven pizza is a local favorite, as is the pan-seared grouper. Other dishes include eggplant Parmesan and cioppino, a seafood stew. For a more casual meal, try the pub. Tauraso's is one of the few restaurants in the area that serve Sunday brunch. | 6 N. East St. | 301/663–6600 | Reservations essential | AE, D, DC, MC, V | $–$$$

Zest. Contemporary. Light pours into this small restaurant and bounces off its caramel-colored wood floors and brightly painted walls. The fairly innovative menu includes such dishes as a bison and gulf shrimp casserole. Trained in popular D.C. kitchens, the chef uses local greens, pork, beef, and lamb. Take a moment to examine the wine collection on display at the back of the space and the impressive collection of cookbooks next to the women's rest room. | 11791 Fingerboard Rd., Monrovia | 301/865–0868 | AE, D, MC, V | Closed Sun. and Mon. | $$–$$$

Lodging

McCleery's Flat. On antiques row, this French-style townhouse has an unbeatable location, just a short walk from restaurants and shops. The home, built in 1876, is furnished with many antiques. Rooms are huge and each is decorated with ornate antiques and vintage furniture; many have balconies and working fireplaces. The Caroline McCleery suite includes an impressive king-size Victorian poster bed and a bathroom with a whirlpool tub, a separate shower, and even a chandelier. No kids under 15, no smoking. | 121 E. Patrick St., 21701 | 301/620–2433 or 800/774–7926 | www.fwp.net/mccleerysflat | 3 rooms, 2 suites | AE, DC, MC, V | BP | $$

Strawberry Inn B&B. This 1840 farmhouse is the oldest B&B in Frederick County. Rooms in the restored home are tastefully decorated with antiques. In summer, the back porch, covered with grapevines, is the setting for the old-fashioned breakfast. The comfortable sitting room has a working fireplace. | 17 W. Main, New Market 21774 | 301/865–3318 | 3 rooms, 1 suite | No credit cards | BP | $–$$

Hagerstown

C&O Canal Museum. Operated by the National Park Service, this small museum runs slide presentations on the history of the canal system. A replica of a canal boat is on display, in addition to photos, artifacts, and books. | 326 E. Main St., Hancock | 301/678–5463 | Free | Tours by appointment.

Fort Frederick State Park. Hiking, camping, canoeing, and cross-country skiing are among the activities in this 550-acre park, which has one of the few surviving stone forts from the French and Indian War. A small museum is dedicated to the Civilian Conservation Corps. | 11100 Fort Frederick Rd., off Rte 56, Exit 12, Big Pool, 20 mi west of Hagerstown | 301/842–2155 | www.dnr.state.md.us | Free | Daily dawn–dusk; visitor center May–Oct., Mon.–Thurs. daily 8–8, Fri. 8–10; Nov.–Apr. weekdays 8–4.

Washington County Museum of Fine Arts. An impressive collection of American paintings, drawings, prints, and sculpture from the 18th century to present are displayed in this small museum. | 91 Key St. | 301/739–5727 | www.washcomuseum.org | Free | Tues.–Fri. 9–5, Sat. 9–4, Sun. 1–5.

Dining

Junction 808. American. Home-style comfort food is served up in this fun family place. Try the spaghetti with homemade sauce, fresh roast turkey, or barbecued ribs. Kids' menu. No smoking. | 808 Noland Dr. | 301/791–3639 | Closed Sun. | MC, V | ¢–$$

Richardson's. American. Greenery and railroad memorabilia abound in this relaxed, woodsy eatery. Crab cakes, prime rib, and Richie's special ham sandwich are some of the menu's best bets. Salad bar. Kids' menu. | 710 Dual Hwy. (U.S. 40) | 301/733–3660 | D, MC, V | ¢–$$

MASSACHUSETTS

HISTORIC CAPE COD
ALONG THE OLD KING'S HIGHWAY

Distance: 40 mi   Time: 1 day
Overnight Breaks: Barnstable, Brewster, Dennis (Although this is a one-day drive, hotels are listed for several towns should you care to stretch out your visit.)

You'll be following an old colonial thoroughfare known as the King's Highway, now Route 6A, from the Cape Cod Canal to Orleans, on the eastern side of Cape Cod. A handful of museums and inns encourage tarrying along the way, and gentle Cape Cod Bay beaches are often just a turn away. Beyond summer, many businesses cut back their hours, some in anticipation of closing completely until the following year; however, spring and fall yield sparser crowds and lovely driving weather.

❶ Begin in **Bourne.** Long, tall **Sagamore Bridge,** a big WPA-era span in the art deco style, carries U.S. 6 over the **Cape Cod Canal,** the world's widest. The first 8-mi canal was completed in 1914 as a private venture, but it proved too narrow for safe passage. The Federal government bought out the first owners in 1928, doubling the width and adding the giant highway and railroad bridges that are Cape Cod's only ground transportation links to the rest of the world. Bluffs on both sides of the canal are surmounted by stretches of U.S. 6.

❷ Your first stop is **Sandwich.** The town's needle-spired church, still-functioning 1654 gristmill, and other historic structures both real and reproduced present the perfect backdrop for a stroll, particularly before or after visiting the **Sandwich Glass Museum.** Continue south of the town hall to **Heritage Plantation,** whose many acres of show gardens and buildings encompass collectible Americana ranging from cigar-store carved totems and military miniatures to antique cars and a working 1912 carousel.

❸ In **Sandy Neck,** Cape Cod's largest salt-marsh ecosystem and miles of barrier dunes provide hours of walking, bird-watching, beachcombing, and swimming.

❹ The approach to **Barnstable** includes many homes designed in the old Cape style, 1½ stories with one or two windows flanking a side or central door. Older, larger, and set back from the road is the **Sturgis Library** in a former parsonage built in 1644.

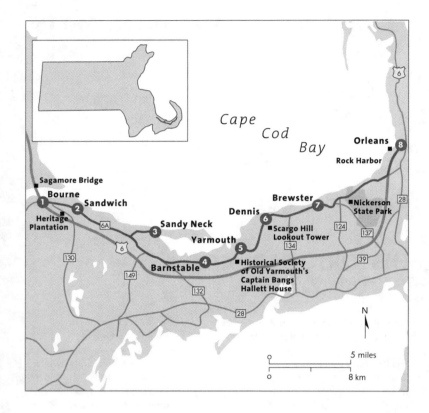

Genealogical collections can be viewed inside. Turn north at the traffic light to admire the harbor, or to take a trip in search of the world's largest mammals with **Hyannis Whale Watcher Cruises.** Barnstable's 1855 brick **Customs House** attests to the tiny community's long-lost importance as a port of entry for foreign shipping. Now the building houses the historical maritime collections of the **Donald G. Trayser Memorial Museum.**

⑤ As you cross from Barnstable into **Yarmouth,** look at the hedge on the right for the 17th-century granite boundary marker inscribed B–Y. Nearly opposite the Yarmouth Port village post office is the circa-1780 **Winslow Crocker House,** an affluent merchant's home moved here in 1936 and turned into a house-size display case for a private antiques collection. Next to the post office, facing the old village common, is the **Historical Society of Old Yarmouth's Captain Bangs Hallet House,** an 1840 residence also open to seasonal tours. Behind the house are 50 wooded acres with ponds and nature trails.

⑥ Not far from the small village green in **Dennis** stands the **Scargo Hill Lookout Tower.** On clear days the panoramic view from the stone parapet encompasses most of the shore of Cape Cod Bay, from Plymouth to Provincetown. Though mostly hidden from the tower by foliage, Dennis's half dozen fine bay-side beaches are easily accessible at the end of nearly every road that turns north from Route 6A. Arts complement recreation at the **Cape Playhouse,** the nation's oldest professional summer theater. Sharing the grounds of the Playhouse are the **Cape Museum of Fine Arts,** showcasing the work of local artists past and present, and the barnlike 1930s **Cape Cinema,** where independent and foreign films are shown.

❼ In **Brewster** houses share the highway with undeveloped tracts of salt marsh as Route 6A skirts the shore of Cape Cod Bay, which is often visible across the treeless wetlands. The **Cape Cod Museum of Natural History** takes advantage of its marshy surroundings with interpretive trails that build on the lessons learned from the museum's indoor exhibits. More scenic walking is found on trails around the old **Stony Brook Mill,** a functioning 1873 gristmill that anchored an area of town once known as Factory Village. **Nickerson State Park** has trails for cycling, horseback riding, and hiking, as well as ponds for swimming, boating, and fishing.

❽ In **Orleans** during the War of 1812 a British landing party from ships anchored in the bay attempted to come ashore at **Rock Harbor,** until persuaded to reconsider by fire from local militiamen's guns. A very different waterfront is found across town on the Atlantic shore at **Nauset Beach,** where the brisk, long surf rolls up the wide sandy strand.

Barnstable

Donald G. Trayser Memorial Museum. The main theme of this town-owned museum is the sea and Barnstable's connection to it. The three-museum complex includes Barnstable's Old Custom House, a carriage shed dominated by a large horse-drawn hearse,

MASSACHUSETTS RULES OF THE ROAD

License Requirements: Drivers in Massachusetts must be at least 18 years old and must have a valid driver's license from their home state or country.

Right Turn on Red: Massachusetts allows right turns at red lights after coming to a complete stop and yielding to all pedestrians, unless otherwise posted. Note that most urban intersections, especially in Boston, are posted with NO RIGHT TURN ON RED signs, although not always conspicuously.

Seat-Belt & Helmet Laws: Massachusetts law requires that everyone riding in a private passenger vehicle wear seat belts. This applies to drivers and all passengers age 12 and over, in cars, vans, and small trucks. State law also requires that motorcyclists and their passengers wear helmets.

Speed Limits: The maximum speed limit in Massachusetts, 65 mph, is only found along the interstates. On the more congested portions of the interstate system in and around Boston, the maximum is 50 mph to 55 mph. Numbered state highways have a maximum speed limit of 55 mph and are frequently posted much lower. Observe speed limits carefully, as speeding tickets are punitively expensive.

Other Regulations: Using handheld mobile phones is permitted while driving in Massachusetts. The legal blood-alcohol concentration limit in Massachusetts is .08%. An open-container law prohibits passengers from possessing open alcohol containers.

For More Information: Massachusetts Highway Department | 617/973–7800 | www.state.ma.us/mhd. Massachusetts State Police | 508/820–2284 | www.state.ma.us/msp/massachu.htm.

and the nation's oldest surviving jail, built in 1690, whose walls still display graffiti from its colonial prisoners. | Main St. (Rte. 6A) | 508/362–2092 | www.barnstablepatriot. com/trayser/museum | $2 donation | 3rd Sun. in June–mid-Oct., Tues.–Sun. 1:30–4:30.

Customs House. The U.S. government built this site in 1855–56 to serve as both a customs house and post office. The second floor now houses maritime artifacts from Barnstable county. The post office, on the first floor, operates only during the Village Stroll in December. | Cobb's Hill (Rte. 6A) | 508/362–2092 | Free with Trayser Museum donation | June 16–Oct. 12, Tues.–Sun. 1:30–4:40.

Hyannis Whale Watcher Cruises. Off the tip of Cape Cod, just north of Provincetown, lies Stellwagen Bank National Marine Sanctuary, whose nutrient-rich waters attract endangered whale species from spring through fall. Excursions to Stellwagen last $3\frac{1}{2}$ hours and include colorful commentary by onboard naturalists. Cruises depart twice a day in summer, once a day in spring and fall. Call for schedules. | Millway Marine Boatyard, Barnstable Harbor | 508/362–6088 or 888/942–5392 | www.whales.net | $29 | May–Oct., daily departure times vary according to tides.

Sandy Neck Beach. Hovering above Barnstable Harbor and the 4,000-acre Great Salt Marsh, this 6-mi-long beach is one of the Cape's most beautiful—dunes, sand, and sea spread endlessly east, west, and north. The marsh is a haven for birds, which are out and about in the greatest numbers morning and evening, at low tide, and during spring and fall migration. The main beach at Sandy Neck has lifeguards, a snack bar, rest rooms, and showers. | Sandy Neck Rd. off Rte. 6A, West Barnstable | 508/362–8300 | Beach free, parking $10 Memorial Day–Labor Day and weekends in June | Daily 9–9, lifeguards and snack bar 9–4.

Sturgis Library. Constructed in 1644 for the Reverend John Lothrop, founder of Barnstable, the house which forms the original part of the Library is the oldest Library building in the United States. Now one of Barnstable's seven public libraries, it has special collections including some of the region's leading genealogical resources, as well as small displays related to local history. | 3090 Main St. (Rte. 6A) | 508/362–6636 | home.capecod.net/~sturgis/links.html | Library free, genealogical research $5 | Mon., Wed., and Fri. 10–5; Tues. 1–8; Thurs. 1–5; Sat. 10–4.

Dining

Barnstable Tavern and Grille. Seafood. In operation since 1799, this cozy colonial tavern is amid a cluster of shops in the historic district. Real New England dishes focus on the fine local seafood. Dine on the patio if weather permits. Live music Friday 5–7. Kids' menu. No smoking. | 3180 Rte. 6A | 508/362–2355 | AE, D, DC, MC, V | $11–$22 | $–$$$

Mattakeese Wharf. Seafood. The casual dining rooms and over-the-water decks provide exceptional views of boats, seagulls, and sunsets. Try the bouillabaisse, baked stuffed shrimp, or lobster. Open-air dining. Sunday brunch. Live music Wednesday–Sunday. No smoking. | 271 Mill Way | 508/362–4511 | Closed Nov.–Apr. | AE, D, MC, V | $13–$25 | $$–$$$$

Lodging

★**Beechwood Inn.** This 1853 Queen Anne is trimmed with gingerbread, wrapped by a wide porch with wicker furniture and a glider swing. Although the parlor is pure mahogany-and-red-velvet Victorian, guest rooms (all with queen- or king-size beds) have antiques in lighter Victorian styles; several have fireplaces, and one has a bay view. Bathrooms have pedestal sinks and antique lighting fixtures. Breakfast is served in the dining room, which has a pressed-tin ceiling, a fireplace, and lace-covered tables. Afternoon tea and homemade snacks are also available. Refrigerators, bicycles; no room phones, no TV in some rooms, no kids under 12, no smoking. | 2839

Main St. (Rte. 6A), 02630 | 508/362–6618 or 800/609–6618 | fax 508/362–0298 | www. beechwoodinn.com | 6 rooms | BP | AE, D, MC, V | $$$

Bourne

Adventure Isle. Two miles south of the Bourne Bridge is Cape Cod's largest amusement park. Among the attractions are New England's largest go-cart track, bumper cars and bumper boats, miniature golf, batting cages, laser tag, and rides for small children. | 343 MacArthur Blvd. | 508/759–2636 or 800/535–2787 | www.adventureisle.com | $12.95 | Apr.–Oct., daily 10 AM–11 PM.

Aptucxet Trading Post Museum. The first free trade in America took place here. Traders bartered for furs from Native Americans, using wampum, strings of beads made from quahog clamshells, as currency. The museum is a replica, rebuilt on the foundation of the small trading house built by the Pilgrim colonists from Plymouth circa 1626. Other historic structures moved to the site include a windmill and the depot used by President Grover Cleveland during his visits to the area. | 24 Aptucxet Rd. | 508/759–9487 | $3.50 | Memorial Day–Columbus Day, Tues.–Sat. 10–4, Sun. 2–5.

Cape Cod Canal Cruises. Two- or three-hour cruises down the Cape Cod Canal departing from the town pier in Victorian-pretty Onset have a live commentary about the history and sights of the area. There are summer sunset and evening cruises with cocktails and live music. | Onset Town Pier, Onset Ave. | 508/295–3883 | www. hy-linecruises.com | $10–$12 | Memorial Day–Oct., daily; call for schedule.

Pairpoint Crystal Co. Inside this nondescript metal warehouse is the oldest glass factory store in the country—it's been handcrafting traditional lead crystal since 1837. You can observe glassblowers at work and purchase their wares. | 851 Sandwich Rd. | 508/888–2344 or 800/899–0953 | www.pairpoint.com | Free | Shop May–Oct., weekdays 9–6, Sat. 10–6, Sun. 11–6; Nov.–Apr., Mon.–Sat. 10–5, Sun. 11–5. Glassblowing May–Dec., weekdays 9–4:30.

Dining

The Bridge. American. Traditional New England with a few Italian and some eclectic menu choices, this Cape restaurant has been run by the same family since the 1930s. Portions are large but prices are small. Stick to the basics like Yankee pot roast and fresh scrod. Kids' menu. Early-bird suppers weekdays. | 21 Rte. 6A, Sagamore, just west of Bourne | 508/888–8144 | D, DC, MC, V | $5–$15 | ¢–$$

Brewster

Cape Cod Museum of Natural History. For nature enthusiasts a visit to this museum is a must. The museum and grounds include guided field walks, a shop, a natural history library, lectures, nature and marine exhibits such as a working beehive, and a pond-and sea-life room with live specimens. Walking trails wind through 80 acres of forest, marshland, and ponds, all rich in birds and other wildlife. The exhibit hall upstairs has a wall display of aerial photographs documenting the process by which the famous Chatham sandbar was split in two. | 869 Main St. (Rte. 6A) | 508/896–3867, 800/479–3867 in MA | www.ccmnh.org | $7 | Mon.–Sat. 9:30–4:30, Sun. 11–4:30.

New England Fire and History Museum. The world's largest collection of fire memorabilia is housed here. Exhibits include everything from a 1929 Mercedes-Benz fire engine to an animated diorama of the Great Chicago Fire. There's also a blacksmith shop and an antique drugstore. | 1439 Main St. | 508/896–5711 | www.nefiremuseum.org | $4 | Memorial Day–mid-Sept., weekdays 10–4; July and Aug., weekends noon–4; mid-Sept.–Columbus Day, weekends noon–4.

Nickerson State Park. The 1,961 acres encompassed by this expansive park were once part of a vast estate belonging to Roland C. Nickerson, son of Samuel Nickerson, a Chatham native who became a multimillionaire and founder of the First National Bank of Chicago. The park consists of acres of forest dotted with seven freshwater kettle ponds that were formed by glacial action. Some ponds are stocked with trout for fishing. You can swim in the ponds, canoe, sail, motorboat, picnic, cross-country ski in winter, and bike along 8 mi of paved trails that have access to the Cape Cod Rail Trail. Flax Pond, in particular, is a kid-friendly freshwater pond surrounded by pines and has picnic areas, a bathhouse, and water-sports rentals. Bird-watchers seek out the many species that frequent the park. Occasionally, red foxes and white-tailed deer are spotted in the woods. Camping is extremely popular here, and nature programs are offered in season. | 3488 Rte. 6A, East Brewster | 508/896–3491 | www.state.ma.us/dem/parks/nick.htm | Free | Daily dawn–dusk.

Punkhorn Parklands. Once home to the Saquatuck Indians, these 800 acres of conservation land encompass 45 mi of trails through lush pine forests and bog land. The short Eagle Point Trail, which begins to the right of the parking lot, leads to a scenic overlook on Upper Mill Pond. There are longer walks of up to six hours. Trail maps are available at Brewster Town Hall (2198 Main St.) and at the beginning of the trails on-site, but note that no phone is available. | End of Run Hill Rd. off Stony Brook Rd. | No phone | Free | Daily dawn–dusk.

Stony Brook Grist Mill. Also known as the Old Grist Mill, this photogenic 1873 mill with its small waterwheel powered by the namesake Stony Brook is only the latest incarnation to occupy this site. The first was erected here in 1663 and helped spawn a small factory village of water-driven local industry along the now-peaceful banks of the small brook. Cornmeal is ground in the mill and is available for purchase in local shops. You can also get a lesson in weaving on a 100-year-old loom. Each spring, herring swim in from Cape Cod Bay up Paine's Creek to Stony Brook, just across from the mill. It's quite a sight. | Stony Brook Rd., West Brewster | No phone | By donation | June–Aug., weekends 10–2.

Dining

Brewster Fish House. Seafood. A long-standing favorite for straightforward seafood, the Fish House has expanded its menu to include more contemporary preparations. Although old favorites like lobster bisque remain on the menu, you might also find pan-roasted lobster with potato gnocchi or an Asian-inspired crispy whole fish. The wine list includes an interesting selection of by-the-glass offerings. Expect long waits for a table on summer weekends. Be sure to call ahead to confirm open hours in the off-season. | 2208 Main St. (Rte. 6A) | 508/896–7867 | Reservations not accepted | MC, V | $18–$26 | $$–$$$$

★ **Chillingsworth.** French. Long regarded as one of the crown jewels of Cape restaurants, Chillingsworth has a formal presentation, excellent (but pricey) French menu, and diverse wine cellar, which combine to create a memorable dining experience. The nightly seven-course menu rotates through an assortment of courses. Super-rich risotto, roast lobster, and grilled venison are among the local favorites. You can also eat in the more casual, patio-style Garden Room. Sunday brunch. | 2449 Main St. (Rte. 6A), East Brewster | 508/896–3640 | www.chillingsworth.com | Jacket required | Closed late Nov.–late May; Mon. mid-June–late Nov.; and some weekdays late May–mid-June and mid-Oct.–late Nov. | AE, DC, MC, V | $55–$67 prix-fixe | $$$$

★ **Hopkins House Gift and Bakery.** American. If you need a quick break, this is the perfect pit stop. Wash down a chewy Hermit cookie—a specialty baked with molasses and raisins—with some strong hot coffee. Have an assortment of cookies, muffins, and snack bars boxed up for the road. A home furnishings shop attached to the bakery might tempt you to stretch your legs a while longer. Meals are not served. | 2727 Main St. | 508/896–9337 | AE, MC, V | $2–$7 | ¢

Lodging

★ **Captain Freeman Inn.** Period furnishings and a wraparound porch punctuate this mid-19th-century home overlooking 2½ acres of gardens and lawns. The innkeepers offer such personal services as arranging private canoe and kayak trips and guided historical tours. A cooking school is held weekends during the off-season. The property is within walking distance of the beach, restaurants, shops, and a bicycle trail. Cable TV, in-room VCRs with movies, pool, massage, bicycles, laundry facilities, airport shuttle; no phones in some rooms, no kids under 10, no smoking. | 15 Breakwater Rd., 02631 | 508/896–7481 or 800/843–4664 | fax 508/896–5618 | www.captainfreemaninn.com | 12 rooms | BP | MC, V | $180–$225 | $$$–$$$$

Dennis

Cape Museum of Fine Arts. Cape Cod's main art museum has a permanent collection of more than 850 works by Cape-associated artists, including Charles Hawthorne, William Paxton, Varujan Boghosian, Karl Knaths, and Hans Hoffman. The museum also hosts film festivals, lectures, art classes, and trips. | 60 Hope La., on grounds of Cape Playhouse, off Rte. 6A | 508/385–4477 | www.cmfa.org | $7, free Sat. 10–1 (donations accepted) | Late May–mid-Oct., Mon.–Sat. 10–5, Sun. 1–5; mid-Oct.–late May, Tues.–Sat. 10–5, Sun. 1–5.

Dining

Ebb Tide Restaurant. Seafood. There are six cozy colonial-style dining rooms at this ocean-side restaurant. The emphasis is on fresh seafood (and lots of it), but steak lovers can find plenty to love, too. The McCormick family opened Ebb Tide in 1959, and all the recipes originate with them. There are many fans of the lower-priced early-bird dinners, which start at 4:30. From Dennis, take Route 6 to Route 134 South; then take exit 9A to Route 28. Turn right on Belmont Road and follow it to the end. | 94 Chase Ave., Dennisport | 508/398–8733 | No lunch. Closed mid-Oct. to early May | AE, MC, V | $18–$28 | $$–$$$$

★ **Gina's by the Sea.** Italian. While this spot by the sea looks unpromising from the outside, the interior is another story: fine northern Italian meals are dished up in a plain but cozy room, which is kept toasty warm in the chilly off-season by fireplaces. Try the scampi à la Gina's (pasta and fresh shrimp in a garlicky butter sauce) or the chicken Gizmundo, in tomato sauce. | 134 Taunton Ave. | 508/385–3213 | Reservations not accepted | Closed Dec.–Mar. No lunch. Open Thurs.–Sun. only after Labor Day, 5–9 | AE, MC, V | $11–$24 | $–$$$

The Marshside. American. Fried clams are the specialty of this casual, down-home eatery. American standards such as burgers, salads, and the like are done well, and the homemade desserts are a highlight. Open year-round. Kids' menu. No smoking. Breakfast served. | 28 Bridge St., East Dennis | 508/385–4010 | Reservations not accepted | AE, D, DC, MC, V | $5–$20 | ¢–$$

Red Pheasant. American. This is one of the Cape's best cozy country-inn kitchens, where hearty American food is prepared with elaborate sauces and herb combinations. Rack of lamb might be served with an intense port-and-rosemary reduction, and exquisitely grilled veal chops come with a red wine and Portobello mushroom sauce. In fall look for the specialty game dishes, including venison and quail. Try to reserve a table in the more intimate Garden Room. Men may want to wear a jacket. | 905 Main St. (Rte. 6A) | 508/385–2133 or 800/480–2133 | Reservations essential | Closed some wks late Feb.–Mar. No lunch | D, MC, V | $18–$30 | $$–$$$$

Swan River Restaurant. Seafood. If the attached fish market doesn't give it away, the menu will: seafood is the story here, told in all its flavorful variations, from simple to creative, framed by views of the eponymous Swan River estuary and the ocean. Try the bouillabaisse, seafood creole, and shrimp and littlenecks on linguine. Raw bar. Live music midweek evenings. Kids' menu. | 5 Lower County Rd., Dennisport | 508/394–4466 | Closed mid-Sept.–late May | AE, D, MC, V | $8–$20 | $–$$

Lodging

Isaiah Hall B&B Inn. Lilacs and pink roses trail along the white picket fence outside this 1857 Greek Revival farmhouse on a residential road near the bay. Guest rooms have country antiques, floral-print wallpapers, and such homey touches as quilts and Priscilla curtains. In the attached carriage house, rooms have three walls stenciled white and one wall of knotty pine, and some have small balconies overlooking a wooded lawn with gardens, grape arbors, and berry bushes. Make-it-yourself popcorn, tea, coffee, and soft drinks are always available. Picnic area, in-room data ports, in-room VCRs with movies, badminton, croquet; no kids under 7, no smoking. | 152 Whig St. | Box 1007, 02638 | 508/385–9928 or 800/736–0160 | fax 508/385–5879 or 800/736–0160 | www.isaiahhallinn.com | 9 rooms, 1 suite | Closed mid-Oct.–early May | CP | AE, D, MC, V | $100–$155 | $$–$$$

Orleans

Academy of Performing Arts. Formerly the town hall, this handsome 1873 building hosts theater, music, and dance performances year-round. There are many shows geared to children in summer, generally Saturday mornings and Thursday. | 120 Main St. | 508/255–3075 | www.apa1.org | Performances $10–$18 | June–mid-Sept., Tues.–Sun.; mid-Sept.–May, Thurs.–Sun. Call for performance times.

French Cable Station Museum. This 1890 museum was the stateside landing point for the 3,000-mi-long transatlantic cable that originated in Brittany. Another cable laid between Orleans and New York City completed the France–New York link, and many important messages were communicated through the station. In World War I it was an essential connection between army headquarters in Washington and the American Expeditionary Force in France, and the station was under guard by the marines. By 1959 telephone service had rendered the station obsolete and it closed. The equipment, however, is still in place. | 41 S. Orleans Rd., East Orleans | 508/240–1735 | www.atlantic-cable.com | By donation | June, Fri.–Sun. 1–4; July–early Sept., Mon.–Sat. 1–4.

Jonathan Young Windmill. This windmill dates from 1700 and is now in its third location in the Orleans vicinity. Meticulously restored, it still grinds corn on occasion. | Rte. 6A and Town Cove | No phone | Free | July and Aug., daily 11–4; Sept.–early Oct., limited weekend hrs.

Nauset Beach. Ten miles of tawny sand face the Atlantic and ensure plenty of elbow room for anyone willing to walk far enough. In summer there are bathhouses with showers and a fried-seafood shack that also rents beach chairs and umbrellas. The nearby Nauset lighthouse was moved from its precarious cliff-top position to a safer site in a notable feat of engineering. The large waves make Nauset good for bodysurfing or board surfing. The beach has lifeguards, rest rooms, showers, and a food concession. | Beach Rd. | 508/240–3775 | Free, parking $10 | Daily sunrise–sunset.

Rock Harbor. Today it hosts a charter fishing fleet and is a nice place to watch the sun set, but this harbor has a storied past. The former packet boat landing was the site of a War of 1812 episode in which the Orleans militia kept a British warship from coming ashore. | Rock Harbor Rd.

Dining

Captain Linnell House. Continental. Come to this Greek Revival home for an intimate dinner of traditional, perfectly prepared meats and fish. Try the rack of roasted baby veal with basil demi-glace, or the monkfish in a Yukon gold potato crust. There's open-air dining on the patio. No smoking. | 137 Skaket Beach Rd. | 508/255–3400 | Closed Mar. and Mon. and Tues. Dec.–Feb. and Apr. and May. No lunch | AE, MC, V | $19–$30 | $$–$$$$

Lobster Claw. Seafood. Fishing nets, brightly painted tables, and happy customers fill this quintessential Cape Cod lobster house, which has been serving ocean-fresh local specialties since 1963. Try the lobster club sandwich, surf-and-turf platter, and mud ice-cream pie. Kids' menu. Early-bird suppers. No smoking. | 42 Rte. 6A | 508/255–1800 | Closed Nov.–Mar. | AE, MC, V | $9–$20 | $–$$

Mahoney's Atlantic Bar & Grill. Contemporary. The creative cuisine here is paired with a fantastic location right in the middle of everything. Try grilled vegetables and polenta or drunken littleneck clams steamed in ale. The 50-foot-long mahogany bar is a nice place to hang out or have a light bite. | 28 Main St. | 508/255–5505 | Closed Jan.–Mar. | AE, MC, V | $15–$28 | $$–$$$$

★ **Nauset Beach Club.** Italian. Flowers, lovely table linen, and an exhaustive wine list helps set the sophisticated, urban-bistro tone in the two small dining rooms of this Cape cottage. The food is contemporary Italian, with specialties such as salmon braised with escarole, prosciutto, and shallots; sun-dried-tomato–crusted halibut with roasted garlic and sage butter; and grilled veal loin with wild mushrooms. Try one of the more than 20 wines by the glass. | 222 E. Main St., 02653 | 508/255–8547 | Reservations essential | Closed Sun. and Mon. mid-Oct.–late May. No lunch | AE, MC, V | $17–$29 | $$–$$$$

Sandwich

★ **Heritage Plantation.** This 76-acre estate was the former home of horticulturist Charles Dexter. Even if you are not interested in the distinctive rhododendrons he cultivated, you might want to explore one of the museums: one displaying antique cars; another devoted to American history, with battle dioramas, the Cape Cod Baseball Hall of Fame, American firearms, and Native American art; and a third with American memorabilia, crafts, and folk art, with notable examples of the unique Nantucket lightship baskets named for the fine and sturdy baskets originated over 150 years ago by captains and crew manning the lightships anchored in strategic locations to warn ship of dangerous shoals off the coast of Nantucket Island, Massachusetts. Walk a labyrinth and see the windmill and working 1912 carousel. | 67 Grove St. | 508/888–3300 | www.heritagemuseumsandgardens.org | $12 | Mid-May–Oct., Fri.–Sun., Tues., Wed. 9–6, Thurs. 9–8; Nov. and Dec., Tues.–Sun. 10–4; Jan.–Apr., call for hrs.

Hoxie House and Dexter Gristmill. Dating from the 1630s, the Hoxie House is supposedly the oldest saltbox house on Cape Cod. Today it's a museum, complete with 17th-century furnishings. In the adjacent 1654 Dexter Mill you can watch live milling demonstrations. | Water St. | 508/888–1173 | $2.50 | Mid-June–mid-Oct., Tues.–Sat. 10–5, Sun. 1–5.

Sandwich Boardwalk. Crossing Mill Creek and acres of salt marsh, the boardwalk leads to one the nicest beaches in the area. Weather permitting, you can see miles of coastline from here. | Jarves St. | Free | Daily dawn–dusk.

Sandwich Glass Museum. The main industry in 19th-century Sandwich was producing vividly colored glass. This museum contains a glinting array of over 5,000 examples of the glassmakers' art and industry. An additional highlight is the museum shop with both contemporary glass and reproductions of antique items. Glassmaking demonstrations are held in summer. | 129 Main St. | 508/888–0251 | www.sandwichglassmuseum.org | $3.75 | Apr.–Dec., daily 9:30–5; Nov., Feb., Mar., Wed.–Sun. 9:30–4.

Thornton W. Burgess Museum. The life and characters of children's author Thornton Burgess is the focus of this charming museum. Burgess is famous for his tales of Peter Rabbit, Reddy Fox, and other assorted animal friends. There's storytelling in July and August. | 4 Water St. | 508/888–4668 | www.thorntonburgess.org | $2 donation | Apr.– Oct., Mon.–Sat. 10–4, Sun. 1–4.

Dining

Aqua Grille. Contemporary. A lively bar scene keeps the atmosphere upbeat in this airy dining room that's more Miami Beach than classic Cape Cod. Fittingly, the wide-ranging menu has more sass than many in the area, from soba noodles with spicy Thai sauce to chipotle aioli or Cajun rémoulade served with fish. Try the tuna sashimi, salads, and grilled fish specials, and wash them down with specialty martinis and margaritas. Open-air dining on porch. Kids' menu. | 14 Gallo Rd. | 508/888–8889 | Closed Nov.–Mar. | AE, MC, V | $12–$20 | $$

Belfry Inne and Bistro. Contemporary. Dining in a converted church can seem odd until you step inside to soaring ceilings and stained glass in this serene space. A regularly changing menu might include duck breast with wild mushroom risotto, lobster-scallop-leek phyllo strudel, filet mignon, crab-stuffed gray sole, or Thai chicken. Unique combinations include lots of fresh vegetables. Open-air dining on patio. Kids' menu. Early-bird suppers. No smoking. Reservations essential in summer. | 8 Jarves St. | 508/888–8550 or 800/844–4542 | Closed Sun. and Mon. No lunch | AE, MC, V | $21–$29 | $$$–$$$$

Dunbar Tea Shop. English. Don't miss a stop at this charming tearoom. In summer enjoy lunch or afternoon tea in a bucolic flower garden or inside the 250-year-old house. Traditional English lunches with Stilton cheese or smoked salmon are served, followed by wonderful home-baked scones, crumpets, shortbread, or nearly a dozen kinds of pie. | 1 Water St. | 508/833–2485 | No dinner | AE, MC, V | $5–$10 | ¢–$

Lodging

Dan'l Webster Inn. Approaching the inn from the curved driveway to the wide portico, you can imagine arriving in a horse-drawn carriage, but inside, updated amenities aim to please the modern traveler. Rooms are decorated in various antique styles, and most have four-poster beds and country fabrics. Some rooms have fireplaces. There are gardens to stroll. Restaurant, some in-room hot tubs, cable TV, pool, gym, wine bar. | 149 Main St., 02563 | 508/888–3622 or 800/444–3566 | www.danlwebsterinn.com | 54 rooms | AE, MC, V | $159–$289 | $$$–$$$$

Yarmouth

Captain Bangs Hallet House. Built in 1840 onto an existing 1740 house for a sea captain in the China trade, then bought by another, who swapped it with a third captain, this white Greek Revival building typifies a well-to-do 19th-century home, with pieces of pewter, china, nautical equipment, antique toys, and clothing on display. The kitchen has the original 1740 brick beehive oven and butter churns. Tours are on the hour. | 11 Strawberry La., off Rte. 6A, Yarmouth Port | 508/362–3021 | $3 | June–mid-Oct., Thurs.–Sun. 1–4.

Winslow Crocker House. This elegantly symmetrical two-story Georgian, built in 1780, has 12-over-12 small-pane windows and rich paneling in every room. Crocker was a well-to-do trader and land speculator; after his death, his two sons built a wall dividing the house in half. The house was moved here from West Barnstable in 1936 by Mary Thacher, who donated it—along with her collection of 17th- to 19th-century furniture, pewter, hooked rugs, and ceramics—to the Society for the Preservation of New England Antiquities, which operates it as a museum. Tours are on the hour. | 250 Main St. (Rte. 6A), Yarmouth Port | 508/362–4385 | www.spnea.org | $4 | June–mid-Oct., weekends 11–5.

ZooQuarium. Both entertaining and educational, this combination zoo and aquarium has a petting area with hoofed creatures, sea-lion shows, wandering peacocks, pony rides, and changing exhibits like "Zoo Nutrition," in which kids prepare meals for their webbed friends. | 674 Main St., West Yarmouth | 508/775–8883 | zooquarium-capecod.net | $9 | Feb.–late June and early Sept.–late Nov., daily 9:30–5; late June–early Sept., daily 9:30–6.

Dining

Hallet's. American. Light breakfasts and lunches are served at a marble soda fountain in this restored 1889 drugstore. Don't miss the homemade ice-cream specialties including frappés, malteds, or sodas. | 138 Main St | 508/362–3362 | No dinner | MC, V | $2–$6 | ¢

Hearth 'N Kettle. American. A wide variety of seafood—lobster, baked salmon, fried clams—as well as chicken and steak dishes are available in this family-owned chain eatery. Desserts and breads are homemade. The dining room overlooks a pond in the backyard. Breakfast served. | 1196 Main St. | 508/394–2252 | AE, D, MC, V | $5–$16 | ¢–$$

Jack's Outback. American/Casual. Tough to find, tough to forget, this eccentric local hangout lives up to its motto, "Good food, lousy service." One of the owners, Jack Braginton-Smith, is a local historian of note, and as far as locals are concerned, if he *doesn't* insult you, you've been insulted. Solid breakfasts give way by midday to thick burgers, freshly concocted sandwiches, pasta salads, homemade soups, and traditional favorites such as Yankee pot roast and fried chicken. Jack's has no liquor license, and you cannot BYOB. | 161 Main St. (Rte. 6A), Yarmouth Port | 508/362–6690 | Reservations not accepted | No dinner | No credit cards | $6–$12 | ¢–$

Lodging

★**Wedgewood Inn.** This handsome 1812 Greek Revival house, on the National Register of Historic Places, is sophisticated but welcoming, with a mix of fine colonial antiques, maritime paintings, and quilts atop handcrafted cherry pencil-post beds. Two spacious suites in the main building have canopy beds, fireplaces, and porches; three additional—and very spacious—suites in the restored barn have king-size beds, TV/VCRs, and large bathrooms. Innkeeper Gerrie Graham cooks elegant breakfasts such as Belgian waffles with strawberries, or eggs with hollandaise sauce. Her husband Milt helps you make plans for the day. Some in-room VCRs; no room phones, no kids under 10, no smoking. | 83 Main St. (Rte. 6A), 02675 | 508/362–5157 or 508/362–9178 | fax 508/362–5851 | www.wedgewood-inn.com | 4 rooms, 5 suites | BP | AE, MC, V | $135–$215 | $$–$$$$

MICHIGAN

THE "MICHIGAN RIVIERA"
FROM LUDINGTON TO TRAVERSE CITY

Distance: Approximately 125 mi   Time: 2 days
Overnight Break: Frankfort

The northwest coast of the Lower Peninsula is sometimes referred to as the "Michigan Riviera." Filled with million-dollar resorts and unmatched natural beauty, it's a land of rolling hills, white sand dunes, peaceful orchards, and dramatic vistas of lake and sky.

❶ Start in **Ludington,** a popular fishing center and port on the eastern shore of Lake Michigan. A huge illuminated cross overlooks the harbor and marks the spot where Père Jacques Marquette is thought to have died in 1675. Nearby is **White Pine Village,** a reconstructed 19th-century community overlooking Lake Michigan, with more than 30 buildings, including a blacksmith shop, a schoolhouse, and logging and maritime museums.

You might spot Ludington's resident car ferry, the SS *Badger,* carrying its 600 passengers across Lake Michigan through Père Marquette Lake by way of the Ludington North Breakwater Lighthouse. Right downtown and at the western end of Ludington Avenue, the stately and attractive light can be seen up to 19 mi out.

❷ Another Ludington favorite is **Ludington State Park.** To get there, turn right at the western terminus of Ludington Avenue onto Lakeshore Drive (M–116), a stunning 8-mi drive through pure white sand dunes. With more than 5,000 acres of forest and an inland lake, the park is known for its scenic hiking trails and dunes, its large campground, and the **Big Sable Point Lighthouse,** accessible only via a 1½-mi beach walk. The attractive lighthouse is one of the most photographed in Michigan due to its unusual black and white stripes. Built in 1867, the 112-foot tower was originally made of brick and later enclosed in steel plates to enable it to withstand the strong Lake Michigan winds.

From Ludington, head north on Route 31 about 20 mi to Forest Trail. This 8-mi road leads to the entrance of the **Nordhouse Dunes,** a 4,300-acre recreation area operated by the National Forest Service, part of the **Huron-Manistee National Forest.**

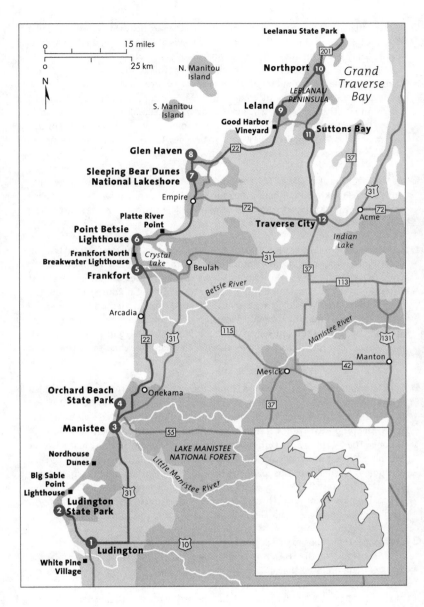

The unspoiled wild dunes are a favorite stop for hikers, campers, shutterbugs, and those looking for a good cardiovascular workout.

❸ About 10 mi north of the dunes is **Manistee,** known today as the Victorian Port City. French and English fur traders inhabited the area that the Chippewa Indians called *Manistee* (spirit of the woods) as early as the late 18th century. A 19th-century logging frenzy produced the town's mix of architectural styles, including Italianate, shingle, and Gothic revival. Manistee's best beaches are Fifth Avenue Beach (follow Memorial Dr., which becomes 5th Ave., to Monroe St.; turn right and follow the signs) and First Street Beach (follow 1st St. until it ends), with great swimming, pure white sand, and free admission. Both beaches have views of the Manistee North Pierhead Light.

❹ About 2 mi north of Manistee on Lakeshore Road is **Orchard Beach State Park,** a popular detour off Route 31. On a bluff with dramatic views of Lake Michigan, the park has a soft, sandy beach, modern campsites, and shady picnic areas.

North of Manistee Route 22 branches off Route 31. Follow Route 22 around Portage Lake and through the small towns of Onekama and Arcadia. Along the way, you're rewarded by views of Lake Michigan on your left and hilly orchards with apple, peach, and cherry trees. About 2 mi north of town take a break at the scenic overlook, clearly marked on the west side of the road, providing views of Portage Point, Portage Lake, and miles of unspoiled Lake Michigan beaches. To expand your view, climb 120 steps to the top of an observation platform.

❺ As you near Frankfort north of the Betsie River, turn left onto Main Street into downtown **Frankfort.** High bluffs surround the harbor, known for its sandy beach and lighthouse (at the western end of Main St.). Frankfort's natural harbor is a favorite of recreational boaters and fishermen.

❻ From Frankfort, follow Route 22 North. The road skirts the shores of Crystal Lake on your right and soon passes the **Point Betsie Lighthouse,** built in 1858. Turn left on Point Betsie Road to reach the landmark light, which still occasionally houses Coast Guard families. Leaving the lighthouse, continue north on Route 22. Follow the highway 8 mi to Lake Michigan Road at the Platte River. Turn left and travel 2½ mi to **Platte River Point** for a dramatic view of the Sleeping Bear Dunes to the north. You can also swim or sun yourself on the beach, unique in Michigan for its river, which empties directly into Lake Michigan, curving through the white-sand beach and providing a calm place to swim if the lake is too choppy.

❼ Back on Route 22, head north toward Empire through rolling hills and meadows filled with apple trees. Two miles north of Empire, Route 109 leads north to Pierce Stocking Scenic Drive, a 7½-mi loop within one of Michigan's most beloved natural attractions, **Sleeping Bear Dunes National Lakeshore.** The drive is open May through October. The Sleeping Bear Dunes take their name from an Ojibway legend. After escaping a forest fire in Wisconsin, a mother bear is said to have swum across Lake Michigan with her two cubs following her. Once she reached the Michigan shore, she sat at the top of a bluff to wait for them. Her cubs never made it. Their bodies are said to have become North and South Manitou islands. The mother bear's body, long since covered with sand, sleeps beneath the giant 400-foot sand dunes.

❽ Exiting the scenic loop proceed north along Route 109 to Route 209, a small spur leading to the ghost town of **Glen Haven** and Glen Haven Beach. Parking for the beach is beside a red storage building that once housed a canning factory. From the beach area, backtrack to Route 109 and continue east to Route 22. Head north, skirting the shore of Sleeping Bear Bay and passing through the resort town of **Glen Arbor.** With lots of interesting boutiques, cafés, and ice-cream shops, it's a nice place to take a break.

Route 22 passes Good Harbor Beach and Good Harbor Bay, both on your left, as it continues north to the **Leelanau Peninsula.** Extending 30 mi into Lake Michigan, the scenic peninsula is a favorite among vacationers for its charming towns, beautiful scenery, and vineyards. A dozen wineries, nearly all of which are on or near Route 22, open their tasting rooms and wine shops to visitors year-round, most commonly offering chardonnays, Rieslings, and pinot grigios. About 6 mi north of Good Harbor Beach you pass **Good Harbor Vineyard,** with a tasting room and a gift shop open daily 9–5 selling local produce and wines.

⑨ About 2 mi past the winery is **Leland,** a popular resort town named by the fishermen who used the harbor. Visit Fishtown, a collection of shops, galleries, and art studios downtown and home to the ferry service that transports visitors to North or South Manitou islands.

⑩ Continue north along Route 22 about 13 mi, winding through hilly terrain of cherry orchards and vineyards. **Northport** sits near the tip of the Leelanau Peninsula, a coastal community with a charming downtown of antiques shops, art galleries, and restaurants. If you love lighthouses, you may want to take a 7-mi side trip on Route 201 to **Leelanau State Park,** home to the Grand Traverse Lighthouse and a pebbled beach. The 1,200-acre state park is a favorite place to watch the sun set and is home to 52 campsites, most reserved well in advance. From Northport follow Route 22 South. The highway hugs the peninsula's eastern shore, skirting Northport Bay on your left. You might enjoy a visit to the **Leelanau Sands Casino,** on Route 22, between Omena and Suttons Bay. The casino-resort has gaming, a hotel, and a restaurant.

⑪ Once a wealthy sawmill town, **Suttons Bay** eventually turned to fruit-growing. Later, art replaced agriculture as craftspeople fled urban areas in search of a slower pace. Today Suttons Bay has tiny boutiques, antiques shops, and coffeehouses. It's also the site of some of the peninsula's finest restaurants.

From Suttons Bay, continue south on Route 22. Several wineries are open to the public along the drive toward Traverse City, northern Michigan's largest town. Check out the tasting rooms and wine shops of Black Star Farms (E. Revold Rd. just west of

MICHIGAN RULES OF THE ROAD

License Requirements: Michigan's minimum driving age is 16 with a valid driver's license.

Right Turn on Red: A right turn on red is permitted throughout the state *after* a full stop, unless posted signs state otherwise.

Seat-Belt & Helmet Laws: Seat belts are mandatory for all front-seat passengers and backseat passengers up to and including age 16. Children under 4 must be in an approved safety seat. Helmets are required for motorcyclists.

Speed Limits: The speed limit on most Michigan roads and highways is 55 mph and 70 mph on freeways unless otherwise posted. The speed limit in residential areas is 25 mph unless otherwise posted. Watch signs carefully—speed limits can change frequently on hilly or curved terrain. Radar detectors are permitted in Michigan.

Other Regulations: Michigan state law allows cell phone use while driving. No open alcohol containers are allowed within a vehicle unless stored in the trunk. Drivers in Michigan must not have a blood-alcohol concentration exceeding .10%.

For More Information: Michigan Department of State | 517/322–1460 | www.michigan.gov/sos. Michigan Department of Transportation | 517/373–2090 | www.michigan.gov/mdot. Michigan State Police | 517/332–2521 | www.michigan.gov/msp.

Rte. 22), Chateau de Leelanau (Rte. 22 at Hilltop Rd.), and Shady Lane Cellars (Shady Lane Rd. just west of Rte. 22), three wineries within view of Rte. 22. All of these wineries, and nearly all others on the Leelanau Peninsula, open their tasting rooms daily 11–5.

⑫ Nestled on the west end of Grand Traverse Bay, **Traverse City** has become a tourist mecca, known for its vibrant arts scene, nearby wineries, trendy shops, and water sports. Clinch Park is the local beach nearest to the city's downtown, on Rte. 37 east of Union Street. It's adjacent to the **Clinch Park Zoo**, filled with animals native to northern Michigan. A bit farther east of town is **Bryant Park Beach.** A long stretch of sandy beach, tall pines, picnic and playground facilities, and gorgeous sunsets make this beach the nicest in town. The 105-foot-tall ship *Manitou* is a replica schooner that runs daily sightseeing trips into the Grand Traverse Bay and functions as a floating bed-and-breakfast. Traverse City is also the home of the annual National Cherry Festival in July, which celebrates the area's status as the world's largest grower of cherries.

To return to Ludington, head south on Route 31.

Empire

★**Sleeping Bear Dunes National Lakeshore.** Many visitors love to run down these massive dunes into Lake Michigan—an easy enough feat. It's the climb up that tests your stamina. Be sure to wear shoes with good traction and take along some water. A National Park Service visitor center near the dune climb and the parking lot has information, rest rooms, and refreshments. Other park highlights include 50,000 acres of hardwood forests, 55 mi of well-marked, scenic hiking and cross-country ski trails, and canoeing on the Platte and Crystal rivers. | 9922 Front St. | 231/326–5134 | www.nps.gov/slbe | $7 weeklong pass | Dune climb and natural areas daily dawn–dusk. Visitor center June–Aug., daily 9–6; Sept.–May, daily 9–4.

Pierce Stocking Scenic Drive. Wind through Sleeping Bear Dunes on this 7½-mi loop, by foot, bike, or car. Pick up a free interpretive guide at the visitor center. | 2 mi north of Empire | May–Oct., daily dawn–dusk.

Frankfort

Point Betsie Lighthouse. The lighthouse once guarded one of northwest Michigan's busiest ports. North of the city of Frankfort, it marks the entrance to the Sleeping Bear Dunes National Lakeshore. You can picnic or swim here, and you can tour the lighthouse, if it isn't occupied by Coast Guard personnel. | Point Betsie Dr. | 800/882–5801 | $2 | Exterior daily dawn–dusk; interior Thurs.–Sat. 10–5, Sun. noon–5.

Dining

★**Coho Cafe.** Contemporary. This hip eatery is decorated with shiny stainless steel, its walls covered with turquoise and brown paint and vinyl. Dishes range from unusual sandwich combinations, like the tasty Border BLT with avocado and chipotle mayonnaise, to interesting entrées. Try the maple-rum–glazed pork tenderloin or the ravioli with wild mushrooms. Kids' menu. | 320 Main St. | 231/352–6053 | MC, V | $–$$

Hotel Frankfort. Continental. Antiques fill the understated dining room at this 1902 gingerbread Victorian hotel. Classic cuisine is the specialty: prime rib and entrées are cooked on a hot marble stone at your table. Pianist. Kids' menu. | 231 Main St. | 231/352–4303 | AE, D, MC, V | $$–$$$$

JoAnn's Restaurant. Continental. Bright yellow table linens and walls and crisp white dishes give this warm restaurant a sunny disposition even on the stormiest of days.

Thursday is Italian night, with a menu heavy on pastas, risotto, and Italian meat dishes. The standard dinner menu includes everything from chicken and seafood to meat loaf and bratwurst. | 411 Main St. | 231/352–4472 | Closed Tues. | MC, V | $–$$

Wharfside. Continental. A favorite of both locals and visitors, this casual Lake Michigan eatery has nice views of Betsie Bay through large picture windows. The menu includes full dinners, sandwiches, and tapas. Try the risotto of the day or the fresh whitefish. Kids' menu. No smoking. | 300 Main St. | 231/352–5300 | AE, MC, V | $–$$$

Lodging

Harbor Lights. Traditional rooms as well as condo-style lodgings are available at this motel with four buildings. Condos have decks and gorgeous views of Lake Michigan and the beach. Double rooms have no lake view. The grounds consist largely of sand dunes and dune grass, a perfect beach getaway. Some in-room hot tubs, some kitchenettes, cable TV with movies, indoor pool, lake, hot tub, beach, laundry facilities, business services, meeting rooms; no a/c in some rooms, no phones in some rooms. | 15 2nd St., 49635 | 231/352–9614 or 800/346–9614 | fax 231/352–6580 | www.harborlightsmotel.com | 57 rooms, 45 condos | D, MC, V | $$–$$$$

Hotel Frankfort. Whether you want a simple hotel-style room or a deluxe, romantic getaway, the Hotel Frankfort oozes Victorian charm throughout, with lots of pastel fabrics, lace, and crystal fixtures. Deluxe rooms include an in-room sauna or steam room and dinner in the restaurant downstairs. Restaurant, some in-room hot tubs, cable TV. | 15 2nd St., 49635 | 231/352–4303 | www.hotelfrankfort.com | 18 rooms | BP | AE, D, MC, V | $–$$$$

Portage Point Inn. On a narrow isthmus of lakeshore, this 1903 inn allows access to the warmer inland waters of Portage Lake on its eastern side and Lake Michigan to the west. Laid-back cottage living is the norm here—children have the run of the shuffleboard courts and the beach area, and families arrive at dinner with their hair still wet from swimming. Cottages and condos must be rented by the week from late June to mid-August, but by the night during the off-season. Restaurant, ice-cream parlor, picnic area, some in-room hot tubs, some kitchens, some kitchenettes, cable TV, 2 tennis courts, indoor pool, 2 lakes, gym, hot tub, beaches, dock, boating, jet skiing, marina, fishing, shuffleboard, snowmobiling, lounge, recreation room, laundry facilities, business services, meeting rooms; no smoking. | 8513 Portage Point Dr., Onekama 49675, 20 mi south of Frankfort | 231/889–4222 or 800/878–7248 | fax 231/889–4260 | www.portagepointinn.com | 30 rooms, 12 cottages, 38 condos | AE, D, MC, V | $$$

R&R Motel. Simple but bright and clean, this inexpensive motel's best feature is its beautifully landscaped grounds. In summer, 6-foot hollyhocks line the parking areas and walkways. Flower beds with lilies, roses, and lavender border footpaths leading to a small stream and a gazebo. Cable TV. | 519 Lake St. (Rte. 22), 49635 | 231/352–9238 | 12 rooms | Closed early Oct.–Apr. | MC, V | $

Ludington

★**Ludington State Park.** Lake Michigan and Hamlin Lake border this park, which has 6 mi of Lake Michigan beach and sand dunes. Hiking and cross-country trails meander for miles, while a canoe trail follows the Hamlin Lake shoreline. The park has a visitor center. | Lakeshore Dr. (M–116), 8 mi north of town | 231/843–8671 or 800/447–2757 | Pedestrians free, vehicles $4 | Daily dawn–dusk.

Big Sable Point Lighthouse. This classic and often-photographed 1867 lighthouse sits right on the Lake Michigan beach. To reach the light, walk north along the shore for 1½ mi from the park entrance. | Lakeshore Dr. (M–116) | 231/845–7343 | www.bigsablelighthouse.org | $2 | May–Oct., daily 10–6.

Père Marquette Memorial Cross. Marking the spot where Father Jacques Marquette is thought to have died in 1675, this huge, illuminated cross overlooks the harbor from the south side of Père Marquette Lake. | S. Lakeshore Dr. | 231/845–5430 or 800/542–4600.

Stearns Park. You can sun on the beach, put your boat in the water, and go fishing at this public park along the city's western border. Don't pass up a walk to the Breakwater Lighthouse adjoining the park. | Lakeshore Dr., at W. Ludington Ave. | 800/542–4600 | Free | Daily dawn–dusk.

White Pine Village. Twenty buildings, including a blacksmith shop, a courthouse, a hardware store, and a school, overlook Lake Michigan from this reconstructed 19th-century community. The site includes logging and maritime museums and sits on the south side of Père Marquette Lake. | 1687 S. Lakeshore Dr. | 231/843–4808 | www.historicwhitepinevillage.org | $6 | Mid-June–Labor Day, Tues.–Sat. 11–5.

Dining

House of Flavors. Ice Cream. White tile and stainless-steel fixtures give this popular ice-cream parlor a 1950s diner look. Burgers, sandwiches, and hot dogs fill out the menu, making this a good stop for lunch or a light supper. But ice cream is the real draw, and you might not be able to resist the enticing array of three dozen flavors. | 402 W. Ludington Ave. | 231/845–5785 | MC, V | ¢

P. M. Steamers. American. Water views are fabulous from the outdoor deck or from a table by the window inside this casual nautical-theme restaurant across from the city marina. Popular dishes include nutty walleye, a lightly breaded panfried fillet, and chicken Caesar salad with lots of Parmesan cheese and a hint of anchovy. | 502 W. Loomis Ave. | 231/843–9555 | No lunch | AE, D, MC, V | $–$$$

Scotty's. American. You can enjoy the street scene on Ludington Avenue while waiting for your meal at this popular bistro. Natives and tourists alike come for seafood, lasagna, spaghetti, and thick cuts of prime rib in three sizes. Kids' menu. | 5910 E. Ludington Ave. (U.S. 10) | 231/843–4033 | AE, MC, V | $$–$$$$

Manistee

Orchard Beach State Park. Grassy picnic areas and a sandy Lake Michigan beach beckon at this park north of Manistee. A ½-mi self-guided nature trail and 1 mi of hiking trails are next to the campground, which has modern campsites. | M–110 | 231/723–7422 or 800/447–2757 | www.dnr.state.mi.us/camping | Pedestrians free, vehicles $4 | Daily dawn–dusk.

Dining

Four Forty West. Steak. Huge windows allow views of the Manistee River at this downtown restaurant. Steak-house classics are on the menu, but the specialty is grilled perch drizzled with an herb-butter sauce. | 440 River St. | 231/723–7902 | AE, D, MC, V | $$–$$$

Roadhouse Mexican Bar & Grill. Tex-Mex. Latin music fills the air in this hip, black-and-wood-tone eatery that serves mean Tex-Mex standards and brews its own beer. Enchiladas, nachos, and burritos fill the menu. As for the brews, ask for the small sampler glasses if you want to try a variety. | 310 River St. | 231/723–4200 | MC, V | $–$$

Suttons Bay

Leelanau Sands Casino. Thousands of visitors flock here for glitzy, Las Vegas–style gaming and shows. The large facility, built to resemble a North Woods lodge, has slots, blackjack, roulette, and craps. Hotel rooms are available on-site and the Double Eagle Restaurant has three-story views of the Leelanau Peninsula through plate-glass windows. | 2521 N.W. Bayshore Dr., Peshawbestown, 5 mi north of Suttons Bay | 231/271–4104 or 800/922–2946 | www.casino2win.com | Daily 10 AM–2 AM.

Dining

Boone's. American. Family-style dining and daily lunch specials attract locals and vacationers. Favorites include whitefish, steaks, and sandwiches. Cozy booths and a wood-and-stone interior create a rustic appeal. Kids' menu. | 102 St. Joseph St. | 231/271–6688 | MC, V | $–$$

Hattie's. Continental. Artwork from local artists accents the spare, elegant interior of this upscale restaurant. Morel ravioli and Thai-style scallops are among the choices from the innovative menu. Don't miss the sinful chocolate paradise with raspberries for dessert. | 111 St. Joseph St. | 231/271–6222 | Reservations essential | AE, D, MC, V | $$$$

★**Leelanau Country Inn.** Continental. Some of the finest food around is produced at this 1890 inn and former country home. The dining room is in what would originally have been the house's front porch. Start off with a salad with a homemade cherry-maple vinaigrette. Entrées include fresh whitefish, poultry, and pasta. | 149 E. Harbor Hwy. (M–22), Maple City, 15 mi west of Suttons Bay | 877/284–3466 | Reservations essential | MC, V | $$–$$$$

Traverse City

Bryant Park Beach. Sugar-white sand, gorgeous blue water, excellent sunset views—Bryant Park is a picture-perfect beach. Additional facilities include a picnic area, playground, rest rooms, grills, and lifeguards from mid-June to August. | M–37 at Peninsula Dr. | Free | Daily dawn–dusk.

Clinch Park Zoo. Animals native to northern Michigan are the focus. The park is downtown, next to the Clinch Park Beach and on the shores of beautiful Grand Traverse Bay. | 400 Boardman Ave. | 231/922–4904 | $3 | Late May–early Sept., daily 9:30–5:30; early Sept.–Oct. and mid-Apr.–late May, daily 10–4.

★**Tall Ship Manitou.** Built after a 19th-century design, this tall ship schooner is a fabulous way to enjoy northern Michigan from the water. Huge white sails flap in the breeze, and passengers are put to work hoisting jibs and steering the ship during the two-hour sail through the beautiful harbor. Small, basic accommodations are available on board. You sleep like a 19th-century sailor, with a narrow, thin bunk and community toilets, but your breakfast is first class, with fresh local berries, maple sausages, and waffles. Noon and evening sails include upscale picnic fare. | 13390 S.W. Bay Shore Dr. | 231/941–2000 or 800/678–0383 | www.traverse.com/tallship | $32–$39 | Memorial Day–Sept., departures daily at noon, 3, 6:30.

MISSISSIPPI

HISTORIC RIVER CITIES & THE NATCHEZ TRACE
FROM VICKSBURG TO ROCKY SPRINGS

Distance: 185 mi   Time: 3 days
Overnight Breaks: Natchez, Vicksburg

On this tour, you will drive many kinds of routes, from winding country roads to four-lane highways and the scenic tree-shaded Natchez Trace Parkway. Your tour stretches from historic Vicksburg to Port Gibson and Natchez. From Vicksburg, travel south on the Great River Road (U.S. 61) to Natchez, then head northeast to Jackson on the scenic parkway. You'll see some of Mississippi's grandest antebellum homes, one of the nation's most important Civil War battlefields, and several marvelous panoramas of the Mississippi River. The best time to visit is in spring, when the dogwoods, redbuds, and azaleas are in bloom, and many historic homes are open for tours. Fall is also a good time to go: skies are generally clear and temperatures are more moderate than in summer.

❶ Begin in **Vicksburg.** High on a bluff overlooking the river, this city is famous for its strategic importance during the Civil War, when it was besieged by the Union Army and Navy for 47 days. Many buildings from the war era are still standing, and much of the battlefield is preserved. Both the soldiers and the public suffered heavy casualties during the siege, which ended with the Confederate surrender on July 4, 1863; the memory was so bitter that the city did not officially celebrate Independence Day until 1976—more than a century later.

The **Vicksburg National Military Park** encompasses a museum, hiking trails, the USS *Cairo* gunboat (with its own museum), the picturesque National Cemetery, and a driving tour of the battlefield with several scenic overlooks.

The **Old Court House Museum,** in one of Mississippi's grandest and most historic buildings, stands atop a high hill near the old center of town; both Confederate president Jefferson Davis and General U. S. Grant delivered speeches from its balconies. The museum has a refreshingly local feel, is crammed with interesting artifacts, and has a friendly, knowledgeable staff.

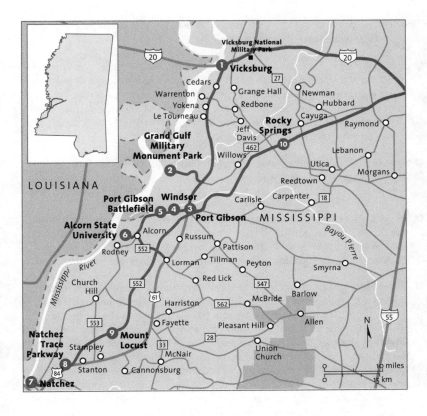

Nearby **Cedar Grove** is a lavish antebellum home that doubles as a bed-and-break-fast inn; a cannonball lodged in the parlor wall testifies to repeated shelling by Union gunboats during the Civil War. Other tour homes include **Anchuca,** where Jefferson Davis visited after his release from prison; and **McRaven,** built in three stages in distinct architectural styles beginning in the 1830s. Several other homes are opened for tours during the March Spring Pilgrimage.

Vicksburg also has four casinos: **Ameristar, Isle of Capri, Rainbow,** and **Harrah's.** You can take hydro-boat tours of the Mississippi and Yazoo rivers to get a wide-angle view of the city.

❷ From Vicksburg, the tour proceeds south on U.S. 61 for approximately 24 mi to Grand Gulf Road (Hwy. 462). Several miles west is the **Grand Gulf Military Monument Park.** It's on the site of a former Mississippi River town where Confederate forces engaged Union gunboats in 1863, and it includes a cemetery, museum, campground, and the best access to the Mississippi River between Vicksburg and Natchez.

❸ Return east on Grand Gulf Road back to U.S. 61, then drive approximately 2 mi south to **Port Gibson.** One of the best-preserved towns in Mississippi, Port Gibson was "too beautiful to burn," according to General U. S. Grant, who passed through on his way to Vicksburg. Drive down tree-lined Church Street, with its stately churches and antebellum homes, and you'll see why. **First Presbyterian Church** may well be the most-photographed church in the state, owing to the golden hand that points skyward from atop the steeple. Nearby churches include **St. Joseph's Catholic Church,** with striking, deep-blue stained-glass windows, and **Temple Gemiluth Chassed,** the oldest synagogue in the state. Port Gibson also has a Spring Pilgrimage, when many of the city's homes are open for tours.

❹ About 14 mi west of Port Gibson via Route 552 (Rodney Rd.) are the Ruins of **Windsor,** once Mississippi's most palatial antebellum plantation home. Today only the ruins of this four-story mansion remain: 23 towering columns and a few sections of cast-iron railing. Once a prominent landmark for steamboat pilots on the nearby Mississippi River, it was used as a Union hospital during the Civil War. Having survived the war, it burned during a party in 1890.

❺ On your way to the Windsor ruins stop by **Port Gibson Battlefield,** off Route 552. Here outmanned rebels were beaten back by the advancing Union Army. The battlefield is on a scenic winding road that's changed little since the war.

❻ From Windsor ruins, continue down Route 552 for a few miles to **Alcorn State University.** Originally a college for planters' sons and later one of the first land-grant colleges for blacks in the United States, the campus has several historic buildings. The ornate iron steps leading to the university chapel came from nearby Windsor.

❼ Follow Route 552 east to back to U.S. 61, and follow it approximately 30 mi to **Natchez.** This is Mississippi's most architecturally significant city, with hundreds of historic buildings, including the opulent **Melrose** (1841–45), which is the centerpiece of Natchez National Historical Park. There are also several federal-style riverfront taverns in what used to be the rowdiest part of town, Natchez-Under-the-Hill, where the paddle wheelers *American Queen, Delta Queen,* and *Mississippi Queen* dock. Atop the hill is Bluff Park, with gazebos, benches, and a sweeping panorama of the Mississippi River.

Several Natchez buildings warrant a closer look. **Longwood** is a rare octagonal mansion. Its construction was interrupted by the Civil War. Not only was it never completed, the tools and paint cans remain where the workers left them when they fled. **Stanton Hall** is an imposing Greek Revival home that occupies an entire city block. **Dunleith** is the quintessential "big house," with colonnades on all four sides. Natchez has the largest and oldest Spring Pilgrimage in the nation, and if you don't mind crowds, it's a good time to tour some of the homes. (There's also a Fall Pilgrimage that's not usually as crowded.) Many of the homes also serve as bed-and-breakfast inns, and the **Eola Hotel** is listed among the Historic Hotels of America.

East of downtown is the **Grand Village of the Natchez Indians,** with large ceremonial mounds, a reconstructed house, and a small museum commemorating the tribe for which the city is named.

❽ Approximately 10 mi northeast of Natchez pick up the **Natchez Trace Parkway,** which follows the route of a trail estimated to be 8,000 years old. It was originally trod by buffalo and by Native Americans, and later used by explorers, settlers, bandits, itinerant preachers, and boatmen traveling between Natchez and Nashville. There are plenty of opportunities to stop and admire the scenery or explore historic sites.

❾ Continuing northeast on the Natchez Trace Parkway, you come to **Mount Locust.** Dating to 1780, this is one of the few surviving frontier inns, or "stands," that offered lodging and food to early travelers on the Trace.

❿ From Mount Locust, continue northeast on the Natchez for approximately 45 mi to **Rocky Springs.** The town this park commemorates was destroyed by erosion and yellow fever. The park has a campground, picnic areas, rest rooms, hiking trails, and some pretty streams. Adjacent to the park is **Rocking Springs Methodist Church,** built in 1837. It is the town's only remaining structure, and its cemetery is worth exploring.

From Rocky Springs, proceed north on the parkway to I–20, which leads east to Jackson, where you could continue the Natchez Trace up to the Alabama border, or back to Vicksburg.

Natchez

Grand Village of the Natchez Indians. The Natchez lived in the southwest Mississippi area from around AD 700 to 1730. Toward the end of that period, Grand Village was their main ceremonial center. The present village is a reconstruction. You will also find exhibits of the life of the Natchez, ceremonial mounds, a typical house, and a small museum. | 400 Jefferson Davis Blvd. | 601/446–6502 | www.mdah.state.ms.us/hprop/gvni.html | Free | Mon.–Sat. 9–5, Sun. 1:30–5.

Isle of Capri Casino and Hotel. Table and video gambling games as well as restaurants are on board this reproduction of a riverboat. | 70 Silver St. | 601/445–0605 or 888/782–9582 | www.isleofcapricasino.com | Free | 24 hrs.

Melrose. Part of the Natchez National Historical Park, Melrose is one of the finest Greek Revival mansions in the country. It contains its original furnishings, outbuildings, and a parklike estate. The house is open for tours only. | 1 Melrose–Montabello Pkwy. | 601/442–7047 | www.nps.gov/natc | $6 | Grounds 8:30–5, tours 9–4.

MISSISSIPPI RULES OF THE ROAD

License Requirements: The legal driving age is 16 in Mississippi.

Right Turn on Red: Right turns are permissible on red unless otherwise posted, and left turns are permissible on red when turning from a one-way street onto another one-way street, unless otherwise posted.

Seat-Belt & Helmet Laws: Seat belts are required for front-seat passengers and driver, and car seats are required for children under four. Motorcycle helmets are required.

Speed Limits: Unless otherwise posted, speed limits are 70 mph on interstate highways, 65 on most other four-lane highways, 55 on other highways, and 50 on the Natchez Trace Parkway, where commercial vehicles are prohibited.

Other Regulations: Headlights must be used before dawn and after dusk, and when weather conditions limit visibility. Handheld-phone use is permitted while driving. The blood-alcohol concentration limit is .08% for drivers over 21; .02% for drivers under 21.

For More Information: Mississippi Department of Public Safety | 601/987–1212 | www.dps.state.ms.us. Mississippi Department of Transportation | 601/359–7001 | www.mdot.state.ms.us.

Natchez Pilgrimage Tours. This information center is your one stop for booking guided visits to the city's many antebellum homes. The company can also make reservations for area B&Bs, evening entertainment, and the city's Fall and Spring pilgrimages, when many private homes open their doors to visitors, in addition to the many full-time house-museums. | Canal Street Depot, Canal and State Sts. | 800/647–6724 | www.natchezpilgrimage.com | Information center free, houses $6 each, $15 for any 3 | Information center 8:30–5, houses daily; call for hrs.

Dunleith. Now an 11-room B&B, Dunleith was built in 1856. This National Historic Landmark building is an archetypal "big house," with Tuscan columns on four sides. The house contains furnishings from 1850 and earlier and has French Zuber wallpaper. The 40-acre former plantation has a lovely garden (note the magnificent magnolia tree). | 84 Homochitto St.

Longwood. The architectural equivalent of an unfinished symphony, Longwood was an octagonal brick mansion under construction when the Civil War began. The work was never completed and its owner, Dr. Haller Nutt, died in 1864, before the war was over. | 140 Lower Woodville Rd.

Rosalie. Built in the early 1820s, Rosalie is a classic Southern plantation home. The mansion was constructed with red brick with a Greek Revival portico. The cautious owner buried the house's antique mirrors in the yard just before the Union Army turned the house into its headquarters. Now restored—both the house and the mirrors— Rosalie's interior furnishings are among the grandest in Natchez. It's a National Historic Landmark. | 100 Orleans St.

Stanton Hall. A National Historic Landmark completed in 1857, Stanton Hall was constructed with the finest materials available, including gas-burning chandeliers, marble mantels, and silver doorknobs. Briefly a girls' school, Stanton Hall now belongs to the Pilgrimage Garden Club. | 401 High St.

Natchez-Under-the-Hill. The city's original waterfront, Natchez-Under-the-Hill was once a notorious draw for pirates, riverboat gamblers, and outlaws. Dwindling use of riverboats brought an end to its infamy. These days Natchez-Under-the-Hill attracts tourists with its restaurants, bars, gift shops, inns, and the Isle of Capri casino. Three paddle wheelers dock here: the *Mississippi Queen,* the *Delta Queen,* and the *American Queen.* | Silver St. off Canal St.

Dining

Biscuits and Blues. Cajun/Creole. This hopping blues joint serves a New Orleans–inspired menu. House specialties are the crawfish-and-mushroom beignet appetizer, smoked chicken and ribs, grilled or fried catfish, and J.P.'s famous gumbo. For lunch, try one of the shrimp, catfish, or beef po'boys. | 315 Main St. | 601/446–9922 | AE, DC, MC, V | $–$$$

Bowie's Tavern. American/Casual. A festive downtown pub with high pressed-tin ceilings, live music, sports on TV, and a lively and noisy crowd, Bowie's specializes in tasty comfort food. Smoked-chicken sandwiches with jalapeño mustard, New Orleans–style muffulettas, seafood gumbo, and andouille sausage po'boys are among the favorites. | 100 Main St. | 601/445–6627 | AE, DC, MC, V | ¢–$

Magnolia Grill. Cajun/Creole. You can get your catfish grilled, amandine, or served with crawfish étouffée at this casual restaurant in Natchez-Under-the-Hill, along the Mississippi River. The Magnolia shrimp, prepared with green onions, mushrooms, and garlic and served over rice or angel hair pasta keeps locals coming back for more. | 49 Silver St. | 601/446–7670 | AE, MC, V | $$–$$$$

Monmouth Plantation. Contemporary. A five-course candlelit dinner from the prix-fixe menu is served at this spectacularly lavish antebellum home. Dinner begins at 7:30; hors d'oeuvres are at 6:30 in the courtyard. The menu changes nightly but has included such captivating creative fare as seared tuna wrapped in bacon with molasses sauce and stuffed quail with crab-cake dressing. | 36 Melrose Ave. | 601/442–5852 | Reservations essential | No lunch | AE, D, DC, MC, V | $$$$

Pearl Street Pasta. Italian. Creative pastas are the main choice on the menu of this intimate storefront café with an outgoing staff. Try the chicken-and-tasso over angle hair, fillet of beef with mushroom-cabernet sauce, or pasta jambalaya. The restaurant has two rooms, one lighter and more traditional, the other darker, with exposed-brick walls. | 105 S. Pearl St. | 601/442–9284 | No lunch Sun. | AE, MC, V | $–$$$

Lodging

The Briars. Built in 1818, this opulent antebellum home affords one of the city's finest views of the Mississippi River. The 19 acres of grounds invite strolling. The mansion was the site of the wedding of Jefferson Davis and Varina Howell. In-room data ports, cable TV, pool; no kids under 12, no smoking. | 31 Irving La., 39120, 1 mi south of town | 601/446–9654 or 800/634–1818 | fax 601/445–6037 | www.thebriarsinn.com | 13 rooms | BP | AE, MC, V | $$$

Cedar Grove Plantation. Built in 1838 by U.S. senator John Sharp Williams, this archetypal Greek Revival plantation house is on 150 acres of forest and farmland. Surrounded by moss-draped trees and landscaped grounds, the plantation enjoys one of the most romantic settings in the state. Pool, ponds, fishing, bicycles, hiking, horseshoes, library, some pets allowed; no smoking. | 617 Kingston Rd., 39120, 21 mi southeast of downtown | 601/445–0585 or 877/508–6800 | fax 601/446–5650 | www.cedargroveplantation.com | 7 rooms | BP | MC, V | $$–$$$$

Dunleith Plantation. Although it stands in the heart of Natchez, this magnificent Greek Revival mansion is surrounded by 40 acres of grounds. Because of its classic Southern look and riverside setting, it has appeared in a number of epic films, including *Showboat*. Rooms have elegant period furnishings, such as four-poster canopy beds, gilt mirrors, fireplaces, and Oriental rugs. Restaurant, in-room data ports, some in-room hot tubs, cable TV, pub; no kids under 14, no smoking. | 84 Homochitto St., 39204 | 601/446–8500 or 800/433–2445 | www.dunleithplantation.com | 22 rooms | BP | D, MC, V | $$–$$$$

Natchez Eola Hotel. An expertly restored early-20th-century hotel, the Natchez Eola is now grander than it was in its heyday. It's in the heart of the city's historic downtown area, only three blocks from the mighty Mississippi. Most rooms are small but some have spectacular views of the city and river, and some have fireplaces. The hotel is listed in the National Register of Historic Places. 2 restaurants, room service, some in-room hot tubs, some microwaves, some refrigerators, cable TV, gym, bar, shop, laundry service, business services, some pets allowed. | 110 Pearl St., 39120 | 601/445–6000 or 866/445–3652 | fax 601/446–5310 | www.natchezeola.com | 131 rooms | AE, D, DC, MC, V | $$–$$$

Ramada Inn Hilltop. Built in the 1970s, this two-story brick hotel is a mile south of town. It is on a bluff with spectacular views the Mississippi River, and is surrounded by 30 beautiful acres. Restaurant, room service, in-room data ports, some refrigerators, cable TV, tennis court, pool, wading pool, bar, laundry facilities, business services, meeting rooms. | 130 John R. Junkin Dr., 39120 | 601/446–6311 or 800/228–2828 | fax 601/446–6321 | www.ramada.com | 156 rooms, 6 suites | AE, D, DC, MC, V | $

Natchez Trace Parkway

Emerald Mound. Thirty-five feet high and covering 8 acres, this rectangular mound of earth was built over several centuries by the Mississippian tribe who lived here between 1250 and 1600. Excavation of this Native American site has been going on since 1838, and the fragments of pottery, bones, and tools offer clues to life along the

Mississippi 500 years ago. The site has been run by the National Park Service since the 1950s. | Natchez Trace Pkwy., MM 10.3, north of Natchez | 601/842–1572 Natchez Trace Parkway Headquarters | Free | Daily dawn–dusk.

Mount Locust. Built in 1779, this home was used as an inn in the mid-1800s and has been restored to its original state with pioneer furnishings. The inn and grounds are open to the public. | Natchez Trace Pkwy., MM 15.5, north of town | 662/680–4025 | Free | Inn Feb.–Nov., daily 8:30–5; grounds daily 8:30–5.

Rocky Springs. The Rocky Springs Methodist Church, built in 1837, is all that remains of this town that fell prey to yellow fever and soil erosion. The adjacent park has a ranger station, scenic streams, picnic areas, nature trails, and a campground. | Natchez Trace Pkwy., MM 54.8, northeast of Natchez | 601/842–1572 Natchez Trace Parkway Headquarters.

Port Gibson

Alcorn State University. Alcorn State University, founded in 1871, was the nation's first land-grant college for blacks. Some of its buildings once belonged to Oakland College, a school for planters' sons that closed at the beginning of the Civil War. Several of its buildings are of architectural note. | 1000 ASU Dr. | 601/877–6100 | www.alcorn.edu.

First Presbyterian Church. Built in 1859, this is probably the most-photographed church in the state because of the unique golden hand atop its steeple. Inside are chandeliers from the steamboat *Robert E. Lee*. | Church St., 39150 | 601/437–4351 | Free | Daily 8–5.

Grand Gulf Military Monument Park. The park, overlooking the Mississippi, commemorates a major Civil War naval battle at what was then the town of Grand Gulf. You can visit Fort Cobun, Fort Wade, log houses, a church, and, in the visitor center, a museum. There are picnic grounds, campsites, and hiking trails. | 12996 Grand Gulf Rd. | 601/437–5911 | www.grandgulfpark.state.ms.us | $2 | Daily 8–5.

Port Gibson Battlefield. The site of this Civil War battle, now enshrouded in pine forest, includes the Greek Revival Shaifer House, which dates to 1840. | Shaifer Rd. | 601/437–4351 | Free | Daily 8–5.

Ruins of Windsor. Completed in 1861, this palatial house had four floors surmounted by a cupola. The roof was used by the Confederates as an observation deck during the Civil War, and it served as a navigational landmark for Mississippi River steamboat pilots. Although it survived the war, Windsor was destroyed by fire in 1890. All that remains today are 22 Corinthian columns, a few sections of balcony railing, one ancient live oak, and a dangerously tilted tenant house. The ruins appeared in the 1950s movie *Raintree County*. | Old Rodney Rd. | No phone | Free | Daily 8–6.

St. Joseph's Catholic Church. The oldest church in Port Gibson, the almost-psychedelic blue windows and altar of this 1849 Gothic Revival structure were carved by a 17-year-old artisan. | Church St. | 601/437–5790 | Free | Daily 9–6.

Temple Gemiluth Chassed. Across the street from St. Joseph's, this 1891 Moorish-Byzantine Revival synagogue is the oldest Jewish place of worship in Mississippi. | 708 Church St. | 601/437–4350 | Free | By appointment only.

Dining

Old Depot. Southern. Not far from the Natchez Trace Parkway, this cozy restaurant is known for its red beans and rice, steak, seafood, and railroad memorabilia. Kids' menu. | 1202 Market St. | 601/437–4711 | Closed Sun. | AE, D, MC, V | $–$$

Vicksburg

Antebellum homes. A number of homes survived the Civil War, and many now serve as bed-and-breakfasts.

Anchuca. Built around 1830, this Greek Revival home was visited by Confederate president Jefferson Davis after his release from prison. It has been restored to its original elegance. | 1010 1st East St. | 601/661–0111 or 888/686–0111 | www.anchucamansion.com | $6 | Daily 9–3.

Martha Vick House. Newitt Vick, the city's founder, built this minimansion in the mid-19th century for an unmarried daughter. The house has been carefully restored, and is notable for its elegant furnishings and collection of French paintings. | 1300 Grove St. | 601/638–7036 | $5 | Mon.–Sat. 9–5, Sun. 1–5.

McRaven. McRaven began as a frontier house around 1797, became a two-story brick Empire-style house 30 years later, and subsequently underwent a Greek Revival renovation. There is visible Civil War cannon damage inside and out. Among its impressive antiques are collections of porcelain and needlepoint. | 1445 Harrison St. | 601/636–1663 | $5 | Mar.–Nov., Mon.–Sat. 9–5, Sun. 10–5.

Biedenharn Coca-Cola Museum. Although it was invented in Atlanta in 1886, the famous soft drink was first bottled in this plant in Vicksburg in 1894. The company had previously sold Coca-Cola syrup and bottled soda water to soda fountains. One day it occurred to Joseph Biedenharn, a local candy merchant, to do the bottling himself— and history was made. The museum features a 1900 soda fountain and a 1890 candy store with Cokes, candy, and ice cream. | 1107 Washington St. | 601/638–6514 | $2.25 | Mon.–Sat. 9–5, Sun. 1:30–4:30.

Casinos. These casinos are open 24 hours a day, and admission is free.
Ameristar | 4116 Washington St. | 601/638–1000 | www.ameristarcasinos.com.
Harrah's Vicksburg | 1310 Mulberry St. | 601/636–3423 | www.harrahs.com.
Isle of Capri | 3990 Washington St. | 601/636–5700 | www.isleofcapricasino.com.
Rainbow Casino | 1380 Warrenton Rd. | 601/636–7575 | www.rainbowcasino.com.

Old Court House Museum. Constructed by slaves in 1858, this Greek Revival building is Vicksburg's most historic site. A fascinating museum documents the speeches delivered by Jefferson Davis and U. S. Grant from the balcony of this building. | 1008 Cherry St. | 601/636–0741 | www.oldcourthouse.org | $3 | Mon.–Sat. 8:30–4:30, Sun. 1:30–4:30.

Vicksburg National Military Park and Cemetery. You can ride in a van with a guide or conduct your own tour of the 1,325 historic monuments and markers along the park's 16-mi driving tour. Along the way you see trenches and earthworks, rifle pits, 144 cannons, and the graves of 17,000 Union soldiers. | 3201 Clay St. | 601/636–0583 | www.nps.gov/vick | $5 | Daily 8–5.

USS *Cairo* Museum. Alongside the military park is a museum that showcases a Union ironclad gunboat with the dubious distinction of being the first ship ever sunk by an electrically detonated torpedo. | 3201 Clay St. | 601/636–0583 | www.nps.gov/vick | Free with admission to military park | Nov.–Mar., daily 8:30–5; Apr.–Oct., daily 9:30–6.

Dining

Beechwood Restaurant & Lounge. American. Don't be put off by the unpromising setting of this frozen-in-time steak-and-seafood joint next to a shabby motel—it serves some of the tastiest food in town, and there's live music many evenings. The retro decor is part of the fun. Try stuffed crab, catfish with hush puppies, fried oysters, or chicken with caramelized onions and mushrooms. The steaks are hefty and charbroiled. | 4451 E. Clay St. | 601/636–3761 | AE, MC, V | ¢–$$

★**Cedar Grove Inn.** Southern. In a stylish restored mansion built in 1840, this restaurant has a cozy split-level dining room. You can eat inside or outside on the veranda. Among the signature dishes are sun-dried-tomato-and-rosemary–crusted salmon, and oysters Rockefeller pasta, with oysters, bacon, onion, and blue cheese over fettuccine. | 2200 Oak St. | 601/636–1000 | Reservations essential | Closed Mon. No lunch | AE, D, MC, V | $$$–$$$$

Eddie Monsour's. American. Imaginative Lebanese and American dishes are served here. Popular dishes include grilled redfish and filet mignon. There is a view of a golf course. | 127 Country Club Dr. | 601/638–1571 | Closed Sun. No lunch Sat. | AE, MC, V | $–$$

Walnut Hills. Southern. Savor some of the best home-style Southern cooking around at this charming downtown restaurant inside a vintage Victorian house. The rib-eye and shrimp platter could feed two hungry adults. Other favorites include crispy fried chicken, fried corn, okra and green tomatoes, and blackberry cobbler. | 1214 Adams St. | 601/638–4910 | Closed Sat. No dinner Sun. | MC, V | ¢–$$

Lodging
Anchuca. Magnificently restored, this 1830 B&B has period furnishings including early-1800s Victorian, Empire, Sheraton, and Hepplewhite pieces. Jefferson Davis spoke on the balcony after the Civil War. Some rooms have fireplaces. Cable TV, pool, hot tub; no kids under 15, no smoking. | 1010 1st East St., 39180 | 601/661–0111 or 888/686–0111 | www.anchucamansion.com | 5 rooms, 2 suites | BP | MC, V | $$

★**Cedar Grove Inn.** One of the largest collections of antiques in the South is displayed in this beautifully restored Greek Revival mansion. A Union cannonball is lodged in its parlor wall. Gazebos, fountains, and statues pepper 4 acres of lush landscaping. The inn is in a residential area of Vicksburg 1 mi from the downtown area. Restaurant, in-room data ports, some in-room hot tubs, cable TV, tennis court, pool, gym, business services; no smoking. | 2200 Oak St., 39180 | 601/636–1000 or 800/862–1300 | fax 601/634–6126 | www.cedargroveinn.com | 10 rooms, 24 suites | AE, D, DC, MC, V | $$–$$$

★**Duff Green Mansion.** Built in 1856, this B&B is one of Mississippi's oldest mansions and a National Historic Landmark. Every room has a fireplace. It's eight blocks northeast of downtown. In-room data ports, cable TV, pool, hot tub, business services, some pets allowed; no smoking. | 1114 1st East St., 39180 | 601/638–6662 or 800/992–0037 | fax 601/661–0079 | www.duffgreenmansion.com | 4 rooms | AE, D, MC, V | $–$$

Hampton Inn Vicksburg. Across from Vicksburg National Military Park and Cemetery and a little more than a mile east of downtown, this well-maintained chain property has bright, functional rooms. In-room data ports, cable TV, pool, business services, no-smoking rooms. | 3332 Clay St., 39180 | 601/636–6100 or 800/426–7866 | fax 601/634–1962 | www.hampton-inn.com | 148 rooms | CP | AE, D, DC, MC, V | $

NEW HAMPSHIRE

WHITE MOUNTAINS LOOP
THROUGH THE WHITE MOUNTAINS NATIONAL FOREST

Distance: 110 mi   Time: 2 days
Overnight Break: Jackson

Explore the heart of the White Mountain National Forest and cover some of New Hampshire's most spectacular scenery. Only a small section of the tour is on the highway—and that stretch is only two lanes in each direction. For the rest of the tour, winding roads cut through rugged mountain passes and deep forests. The last section of the trip traverses the Kancamagus Highway, known for its fall splendor. In early summer, wildflowers mix with the trees at the edges of the roads. Winter can bring heavy snow, and it seems that every other car carries a ski rack. Spring, which tends to be wet and muddy, is the least desirable time to visit.

❶ Begin your tour at **Franconia Notch State Park** (access from Franconia Notch State Pkwy., Exits 1–3). This narrow notch through the White Mountains is one of the New Hampshire's prettiest state parks. The park's **information center** (Exit 1) has trail maps for visitors and is also the access point for the **Flume,** one of the park's natural wonders. Off Exit 2 you come to the viewing area for the ruins of the **Old Man of the Mountain,** a natural rock profile that collapsed in spring 2003 but remains the state's symbol on everything from license plates to the New Hampshire commemorative quarter. In summer, a trip to the top of **Cannon Mountain Ski Area** on a tram affords panoramic views of the White Mountains.

❷ Continue north along I–93 to **Franconia,** where you find **Frost Place** (I–93, Exit 38, 1 mi south on Rte. 116 to Bickford Hill Rd., right over bridge, left at fork onto Ridge Rd.). Poet Robert Frost lived here from 1915 to 1920.

❸ Continue north on I–93 to Exit 40, and pick up U.S. 302 heading east. In **Bretton Woods,** stop at the historic marker in front of the **Mount Washington Hotel** (U.S. 302) to read about the role this grand resort played in the International Monetary Conference of 1944. If you visit in summer or fall, you may want to take a ride to the top of **Mt. Washington,** the highest mountain in the northeast, aboard the **Cog Railway** (Base Station Rd., 4 mi east of junction U.S. 3 and U.S. 302). This steam-powered railway

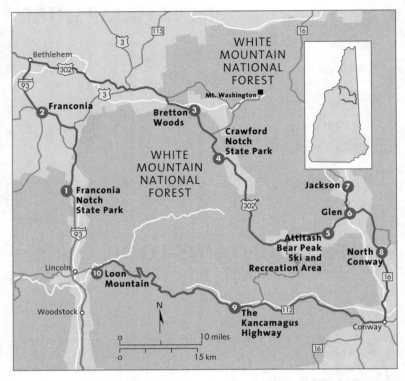

provides a scenic trip to the top of the mountain. Mt. Washington is known for its extreme weather and high winds, so a jacket is advisable no matter what the temperature is at the base.

4 **Crawford Notch State Park** (U.S. 302, beginning about 6 mi east of the Mount Washington Hotel and continuing for another 6 mi) is the second of the mountain passes, or "notches," you travel through on this tour. Hiking trails from either side of U.S. 302 lead to several waterfalls.

5 **Attitash Bear Peak Ski and Recreation Area** (U.S. 302) in Bartlett has nearly year-round activities. Winter is devoted to alpine and cross-country skiing and snowshoeing. In warm weather try the water slides or dry alpine slide or go horseback riding.

6 Continue on U.S. 302 to **Glen,** where the theme park **Story Land** (Rte. 16) and historic village **Heritage New Hampshire** (Rte. 16) provide entertainment for families.

7 Head north on Route 16 to **Jackson** (off Rte. 16A), perhaps the most charming of the White Mountains towns. The **Honeymoon Covered Bridge** spanning the Ellis River marks the entrance to the village off Route 16, and the White Mountains surround the town, giving it a sheltered and timeless air. Activities are geared toward the outdoors, as Jackson is one of the nation's top cross-country skiing destinations. Hiking, golfing, and tennis are popular in summer.

8 From Jackson, take Route 16 south to **North Conway.** Shopping is one of the primary activities in North Conway. Outlet stores line both sides of Route 16. In the town center, also on Route 16, some nice shops sell local and regional crafts and sporting goods.

Conway Scenic Railroad (38 Norcross Circle, off Rte. 16 in the center of town; look for the Victorian train station) uses vintage coaches, including a dome observation coach, for scenic trips through the White Mountain National Forest.

9 Continue south on Route 16 to Conway, and make a right turn onto the **Kancamagus Highway** (Rte. 112 between Conway and Lincoln), probably the state's best-known roadway. It cuts through the **White Mountain National Forest** for 32 mi, paralleling the Swift River. Although the trip is beautiful any time, traffic is heavy on weekends during foliage season and snow can cause closings in winter. You can get hiking information and check on winter road conditions at the **Saco Ranger Station** at the Conway end of the route (Rte. 112). There are a number of scenic overlooks and other stopping points along the road.

10 In Lincoln and North Woodstock, **Loon Mountain** (Rte. 112) is a year-round resort area with skiing in winter and activities that range from mountain biking to a wildlife theater in summer. This is also a popular base from which to hike in the surrounding White Mountain National Forest.

Bretton Woods

Attitash Bear Peak. This high-profile resort continues to expand and improve its infrastructure. Attitash has a computerized lift-ticket system that allows downhill skiers to pay as they run. Enhanced with massive snowmaking (98%), the trails number 70

NEW HAMPSHIRE RULES OF THE ROAD

License Requirements: To drive in New Hampshire you must be at least 16 years old.

Right Turn on Red: Everywhere in the state, you can make a right turn at a red light *after* a complete stop unless the intersection is posted to the contrary.

Seat-Belt & Helmet Laws: New Hampshire is the only state not to require seat-belt use; however, restraints are required for children under 12. Children under 4 must be secured in a federally approved safety seat. Motorcycle helmets are required for riders under 18.

Speed Limits: Most interstates have speed limits of 65 mph, except in congested areas where the limit is typically 55 mph. Secondary roads occasionally have speed limits as high as 50 mph or 55 mph but more often average 40 mph to 45 mph.

Other Regulations: The legal blood-alcohol concentration limit in New Hampshire is .08%. It is illegal for vehicle passengers to have open alcoholic containers.

For More Information: New Hampshire Department of Transportation | 603/271–3734 | www.state.nh.us/dot. New Hampshire State Police | 603/271–2575 information, 603/271–3636 or 800/852–3411 emergency | www.nh.gov/safety/nhsp.

on two peaks, both with full-service base lodges. The bulk of the skiing and boarding is geared to intermediates and experts, with some steep pitches and glades. | U.S. 302, Bartlett, 18 mi southeast of Bretton Woods | 603/374–2368, 800/223–7669 snow conditions, 800/223–7669 lodging | www.attitash.com.

Bretton Woods Mountain Resort. The pristine setting of this ski area and its lack of crowds make it popular among families. Most slopes are rated for beginners and intermediates, with a few steeper sections near the peak. | U.S. 302 | 603/278–3320, 603/278–3333 weather conditions, 800/232–2972 recorded information | www.brettonwoods.com.

Crawford Notch State Park. This state park encompasses the 6-mi mountain pass that is one of the most scenic in the state. Hiking trails have views of the Presidential Mountain range and lead to several waterfalls. | U.S. 302, 6 mi southeast of town | 603/374–2272 | www.nhparks.state.nh.us | Free | Mid-May–mid-Oct., daily dawn–dusk.

Arethusa Falls. Accessible by hiking trail, this waterfall is one of the highest in New Hampshire. Frankenstein Cliff, near the falls, is named for George L. Frankenstein, a late-19th-century artist who frequently painted the White Mountains. | Crawford Notch Park, off U.S. 302, ½ mi south of Dry River Campground, 6 mi north of Bartlett | Mid-May–mid-Oct., daily dawn–dusk.

Silver Cascade. Actually a series waterfalls, these cascades vary in intensity as the water level changes over the course of the year. | U.S. 302 at north end of the park.

★ **Mt. Washington Cog Railway.** The Cog Railway went up on the great mountain's western flank in 1869 and has been providing a thrilling alternative to climbing or driving to the top of Mt. Washington ever since. The climb takes about three hours round-trip, with a 20-minute stop at the top. | U.S. 302, 6 mi northeast of town | 603/846–5404 or 800/922–8825 | www.thecog.com | $49 | Early–mid-May, weekends; late May–early Nov., daily; call for train schedules.

Mount Washington Hotel. The sparkling white facade of this historic turn-of-the-20th-century grande dame is breathtaking against the backdrop of Mt. Washington. The hotel was the meeting place for the International Monetary Conference of 1944, which set the American dollar as the standard currency for international exchange. The large porch is the best place to contemplate the view. The hotel is very informal and you can explore freely. | U.S. 302 | 603/278–1000 or 800/258–0330 | www.mtwashington.com.

Dining

Cold Mountain Cafe. Eclectic. Slick halogen lights focus on the rotating art exhibits gracing the frescoed walls of this friendly, popular, local coffeehouse. The diverse menu includes ethnic favorites like Thai noodle salad and hummus plates for lunch and Thai chicken curry and stuffed flounder for dinner. | 2015 Main St., Bethlehem, 15 mi west of Bretton Woods | 603/869–2500 | No credit cards | ¢–$$

Fabyan's Station. American. Railroad mementos permeate this noisy and festive former train station that's a good bet for hamburgers, sandwiches, and similarly uncomplicated pub fare. Kids' menu. | U.S. 302 at Cog Railway Base Rd. | 603/278–2222 | AE, D, MC, V | $–$$

Tim-bir Alley. Contemporary. Regional American ingredients are used in creative ways at this elegant restaurant in the Adair Country Inn whose menu changes weekly. Main dishes might include pork tenderloin with maple-balsamic glaze and apple-almond relish or sunflower seed–encrusted salmon with a smoked-tomato puree. The hours change seasonally (and they're sometimes sporadic within a given season); it's best to call ahead. | 80 Guider La., Bethlehem, 14 mi west of Bretton Woods | 603/444–6142 | Closed Jan.–Apr. and Mon. and Tues. No lunch | No credit cards | $$–$$$

Franconia

★**Franconia Notch State Park.** Some of New Hampshire's best-loved attractions are contained in this park. It's also the site of what had been the icon of New Hampshire, the granite profile of the Old Man of the Mountain, which crumbled due to erosion in spring 2003. | Access via Rte. 18 or the Franconia Notch State Pkwy. (I–93), 7 mi south of Franconia | 603/823–5563 | www.nhparks.state.nh.us | Free | Daily dawn–dusk.

The Basin. Twenty feet in diameter, this deep glacial pothole is at the base of a waterfall. South of Profile Lake, below the Basin, the Pemigewasset River splashes through a gorge that is a smaller version of the Flume. The Basin is reached from the Basin Cascades hiking trail. | Franconia Notch State Pkwy. (I–93), Exit 1 | 603/823–5563 | Free | Daily dawn–dusk.

Cannon Mountain Ski Area. One of the most rugged and scenic ski mountains in New Hampshire, this state-owned and -operated ski area has narrow trails that wind down 2,145 vertical feet, in a thoroughly New England style. | Franconia Notch State Pkwy. (I–93), Exit 2 or 3, 5 mi south of town | 603/823–8800, 603/823–7771 snow conditions | www.cannonmt.com.

The Flume. A chasm at the southern end of Franconia Notch, the Flume extends 800 feet at the base of Mt. Liberty. Granite walls that rise 70 feet to 90 feet are only 12 feet to 20 feet apart and a mountain stream flows between them. A boardwalk takes you through the Flume, which remains cool even on the hottest day of the year. | Franconia Notch State Pkwy., Exit 2 | 603/745–8391 | www.flumegorge.com | $8 | Early May–late Oct., daily 9–5.

Flume Bridge. One of two covered bridges in Franconia Notch State Park, this structure is used both by hikers and by buses bringing visitors to the Flume. The shingles that roofed the bridge when it was built in 1871 were replaced in 1951. | Rte. 175 at U.S. 3, spanning the Pemigewasset River.

New England Ski Museum. At the foot of the Cannon Mountain Tramway, this member-owned and -operated museum displays old photos, trophies, skis and bindings, and clothing dating from the late 1800s. | Franconia Notch State Pkwy. (I–93), Exit 2 | 603/823–7177 | www.skimuseum.org | Free | Dec.–Mar. and Memorial Day–Columbus Day, daily noon–5.

Sentinel Pine Bridge. The Society for the Protection of New Hampshire Forests built this footbridge in 1939 over the pool in the Flume Gorge. The year before the bridge was built, a major hurricane blew down the pine tree that stood near the rear of the pool like a sentinel; a 60-foot section of the tree was built into the base of the bridge. | Franconia Notch State Pkwy. (I–93), Exit 1.

Frost Place. Robert Frost's home from 1915 to 1920, this rambling farmhouse is where the poet wrote one of his most-remembered works, "Stopping by Woods on a Snowy Evening." Two rooms host occasional readings and contain memorabilia and signed editions of his books. Outside, you can follow short trails marked with lines from Frost's poetry. | Ridge Rd. off Rte. 116 | 603/823–5510 | www.frostplace.com | $3 | Memorial Day–June, weekends 1–5; July–Columbus Day, Wed.–Mon. 1–5.

Dining

Beal House Inn. Contemporary. This cozy restaurant inside a charming farmhouse inn has an eclectic menu. From a classic escargots appetizer you might move on to roast duck with a blueberry brandy and crème de cassis sauce. Chef-owners José Luis and Catherine Pawelek prepare everything from scratch, including banana-buttermilk pancakes for breakfast. | 2 W. Main St., Littleton, 7 mi north of Franconia | 603/444–2661 | MC, V | $$–$$$

Franconia Inn. Contemporary. The setting is casually elegant, and the unusual dining room features a lofted ceiling. Try the Atlantic salmon fillet with spicy corn-and-mango relish and roasted new potatoes, or the vegetarian spinach-and-eggplant–stuffed peppers with couscous and a spicy curry aioli. Kids' menu. No smoking. | 1300 Easton Rd. (Rte. 116) | 603/823–5542 or 800/473–5299 | Closed Apr.–mid-May | AE, MC, V | $$–$$$$

Miller's Fare. American. Beside the Littleton Grist Mill, this homey café serves coffees, microbrews, wines, baked goods, sandwiches, and salads. In warm weather dine on a deck overlooking the Ammonoosuc River. | 16 Mill St., Littleton, 7 mi northeast of Franconia | 603/444–2146 | MC, V | ¢

Polly's Pancake Parlor. American. Built in 1830, this building was originally a carriage shed and then was converted to a tearoom during the Great Depression, when the Dexters began serving all-you-can-eat pancakes, waffles, and French toast for 50¢. The prices have gone up a bit, but the descendants of the Dexters continue to serve pancakes and waffles made from grains ground on the property, their own country sausage, and pure maple syrup. | Rte. 117, Sugar Hill, 3 mi west of Franconia | 603/823–5575 | No dinner | D, MC, V | ¢–$

Glen

Heritage New Hampshire. A trip to Heritage New Hampshire is as close as you may ever come to experiencing time travel. Special effects usher you aboard the HMS *Reliance* and carry you from a village in 1634 England over tossing seas to the New World. Saunter along Portsmouth's streets in the late 1700s, hear a speech by George Washington, then continue on to the present day. | Rte. 16 | 603/383–4186 | www.heritagenh.com | $10 | Memorial Day–mid-June and Sept.–mid-Oct., weekends 9–5; mid-June–Aug., daily 9–5.

Story Land. Stroll through this children's theme park, which has life-size storybook and nursery-rhyme characters. High points include the 16 rides and four shows, the Victorian-theme river-raft ride, a farm family variety show, and a simulated voyage to the moon. | Rte. 16 at U.S. 302 | 603/383–4186 | www.storylandnh.com | Mid-June–early Sept. $20; late May–mid-June and early Sept.–mid-Oct. $15 | Mid-June–early Sept., daily 9–6; late May–mid-June and early Sept.–Columbus Day, weekends 10–5.

Dining

Rare Bear Bistro. Eclectic. At the alpine Bernerhof Inn in Glen, this dark wood–paneled, candlelit restaurant specializes in such Swiss specialties as fondue and Wiener schnitzel as well as contemporary American dishes—oven-roasted haddock with brown-butter citrus sauce is a top choice. Sample the chef's full repertoire with the five-course tasting menu. | Bernerhof Inn, U.S. 302 | 603/383–9132 | AE, D, MC, V | $$–$$$

Red Parka Pub. American. Practically an institution, the Red Parka Pub has been in downtown Glen for more than two decades. The menu has everything a family could want, from an all-you-can-eat salad bar to scallop pie. The barbecued ribs are favorites, and you can find hand-carved steaks of every type, from aged New York sirloin to prime rib. Entertainment weekends. Kids' menu. | U.S. 302 | 603/383–4344 | No lunch | AE, D, DC, MC, V | $–$$$

Jackson

Black Mountain. The atmosphere is fun, friendly, and informal at this ski area 2½ mi from Jackson. The mountain's 38 trails and two glades have good sections for beginners and intermediates, as well as a number of trails that keep experts happy. The southern exposure is welcome on cold days, and the view of Mt. Washington from the top of the double chair is breathtaking. | Rte. 16B | 603/383–4490, 800/475–4669 snow conditions | www.blackmt.com.

Honeymoon Covered Bridge. Built around 1876, this bridge across the Ellis River is the first landmark most visitors see when entering Jackson. A pedestrian sidewalk was added in 1930. | Rte. 16A at Rte. 16.

★**Jackson Ski Touring Foundation.** Rated one of the nation's top cross-country skiing areas and by far the largest in New Hampshire, Jackson has 97 mi of trails maintained by the Ski Touring Foundation. Sixty miles are track groomed, 53 mi are skate groomed, and there are 39 mi of marked and mapped backcountry trails. The foundation headquarters, easy to find in the center of town, serves skiers in winter and golfers in summer. Here you pay a daily fee ($14) for using trails. You can also rent skis and use showers and lockers in the attractive and well-designed building. Trails leave from the door. | Main St. (Rte. 16A) | 603/383–9355 or 800/927–6697 | www.jacksonxc.com.

Wildcat Mountain Gondola. This gondola journeys to the 4,100-foot peak of Wildcat Mountain, where you have views of Mt. Washington, the Presidential Range, and—on a clear day—the Atlantic Ocean. The trip is 15 minutes each way. Buy tickets at the base. | Rte. 16, 10 mi north of Jackson | 603/466–3326 | www.skiwildcat.com | $9.50 | Late May–mid-June, weekends, 10–5; mid-June–mid-Oct., daily 10–5.

Dining

Thompson House Eatery. American. One of the most innovative restaurants in generally staid northern New Hampshire, this romantic eatery in a rambling red farmhouse serves worldly fare like apple-wood–smoked skewered shrimp over baby greens. The grilled lamb chop entrée with cucumber-tomato relish over Israeli couscous, Greek olives, and pancetta wins raves all around. | Rte. 16A | 603/383–9341 | AE, D, MC, V | $$–$$$$

Wentworth. Contemporary. This acclaimed restaurant inside the charming Victorian inn overlooking Jackson's quaint green serves a five-course candlelit dinner with a menu that changes seasonally. Good choices are herb-roasted rack of lamb over roasted shallots and asparagus, and grilled farm-raised salmon with potato scallion pancakes and a baby-spinach–and–bacon salad. | Rte. 16A | 603/383–9700 | AE, D, DC, MC, V | $$–$$$$

Wildcat Tavern. Contemporary. A cozy antiques-filled spot in Jackson Village, Jackson's town center, the tavern is known for fresh seafood and casual pub fare. Open-air dining. Kids' menu. | Rte. 16A | 603/383–4245 | AE, MC, V | $–$$

Lodging

Eagle Mountain House. With downhill slopes nearby and cross-country trails beginning at this 1879 country estate, skiing is the order of the day. Public areas are rustic but elegant, and the large guest rooms are furnished with late-Victorian pieces. On a warm day, you can nurse a drink in a rocking chair on the wraparound deck. 2 restaurants, some refrigerators, driving range, 9-hole golf course, tennis court, pool, gym, hot tub, sauna, cross-country skiing, video game room, playground, meeting rooms. | Carter Notch Rd. (Rte. 16B), 03846 | 603/383–9111 or 800/966–5779 | fax 603/383–0854 | www.eaglemt.com | 96 rooms | AE, D, DC, MC, V | $$–$$$

Inn at Jackson. A Stanford White design was the blueprint for this 1902 Victorian overlooking the village. Although the foyer's staircase is grand, everything else—from the braided rugs on the hardwood floors to the smattering of antiques—is unpretentious and exceedingly comfortable. Airy guest rooms have oversize windows; six have fireplaces. The exceptional full breakfast can include egg soufflé casserole or blueberry pancakes. Hot tub, cross-country skiing, some pets allowed.

| Thorn Hill Rd. | Box 807, 03846 | 603/383–4321 or 800/289–8600 | fax 603/383–4085 | www.innatjackson.com | 14 rooms | BP | AE, D, DC, MC, V | $$–$$$$

Wentworth. Individually decorated rooms in this pale-yellow 1869 Victorian inn are accented with antiques; many have fireplaces. The inn overlooks the Wildcat River and the village green in Jackson, and is a 10-minute stroll from the often-photographed covered bridge. The menu for the five-course candlelit dinner changes seasonally. Two condos are available for nightly or seasonal rentals. Restaurant, some in-room hot tubs, tennis court, pool, billiards, cross-country skiing, ice-skating, sleigh rides, bar. | Rte. 16A, 03846 | 603/383–9700 or 800/637–0013 | fax 603/383–4265 | www.thewentworth.com | 60 rooms, 2 condos | MAP | AE, D, DC, MC, V | $$$–$$$$

Wildcat Inn & Tavern. After a day of skiing you can collapse on a comfy sofa by the fire at this 19th-century inn. The fragrance of home baking permeates into the eclectically decorated guest rooms, which are full of knickknacks and furniture of various periods. The tavern, where bands often perform, attracts skiers. In summer you can dine in the garden. 2 restaurants, some kitchenettes, in-room VCRs, bar. | Rte. 16A, 03846 | 603/383–4245 or 800/228–4245 | fax 603/383–6456 | www.wildcattavern.com | 6 rooms, 4 with bath; 7 suites; 1 cottage | BP | AE, MC, V | $–$$

North Conway

Conway Scenic Railroad. Vintage coaches pulled by steam or diesel engines, including a dome observation coach, travel through some of the finest scenery in the Northeast. The trip through Crawford Notch is especially scenic. The 1874 Victorian train station has displays of railroad artifacts, lanterns, and old tickets and timetables. Foliage-season trains and special December trains sell out early, sometimes months in advance. | 38 Norcross Circle, just behind Schouler Park, off Rte. 16 (U.S. 302) | 603/356–5251 or 800/232–5251 | www.conwayscenic.com | $10–$50 | Mid-Apr.–late Dec; call for schedule.

Cranmore Mountain Resort. Opened in 1938, this ski mountain has 39 well-laid-out trails that are fun to ski. Snowboarders have a terrain park and a half-pipe. There's also outdoor skating, snowshoeing, and, on Friday and Saturday until 9 and Sunday until 4, snow tubing. | 1 Skimobile Rd., 1 mi east of Rte. 16 (U.S. 302), on the outskirts of town | 603/356–5543, 603/356–8516 snow conditions | www.cranmore.com.

Echo Lake State Park. A paved road leads to the top of scenic White Horse Ledge. From there you have a panoramic view of the White Mountains, the Saco River valley, and Echo Lake at the base of the ledge. Swimming is allowed in the lake and there are picnic sites scattered throughout the park. | Off Rte. 16 (U.S. 302), 2 mi west of North Conway | 603/356–2672 | www.nhparks.state.nh.us | $3 | Late May–mid-June, weekends dawn–dusk; mid-June–early Sept., daily dawn–dusk.

Factory outlet stores. North Conway is famous among outlet shoppers, who can choose from more than 150 stores. | Rte. 16 (U.S. 302), center of town.

Saco Bound Canoe & Kayak. River outfitter Saco Bound Canoe & Kayak leads gentle canoeing expeditions, guided kayak trips, and white-water rafting on seven rivers and provides lessons, equipment, and transportation. | Rte. 113 (U.S. 302), 7 mi southeast of North Conway | 603/447–2177 | www.sacobound.com.

Weather Discovery Center. The hands-on exhibits at this meteorological educational facility teach how weather is monitored and how it affects us. The facility is a collaboration between the National and Atmospheric Administration Forecast Systems lab and the Mt. Washington Observatory at the summit of Mt. Washington. | Rte. 16 (U.S. 302), ⅕ mi north of rail tracks | 603/356–2137 | www.mountwashington.org | $5 | Fri.–Tues. 10–5.

Dining

Darby Field Inn. American. The restaurant at this rambling 1820s inn serves haute regional American fare. Roast duckling is topped with a Chambord sauce and calvados-glazed chicken is stuffed with cheddar and apples. The dark-chocolate pâté with white-chocolate sauce is a knockout dessert. | 185 Chase Hill, Albany, 8 mi southwest of North Conway | 603/447–2181 | Closed Apr. | AE, MC, V | $$–$$$

Delaney's Hole in the Wall. American/Casual. This casual restaurant has eclectic memorabilia that includes autographed baseballs and an early photo over the fireplace of skiing at Tuckerman Ravine. Entrées range from fish-and-chips to fajitas to mussels and scallops sautéed with spiced sausage and Louisiana seasonings. | Rte. 16 (U.S. 302), ¼ mi north of town | 603/356–7776 | D, MC, V | $–$$

Muddy Moose. American/Casual. Especially popular with young professionals and families, the Muddy Moose is inviting and rustic, thanks to its fieldstone walls, exposed wood, and understated lighting. Dig into a Greek salad, grilled-chicken Caesar wrap, char-grilled pork chops with a maple-cider glaze, or Muddy Moose pie. | Rte. 16 (U.S. 302), just south of town | 603/356–7696 | AE, D, MC, V | $–$$

NEW HAMPSHIRE'S SEACOAST & LAKES
FROM EXETER TO WOLFEBORO

Distance: 125 mi   Time: 3 days
Overnight Breaks: Meredith, Portsmouth

Drive along New Hampshire's short but lovely seacoast and around the largest of the state's many lakes. You'll also see some of the smaller lakes and the rivers that feed them. Many of the towns along the way have museums that highlight New Hampshire's long and varied history. Summer and fall are the best times for this drive since many of the attractions are closed in winter and spring. Summer is the best choice if you want to swim or sunbathe, but fall ushers in cool sunny days, crisp nights, and colorful foliage.

❶ Begin at colonial **Exeter,** on the Swamscott River. One of the state's earliest towns, it was the capital before the political center was moved inland to Concord. The **American Independence Museum** explains the state's early history with exhibits such as a draft of the U.S. Constitution. The nearby **Gilman Garrison House** was built around 1690 as a fortified garrison.

❷ From Exeter, head north on Route 108 until you reach Route 101. Then take Route 101 southeast to **Hampton Beach,** which has the state's longest stretch of sand, weekly fireworks in summer, arcades, shops, ice-cream stands, and other traditional seacoast fun. **Fuller Gardens** blooms all summer long with 2,000 rosebushes of every shade and type.

❸ Head north along Route 1A and stop at **Odiorne Point State Park** in Rye to walk along the rocks at the water's edge and examine tide pools or visit the **Seacoast Science Museum.** The Science center has guided nature walks and exhibits on the area's natural history and marine life.

❹ Follow Route 1A north to **Portsmouth.** Enjoy a walk through Portsmouth's historic district and stop in at least one or two of the half dozen or so historic houses open

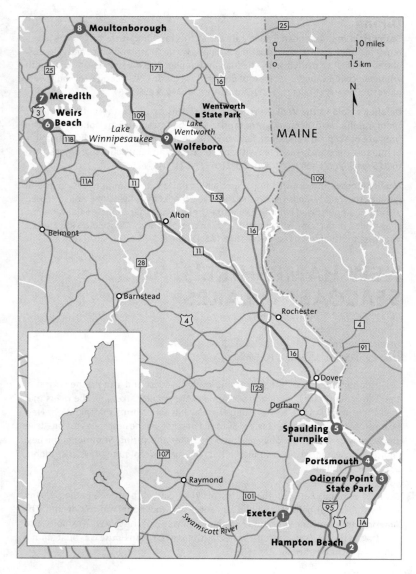

to visitors. The **Moffatt-Ladd House** and the **John Paul Jones House** are good choices. Pick up a brochure for a walking tour and information on multiple-house tickets at any of the houses. For a more comprehensive look at Portsmouth's history, spend some time at **Strawbery Banke Museum,** where a series of renovated and furnished houses provide a peek at 300 years of history in one neighborhood. Consider a cruise to the **Isles of Shoals.** These nine islands (eight at high tide) are divided between New Hampshire and Maine. Two companies offer harbor tours and island cruises from the waterfront near the center of town: **Isles of Shoals Steamship Co.** and **Portsmouth Harbor Cruises.**

⑤ From Portsmouth, take the **Spaulding Turnpike (Rte. 16)** north to Route 11 (at Exit 15). This route leads first through small towns and countryside as it heads toward **Lake**

Winnipesaukee, the state's largest lake, which covers 72 square mi and has 274 islands. Routes 11 and 11B follow the western shoreline, offering both quick glimpses of the water between the trees and wide-open vistas from higher points.

⑥ Off Route 11B is **Weirs Beach,** the lakefront equivalent of Hampton Beach; the town has a a public beach, the **Surf Coaster** water park, and two lake cruise boats, including the **MS Mt. Washington.**

⑦ Take U.S. 3 north to **Meredith,** the site of one terminus of the **Winnipesaukee Scenic Railroad,** which runs along the lakeshore.

⑧ From Meredith, take Route 25 northeast to **Moultonborough.** The **Loon Center** is a great place to learn about the pretty black-and-white birds whose haunting calls drift across New Hampshire's lakes in the evening and early morning. The view alone is reason enough to visit **Castle in the Clouds.** This odd, elaborate mansion took three years to build and cost nearly $7 million in 1911.

⑨ Head southeast on Route 109 to **Wolfeboro,** a pretty Lake Winnipesaukee resort town, with a main street that runs along the waterfront. Wolfeboro also has shoreline on **Lake Wentworth,** named for an early governor, where you find **Wentworth State Park.** The park has a beach, picnic areas, and a bathhouse. Also worth a stop is the **Wright Museum,** which overflows with artifacts illustrating the contributions of those on the home front to World War II.

Exeter

American Independence Museum. The story of the American Revolution unfolds during each tour of the Ladd Gilman House. Drafts of the U.S. Constitution and the first Purple Heart are some of the items on display. The house served as the state treasury from 1775 to 1789 and as the governor's mansion during the 14-year term of John Taylor Gilman. | 1 Governors La. | 603/772–2622 | www.independencemuseum.org | $5 | May–Oct., Wed.–Sat. 10–4, Sun. 11–4; last tour at 3 each day.

Gilman Garrison House. Built around 1690 as a fortified garrison, this historic house is one of the oldest remaining structures in Exeter. Massive logs form the walls and a portcullis was installed behind the main door. | 12 Water St. | 603/436–3205 | www.spnea.org | Free | By appointment only.

Kingston State Park. Relax by Great Pond, or take a leisurely dip, in this 44-acre park. No pets. | Rte. 125, Kingston, 8 mi southwest of Exeter | 603/642–5471 | www.nhparks.state.nh.us | $3 | May–Sept., daily dawn–dusk.

Phillips Exeter Academy. Founded in 1783, this is one of the most esteemed prep schools in the nation. The buildings, with architectural styles spanning several centuries, are mainly along Front Street in the historic district. | Front St. | 603/777–3437 | www.exeter.edu | Free | Tours by appointment.

Dining

Inn of Exeter's Terrace Restaurant. Contemporary. Quintessential New England furnishings and innovative food make for a memorable dining experience. Try mustard-glazed American bison and pecan-encrusted Atlantic salmon with a pineapple salsa. On Sunday the line forms early for brunch. | 90 Front St. | 603/772–5901 or 800/782–8444 | AE, D, DC, MC, V | $$–$$$$

Loaf and Ladle. American/Casual. Chowders, soups, and stews as well as huge sandwiches on homemade bread are served cafeteria-style at this understated eatery overlooking the river. Check the blackboard for the ever-changing rotation of specials, breads, and desserts, and don't miss the fresh salad bar. | 9 Water St. | 603/778–8955 | Reservations not accepted | AE, D, DC, MC, V | ¢–$

Tavern at River's Edge. American. A convivial downtown gathering spot on the Exeter River, this tavern pulls in parents of prep school kids, UNH students, and suburban yuppies. It can be informal, but the kitchen turns out surprisingly sophisticated chow. Try the gingered Atlantic salmon with a *ponzu* glaze and lemon-jicama slaw. | 163 Water St. | 603/772–7393 | No lunch | AE, D, DC, MC, V | $$–$$$

Hampton Beach

Fuller Gardens. Arthur Shurtleff designed this turn-of-the-20th-century estate garden in the colonial-revival style. In the 1930s, the Olmsted brothers added to it. Now the garden blooms all summer long with 1,700 rosebushes. Other plantings include a hosta display garden and a serenity-inspiring Japanese garden. | 10 Willow Ave., North Hampton, 4 mi north of Hampton Beach | 603/964–5414 | www.fullergardens.org | $6 | May–mid-Oct., daily 10–6.

Hampton Beach Casino Ballroom. On summer evenings, this live performance venue is packed with vacationers and locals who come to see name entertainers. Tina Turner, Jay Leno, and Loretta Lynn are just a few who have played here. | 169 Ocean Blvd. | 603/929–4100 | www.casinoballroom.com | Apr.–Oct.

Hampton Beach State Park. This state park has a beach with a bathhouse and lifeguards in summer. The beach is within walking distance of all the honky-tonk amusements of Hampton Beach (the town), and has an amphitheater and band shell, both of which have live concerts throughout the summer. Crowds are thick on summer weekends. | Rte. 1A, 3 mi south of Hampton Beach | 603/926–3784 | Weekdays $5 per car, weekends $8 per car | Daily dawn–dusk. Lifeguards weekends only early May–mid-June; daily mid-June–Labor Day.

Dining

Ashworth by the Sea. American. Enjoy views of the sea beyond Hampton Beach while sampling from an eclectic menu of casual café cuisine, elaborate buffets, and sophisticated seafood fare with an emphasis on rich cream sauces. Of the seven lobster variations, the lobster meat wrapped in haddock with a crawfish-sherry sauce stands out. | 295 Ocean Ave. | 603/926–6762 or 800/345–6736 | fax 603/926–2002 | AE, D, DC, MC, V | $$–$$$$

Ron's Landing at Rocky Point. Contemporary. In an oceanfront setting with a view of Hampton Beach, this restaurant serves seafood, pasta, veal, and beef. Try the seafood Florentine pie (sea scallops, shrimp, and lobster baked in Florentine sauce with bacon and a Parmesan-cracker crust). Sunday brunch. | 379 Ocean Blvd. | 603/929–2122 | No lunch Mon.–Sat. | AE, D, DC, MC, V | $$–$$$$

Meredith

Annalee's Doll Museum. Come see the world's largest collection of Annalee dolls at this museum with more than 800 pieces spanning the creative career of Annalee Thorndike, the doll's creator and museum curator. | Hemlock Dr., off Rte. 104 | 603/279–4144 | www.annalee.com | Free | Memorial Day–mid-Oct.; call for hrs.

Lakes Region Summer Theatre. This acclaimed seasonal stage presents Broadway-style musicals. | Interlakes Auditorium, Rte. 25 | 603/279–9933 or 800/643–9993 | www.lakesregionsummertheatre.com | Tickets $20 | Late June–Aug.; call for performance times.

Meredith Marina. If you want to explore Lake Winnipesaukee, you can rent a power-boat here. | Bay Shore Dr. | 603/279–7921 | June–Sept., daily 9–6.

Mill Falls Marketplace. This delightful set of shops includes boutiques, galleries, restaurants, and an ice-cream parlor. | U.S. 3 at Rte. 25 | 603/279–7006 or 800/622–6455 | Mon.–Thurs. 10–5:30, Fri. and Sat. 10–8, Sun. 10–4.

Wellington State Beach. A ½-mi stretch on Newfound Lake, this beach is ideal for swimming, sunning, or picnics. | Rte. 3A, Bristol, 12 mi west of Meredith | 603/744–2197 | $3 | Mid-May–mid-June, weekends dawn–dusk; mid-June–Columbus Day, daily dawn–dusk.

Winnipesaukee Scenic Railroad. Take one- to two-hour rides in these early-19th-century railroad cars that carry passengers along the shores of Lake Winnipesaukee. Board at Weirs Beach or Meredith. Santa trains, on which a costumed Santa passes out gifts, run some weekends in December. | U.S. 3 | 603/279–5253 or 603/745–2135 | www.hoborr.com | $10–$26 | Late June–early Sept., daily; late May–late June and early Sept.–mid-Oct. weekends only. Call for Santa train schedule.

Dining

Boathouse Grill. Contemporary. An upscale lakeside restaurant on the ground floor of the Inn at Bay Point, part of the Inns at Mills Falls, the Boathouse Grill has seating in a sunny dining room overlooking Lake Winnipesaukee and the dock for the MS *Mt. Washington.* The kitchen turns out some of the most sophisticated cuisine in the area, including lobster-corn chowder with sherry, and grilled salmon over seasonal greens with roasted-garlic vinaigrette. | U.S. 3 at Rte. 25 | 603/279–2253 | AE, D, DC, MC, V | $$–$$$

Coe House Restaurant. Contemporary. In a handsomely restored 18th-century mansion in tranquil Center Harbor, this grand restaurant turns out expertly prepared contemporary American and Continental fare. Start with the glazed cherrywood-smoked duck breast with toasted pecans and a cognac blackberry sauce, before moving on to grilled maple porterhouse pork chops with garlic-mashed potatoes and a black pepper–cider sauce. | Rte. 25B, Center Harbor, 5 mi northeast of Meredith | 603/253–8617 | Closed Mon.–Wed. Nov.–Apr. No lunch | AE, MC, V | $$–$$$

Mame's. American. This 1820s tavern, once the home of the village doctor, now contains a warren of convivial dining rooms with exposed-brick walls, wooden beams, and wide-plank floors. Expect American standbys of the seafood, steak, veal, and chicken variety; the mud pie is highly recommended. | 8 Plymouth St. | 603/279–4631 | AE, D, MC, V | $–$$

Lodging

Gunstock Inn & Fitness Center. The original building of this colonial-style inn, just up the road from the Gunstock ski area, was constructed in the 1930s by Civilian Conservation Corps workers who cut the area's first ski trails. Rooms are individually decorated, and some are large enough to accommodate families. Many have views of the mountains and Lake Winnipesaukee. The snug tavern serves everything from seafood to burgers. In the fitness center you can take water aerobics and body-toning classes free of charge. Restaurant, some refrigerators, indoor pool, health club, sauna, steam room. | 580 Cherry Valley Rd., Gilford 03246, 11 mi southeast of Meredith | 603/293–2021 or 800/654–0180 | fax 603/293–2050 | www.gunstockinn.com | 23 rooms, 2 suites | BP | AE, MC, V | $–$$

Inns at Mill Falls. Overlooking Lake Winnipesaukee and incorporating sections of the 19th-century Meredith Linen Mills, this stunning complex is a full resort with warmth and personality. There are four lodging options here. The Inn at Mills Falls, which adjoins an 18-shop market, has a pool and 54 spacious rooms. The lakefront Inn at Bay Point has

24 rooms—most with balconies, some with fireplaces. The 20 rooms and three suites at the lake-view Chase House at Mill Falls all have fireplaces; some have balconies. All three buildings have excellent restaurants. An additional inn, Church Landing, at this writing set to open in spring 2004, will add 70 lakefront rooms and suites. 3 restaurants, some in-room hot tubs, indoor pool, sauna, beach, dock, boating, ice-skating, bar, shops, meeting rooms. | U.S. 3 at Rte. 25, 03253 | 603/279–7006 or 800/622–6455 | fax 603/279–6797 | www.millsfalls.com | 98 rooms, 3 suites | AE, D, DC, MC, V | $$–$$$$

Pressed Petals Inn. Graceful, simple Victorian furnishings fill the eight floral-theme rooms at this peaceful farmhouse inn that's a short stroll from Squam Lake. Each room has Crabtree & Evelyn bath amenities and downy bathrobes. The inn is well away from the bustle of Winnipesaukee's amusements but within an easy drive of eateries and shops. A full country breakfast and Saturday-afternoon hors d'oeuvres are served by candlelight. No room phones, no room TVs, no kids under 10, no smoking. | Shepard Hill Rd., Holderness 03245, 7 mi north of Meredith | 603/968–4417 | fax 603/968–3661 | www.pressedpetalsinn.com | 8 rooms | BP | AE, D, MC, V | $$–$$$

Moultonborough

Castle in the Clouds. The odd, elaborate stone mansion high in the Ossipee Mountains was built by Thomas Gustave Plant between 1911 and 1914. Plant spent $7 million, the bulk of his fortune, to build the 16-room house. The 5,200-acre estate is now a recreation area. Tours are given of the house, the Castle Springs Microbrewery, and the Castle Springs water-bottling facility. You can also ride a paddleboat, picnic, or take a guided horseback ride. | Rte. 171 | 603/476–2352 or 800/729–2468 | www.castlesprings.com | With tour $12, without tour $6 | Mid-May–mid-June, weekends 9–4:30; early June–mid-Oct., daily 9–4:30.

The Loon Center. At the Frederick and Paula Anna Markus Wildlife Sanctuary, this headquarters of the Loon Preservation Committee is administered by the Audubon Society. This common loon, recognizable for its eerie calls and striking black-and-white coloring, resides on many New Hampshire lakes but is threatened by boat traffic, poor water quality, and habitat loss. The center presents changing exhibits about the birds. Two trails wind through the 200-acre property; vantage points on the Loon Nest Trail overlook the spot resident loons sometimes occupy in late spring and summer. | Lees Mills Rd. | 603/476–5666 | www.loon.org | Free | July–mid-Oct., daily 9–5; mid-Oct.–June, Mon.–Sat. 9–5.

Old Country Store and Museum. Since it opened in 1781, this local landmark has been selling everything from penny candy and homemade jams to coonskin caps and weather vanes. The upstairs museum is filled with old-time farming equipment. | Moultonborough Corner, Rtes. 25 and 109 | 603/476–5750 | Free | Daily 10–5.

Dining

The Woodshed. American. Tucked ½ mi down a quiet country road, this 1860s barn and farmhouse has become a local legend, serving delicious fare to a steady stream of celebrities and local folks. Old farm implements on the walls create a rustic look. The fare is mostly traditional New England—sea scallops baked in butter and lamb chops with mint sauce; ingredients are exceptionally fresh. Kids' menu. | 128 Lee Rd., off Rte. 109, 1 mi south of town | 603/476–2311 | Closed Mon. No lunch | AE, D, DC, MC, V | $$–$$$

Portsmouth

Children's Museum of Portsmouth. Kids don rain slickers, haul lobster traps, and work the counter of a fish market at this child-friendly museum, housed in an 1866 schoolhouse. Nineteen hands-on exhibits explore lobstering, sound and music, computers, space travel, and other subjects. Many kids never make it past the big yellow submarine, a three-story play structure with tunnels, platforms, peek holes, slides, and more. | 280 Marcy St. | 603/436–3853 | www.childrens-museum.org | $5 | Tues.–Sat. 10–5, Sun. 1–5; also Mon. 10–5 in summer and during school vacations.

Fort Constitution. Originally called Fort William and Mary, this National Historic Site 4 mi east of Portsmouth was once a British stronghold overlooking Portsmouth Harbor. Rebel patriots raided the fort in 1774 in one of revolutionary America's first overt acts of defiance against the king of England. The rebels later used the captured munitions against the British at the Battle of Bunker Hill. Only the base of the walls remains. It's a great place to snap photos of the Portsmouth Harbor Lighthouse, resting out on the rocky point. | Rte. 1B at Coast Guard Station, New Castle, 4 mi east of Portsmouth | 603/436–1552 | www.nhparks.state.nh.us | Free | Daily dawn–dusk.

★ **Historic District.** The first European settlers encamped here in 1623, making Portsmouth one of the oldest cities in New Hampshire, and in the United States. The Old Harbor area, along Bow and Ceres streets, was once the focus of this thriving seaport. Shops and restaurants now occupy its chandleries and warehouses, but the tugboats and container ships are a reminder that this is still a busy port. Marcy Street, Prescott Park, and the narrow streets surrounding the Strawbery Banke Museum are in the oldest part of the city. Point of Graves, the city's oldest cemetery, has headstones dating from 1682. | Take Exit 7 from I–95 and follow signs for historic district.

Isles of Shoals. Five of these islands belong to Maine, four to New Hampshire. Many, like Hog Island, Smuttynose, and Star Island, retain the earthy names given by the transient fishermen who visited them in the early 17th century. Celia Thaxter, a native islander, romanticized these islands with her poetry in *Among the Isles of Shoals* (1873). In the late 19th century, Appledore Island became an offshore retreat for her coterie of writers, musicians, and artists. You reach the islands via either of two harbor cruise companies, Isles of Shoals Steamship Co. or Portsmouth Harbor Cruises.

Portsmouth Harbor Cruises. Sunset cruises, foliage trips, and trips to the Isles of Shoals and Portsmouth Harbor aboard the MV *Heritage* are among the popular offerings of this cruise company. | 64 Ceres St. | 603/436–8084 or 800/776–0915 | www.portsmouthharbor.com | $14–$18 | Mid-May–Oct., daily; call for schedules.

John Paul Jones House. The bright yellow, hip-roof house, minutes from Market Square, was a boardinghouse when the Revolutionary War hero lived here while supervising shipbuilding for the Continental Navy. The 1758 structure, now the headquarters of the Portsmouth Historical Society, contains furniture, costumes, glass, guns, portraits, and documents from the late 18th century. | 43 Middle St. | 603/436–8420 | www.portsmouthhistory.org | $4 | June–mid-Oct., Mon.–Sat. 10–4, Sun. noon–4.

Moffatt-Ladd House. Built in 1763, this historic home tells the story of Portsmouth's merchant class through portraits, letters, and fine furnishings. Take a stroll through the colonial revival garden, which includes a horse chestnut tree planted by General William Whipple when he returned home after signing the Declaration of Independence in 1776. | 154 Market St. | 603/436–8221 | $6 | Mid-June–mid-Oct., Mon.–Sat. 11–5, Sun. 1–5.

Portsmouth Harbour Trail. The trail is a great way to view the historic homes and major sites of Portsmouth. You can either do it yourself with an informative map purchased for $2 at the information kiosk at Market Square, the Chamber of Commerce at 500 Market Street, or from homes on the tour route, or you can take a guided tour. Local experts take groups through the trail. | 603/436–3988 | www.seacoastnh.com/harbourtrail | Trail free, tours $8 | Tours July 4th weekend–Columbus Day, Mon. and Thurs.–Sat. 10:30 and 5:30, Sun. at 1:30.

★**Strawbery Banke Museum.** The city's largest and most impressive museum was named for the wild strawberries once abundant along the shores of the Piscataqua River. The 10-acre compound has 46 buildings that date from 1695 to 1820, as well as period gardens, exhibits, and craftspeople. Ten furnished homes represent 300 years of history in one continuously occupied neighborhood. Half the interior of the Drisco House, built in 1795, depicts its history as a colonial dry-goods store, while the living room and kitchen are decorated as they were in the 1950s. The Shapiro House has been restored to reflect the life of the Russian Jewish immigrant family who lived in the home in the early 1900s. Perhaps the most opulent house, done in decadent Victorian style, is the 1860 Goodwin Mansion, former home of Governor Ichabod Goodwin. | Marcy St. | 603/433–1100 | www.strawberybanke.org | $12 | May–Oct., Mon.–Sat. 10–5, Sun. noon–5; Nov., Dec., Feb., and Apr., Thurs.–Sat. 10–2, Sun. noon–2.

Dining

B.G.'s Boathouse Restaurant. Seafood. It might look like an old bait shack on the outside, but this busy spot serves up surprisingly large portions of fresh seafood such as lobster and fried clams. | 191 Wentworth Rd. | 603/431–1074 | Reservations not accepted | Closed Nov.–Mar. | AE, D, MC, V | $–$$

Blue Mermaid World Grill. Caribbean. The chefs at Blue Mermaid prepare Caribbean-influenced fare on a wood-burning grill. Specialties include wood-grilled seafood dishes and specialty pizzas, pan-seared cod with coconut curry sauce, and seasoned hangar steak with papaya-pineapple salsa and sweet-potato hash. In summer you can eat on a deck that overlooks the historic Hill neighborhood. Entertainers perform (outdoors in summer) on Friday and Saturday. | 409 Hanover St. | 603/427–2583 | AE, D, DC, MC, V | $$

Forty-Three Degrees North. Contemporary. Sage-green and mustard-yellow walls, dark woods, and large framed artworks give this popular, upscale restaurant a European look. The menu changes daily, but there are some standbys like the crispy duck spring rolls with ginger-jalapeño sauce, Maine crab cakes, pan-seared tuna with wasabi vinaigrette, and porcini-dusted veal medallions. | 75 Pleasant St. | 603/430–0225 | Closed Sun. | AE, MC, V | $$–$$$$

★**Library Restaurant.** Continental. At the turn of the 20th century, the Russo-Japanese peace treaty was signed in this building, which today feels like a fine gentlemen's club, with its shelves of books, hand-carved mahogany, and pressed-linen ceiling. Although the kitchen churns out such light dishes as sesame-encrusted tuna with a soy reduction, the mainstays are traditional dishes like char-grilled rib chop and pan-seared rack of lamb with a blackberry sauce. Live music. | 401 State St. | 603/431–5202 | AE, D, DC, MC, V | $$–$$$$

★**Poco's Bow Street Cantina.** Latin. Poco's boisterous downstairs bar and outside waterfront draws hordes of folks slurping down pitchers of margaritas and noshing on platters of chips and salsa. The upstairs dining room caters to more serious diners, turning out exceptional Southwestern and pan-Latin cuisine at great prices. Avocado-wrapped fried oysters with chipotle tartar sauce and lobster quesadilla with Brie, caramelized onions, and roasted corn–tomato salsa are among the better choices. Most tables have great views of the Piscataqua River. | 37 Bow St. | 603/431–5967 | AE, D, MC, V | $–$$

Lodging

Inn at Strawbery Banke. Small, simply decorated rooms (think white walls, white bedspreads, and patchwork quilts on double beds) give guests a hint of life in an early colonial home at this downtown property. Breakfast is served in a sunny room overlooking the gardens; there's also a cozy sitting room with a TV and plenty of books and magazines to peruse. It's a short stroll to restaurants and shops. No room phones, no room TVs, no children under 10. | 314 Court St., 03801 | 603/436–7242 or 800/428–3933 | www.innatstrawberybanke.com | 7 rooms | BP | AE, D, MC, V | $$

Port Motor Inn. This attractive motel has an old New England feel. Although the building looks like an inn from the front, all the rooms are off an exterior corridor. If you choose to go into the lobby, you can relax by the fireplace. The grounds are well maintained and landscaped. Picnic area, some microwaves, some refrigerators, cable TV, pool. | 505 U.S. 1 Bypass, at I–95, Exit 5, 03801 | 603/436–4378 or 800/282–7678 | fax 603/436–4378 Ext. 200 | www.theportinn.com | 33 rooms, 20 studios, 4 suites | AE, D, DC, MC, V | $–$$

Sise Inn. Each room at this 1881 Queen Anne–style town house is decorated in Victorian style, with designer fabrics, antiques, and reproductions; some rooms have fireplaces. About half the rooms are in a modern addition, which was completed in the 1980s, that blends well with the older section. The inn is close to Market Square. Some in-room hot tubs, cable TV, in-room VCRs, laundry service, meeting rooms, no-smoking rooms. | 40 Court St., 03801 | 877/747–3466 | phone/fax 603/433–1200 | www.siseinn.com | 26 rooms, 8 suites | CP | AE, DC, MC, V | $$$–$$$$

Wentworth by the Sea. New Hampshire's only seaside resort hotel, this luxury property, which dates to 1874, was once a summer resort for East Coast socialites, wealthy patrons, and former presidents. The resort and spa, on New Castle island, a few minutes' drive from downtown Portsmouth, was boarded up for years; it reopened in spring 2003 after major renovations. Most of the bright airy rooms have ocean and harbor views. 2 restaurants, room service, in-room data ports, 18-hole golf course, pro shop, 4 tennis courts, 2 pools (1 indoor), health club, hot tub, spa, bar, lobby lounge, dry cleaning, laundry service, concierge. | 860 Wentworth Rd., New Castle 03854, 4 mi east of Portsmouth | 603/422–7322 or 866/240–6313 | fax 603/422–7329 | www.wentworth.com | 161 rooms, 34 suites | AE, D, DC, MC, V | $$–$$$$

Weirs Beach

Ellacoya State Beach. This 600-foot beach on the southwestern shore of Lake Winnipesaukee has a bathhouse and picnic tables. | Rte. 11, Gilford, 7 mi southeast of Weirs Beach | 603/293–7821 | $3 | Mid-May–mid-June, weekends dawn–dusk; mid-June–Columbus Day, daily dawn–dusk.

Funspot. The mother ship of Winnipesaukee's several giddy family-oriented amusements parks, Funspot claims to be the second-largest arcade in the country, but it's much more than just a video-game room. You can work you way through a miniature golf course, a golf driving range, an indoor golf simulator, 20 lanes of bowling, cash bingo, and more than 500 video games. | Rte. 11B at U.S. 3 | 603/366–4377 | www.funspotnh.com | Entrance is free, rates differ for each activity | Mid-June–early Sept., daily 9 AM–midnight; early Sept.–mid-June, Sun.–Thurs. 10–10, Fri. and Sat. 10 AM–11 PM; some outdoor attractions closed in winter.

Mt. Washington Cruises. The 230-foot MS *Mt. Washington* makes 2½-hour scenic cruises of Lake Winnipesaukee, leaving from Weirs Beach with stops in Wolfeboro, Alton Bay, Center Harbor, and Meredith. Evening cruises include live music and a buffet dinner. | On the boardwalk | 603/366–5531 or 888/843–6686 | www.cruisenh.com | $15–$45 | Mid-May–mid-Oct.

Surf Coaster. The lake's ultimate water park, Surf Coaster has seven water slides, a wave pool, and the large Barefoot Action Lagoon, for young children. Teams of six can duke it out in a massive inflatable maze for a game of water tag. | U.S. 3 | 603/366–5600 | www.surfcoasterusa.com | $24.95, afternoon only $16.95 | Late June–early Sept., daily 10–6.

Dining

Hickory Stick Farm. American. The scent of duckling roasting (before being served with an herb stuffing and an orange-sherry sauce) frequently fills this restaurant in a 200-year-old Cape-style house. In fact, the duck dinners have become so renowned that the restaurant has developed a mail-order business for them. Other favorites from the mostly Continental and American menu include filet mignon and vegetarian lasagna. | 66 Bean Hill Rd., Belmont, 9 mi south of Weirs Beach | 603/524–3333 | Closed Mon. No lunch Tues.–Sat. | AE, D, MC, V | $$–$$$

Nothin Fancy Mexican Bar and Grill. Mexican. Popular with boaters and motorcyclists, this friendly, hopping joint is a short walk from the public docks. Try the deep-fried chimichanga or the steak-and-cheese burrito. The canning jar margarita is a local legend. | 306 Lakeside Ave. | 603/366–5764 | AE, D, MC, V | ¢–$

Wolfeboro

Hampshire Pewter Company. The artisans here use 16th-century techniques to make pewter tableware and accessories. Free tours are conducted most days from Memorial Day to Columbus Day and by appointment at other times. The gift shop is open year-round. | 43 Mill St. | 603/569–4944 or 800/639–7704 | www.hampshirepewter.com | Free | Call for hrs.

Wentworth State Park. This park has a beach on Lake Wentworth with good swimming, picnic areas, and a bathhouse. | Rte. 109, 6 mi east of Wolfeboro | 603/569–3699 | www.nhparks.state.nh.us | $3 | Mid-May–mid-June, weekends dawn–dusk; mid-June–Columbus Day, daily dawn–dusk.

Wright Museum. Uniforms, vehicles, period advertisements, and other artifacts commemorate World War II. Exhibits cover major events and the impact of the war. | 77 Center St. | 603/569–1212 | www.wrightmuseum.org | $6 | May–Oct., Mon.–Sat. 10–4, Sun. noon–5; Apr. and Nov., Sat. 10–4, Sun. noon–4.

Dining

Lydia's. American/Casual. Brewster Academy students and summer folk converge upon this groovy little spot, which serves espresso, hearty sandwiches, homemade soups, bagels, and desserts. | 30 N. Main St. | 603/569–3991 | No dinner | No credit cards | ¢

Wolfetrap Grill and Raw Bar. Seafood. The seafood at this festive shanty on Lake Winnipesaukee comes right from the adjacent fish market. All the favorites are here, including a renowned clam boil for one with steamers, corn on the cob, onions, baked potatoes, sweet potatoes, sausage, and a hot dog. The raw bar has oysters and clams on the half shell. The fried seafood dinners, steaks, and lobster Caesar salads are also great. | 19 Bay St. | 603/569–1503 | Closed mid-Oct.–mid-May | MC, V | $–$$$

SOUTH JERSEY SHORE
FROM ATLANTIC CITY TO CAPE MAY

Distance: Approximately 50 mi, depending on detours   Time: 2 days
Overnight Breaks: Cape May, the Wildwoods

Take a drive from Atlantic City to the southernmost tip of the state. You can see some of the best of the Jersey Shore, including sterling examples of its boardwalks, natural habitats, historic architecture, and kitsch. While you can spend plenty of time on the beach, there are also some great attractions and diversions inland, including horseback riding, touring the Intracoastal Waterway, and hiking. Summer is peak season, and traffic can be nightmarish on Friday going south and Sunday going north. Try visiting in spring or fall when the crowds have thinned and the birds are stopping by along the Atlantic Flyway.

❶ In **Atlantic City** you can park for a modest fee in one of the casino lots and walk to other casinos and boardwalk sights. If you want to experience (or just witness) gambling at its most frantic, visit the casinos in the evening; for a more subdued gaming experience, go in late morning or afternoon, when the crowds are appreciably thinner and the pace is more subdued. If gambling is not your thing, it's still fun to walk the boardwalk and ogle the over-the-top casino architecture. At the **Garden Pier** visit the Atlantic City Historical Museum, small but with a wonderful array of memorabilia from the times of Mr. Peanut and full-body bathing suits. Once you've exhausted your capacity for glitz and ballyhoo, north of Atlantic City is the pristine **Edwin B. Forsythe National Wildlife Refuge,** which has an 8-mi driving loop as well as two short hiking trails and watchtowers. To get there take the Garden State Parkway north, exit at Atlantic City Service Plaza, MM 41, and follow signs for Jim Leeds Road. Turn right onto Leeds and left at Great Creek Road, then continue 3 mi to Route 9. Go south on Route 9 and take a left onto Lily Lake Road.

❷ In **Ocean City** you can play games and try amusement park rides on the boardwalk of "America's Greatest Family Resort," as the town calls itself. Ocean City has 2 mi of beach and boardwalk. Founded by Methodists, the city remains a dry town, with values in stark contrast to that of nearby Atlantic City.

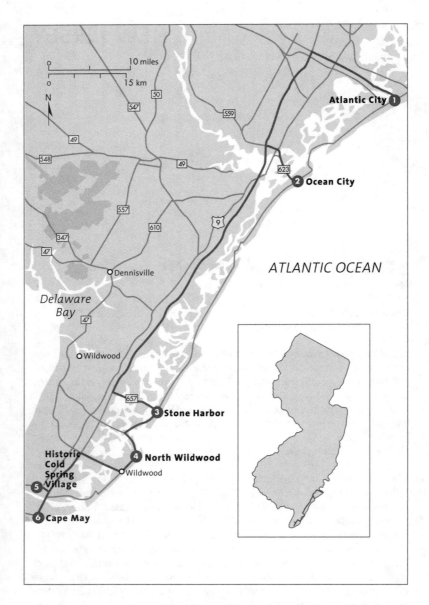

❸ Return to the Garden State Parkway via Route 623 and proceed south to Exit 10 (Rte. 657 [Stone Harbor Blvd.]), which takes you into **Stone Harbor.** Visit the **Wetlands Institute** which has easy flat hikes as well as exhibits of marine life in the wetlands environment. On the second weekend in September the institute sponsors a huge **Wings 'n' Water Festival** in Stone Harbor and several of the surrounding towns.

❹ In **North Wildwood** you begin to see the kitschy 1950s "mid-century modern" architecture of the diners and motels that line block after block near the beach. You can take an official tour, called the **Doo-Wop Trolley Tour,** on Tuesday or Thursday, or drive by and enjoy it on your own anytime; the buildings are particularly photogenic at sunrise and sunset. Next you can head for Morey's Piers and check out the biggest

Ferris wheel on the East Coast, along with a slew of other rides at not only Morey's but at four other piers. The boardwalk really rocks most nights in season, which has grown to include part of October, when the crowds are not as thick. Buy some curly fries or some Kohr's custard (after you go on the rides) then pick up a paddle-wheeler cruise of the Intracoastal Waterway. Consider spending the night in the Wildwoods.

❺ Proceed west on Wildwood Boulevard (Rte. 47) to Garden State Parkway South. Continue on the Parkway to Route 109 (U.S. 9) West to Cold Spring, where you find the **Historic Cold Spring Village,** a collection of vintage houses from around the state. Often on weekends there are craft fairs and entertainment suitable for kids.

❻ From Cold Spring Village take U.S. 9 East to Route 633 South into **Cape May,** where you find an awesome collection of restored Victorian houses in a city that reestablished its National Historic Landmark status in the 1970s. Be aware that hotel parking for guests is almost nonexistent, street parking is scarce, and free parking is even scarcer, so have plenty of quarters on hand for the meters and look for parking early, especially if you want to leave your car near the beach in summer.

The Mid-Atlantic Center for the Arts (MAC) offers architectural tours of Cape May, most of which include the **Emlen Physick Estate,** a carefully restored mansion. Cape May's strategic position along the Atlantic Flyway makes for great bird-watching, from a hawk-sighting watch point on the boardwalk at the **Cape May Point State Park** to sightings of songbirds and even monarch butterflies.

NEW JERSEY RULES OF THE ROAD

License Requirements: To drive in New Jersey you must be at least 17 years old and have a valid driver's license.

Right Turn on Red: Everywhere in the state you can make a right turn at a red light *after* a full stop unless otherwise posted.

Seat-Belt & Helmet Laws: All drivers and front-seat passengers must wear seat belts. Children under age 10 must wear a seat belt at all times, whether they are in the back or the front. Children under age 4 must be in a federally approved child safety seat. Motorcyclists must wear helmets and are required to keep their headlights and taillights on at all times.

Speed Limits: The speed limit is 65 mph on many major highways. In areas of heavier traffic, 55 mph is the speed limit, and, of course, on local roads the limit is usually 30 mph. Speed limits often change from town to town, so be sure to check the speed limit signs carefully.

Other Regulations: To drive in New Jersey, your blood-alcohol concentration must not exceed .10%. Passengers cannot possess open containers of alcohol in a vehicle. The use of handheld phones is prohibited while driving.

For More Information: New Jersey State Department of Transportation | 609/292–6500, 888/486–3339 in NJ | www.state.nj.us/transportation. New Jersey State Police | 609/882–2000 | www.njsp.org.

At the other end of the parking lot from the birders is the **Cape May Point Lighthouse,** open to the public after a $2 million restoration. You can climb the 199 steps to the top, where you're rewarded with great views of the ocean and the shoreline. If you keep your eyes peeled you may even see some dolphins splashing about in the ocean. If not, take a whale-and-dolphin-watch cruise aboard any of several sightseeing boats in the Cape May marina near the bridge on Route 9 coming into town. Spend the night in Cape May if you didn't already bed down in the Wildwoods.

To return to your starting point take the Garden State Parkway north to the Atlantic City Expressway, and then drive east to Atlantic City.

Atlantic City

Absecon Lighthouse. This 1857 lighthouse was designed by George Meade, stands 171 feet tall, and is the oldest man-made tourist attraction on the Jersey shore. You can tour the adjacent light keeper's house and climb to the top for a great view of the city. | Pacific and Rhode Island Aves. | 609/927–5218 or 609/449–1360 | Free | Mar., weekends 11–4; Memorial Day–June and early Sept.–Labor Day, Thurs.–Mon. 11–4; July–Aug., daily 11–4.

Atlantic City Art Center. Exhibition and sale galleries are housed here, and the art center regularly hosts concerts and readings. | Garden Pier, Boardwalk and New Jersey Ave. | 609/347–5837 | www.aclink.org/acartcenter | Free | Daily 10–4.

Atlantic City Historical Museum. With its vast collection of photographs and kitschy memorabilia, the museum tells the story of the resort's rise from barren sand dune to the "Queen of Resorts." | Garden Pier, Boardwalk and New Jersey Ave. | 609/347–5837 | www.acmuseum.org | Free | Daily 10–4.

Boardwalk. Part thoroughfare, part three-ring circus, the Boardwalk is center stage for every imaginable oddity. Conceived in 1870 as a way to allow Victorian-era visitors to experience nature without getting sand in their shoes, the Boardwalk became the place to see or be seen. Named for Alexander Boardman, the promenade's inventor, and not as you might think, for its wooden boards, the 4-mi-long Boardwalk begins in the resort's Inlet section, and heads south into neighboring Ventnor where it continues for another 1 1/2 mi. Saltwater taffy was invented on the Boardwalk in 1883, as the legend has it, when a storm flooded a candy dealer's wares. The Boardwalk's attractions include amusement piers, museums, arcades, bars, restaurants, carnival games, and miniature golf. The Steel Pier, which once hosted the best music acts of the day, as well as the famed diving horse show, is now home to rides and carnival games. On the Central Pier, you can ride go-carts or fire paintball rounds at human targets. Aside from strolling, the traditional way to experience the Boardwalk is being pushed in a rolling wicker chair, which evolved from the wheelchairs used by infirm visitors back when the city's promoters claimed the salty ocean air could cure diseases. The Boardwalk stretches the length of the city, from Absecon Inlet (Maine Avenue) to Ventnor City (Jackson Avenue).

Edwin B. Forsythe National Wildlife Refuge, Brigantine Division. Nearly 40,000 acres of coastal habitats—including 3,000 acres of woodland—are protected in this refuge. Peregrine falcons and bald eagles are among the winged visitors. You can take an 8-mi wildlife drive or walk the Leeds Eco-Trail, a 1/2-mi loop through salt marsh and woodlands, or the Akers Woodland Trail, an easy 1/4 mi through the woodlands. | Great Creek Rd. and Rte. 9, Oceanville, 11 mi northwest of town; head west on Rte. 30, then right on Rte 9; after 5 mi, make a right on Great Creek Rd. | 609/652–1665 | forsythe.fws.gov | $4 per vehicle | Daily dawn–dusk.

Lucy the Margate Elephant. Built in 1881 as a publicity stunt to sell real estate in what was then known as "South Atlantic City," Lucy is a six-story-tall, 90-ton elephant.

Before being designated a national historic landmark, this palatial pachyderm had a stint as a hotel. You can tour the elephant's innards and climb to the top of its howdah, for a view of the ocean. | 9200 Atlantic Ave., Margate, 3 mi south of Atlantic City | 609/823–6473 | www.lucytheelephant.org | $4 | Apr.–mid-June, weekends 10–4; mid-June–Labor Day, Mon.–Thurs. 10–8, Fri. and Sat. 10–5.

Ripley's Believe It or Not! Museum. In a bizarre building that looks as if it's about to be destroyed by a wrecking ball, this eclectic museum has, among its equally bizarre treasures, a lock of George Washington's hair and a collection of actual shrunken heads. | 1441 Boardwalk | 609/347–2001 | Memorial Day–Labor Day, daily 10–10; rest of year, weekdays 11–5, weekends 10–8.

Storybook Land. Fifty larger-than-life buildings and displays illustrate the tales of popular childhood stories at this 20-acre theme park. There are also rides and a picnic area. The park is geared for younger children. | 6415 Black Horse Pike, Egg Harbor Township, 10 mi west of Atlantic City | 609/641–7847 or 609/646–0103 | fax 609/646–4533 | www.storybookland.com | $14.95 | Daily 10–5.

Dining

Angelo's Fairmount Tavern. Italian. A popular hangout for locals since 1935, this no-frills Italian restaurant lies at the center of the city's Ducktown neighborhood. Angelo's is known for its Italian dishes, steaks, and seafood, and for its owner's predilection for New York Yankees memorabilia. | 2300 Fairmount Ave. | 609/344–2439 | No lunch weekends | AE, D, MC, V | $–$$$

★**Dock's Oyster House.** Seafood. Owned and operated by the Dougherty family since 1897, the city's oldest and arguably best restaurant serves seafood in a classy but understated wood-and-glass dining room. A portion of the menu appears exactly as it did in 1897. Try the pan-seared ahi tuna and fresh soft-shell crab. Piano bar. Kids' menu. | 2405 Atlantic Ave. | 609/345–0092 | Closed Dec. and Jan. No lunch Mon. | AE, DC, MC, V | $$–$$$$

Grabel's. Continental. Veal chops, steak, jumbo shrimp, and crab cakes are the attractions at this restaurant. There are a kids' menu, a piano bar from Thursday through Sunday, and a large dance floor to hit between courses. | 3901 Atlantic Ave. | 609/344–9263 | No lunch | AE, DC, MC, V | $$–$$$$

★**White House Sub Shop.** Delicatessens. More than 17 million hefty sandwiches have been served at the White House since 1946. The Italian or cheesesteak subs are well worth the wait. The fresh Atlantic City bread is baked right around the corner. You can cram into one of the booths or request a take-out order. Almost every bit of wall space is obscured by celebrity photos scrawled with effusive testimonials about the satisfying fare. | 2301 Arctic Ave. | 609/345–1564 or 609/345–8599 | No credit cards | ¢–$

Cape May

Cape May–Lewes (DE) Ferry. A 70-minute trip aboard one of five modern ferries in the fleet shuttles foot passengers and cars between the two resort areas. Sometimes dolphins swim along for company. Food is available on board. | Cape May: board Terminal Bldg., Lincoln Dr.; Lewes, DE: board at 43 Henlapen Dr. | 609/886–1725, 302/645–6313, or 800/643–3779 | www.capemay-lewesferry.com | $20 per car | Daily 8:30–4:30; call or check Web site for departure times.

Cape May Lighthouse. Built in 1859, this lighthouse in Cape May Point State Park is one of the oldest operating lighthouses in the United States. The 157½-foot structure includes a small museum and has wonderful views of the shoreline. | Cape May Point State Park, Lighthouse Ave. | 609/884–5404 | www.capemaymac.org | $5 | Apr.–Nov., daily 10–4; Dec.–Feb., weekends 11–4.

Emlen Physick Estate. Built in 1879, this Stick-style mansion is attributed to architect Frank Furness. The house has many of the original furnishings as well as textiles and objets d'art. It is home to the Mid-Atlantic Center for the Arts, which was formed in an effort to save the structure. It offers a look at Victorian architecture, decorative arts, customs, and the lives of one particular Cape May family, the Physicks. The Physick Estate is also home to the restored Carriage House Gallery, which hosts changing exhibits. | 1048 Washington St. | 609/884–5404 | www.capemaymac.org | $8 | Tours daily; call for schedule.

Historic Cold Spring Village. More than 20 antique structures, built between 1702 and 1897, were brought in from sites throughout Cape May County and laid out to represent a small 19th-century south Jersey farming village. Village craftspeople in period costumes demonstrate age-old crafts using traditional tools, methods, and materials. | 720 Rte. 9 | 609/898–2300 | www.hcsv.org | $7 | Late June–Sept., daily 10–4:30.

The Mid-Atlantic Center for the Arts tours. There are almost as many ways to see Cape May as there are things to do here, and the Mid-Atlantic Center for the Arts offers a wide variety of tours almost every day of the year. Boat tours include sightseeing cruises around Cape May, tours of Delaware Bay (July and August), and, on D-Day, a morning cruise to see historic sites on both sides of the Delaware Bay. | Tours depart from Miss Chris Fishing Center, marina at entrance to Cape May | 609/884–5404 | www. capemaymac.org | Late Apr.–mid-Oct., tours daily at 10 AM.

Nature Center of Cape May. Explore 18 acres of beach, meadow, and marsh habitat at this New Jersey Audubon Center. Tours, exhibits, and educational activities are also available. | 1600 Delaware Ave. | 609/898–8848 | Free | Tues.–Sat. 10–3.

Dining

410 Bank Street. Cajun/Creole. Inside this 1850s summer cottage is one of southern New Jersey's most enduring restaurants. Most people dine outside, either on the partially covered patio or on the front porch. It's known for mesquite-grilled fish and steaks and home-smoked meats. Try smoked prime rib, barbecued jumbo shrimp, blackened striped bass, or fresh Maine lobster tails. BYOB. | 410 Bank St. | 609/884–2127 | Closed Nov.–Apr. No lunch | AE, D, DC, MC, V | $$–$$$$

Lobster House. Seafood. You can order shellfish and sit either inside or outside at this large, popular spot on the wharf. Inside there's a cocktail lounge with a lot of nautical touches. Outside you can sit on the dock and watch the ships come in. There's a raw bar and a kids' menu. | Fisherman's Wharf, Shillenger Landing Rd. | 609/884–8296 | No lunch Sun. | AE, D, MC, V | $$$$

Mad Batter. Contemporary. Housed in a lovely old building, this restaurant is known for fresh seafood and desserts. Try classic crab *mappatello* (a pastry puff filled with fresh crabmeat, spinach, and ricotta cheese, baked and served with a roasted-red-pepper–white-wine cream sauce), the Jackson Street crab cakes, or the orange-almond French toast. The dining room has purple walls, a green ceiling, Victorian lamps, and art that changes monthly. Dine outside on the front porch or garden terrace. Kids' menu. Sunday brunch. BYOB. Breakfast served. | 19 Jackson St. | 609/884–5970 | Closed Jan. | AE, D, DC, MC, V | $$–$$$$

★**Peaches at Sunset.** Contemporary. All the tropically inspired dining rooms are cozy here, but ask to sit on the serene screened porch overlooking gardens. Try the sea bass with a jade sauce (spinach, cilantro, basil, and ginger), avocado crab cake, grilled breast of duck with Mexican orange chipotle glaze, or the rack of lamb. Kids' menu. BYOB. No smoking. | 1 Sunset Blvd. | 609/898–0100 | Closed Mon.–Thurs. Oct.–May. No lunch | AE, D, DC, MC, V | $$–$$$

Lodging

Atlas Inn. Although the name might suggest otherwise, this "Inn" is really a full-service, kid-friendly beach resort. There's a pool with a sundeck and kids' area, barbecue grills, and a baseball-theme restaurant loaded with Babe Ruth memorabilia. Modern and airy guest rooms all have private balconies, many with ocean views. Restaurant, microwaves, refrigerators, cable TV, pool, gym, sauna, bar, laundry facilities, no-smoking rooms. | 1035 Beach Dr., 08204 | 609/884–7000 or 888/285–2746 | fax 609/884–0301 | www.atlasinn.com | 90 rooms | BP | AE, D, MC, V | $$$

Chalfonte. Loyal guests return yearly to stay in this 1876 Victorian Inn, with its rocking chairs, sweeping veranda, original furnishings, and Southern-style courtesy. Restaurant, bar; no room phones, no room TVs, no smoking. | 301 Howard St., 08204 | 609/884–8409 | fax 609/884–4588 | www.chalfonte.com | 78 rooms, 2 cottages | BP | MC, V | $$–$$$$

★**Mainstay Inn.** Two blocks from the historic district, this bed-and-breakfast consists of two restored Victorian buildings. Although the rooms are furnished with period antiques, the luxury suites have a more contemporary look, with hot tubs, kitchens, and fireplaces. All guests get beach passes. Some in-room hot tubs, some kitchens; no smoking. | 635 Columbia Ave., 08204 | 609/884–8690 | www.mainstayinn.com | 9 rooms, 7 suites | BP | No credit cards | $$$–$$$$

Montreal Inn. Within walking distance of Cape May's historic district and the Washington Mall, this hotel is right near the ocean. Although the structure is a basic concrete building, the Inn remains is hopping all summer long. Restaurant, room service, in-room data ports, some kitchenettes, microwaves, refrigerators, cable TV, miniature golf, putting green, pool, wading pool, gym, hot tub, bar, laundry facilities, business services, airport shuttle, no-smoking rooms. | 1028 Beach Dr., 08204 | 609/884–7011 or 800/525–7011 | fax 609/884–4559 | www.capemayfun.com | 70 rooms | Closed late Oct.–mid-Mar. | AE, D, MC, V | $$–$$$

Ocean City

Boardwalk. This may be the most family-friendly boardwalk at the shore, with a seemingly endless row of rides, pizzerias, ice-cream parlors, movie theaters, rides, and shops. Rent a surrey and pedal down the boards.

Ocean City Historical Museum. Here you'll find exhibits of local artifacts and old postcards. The Sindia Room highlights Ocean City's most famous shipwreck. | 1735 Simpson Ave. | 609/399–1801 | Donations accepted | Weekdays 10–4, Sat. 1–4, and by appointment.

Dining

Chef Paolo's That's Amore Italian Restaurant. Italian. Everything from soup to pasta is made from scratch at this 10-table eatery whose chef-owner used to own a restaurant in Florence. Try the ravioli, with such fillings as lobster, crab, shrimp, and, in fall, sweet potato and pumpkin. | 506 9th St. | 609/399–5800 | Closed mid-Oct.–Apr. | AE, MC, V | $$–$$$$

Cousin's. Italian. Since the Carnuccio family opened this homey family-style restaurant in 1980, they have taken on catering duties and even published their own cookbook. Seafood, chicken, and steak are staples. Try the chicken saltimbocca or the jumbo fried shrimp. Family-size takeout is available. Kids' menu. Early-bird dinners. | 104 Asbury Ave. | 609/399–9462 or 800/286–1963 | AE, MC, V | $–$$$

Deauville Inn. American. If you're looking for the perfect sunset dining experience, try this waterfront restaurant in a former hotel built in 1880. The main fare is seafood and there are daily specials. Eat outdoors overlooking the water, and enjoy live music on summer weekends. Kids' menu. Early-bird dinners. | 201 Willard Rd., Strathmere, 7 mi south of town | 609/263–2080 | www.deauvilleinn.com | Closed 2 days a wk Nov.–Mar. (check Web site for days) | AE, MC, V | $$–$$$$

Stone Harbor

Stone Harbor Bird Sanctuary. Hundreds of species of shorebirds can be viewed from this open-air sanctuary. | 3rd Ave. and 114th St. | 609/368–5102 | Free | Weekdays 9 AM–8 PM, weekends 10 AM–8 PM.

Wetlands Institute. The facility offers exhibits and hiking trails geared towards appreciation of the Jersey Shore's highly prized wetlands ecology. | 1075 Stone Harbor Blvd. | 609/368–1211 | www.wetlandsinstitute.org | $5 | Mid-Oct.–mid-May, Tues.–Sat. 9:30–4:30; mid-May–mid-Oct., Mon.–Sat. 9:30–4:30, Sun. 10–4.

Dining

Back Yard Restaurant. Contemporary. Dine outside under a grape arbor surrounded by flowers, or inside in air-conditioned glass-walled comfort. Either way you're in for a romantic treat. Try the curried shrimp or the roast duck, but save room for the key lime tart. | 222 81st St. | 609/368–2627 | Closed Sun. No lunch | AE, V | $–$$

The Mirage. Continental. The three dining rooms in this restaurant have touches of ancient Egypt. Try the seafood martini, the honey-marinated port medallions, and the corn-bread pudding. Pianist Friday–Sunday. Kids' menu. Breakfast available. | 7888 Dune Dr., Avalon, 4 mi north of Stone Harbor | 609/368–1919 | www.desertsand.com/miragemenu.htm | Closed Nov.–Mar. | MC, V | $$–$$$$

The Wildwoods

Boardwalk. Encompassing more than 2 mi of boards, the Boardwalk has five amusement piers, the bulk of them owned by the Morey family. Morey's Piers has the tallest Ferris wheel in America. There are water parks, bumper cars, and five major roller coasters, along with some bungeelike thrill rides. Despite beach erosion elsewhere in the state, Wildwood seems to attract more and more sand every year, making the trek to the sea seem like crossing the Sahara. | On the ocean, Wildwood | 800/786–4546 boardwalk information, 888/667–3971 Morey's Piers | www.wildwoods.org | Free | Boardwalk 24 hrs, rides open between noon and 3 and close at midnight.

Doo-Wop Trolley Tours. So-called "doo-wop" 1950s-era architecture, preserved in the town's rich stock of old-fashioned motels, is the focus of this 45-minute tour. Learn about the shapes, images, and symbols associated with the designs, "fractured geography," and the space-age infatuation of the day. There are pickups for the tour in both Cape May and Wildwood. Reservations are not necessary, but best to call ahead. | Information booth at Washington St. Mall on Washington and Ocean Sts., North Wildwood | 609/884–5404 | $8 | June–Sept., Tues. and Thurs. 7:45 PM.

Sunset Lake & Turtle Gut Park and Memorial. An American Revolution battle fought in Cape May County is marked on this site. | New Jersey and Miami Aves., Wildwood Crest | No phone.

Wyland's Whaling Wall. Painted by acclaimed marine artist Wyland, this huge wall mural (220 feet by 30 feet) depicts life-size whales and dolphins. | Boardwalk Mall at Garfield Ave., Wildwood.

Dining

Groff's. American. You can find old-fashioned comfort food at its best at this restaurant, which first opened in 1932 and is still owned and run by the original family. Try pork chops with apple sauce, fried chicken, and lemon meringue and coconut cream pies. One of the original waitresses, a former Miss Wildwood, now in her eighties, still works here in summer. | 423 E. Magnolia, Wildwood | 609/522–5474 | Closed late Sept.–mid-May. No lunch | AE, D, DC, MC, V | $–$$$

Papa Joe's Bayside Pizza Pasta House. Pizza. Loved by locals, this neighborhood pizza joint is known for its white pizza, seafood pasta dishes, hoagies, and milk shakes. Takeout and delivery are available. | 6710 New Jersey Ave., Wildwood Crest | 609/729–3236 | AE, V | $–$$

Snuffy's. American. Opened in 1940 by Snuffy and Flo Smith, this corner luncheonette is still run by the Smiths and their children. There is a different $3.95 soup-sandwich-and-small-beverage lunch special every day. Breakfast served. | 101 E. Aster Rd., Wildwood Crest | 609/522–1825 | No dinner Sept.–June | No credit cards | $–$$

Lodging

Ivanhoe. The Ivanhoe Panoramic Hotel, 5 minutes from Cape May and 30 minutes from Atlantic City, rents family suites (bungalows) as well as standard rooms. You can't get much closer to the beach—you don't even have to cross the street. The room decor is early 1980s. Microwaves, refrigerators, cable TV, pool, wading pool, laundry facilities, business services, no-smoking rooms. | 430 E. 21st Ave., North Wildwood 08260 | 609/522–5874 | www.ivanhoemotel.com | 40 rooms, 3 suites | AE, D, DC, MC, V | $–$$

Le Voyageur. A block from the beach and boardwalk, this three-story hotel has many rooms overlooking the pool. Picnic area, some kitchenettes, refrigerators, cable TV, pool, wading pool, laundry facilities. | 232 E. Andrews Ave., Wildwood 08260 | 609/522–6407 or 800/348–0846 | fax 609/523–1834 | www.levoyageurmotel.com | 33 rooms | Closed Nov.–mid-Apr. | AE, MC, V | $–$$$

Park Lane. All rooms at this three-story hotel have views of the pool or of Wildwood Crest beach. A sundeck overlooks the ocean. Rooms are modern and standard. Picnic area, some kitchenettes, refrigerators, cable TV, pool, wading pool, laundry facilities, no-smoking rooms. | 5900 Ocean Ave., Wildwood Crest 08260 | 609/522–5900 | www.parklanemotel.net | 36 rooms | Closed late Sept.–Apr. | MC, V | $–$$

Rio Motel. An ocean observation deck, shuffleboard court, and miniature golf course are draws at this waterfront motel. It's two blocks from a municipal beachfront playground and tennis court, and guests have golf privileges at both the public or Greater Wildwood Club courses. Rooms are cheerful and sunny with private balconies. Restaurant, cable TV, golf privileges, miniature golf, pool, baby-sitting, laundry facilities, no-smoking rooms. | Rio Grande Ave. at the ocean, Wildwood 08260 | 609/522–1461 or 800/900–8876 | www.beachcomber.com/Wildwood/rio.html | 115 rooms | MC, V | $–$$$

NEW YORK

FINGER LAKES & THOUSAND ISLANDS
FROM ITHACA TO ALEXANDRIA BAY

Distance: 290 mi   Time: 4 days
Overnight Breaks: Corning, Geneva, Sackets Harbor

Explore the Finger Lakes Region, the southern shore of Lake Ontario, and part of the state's Seaway Trail, which hugs what some consider to be the nation's "North Coast": the Great Lakes and St. Lawrence River.

❶ Begin in **Ithaca,** a city of gorges that sits on the southern end of Cayuga Lake, the longest of the Finger Lakes. Here, you can enjoy an early-morning stroll at Ithaca Falls, **Buttermilk Falls State Park,** which is just south of the city on Route 13, or at some of the gorges that cut through the **Cornell University** campus on a hillside east of the city. One of the best views of the lake and city is from the **Herbert F. Johnson Museum of Art** (on University Ave., on northwest side of the campus), which was designed by I. M. Pei. If you have time see Cornell Plantations and Sapsucker Woods.

❷ From Ithaca take a quick drive north on Route 89, which climbs out of the city and follows the west bank of Cayuga Lake. Stop at **Taughannock Falls State Park** (8 mi north of Ithaca on Rte. 89). A short walk brings you to the highest waterfall in the state. At 215 feet, it eclipses Niagara by approximately 30 feet.

❸ Retrace your route back through Ithaca and head south on Route 13 toward **Elmira.** There you find **Mark Twain's Study** (on the campus of Elmira College, off Park Ave.), an unusual octagonal building where the author wrote *The Adventures of Huckleberry Finn* and other books. Twain is buried in the city's **Woodlawn Cemetery.** Next door to that graveyard is the **Woodlawn National Cemetery,** in which about 3,300 Confederate prisoners and Union soldiers are buried. Move from somber to soaring with a visit to the **National Soaring Museum** at Harris Hill Park, where gliding began in this country. Take a ride or simply enjoy the world's largest exhibit of sailplanes and historic gliders.

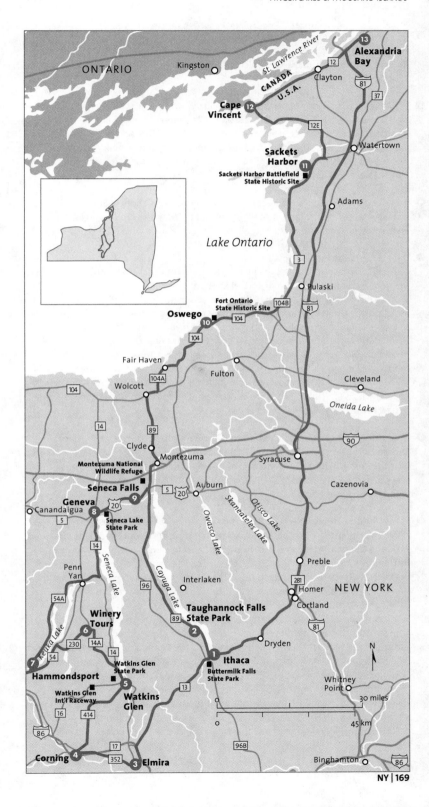

❹ Head west on Route 352 to **Corning** where the **Corning Glass Center** beckons. The center is one of New York State's major tourist attractions. Also worth seeing are the **Rockwell Museum** and the city's historic **Market Street district** (between Denison Pkwy. and Tioga Ave.)

❺ **Watkins Glen** is to the northeast, on Route 414. If you're a fan of auto racing, take a peek at the layout of the famous **Watkins Glen International Raceway.** Without question the main attraction of the area is the glen itself, in **Watkins Glen State Park,** which stretches west from the city's main street and includes nearly 20 waterfalls and a deep walk-through canyon. You can leave from here for a cruise on one of the Finger Lakes with **Captain Bill's Seneca Lake Cruises.**

❻ A pretty drive north on Route 14 takes you along the west shore of Seneca Lake and past several wineries. Many have regularly scheduled **winery tours** and tastings, as well as restaurants and views of the lake.

❼ Cut over to Route 230 and go west along a swooping curve toward Keuka, whose forks make it the most unusual of the Finger Lakes. At Route 54 head south toward the delightful village of **Hammondsport,** at the southern end of the lake. You can easily spend a day here with the **Glenn H. Curtiss Museum** (dedicated to the father of naval aviation), the **Great Western Winery Visitor Center,** and the peaceful village square. The *Keuka Maid* offers a chance for a lake cruise if you haven't taken one.

Wineries continue to beckon. Try **Heron Hill Winery** (9249 Rte. 76) or **Bully Hill Vineyards,** which has its own museum dedicated to charting the growth of the wine industry. Head north from the village along Route 54A and enjoy a drive that will make you grateful that cars were invented. You'll see the lake and Bluff Point, which splits the lake's northern arms. You'll also pass through **Penn Yan** and rejoin Route 54 as it swings east back toward Seneca Lake.

❽ Go north on Route 14 and head for **Geneva,** where you can picnic at the expansive **Seneca Lake State Park** (1 mi east of Geneva on Rtes. 5 and 20). You may choose to visit the **Rose Hill Mansion** (3 mi east of Geneva, on the northeast shore of Seneca Lake on Rte. 96A, just south of Rtes. 5 and 20), one of the best examples of Greek Revival architecture in America.

❾ Follow Route 20 East to **Seneca Falls** and key places in the history of the women's rights movement: the **Elizabeth Cady Stanton House, Wesleyan Chapel Declaration Park,** and **National Women's Hall of Fame.** You can stretch your legs at the **Montezuma National Wildlife Refuge** (5 mi east of Seneca Falls on Rtes. 5 and 20), which is perched on the north end of Cayuga Lake. The refuge is a major stopover for migrating birds and includes a walking tour that takes you close to the waterfowl.

❿ Head north on Route 89 and meet the nationally recognized scenic byway Seaway Trail at Wolcott. Follow the signs (along Rte. 104A) to Fair Haven, on the shore of Lake Ontario. The road goes through **Oswego** right by the **Ft. Ontario State Historic Site,** where you can catch daily military drills from mid-spring through early autumn. From Oswego the Seaway Trail follows Routes 104, 104B, and 3, which takes you north along the beautiful eastern end of Lake Ontario. At the Pulaski River, depending upon the season and your inclination, you might want to watch the anglers, who come from all over the world. (The county sells more than 65,000 fishing licenses a year.) The eastern shore of Lake Ontario has some fragile barrier beaches, dunes, and lagoons.

⑪ At **Sackets Harbor** stroll the battlefield where two engagements of the War of 1812 took place. In summer the harbor is likely to be bustling with cruising activity. In winter, the town belongs to hardy cross-country skiers and snowmobilers.

⑫ The Seaway Trail leaves Route 3, eventually links with Route 12 East, and takes you to **Cape Vincent,** where Lake Ontario meets the St. Lawrence River. The **Tibbetts Point Lighthouse** marks the spot. Farther along Route 12 is **Clayton,** which retains a genuine river-city feel and features the must-see **Antique Boat Museum.** The local **Thousand Islands Inn** is the birthplace of Thousand Island dressing.

⑬ Commercial and busy **Alexandria Bay** lies in the center of the 50-mi-long Thousand Islands area. Attractions include historic **Boldt Castle** (on Heart Island) and many opportunities to get out on the water and begin counting the islands.

The simplest way back is to head south on I–81 to Exit 13 in Preble. Go south on Route 281 until it hits Route 13, which takes you to Ithaca.

Alexandria Bay

★**Antique Boat Museum.** Boats and river memorabilia depict life on the St. Lawrence River. The collection of 205 craft includes an 8-foot canoe and a 65-foot yacht. Landlubbers may appreciate an exhibit that shows the Thousand Islands as a vacation destination; in its heyday, 15 trains a day arrived from New York City and Boston. | 750 Mary

NEW YORK RULES OF THE ROAD

License Requirements: Licensed 16-year-olds can drive in New York state (outside New York City, where the minimum driving age is 18), with restrictions. Those 18 and older have no restrictions. Foreign drivers need only a valid license from their home country to drive in New York.

Right Turn on Red: In most areas (and outside New York City), right turns on red are permitted, unless otherwise posted.

Seat-Belt & Helmet Laws: Seat belts are required for driver, front-seat passengers, and backseat passengers between the ages of 4 and 10. Children younger than 4 must be in federally approved child restraints. Motorcyclists are required to wear helmets.

Speed Limits: The speed limit on rural interstates is 65 mph; 55 mph on nonrural interstates. Watch signs on all roads.

Other Regulations: Headlights must be used before dawn and after dusk or before dawn or when weather conditions affect visibility. It is illegal to operate a motor vehicle in New York if your blood-alcohol concentration exceeds .10%. Using a handheld phone is prohibited while operating a vehicle.

For More Information: New York State Department of Transportation | 716/847–3238 Buffalo, 315/428–4351 Syracuse | www.dot.state.ny.us. New York State Police | 716/343–2200 Buffalo, 585/398–4100 Finger Lakes, 315/366–6000 Syracuse | www.troopers.state.ny.us.

St., Clayton, 12 mi west of Alexandria Bay | 315/686–4104 | www.abm.org | $8 | Mid-May–mid-Oct., daily 9-5; other times call for hrs.

Aqua Zoo. More than 50 exhibits show creatures from lakes, oceans, and rivers around the world. | 43681 Rte. 12, $^3/_4$ mi off Rte. 81 | 315/482–5771 | $5 | Daily; call for hrs.

Boat trips. Narrated cruises run throughout the islands. Some companies run dinner cruises.

Empire Boat Lines. Empire offers a shuttle to Boldt Castle every 30 minutes, as well as narrated 90-minute cruises to the castle. Dinner cruises are also available. | 5 Fuller St. | 315/482–8687 or 888/449–2539 | www.empireboat.com | $12.50 | Memorial Day–Labor Day, tours daily at 10, noon, 2, and 4.

Rockport Boat Line. Hour-long tours by this Canadian cruise line bring passengers within sight of Boldt Castle and Millionaire's Row. | 23 Front St., Rockport, ON, Canada; head east across the Thousand Islands bridge, go 3 mi east to Rockport | 613/659–3402 or 800/563–8687 | www.rockportcruises.com | C$12 | Mid-Apr.–June, tours leave daily at 10, noon, and 2; July–Oct., tours leave every hr 9–5.

Uncle Sam Boat Tours. July and August are the peak months for the 2$^1/_4$-hour tours that go through the Canadian side of the islands, but fall foliage is also worth catching. Sightseeing cruises last 2$^1/_4$ hours, and there is a stopover at Boldt Castle. Boats have heated, enclosed lower decks. Lunch cruises leave at 12:30 PM. Dinner cruises run at 7 PM Tuesday, and Thursday through Sunday. Reservations are required. | 47 James St. | 315/482–2611 or 800/253–9229 | www.usboattours.com | $14 | May, June, Sept., Oct., tours daily at 10, 10:30, 12:30, 1, 3, and 3:30; July and Aug., tours daily at 10, 11:30, 12:30, 2, 3, and 4:30.

★ **Boldt Castle.** George C. Boldt, proprietor of the Waldorf-Astoria Hotel in New York, began building this 120-room Rhineland-style castle on Heart Island for his wife, Louise, in 1900. Four years later, when she died suddenly, he ceased work on the castle. The building remained deserted for 73 years, abused by vandals and weather. Since 1977, millions of dollars have been poured into restoration work. It's worth a trip to the island to see the castle and its fleet of wooden boats. Shuttle boats run from Alexandria Bay and Wellesley Island for a fee. | Box 428, 13607 | 315/482–2501 or 800/847–5263 | www.boldtcastle.com | $4.75, not including shuttle | May, June, Sept., Oct., daily 10–6:30; July and Aug., daily 10–7:30.

Dining

Captain's Landing. American. This family-oriented restaurant actually floats on the water. The foundation was once used as a dredge on the New York State Canal system. The oak-trimmed dining room has antique buffet tables. Try the prime rib (also served Cajun style), seafood pasta, porterhouse steak, or shrimp scampi. The restaurant is part of Captain Thompson's Resort. Kids' menu. Open-air dining on the deck. All-you-can-eat breakfast buffet July–August. | 49 James St. | 800/253–9229 | Closed mid-Oct.–May | AE, D, MC, V | $$–$$$

Chez Paris Restaurant. Eclectic. Run by the same family since 1945, this lunch spot specializes in fresh-pressed hamburgers and homemade peach or blueberry cobblers. Breakfast is available all day. Takeout menu. Kids' menu. | 24 Church St. | 315/482–9825 | No dinner | No credit cards | ¢

Dockside Pub. American. Despite billing itself as the village's "best-kept secret," this sports bar and restaurant near the shore always seems to be hopping. The daily menu includes pizzas, burgers, appetizers, and dinner specials where the chef gets creative with what's in the kitchen. Cheese sauces are common. There's fish on Friday and prime rib on Saturday. | 17 Market St. | 315/482–9849 | MC, V | ¢–$$

Jacques Cartier Dining Room. French. A pianist sets a romantic mood at this elegant restaurant at the Riveredge Resort Hotel that has views of Boldt Castle and the St.

Lawrence River. Salads, broiled sea bass, veal, New York–cut prime rib, and lobster are worth trying, as are the flaming desserts. Kids' menu. Sunday brunch. | 17 Holland St. | 315/482–9917 | AE, D, DC, MC, V | $$$$

Corning

Benjamin Patterson Inn Museum Complex. Guides in period dress take you through this complex of buildings that include a log cabin, one-room schoolhouse, barn, and blacksmith shop. The centerpiece is a restored 1796 inn. | 59 W. Pulteney St. | 607/937–5281 | www.corningny.com/bpinn | $3.50 | Mid-Mar.–mid-Dec., weekdays 10–4.

★ **Corning Museum of Glass.** About 10,000 of the more than 35,000 glass objects in the museum's collection are on display at any one time. The works range from contemporary pieces to glassware crafted by Egyptians 3,500 years ago. Catch the Hot Glass Show, a live glassmaking demonstration. A workshop encourages you to make your own glass souvenir. Interactive exhibits show the history, beauty, and creativity of 35 centuries of glasswork. | 1 Museum Way | 607/937–53271 or 800/732–6845 | www.cmog.org | $12 | Sept.–June, daily 9–5; July and Aug., daily 9–8.

Market Street. Flooded by Hurricane Agnes in 1972, the city's main street was restored to evoke the late 19th century with brick sidewalks and plenty of trees, more than 20 restaurants, and a number of glass-art studios. A shuttle bus leaves the area for the Corning Glass Center every 20 minutes. | Between Denison Pkwy. and Tioga Ave. | 607/962–8997 chamber of commerce.

Rockwell Museum of Western Art. The West is so close, you might feel like riding off into the sunset. Art from the 19th and 20th centuries and Native American works show the people, places, and ideas of the West. Works are displayed by three themes and invite comparison of the past to the present. | 111 Cedar St. | 607/937–5386 | www.rockwellmuseum.org | $6.50 | Early Sept.–June, Mon.–Sat. 9–5, Sun. 11–5; July–early Sept., Mon.–Sat. 9–8, Sun. 11–8.

Dining

London Underground Cafe. Continental. The café is named after the London subway, and the British theme carries throughout. Paintings of the Underground adorn the walls, and teapots and British china are displayed. The three-level dining room provides plenty of space, and the menu includes fish-and-chips, burgers, and generous salads. Open-air dining is available. A pianist plays on Saturday evenings. Kids' menu. | 69 E. Market St. | 607/962–2345 | Closed Sun. | AE, D, DC, MC, V | $$–$$$$

Market Street Brewing Company and Restaurant. Eclectic. Five beers, two lagers, and a red, pale, and dark ale, are brewed on-site throughout the year. Each season brings its own specialty brew. The food menu consists of upscale dinner entrées and chicken wings and burgers. Owners won an award for their renovation of a historic building in the city's business district. | 63–65 W. Market St. | 607/936–2337 | Closed Sun. and Mon. Nov.–Mar. | AE, MC, V | $–$$

Medley's Cafe. Eclectic. Indian, Indonesian, French, and Italian are just some of the international flavors used to prepare vegetarian and vegan dishes. Seafood and organic meats also are served. Kids' menu. | 88 W. Market St. | 607/936–1685 | fax 607/936–0507 | AE, D, DC, MC, V | ¢–$$

Old World Cafe & Ice Cream. Café. Grilled panini, homemade quiche, homemade soup, and imported cheeses are the preludes to dessert at this Victorian ice-cream parlor. Ice cream, of course, finishes a meal, as does old-fashioned candy. | W. Market St. and Centerway | 607/936–1953 | Closed Sun. Labor Day–May | D, MC, V | ¢–$

Spencer's Restaurant and Mercantile. American. This rustic, family-oriented restaurant is popular with the locals and has a large and varied menu that includes chicken and biscuits, steak chops, fish fry, taco salads, seafood, and Italian dishes. Kids' menu. | 359 E. Market St. | 607/936–9196 | AE, D, DC, MC, V | $–$$$$

Lodging
Best Western Lodge on the Green. Built in the early 1970s, this two-story chain hotel has rooms larger than standard accommodations. Rooms have queen-size beds and there's still space to move around. The hotel sits on a 12-acre, parklike lot with a river for fishing just 45 feet from the door. Restaurant, room service, in-room data ports, some kitchenettes, cable TV, pool, laundry service, airport shuttle, some pets allowed. | 3171 Canada Rd., Painted Post 14870; ½-mi west of town | 607/962–2456 or 800/528–1234 | fax 607/962–1769 | www.bestwestern.com | 135 rooms | CP | AE, D, DC, MC, V | ¢–$

Comfort Inn. In a quiet residential neighborhood, this two-story hotel is within walking distance of Market Street, the Rockwell Museum, and the Benjamin Patterson Inn Museum Complex. Rooms were renovated in 2002. In-room data ports, some refrigerators, cable TV, pool, gym, business services. | 66 W. Pulteney St., 14830 | 607/962–1515 | fax 607/962–1899 | www.comfortinn.com | 62 rooms | CP | AE, D, DC, MC, V | $–$$

Rosewood Inn. This 1855 neighborhood home has off-street parking and is three blocks from downtown and less than 1 mi from the Corning Museum of Glass. Each of the seven rooms is themed. Plush towels and 300-count sheets await. Porch-sitting in summer is replaced by 4 PM tea and cookies by the parlor fireplace in winter. Only the suites have phones. No phones in some rooms, no TV in some rooms. | 134 E. 1st St., 14830 | 607/962–3253 | www.rosewoodinn.com | 5 rooms, 2 suites | BP | AE, D, DC, MC, V | $–$$$

Elmira
Arnot Art Museum. The core collection at this museum comes from 1890s Elmira banker Matthias Arnot, who acquired paintings by Brueghel, Rousseau, and others. European paintings from the 17th to the 19th centuries and American paintings from the 19th and 20th centuries are also in the collection. | 235 Lake St. | 607/734–3697 | $5 | Tues.–Sat. 10–5, Sun. 1–5.

Chemung Valley History Museum. Exhibits on the Seneca Nation, Mark Twain, and Elmira's Civil War prison camp are part of this local downtown museum. | 415 E. Water St. | 607/734–4167 | Donations accepted | Tues.–Sat. 10–5, Sun. 1–5.

Mark Twain's Study. Twain wrote *The Adventures of Huckleberry Finn* and *The Adventures of Tom Sawyer* at this study built for him by his sister-in-law. The octagonal shape was inspired by a Mississippi riverboat pilothouse. | Elmira College campus at Park Ave. | 607/735–1941 | Donations accepted | Apr. 15–Oct. 31; Mon.–Sat. 9–5, Sun. noon–5.

★ **National Soaring Museum.** Dozens of sailplanes are on display. Movies and exhibits help explain and explore the heritage of gliding. | Harris Hill Park, 51 Soaring Hill Dr., off Rte. 17, 15 mi west of downtown Elmira | 607/734–3128 | www.soaringmuseum.org | $6 | Daily 10–5.

Woodlawn Cemetery. Mark Twain rests in the Langdon family plot, with his son-in-law, Ossip Gabrilowitsch, at his feet. A 12-foot-high monument marks the spot (12 feet, in river terminology, is 2 fathoms, or "mark twain"). | 1200 Walnut St. | 607/732–0151 | Free | Daily dawn–dusk.

Woodlawn National Cemetery. Next to the main cemetery, this cemetery has the graves of 2,963 Confederate prisoners who died in the prison in Elmira, as well as the graves of 322 Union soldiers. The Elmira Correctional Facility, at Davis Street and

Bancroft Road, sits on the site of the city's Civil War prison camp. | 1825 Davis St. | 607/732–5411 | www.cem.va.gov | Donations accepted | Grounds daily dawn–dusk, office weekdays 8–4:30.

Dining

Anne's Pancakes. American. Home cooking is the star here. Try the country-fried steak, burgers, homemade pies, rice pudding, or the tasty pancakes. Breakfast served. | 114 S. Main St. | 607/732–9591 | Closes at noon weekends | No credit cards | ¢–$

Hilltop Inn. American. A giant wreath with a shamrock beckons from a hill, making Elmira's oldest restaurant hard to miss. The Hilltop has been in the same family since 1933. Steak and seafood are popular choices. Open-air dining. Kids' menu. | 171 Jerusalem Hill Rd. | 607/732–6728 | Closed Sun. No lunch | AE, D, DC, MC, V | $–$$$$

Moretti's. Italian. Established in 1917, this neighborhood restaurant in downtown Elmira serves generous portions of Italian food, steaks, and chops. Kids' menu. | 800 Hatch St. | 607/734–1535 | No lunch | AE, D, MC, V | $$–$$$$

Pierce's 1894 Restaurant. Continental. Fifteen minutes from downtown, this Old English–style village inn is known for its seafood, roasted rack of lamb, and chateaubriand. The bar has 52 martinis. Frequent patrons can get a card to keep track of how many they've sampled. Kids' menu. | 228 Oakwood Ave. | 607/734–2022 | AE, D, MC, V | $–$$$$

Geneva

Geneva Historical Society Museum. Also known as the Prouty-Chew Museum, this 1829 mansion houses four exhibits of costumes and local history. You can also stop here to pick up directions for walking and driving tours. | 543 S. Main St. | 315/789–5151 | Donations accepted | Tues.–Fri. 9:30–4:30, Sat. 1:30–4:30.

Rose Hill Mansion. Six Ionic columns punctuate this restored 1839 Greek Revival mansion overlooking Seneca Lake. Many of the Empire-style furnishings were used from 1850 to 1890 by the prosperous farm family the Swans, whose patriarch Robert was a pioneer in the use of tile drainage systems. Guided tours show off the 24 rooms. | Rte. 96A | 315/789–3848 | $3 | May–Oct., Mon.–Sat. 10–4, Sun. 1–5.

Sampson State Park and Naval Museum. You can swim, fish, boat, and camp at this 1,852-acre park. The on-site museum honors the program that brought navy trainees to the shore of Seneca Lake at the outbreak of World War II. | Rte. 96A | 315/585–6392, 800/357–1814 museum | www.nysparks.state.ny.us/parks | $7 per car 3rd weekend in June–early Sept.; free early Sept.–May | Park daily dawn–dusk, museum Wed.–Sun. 10–3:30.

Seneca Lake State Park. The popular park has a marina, swimming beach, picnic areas, and onshore fishing spots. | Rtes. 5 and 20 | 315/789–2331 | www.nysparks. state.ny.us/parks | $7 per car mid-June–early Sept.; $6 early Sept.–last weekend in Oct. | Daily dawn–dusk.

Smith Opera House. Since 1894 this theater has been presenting stage productions, concerts, and films. Tours are given by appointment. Call for schedule and ticket information. | 82 Seneca St. | 315/781–5483 or 866/355–5483.

Dining

Belhurst Castle. Continental. The six ornate dining rooms have beamed cathedral ceilings and mosaic tiled fireplaces. Extensive wine list suits any taste. Its 250 choices emphasize Finger Lakes wines and other New York state vintages. The Hunter's Plate features the season's wild game. Lunch buffet. Sunday brunch. | Rte. 14 S | 315/781–0201 | fax 315/781–0201 | www.belhurstcastle.com | MC, V | $$–$$$$

Hamilton 258. American. Coffee-rubbed rib-eye steak, fillet with balsamic glaze, and tuna with sesame-soy marinade give American cuisine a creative spin. Martinis and Finger Lakes wines complement entrées. Dining is intimate in the remodeled turn-of-the-20th-century home. | 258 Hamilton St. | 315/781–5323 | Closed Sun. and Mon. | AE, D, MC, V | $$–$$$

Pasta's Only Cobblestone Restaurant. Italian. Gourmet pasta, veal, Angus beef, and fresh fish are served with contemporary flair. The building was a stagecoach stop in the 1880s and has the original planking. Fireplaces and in-season balcony dining and porch dining add to the ambience. It's co-owned by a former lieutenant governor of the state of New York. | Rtes. 5 and 20 | 315/789–8498 | Closed Mon. | AE, D, DC, MC, V | $$–$$$

Water St. Cafe. American. Photos of tourists from around the world give this local eatery an international flavor. A special low-carbohydrate menu mirrors the Dr. Atkins diet plan. But protein junkies may not be able to resist the aroma of the home fries. The café has counter service, booths, tables, and, in season, outdoor seating. Breakfast served. | 467 Exchange St. | 315/789–2560 | No dinner | No credit cards | ¢

Lodging

Belhurst Castle and White Springs Manor. Sister properties sit 1½ mi apart overlooking Seneca Lake. Belhurst is an 1880s castle with 11 rooms and 3 suites, including the tower, furnished with antiques. White Springs is a 13-room Georgian revival mansion where each room is architecturally distinct. Restaurant, cable TV, bar, business services. | Rte. 14 S, 14456 | 315/781–0201 | www.belhurstcastle.com | 24 rooms, 3 suites | MC, V | $$–$$$$

Clark's Motel. The single-story motel sits back from busy Routes 5 and 20 and has been a landmark since the 1950s. The current owners took over in 1979 and have updated the rooms, but the decor is simple and the technology is late 20th century. Two acres of land, with a garden and gazebo, stretch behind the units. Retirees and travelers who prefer byways to highways frequent the motel. Cable TV, no-smoking rooms; no room phones. | 824 Canandaigua Rd. (Rtes. 5 and 20), 14456 | 315/789–0780 | 10 rooms | Closed Dec. 1–Mar. 31 | MC, V | ¢

Geneva on the Lake. The manicured grounds and Italian Renaissance architecture give this villa European flavor. Rooms are furnished with different styles of Stickley furniture. Pass a summer afternoon playing lawn games or taking a pontoon boat ride on Seneca Lake. Ten suites have two bedrooms. Suites also have kitchen. Studios have living rooms and Murphy beds, also separate baths; one studio has a kitchenette. Restaurant, cable TV, pool, gym, laundry service. | 1001 Lochland Rd. (Rte. 14), 14456 | 315/789–7190 | fax 315/789–0322 | www.genevaonthelake.com | 23 suites, 6 studios | CP | AE, D, MC, V | $$$–$$$$

Ramada Inn Geneva Lakefront. The anchor of the Geneva skyline, this hotel is on the shore of Seneca Lake. First floor lakeside rooms have patios that enhance the view. Four minisuites have pull-out sofas. Reservations are a must in summer. Restaurant, in-room data ports, some in-room hot tubs, cable TV, pool, gym, bar, laundry service, some pets allowed, no-smoking rooms. | 41 Lakefront Dr., 14456 | 315/789–0400 | fax 315/789–4351 | 148 rooms | AE, D, MC, V | $–$$

Hammondsport

Glenn H. Curtiss Museum. Just outside of Hammondsport is this museum honoring Curtiss and his early aviation experiments. He made the first public preannounced flight when he flew his *June Bug* plane more than 5,000 feet outside the village on July 4, 1908. The exhibits include aircraft, engines, and a collection of antique motorcycles. | 8419 Rte. 54 | 607/569–2160 | fax 607/569–2040 | $6 | May–Oct., Mon.–Sat. 9–5, Sun. 11–5; Nov.–Apr., Mon.–Sat. 10–4, Sun. noon–5.

Great Western Winery Visitor Center at the Pleasant Valley Wine Co. The Great Western Winery was the first in the country to have a license to make and sell wine on the premises and the first to pay Federal taxes. One of the highlights of its visitor center is a slide show you can watch from inside a 35,000-gallon wine tank. | 8260 Pleasant Valley Rd., 3 mi south of Hammondsport | 607/569–6111 | Visitor center and tastings free, guided tour $3 | Jan.–Mar., Tues.–Sat. 10–4; Apr.–Dec., daily 10–5.

Wine and Grape Museum of Greyton H. Taylor. The first wine museum in the nation focuses on 18th-century wine-making equipment. | Bully Hill Vineyards, 8843 Greyton H. Taylor Memorial Dr., off Rte. 54A | 607/868–4814 | www.bullyhill.com | Donations accepted | May–Oct., Mon.–Sat. 9–5, Sun. noon–5.

Dining

Bully Hill Restaurant. Fusion. A spectacular view of Keuka Lake awaits you at this breezy café, which serves sandwiches, salads, and a full dinner menu. The restaurant is part of the Bully Hill Vineyards, giving it a diverse wine selection. | 8843 Greyton H. Taylor Memorial Dr. | 607/868–3490 | Closed Dec.–Apr. No dinner Sun.–Thurs. | AE, D, MC, V | $–$$

Lakeside Restaurant. American. On the west side of Keuka Lake, this 1880s cottage inn was converted into a delightful Victorian-era restaurant. Outside there is a fire pit and 150 seats overlooking the bluff of the lake. On the menu are prime rib, shrimp, steaks, and bacon-wrapped beef tenderloin. | 800 W. Lake Rd. | 607/868–3636 | Closed weekdays and some weekends mid-Oct.–late May; call ahead | AE, D, MC, V | $–$$$

Three Birds Restaurant. Eclectic. Crisp waitstaff is as impressive as the meal—both are presented in fine style. Servers are educated about food and wine and the chef is trained in the classical French style. Pecan-encrusted pork tenderloin, New Zealand rack of lamb, and crab cakes are favorites. Lift your eyes from the plate long enough to take in the view of Keuka Lake from this Victorian-style building. Docking for boats is available. | 144 W. Lake Rd. | 607/868–7684 | AE, D, MC, V | $$–$$$$

Lodging

Esperanza Mansion. On a hill overlooking Keuka Lake, this stately 19th-century restored Greek Revival mansion and separate inn have rooms with spectacular views. The mansion, a National Historic Landmark, was a link in the Underground Railroad. Linger over a cocktail on the outdoor terrace and drink in the lake, surrounding hills, and farms. Rooms have four-poster and sleigh beds, armoires, and decorative fireplaces. Whitewashed furniture and quilted bedspreads give the two-story inn (built in 2003) a casual "cottage" feel. Sun. brunch. Restaurant, bar, in-room data ports, cable TV, business services, meeting room, library, shop; no smoking. | 3456 Route 54A, Bluff Point, 14478, 16 mi north of Hammondsport, 30 mi northwest of Watkins Glen | 315/536–4400 | fax 315/536–4900 | www.esperanzamansion.com | 9 mansion rooms, 21 inn rooms | AE, D, DC, MC, V | BP | $$$–$$$$

Ithaca

Buttermilk Falls State Park. Water cascades over 10 falls through a 3/4-mi gorge, dropping close to 500 feet at this park on the southern end of Ithaca. At the base of the falls there is a swimming hole, as well as playing fields and a campground. | Rte. 13 | 607/273–5761, 800/456–2267 for camping reservations | www.nysparks.state.ny.us/

parks | $7 per car late May–early Sept.; $6 weekends early Sept.–mid-Oct. and Apr.–late May | Daily dawn–dusk.

Cornell University. With its historic buildings, views of Cayuga Lake, open spaces, and gorges, the campus at this private university founded in 1865 is considered one of the most beautiful in the country. Seventy-five-minute tours of the campus leave from Day Hall, Tower Road, and East Avenue. | 607/254–4636 | www.cornell.edu | Free | Tours daily at 9, 11, 1, and 3.

    Cornell Lab of Ornithology. Four miles of trails lead through Sapsucker Woods Sanctuary. Bird artist Louis Agassiz Fuertes named the woods after two yellow-bellied sapsuckers he spotted in the area. A computer touch screen walks you through interpretive displays. | 159 Sapsucker Woods Rd. | 607/254–2473 | Donations accepted | Mon.–Thurs. 8–5, Fri. 8–4, Sat. 9:30–4, Sun. 11–4.

    Cornell Plantations. Just north of the university, the Cornell Plantations include an arboretum, specialty gardens, nature trails, and an herb garden. | 1 Plantations Rd., off Rte. 366 | 607/255–2400 | Free | Grounds daily dawn–dusk. Gift shop Oct.–Apr., weekdays 9–4; May–Sept., weekdays 9–4 and weekends 11–4.

    Herbert F. Johnson Museum of Art The I.M. Pei–designed museum houses collections of Asian and modern art. The 5th floor has a wonderful view of Cayuga Lake and the surrounding area. | University Ave. | 607/255–6464 | www.museum.cornell.edu | Free | Tues.–Sun. 10–5.

Ithaca Farmer's Market. Open-air market houses 88 stalls where plants, artwork, food, and flowers all come from local residents. | Steamboat Landing on Cayuga Lake | 607/273–7109 | Free | June–Oct., Sat. 9–2, Sun. 10–2; Nov.–Christmas, Sat. 9–2.

★ **Museum of the Earth.** Extinct and fossilized species moved into modern digs when this museum, formerly known as the Paleontological Research Institution, opened in its current form in September 2003. The expanded museum has three main exhibit areas that show the very early days of what is now New York state: Beneath an Ancient Sea, Where Dinosaurs Walked, and A World Carved By Ice. The whale and mastodon skeletons are eye-catchers. | 1259 Trumansburg Rd. (Rte. 96) | 607/273–6623 | www.museumoftheearth.org | $8 | Wed.–Mon. 10–6.

★ **Taughannock Falls State Park.** Thirty feet higher than Niagara, these 215-foot falls are surrounded by walls that rise up to 400 feet. Camping and swimming are allowed in season. The park has playgrounds for children. | Rte. 89 | 607/387–6739 | www.nysparks.state.ny.us/parks | $7 per car late May–early Sept.; $6 weekends early Sept.–Oct. | Daily dawn–dusk.

Dining

The Antlers. American. Grilled fare is the specialty at this country inn. Shrimp, chicken, and contemporary pasta dishes are among the extensive choices. Sit in front of the fireplace and drink local wine within the watchful gaze of a large mounted deer head looming above the doorway. | 1159 Dryden Rd. | 607/273–9725 | No lunch | AE, DC, MC, V | $–$$$

John Thomas Steak House. Steak. A two-story 1848 farmhouse is home to this restaurant that serves steak, chicken, and lobster. In summer, you can eat outside on the deck. | 1152 Danby Rd. (Rte. 96B) | 607/273–3464 | Reservations essential | No lunch | D, MC, V | $$–$$$$

Moosewood. Vegetarian. Since its founding in 1973, this restaurant downtown has been a pacesetter in the field of creative vegetarian cooking; its cookbooks are known worldwide. The setting is simple and casual. The menu changes daily and everything is prepared from fresh ingredients. A vegan option is always available. You can dine outside on a patio. Full bar. | 215 N. Cayuga St. | 607/273–9610 | www.moosewoodrestaurant.com | MC, V | $$

Station Restaurant and Sleeping Cars. American. The main dining room is in the waiting area of an old Lehigh Valley Railroad station. Dining is available in a railcar. On the menu are steaks, prime rib, seafood, pasta, and salad. Three overnight sleeping "cars" are available by reservation ($$). | 800 W. Buffalo St. | 607/272–2609 | Closed Mon. Sept.–June. No lunch | AE, D, MC, V | $$–$$$

Willow. The cuisine starts out American, but influences of other cuisines can't keep it in that box. Homemade pasta, fresh fish, and vegetarian dishes are specialities. A husband-and-wife team runs the place. Finish the evening in the martini lounge where the bartender's special is the Gorgy, a concoction with Gorgonzola-filled olives. | 202 E. Falls St. | 607/272–0656 | www.willowithaca.com | Closed Sun. and Mon. No lunch | AE, MC, V | $$–$$$

Oswego

Ft. Ontario State Historic Site. The British built a fort, which the French captured and destroyed in the 1740s. The British then built another fort, which they eventually handed over to the United States in the late 1700s. Reenactments and festivals are staged throughout the summer. Military drills are performed July 1–Labor Day. | 1 E. 4th St. | 315/343–4711 | $4 | May–Oct., Tues.–Sun. 10–4:30.

    Safe Haven Museum and Education Center. The story of the United States' only camp for Holocaust survivors during World War II is presented here. In 1944 the United States allowed 982 European Holocaust escapees and survivors to seek shelter here at Ft. Ontario, a former army camp surrounded by a chain-link fence topped with barbed wire. The museum may not be suitable for younger children. | 2 E. 7th St. | 315/342–3003 | www.oswegohaven.org | $4 | Memorial Day–Labor Day, Tues.–Sat. 10–5, Sun. 1–5; off-season call for hrs.

H. Lee White Marine Museum. Artifacts reflect local history and include a real birch-bark canoe, an old dugout canoe, and some wall-size murals. Parked outside is the *Nash*, a U.S. Army tug (an LT-5) that is a veteran of the D-Day invasion of Normandy. | W. 1st St. | 315/342–0480 | $3 | June and Sept., daily 1–5; July and Aug., daily 10–5.

Dining

Canale's Ristorante. Italian. Gorge on pasta at this relaxed restaurant known for generous portions. Private booths and a bar add intimacy. Kids' menu. | 156 W. Utica St., 13126 | 315/343–3540 | No lunch weekends May–Sept. | AE, D, DC, MC, V | $–$$$

Rudy's Lakeside Drive-In. American. For more than half a century, this casual eatery on the shores of Lake Ontario has been a local institution. Fresh fish, sandwiches, burgers, and ice cream are staples. If you're brave, try Rudy's signature Texas Hot Sauce. Takeout available. | Washington Blvd. | 315/343–2671 | Closed Oct.–Feb. | No credit cards | ¢–$

Vona's. Italian. Southern Italian dishes like veal parmigiana and baked lasagna are the specialties of this pleasant family-style restaurant. There's also a cocktail lounge. Kids' menu. | W. 10th and Utica Sts. | 315/343–8710 | No lunch weekends | AE, D, DC, MC, V | $–$$$$

Lodging

Redwood Motel. The fish run fast and furious from mid-August to mid-November in the Salmon River, accessible by a right-of-way from this motel. Lake Ontario is 3½ mi away. The motel is a single-story building with units on both sides of the road and basic lodging. Cable TV, some in-room data ports. | 3723 Rte. 13, Pulaski 13142, off Rte. 13 exit from I-81, 23 mi east of Oswego | phone/fax 315/298–4717 | www.gisco.net/redwoodmotel | 50 rooms, 1 suite | AE, MC, V | ¢–$

Sackets Harbor

Robbins' Farm and Old McDonald's Children's Farm. Walk up and say hello to cows, camels, and more than 200 other animals. Old McDonald's has been educating children about farm life since 1986. The complex includes a calf-raising facility as part of a 1,200-acre working farm. There's also a miniature golf course. | 14471 Rte. 145, 13685 | 315/583–5737 | www.oldmcdonaldhasafarm.com | $5; additional fees for tour of calf-raising facility and pony rides | Mid-June–early Sept., Mon.–Sat., 10–6, Sun. 10–4; early Sept.–Sept. 30, weekdays 10–4, weekends 10–5; May–mid-June, Sun.–Thurs. 10–4, Fri. and Sat. 10–6.

Sackets Harbor Battlefield State Historic Site. During the War of 1812, two battles were fought here between the British and the Americans. The harbor served as headquarters for divisions of the army and navy. Today the site includes a nicely restored commandant's house, which dates to 1850. In summer, guides reenact camp life. | 505 W. Washington St., 13685 | 315/646–3634 | $3 | Commandant's house and gift shop late May–early Sept., Mon.–Sat. 10–5, Sun. 11–5; early Sept.–Columbus Day, Fri. and Sat. 10–5; Sun. 11–5.

Sackets Harbor Heritage Area Visitors Center. Displays focus on the harbor's role in the War of 1812. | 301 W. Main St., 13685 | 315/646–2321 | www.sacketsharborny.com | Free | Memorial Day weekend–Columbus Day, daily 10–5.

Seaway Trail Discovery Center. The Seaway Trail is a 454-mi federally recognized scenic byway along the shores of lakes Erie and Ontario and the St. Lawrence River. Nine rooms in the Discovery Center present interactive exhibits that explain life along the water. Displays include agriculture, history, culture, lighthouses, architecture, and recreation. Fully accessible. | Corner of Ray St. and W. Main St., 13685 | 315/646–1000 or 800/732–9298 | fax 315/646–1004 | www.seawaytrail.com | $4 | May–Oct., daily 10–5; Nov.–Apr. call for hrs.

Dining

1812 Steak and Seafood Co. Contemporary. Try the London broil à la 1812 at this restaurant in the middle of the village's historic district. Kids' menu. Early-bird dinners. Sunday breakfast buffet. | 212 W. Main St. | 315/646–2041 | AE, D, MC, V | $–$$$

Tin Pan Galley. Contemporary. Actually two restaurants in one, Tin Pan has an upstairs dining room that begins service at 5:30 PM daily; breakfast and lunch are served downstairs or outside. Salads and sandwiches are popular; try the grilled Portobello mushroom sandwich. Alfresco dining is in a New Orleans–style flower garden with wrought-iron gates and a stone archway. | 110 W. Main St. | 315/646–3812 | AE, D, MC, V | $–$$$$

Lodging

Candlelight Bed and Breakfast. Built in 1832, this Georgian redbrick home is next door to the Sackets Harbor Battlefield State Historic Site and a three-minute walk from restaurants, shops, and the Seaway Trail. Rooms have period antiques, four-poster beds, and quilts; two have water views, the other looks out onto the village. Business services; no kids under 18, no smoking. | 501 W. Washington St., 13685 | 315/646–1518 or 800/306–5595 | www.imcnet.net/candlelight | 3 rooms | BP | MC, V | $–$$

Ontario Place Hotel. Some rooms have views of the harbor at this hotel with a range of accommodations. In addition to standard rooms, there are larger minisuites with rollaway beds that can accommodate up to five people. Minisuites have refrigerators, microwaves, and in-room hot tubs. In-room data ports, some in-room hot tubs, some microwaves, some refrigerators, cable TV. | 103 General Smith Dr., 13685 | 315/646–8000 | fax 315/646–2506 | www.imcnet.net/ontario_place/hotel.htm | 38 rooms, 1 suite, 1 apartment | AE, D, DC, MC, V | $–$$$

Seneca Falls

Cayuga Lake State Park. A swimming beach, bathhouse, boat launch, playground, campground, and trails are the key attractions in this 190-acre park. You can also fish. | 2678 Lower Lake Rd. | 315/568–5163 | www.nysparks.state.ny.us/parks | $7 per car late May–early Sept.; $6 per car weekends early Sept.–Oct. | Daily dawn–dusk.

Cayuga-Seneca Canal. The Cayuga-Seneca connects the Erie Canal near the Montezuma Wildlife Refuge with Cayuga Lake. Boaters can lock through to Seneca Lake. The New York State Canal Corp provides information on cruising the canal. | 9 Seneca St. | 315/568–5797, 800/422–6254 Canal Corp. | Fee for locking through | Locks in service May–mid-Nov., daily 8:15–10:15.

Cayuga Wine Trail. Fifteen wineries are part of this trail that circles Cayuga Lake. The Cayuga Wine Trail organization sponsors various events throughout the year. Call for information and maps, or check the Web site. Admission prices and hours vary by winery. | Fayette | 800/684–5217 | www.cayugawinetrail.com | Tours and tastings May–Dec., daily.

★**Montezuma National Wildlife Refuge.** For an introduction to these wetlands, take the 3½-mi Wildlife Drive, which begins at the visitor center. The center also has exhibits and is a good way to orient yourself to the wildlife you'll see. Pick up a brochure listing the 320 species of birds that have been identified at the 8,000-acre Montezuma site since 1938. | Rtes. 5 and 20; entrance at north end of Cayuga Lake, 5 mi east of Seneca Falls | 315/568–5987 | www.fws.gov/r5mnwr | Free | Daily dawn–dusk; visitor center Apr.–Nov. 1, weekdays 10–3, weekends 10–4; limited winter access, call for information.

★**National Women's Hall of Fame.** The hall honors distinguished American women, with portraits, recordings, and photographs. | 76 Fall St. | 315/568–8060 | www.greatwomen.org | $3 | May–Oct., Mon.–Sat. 9:30–5, Sun. noon–4; Nov.–Apr., Wed.–Sat. 10–4, Sun. noon–4.

Seneca Falls Historical Society Museum. Victorian-era rooms and local history exhibits are the highlights of this museum. | 55 Cayuga St. | 315/568–8412 | $3 | Sept.–June, weekdays 9–4; July and Aug., weekdays 9–4, weekends 1–4.

★**Women's Rights National Historical Park.** Exhibits, films, and talks explore the development of the women's rights movement. | 136 Fall St. | 315/568–2991 | $3 | Daily 9–5.

    Elizabeth Cady Stanton House. This meticulously restored home belonged to one of the leaders of the women's rights movement. Amelia Bloomer, the reformer who first introduced pants for women, and noted suffragist Susan B. Anthony were frequent guests. | 32 Washington St. | 315/568–2991 | $1 | Mar.–Oct., Wed.–Sun. noon–4.

    Wesleyan Chapel Declaration Park. This was the site of the 1848 women's rights convention, which produced the Declaration of Sentiments. Its words are etched on a 140-foot-long wall along which a continuous stream of water flows. nearby along with the names of the 300 signers (both men and women). All that remains of the chapel are a piece of the roof and fragile walls. | 126 Fall St. | 315/568–2991 | www.nps.gov/wori | Free with admission to Women's Rights National Historic Park | Daily 9–5.

Dining

Knapp Vineyard and Restaurant. Contemporary. A vineyard with flower and vegetable gardens is the setting for the restaurant on the Cayuga Wine Trail, which uses the fresh produce in its cooking. Menu changes every six weeks. Dine on the outdoor patio in season. | 2770 County Rd. 128 (Ernsberger Rd.), Romulus, 14541, 14 mi south of Seneca Falls | 607/869–9271 | www.knappwine.com | Closed Jan.–Mar. No dinner Mon.–Wed. | AE, D, MC, V | $$–$$$

Watkins Glen

Captain Bill's Seneca Lake Cruises. The Captain runs meal cruises and 10-mi lake trips from the bottom of Franklin Street. | 1 N. Franklin St. | 607/535–4541 | Sightseeing $8.50, lunch $25, dinner $33–$38 | Cruises depart May–Oct., daily on the hr 10–8.

Farm Sanctuary. A 175-acre working farm and educational center, the sanctuary houses hundreds of livestock and other animals brought from slaughterhouses and stockyards and nursed back to health. You are encouraged to pet the animals. | 3100 Aikens Rd. | 607/583–2225 | www.farmsanctuary.org | Visitor center free, tours $2 | June–Aug., Wed.–Sun. 10–4; May, Sept., Oct., weekends 10–4. Tours daily 11–3 on the hr.

Finger Lakes National Forest. The only real forest in the region runs along a ridge between Cayuga and Seneca lakes. At 16,000 acres, it is one of the smallest of the 76 national forests. There are around 33 mi of easy-to-moderate hiking trails, and spaces for camping, horseback riding, fishing, and hunting. In winter you can cross-country ski and ride a snowmobile. | 5218 Rte. 414, Hector, 9 mi north of Watkins Glen | 607/546–4470 | Free | Daily dawn–dusk; visitor center weekdays 8–4:30, Sat. 10–4:30.

Watkins Glen International Raceway. "New York's Thunder Road" rumbles from June to September. The season's highlight is the NASCAR Winston Cup Series at the Glen in mid-August. On a Thunder Road tour, drive the track in your own vehicle behind a pace car. Call for event schedules and prices. | 2790 Rte. 16 | 607/535–2481 | www.theglen.com | Thunder Road tours $25 | May–Oct.

★**Watkins Glen State Park.** The main entrance to this park is in Watkins Glen. Campgrounds are scattered around the beautiful creek and its waterfalls. The waters of Glen Creek drop about 500 feet in 2 mi, in nearly 20 waterfalls. The 1½-mi gorge trail runs parallel to the water and 300-foot cliffs border the creek. One bridge spans 165 feet over the water. There is also an Olympic-size pool. The gorge is not accessible in winter. | Franklin St. | 607/535–4511 | www.nysparks.state.ny.us/parks | $7 per car late May–early Sept.; $6 early Sept.–Oct. | Daily dawn–dusk.

Winery tours. The Seneca Lake Wine Trail includes most of the area's wineries. Several offer tours and all offer tastings. Member wineries are located along both shores of the lake. Winery hours vary. | 877/536–2717 Wine Association Trail | www.senecalakewine.com | Some tours free, others up to $4; call ahead for groups of 10 or more.

Chateau Lafayette Reneau. The view of Seneca Lake is gorgeous from this beautiful friendly winery, and the wine has won awards in international competition. | 14841 Rte. 414 N, Hector, 9 mi north of Watkins Glen | 607/546–2062 | May–Oct., Mon.–Sat. 10–6, Sun. 11–6; Nov.–Apr., Mon.–Sat. 10–5, Sun. 11–5.

Glenora Wine Cellars. A tour of this winery includes a "Vine to Wine" video tour. | 5435 Rte. 14, Dundee, 9 mi north of Watkins Glen | 607/243–5511 or 800/243–5513 | www.glenora.com | Free | Daily 10–5.

Dining

Castel Grisch. Continental. The restaurant is part of Castel Grisch winery. Strudel and Swiss fondue highlight the Bavarian deli lunches. | 3380 County Rd. 28 | 607/535–9614 | www.fingerlakes-ny.com/castelgrisch | No dinner | AE, D, MC, V | ¢–$$

Wildflower Cafe. Contemporary. Close to the entrance of Watkins Glen State Park is this upscale-yet-casual eatery in a brick-and-wood building. Oak, brass, and stained-glass windows accent the interior. Louisiana scampi, jambalaya, ribs, and duck are specialties. Kids' menu. | 301 N. Franklin St. | 607/535–9797 | Closed Sun. and Mon. Nov.–Apr. | AE, MC, V | $$

SEAWAY TRAIL ALONG LAKE ERIE
*FROM THE NEW YORK–PENNSYLVANIA BORDER TO
HISTORIC OLD FT. NIAGARA*

Distance: Approximately 110 mi, excluding detours   Time: 1–3 days
Overnight Breaks: Buffalo, Chautauqua, Niagara Falls

Follow the green-and-white signs of the Seaway Trail through three of western New York's picturesque and historic counties—Chautauqua, Erie, and Niagara. The drive starts near the New York–Pennsylvania border and could be called "Grape Alley" for the number of vineyards lining the route. The trip ends at Old Ft. Niagara in the northwestern part of Niagara County. Drive between May and November and enjoy cool lake breezes and the foliage and grape harvest in Chautauqua County's wine country. Along the way enjoy beautiful countryside, breathtaking lake views, many beaches and boat launches, lighthouses, quaint villages, an historic fort, and the awesome power of Niagara Falls.

1 Begin near the New York–Pennsylvania border, heading north on Route 5. At Barcelona Harbor, look for a National Landmark lighthouse. The structure, built in 1829, was the first to be fueled by natural gas. It is now privately owned.

Continue heading away from Lake Erie by driving southeast on Route 394, past I–90, until you come to the historic town of **Westfield,** which is home to Welch's grape juice. Near Westfield's town square are antiques and craft shops, as well as the federal-style **McClurg Mansion,** which was built in 1820. Guided tours are offered from May through November for a modest fee.

2 Traveling farther inland along Route 394 toward **Chautauqua,** you come to Mayville, on Chautauqua Lake. Here is the ***Chautauqua Belle,*** an old steamboat that once carried passengers the length of the lake; today the boat offers 1½-hour narrated cruises from Memorial Day through Labor Day. From Mayville, take Route 394 back towards Barcelona and proceed north on Route 5. A few miles north of Barcelona is Blue Water Beach, a place to camp, fish, or picnic while looking across the seemingly endless lake toward Canada.

3 Driving 15 mi north on Route 5 to **Dunkirk,** you can visit the **Dunkirk Historical Lighthouse and Veterans Park Museum.** The lighthouse was built in 1875 and the keeper's house is filled with memorabilia from various branches of the military.

4 From Route 5 take Route 60 South to the **Lily Dale Assembly** on Cassadaga Lake. This is the largest spiritualist center in the world. Throughout the summer, people flock here for lectures, workshops, and services on such subjects as spiritual healing and clairvoyance.

Backtracking to Route 5, drive north just past the town of Silver Creek. Make a left on Allegheny Road and continue north to the hamlet of Sunset Bay. This seasonal town has a warren of summer cottages, a sandy beach, and restaurants that take advantage of the fantastic sunsets over Lake Erie.

Return to Route 5 and you soon enter the northern end of the **Cattaraugus Indian Reservation.** Native American homes are visible when driving south on Route 438 along Cattaraugus Creek. Leaving the reservation, head north on Route 5. Travel west on Lotus Point Road, then north on Lakeshore Road.

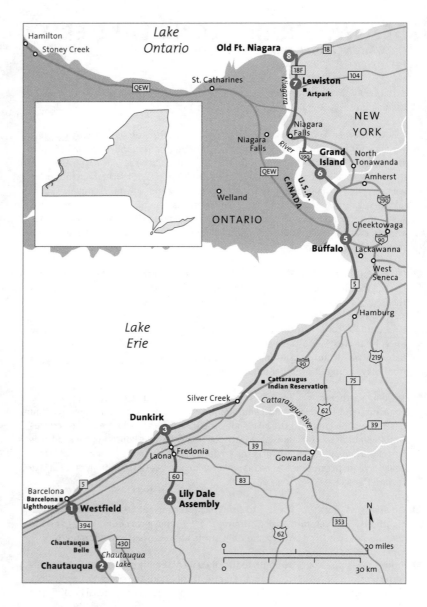

⑤ At the town of Pinehurst, Lakeshore Road joins Route 5. As you stay on Route 5, you start to see industrial **Buffalo,** with old steel factories on either side of the highway.

Route 5 is nicknamed the "Skyway" because it rises above the magnificent grain elevators lining Buffalo Creek on the way to downtown Buffalo. (Note: you don't want to be on the Skyway in a driving rain or during a high-wind warning.) To the west of the roadway are expansive views of Lake Erie and Buffalo's inner harbor, while to the east you have a bird's-eye view of downtown Buffalo.

High above **Buffalo and Erie County Naval and Military Park,** Route 5 joins I–190 from the east. Stay on I–190 North as you approach the Peace Bridge, which crosses over into Canada.

⑥ Now you are leaving Lake Erie as it spills into the Niagara River. You'll soon have more breathtaking views as you take I–190 over bridges that lead on and off **Grand Island.** The first exit off the island puts you on the Robert Moses Parkway (which hugs the river known for its ever-mounting rapids), and leads to the city of **Niagara Falls.**

⑦ After experiencing the falls, continue north on Robert Moses Parkway to the historic village of **Lewiston,** which was settled in 1796. The Niagara Power Project Visitors Center has exhibits that explain how the river was harnessed for electricity. Taking Route 18F due west from the parkway you find **Artpark,** at the foot of South 4th Street. This 200-acre state park on a bluff overlooking Niagara Gorge is the only New York state park dedicated to the performing arts.

⑧ Continue north on Route 18F for your last stop on this driving adventure—the New York State Historic Site of **Old Ft. Niagara,** at the mouth of the Niagara River where it empties into Lake Ontario. The earliest part of the fort was built as a French castle in 1726 and the fort later played a critical role in the French and Indian War (1754–63). Self-guided tours are available throughout the year, and living-history demonstrations and reenactments are held from spring through fall.

To return to your starting point, take Route 18F to I–190 to Route 5.

Buffalo

Albright-Knox Art Gallery. Twentieth-century art is well represented here. The gallery's collections are especially rich in postwar American and European art, including Pollock, Johns, and Warhol. Works by Picasso, van Gogh, Monet, Matisse, and Renoir are here as well. On Sunday afternoons in July and August, find free jazz performances on the massive front steps. | 1285 Elmwood Ave. | 716/882–8700 | www.albrightknox.org | $6 | Tues.–Sat. 11–5, Sun. noon–5.

Buffalo and Erie County Botanical Gardens. Even in the middle of winter, soak in the sights and scents of the tropics under the domes of this Victorian glass conservatory. The 12 greenhouses shelter cacti, fruit trees, palms, and orchids. The American Ivy Association certified the claim of the largest ivy collection of any botanical garden in the world. Guided tours are given by reservation. | 2655 S. Park Ave. | 716/827–1584 | www.buffalogardens.com | Free | Mon., Tues., Thurs., Fri. 9–4, Wed. 9–6, weekends 9–5.

Buffalo and Erie County Naval and Military Park. A guided missile cruiser, destroyer, and a World II submarine are on display at this 6-acre waterfront site, the largest inland naval park in the nation. | 1 Naval Park Cove | 716/847–1773 | www.buffalonavalpark.org | $6 | Apr.–Oct., daily 10–5; Nov., weekends 10–4.

Buffalo Zoological Gardens. Endangered Siberian tigers, Asian elephants, and Indian rhinos are among the more than 1,000 wild and exotic animals found in this natural setting in Delaware Park. The grounds include Vanishing Animals, six large outdoor enclosures built in 2002 to house endangered wildlife, and Eco Station, an interactive mock field research station built in 2003. | 300 Parkside Ave. | 716/837–3900 | www.buffalozoo.org | $7 | June–Sept. 1, daily 10–5; Sept. 2–May, daily 10–4.

City Hall. The broad-shouldered art deco architectural masterpiece rises from the heart of downtown. An elevator and three flights of stairs take you to an observation deck with spectacular views of the city and the Lake Erie waterfront. | Niagara Sq. | 716/851–5891 | Free | Weekdays 8–4.

★**Pedaling History Bicycle Museum.** More than 400 rare and unique bicycles and antiques with a bicycle motif are on display at one of the largest bicycle museums in the world. | 3943 N. Buffalo Rd., Orchard Park, 12 mi south of Buffalo | 716/662–3853 | www.pedalinghistory.com | $6 | Mon.–Sat. 11–5, Sun. 1:30–5.

Steel Plant Museum. Photos, exhibits, and memorabilia pay tribute to western New York's steel workers, and what was once the largest steel plant in the world, Bethlehem Steel. A themed café sits inside the museum. | Carnegie Library, 560 Ridge Rd., Lackawanna, 6 mi south of Buffalo | 716/823–0630 | Free | Mon. and Wed. 1–9, Tues. and Thurs.–Sat. 9–5; closed Sat. July–early Sept.

Wilcox Mansion: Theodore Roosevelt Inaugural National Historical Site. After President William McKinley was assassinated at the Pan-American Exposition in 1901, Theodore Roosevelt was inaugurated as the nation's 26th president in the library of this mansion. You can take guided tours and view exhibits and gardens. Architectural walking tours are also available. | 641 Delaware Ave. | 716/884–0095 | www.nps.gov/thri | $3 | Weekdays 9–5, weekends noon–5.

Dining

Anchor Bar and Restaurant. American. Anchor claims to have originated Buffalo wings. Some people dispute that, but many come to sample the groundbreaking invention in bar food. Try them hot for the full experience. A buffalo's head hanging on the wall is about all the atmosphere you need. Jazz Friday and Saturday. | 1047 Main St. | 716/886–8920 | AE, D, DC, MC, V | ¢–$$

Coles. American. Sandwiches are the speciality of this restaurant, which was established in 1934. Among the mouthwatering favorites is the ham, turkey, and Swiss sandwich with onions and Russian dressing on marble rye. | 1104 Elmwood Ave. | 716/886–1449 | AE, D, DC, MC, V | $–$$

Rue Franklin West. French. French doors open onto a beautiful landscaped courtyard for summer dining. The changing menu offers modern French dishes such as fresh seafood, fresh game, wild mushrooms, wild striped bass, and rack of lamb, and fresh baked desserts. | 341 Franklin St. | 716/852–4416 | www.ruefranklin.com | Closed Sun. and Mon. No lunch | AE, DC, MC, V | $$–$$$$

Lodging

Adam's Mark Hotel. Stay here for spacious rooms and suites convenient to downtown activities. The lounge has live music and a pianist. Restaurant, some in-room hot tubs, cable TV, pool, health club, bar, shops, parking (fee). | 120 Church St., 14202 | 716/845–5100 or 800/444–2326 | fax 716/845–5377 | www.adamsmark.com | 486 rooms, 7 suites | AE, D, DC, MC, V | $$–$$$

Holiday Inn–Downtown. In the historic Allentown neighborhood, across from the Wilcox Mansion, where Theodore Roosevelt was inaugurated, this hotel is also near the downtown business district. Restaurant, room service, in-room data ports, cable TV, pool, wading pool, bar, laundry facilities, business services, airport shuttle, free parking, some pets allowed. | 620 Delaware Ave., 14202 | 716/886–2121 or 800/465–4329 | fax 716/886–7942 | www.holiday-inn.com | 168 rooms | AE, D, DC, MC, V | $–$$

Lenox. In the Allentown district around the corner from the Theodore Roosevelt Inauguration National Historic Site is this 19th-century hotel. Although it has been renovated several times, it retains its charm with high ceilings, hardwood floors, and spacious rooms. In-room data ports, some kitchenettes, cable TV, laundry facilities, business services, parking (fee); no a/c in some rooms. | 140 North St., 14201 | 716/884–1700 or 800/825–3669 | fax 716/885–8636 | 156 rooms | AE, D, DC, MC, V | $–$$

Chautauqua

★**Chautauqua Institution.** Founded in 1874 as a vacation school for Sunday-school teachers, this lakeside Victorian village is a summer home for the mind. More than 2,000 events take place from mid-June through August, including the symphony, opera, chamber music, visual arts, dance, theater, open-enrollment classes, lectures, and programming for young people. | 1 Ames Ave., Chautauqua | 716/357–6200 or 800/ 836–2787 | www.ciweb.org | Event tickets $7–$36 | June–Aug.; call for performance times.

Lodging

Athenaeum Hotel. Opened in 1881 on the grounds of Chautauqua Institution, this hotel frequently hosted Thomas Edison and is believed to be the first electrified hotel in the United States. Modern guests stay for the architectural splendor rather than the technological advances. Rooms are furnished in Victorian and arts and crafts styles. The hotel is on the National Registry of Historic Places. Some in-room data ports, cable TV, gym. | 26 S. Lake Dr. (Box 66), 14722 | 800/821–1881 | fax 716/357–2833 | www. athenaeum-hotel.com | 57 rooms | Closed early Sept.–late June | AE, D, MC, V | $$$$

Webb's Lake Resort. This motel–restaurant–candy-shop complex sits across from Chautauqua Lake. After a day of sightseeing there's plenty to entertain the family in the evening, with an on-site candy store and mini-golf course. Stargazers can check out the wall of fame off the main lobby and see who else might have slept here. Restaurant, pool, miniature golf, gym, shops, laundry facilities. | Rte. 394, Mayville 14757 | 716/ 753–2161 | fax 716/753–1383 | www.webbsworld.com | 53 rooms | AE, D, MC, V | $$

Dunkirk

ALCO-Brooks Railroad Display. Ring the bell of the No. 444, a steam locomotive built in 1916. A 1907 wood-sided boxcar, a locomotive built in Dunkirk, and a restored 1905 wooden New York Central caboose also are part of this museum's displays, which showcase the railroading history of western New York. | Chautauqua County Fairgrounds, 1089 Central Ave. | 716/366–3797 | Donations accepted | Call for hrs.

Dunkirk Historical Lighthouse and Veterans Park Museum. The lighthouse has been a beacon in the dark since 1826, and the staircase from the original is part of the "new" light, built in 1857. The downstairs of the keeper's house is a museum that depicts how the keeper and his family would have lived. The upstairs rooms are devoted to exhibits about lighthouses, shipping, and the military. There are Coast Guard boats on display, including a 45-foot buoy tender. You can take a guided tour up to the tower. | 1 Lighthouse Point, off Rte. 5 | 716/366–5050 | $5 | Apr.–June, Sept., Oct., Mon., Tues., and Thurs.– Sat. 10–2; July and Aug., Mon., Tues., and Thurs.–Sat. 10–4.

Lake Erie State Park. On bluffs overlooking the lake, this park has spectacular scenery. If you come for the day, you can swim, picnic, hike, or enjoy the playgrounds. There are also 102 campsites, 10 cabins, and camping amenities. Picnic areas have shelters. | Rte. 5, 8½ mi west of Dunkirk | 716/792–9214 or 800/456–2267 | www.nysparks.state.ny.us/parks | $7 per vehicle late May–early Sept.; $7 per vehicle weekends early Sept.–Oct.; free weekdays early Sept.–Oct. and daily early Sept.–late May | Daily dawn–dusk.

Grand Island

Grand Lady Cruises. Cruise the upper Niagara River above the falls while enjoying a breakfast, lunch, or dinner. Charters are also available. | 100 Whitehaven Rd. | 716/774– 8594 or 888/824–5239 | www.grandlady.com | $15–$22 cruises; $30–$33 lunch cruises; $42–$44 dinner cruises | May–Oct., daily 10–11:30, noon–1:30, and 7–9:30.

Martin's Fantasy Island. A wooden roller coaster is one of the more than 100 rides at this 80-acre family theme park. The water park includes a wave pool and there is a petting zoo. | 2400 Grand Island Blvd. | 716/773–7591 | $19 | May–Sept., daily 11:30–8:30.

Dining

Beach House. American. This family-style eatery serves acclaimed Wednesday and Friday fish fries. The menu also includes tacos, subs, and Buffalo wings. Kids' menu. Beer and wine available. | 5584 E. River Rd., 2 mi north of downtown | 716/773–7119 | AE, D, MC, V | $

Niagara Falls

Artpark. Niagara's premier performing arts center has reasonably priced, world-class professional musical theater, dance, and headline musical acts. The center is in a 150-acre state park. Call for schedules and fees. | 450 S. 4th St., Lewiston, 7 mi north of Niagara Falls | 716/754–4375 or 800/659–7275 | www.artpark.net.

★ *Maid of the Mist* **Boat Tour.** View the three falls from up close during a spectacular 30-minute ride on this world-famous boat tour. Waterproof clothing is provided. To get to the boat launch, take the elevator in the Prospect Point Observation Tower, which descends to the base of the falls. Call for special hours in summer and on holidays. | Prospect Park, 151 Buffalo Ave. | 716/284–8897 | www.maidofthemist.com | $10.50 | Apr.–mid-Oct., weekdays 9:45–4:45, weekends 9:45–5:45; boats depart every 15 minutes daily.

★ **Niagara Power Project Visitors Center.** See how the Niagara River is harnessed into one of the largest producers of electricity in the Western world. Kids can play with 50 interactive exhibits. A 3-D photo displays depicts the construction of the power plant. | 5777 Lewiston Rd., Lewiston, 6 mi north of Niagara Falls | 866/697–2386 or 716/286–6661 | www.nypa.gov | Free | Daily 9–5.

Old Ft. Niagara. The fort's 300-year history is acknowledged through cannon and musket firings, historical reenactments, 18th-century military demonstrations, and archaeological programs. The fort's buildings date from 1726, and include a French castle. The fort is at the river's edge; follow signs from Robert Moses Parkway. | Ft. Niagara State Park, Youngstown, 10 mi north of Niagara Falls | 716/745–7611 | $7 | July–early Sept., daily 9–7:30; early Sept.–June, weekdays 9–5:30, weekends 9–6:30; Nov.–Mar., daily 9–4:30.

Seneca Niagara Casino. The Native American Seneca Nation runs this 82,000-square-foot casino. There are 2,625 slot machines and 112 table games, including baccarat, craps, roulette, and several styles of poker. You must be at least 21 years old to enter. | 310 4th St. | 716/299–1100 or 877/873–6322 | www.snfgc.com | Free | Daily 24 hrs.

Dining

Clarkson House. American. Along with delicious steaks and lobsters, there's a lot of history in this restaurant housed in an antiques-filled 19th-century building. Reservations are essential on weekends. Kids' menu. | 810 Center St., Lewiston, 12 mi north of Niagara Falls | 716/754–4544 | AE, D, MC, V | $$–$$$$

Olde Fort Inn. Continental. Barbecued ribs, Cajun pork tenderloin, and Maryland crab cakes are the specialties of this colonial inn. Bread and desserts are homemade. Early-bird dinners. Friday fish fry. Kids' menu. | 110 Main St., Youngstown, 15 mi north of Niagara Falls | 716/745–7141 | www.oldefortinn.com | Closed Mon. | AE, D, MC, V | $–$$$

Red Coach Inn. Continental. A spectacular view of the falls' upper rapids is the draw of this cozy English tavern. Try the slow-roasted prime rib of beef or a broiled, 8-ounce lobster tail with black-pepper fettuccine. The main dining room has a stone fireplace;

the patio, for outdoor dining in summer, is strewn with flowers. Kids' menu. | 2 Buffalo Ave. | 716/282–1459 or 800/282–1459 | www.redcoach.com | D, MC, V | $$$–$$$$

Riverside Inn. Continental. Breathtaking views of Niagara Gorge and amazing sunsets make this a popular honeymooners' dining spot. Try the aged Angus beef or the Brazilian lobster tails. The pub has a more casual menu. Entertainment. Kids' menu. Pub and formal dining. Early-bird dinners September–May. | 115 S. Water St., Lewiston, 8 mi north of Niagara Falls | 716/754–8206 | AE, D, DC, MC, V | $15–$22 | $$–$$$

Lodging

Comfort Inn at The Pointe. This is the closest hotel to the Falls in the United States and half the rooms overlook the Niagara River on its breathtaking tumble. The rooms are standard, but with such scenery about 500 feet away, you won't spend much time in them. Restaurant, some in-room hot tubs, cable TV, shops, business services. | 1 Prospect Pointe, 14303 | 716/284–6835 or 800/284–6835 | fax 716/284–5177 | 118 rooms | CP | AE, D, DC, MC, V | $–$$$

Red Coach Inn. Established in 1923 and modeled after an old English inn, the decor includes wood-burning fireplaces and a spectacular view of Niagara Falls' upper rapids. Unique guest units—with names like the London Room, Bristol Suite, and Windmere Suite—are furnished with antiques, and there are 13 luxurious suites. Old-world service includes champagne and a cheese tray presented when you arrive. Restaurant, room service, some kitchenettes, cable TV, bar, business services. | 2 Buffalo Ave., 14303 | 716/282–1459 or 800/282–1459 | fax 716/282–2650 | www.redcoach.com | 2 rooms, 13 suites | CP | D, MC, V | $$$

Sands Motel. For a comfortable room and a convenient sightseeing location, try this budget alternative. Not just a cookie-cutter roadside motel, this place has retro charm with low-key friendly service. Picnic area, refrigerators, cable TV, pool. | 9393 Niagara Falls Blvd., 14304 | 716/297–3797 or 800/277–3741 | www.travelbase.com/destinations/niagara-falls/sands-motel | 17 rooms | AE, D, DC, MC, V | ¢–$

NORTH CAROLINA

OUTER BANKS
FROM KITTY HAWK TO OCRACOKE ISLAND

Distance: 96 mi   Time: 3 days
Overnight Break: Manteo

This drive covers most of the Outer Banks, from Kitty Hawk at the north end to Ocracoke in the south, primarily along Route 12. After coming in from the mainland on U.S. 158, continue south, with a detour to Roanoke Island. A summer trip finds beach life in full swing, but if you want to avoid crowds, try spring or fall.

❶ Kitty Hawk (off U.S. 158), with a few thousand permanent residents, is among the quieter of the beach communities. The **Aycock Brown Welcome Center,** operated by the Outer Banks Visitors Bureau, provides extensive resources, including area maps, tide charts, and ferry schedules.

❷ Kill Devil Hills is home to the **Wright Brothers National Memorial,** a granite monument that resembles the tail of an airplane and stands as a tribute to the two bicycle mechanics from Ohio who took to the air on December 17, 1903. You can see a replica of the *Flyer* and stand on the spot where it made four takeoffs and landings. **Nags Head Wood Preserve** is a quiet 1,400-acre maritime forest dedicated to preserving a barrier-island ecosystem.

❸ Nags Head has 11 mi of beach with 33 public access areas, all with parking and some with rest rooms and showers. **Coquina Beach** is considered by many to be the best swimming hole on the Outer Banks. The wide-beam ribs of the shipwreck *Laura Barnes* rest in the dunes here. **Jockey's Ridge State Park** has the tallest sand dune in the East (about 90 feet). It is popular for hang gliding, kite flying, and sandboarding.

❹ Roanoke Island is a sleepy well-kept place that hasn't succumbed to full-scale commercialism—much of the 12-mi-long island remains wild. The town of **Manteo** is the focal point. A history, education, and cultural arts complex opposite the waterfront in Manteo, **Roanoke Island Festival Park,** includes the *Elizabeth II* State Historic Site. Clustered together on the outskirts of Manteo are the lush **Elizabethan Gardens,** a re-creation of a 16th-century English garden, established as a memorial to the first

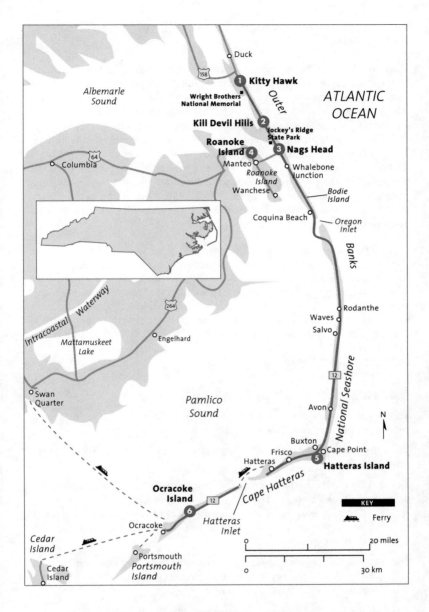

English colonists. Next door is the **Fort Raleigh National Historic Site.** The **North Carolina Aquarium at Roanoke Island,** next to the Dare County Regional Airport, is one of three aquariums in the state; it has wetlands and shark exhibits. Spend one or two nights in Manteo.

Cape Hatteras National Seashore has 75 mi of unspoiled beaches stretching from south Nags Head to Ocracoke Inlet across three narrow islands: Bodie, Hatteras, and Ocracoke. The islands are linked by Route 12 and the Hatteras Inlet ferry. This coastal area is ideal for swimming, surfing, windsurfing, diving, boating, and many other water activities. It's easy to find a slice of beach all your own as you drive south down Route 12, but park only in designated areas. If you want to swim, beware of strong tides and currents—there are no lifeguard stations. Fishing piers are in Rodanthe, Avon, and Frisco.

❺ The Herbert C. Bonner Bridge arches for 3 mi over Oregon Inlet and carries traffic to **Hatteras Island,** known as the "blue marlin capital of the world." This 60-mi-long ribbon of sand is 25 mi from the mainland at its most distant point (Cape Hatteras). About 85% of the island belongs to Cape Hatteras National Seashore, and the remainder is privately owned in seven small, quaint villages strung along Route 12, the island's fragile lifeline to points north. **Pea Island National Wildlife Refuge,** between Oregon Inlet and Rodanthe, is made up of more than 5,000 acres of marsh. This birder's paradise is on the Atlantic Flyway: more than 250 species are spotted regularly, including endangered peregrine falcons and piping plovers. Route 12 travels through marsh areas, and you can hike or drive, depending on the terrain. In Rodanthe, about 15 mi south of Pea Island, is the restored 1911 **Chicamacomico Lifesaving Station.**

❻ Much of **Ocracoke Island** is part of Cape Hatteras National Seashore. A free ferry that runs roughly every half hour from May to October, and every hour from November to April takes you from Hatteras to the island in 40 minutes. Ocracoke was cut off from the world for so long that locals still speak in quasi-Elizabethan accents; today, however, the island is a refuge for visitors. A village of shops, motels, and restaurants has grown around Silver Lake Harbor, where the pirate Blackbeard met his death in 1718. You can ride bikes all over the island. The white brick **Ocracoke Lighthouse** is

NORTH CAROLINA RULES OF THE ROAD

License Requirements: To drive without restrictions in North Carolina you must be at least 18 years old and have a valid driver's license.

Right Turn on Red: Everywhere in the state you can make a right turn at a red light *after* a full stop.

Seat-Belt & Helmet Laws: All drivers and front-seat passengers must wear safety belts. All children between the ages of 5 and 12 must wear a belt. Children under 5 years and less than 40 pounds must by properly secured in a weight-appropriate child-restraint system. Motorcyclists are required to wear helmets and to keep their headlights and taillights on at all times.

Speed Limits: The maximum speed limit in cities and towns is 35 mph. Outside cities and towns, the maximum is 55 mph, and on interstates it's 70 mph. Speed limit signs change rather abruptly, though, so stay alert.

Other Regulations: The legal blood-alcohol concentration limit in North Carolina is .08%. No passenger in a vehicle may have an open container of alcohol.

For More Information: North Carolina Department of Transportation | 877/368–4968 | www.ncdot.org. North Carolina State Police, Division of Highway Patrol | 919/733–7952 | www.ncshp.org.

located in the southwest corner of the village. Ocracoke Island beaches are among the least populated and most beautiful in the Cape Hatteras National Seashore. Four public access areas have parking, as well as off-road vehicle access. At the **Ocracoke Pony Pen** you can observe from a platform the direct descendants of Spanish mustangs that once roamed wild on the island.

Hatteras Island

Chicamacomico Lifesaving Station. This restored 1911 structure has a museum that tells the story of the 24 stations that once lined the Outer Banks. Summer programs might include knot-tying classes, scavenger hunts, or shipwreck storytelling. | Rte. 12, Rodanthe | 252/987–1552 | www.chicamacomico.org | Free | Apr.–Nov., Tues.–Sat. 9–5.

Pea Island National Wildlife Refuge. More than 265 species, some of them endangered, regularly visit this 5,000-acre refuge between Oregon Inlet and Rodanthe. Guided canoe tours, special wildlife and children's tours, and bird and turtle walks are available. A visitor center, 5 mi south of Oregon Inlet, has an informational display. | Pea Island Refuge Headquarters, Rte. 12, between Rodanthe and Oregon Inlet | 252/473–1131 | www.hatteras-nc.com/peaisland | Free | Refuge daily dawn–dusk. Visitor center May–Sept., daily 9–4; Oct.–Apr., weekdays 9–4.

Dining

Breakwater Restaurant. Seafood. Fat daddy-crab cakes rolled in potato chips, then fried and served on pineapple-jalapeño salsa, as well as Carolina shrimp served either fried or broiled in white wine and butter are the menu toppers at this restaurant, which overlooks Oden's Dock. Seafood pastas, fried oysters, and roast duck are also on the menu. | Hwy. 12, Oden's Dock, Hatteras Village | 252/986–2733 | Closed Wed. No lunch | AE, D, MC, V | $$–$$$

Channel Bass. Seafood. Fish are mounted on the walls of this casual family-style seafood spot known for its fresh fish, though a nod is given to steaks, chicken, and ribs. The seafood platters are very popular, as is the homemade crab imperial. The seafood delight—scallops, shrimp, and crabmeat with mushrooms and onions topped with cheese—is also a favorite. Kids' menu. | Rte. 12, Hatteras Village | 252/986–2250 | Closed Dec.–Mar. and Tues. No lunch | D, MC, V | $$–$$$$

Down Under. Seafood. On the pier at Hatteras Island Resort, this spot is known for some of the best fried shrimp on Hatteras. You can also find ocean views and a very casual atmosphere. À la Australia, try spicy fish burgers and the "Great Australian Bite"— a beef burger with fried egg, grilled onions, cheese, and bacon. | Rte. 12, Waves | 252/987–2277 | Closed Dec.–Mar. | AE, MC, V | $$–$$$

Quarterdeck. Seafood. Find all varieties of local fish and shellfish at this unpretentious local favorite. Try the crab cakes with jumbo crab or the fish of the day, and save room for the coconut cream pie. Beer and wine only. | Rte. 12, Frisco | 252/986–2425 | Reservations not accepted | Closed late Nov.–mid-Mar. | D, MC, V | $$–$$$

Kill Devil Hills

Nags Head Wood Preserve. Owned by the Nature Conservancy, this quiet 1,400-acre maritime forest is dedicated to preserving a barrier-island ecosystem. More than 5 mi of hiking trails wind through forest, dune, swamp, and pond habitats. No camping, bicycling, picnicking, or pets are allowed. Educational programs are offered; the preserve has a small visitor center. | 701 Ocean Acres Dr. | 252/441–2525 | Free | Preserve daily dawn–dusk; visitor center weekdays 10–3.

★**Wright Brothers National Memorial.** Orville and Wilbur Wright camped on this windswept spot as they prepared to take flight in 1903. The visitor center has a full-scale reproduction of their plane and glider, and on the grounds are the brothers' camp buildings. | Off U.S. 158 between MM 7 and MM 8 | 252/441–7430 | www.nps.gov/wrbr | $3 | Daily 9–5.

Dining

Colington Café. Eclectic. Nestled amid oak trees, this café is known for seafood, steaks, and French dishes. Try the crab bisque and crab dip. Beer and wine only. | 1029 Colington Rd. | 252/480–1123 | Reservations essential | Closed Dec.–Feb. | D, MC, V | $$–$$$

J.K.'s. Contemporary. You can dine privately in large booths and enjoy simply prepared food. Try the mesquite-grilled dishes: beef, veal, chicken, and fresh seafood. | U.S. 158 Bypass, MM 9 | 252/441–9555 | fax 252/441–8079 | www.jksfoods.com | Reservations not accepted | No lunch | AE, D, MC, V | $$–$$$

Jolly Roger. American. Nautical motifs and pirate-era artifacts dominate here. Live music and karaoke livens up the place, which is open nearly all day, on weeknights. | 1336 N. Virginia Dare Trail | 252/441–6530 | Reservations not accepted | AE, D, DC, MC, V | $–$$

Mako Mike's. American. Murals, local artwork, and big-game fish hang on the walls of this restaurant, which is open year-round. Favorites include chicken marsala, Cajun pasta, shrimp scampi, and Mediterranean fresh spinach. Kids' menu. | 1630 N. Croatan Hwy. | 252/480–1919 | AE, D, DC, MC, V | $–$$

Port O' Call. Continental. Near the beach, you can listen to live music nightly in season and enjoy grilled fresh catches and crab cakes at this casual place. Kids' menu. Sunday brunch. | 504 S. Virginia Dare Trail | 252/441–7484 | Closed Jan.–mid-Mar. | AE, D, MC, V | $$–$$$

Kitty Hawk

Aycock Brown Welcome Center. Maps, tide charts, and ferry schedules are available here. | U.S. 158 | 252/261–4644 | www.outerbanks.org | Free | Daily 9–5:30.

Kitty Hawk Public Beach and Bathhouse. Across the road from the ocean rests a small parking area and bathhouse with rest rooms and showers. People who arrive too early for check-in to their room or condo will often change into bathing suits here and spend time in the water before heading to their lodgings. | Rte. 12 | 252/261–3552 | Free | Memorial Day–Labor Day, daily 10–6.

Dining

Rundown Café. Caribbean. A popular and fun place with a Caribbean flair, this restaurant's specialties include fish tacos, Jamaican stew, and conch fritters. Kids' menu. | 5300 Beach Rd. | 252/255–0026 | Reservations not accepted | Closed Dec. and Jan. | AE, D, MC, V | $$

Lodging

Outer Banks Hostel. Formerly the island's 1918 schoolhouse, this hostel is clean and family-oriented, with a large community kitchen, a common room with Internet access, front porch with Adirondack chairs, bathhouse, and outside hot showers. Lots of games and toys like volleyball, Boogie boards, bikes, and crab fishing lines keep the place lively. It's a 1½-mi walk from the beach. Picnic area, bicycles, shuffleboard, volleyball, laundry facilities, Internet; no room TVs. | 1004 W. Kitty Hawk Rd., 27949 | 252/473–5619 | www.outerbankshostel.com | 2 male dorms and 2 female dorms with shared bath; 6 private rooms | AE, MC, V | ¢–$

Manteo

Elizabethan Gardens. Established as a memorial to the first English colonists who arrived between 1584 and 1587, these are lush recreations of 16th-century English gardens. | 1411 U.S. 64 (U.S. 264) | 252/473–3234 | www.elizabethangardens.org | $6 | Dec.–Feb., daily 10–4; Mar. and Nov., daily 9–5; Apr., May, Sept., and Oct., daily 9–6; June–Aug., Mon.–Sat. 9–8, Sun. 9–7.

Fort Raleigh National Historic Site. A restoration of the original 1585 earthworks mark the beginning of English-colonial history in America. You can view the orientation film and then take a guided tour of the fort. A nature trail leads to an outlook over Roanoke Sound. | Off U.S. 64 (U.S. 264) W, 3 mi north of Manteo | 252/473–5772 | www.nps.gov/fora | Free | Grounds daily dawn–dusk; visitor center daily 9–5; extended hrs June–Aug.

North Carolina Aquarium at Roanoke Island. One of three aquariums in the state, this one has a wetlands exhibit with turtles and amphibians, a shark exhibit, and a hands-on observation tank that is the aquatic equivalent of a petting zoo. | 374 Airport Rd., off U.S. 64 | 252/473–3493 | www.ncaquariums.com | $6 | Daily 9–5.

Roanoke Island Festival Park. The *Elizabeth II* State Historic Site is across the street from the waterfront in Manteo. Costumed interpreters conduct tours of the 69-foot ship—which is modeled after a 16th-century vessel—except when it is on educational voyages in the off-season (call ahead). A film about the area's history runs several times daily; there are blacksmithing and other demonstrations as well as plays, concerts, art exhibitions, and special programs. | 1 Festival Park | 252/475–1506, 252/475–1500 information | www.roanokeisland.com | $8 | Apr.–Oct., daily 9–6; Mar., Nov., and Dec., daily 10–5.

Tuna Fever Charters. Fish all day for tuna, dolphin fish, wahoo, sailfish, and blue marlin. Boats go out when at least six people have made reservations; reserve at least one week in advance. Charters begin at around $1,000 for a full-day trip and run March through November. | 111 Gilbert St. | 800/272–5199.

Dining

1587. Contemporary. In the Tranquil House Inn, this dining spot is surrounded by beautiful boardwalks, sailboats, and the lulling sounds of the Shallowbag Bay lapping the shore. Inventive, artistically prepared entrées change weekly and can include sesame-crusted tuna with wasabi vinaigrette and shiitake mushrooms. Kids' menu. | 405 Queen Elizabeth Ave. | 252/473–1587 or 800/458–7069 | www.1587.com | No lunch | AE, D, MC, V | $$$–$$$$

Clara's Seafood Grill. Steak. Three dining rooms with an art deco look have spectacular views of the bay. You can feel the ocean breeze if you dine on the porch. Favored dishes are the she-crab soup, tuna, and baked Atlantic salmon. Kids' menu. Beer and wine only. | Sir Walter Raleigh St. | 252/473–1727 | Reservations not accepted | Closed Jan. and Feb. | AE, D, MC, V | $$–$$$

Weeping Radish Brewery and Restaurant. German. A Bavarian-style restaurant and microbrewery known for its schnitzel and sausages, the restaurant holds an annual post–Labor Day Oktoberfest weekend showcasing German and blues bands. Brewery tours are offered. | Rte. 64 | 252/473–1157 | D, MC, V | $$

Lodging

Island House of Wanchese B&B. Built in 1902, this two-story bed-and-breakfast with wraparound porch is on the northern, inner portion of Roanoke Island, surrounded by Roanoke Sound. Though on an acre of woods, it's in the center of this small fishing town, a short walk to shops, restaurants, and beaches. Fishing, boating, and water sports are available in town. Cable TV, laundry facilities; no smoking. | 104 Old Wharf Rd.,

Wanchese, about 4 mi south of Manteo, 27981 | 252/473–5619 | fax 252/473–6163 | www.islandhouse-bb.com | 4 rooms, 1 suite | BP | V | $$

Tranquil House Inn. On the Manteo waterfront, the Inn has views of Roanoke Sound and Shallowbag Bay. Rooms have queen- or king-size beds; minisuites have cozy sitting areas. Whitewashed furniture, earth tones, hardwood floors, plantation shutters, and matelasse coverlets give the place a beach cottage feel. Restaurant, cable TV, business services; no smoking. | 405 Queen Elizabeth St., 27954 | 252/473–1404 or 800/458–7069 | fax 252/473–1526 | www.tranquilinn.com | 25 rooms | CP | AE, D, MC, V | $$$

Nags Head

Bodie Island Lighthouse. The third-oldest working lighthouse in the Outer Banks, this black-and-white banded tower dates to 1872 and stands 156 feet above the ground. Though the lighthouse itself is not open to the public, the keeper's house below serves as an information center, and the surrounding marshland is open for self-guided nature and bird-watching tours. | Hwy. 12, between Nags Head and the Oregon Inlet | 252/473–2138 | Free | Keeper's house daily 9–5.

Jockey's Ridge State Park. Home to the largest "living" sand dune on the East Coast, this 400-acre park (and its 90-foot dune) is a favorite among kite-flyers and hang-gliders. A visitor information center is on-site. | U.S. 158 Bypass, 5 mi north of Nags Head | 252/473–2138 | Free | Daily dawn–dusk.

Dining

Bacu Grill. Seafood. There's not much ambience in this dark restaurant with a large bar area and adjoining dining room, but locals love it for the convivial atmosphere, fresh seafood, large portions, and reasonable prices. Try the fish sandwich, soft-shelled crab, or one of the mojo roast pork dishes. | Outer Banks Mall, 158 Bypass | 252/480–1892 | AE, D, MC, V | $$

Nags Head Fishing Pier. Seafood. Perched on one end of the oldest and longest pier on the Outer Banks, the dining room here commands some serious water views. The room is very casual, with lots of light pine planking and plastic deck furniture. The menu includes crab, shellfish, and fish fillets, but the real bonus is that after a successful day on the end of the pier, you can bring in your own pre-cleaned catch and have it cooked to your specifications. | Fishing pier, downtown Nags Head | 252/441–5141 | AE, D, MC, V | $–$$

Tortuga's Lie. Seafood. Hunkered down against the dunes in a bright aqua-blue building, this smallish spot has a distinct Caribbean flavor. Colored pennants and wooden beams shade the spacious patio, and the varied menu has such items as pork loin chops rubbed with jerk sauce, grilled, and topped with habanero pepper jelly. You can get fresh local seafood, too, and there's a sushi bar on Wednesday nights. Sand volleyball courts out back provide friendly premeal competition. | At MM 11.5 on Beach Rd. | 252/441–7299 | AE, D, MC, V | $–$$

Ocracoke Island

Hatteras to Ocracoke Ferry. The trip between Hatteras and Ocracoke takes 40 minutes. Reservations for autos are recommended. | Rte. 12 | 252/928–3841 or 800/345–1665 | www.ncferry.org | Auto $15, motorcycle $10, bicycle $3, pedestrian $1 | Ferrys depart May–Oct. every hr 5 AM–7 AM and 7 PM–midnight, every 30 mins 7–7; Nov.–Apr. every hr. 5 AM–midnight.

Ocracoke Island Visitor Center. Operated by the National Park Service as part of the Cape Hatteras National Seashore, the center has an information desk, a small bookshop, and exhibits. | Near the Cedar Island and Swan quarter Ferry docks, Ocracoke | 252/928–4531 | Free | Daily 9–6 Memorial Day–Labor Day, 9–5 rest of year.

Ocracoke Lighthouse. Built in 1823, this is the state's oldest and, at 75 feet, shortest operating lighthouse. You can walk up close to the light, but you cannot enter. There's an old graveyard behind the lighthouse. | Point Rd., Ocracoke | 252/473–2111 | Free | Daily dawn–dusk.

Ocracoke Pony Pen. From a platform you can observe the direct descendants of Spanish mustangs that once roamed the island. The unruly herd is now cared for by the National Park Service. During rough weather these rugged horses take shelter near the southwest end of the island, where they have a retreat. | Rte. 12, Ocracoke | 252/928–4531 | Free | Daily dawn–dusk.

Dining

Back Porch. Seafood. Crab beignets, smoked local fish, and lime cilantro scallops are the stars in the juniper-paneled dining room. You can eat on the screened porch. Beer and wine only. | 110 Back Rd. | 252/928–6401 | Reservations not accepted | Closed Dec.–Mar. No lunch | D, MC, V | $$–$$$

Café Atlantic. Seafood. Known for grilled and sautéed local seafood, this restaurant serves meals in simple surroundings on two levels. Beer, wine, and spirits are available. Sunday brunch. Kids' menu. Reservations accepted for parties of five or more. | Rte. 12 | 252/928–4861 | Closed late Oct.–early Mar. | AE, D, MC, V | $–$$

Creekside. American/Casual. There's a great view of the harbor from this 2nd-floor space that's accented with nautical attire. Crab cakes, fresh fish, and local catches of the day are all on the menu. Oyster burgers and shrimp-salad pitas make for something a little different. | 368 Rte. 12 | 252/928–3606 | Closed Nov.–Mar.; call for hrs in spring and fall | D, MC, V | $

Howard's Pub and Raw Bar. American/Casual. Large oak and walnut tables accommodate larger groups for a hearty lunch or dinner. Live music attracts a younger set at night. Burgers, sandwiches, and seafood are served along with home-smoked ribs and local catches. Come for a full meal or just for the raw bar and a beer. | Rte. 12 | 252/928–4441 | Reservations not accepted | D, DC, MC, V | $$

Island Inn and Dining Room. Seafood. Central to the village, this eatery specializes in crab cakes, hush puppies, and oyster omelets. Piano and fiddle music is performed on Tuesday nights. Breakfast available. | 100 Lighthouse Rd. (Rte. 12) | 252/928–7821 | Closed Dec.–Feb. No lunch | D, MC, V | $$–$$$

OHIO

NORTH LOOP CITIES

FROM CANTON TO AKRON, CLEVELAND, ELYRIA, SANDUSKY, AND PORT CLINTON

Distance: 135 mi   Time: 5–6 days
Overnight Breaks: Akron, Cleveland, Port Clinton, Sandusky

The bustling cities of northern Ohio shape this drive that begins in the Akron-Canton area, continues to the rocking city of Cleveland, and concludes with a ride to the more serene Port Clinton peninsula.

❶ Canton is home to the **National Football League Hall of Fame,** where the gridiron's greatest are enshrined. Highlights include interactive exhibits, a two-story movie theater, and impressive memorabilia. Another fun stop is **Harry London Candies,** a factory where you can watch the creation, packaging, and shipping of chocolate candy.

❷ In **Akron** (20 mi north on I–77), if your timing is right, visit Canal Park, the home of the Akron Aeros, the Cleveland Indians' Double-A affiliate. Before the game, scoot over to **Quaker Square,** the home of the Quaker Oats Company, the first company to register a cereal trademark and the first to nationally advertise food. The original Quaker Oats mills are now a shopping area with restaurants. The silos are part of the 173-room **Crowne Plaza Hotel at Quaker Square.**

❸ Cleveland (30 mi north on I–77) is home to the **Rock and Roll Hall of Fame and Museum.** With its head-turning collection of objects, clothing, and memorabilia once belonging to rock celebrities, this museum puts a personal twist on rock history. If you're in Cleveland during basketball or baseball season, try to get tickets to see the Cavaliers or Indians. The Cavs take to the basketball court at **Gund Arena** and the Indians play baseball at **Jacobs Field.**

❹ In **Elyria** (25 mi west on I–90) check out the **Hickories Museum,** in a 1894 Tudor home built by inventor Arthur Garford, the man who brought us the padded bicycle seat. Two wineries in nearby Avon Lake—**John Christ** and **Klingshirn**—provide a respite from driving, and offer tours and several quality vintages.

⑤ Superlatives are the norm in describing the most famous **Sandusky** attraction, **Cedar Point**—an amusement park on a Lake Erie peninsula that has the highest, fastest, steepest, and most breathtaking roller coaster in the universe. There's plenty of fun for the younger kids, too.

⑥ The scenery and low-key sightseeing in **Port Clinton** permits you to cool down after the intensity of the big cities. Attractions include the oldest lighthouse on the Great Lakes. **Kelleys Island** and **Put-In-Bay** are just north of Port Clinton and are accessible by ferry. These two scenic agricultural areas are also serene places to wind down. Spend the last night of the tour in Port Clinton.

If you're returning to Canton, take Route 2 East to I–80 East (off Rte. 57 S). Proceed east for about 90 mi to Exit 173 (old Exit 12) and head south on I–77 for about 35 mi.

Akron

Cuyahoga Valley National Park. Ohio's only national park, along with the waters of the crooked Cuyahoga River, is an escape from the growing metro areas of Cleveland and Akron. Year-round outdoor activities abound. | Bolanz Rd. between Riverview and Akron–Peninsula Rds., Peninsula, 13 mi north of Akron | 216/524–1497, 330/650–4636, or 440/546–5991 | www.nps.gov/cuva/ | Free | Daily dawn–dusk.

Boston Mills/Brandywine Ski Resort. This is the hub of skiing, snowboarding, and tobogganing within the Cuyahoga Valley National Park. The resort is open some late nights until 3 AM; call ahead. | 7100 Riverview Rd., Peninsula | 800/875–4241 | www.bmbw.com | Dec.–Mar., daily 9:30 AM–10:30 PM.

Happy Days Visitors Center. This is the park's information and entertainment hub, hosting lectures, concerts, poetry readings, and other activities nightly year-round. | Rte. 303, Peninsula, ½ mi west of Rte. 8 | 330/650–4636 or 800/257–9477 | Wed.–Sun. 10–4.

Cuyahoga Valley Scenic Railroad. The only operating touring railroad in northeast Ohio, this line offers a smorgasbord of themed tours: wine-tasting, train-and-hike, foliage, murder-mystery, and plain old see-the-countryside. As a mid-20th-century locomotive pulls you through the Cuyahoga River dale, you wonder why more railroads like this don't sprout up. The wine-tasting tour is particularly popular, selling out weeks—and sometimes months—in advance. There are several boarding areas for the trains, and tours range from 2½ hours to 7 hours in length. | Peninsula Depot Boarding Station, Akron–Peninsula Rd. and Rte. 303, Peninsula | 330/657–2000 or 800/468–4070 | www.cvsr.com | $8–$20 | Feb.–Dec., daily. Departure times vary; check Web site or call for information.

Goodyear World of Rubber. In this interactive museum across the street from Goodyear headquarters, you learn about the history and versatility of rubber. Highlights include an Indy race car, an artificial heart, and a plethora of Goodyear products. | Goodyear Hall, 1144 E. Market St., 4th fl. | 330/796–7117 | www.goodyear.com | Free | Weekdays 8–4:30.

Hale Farm and Village. The buildings on this farmstead north of Akron are original structures, more than 170 years old. They've been moved here from other locations over the past century and a half. The original farm was founded by pioneer Jonathan

OHIO RULES OF THE ROAD

License Requirements: The legal driving age in Ohio is 18.

Right Turn on Red: Unless posted otherwise, it is legal to make a right turn at a red light *after* a full stop.

Seat-Belt & Helmet Laws: Drivers and front-seat passengers must wear seat belts. Kids under age 4 or less than 40 pounds must use a child-safety restraint. Motorcyclists under age 18 or with less than one-year's driving experience must wear helmets.

Speed Limits: Speed limits are 25 mph to 35 mph in most cities and towns; 55 mph on township, county, and state roads; and 55 mph to 65 mph on expressways and the Ohio Turnpike.

Other Regulations: Passengers cannot possess open containers of alcohol in a vehicle. The blood-alcohol concentration of a driver in Ohio must be below .10%.

For More Information: Ohio Department of Transportation | 614/466–7170 | www.dot.state.oh.us. Ohio State Highway Patrol | 877/782–8765 in Ohio | www.state.oh.us/ohiostatepatrol.

Hale during the canal years in Ohio. Crafters, including a glassblower, candle maker, potter, and blacksmith, demonstrate the industries of the mid-1800s. On spring weekends there are maple-sugar festivities. | 2686 Oak Hill Rd., Bath, 11 mi north of Akron | 330/666–3711 | www.wrhs.org/sites/hale.htm | $12 | Memorial Day weekend–Oct., Wed.–Sat. 11–5 and Sun. noon–5.

National Inventors Hall of Fame. Exhibits at the National Inventors Hall of Fame celebrate the creative and entrepreneurial spirit of great inventors who have been inducted into this organization since its founding in 1973, from Thomas Edison to Apple Computer's Steve Wozniak. In addition, water play, a K'NEX model-building table, and other hands-on attractions let you explore your own creativity. | 221 S. Broadway | 330/762–4463 | www.invent.org | $7.50 | Tues.–Sat. 10–4:30, Sun. noon–5.

Portage Lakes State Park. You can swim, camp, hike, fish, and boat at this 4,963-acre lake area. Its wetlands attract waterfowl and shorebirds. | 5031 Manchester Rd. | 330/644–2220 | www.dnr.state.oh.us/parks/parks/portage.htm | Free | Daily dawn–dusk.

Quaker Square. Originally a working facility, built in 1854, the Quaker Oats mills have been converted into a shopping, restaurant, and entertainment complex. | 135 S. Broadway | 330/253–5970 | www.quakersquare.com | Free | Mon.–Thurs. 10–8, Fri. and Sat. 10–10, Sun. noon–5.

Stan Hywet Hall and Gardens. Built on a stone quarry, this English Tudor mansion was the home of the Seiberling family—the founders of the Goodyear Tire and Rubber Company. It has 23 fireplaces and a number of concealed telephones. | 714 N. Portage Path | 330/836–5533 | www.stanhywet.org | Self-guided tours $10, guided tours $12 | Apr.–Dec., daily 9–6; Feb. and Mar., Tues.–Sat. 10–4, Sun. 1–4; tours Apr.–Dec., daily 10–4:30.

Dining

Ken Stewart's Grille. Contemporary. Near-capacity crowds flock to this art-filled restaurant known for steaks, lobster, and imaginative daily specials, ranging from the latest trends to variations on old favorites. Chicken breast in phyllo with a light pepper-cream sauce, grilled pork tenderloin, potato-crusted halibut, and penne pasta with artichoke hearts, sun-dried tomatoes, and garlic are among the offerings. Kids' menu. | 1970 W. Market St. | 330/867–2555 | Reservations essential | Closed Sun. | AE, D, DC, MC, V | $$$–$$$$

Lanning's. Steak. Windows with a view of a nearby wooded creek, low lighting, and an open-flame grill in the intimate dining room make this a popular spot for special occasions. The delicious Lanning's Secret Sauce is brushed onto all steaks prior to cooking. Seafood dishes range from shrimp scampi to fillet of salmon. Pianist Saturday. | 826 N. Cleveland–Massillon Rd. | 330/666–1159 | www.lannings-restaurant.com | Closed Sun. No lunch | AE, D, DC, MC, V | $$–$$$$

Mustard Seed Market Cafe. Eclectic. Known for healthful and creative combinations of grains, beans, vegetables, and macrobiotic fare, this deli-café on a mezzanine overlooking the market serves appetizers, salads, and sandwiches. Influences range from Asian (peanut Thai shrimp) to Mexican (bean quesadillas). Daily specials might include almond-crusted sea bass with a pesto pierogi. Entertainment Friday–Sunday. Sunday brunch. No smoking. | 3885 W. Market St. | 330/666–7333 | No dinner Sun. | MC, V | ¢–$$

Swensons. American. For a taste of the 1950s and '60s—as well as a darn fine hamburger—Swensons drive-up restaurants can't be beaten. The local chain has been around since 1934, and with six restaurants in and around the Cuyahoga Valley, its popularity has certainly not waned. After a long day of hiking, the so-named "America's best cheeseburger" is a fitting trophy. Try the quirky milk shakes: grape flavoring and milk *do* match. | 7635 Broadview Rd., Seven Hills | 216/986–1934 | No credit cards | ¢

Lodging

★**Crowne Plaza Hotel at Quaker Square.** In the early 1930s the structure that now hosts travelers housed grain for the Quaker Oats Company. The eight-story building has several grain storage silos that were converted into unique, round hotel rooms in the 1980s. Don't expect to wake up with oat hulls in your hair, however. Guest rooms are modern in every way and betray little of the structure's original purpose. The hotel is a historic site; it has hand-sculpted wall murals and history displays. Restaurant, cable TV, indoor pool, gym, business services, Internet, parking (fee). | 135 S. Broadway | 330/253–5970 or 800/445–8667 | fax 330/253–2574 | www.crowneplaza.com | 190 rooms | AE, D, DC, MC, V | $$

Hilton Akron/Fairlawn. With two swimming pools, a shopping mall across the street, and downtown Akron just 5 mi away, this hotel is a good choice for families. Guest rooms are spare and furnished with unassuming wood-veneer pieces. Restaurant, room service, in-room data ports, some refrigerators, cable TV, indoor pool, gym, bar, laundry facilities, business services, airport shuttle, free parking, some pets allowed. | 3180 W. Market St. | 330/867–5000 | fax 330/867–1648 | www.hilton.com | 204 rooms | AE, D, DC, MC, V | $

Holiday Inn Akron/Fairlawn. This hotel's location, in Akron's quiet Fairlawn suburb just off I–77, 12 mi north of downtown Akron, makes it a likely suspect if you're just passing through the area and don't want to deal with city traffic. There are numerous restaurants and shopping complexes within a mile or two of the hotel. Restaurant, room service, in-room data ports, cable TV, pool, gym, laundry facilities, business services, free parking. | 4073 Medina Rd. | 330/666–4131 | fax 330/666–7190 | www.holiday-inn.com | 166 rooms | AE, D, DC, MC, V | $

Inn at Brandywine Falls. Built in 1848, this inn offers proximity to charming Brandywine Falls, as well as a retreat from the daily grind. Plenty of strolling grounds surround the inn, and its porches and library offer pacific solitude. Some in-room hot tubs, some refrigerators, free parking; no TV in some rooms. | 8230 Brandywine Rd., Sagamore Hills 44067 | 330/467–1812 or 888/306–3381 | fax 330/467–2162 | www.innatbrandywinefalls.com | 6 rooms | AE, D, MC, V | $$$–$$$$

Canton

Canton Classic Car Museum. More than 35 classic automobiles are on view, among them cars featured in movies and vehicles once owned by celebrities. Ohio's first Ford dealership now houses this museum where cars are displayed alongside advertisements and fashions from their time period. | 555 Market Ave. SW | 330/455–3603 | www.cantonclassiccar.org | $7.50 | Daily 10–5.

Harry London Candies. Watch chocolate candy being made from cocoa beans, and see how it is packaged, prepared, and shipped out on a 45-minute factory tour that includes a visit to the "Chocolate Hall of Fame." Reservations are essential. | 5353 Lauby Rd. | 330/494–0833 or 800/321–0444 | fax 330/499–6902 | www.londoncandies.com | $2 | Mon.–Sat. 9–4.

Hoover Historical Center. One of only two vacuum cleaner museums in the world, the center chronicles how the suction cleaner developed during the past century. The museum is in the boyhood home of William Henry Hoover, founder of the Hoover Company. A variety of early vacuum cleaners is on display, including a 1910 model that users had to pump with their feet. | 1875 Easton St. NW, North Canton | 330/499–0287 | www.hoover.com | Free | Tues.–Sun. 1–5.

McKinley National Memorial. A national landmark dedicated to William McKinley, the 25th president of the United States, this is also his and his family's burial site. An adjacent museum chronicles McKinley's life. | 800 McKinley Monument Dr. NW | 330/455–7043 | www.mckinleymuseum.org | Free | Landmark and museum Sept.–May, Mon.–Sat. 9–5, Sun. noon–5; June–Aug., Mon.–Sat. 9–6, Sun. noon–6.

The interactive history and science exhibits at the **McKinley Museum of History, Science and Industry** encourage people of all ages to explore fossils, dinosaurs, and the life of early man. You can hunt for baby maisaurus dinos, meet Alice the robotic allosaurus, check out chinchillas in their simulated mountain habitat, and learn about stars at the Hoover-Price Planetarium. The history exhibits include the Street of Shops, which include a pioneer house and general stores. | 800 McKinley Monument Dr. NW | 330/455–7043 | www.mckinleymuseum.org | $7 | Museum Mon.–Sat. 9–5, Sun. noon–5; extended hrs until 6 mid-June–mid-Aug. Planetarium shows Sat. at 2 and 3, Sun. at 2.

★ **Pro Football Hall of Fame.** Joe Montana, Jim Brown, and Vince Lombardi are just a few of the stars and coaches honored at this famous facility. The hall's highlights include the Enshrinees Mementos Room, the Super Bowl Room, and the hall's revolving stadium, which has regular big-screen showings of a "bone-crunching" NFL documentary. Also part of the complex is the Fawcett Stadium, home of the annual Hall of Fame Game. | 2121 George Halas Dr. NW | 330/456–8207 | www.profootballhof.com | $12 | Late May–early Sept., daily 9–8; early Sept.–late May, daily 9–5.

Dining

John's Grille. American. If you're looking for cheap eats and an informal, relaxed, and friendly bar, this is the spot. The supersize burgers, fresh-cut fries, and hearty steaks draw praise from locals. The minimal furnishings in the dark dining room include wooden tables and booths and sports pictures scattered across the walls; there's also a sunny "garden" room with windows and plants. | 2749 Cleveland Ave. NW | 330/454–1259 | Closed Sun. | AE, D, MC, V | $–$$

Lolli's. Italian. Dine by candlelight in intimate booths. Popular dishes include garlic chicken and angel-hair pasta topped with smoked salmon and shrimp in a dill cream sauce. Early-bird dinners. | 4801 Dressler Rd. NW | 330/492–6846 | Closed Sun. and Mon. No lunch | AE, D, MC, V | $$

Spread Eagle Tavern and Inn. Continental. Built as an inn in 1837, this restaurant contains several romantic, candlelit dining rooms, including the Barn Room, with a large stone fireplace; the Patriot's Room, decorated with Civil War–era memorabilia; and the Barbara Bush Room, filled with pictures and memorabilia of the former First Lady. On the menu is fresh fish, smoked rack of lamb, and beef and chicken entrées as well as lobster and Maryland-style crab cakes. Meats are smoked in the restaurant's own smokehouse. Entertainment Saturday. Kids' menu. No smoking. | 10150 Plymouth St., Hanoverton, 20 mi east of Canton | 330/223–1583 | AE, D, MC, V | $$–$$$$

Cleveland

Cleveland Metroparks Zoo and Rainforest. Home to 3,300 animals that live in naturalistic habitats, the zoo includes giraffes and zebras roaming in the African savanna and kangaroos hopping in the Australian children's area. There's a thunderstorm every 15 minutes in the Rainforest, a simulated tropical habitat with waterfalls, rainforest animals, and plants from jungles around the world. | 3900 Wildlife Way, east of Fulton Rd. off I–71 | 216/661–6500 | www.clemetzoo.com | $9 | Daily 10–5.

Cleveland Museum of Art. In its 70 galleries the museum presents art chronologically, from the ancient Mediterranean times to the present. The museum is known for its medieval European, Asian, and pre-Columbian collections. Its holdings include works by Picasso, Michelangelo, Monet, and Van Gogh. Other popular exhibits feature mummies, African masks, and weapons. | 11150 East Blvd. | 216/421–7340 | www.clevelandart.org | Free | Tues., Thurs., and weekends 10–5; Wed. and Fri. 10–9.

Cleveland Museum of Natural History. A 70-foot-long dinosaur skeleton and "Lucy," the world's oldest human fossil, are among the treasures here. The collection contains artifacts and environmental samples from nearly 1,700 sites and documents more than 10,000 years of prehistoric life in Ohio. The largest specimen is the 3,600-year-old Ringler dugout, one of the oldest watercraft found in North America. The museum is known for its 1,500-piece collection of rare gems and the Shafran Planetarium & Astronomy Exhibit Hall. | 1 Oval Wade Dr., at University Circle | 216/231–4600 | Museum $6.50, planetarium $3 (in addition to museum fee) | Mon.–Sat. 10–5, Sun. noon–5.

Great Lakes Science Center. There are more than 300 interactive exhibits and daily demonstrations at this indoor-outdoor educational center. Science and technology displays include a bridge of fire, an indoor tornado, and an area that focuses on the environment of the Great Lakes region. There's a six-story OMNIMAX theater on the premises. | 601 Erieside Ave. | 216/694–2000 | Center $7.95, OMNIMAX $7.95, combo ticket $10.95 | Sun.–Thurs. 9:30–5:30, Fri. 9:30–5:45, Sat. 9:30–6:45.

★ **Rock and Roll Hall of Fame and Museum.** The I.M. Pei–designed building hosts everything from the ridiculous (Jim Morrison's Cub Scout uniform) to the sublime (John Lennon's "Lucy In the Sky With Diamonds" handwritten lyrics). Other exhibits include interactive video and sound kiosks and a collection from Sun Studio, where Elvis Presley, Carl Perkins, and Roy Orbison made their first records. Stage costumes that once belonged to Chuck Berry and Iggy Pop, handwritten lyrics by Jimi Hendrix, Janis Joplin's Porsche, and some thought-provoking films are among the museum's holdings. | 1 Key Plaza | 216/781–7625 | www.rockhall.com | $18 | Thurs.–Tues. 10–5:30, Wed. 10–9.

Dining

Don's Lighthouse Grille. Seafood. Known for its legendary happy hours, this west-end eatery across from Eden Park is in a 1929 building with a steeple. The dining room has large windows, a high ceiling, chandeliers, and nautical murals. The catch of the day may be scrod, tuna, or salmon, but jumbo sea scallops, halibut, and sea scallop ravioli are always on the menu. | 8905 Lake Ave. | 216/961–6700 | No lunch weekends | AE, D, DC, MC, V | $$–$$$$

Empress Taytu Ethiopian Restaurant. Ethiopian. Vegetarian meals, chicken, lamb, and beef are married with northern African music and culture to create a dining experience you won't soon forget. Meals are served without silverware. Reservations are essential on weekends. | 6125 St. Clair Ave. | 216/391–9400 | Closed Sun. and Mon. No lunch | AE, D, MC, V | $$–$$$$

Great Lakes Brewing Co. American. The traditional grub at this pub southwest of downtown in Ohio City includes calamari, a sausage sampler, chili, black-bean ravioli, and ribs. A specialty is the brewmaster's pie—hot and mild Italian sausage, spinach, and mozzarella and ricotta cheeses baked in a flaky pie crust and served on a bed of marinara sauce. Wash it down with one of the home-brewed beers. Open-air dining is available in a courtyard with 25 tables. Kids' menu. No smoking. | 2516 Market St. | 216/771–4404 | AE, DC, MC, V | $–$$

Heck's Cafe. American. In historic Ohio City, this publike eatery has an open kitchen and glass garden atrium filled with plants. It's known for its bouillabaisse and for what is arguably the best burger in town. Dine at tables or in booths. | 2927 Bridge Ave. | 216/861–5464 | AE, D, MC, V | $$

Johnny Mango. Eclectic. Burritos, wraps, coleslaw with a kick, and fried bananas never tasted so good. The chips and salsa before dinner are notable, and the guacamole is outstanding. Make sure to get a booth toward the back of the restaurant to avoid incoming patrons. | 2130 Bridge Ave. | 216/575–1919 | AE, MC, V | $–$$

Lodging

Cleveland Marriott Key Center. Attached to Key Tower, the tallest building in Cleveland, this hotel faces the historic Mall "C" and abuts Public Square. Plush accommodations have fantastic views of Lake Erie and the downtown skyline. Restaurant, gym, lounge, laundry service, laundry facilities, concierge, business services, parking (fee). | 127 Public Sq. | 216/696–9200 | fax 216/696–0966 | www.marriott.com | 400 rooms, 15 suites | AE, D, DC, MC, V | $$$

Hampton Inn Cleveland-Downtown. Cleveland's business district provides the backdrop for this 15-story hotel. The city bustles during the week, and restaurants and activities—such as the Rock and Roll Hall of Fame and shopping at the Avenue at Tower City Center—are within a 10-minute walk. Two-room suites are available. Cable TV, in-room data ports, gym, shop, laundry service, business services, meeting rooms, parking (fee). | 1460 E. 9th St. | 216/241–6600 | fax 216/621–4274 | www.hampton-inn.com | 194 rooms, 6 suites | BP | AE, D, DC, MC, V | $$

Hilton Garden Inn Gateway. Within walking distance of Jacobs Field, Cleveland State University Convocation Center, Tower City, and Gund Arena, this state-of-the-art facility has rooms and suites with desks and Internet for business guests, and is within walking distance of several of Cleveland's entertainment districts. Restaurant, indoor pool, gym, bar, Internet, business services, meeting rooms, parking (fee). | 1100 Carnegie Ave. | 216/658–6400 | fax 216/658–6400 | www.hiltongardeninn.com | 240 rooms, 8 suites | AE, D, DC, MC, V | $$–$$$

Renaissance Cleveland Hotel. This grand 14-story hotel built in 1851 is within walking distance of the Cleveland Convention Center, the Flats, the Theater District, and the Rock and Roll Hall of Fame and Museum. Each tastefully furnished room has one or two queen-size beds or a king-size bed, a dark-wood entertainment center, a plush chair with ottoman, and a work desk. 2 restaurants, some in-room hot tubs, shops, business services, parking (fee). | 24 Public Sq. | 216/696–5600 | fax 216/696–0432 | www.renaissancehotels.com | 491 rooms, 50 suites | AE, D, DC, MC, V | $$–$$$

Elyria

Hickories Museum and Lorain County Historical Society. Inventor and Elyria native Arthur Garford owned this 1895 mansion, which is surrounded by hickory trees. Among the museum's major collections are Victorian-era clothing and furniture. Exhibits include brilliant glassware and early woodworking tools. | 509 Washington Ave. | 440/322–3341 | $3.50 | Museum Tues.–Sat. 10–4; tours at 1 and 2:30. Library daily 1–4.

John Christ Winery. Alfresco seating, a warm brick-and-wood–laden tasting room, and two amiable and knowledgeable managers make John Christ a must. Try the Vidal Blanc and the ice wine. | 32421 Walker Rd., Avon Lake, 10 mi east of Elyria | 440/933–9672 | Free | Mon.–Wed. 10–6, Thurs.–Sat. 10–midnight.

Klingshirn Winery. Lee Klingshirn is a third-generation winemaker, and his mature Riesling, pinot grigio, and cabernet sauvignon are proof: *Wine Spectator* has rated each wine "good," a feat of some importance for Ohio's burgeoning wine industry. Tours of the Klingshirns' vast vineyard are available. | 33050 Webber Rd., Avon Lake, 10 mi east of Elyria | 440/933–6666 | Free | Mon.–Sat. 10–6.

Dining

Hometown Buffet. American. Norman Rockwell prints line the entrance to the restaurant and are scattered throughout the dining room. This hearty slice of America is just 10 minutes from central Elyria. There's a salad bar, a hot food bar, a beverage bar, and a dessert bar, whose offerings change with each meal. | 1565 W. River Rd. N | 440/ 324–2177 | D, MC, V | $

Sugarcreek. American. Hamburgers, liver and onions, and turkey dinners are some of the items you find at this comfortably subdued family restaurant. At lunch, local businesspeople pack the place, so try to arrive before or after the rush. Breakfast served. | 5196 Detroit Rd., Sheffield Village | 440/934–5059 | D, MC, V | $–$$

Port Clinton

African Safari Wildlife Park. More than 400 wild animals wander freely as you drive through this 100-acre park. | Lightner Rd., 4½ mi east of town | 419/732–3606 or 800/ 521–2660 Ext. 3 | www.africansafariwildlifepark.com | Apr.–late May and early Sept.– late Oct. $12.95, late May–early Sept. $15.95 | Apr.–late May and early Sept.–late Oct., daily 10–5; late May–early Sept., daily 9–7.

Catawba Island State Park. Along Lake Erie, this small park has camping, fishing, and boating. Take a picnic and a swimsuit, or walking shoes to explore the Marblehead Lighthouse, the oldest continually operating lighthouse on the Great Lakes. | 4049 E. Moore's Dock Rd., off Rte. 53, 6 mi north of town | 419/797–4530 | www.dnr.state.oh. us/parks | Free | Daily dawn–dusk.

Heineman Winery. Some of the best-value vintages in the state are produced at this family-run winery. The majority of the grapes used in Heineman's wines are grown on South Bass Island, and the Riesling, Vidal Blanc, and ice wine are especially tasty. To get to Put-in-Bay from Port Clinton, take the *Jet Express* ferry. | 978 Catawba Ave., Put-in-Bay, 6 mi north of Port Clinton (by ferry) | 419/285–2811 | Free | Apr.–Oct., Mon.– Sat. 11–7 and Sun. noon–7.

Jet Express. Take a ferry ride from Port Clinton to the happening, sometimes rambunctious town of Put-in-Bay, which is on South Bass Island. Wear good walking shoes or take bicycles; driving a car around South Bass Island can be difficult. Bicycle rental is available in Put-in-Bay. The ferry ride is just over 20 minutes. | 3 N. Monroe St. | 800/ 245–1538 | www.jet-express.com | $20 round-trip | June–Aug., daily 8–midnight; May, daily 9–midnight; Sept., daily 9–11:30; Oct., Fri.–Sun. 9–11:30.

Ottawa County Historical Museum. Fossils, Indian artifacts, and the military history of Ohio are among the topics covered at this northern Ohio museum. | W. 3rd and Monroe Sts. | 419/732–2237 | Free | Late May–early Sept., weekdays 1–4; early Sept.–late May, Wed. 1–4 or by appointment.

Ottawa National Wildlife Refuge. More than 9 mi of pathways and an observation deck give you a bird's-eye view of the migratory birds that stop here on the journey south for the winter and north for the summer. In February and October you can see thousands of birds. | 14000 W. Rte. 2, Oak Harbor, 15 mi west of Port Clinton | 419/898– 0014 | midwest.fws.gov/ottawa/ottawa.html | Free | Refuge daily dawn–dusk, office weekdays 8–4.

Dining

Garden at the Lighthouse. Continental. The main dining room has floor-to-ceiling windows and a view of Lake Erie. Seafood dishes dominate. Try the *poulet d'élégance,* a chicken breast stuffed with lobster tail and Swiss cheese and baked in a puff-pastry shell. Open-air dining is available from Memorial Day to Labor Day. Kids' menu. | 226

E. Perry St. (Rte. 163) | 419/732–2151 | Closed Sun. and Mon. Sept.–May | AE, D, DC, MC, V | $–$$$

Mon Ami Restaurant and Winery. Contemporary. Antique chandeliers and dark-wood detailing fill the elegant dining room. The more casual chalet has a round fireplace in the center of the room. Seafood, ribs, chicken, steaks, and chops are served; each menu item has a suggested wine pairing. Open-air dining on patio. Entertainment Friday and Saturday. Kids' menu. Sunday brunch. | 3845 E. Wine Cellar Rd. | 419/797–4445 or 800/777–4266 | AE, D, MC, V | $$–$$$$

Lodging

Country Hearth Inn. On the shores of Lake Erie, this modern hotel is 10 minutes from Port Clinton and 20 minutes from Cedar Point Amusement Park, and offers excellent views of Lake Erie. In-room data ports, in-room safes, some refrigerators, cable TV, pool, laundry facilities, some pets allowed. | 1815 E. Perry St. (Rte. 163), off Rte. 2 | 419/732–2111 or 800/282–5711 | 66 rooms | CP | AE, D, DC, MC, V | $$$

Fairfield Inn by Marriott. There are several eating and drinking establishments less than a mile north of this hotel, which is adjacent to Keller Field, Port Clinton's airport. The rooms are bright and clean, with modern furniture. Restaurant, some refrigerators, cable TV, indoor pool, laundry facilities, business services, airport shuttle. | 3760 E. State Rd. | 419/732–2434 | www.marriott.com | 64 rooms | CP | AE, D, DC, MC, V | $$

Island House Inn. Smartly appointed rooms with a mix of country and modern furnishings and a friendly staff highlight this historic inn. Rooms are tastefully decorated but snug. Two restaurants are attached, one is a year-round steak house and the other a seasonal Italian eatery. 2 restaurants, cable TV, bicycles, 2 bars, meeting rooms. | 102 Madison St. | 419/734–2166 or 800/283–7307 | 39 rooms | Closed Mon.–Thurs. Oct. 15–Apr. 15 | BP | AE, D, DC, MC, V | $$$

Sandusky

Battery Park. Try to take in the breathtaking view of Sandusky Bay at either sunrise or sunset. | 701 E. Water St. | 419/625–6142 | Free | Daily dawn–dusk.

Cedar Point. One of the country's largest amusement parks, Cedar Point opened in 1870. Its 15 roller coasters include the 310-foot Millennium Force and the mind-blowing 420-foot Top-Thrill Dragster—a coaster that speeds 120 mph, straight up and straight down. There are also kiddie rides, a picnic area, an IMAX theater, live entertainment, a water park, and a stretch of Lake Erie beach. Next door is Challenge Park, with race cars and miniature golf courses. | 1 Cedar Point Rd. | 419/627–2350 | www.cedarpoint.com | $43.95 | Mid-May–Labor Day, daily from 10 AM; after Labor Day–mid-Oct., weekends only; closing hrs vary.

Follett House Museum. The 1830s home of Oran Follett, one of the founders of the Republican Party, is now a research center where you can view artifacts and drawings from Johnson's Island Prison, which held captured Confederate officers during the Civil War. The house has a widow's walk that overlooks Sandusky. | 404 Wayne St. | 419/627–9608 | Free | www.sandusky.lib.oh.us | June–Aug., Tues.–Sat. noon–4; Apr., May, and Sept.–Dec., Sat. noon–4 and Sun. 1–4.

Merry-Go-Round Museum. Carnival memorabilia is displayed in this colorful gallery. Take the tour to watch craftsmen carve carousel horses. Top off your visit with a ride on a 1930s carousel. | W. Washington and Jackson Sts. | 419/626–6111 | $4 | Late May–early Sept., Mon.–Sat. 11–5, Sun. noon–5; Jan. and Feb., weekends noon–5; early Sept.–Dec. and Mar.–late May, Wed.–Sat. 11–5, Sun. noon–5.

Dining

Damon's at Battery Park. American/Casual. Wall-size big-screen televisions, local sports team memorabilia, and electronic trivia games fill this sports bar, but the fine view of Lake Erie—including a sliver of Cedar Point—is what Damon's is known for. Try the onion loaf appetizer, a tasty tangle of thin onion straws that are breaded and deep-fried. | 701 E. Water St. | 419/627–2424 | AE, D, MC, V | $$–$$$

DeMore's Fish Den. Seafood. The fish, sold as dinners or by the pound, comes fresh from DeMore's wholesale distributorship, the largest for yellow perch in the Midwest. Clam chowder and Lake Erie fish—perch and walleye—are favorites here. Open-air dining. Cafeteria service. Kids' menu. | 302 W. Perkins Ave. | 419/626–8861 | MC, V | $–$$

Lodging

Best Western–Cedar Point. After a day of frolicking at Cedar Point amusement park, many families retire to this comfortable motel for its affordable rates and proximity to the amusement park. Large suites with full kitchens are also available. Restaurant, cable TV, pool, video game room, laundry facilities. | 1530 Cleveland Rd. | 419/625–9234 or 800/528–1234 | fax 419/625–9971 | www.bestwestern.com | 105 rooms | AE, D, DC, MC, V | $$

Clarion Inn. Across the street from the Sandusky Mall and within minutes of Cedar Point is this New Orleans–style hotel. Gaslights flicker throughout the complex, and interspersed topiaries and fountains are reminiscent of New Orleans' Garden District. Rooms are neat and comfortable, but dim. Restaurant, room service, in-room data ports, cable TV, indoor pool, exercise equipment, hot tub, bar, recreation room, business services, meeting rooms, some pets allowed. | 1119 Sandusky Mall Blvd. | 419/625–6280 or 800/252–7466 | fax 419/625–9080 | www.clarioninn.com | 143 rooms | AE, D, DC, MC, V | $$

Fairfield Inn by Marriott. This hotel is less than 5 mi from three golf courses, within walking distance to two restaurants, and 4 mi from Cedar Point. Its rooms are clean and quiet, although the hotel is on busy U.S. 250. Some in-room hot tubs, cable TV, indoor pool, sauna, laundry facilities, business services, meeting room. | 6220 Milan Rd. | 419/621–9500 or 800/288–2800 | www.marriott.com | 63 rooms | CP | AE, D, DC, MC, V | $$$

★ **Hotel Breakers.** Every room has a balcony—most have a view of Lake Erie—at this hotel with a rotunda and waterfall. Kids like the Peanuts floor, where rooms have Peanuts characters on the walls. Adults can take advantage of the lake cruises, boardwalk, spa, and murder-mystery weekend dinner packages. Restaurant, cable TV, indoor-outdoor pool, hot tub, spa, beach, shops, laundry facilities, business services, meeting rooms. | 1 Cedar Point Dr. | 419/627–2109 | resorts.cedarpoint.com | 650 rooms | Closed mid-Oct.–Apr. | CP | D, MC, V | $$$$

Radisson Harbour Inn. Most of the rooms at this hotel have breathtaking views of the Sandusky Bay waterfront, and all rooms have private balconies. The hotel is within a five-minute drive of Cedar Point. Restaurant, room service, in-room data ports, cable TV, indoor pool, gym, hot tub, bar, laundry facilities, business services, airport shuttle, some pets allowed. | 2001 Cleveland Rd. | 419/627–2500 | fax 419/627–0745 | www.radisson.com | 237 rooms, 49 suites | CP | AE, D, DC, MC, V | $$$

BUCKS COUNTY

RIVER RAFTING, ANTIQUES & COVERED BRIDGES

Distance: Approximately 50 mi (one way)   Time: 4 days
Overnight Breaks: Doylestown, New Hope

Bucks County, about an hour's drive northeast of Philadelphia and a short drive from New York City, was unspoiled countryside until the 1930s, when weekend escapees from nearby cities started to build country homes in the area. This slice of the Delaware River valley has, indeed, experienced the effects of urban sprawl, but many small-town communities, historic towns, and pastoral landscapes continue to make Bucks County a great weekend getaway for Philadelphians.

The area is known for antiques shops, many of which fall along a 4-mi stretch of U.S. 22 between Lahaska and New Hope and on intersecting country roads. Eleven covered bridges remain in the area—the **Bucks County Tourist Commission** has a good map with concise details and information about the sites. There are also many charming inns and restaurants in the region.

Summer and fall weekends are very busy, so you need to make reservations ahead of time and be ready for crowds; a weekday trip could be more relaxing. Winter has its appeal here, though, especially around the holidays; the snow-covered buildings and fields are lovely.

❶ Begin your tour in **Point Pleasant** (on Rte. 32 [River Rd.], approximately 8 mi north of New Hope). If you want a more scenic route take the Delaware Canal towpath (which runs parallel to River Rd.). This is the section of Bucks County that is reminiscent of the Cotswolds of England, with bridge-keeper-lodges, corkscrew bends in the road, and gorgeous vistas (drivers, beware of the artists often painting at easels by the side of the road).

Point Pleasant is a popular base for exploring the Delaware River. More than 100,000 people a year—from toddlers to senior citizens—negotiate the Delaware on inner tubes or in canoes from **Bucks County River Country Canoe and Tube.** Rafts and kayaks are also available from April through October.

❷ Drive south on Route 32 (River Rd.) for approximately 2 mi until you reach tiny **Lumberville.** The town is centered around the Lumberville Store, established in 1770.

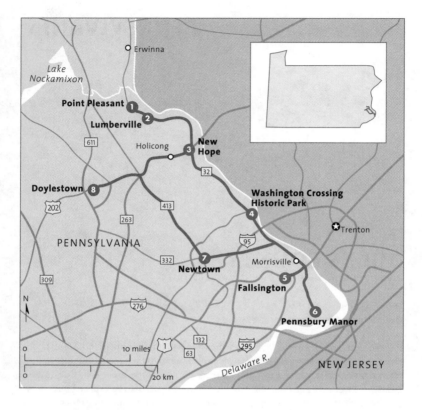

This is the place to pick up groceries or rent a bicycle for a ride on the pastoral river-front towpath.

❸ From Lumberville, drive south on Route 32 (River Rd.) for 3 mi to **New Hope.** The cosmopolitan village is a mecca for artists, shoppers, and lovers of old homes—and hordes of day-trippers and backpackers on summer weekends. The most interesting sights and stores are clustered along four blocks of Main Street and on the cross streets—Mechanic, Ferry, and Bridge—which lead to the river. The **Parry Mansion,** a stone house built in 1784, displays furnishings that reflect decorative changes from 1775 to the Victorian era. The **New Hope Canal Boat Company** provides one-hour narrated barge excursions that take you past Revolutionary-era buildings. Dinner and one or two nights in New Hope are worth your time. And if you get the urge to walk to another state, consider strolling across the bridge that leads from New Hope to Lambertville, New Jersey, which has fun shops and restaurants.

❹ From New Hope continue south on Route 32 (River Rd.) for approximately 7 mi to **Washington Crossing Historic Park.** It was here on Christmas night in 1776 that General George Washington and 2,400 of his men crossed the Delaware River, surprised the mercenary Hessian soldiers, and captured Trenton. A tall granite shaft surrounded by 13 cedar trees marks the point from which the soldiers embarked that snowy night. Spend half a day exploring the park and then continue south on Route 32 (River Rd.) to I–95 South to Route 1 into Morrisville and the nearby attractions of Fallsington and Pennsbury Mansion.

⑤ The pre-Revolutionary village of **Fallsington** is where William Penn attended Quaker meetings. Exhibits at the village cover 300 years of American architecture, from a simple 17th-century log cabin to the Victorian excesses of the late 1800s. Ninety period homes surround the village, which is listed on the National Register of Historic Places. Three buildings, including a log cabin, have been restored and opened for guided tours by **Historic Fallsington, Inc.**

⑥ **Pennsbury Manor,** on a slope 150 yards from the Delaware River, is a reconstruction of the Georgian-style mansion and plantation William Penn built as his country estate. Formal gardens, orchards, an icehouse, a smokehouse, a bake-and-brew house, and collections of tools attest to the self-sufficient nature of Penn's early community, and living-history demonstrations provide a glimpse into daily life in 17th-century America.

⑦ From Pennsbury Manor, take I–95 North to Route 332 West into **Newtown** (approximately 10 mi), with its many 18th- and 19th-century homes and inns. Downtown Newtown is on the National Register of Historic Places. The **Newtown Historical Association** has regional antiques and paintings by the late local artist Edward Hicks. An association brochure provides a walking tour of the town.

⑧ Continue north on Route 413 for approximately 12 mi to U.S. 202 West, and proceed for 3 mi into **Doylestown,** the county seat. The town is a showcase of American architecture, with stately federal brick buildings, and gracious Queen Anne–, Second

PENNSYLVANIA RULES OF THE ROAD

License Requirements: To drive in Pennsylvania, you must be at least 16 years old and have a valid driver's license.

Right Turn on Red: Everywhere in Pennsylvania, you can make a right turn on red *after* coming to a complete stop, unless a sign is posted prohibiting it.

Seat-Belt & Helmet Laws: Seat belts are required for all passengers in the front seats. Children under four years must be in an approved passenger restraint everywhere in the vehicle and must use an approved safety seat in the front seat; children ages one to three can use a regulation seat belt in the backseat only; under age one, an approved safety seat must be used everywhere in the vehicle. Children four and older can use a regulation seat belt.

Speed Limit: The speed limit is 65 mph on rural interstate highways and 55 mph on heavily congested highways in and around urban areas.

Other Regulations: The use of handheld mobile phones by drivers is prohibited in some cities. The legal blood-alcohol limit is .10%. Passengers in a vehicle cannot possess open containers of alcohol.

For More Information: Pennsylvania Department of Transportation | 717/391–6190 or 800/932–4600 | www.dot.state.pa.us. Pennsylvania State Police | 717/783–5517 highway patrol | www.psp.state.pa.us.

Empire–, and Italian-style homes. The historic district includes nearly 1,200 buildings and is listed on the National Register of Historic Places.

Stop at the **Central Bucks Chamber of Commerce** for a map highlighting three walking tours of the area. A main feature of Doylestown is Mercer Mile, consisting of three National Historic Landmark buildings—the stone mansion **Fonthill, Mercer Museum,** and the **Moravian Pottery and Tile Works**—conceived by talented resident Henry Chapman Mercer in the early 1800s. The **James A. Michener Art Museum** focuses on 19th- and 20th-century American art and Bucks County art. It was endowed by the late best-selling author, a Doylestown native. Have dinner and stay overnight in Doylestown before heading back to Erwinna or Point Pleasant.

To return to Point Pleasant, drive east on U.S. 202 for about 10 mi, then north on Route 32 (River Rd.) for another 10 mi.

Doylestown

Central Bucks Chamber of Commerce. This is a good place to stop for maps, brochures, and information on restaurants, lodging, and local businesses. | Wachovia Bank Building, 2nd fl., 115 West Court St., 18901 | 215/348–3913 | fax 215/348–7154 | www.centralbuckschamber.org | Weekdays 8–4:30.

Covered bridges. Bucks County has 11 covered bridges. The oldest was built in 1832. The longest bridge—Schofield Ford Covered Bridge—is 170 feet long. Only two have no vehicle access: Schofield and the South Perkasie Covered Bridge. Uhlerstown Bridge is closed in winter. The Bucks County Conference and Visitors Bureau has maps, brochures, and other information for visitors. | 215/345–4552 or 800/836–2825.

James A. Michener Art Museum. Named in honor of the Pulitzer prize–winning author and Doylestown native, the museum showcases his career as a writer, public servant, art collector, and philanthropist. Other exhibits include Bucks County regional art from colonial times to the present. Café on premises. | 138 S. Pine St. | 215/340–9800 | www.michenerartmuseum.org | $6 | Tues., Thurs., and Fri. 10–4:30, Wed. 10–8, weekends 10–5.

Mercer Mile. Three National Historic Landmarks—Mercer Museum, Fonthill Museum, and Moravian Pottery and Tile Works—make up what is known as the Mercer Mile, the work of historian and archaeologist Henry Chapman Mercer.

★ **Fonthill Museum.** The former home of Henry Mercer was built in 1910 and designed after a 13th-century Rhenish castle. The stone mansion bristles with turrets and balconies on the outside while the inside is a veritable maze of Gothic doorways, sudden stairways, and dead ends. | E. Court St. | 215/348–9461 | www.mercermuseum.org | $7 | Mon.–Sat. 10–5, Sun. noon–5.

Mercer Museum of the Bucks County Historical Society. Mercer's original collection of everyday early-American objects is constantly expanding and includes furnishings, folk art, and implements of early America. Also in the seven-story building is the Spruance Library, a research collection with more than 20,000 volumes, including Mercer's papers. | 84 S. Pine St. | 215/345–0210 | www.mercermuseum.org | $6 | Mon. and Wed.–Sat. 10–5, Tues. 10–9, Sun. noon–5.

Moravian Pottery and Tile Works. The shop still produces unique arts-and-crafts-style picture tiles, with scenes from mythology, the Bible, and history. These "Mercer" tiles adorn such structures as Graumann's Chinese Theater in Hollywood, the Pocantico Hills residence of John D. Rockefeller, and the Harvard Lampoon Building. Self-guided tours are offered every half hour. | 130 Swamp Rd. | 215/345–6722 | www.mercermuseum.org | $3 | Daily 10–4:45.

Pearl S. Buck House. The Pulitzer prize–winning author moved to this Green Hills farmhouse in 1934 and lived there until her death in 1973, two months before her 81st birthday. She is buried on the 60-acre farm. Guided tours of the house are available. | 520 Dublin Rd., Dublin, 7 mi northwest of Doylestown | 215/249–0100 or 800/220–2825 Ext. 170 | fax 215/249–9657 | www.pearl-s-buck.org | $6 | Call for hrs.

Dining

Black Walnut Cafe. Contemporary. Inside an 1846 town house, this restaurant, with original plank hardwood floors and white tablecloths, looks traditional. However, the American cooking includes innovative global touches, such as Brazilian lobster tails with shiitake mushroom dumplings. | 80 W. State St. | 215/348–0708 | Closed Mon. and Tues. No lunch | AE, D, DC, MC, V | $$–$$$$

★ **Cafe Arielle.** French. This French bistro serves delicious grilled seafood dishes, including tuna steaks, as well as prime meats. The interior is furnished in a country-French style, with striking artwork. | Doylestown Agricultural Works, 100 S. Main St. | 215/345–5930 | Closed Mon. and Tues. No lunch weekends | AE, DC, MC, V | $$$–$$$$

Los Sarapes. Mexican. The surroundings are simple, the menu inventive. Try the filet mignon with shrimp and chipotle sauce or the fillet huachinango (red snapper) cooked in garlic oil. No smoking. | 17 Moyer Rd., Kulpsville, 2 mi south of town, 15 mi west of Doylestown | 215/822–8858 | Closed Mon. No lunch Sun. | AE, D, MC, V | $$–$$$

Lodging

Bucksville House Bed & Breakfast. A stop for stagecoaches for over a century, this inn became a speakeasy during Prohibition. The original 1795 building has fireplaces in some guest rooms; plenty of antique quilts, baskets, and colonial furniture add warmth. On the inn's 4¹/₂ acres are a large pond and an herb and perennial garden. In summer the breakfast, which includes such dishes as three-cheese puffy omelets or fresh fruit parfait, is served on a modern octagonal deck; at other times you eat in an enclosed gazebo. Lounge, library; no room phones, no room TVs, no kids under 12, no smoking. | 4501 Durham Rd., Kintnersville 18930, 16 mi north of Doylestown | phone/fax 610/847–8948 or 888/617–6300 | www.bucksvillehouse.com | 5 rooms | BP | AE, D, MC, V | $$

Doylestown Inn. In the middle of town at the crossroads of Route 611 and U.S. 202, this Victorian hotel dates to 1902. It has been completely refurbished, with guest rooms on the third floor. Dark woods and traditional furniture set the tone in the guest rooms, some of which have whirlpool tubs and fireplaces. Mercer tiles are in the lobby. Restaurant, in-room data ports, minibars, free parking. | 18 W. State St., 18901 | 215/345–6610 | fax 215/345–4017 | www.doylestowninn.com | 11 rooms | CP | AE, D, DC, MC, V | $$–$$$

Pine Tree Farm. This colonial farmhouse from 1730 has light and airy guest rooms that have been decorated with cheerful country antiques. The largest and most popular room has a white twig bed and a dressing table in the bathroom. The glass-enclosed garden room in the rear of the house overlooks 16 acres of pine trees. Breakfast, served poolside in summer, can include Grand Marnier French toast and fresh-baked muffins; lighter fare is also available. There's a two-night minimum stay. Pool, pond; no smoking. | 2155 Lower State Rd., 18901 | 215/348–0632 | 3 rooms | BP | AE, MC, V | $$$

New Hope

New Hope Canal Boat Company. The one-hour narrated excursion on a mule-drawn barge travels past Revolutionary-era cottages, gardens, and artists' workshops, as a barge historian–folksinger entertains and educates onboard. | 149 S. Main St. | 215/862–0758 | $8 | Boats depart Apr., Fri.–Sun. at 12:30 and 3; May–Oct., daily at noon, 1:30, 3, and 4:30.

New Hope and Ivyland Rail Road. A vintage locomotive and restored 19th-century cars cover a 9-mi trip through the countryside of New Hope and Lahaska. The tour takes about an hour. Special schedules may be in effect during November and December, so call ahead. | 32 W. Bridge St. | 215/862–2332 | www.newhoperailroad.com | $10 | May 28–Nov. 4, weekdays 11–4, weekends 11–5.

Parry Mansion Museum. The museum has decorative art from 1775 to 1900 and details the life of the Parry family, some of the area's original founders. | 45 S. Main St. | 215/862–5652 | $5 | May–Dec., Fri.–Sun. 1–5.

Washington Crossing Historic Park. On Christmas night 1776, George Washington and the Continental Army crossed the icy Delaware River here and assaulted the unsuspecting Hessians at Trenton. Every year on Christmas Day the town conducts a reenactment of this famous crossing. The 500-acre site has a number of homes used by Washington and his troops, including McKonkey's Ferry Inn, which served as a guard post during the Continental Army's encampment in Bucks County. According to traditional lore, this is where Washington and his aides ate their Christmas dinner prior to the crossing. | 1112 River Rd. (Rte. 32) | 215/493–4076 | Park free, 45-min walking tour $4 | Tues.–Sat. 9–5, Sun. noon–5.

Dining

Havana Bar and Restaurant. Eclectic. Grilled specialties are what stand out amid the American and contemporary fare here. Options include sesame onion rings, a grilled eggplant and Brie sandwich, and a newfangled hamburger with Gorgonzola cheese and spiced walnuts. The bar is enlivened by jazz, blues, and dance bands from Thursday through Sunday nights and by karaoke on Monday. The view of Main Street you get here, especially from the patio, makes Havana ideal for people-watching. | 105 S. Main St. | 215/862–9897 | AE, D, DC, MC, V | $–$$

★ **La Bonne Auberge.** French. Inside a pre-Revolutionary farmhouse, La Bonne Auberge serves classic French cuisine. Some specialties include rack of lamb and poached Dover sole with a champagne and lobster sauce. The four-course prix-fixe menu ($50; available Wednesday and Thursday) is a good deal. The restaurant is within a development called Village 2; travel directions are provided when you call for a reservation. | Village 2 off Mechanic St. | 215/862–2462 | www.bonneauberge.com | Reservations essential | Jacket required | Closed Mon. and Tues. No lunch | AE, MC, V | $$$$

Mother's. Eclectic. At one of New Hope's most popular dining spots, it's the desserts, including chocolate mousse pie and apple walnut cake, that really stand out. Homemade soups, pastas, and unusual pizzas are also on the extensive menu, but your best bet for good food is to visit for breakfast. In summer meals are also served in the garden. Expect to wait; it's often crowded here. | 34 N. Main St. | 215/862–9354 | AE, D, MC, V | $$–$$$

Spotted Hog. Continental. A mural in the Pasture Room has information on the family that started this restaurant and on the family's pet pig Barbi Q, for whom the establishment is named. There are four seating areas: Pig Pen, Pasture, Corn Crib, and the Tavern, where you can eat peanuts and toss the shells on the floor. Try the Foxbriar chicken sandwich, a sautéed chicken breast served with a cherry wine sauce and mushrooms and onions on a baguette. Kids' menu. | U.S. 202 and Street Rd., Lahaska, 3 mi west of New Hope | 215/794–4040 | Reservations not accepted | AE, D, DC, MC, V | $–$$$

Lodging

Aaron Burr House. Hardwood floors, tall arched windows, and a screened-in patio accent this circa-1873 Victorian bed-and-breakfast. A classic "painted lady," this inn has interior rooms that are hand-painted and -stenciled by a New Hope artist. Rooms showcase period antiques and brass ceiling fans. Some have hot tubs, canopy four-poster beds, fireplaces, and private porches. All have private baths and air-conditioning. Business services, some pets allowed; no smoking. | 80 W. Bridge St., at Chestnut St., 18938 | 215/862–2570 | fax 215/862–3937 | www.new-hope-inn.com/aaron | 7 rooms, 1 suite | BP | MC, V | $–$$$

Hotel du Village. French. The large old stone boarding school has been transformed into an inn surrounded by flowers, creating the feel of an English manor house. The guest rooms have wrought-iron beds, period antiques, quilts, and crocheted fabrics. Dining room, 2 tennis courts, pool, bar; no room phones, no smoking. | 2535 N. River Rd. (Rte. 32), 18938 | 215/862–9911 | fax 215/862–9788 | www.hotelduvillage.com | 19 rooms | CP | AE, DC | $–$$

Logan Inn. Eclectic. George Washington is said to have stayed at least five times at this 1727 inn. Rooms have original and reproduction colonial and Victorian furnishings and canopy beds; some also have river views. The Continental breakfast of muffins, fruit, cereals, and juices is served on the tented patio. Restaurant, in-room data ports, cable TV. | 10 W. Ferry St., 18938 | 215/862–2300 | www.loganinn.com | 16 rooms | CP | AE, D, DC, MC, V | $$–$$$

★**Mansion Inn.** This elegant Victorian inn was built in 1865. Even the English gardens feel pleasantly private. Inside, Depression glass, local art, antiques, and comfortable furniture fill the high-ceiling yellow and beige sitting rooms. Guest rooms have antique pieces, plush linens, and modern baths; some have fireplaces and whirlpool tubs. Breakfast can include fresh muffins, an egg dish, or French toast. There's a two-night minimum on weekends and three on holidays. Cable TV, pool, business services; no kids under 16, no smoking. | 9 S. Main St., 18938 | 215/862–1231 | fax 215/862–0277 | www.themansioninn.com | 7 rooms, 5 suites | BP | AE, MC, V | $$$–$$$$

★**Wedgwood Inn.** Three buildings make up the Wedgwood Inn B&B: a federal-style 1840 stone manor house; the 1870 Aaron Burr House; and a blue 1870 Victorian, with a porch and gabled roof. Outside are lush gardens; the interiors are furnished with Wedgwood pottery and fireplaces. Five rooms have two-person whirlpool tubs. Breakfast is served on the sunporch, gazebo, or in your room. Tennis and pool privileges are available. Some cable TV, concierge, some pets allowed; no phones in some rooms, no TV in some rooms, no smoking. | 111 W. Bridge St., 18938 | 215/862–2570 | www.new-hope-inn.com/wedgwood | 15 rooms, 4 suites | CP | AE, MC, V | $–$$$

Point Pleasant

Bucks County River Country Canoe and Tube. The company has equipment for rafting, canoeing, tubing, and kayaking on the Delaware River. All tours are self-guided; the company takes you to the drop-off point and picks you up after the trip. | Rte. 32 N to Byram Rd.; follow signs | 215/297–5000 | www.rivercountry.net | Price varies with equipment | Apr.–Oct., daily 9–7.

Lodging

Evermay on-the-Delaware. Guest rooms have antiques and fresh flowers in this clapboard Victorian house. A breakfast of fresh fruit compote, croissants, cereal, juice, and coffee is served in the garden room, and a predinner sherry or afternoon tea is served in the stately parlor, which has twin fireplaces. Dining room, in-room data ports; no room TVs, no smoking. | River and Headquarters Rds., Box 60, Erwinna 18920, 6 mi north of Point Pleasant | 610/294–9100 | www.evermay.com | 18 rooms | CP | MC, V | $$$–$$$$

LANCASTER COUNTY
FROM COLUMBIA TO GETTYSBURG

Distance: Approximately 175 mi (one way)   Time: 6 days
Overnight Breaks: Gettysburg, Hershey, Lancaster, Lititz, Strasburg

Lancaster County can be hectic, especially on summer weekends and in October, when the fall foliage attracts crowds and farmers' markets and family-style restaurants overflow with people. Its main arteries, U.S. 30 (also known as the Lincoln Hwy. and Lancaster Pike) and Route 340 (sometimes called the Old Philadelphia Pike), are lined with gift shops and outlets. If possible, plan your trip for early spring, September, or Christmas season, when it is less crowded. Note that although many restaurants, shops, and farmers' markets close Sunday for the Sabbath, commercial attractions remain open.

❶ Begin in **Strasburg** (Rtes. 741 and 896), the railroad center of eastern Pennsylvania. The **Strasburg Rail Road** provides a scenic 9-mi round-trip excursion from Strasburg to Paradise on a rolling antique train originally chartered in 1832 to carry milk, mail, and coal. The train has wooden coaches and is pulled by an iron steam locomotive. You can buy a box lunch at the station and have a picnic at Groff's Grove along the way. Across the road from the Strasburg Rail Road is the **Railroad Museum of Pennsylvania,** which includes 12 railroad cars, among them a Pullman sleeper that operated from 1855 to 1913; sleighs; and railroad memorabilia documenting the history of Pennsylvania railroading. The **National Toy Train Museum** includes huge moving setups and hundreds of locomotives and cars on display, and the **Choo-Choo Barn, Traintown USA,** has a 1,700-square-foot display of Lancaster County in miniature, with 20 trains and 150 scenes with figures and vehicles.

❷ From Strasburg head west on Route 741 for about 2 mi and then south on U.S. 222 to the **Hans Herr House.** This is the oldest house in Lancaster County, considered the best example of medieval-style German architecture in North America.

❸ From the Hans Herr House, return to Route 741 and drive west for approximately 5 mi to Route 272, then north on Route 272 for about 6 mi to **Lancaster** (on Rte. 272 just south of Rte. 283). In the early 1700s this was one of the largest inland cities in the 13 colonies. Today it is the heart of Pennsylvania Dutch Country. To get a good feel for the town, take the 90-minute **Historic Lancaster Walking Tour,** led by costumed guides and covering a six-block radius filled with points of architectural and historical interest. One of the stops on the tour is the **Central Market,** which began with open-air stalls in 1742. You can find everything from shoofly pie and sticky buns to fresh-grown produce from area farms.

❹ After you've had your tour and maybe a snack or lunch from the market, head to **Wheatland,** home of the only U.S. president from Pennsylvania, James Buchanan. The restored 1828 federal mansion displays the 15th president's furniture just as it was during his lifetime.

❺ From Wheatland return to Lancaster and continue north for approximately 4 mi on Route 272 to the **Landis Valley Museum,** an outdoor museum of Pennsylvania's German rural life and folk culture before 1900. There are more than 15 structures on the grounds, from a farmstead to a country store, and from May through October there are demonstrations of crafts of the era. Head back to Lancaster for dinner and overnight.

6 Next day, drive to **Ephrata** (12 mi northeast of Lancaster, on Rte. 501 to Rte. 272 into town). Visit the popular **Green Dragon Market and Auction.** The market, one of the largest in the state, is on 30 acres and includes an auction, flea market, and plenty of goods from local Amish and Mennonite farmers. Be sure to see the remains of the 18th-century **Ephrata Cloister.** There's a 45-minute tour of three restored buildings, after which you can wander unescorted through the stable, print shop, and craft shop.

7 From the Cloister, drive west on Route 772 for approximately 8 mi to **Lititz.** Lititz was founded in 1756 by Moravians who settled in Pennsylvania to do missionary work among the Native Americans. Its tree-shaded main street, lined with 18th-century cottages and shops selling antiques, crafts, clothing, and gifts, is a fine place for a walk. Around the main square are the Moravian communal residences, a church dating from 1787, and a hospital that treated the wounded during the Revolutionary War. You can pick up a Historical Foundation walking tour brochure at the **General Sutter Inn,** at the **Johannes Mueller House,** or at the **Lititz Museum.**

8 From Lititz, drive west on Route 772 for approximately 15 mi to **Marietta.** Close to half of the buildings in this restored river town, ranging in architectural style from log cabins to federal and Victorian homes, are listed on the National Historic Register. In the past 20 years or so, it has become an artists' community, and is a nice place for a stroll past well-preserved facades, art galleries, and antiques shops.

9 When you're tired of walking or just ready for a break, head to **Mount Joy** (5 mi northeast of Marietta on Rte. 772) for lunch or a snack. If you're interested in beer and beer making, be sure to take the tour of **Bube's Brewery.** It takes you 43 feet below the street into the brewery's vaults and passages, which were built in a cave and served as part of the Underground Railroad.

10 From Mount Joy, drive west on Route 230 for approximately 2 mi to Route 743 and proceed north for about 10 mi to the "chocolate town" of **Hershey.** Founded in 1903 by confectioner Milton S. Hershey, the town flaunts streetlights shaped like foil-wrapped kisses and avenues named Chocolate and Cocoa. At **Hershey's Chocolate World,** a 10-minute automated ride takes you through the steps of producing chocolate— from picking the cocoa beans to making candy bars. It also serves as the town's official visitor center. Taste-testing is a favorite part of the tour. Be sure to visit the **Hershey Museum,** which preserves the history of the town and its founder as well as that of Pennsylvania Germans and the Native Americans of the area. Have dinner and stay overnight in Hershey.

11 From the fanciful "World of Chocolate," drive 20 mi west on U.S. 322 to U.S. 15 South and proceed for 30 mi to the stark battlefields and monuments of **Gettysburg,** jarring testimonials to a darker chapter in American history. On this site, on July 1– 3, 1863, 51,000 Americans were killed, wounded, or counted as missing in the bloodiest battle of the Civil War. The Gettysburg National Military Park **Visitor Center** provides a free map with a driving tour through the battlefield, as well as an orientation program, Civil War exhibits, and current schedules of ranger-conducted programs and talks. Free walking-tour maps, outlining short 1-mi loops that include the sites of some of the battle's most pivotal engagements, are available at the center. Spend at least a day exploring the park.

12 From Gettysburg, drive approximately 45 mi east on U.S. 30 to the once-bustling river town of **Columbia.** Today Columbia is tranquil, with several museums worth exploring.

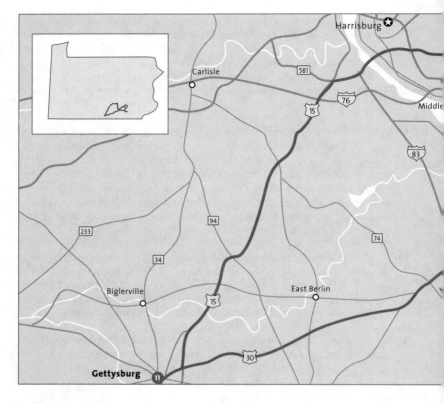

The **National Watch and Clock Museum** displays a large and varied collection of timepieces, specialized tools, and related items from the primitive to the modern. You can capture a bit of the state's history at **Wright's Ferry Mansion,** the former residence of English Quaker Susanna Wright. The 1738 stone house showcases period furniture and English needlework, ceramics, and glass, all predating 1750. Before heading back to Lancaster, stop for lunch and a bit of shopping at the **Market House and Dungeon,** one of the oldest continuously operating farmers' markets in the state.

To return to Lancaster, drive west on U.S. 30 for approximately 10 mi.

Columbia

Market House and Dungeon. Built in 1869, this is one of the oldest continuously operating farmers' markets in the state. The basement of the market used to be a dungeon, and you can still see the ground-level windows through which the prisoners were shoved down a chute into the darkness. For appointments to view the dungeon, contact the Susquehanna Heritage visitor center (3rd and Linden Sts., 717/684–5249). | 308 Locust St., off Rte. 441 | 717/684–2468 | Farmers' market: Fri. 7–4, Sat. 7–noon. Dungeon by appointment only.

National Watch and Clock Museum. Take an entertaining trip through the history of timekeeping. The museum displays more than 10,000 timepieces and time-related items, including early sundials; a 19th-century Tiffany globe clock; and the showstopper, the Engle Clock, an 1877 timepiece designed to resemble the famous astronomical cathedral clock of Strasburg, France. | 514 Poplar St. | 717/684–8261 | www.nawcc.org | $6 | Tues.–Sat. 10–5, Sun. noon–4.

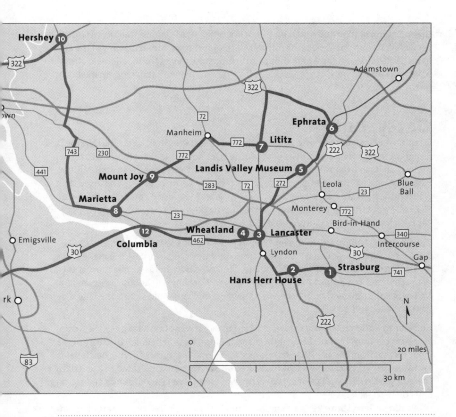

Wright's Ferry Mansion. The 1738 stone house was the residence of English Quaker Susanna Wright, a silkworm breeder whose family helped open Pennsylvania west of the Susquehanna River. The collection showcases period furniture in the Philadelphia William & Mary and Queen Anne styles and a great collection of English needlework, ceramics, and glass, all predating 1750. | 38 S. 2nd St. | 717/684–4325 | $5 | May–Oct., Tues., Wed., and Fri. 10–3.

Dining

Prudhomme's Lost Cajun Kitchen. Cajun. Transplanted Southerners and other Cajun food fans come from as far away as Philadelphia and Baltimore to dine at the only restaurant for miles where you can taste crawfish étouffée, blackened catfish, fried alligator, and other specialties. They are prepared as hot as you like by David Prudhomme, whose famous Uncle Paul perfected these New Orleans flavors. | Rte. 462 and Cherry St. | 717/684–1706 | No dinner Sun., no lunch Mon. | AE, D, MC | $$–$$$

Ephrata

Ephrata Cloister. Founded in 1732 by Conrad Beissel, the Ephrata Cloister was one of America's earliest communal societies. The membership declined after the Revolution, following Beissel's death in 1768. By 1800, the celibate orders were nearly extinct, and in 1814, the remaining householders incorporated with the Seventh Day German Baptist Church. Today you can see many of the medieval-style buildings, and there are a slide show and exhibits about the religious order at the visitor center. | 632 W. Main St. | 717/733–6600 | $6 | Mar.–Dec., Mon.–Sat. 9–5, Sun. noon–5; Jan. and Feb., Tues.–Sat. 9–5, Sun. noon–5.

★ **Green Dragon Market and Auction.** Here, at one of the state's largest traditional agricultural markets on 30 acres, local Amish and Mennonite farmers tend to many of the 400 indoor and outdoor stalls, where shoppers can purchase meats, fruits, vegetables, fresh-baked pies, and dry goods. | 955 N. State St. | 717/738–1117 | www.greendragonmarket.com | Free | Fri. 9 AM–10 PM.

Gettysburg

★ **Eisenhower National Historic Site.** See the only place President and Mrs. Dwight D. Eisenhower ever owned as a home. In 1951, the Eisenhowers, looking forward to retirement, purchased the Allen Redding farm adjoining Gettysburg National Military Park. During Eisenhower's presidency, the 230-acre country estate was used as a weekend retreat and as a meeting place for world leaders. There are exhibits on Eisenhower's life. | 250 Eisenhower Farm La. | 717/338–9114 | www.nps.gov/eise | $5.75 | Apr.–Oct., daily 9–4; Nov.–Mar., Wed.–Sun. 9–4.

General Lee's Headquarters. General Robert E. Lee established his personal headquarters in this old stone house, which dates from the 1700s. On July 1, 1863, Lee made plans for the Battle of Gettysburg in this house. The home now holds a collection of Civil War artifacts. | 401 Buford Ave. | 717/334–3141 | www.civilwarheadquarters.com | $3 | Mid-Mar.–mid-Apr. and mid-Oct.–Nov., daily 9–5; mid-Apr.–mid-Oct., Sun.–Thurs. 9–7, Fri. and Sat. 9–8:30.

★ **Gettysburg National Military Park.** Touching, jarring, and riveting all at once, the 6,000-acre park contains hundreds of markers and memorials that help tell the story of the bloodiest battle of the Civil War. Cannons stand along the 35 mi of scenic battlefields and avenues, and you can visit 20 museums and attractions dedicated to the battle. | 97 Taneytown Rd. | 717/334–1124 | www.nps.gov/gett | Free | Park grounds and roads, daily 6 AM–10 PM.

Battle of Gettysburg Reenactments. In the first week of July, thousands of volunteers dress in period uniforms and reenact the three-day battle, which began on July 1, 1863. Reenactments take place at various locations around Gettysburg—usually in a farmer's field. Call the Gettysburg Reenactment Committee or check the Web site for information. | 717/338–1525 | www.gettysburgreenactment.com.

Battle of Gettysburg Visitor Center. The Gettysburg Museum of the Civil War is here. The museum has one of the world's largest collections of Civil War items, Gettysburg-related memorabilia, and an electric-map battle-orientation program, which gives an overview of the field, the battle, and its participants. | 89 Steinwehr Ave. | 717/334–2100 | www.gettysburg.com | Free, $3 for tour map | Mid-June–mid-Aug., daily 8–6; mid-Aug.–mid-June, daily 8–5.

Gettysburg Railway. You can take 90-minute and four-hour trips on a diesel train. The theme rides include Civil War raids, a ride with Lincoln, dinner trips, fall foliage, a Santa train, an Easter bunny train, and a Halloween ghost train. | 106 N. Washington St. | 717/334–6932 or 888/948–7246 | www.gettysburgrail.com | $10 | Thurs.–Sun. 10–3.

Hall of Presidents and First Ladies. The U.S. presidents are meticulously reproduced in wax. The wax replicas of the first ladies wear copies of their inaugural gowns. | 789 Baltimore St. | 717/334–5717 or 800/447–8788 | www.gettysburgbattlefieldtours.com | $5.95 | Late May–early Sept., daily 9–9; early Sept.–Oct. 15 and Apr., daily 9–7; Oct. 16–Thanksgiving and Mar., daily 9–5.

National Civil War Wax Museum. The Civil War audiovisual presentation has more than 200 life-size figures in 30 scenes including a battle-room auditorium, a reenactment of the Battle of Gettysburg, and an animated Abraham Lincoln giving the Gettysburg Address. | 297 Steinwehr Ave. | 717/334–6245 | www.e-gettysburg.cc | $5.50

| Late May–early Sept., daily 9–9; early Sept.–Dec., Mar., and Apr., daily 9–5; Jan. and Feb., weekends 9–5, weather permitting.

Schriver House. George Washington Schriver was a local hero during the Civil War. His home has been restored to show what civilian life was like in the Battle of Gettysburg. The home tour showcases an area where sharpshooters perched (and were killed), as well as Schriver's Saloon, operated out of the basement. | 309 Baltimore St. | 717/ 337–2800 | www.schriverhouse.com | $5.75 | Apr.–Nov., Mon.–Sat. 10–5, Sun. noon–5; Dec., Feb., and Mar., weekends noon–5.

Soldiers' National Museum. The headquarters for Union General Oliver O. Howard during the Battle of Gettysburg, this building became the Soldiers National Orphanage after the war and now has 60 displays of more than 5,000 Civil War items. | 777 Baltimore St. | 717/334–4890 or 717/334–6296 | gettysburgaddress.com | $5.95 | June–early Sept., daily 9–9; early Sept.–mid-Oct. and May, daily 9–7; mid-Oct.–Thanksgiving and Mar.–Apr., daily 9–5.

Dining

Blue Parrot Bistro. Eclectic. A great place for groups with differing tastes in food, the Blue Parrot is all over the culinary map, with pita pizza, creative soups and salads, eggs Benedict, fried rice with vegetables, and porterhouse steaks. There are white linen cloths on all the tables in the main dining room and a smaller side room, and, as you'd expect, parrot decorations are prevalent. Both rooms have bars, and there's even a pool table. | James Getty Hotel, 35 Chambersburg St. | 717/337–3739 | Closed Sun. year-round; closed Mon. in cold weather (usually Nov.–mid-May) | AE, D, DC, MC, V | $–$$$

Dobbin House. Continental. Listed on the National Register of Historic Places, this tavern and inn puts its waiters in period clothing. The building, the oldest in Gettysburg, was a stop on the Underground Railroad and a hospital during the Civil War. You can eat your meal while reclining under a bed canopy, part of the restaurant's seating area. The food, a nod to the colonial past, includes prime rib, roast duck over apples with a citrus-orange sauce, or a pork tenderloin with raspberry sauce. The more casual Springhouse Tavern, in the basement, serves sandwiches, salads, ribs, and roast chicken. | 89 Steinwehr Ave. | 717/334–2100 | Reservations essential | No lunch | AE, D, MC, V | $$–$$$$

★**Farnsworth House Inn.** Southern. You can eat like a fortunate Civil War soldier here: wild game pie, peanut soup, pumpkin fritters, and spoon bread are all served in the antiques-filled dining room. The historic home, riddled by bullets during the war, has an attic full of war memorabilia that you can examine. | 401 Baltimore St. | 717/334–8838 | www.farnsworthhousedining.com | Reservations essential | AE, D, MC, V | $–$$

Gettysbrew Restaurant and Brewery. Contemporary. In a building used as a field hospital by the Confederates during the Civil War, Gettysbrew has a patio overlooking the surrounding farmland. Standouts include beer-cheese soup, sandwiches on focaccia bread, buffets with 10 cold salads and 6 hot entrées, and handcrafted root beer and sodas. | 248 Hunterstown Rd. | 717/337–1001 | No lunch weekdays | D, MC, V | $–$$

Hickory Bridge Farm. American. Meals in the 150-year-old barn, accented with antiques and knickknacks, are home-cooked and large, often served family-style. Dishes might include oven-fried chicken, barbecued ribs, country steak, or crab imperial. | 96 Hickory Bridge Rd. | 717/642–5261 or 800/642–1766 | Reservations essential | www.hickorybridgefarm.com | Closed Mon.–Thurs. No lunch Fri. and Sat., no dinner Sun. | MC, V | $–$$

Lodging

Baladerry Inn. During the Battle of Gettysburg this 1812 home on 4 acres with a gazebo served as a field hospital. You can stay in the original home or a newer addition. The rooms, given floral names like Primrose and Garden, are bright and airy;

some have private patios and fireplaces. Tennis court; no room TVs, no kids under 12. | 40 Hospital Rd., 17235 | 717/337–1342 | fax 717/337–1342 | www.baladerryinn.com | 8 rooms, 1 suite | BP | AE, D, DC, MC, V | $$–$$$

★ **Best Western Gettysburg Hotel.** The hotel is a pre–Civil War structure in the heart of the downtown historic district; prominent guests have included Carl Sandburg, Henry Ford, and General Ulysses S. Grant. During the Cold War, the hotel served as President Eisenhower's national operations center while he was recuperating from a heart attack at his nearby home. Rooms are furnished in traditional style, and suites have fireplaces and whirlpool baths. Ask about the cannonball from the battle that is still embedded in the brick wall across the street. Suites are available in summer only. Restaurant, room service, in-room data ports, in-room hot tubs, microwaves, refrigerators, cable TV, pool, hot tub, bar, laundry service, business services, no-smoking rooms. | 1 Lincoln Sq., 17325 | 717/337–2000 | fax 717/337–2075 | www.gettysburg-hotel.com | 99 rooms, 30 suites | AE, D, DC, MC, V | $$–$$$

Brafferton. The original stone town house, a half block from Lincoln Square, was built in 1786, the brick addition in 1815. The town house once served as a chapel. Some suites have their own entrance and exposed-brick walls. No room phones, no TV in some rooms, no smoking. | 44 York St., 17325 | 717/337–3423 | fax 717/334–8185 | www.brafferton.com | 9 rooms, 5 suites | BP | AE, D, MC, V | $–$$$

★ **Farnsworth House Inn.** This inn is an early-19th-century federal brick house that Confederate sharpshooters occupied during the Battle of Gettysburg. You can take a tour of the house and cellar, rumored to be haunted. Each Victorian guest room is lushly decorated with period sewing machines, Victrolas, and antique clothing; some have claw-foot bathtubs. An art gallery and bookstore are on the premises. Restaurant, library, shops, business services; no room phones. | 401 Baltimore St., 17325 | 717/ 334–8838 | fax 717/334–5862 | www.farnsworthhousedining.com | 11 rooms | CP | AE, D, MC, V | $$–$$$

James Gettys Hotel. Just off the town square, this four-story all-suites hotel was established in 1804; the main staircase is original. The individually decorated rooms are decorated in a country style. When you've had enough sightseeing, you can relax with full English afternoon tea at the neighboring Thistlefields tearoom. Restaurant, kitchenettes, microwaves, refrigerators, cable TV, laundry service, business services; no smoking. | 27 Chambersburg St., 17325 | 717/337–1334 | fax 717/334–2103 | www.jamesgettyshotel.com | 11 suites | CP | AE, D, MC, V | $$

Hershey

★ **Hershey Museum.** You can hear the story of Milton Hershey's world of candy making here. There are exhibits of Pennsylvania German furniture, folk art, and Hershey's Native American doll collection. | 170 W. Hersheypark Dr. | 717/534–3439 or 800/437–7439 | www.hersheymuseum.org | $6 | Mid-May–early Sept., daily 10–6; early Sept.–mid-May, daily 10–5.

Hersheypark. Thrilling rides and nostalgic rides are found at this park, along with the opportunity to socialize with Hershey Bar and Reese's Peanut Butter Cup costumed characters. Known as "the Sweetest Place on Earth," the park has more than 100 landscaped acres, with more than 60 rides, five theaters, and ZooAmerica, with animals from North America. Opened in 1907, Hersheypark is prized as one of America's cleanest and greenest theme parks. Among its historical rides are the Comet, a 1946-vintage wooden roller coaster, and a carousel built in 1919 with 66 hand-carved wooden horses. For thrill seekers, some of the newer rides include the exciting Lightning Racer double-track wood racing coaster, the Great Bear steel inverted roller coaster, and the Roller Soaker that is half roller coaster and half water ride. Hershey

Stadium and the brand new Giant Center are venues for concerts, musicals, and sporting events. | 100 W. Hersheypark Dr. (Rte. 39), between Rte. 743 and U.S. 422 | 717/534–3090 | www.hersheypa.com | $35.95 | Late May–early Sept., daily 10–10 (some earlier closings); early May and late Sept., weekends only, call for hrs.

ZooAmerica. This 11-acre zoo showcases the plants and animals that are native to North America, with gray wolves, prairie dogs, bison, deer, black bear, owls, and animals of the desert. | 100 W. Hersheypark Dr. | 717/534–3860 or 800/437–7439 | $7.50, free with Hersheypark admission | Daily 10–8.

★ **Hershey's Chocolate World.** Hershey's chocolate experience is told through a tour ride that shows how chocolate is made and also gives some company history. There are a gift shop and restaurants highlighting Hershey products. | 800 Park Blvd. | 717/534–4900 or 800/437–7439 | www.hersheypa.com | Free | Daily 9–5.

Dining

Chocolate Town Cafe. American. Connected to Chocolate World, this kids' café is painted in bright colors with Hershey's characters on the walls. The half-pound burger and the chicken fingers are favorites. The café claims to have the world's thickest milk shakes. | 800 Park Blvd. | 717/533–2917 | No dinner | AE, D, MC | $–$$

Circular Dining Room. Continental. This stylish glass-enclosed formal dining room overlooks the gardens at the back of the elegant Hotel Hershey. You might find lobster, salmon, filet mignon, or roast leg of lamb on the menu, and an amazing chocolate buffet of desserts such as chocolate cream pie and chocolate mousse. Breakfast served. | Hotel Hershey, 400 Hotel Rd. | 717/533–2171 | Jacket and tie | AE, D, DC, MC, V | $$$–$$$$

Hershey Pantry. American. The charm of lace curtains accents this popular family restaurant that has been honored for serving the best breakfast in the area. Be sure to try the delicious stuffed French toast. You can eat on an enclosed porch. | 801 E. Chocolate Ave. | 717/533–7505 | Closed Sun. | No credit cards | $–$$$

Isaac's. American. There are exposed ceilings, aquariums, and paintings of wildlife in this roadside restaurant. The extra-thick deli sandwiches are named after birds, such as the Whooping Crane with turkey, onions, and spinach grilled with Swiss cheese and honey-Dijon dressing, or the Jamaican Tody, grilled chicken breast seasoned with Caribbean jerk spices on pumpernickel with ranch dressing, pineapple, and melted cheddar. | 1201 W. Chocolate Ave., off Hwy. 422, 1 mi northeast of downtown | 717/533–9665 | AE, D, MC, V | ¢–$

Lodging

Best Western Inn. A two-story modern concrete-and-limestone building, this hotel is only minutes from Hersheypark. This an affordable choice for the family, with large comfortable rooms and a great outdoor pool area in warm months. In-room data ports, refrigerators, cable TV, pool, spa, video game room, laundry facilities, business services, no-smoking rooms. | Rte. 422 and Sipe Ave., 17033 | 717/533–5665 | fax 717/533–5675 | www.bestwestern.com | 123 rooms | CP | AE, D, DC, MC, V | $$–$$$$

Hershey Lodge. This modern five-level lodge and convention center is across the road from Hershey Medical Center. Free shuttles are provided from Hersheypark, which is 2 mi away. Rooms are nicely appointed with attractive colors, artwork, and coordinating bedspreads and draperies. Restaurant, dining room, in-room data ports, cable TV, miniature golf, tennis court. 2 pools (1 indoor), wading pool, gym, hot tub, bar, playground, business services, airport shuttle. | W. Chocolate Ave. and University Dr., 17033 | 717/533–3311 or 800/533–3131 | fax 717/533–9642 | www.hersheypa.com | 665 rooms | AE, D, DC, MC, V | $$$$

Hotel Hershey. The grande dame of Hershey, this gracious Mediterranean villa–style hotel is a sophisticated resort with plenty of options for recreation, starting with the golf course that surrounds the hotel. Inspired by the fine European hotels Milton S. Hershey encountered in his travels, the hotel abounds in elegant touches, from the mosaic-tile lobby to rooms with maple armoires, paintings from local artists, and tile baths. Dining options include the Iberian Lounge, Fountain Café, the casual Clubhouse Café, and the formal Circular Dining Room, which overlooks the gardens, fountains, and reflecting pools. The spa's treatments here include a chocolate bean polish, a cocoa butter scrub, a chocolate fondue wrap, and whipped cocoa bath. Carriage rides, a ropes course, and nature trails are all on the property. 3 restaurants, coffee shop, room service, 2 18-hole golf courses, 9-hole golf course, 3 tennis courts, 2 pools (1 indoor), gym, sauna, spa, bicycles, basketball, lounge, baby-sitting, laundry service, concierge, business services, meeting rooms. | Box 400, Hotel Rd., 17033, of Rte. 39 W to Sandbeach Rd. | 717/533–2171 or 800/533–3131 | www.hersheypa.com | 234 rooms, 20 suites | AE, D, DC, MC, V | $$$$

Lancaster

Amish Farm and House. Tour an Amish house on a 25-acre farm. The house was built in 1805 and is a replica of an "Old Order" Amish home. The farm dates back to 1715. You can examine a stone-lined well, windmill, waterwheel, tobacco shed, and other buildings. | 2395 Lincoln Hwy. E | 717/394–6185 | www.amishfarmandhouse.com | $6.95 | Daily 8:30–6.

★**Central Market.** In the heart of town, the market began as open-air in 1742 and is now in an 1889 Romanesque building. It's one of the oldest covered markets in the country and a good place to pick up everything from bologna to shoofly pie. | Penn Sq. | 717/291–4723 | Free | Tues. and Fri. 6–4, Sat. 6–2.

Dutch Wonderland. The 48-acre park has two roller coasters, a water coaster, log flume shows, botanical gardens, and 19th-century paddleboats. You can also see Acapulco cliff divers plummet 90 feet. | 2249 U.S. 30 E | 717/291–1888 | www.dutchwonderland.com | $25.95 | Memorial Day–Labor Day, daily 10–7; other times, call for hrs.

★**Hans Herr House.** Built in 1719, this is the oldest building in Lancaster County and the oldest remaining site of Mennonite worship in North America. The stone house also has a reconstructed blacksmith shop, an outdoor baking oven, and a smokehouse. | 1849 Hans Herr Dr., at Willow St. | 717/464–4438 | www.hansherr.org | $4 | Apr.–Nov., Mon.–Sat. 9–4.

Historic Lancaster Walking Tour. Costumed guides comment on points of historical and architectural interest during a 90-minute tour through the six-block heart of the old city. Tours depart from the visitor center at Old Southern Market. | Visitor Center, 100 S. Queen St., at Vine St. near Penn Sq. intersection | 717/392–1776 | $7 | Apr.–Oct., Tues., Fri., and Sat. at 10 and 1, Sun., Mon., Wed., and Thurs. at 1; Nov.–Mar., by reservation only.

Historic Rock Ford Plantation. Eighteenth-century antiques and folk art are displayed in a 1794 Georgian-style mansion, the restored home of General Edward Hand, Revolutionary War commander, George Washington's adjutant, and member of the Continental Congress. Changing exhibits are displayed at the Kauffman Barn. | Lancaster County Park, 881 Rock Ford Rd. | 717/392–7223 | www.rockfordplantation.org | $5 | Apr.–Oct., Tues.–Fri. 10–4, Sun. noon–4. Yuletide tours weekends Thanksgiving–Christmas.

Landis Valley Museum. Experience the rural lifestyle of the Pennsylvania Germans by exploring more than 15 historic buildings with crafts demonstrations, a mid-

1800s country hotel, and a museum shop. | 2451 Kissel Hill Rd. | 717/569–0401 | www. landisvalleymuseum.org | $9 | May–Oct., Mon.–Sat. 9–5, Sun. noon–5.

★ **Wheatland.** See the former home of James Buchanan, the 15th president of the United States. The 4½-acre 1828 national historic landmark, part of the Civil War Discovery Trail, is also where Buchanan wrote his inaugural address. | 1120 Marietta Ave. | 717/ 392–8721 | www.wheatland.org | $5 | Apr.–Nov., daily 10–4.

Dining

Carr's Restaurant. French. Owner Tim Carr and chef Kathy Walls have created a simple and appealing restaurant with the look of a French café. Fresh meats, vegetables, fruit, and fowl are all featured. A signature dish is the shrimp and basil ravioli in Provençale sauce. | Market and Grant Sts. across from Central Market | 717/299–7090 | Closed Mon. | AE, D, DC, MC, V | $$$–$$$$

Catacombs, Alois's, and The Bottling Works. Continental. Dine in the original dining rooms of this 19th-century brick brewery or its cellars; cellar staff are dressed in medieval-style clothing. Shrimp and roast duck are among the choices. You can take a guided tour of the old bottling works. Open-air dining on a patio. Live entertainment, acoustic guitar Friday and Saturday. | 102 N. Market St., Mount Joy, 12 mi west of Lancaster | 717/653–2056 | No lunch Sun. | AE, D, MC, V | $$–$$$$

Gibraltor. Seafood. An unexpected addition to Lancaster County, Gibraltor's Mediterranean cuisine emphasizes fresh, beautifully prepared seafood. The enticing tapas include flash-fried calamari and steamed mussels. The menu changes every few weeks, but might include lobster risotto, seared Chilean sea bass, and grilled yellowfin tuna with basil pesto. The golden yellows used throughout the restaurant are complemented by striking blue goblets. The restaurant's Aqua Bar is a big hit with the Friday-evening crowd, which comes for cocktails and tapas. | 931 Harrisburg Pike, at College Sq. across from Franklin & Marshall College | 717/397–2790 | fax 717/397–3622 | AE, MC, V | Closed Sun. | $$–$$$$

★ **Log Cabin.** Steak. Consistency is the appeal here: several generations have made this their special-occasion place for classic fare such as filet au poivre with brandy Dijon sauce. The steaks, as well as lamb chops and seafood, are prepared on a charcoal grill in this 1928 expanded log cabin on a wooded hillside. An impressive collection of 18th- and 19th-century American paintings help make the 10 candelit dining rooms elegant. | 11 Lehoy Forest Dr., off Rte. 272, Leola, 6 mi north of Lancaster | 717/626–1181 | www.logcabinrestaurant.com | No lunch | AE, MC, V | $$–$$$$

Lodging

★ **Eden Resort Inn.** Attractive grounds and spacious rooms with cherrywood colonial furnishings make a stay here pleasant. The inn has a tropical indoor pool and a whirlpool under a retractable roof; you can request a poolside room. The chef at Arthur's is noted for seafood and pasta dishes; casual fun food is presented in Garfield's. If you're spending a few days in the area, consider one of the extended-stay suites. 2 restaurants, room service, in-room data ports, in-room safes, refrigerators, tennis court, 2 pools (1 indoor pool), gym, sauna, lounge, parking (fee). | 222 Eden Rd., U.S. 30 and Rte. 272, 17601 | 717/569–6444 or 800/528–1234 | fax 717/569–4208 | www.edenresort.com | 276 rooms, 40 suites | CP | AE, D, DC, MC, V | $$–$$$

King's Cottage. An elegant 1913 Spanish Mission Revival mansion on the National Register of Historic Places is now a B&B. The blend of decorative and architectural elements encompasses Chippendale-style furniture in the dining room and an art deco fireplace and stained-glass windows. Several rooms have whirlpools and fireplaces, including the first-floor bedroom chamber. An outdoor goldfish pond and a patio with seating are pleasant in warmer weather. The price includes full breakfast and afternoon tea;

a small kitchen is available for those staying here. Dining room, in-room data ports, library, free parking; no smoking. | 1049 E. King St., 17602 | 717/397–1017 or 800/747–8717 | fax 717/397–3447 | www.kingscottagebb.com | 7 rooms, 1 cottage | BP | D, MC, V | $$–$$$$

Lancaster Host Resort and Conference Center. This sprawling family resort has a striking marble lobby and comfortable, contemporary rooms with cherrywood furnishings. You can jog or rent a bike and ride around the beautifully landscaped golf course and grounds. 2 restaurants, room service, in-room data ports, driving range, 18-hole golf course, miniature golf, putting green, 2 tennis courts, basketball, 2 pools (1 indoor), bicycles, piano bar, convention center, meeting rooms, free parking. | 2300 Lincoln Hwy. E (U.S. 30), 17602 | 717/299–5500 or 800/233–0121 | www.lancasterhost.com | 330 rooms, 8 suites | AE, DC, MC, V | $$–$$$

Willow Valley Family Resort and Conference Center. Smorgasbord meals, large rooms, a duck pond, and indoor pools make this large, stylish resort a great family place. Rooms are spread out over three buildings; those in the Atrium Building surround a striking skylighted lobby. The extensive Sunday brunch in the Palm Court is a favored feast. Since the resort is owned by Mennonites, liquor isn't permitted on the premises. 2 restaurants, 9-hole golf course, 2 tennis courts, 3 pools (2 indoor), gym, hot tub, sauna, steam room, basketball, recreation room, playground, business services, meeting rooms, free parking. | 2416 Willow St. Pike, 17602 | 717/464–2711 or 800/444–1714 | fax 717/464–4784 | www.willowvalley.com | 342 rooms, 50 suites | AE, D, DC, MC, V | $$$

Lititz

Johannes Mueller House. Step back into late-18th- to early-19th-century Moravian life as you visit the restored 1792 home of tradesman Johannes Mueller. | 137–145 E. Main St. | 717/627–4636 | www.lititzmutual.com/public/lhf.nsf/museum | $5 | Memorial Day–Oct., some weekends in May, and Nov. and Dec., Mon.–Sat. 10–4.

Julius Sturgis Pretzel House. At the nation's oldest pretzel bakery, the treats are twisted by hand and baked in brick ovens the same way Julius Sturgis did it in 1861. You can try your hand at the almost extinct art of pretzel twisting at the end of the 20-minute tour. | 219 E. Main St. | 717/626–4354 | www.sturgispretzel.com | $2 | Mon.–Sat. 9–5.

Lititz Museum. Next door to the Johannes Mueller House is the Lititz Museum, with historical artifacts from Lititz. | 137–145 E. Main St. | 717/627–4636 | www.lititzmutual.com/public/lhf.nsf/museum | $5 | Memorial Day–Oct., some weekends in May, and Nov. and Dec., Mon.–Sat. 10–4.

Wilbur Chocolate Factory's Candy Americana Museum and Factory Outlet. The first thing you notice in Lititz is the smell of chocolate coming from the Wilbur Chocolate Factory, which produces 150 million pounds of the luscious product each year. There's a small museum of candy-related memorabilia and a large retail store. | 48 N. Broad St. | 717/626–3249 | www.wilburbuds.com | Free | Mon.–Sat. 10–5.

Dining

★ **1764 Restaurant.** American. In the General Sutter Inn, this restaurant has fine dining with an artistic flourish; favorite selections include crab cakes, elk medallions, and Pennsylvania trout. There are also twilight menus and Wine Wednesday menus. In warm weather the brick patio is a favorite dining spot. The Zum-Anker Cafe is the Sutter Inn's casual eatery, which serves eggs with Canadian bacon and grilled cinnamon buns for breakfast, and soups, stews, and salads for lunch. The fun-filled Friday-evening seafood fest in the cool-weather months features whole lobster, clam chowder, and fish-and-chips. | 14 E. Main St., on the square, at Rtes. 501 and 772, corner of Rtes. 501 and 772 | 717/626–2115 | AE, D, MC, V | $$–$$$$

Lodging

Alden House. In the heart of the historic district, this B&B offers period rooms with modern baths in an 1850 redbrick Victorian-colonial house. Much care has gone into the decorating of each room, some with canopy beds or four-poster beds, local quilts, and hand stenciling. Free parking. | 62 E. Main St., 17543 | 717/627–3363 or 800/584–0753 | www.aldenhouse.com | 5 rooms | MC, V | $–$$

★**General Sutter Inn.** Built in 1764, the oldest continuously run inn in Pennsylvania was named after the man who founded Sacramento in 1839, 10 years before the discovery of gold on his California property started the gold rush. Sutter retired in Lititz and the inn named after him is a delight with charming Victorian furnishings and color-coordinated fabrics. The buildings of the historic district are within easy walking distance. The elegant 1764 Restaurant offers artistically prepared lunches, dinners, and Sunday brunch, while the cozy wood-trimmed Zum-Anker Cafe has tasty breakfasts, lunches, and casual seafood fare. Restaurants, café, bar, no-smoking rooms. | 14 E. Main St., on the square at Rtes. 501 and 772, 17543 | 717/626–2115 | fax 717/626–0992 | www.generalsutterinn.com | 16 rooms, 3 suites | AE, D, MC, V | $–$$

★**Swiss Woods.** On the edge of 30 acres of woods overlooking Speedwell Forge Lake is this open and airy European-style B&B. Each room has its own balcony or patio. Boating, fishing, hiking. | 500 Blantz Rd., 17543 | 717/627–3358 or 800/594–8018 | fax 717/627–3483 | www.swisswoods.com | 6 rooms, 1 suite | BP | AE, D, MC, V | $$–$$$

Strasburg

Amish Village. Guided tours are given through an authentically furnished Amish house, and afterward you can wander around the village, which includes a barn and house, a one-room schoolhouse, a blacksmith shop, a village store, and an operating smokehouse built by Amish craftsmen. | Rte. 896 between U.S. 30 and Rte. 741 | 717/687–8511 | $6.50 | Mar.–mid-May, Sept., and Oct., daily 9–5; mid-May–Aug., daily 9–6. House tours Nov.–Feb., weekends 10–4.

Choo-Choo Barn, Traintown, USA. What started as a family hobby in 1945 with a single train chugging around the Groff family Christmas tree is now a 1,700-square-foot display of Lancaster County in miniature, with 20 trains, mainly in O-gauge, with 150 animated scenes, including an authentic Amish barn raising, a huge three-ring circus with animals and acrobats, and a blazing house fire with fire engines rushing to the disaster. Periodically, the overhead lights dim, and it becomes night, when streetlights and locomotive headlights glow in the darkness, and a nighttime baseball game gets underway. | Rte. 741 | 717/687–7911 | www.choochoobarn.com | $5 | Apr.–Dec., daily 10–5.

★**National Toy Train Museum.** The showplace of the Train Collectors Association, this museum has five huge operating layouts, with toy trains from the 1800s to present, plus nostalgia films and hundreds of locomotives and cars in display cases. | Paradise La. just north of Rte. 741 | 717/687–8976 | www.traincollectors.org/toytrain.html | $3 | May–Oct. and Christmas wk, daily 10–5; Apr. and Nov.–late Dec., weekends 10–5.

★**Railroad Museum of Pennsylvania.** Across the road from Strasburg Rail Road, this museum displays 75 pieces of train history, with 13 colossal engines built between 1888 and 1930; 12 railroad cars, among them a Pullman sleeper; sleighs; and railroad memorabilia documenting the history of Pennsylvania railroading. | Rte. 741 | 717/687–8628 | www.rrmuseumpa.org | $7 | May–Oct., Mon.–Sat. 9–5, Sun. noon–5; Nov.–Apr., Tues.–Sat. 9–5, Sun. noon–5.

Strasburg Rail Road. The Strasburg Rail Road can take you on a scenic 45-min round-trip excursion through Amish farm country from Strasburg to Paradise on a rolling antique train. Called America's oldest short line, the Strasburg run has wooden coaches pulled by an iron steam locomotive. Picnic lunches are available for the stop at the picnic grove. | Rte. 741 | 717/687–7522 | www.strasburgrailroad.com | $9.25 | Apr.–June and Sept., daily 11–4; July and Aug., daily 10–7; Oct.–Dec. and mid-Jan.–Mar., weekends noon–3; closed 1st 2 wks in Jan. Trains depart every 30–60 mins depending on season; call for schedule.

Dining

By George Tavern and Washington House Restaurant. American. Steaks, jumbo lump crab cakes, sandwiches, and bistro fare fill the menu at the casual By George Tavern. There's a full ale, beer, and wine menu. The elegant Washington House Restaurant serves breakfast only, including a Sunday brunch with a full array of breakfast specialties and breads. | Historic Dr., off Rte. 896 | 717/687–9211 | No dinner at Washington House | AE, D, DC, MC, V | $$–$$$

Hershey Farm Restaurant. American. Bountiful buffets are available at breakfast, lunch, and dinner, or you can order from the à la carte menu. The decor is warm and folksy, with quilt-patterned accents and wooden furnishings | 240 Hartman Bridge Rd. | 800/827–8635 | $$–$$$$

Lodging

Historic Strasburg Inn. The five buildings of this colonial-style inn are set on 58 peaceful acres overlooking farmland. The rooms, simply and comfortably furnished, have rocking chairs. There are two restaurants, including the elegant Washington House Restaurant that features breakfast and the casual By George Tavern with appetizers, lunch, dinner, and beer and ale selections. 2 restaurants, in-room data ports, cable TV, in-room VCRs, pool, gym, hot tub, sauna, bicycles, business services. | Historic Dr., off Rte. 896, 17579 | 717/687–7691 or 800/872–0201 | fax 717/687–6098 | www.historicstrasburginn.com | 102 rooms, 9 suites | BP | AE, D, DC, MC, V | $$$–$$$$

Limestone Inn Bed and Breakfast. Listed on the National Register of Historic Places, this 1786 Georgian home has a formal living room, a library, and a sitting room and fireplace, plus a small garden with a fish pond. Bedrooms are in colonial colors with Amish quilts and four-poster beds. Dining room, library. | 33 E. Main St., 17579 | 717/687–8392 | www.thelimestoneinn.com | 6 rooms | BP | No credit cards | $–$$

★**Strasburg Village Inn.** Built around 1788, the inn is in the heart of town and has rooms appointed in the Williamsburg style. A sitting–reading room is on the second floor; an old-fashioned porch overlooks Main Street. Breakfast is served at the adjacent Strasburg Creamery. Some in-room hot tubs; no room phones, no smoking. | 1 W. Main St., 17579 | 717/687–0900 or 800/541–1055 | www.strasburg.com | 10 rooms | BP | AE, D, MC, V | $$–$$$

RHODE ISLAND COAST

FROM WESTERLY TO NEWPORT

Distance: 59 mi   Time: 2½ hours
Overnight Break: Newport

Dazzling nature preserves, beaches, architecturally significant homes, and lighthouses are the highlights of this drive. Westerly, Jamestown, and Newport are famous summer places, so this tour is best in warmer weather. However, fall foliage season, with smaller crowds and fewer tour buses, is an excellent alternative, especially for Newport, though some sights will be closed.

❶ In Westerly (I–95, Exit 1, Rte. 3 S, Rte. 78 W, to U.S. 1) the coastal village of **Watch Hill** (Rte. 1A to Watch Hill Rd.) is at Rhode Island's southwestern extreme. This Victorian-era resort village has a harbor and miles of beautiful beaches. The area's many summer homes are renowned for their stylish beauty (look for their trademark foundations of beach stone). Statues commemorating the Native Americans of this region, the Niantics (a branch of the Narragansett tribe), stand on the shores of Watch Hill Cove. Also at the heart of Watch Hill is the **Flying Horse Carousel,** the oldest merry-go-round in America. Built in 1867, its hand-carved horses are suspended from above and swing out when in motion. The 1-mi-long spit of sand known as **Napatree Point** (off Watch Hill Rd.) is a conservation area teeming with birdlife. It is open to the public daily. The **Watch Hill Lighthouse** (Lighthouse Rd. off Watch Hill Rd.) has great views of the ocean and of Fishers Island, New York. It houses a tiny museum that contains exhibits about Rhode Island lighthouses. There is a small parking area for people with disabilities; everyone else must walk from the public lot that serves Watch Hill and Napatree Point.

❷ **Misquamicut State Beach,** just east of Westerly, is the New England equivalent of Coney Island.

❸ Head northeast on Route 1A, which becomes U.S. 1. One of the state's most tranquil areas is **Charlestown Beach,** in Charlestown. A barrier beach, it is bordered by tidal and freshwater marshes. If you have time, walk the beach to the breach way—you can wade across.

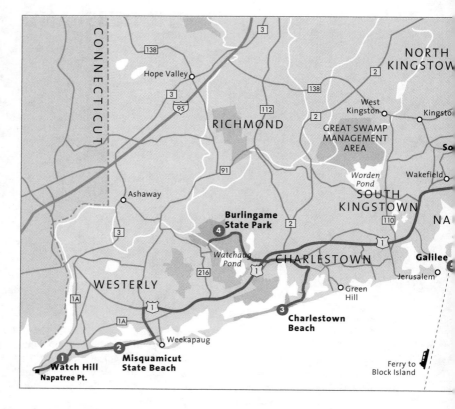

④ North of U.S. 1, **Burlingame State Park** has nature trails and picnic and swimming areas. There are 755 campsites in the 2,100-acre park on the banks of Watchaug Pond.

⑤ Continue northeast on U.S. 1, then take Route 108 South. In **Galilee** there is a slew of seafood restaurants. The **Frances Fleet** leads fishing and whale-watching excursions, if you are extending your tour. The **Block Island Ferry** runs to the island daily. Day trips to the island are best planned in summer and fall when there are numerous ferry trips; to bring a car you will need a hard-to-come-by reservation. **Roger Wheeler State Beach** has a beach pavilion that has won a variety of architectural awards. The calm protected beach is great for families with small children.

⑥ **Point Judith Lighthouse** in **Narragansett** marks the western mouth of the Narragansett Bay. The lighthouse itself and the active Coast Guard Station are restricted, but the expansive views make this a worthwhile stop. Farther north in Narragansett are **The Towers.** This is the last remaining section of the once-famous Narragansett Pier Casino, which in its heyday was the center of a seaside resort. The ground floor houses the chamber of commerce visitor center.

⑦ Nearby is the **Narragansett Town Beach,** which is convenient to many shops and restaurants.

⑧ **South County Museum** (off Rte. 1A) has over 30,000 artifacts that date from 1800 to 1950. Historically accurate exhibits include a country kitchen, a cobbler's shop, a tack shop, a working printer's shop, and an antique carriage collection.

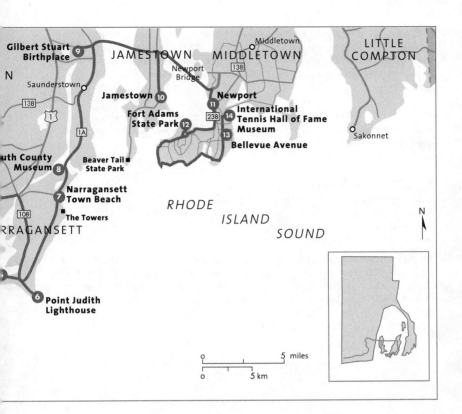

⑩ Head east on Route 138 across the bridge to **Jamestown,** where you can explore 153-acre **Beavertail State Park,** at the southern tip of Conanicut Island, and the small **Beavertail Lighthouse Museum,** which has a simple exhibit about Rhode Island lighthouses.

⑪ Continue east on Route 138 across the Newport Bridge, then south to Ocean Drive in **Newport.** The 5-mi drive passes dozens of the huge private mansions that evoke the "Gilded Age" of the late 19th century. There's much to do in Newport—historical sightseeing, fun shopping, good food, and in-town beaches. In summer, especially on weekends, the narrow roads can be choked with sightseers. Consider parking and getting around town on the frequent trolleys.

⑫ **Fort Adams State Park** presents magnificent panoramas of Newport Harbor and is a great place to take sailing or windsurfing lessons. A massive stone fort built in the early 1800s stands here, but it is closed to the public.

⑬ Ocean Avenue ends at world-famous **Bellevue Avenue.** The wide street is lighted by gas lamps and fronts seven Gilded Age mansions that are open to the public. To avoid long lines on summer days, go early or choose the less popular but still amazing mansions—**The Elms, Kingscote,** and **Belcourt Castle.** Plan on spending one hour at each mansion.

⑭ Built in 1888, the **International Tennis Hall of Fame Museum** at the landmark Newport Casino chronicles the game's greatest moments and players. The magnificent shingle-style club is considered the birthplace of modern tennis.

Charlestown

Charlestown Beach. A calm contrast to other area beaches, this barrier beach is rarely crowded. Rest rooms and parking are available, but there are no dining options in the immediate vicinity. | Charlestown Beach Rd. | 401/364–1222 | Beach free, parking $12 per car | Apr. 15–Oct. 31, daily dawn–dusk.

Kimball Wildlife Refuge. Bordering the second-largest natural pond in the state, this 29-acre wildlife preserve is especially attractive to waterfowl and migrating birds. It's maintained by the Audubon Society of Rhode Island. It is off U.S. 1 near Watchaug Pond. | Sanctuary Rd. | 401/949–5454 | fax 401/949–5788 | www.asri.org | Free | Daily dawn–dusk.

RHODE ISLAND RULES OF THE ROAD

License Requirements: To drive in Rhode Island you must be at least 16 years old and have a valid driver's license.

Right Turn on Red: A right turn on red is permitted after a complete stop, unless posted otherwise.

Seat-Belt & Helmet Laws: Seat belts are required for all operators and passengers. All children under age five must ride in the backseat. Helmets are not required for operators of motorcycles but are required for passengers. Protective goggles, glasses, or windscreen are required of operators and passengers.

Speed Limit: The maximum legal speed in Rhode Island is 65 mph; 25 mph in business and residential areas; elsewhere, 50 mph in day, 45 mph at night, or as posted.

Other Regulations: The legal blood-alcohol concentration is below .08%. Rhode Island enforces an open container law, meaning passengers cannot carry open alcoholic containers. The use of handheld phones is prohibited while driving.

For More Information: Rhode Island Department of Transportation | 401/222–2481 | www.dot.state.ri.us. Rhode Island State Police | 401/444–1000 | www.risp.state.ri.us.

Ninigret National Wildlife Refuge. About 9 mi of trails weave through 400 acres of beach lands and marshes at this wildlife refuge, which also includes freshwater ponds. | Rte. 1A | 401/364–9124 | Free | Daily dawn–dusk.

Ninigret Park. Picnic grounds, ball fields, a 10-speed bike course, and tennis and basketball courts are among the features of this 227-acre park. In addition there is a 3-acre spring-fed swimming pond. On Friday nights an observatory is open for public use of the telescopes. | Rte. 1A | 401/364–1222 | Free | Daily dawn–dusk.

Quonochontaug Beach. A white-sand beach, Quonochontaug straddles the Westerly town line. There are no concession stands in the immediate area, so pack a lunch if you plan to linger. | Spring Ave. | 401/364–7718 | Free | Daily dawn–dusk.

Trustom Pond National Wildlife Refuge. A haven for waterfowl, this 642-acre refuge is one of the best places in the state to observe wild birds. The 161-acre coastal pond is a stopover for migrating duck, including canvasback, scaup, goldeneye, and bufflehead. In the upland areas, nesting birds include brown thrasher, bobolink, and red-winged blackbird. You can stroll along several walking trails. | Matunuck Schoolhouse Rd., South Kingstown, 1½ mi east of Charlestown | 401/364–9124 | Free | Daily dawn–dusk.

Galilee

Block Island Ferry. Interstate Navigation Company operates ferry service from Galilee to Block Island on the Point Judith Ferry. Make auto reservations well ahead; foot passengers cannot reserve space. In summer, arrive early in the day; the boats are often filled to capacity. There are eight boats daily in summer, limited service the rest of the year. The ferry crossing takes about an hour. | Galilee State Pier, Great Island Rd. (Point Judith Rd.), off Rte 1 N | 401/783–4613 | www.blockislandferry.com | Round-trip on foot $13.65, round-trip by car $51.90 | Ferries depart frequently; call or check Web site for schedules.

Roger Wheeler State Beach. This calm protected beach with a lifeguard is a draw for families with kids. Amenities include a children's playground, picnic tables, showers, and a pavilion that has won a number of architectural awards. | 100 Sand Hill Cove Rd. | 401/789–3563 | www.riparks.com | Weekdays $12 per car, weekends $14 per car | Early–late May, weekends dawn–dusk; late May–early Sept., daily dawn–dusk, weather permitting.

Southland Cruises. Take 1¾-hour narrated sightseeing cruises or 2½-hour sunset cruises in the port of Galilee on this midsize passenger boat. Sights on the tours include the Point Judith Lighthouse, Block Island, and the largest salt pond in Rhode Island. There are foliage cruises in October and special events cruises throughout the summer. | State Pier, 304 Great Island Rd. | 401/783–2954 | www.southlandcruises.com | Sightseeing cruise $12, sunset cruise or foliage cruise $14 | May–Oct.; call or check Web site for schedules.

Dining

George's Restaurant. Seafood. At the mouth of Point Judith Harbor, this restaurant has been a "must" for tourists since 1948. The "stuffies" (baked stuffed quahogs) are popular, and the menu has a wide variety of fried and broiled seafood, as well as chicken, steak, and pasta. Its proximity to the beach and its large outdoor bar on the second floor make George's a busy place all summer. You can take food out for a beach picnic. There's often live music. | 250 Sand Hill Cove Rd. | 401/783–2306 | www.georgesofgalilee.com | Closed Dec. and weekdays Nov. and Jan. | AE, D, MC, V | ¢–$$

Jamestown

Beavertail State Park. A 153-acre park at the southern tip of Conanicut Island, Beavertail is a favorite destination for Rhode Island residents. Look for garnet and fool's gold in the outcroppings of slate and granite that line the shore. Hermit crabs, periwinkles, sea anemones, and sea stars can be seen in the tide pools. | Beavertail Rd. | 401/423–9941 or 401/884–2010 | www.riparks.com | Free | Daily dawn–dusk.

The **Beavertail Lighthouse Museum.** Inside the third-oldest lighthouse in the United States, built in 1749 and later moved to the grounds of the park, resides a small museum with an exhibit about all of Rhode Island's lighthouses. | 401/423–3270 | www.beavertaillight.org | Free | Late May–mid-June and early Sept.–mid-Oct., weekends noon–3; mid-June–early Sept., daily 10–4.

Fort Wetherill State Park. Spectacular views beckon from this park on an outcropping of cliffs. From the east you can see Newport's Fort Adams, and from the south, the ocean. Many a wedding picture has been shot here, and picnicking and scuba diving are popular activities. | Ocean St. | 401/423–1771 | www.riparks.com | Free | Daily dawn–dusk.

Old Windmill (Jamestown Windmill). Operated by the Jamestown Historical Society and restored in 2001, the mill was in use from 1789 to 1896. The gears, the stone for grinding corn, and the granary can all be viewed inside. | 280 N. Main Rd. | 401/423–1798 | Free | June–Aug., weekends 1–4.

Sydney L. Wright Museum. Conanicut Island (Jamestown) was used by the Narragansett tribe as a summer camp. Certain areas of the island are being excavated by archaeologists to learn more about the Narragansetts. This small museum, in the Philomena Library, houses some of the finds. | 26 North Rd. | 401/423–7280 | Free | Mon. 10–9, Tues. and Thurs. noon–5 and 7–9, Wed. 10–5 and 7–9, Fri. and Sat. 10–5.

Dining

Bay Voyage. Continental. Once on the other side of the bay, this lovely inn was moved across by ship many years ago. The pleasant bright dining room with a panoramic view over Newport is packed for the popular Sunday brunch. Sophisticated dinner menu choices include beet-crusted salmon and coriander–and–pepper-rubbed rack of lamb. Save room for the fresh-baked fruit tarts. | 150 Conanicus Ave. | 401/423–2100 | Reservations essential | AE, D, DC, MC, V | $$$–$$$$

East Ferry Deli. Café. Homemade muffins, cakes, and cookies are the draws here. Deli sandwiches, quiches, burgers, and salads are also available. There's a good selection of vegetarian sandwiches. Tables inside and out provide splendid views of Jamestown Harbor and Narragansett Bay. Breakfast served. | 47 Conanicus Ave. | 401/423–1592 | www.jamestownri.com/efdeli | No dinner | No credit cards | ¢

★**Jamestown Oyster Bar.** Seafood. Fresh seafood—from oysters and littlenecks to lobster and steamed mussels—is on the menu at this rustic place. The french fries are hand-cut, and the mashed potatoes rise to new heights with roasted garlic and shallots. Chicken, steaks, and hefty burgers can be ideal if you're not in the mood for the latest catch. | 22 Narragansett Ave. | 401/423–3380 | No lunch weekdays | AE, MC, V | $–$$

Trattoria Simpatico. Italian. This restaurant is popular for its sunny Caribbean atmosphere, lively crowd, and good food. Fresh seafood comes from local boats, or try specialties like ravioli stuffed with duck breast. Outside you sit in the stone-walled garden under a three-century-old beech tree. Inside, your choices include the garden room, an enclosed porch, or the charming house itself. Live jazz accompanies most evenings. | 13 Narragansett Ave. | 401/423–3731 | AE, D, MC, V | $$–$$$$

Narragansett

Narragansett Pier–The Towers. The Narragansett summer beach community was once known for its Stanford White–designed Pier Casino, which burned in 1900. All that remains are the stone towers and the looming eight-story stone entrance that spans

Route 1A. You can dance on the wooden floor of the tower bridge Thursday nights from 7 to 10, June through September. There's a gift shop and information service on the ocean side of the building. | Rte. 1A | 401/782–2597 | Free | Towers weekends noon–4, or by appointment.

Narragansett Town Beach. The pavilion has a bathhouse, concessions, and activities for kids. The south end is great for surfing, while the north end is quieter. | 39 Boston Neck Rd. (Rte. 1A) | 401/782–0658 | Beach free, parking $12 per car | Early–late May, weekends 9–6; late May–early Sept., daily dawn–dusk, weather permitting.

South County Museum. The seven buildings on Canochet Farm contain 30,000 artifacts dating from 1800 to 1950. Exhibits include a country kitchen, a living-history farm, carpentry, blacksmith, and letterpress printing exhibits, and an antique carriage collection. | Canochet Farm, Strathmore St. | 401/783–5400 | www.southcountymuseum.org | $5 | May, June, Sept., and Oct., Fri. and Sat. 10–4, Sun. noon–4; July and Aug., Wed.–Sat. 10–4, Sun. noon–4.

Dining

Aunt Carrie's Restaurant. Seafood. Serving fresh seafood since 1920 on the beach at Point Judith, rustic Aunt Carrie's is revered for its lobster, lobster rolls, steamers, and steak. Try the odd local delicacy called clamcakes—deep-fried dough studded with bits of clam. You can eat inside or take your catch out to the large waterside picnic area. | 1240 Ocean Rd. | 401/783–7930 | Closed Tues. | MC, V | $–$$

Crazy Burger Cafe & Juice Bar. American. An old vegetable market ½ mi from Narragansett Beach has been converted into a funky and fun year-round restaurant that serves an array of burger-shape patties with funny names and unusual ingredients. Examples include neurotic (tofu, black beans, and couscous) and Luna-Sea (salmon with orange pistachio pesto in puff pastry). The ketchup is homemade, and the waffle chips are awesome. Dine alfresco on the garden patio. BYOB. Breakfast served. | 144 Boon St. | 401/783–1810 | D, MC, V | $$

Newport

★**Cliff Walk.** The 3½-mi Cliff Walk began as a footpath in the late 1700s. Today you find backyard glimpses of many of Newport's mansions on one side, and open ocean on the other. Although mostly smooth, parts can be a bit rocky, so wear proper walking shoes—this is not an outing for flip-flops. | Memorial Blvd. at Eustis Ave. | 401/849–8098 or 800/326–6030 | Free | Daily dawn–dusk.

Fort Adams State Park. Take in Newport Harbor from this 105-acre seaside park, also a good place to take sailing or windsurfing lessons; sailboat rentals are available. The park is home to the legendary Newport Jazz Festival and Folk Festival, held annually during the first and second weeks of August. | Harrison Ave. and Ocean Dr. | 401/847–2400 | www.riparks.com | Free | Daily dawn–dusk.

★**Great Friends Meeting House.** In 1657 a ship bearing Quakers arrived in Newport after their failed attempts to settle in New York and Boston. This meetinghouse was built in 1699, when the Friends made up 60% of Newport's population. It has been called the finest medieval structure in America, and its weathered exterior belies the soaring post-and-beam construction of the interior. | Farewell and Marlborough Sts. | 401/846–0813 | www.newporthistorical.com | $4 | Tours mid-June–Aug., Thurs.–Sat. at 10, 11, 1, and 3, or by appointment.

★**Preservation Society of Newport historic mansions and houses.** Eleven mansions are maintained by the Preservation Society, some of which are described below. Guided tours are given of each; you can purchase a combination ticket at any of the mansions. The society also runs various tours throughout the year including walking tours in the summer, holiday decoration tours, and a Behind-The-Scenes tour. Call or check the Web site for schedule and prices. | 401/847–1000 | www.newportmansions.org | $10–$25.

Belcourt Castle. Richard Morris Hunt based this 1894 Gothic Revival mansion, built for banking heir Oliver H. P. Belmont (of the Belmont Race Track), on Louis XIII's hunting lodge. The house is filled with so many priceless European and Asian treasures that locals have dubbed it the "Metropolitan Museum of Newport." Don't miss the Golden Coronation Coach. This is the only Newport mansion in which the owners still reside. | 657 Bellevue Ave. | 401/846–0669 or 401/849–1566 | www.belcourtcastle.com | $10 | June–mid-Oct., Mon.–Sat. 9–5, Sun. 10–5; mid-Oct.–May, weekends 10–4.

★   **The Breakers.** The grandest of the mansions their owners called "cottages" was built for steamship and railroad heir Cornelius Vanderbilt II, amazingly in just two years. Designed by Richard Morris Hunt as a Renaissance-style palace, the Breakers has an acoustically perfect music room complete with gold ceiling, a blue marble fireplace in the ballroom, rose alabaster pillars in the dining room, and a porch with a mosaic ceiling that took Italian workers six months to complete. | Ochre Point Ave. | 401/847–1000 | www.newportmansions.org | $15 | Daily 9–5.

The Elms. In 1901, architect Horace Trumbauer built the Elms for Philadelphian coal baron Edward Julius Berwind. Trumbauer paid homage to the French neoclassical style of the Château d'Asnières near Paris. The house was intended as a setting for the Berwind's extensive art collections. The gardens are the finest in Newport and are labeled, providing an exemplary botany lesson. On the behind-the-scenes tour you learn about the inner workings of the house and the staff who kept it all running smoothly. Reserve 24 hours in advance for this tour. | Bellevue Ave. | 401/847–1000 | www.newportmansions.org | $10, behind-the-scenes tour $15 | Daily 10–6 (last tours at 5), behind-the-scenes tour daily 10–4 on the hr.

★   **Hunter House.** The French admiral Charles Louis d'Arsac de Ternay used this fine Georgian-colonial house, built in 1748, as his Revolutionary War headquarters. The carved pineapple over the door was a symbol of hospitality throughout colonial America; a fresh pineapple placed out front signaled an invitation to neighbors to visit a returned seaman or to look over a shop's new stock. Pieces made by the very best Newport colonial cabinetmakers furnish much of the house. | 54 Washington St. | 401/847–7516 | www.newportmansions.org | $10 | May–Oct., daily 10–6 (last tours at 5).

Kingscote. The first of the mansions on Bellevue Avenue, Kingscote was built in 1839 for Georgia planter George Noble Jones. The Gothic Revival property was sold to the King family of the China trade during the Civil War and expanded under the direction of McKim, Mead & White. Today it is filled with antique furniture, glass, and Asian art, and contains a number of unusual features including a cork ceiling and several Tiffany windows. | Bowery St. off Bellevue Ave. | 401/847–1000 | fax 401/847–1361 | www.newportmansions.org | $10 | May–Oct., daily 10–6 (last tours at 5).

★   **Rough Point.** Originally built for Frederick W. Vanderbilt, tobacco magnate James Duke bought this house in 1922. His daughter, Doris Duke, hosted such celebrities as Elizabeth Taylor here. Furnishings range from the grand to peculiar (count the mother-of-pearl bedroom suite among the latter), but Duke's taste in art, especially English portraiture, was pretty sharp: of all the Newport mansions, Duke's has the best art collection. Tours leave from the Newport Gateway Visitor's Center (23 America's Cup Ave.). Reservations can also be made on the Web site. | 680 Bellevue Ave., at Ocean Dr. | 401/845–9124 | www.www.newportrestoration.com | $25 | Daily 10–6. Tours Tues.–Sat. 10–3:20, every 20 mins.

Touro Synagogue. Founded in 1658, this is the oldest synagogue in the United States, and the only one surviving from colonial times. Designed by respected colonial architect Peter Harrison, it is considered his best work, and it ranks among the best examples of 18th-century architecture in America. Washington's letter to the synagogue in 1790 is the classic expression of religious freedom in America. He wrote: ". . . to bigotry no sanction, to persecution no assistance . . ." | 85 Touro St. | 401/

847–4794 | www.tourosynagogue.org | Free | Daily 10–5. Guided tours July and Aug., Sun.–Fri. 10–5; May, June, Sept., and Oct., weekdays 1–3, Sun. 11–3.

Dining

Asterisk. Contemporary. A former garage, this restaurant has been renovated as a Parisian-style café, with silver mirrors and paintings hanging on the brightly painted walls of the loft-style dining room. Try the crispy salmon with mushrooms and asparagus, or the steak au poivre, or vegetable-filled ravioli. Entertainment some evenings. | 599 Thames St. | 401/841–8833 | No lunch | AE, D, DC, MC, V | $$–$$$$

Atlantic Beach Club. American/Casual. Newport's only restaurant with beachfront dining has great live entertainment inside and outside. Summer days of beach volleyball, live bands, and buff bodies—all visible as you eat at the outdoor deck—seem more like Miami Beach than Easton's Beach. The house cocktail, the A Bomb ($6.50) is a patriotic red, white, and blue mixture of raspberry vodka, lemonade, and curaçao. The outdoor deck has sandwiches and burgers, but head inside to the more formal dining room for huge portions of delicious fresh fish, good salads, and a huge Sunday brunch buffet. | 55 Purgatory Rd., Middletown, just south of Newport | 401/847–2750 | AE, MC, V | $–$$$$

Black Pearl. Continental. Whether you dine in the venerable Commodore's Room ($$$–$$$$) or opt for the casual Tavern or waterside patio ($$–$$$), this favorite old Newport restaurant is sure to please. The water-view Commodore's Room is reminiscent of an elegant ship's interior and has black-tie service. It is famous for its creamy clam chowder and the classic menu includes fried Brie, swordfish with tomato-basil beurre blanc, and New England lobster tail stuffed with Maryland jumbo lump crabmeat. Jacket is required and reservations are essential in the Commodore's Room, and no jeans, shorts, or sneakers are allowed. | Bannister's Wharf | 401/846–5264 | Closed Jan.–mid-Feb. | AE, MC, V | $–$$$$

Brick Alley Pub. American. The lines start forming early at this midtown favorite, but fortunately a bar, four dining rooms, and a brick walled patio offer a lot of seating. A real 1938 Red Chevrolet truck divides two rooms, and artifacts and memorabilia of old Newport abound. Try the generous ultimate nachos. Kids under nine have a special menu and are supplied with free beverage and dessert, crayons, and a selection from a treasure chest. | 140 Thames St., 02840 | 401/849–6334 | fax 401/848–5640 | www.brickalley.com | AE, D, DC, MC, V | $–$$$

Clarke Cooke House. American. If you had to pick the quintessential Newport eatery it would be the ever-classic Clarke Cooke House in the middle of the Bannister Wharf tourist and shopping district. With more than 20 shops, the area was as bustling 150 years ago as it is today. There are several different restaurants in the building, from a casual sushi spot to the more formal Porch, where you can savor delicacies like wood-grilled native swordfish. A similar menu is served in the Candy Store (named for the cigars that, at this writing, are still allowed there). In any case, don't miss the clam chowder—probably the best anywhere. Sunday brunch. | Bannister's Wharf | 401/849–2900 | No lunch weekdays | AE, D, DC, MC, V | $$$$

White Horse Tavern. American. Dine in a beautifully decorated colonial home in the oldest continually operating restaurant in America. Charming in summer and cozy in winter, White Horse has well-prepared, old-fashioned American classics like roasted breast of free-range chicken with lemon and rosemary, and a traditional preparation of lobster poached in butter. At this writing, the tavern plans to open for lunch; call ahead. | 26 Marlborough St., at Farewell St. | 401/849–3600 | Reservations essential | No lunch | AE, D, DC, MC, V | $$$–$$$$

Lodging

Best Western Mainstay Inn. This grand house near the beach, which was designed and built in 1866 by George Champlin Mason, has an impressive collection of the work of Newport's women artists. The inn's guests are pampered with a choice of 17 different pillows, elaborate bath amenities, or more than a dozen bottled waters. Each rooms has a fireplace and a two-person whirlpool tub; one has secret doors. Personal service is a hallmark here. There's musical entertainment in summer. Children under 12 stay free. Restaurant, room service, cable TV, pool, bar, business services, airport shuttle, no-smoking rooms. | 151 Admiral Kalbfus Rd., 02840, 1 mi west of downtown | 401/849–9880 or 800/528–1234 | fax 401/849–4391 | www.bestwestern.com | 165 rooms | AE, D, DC, MC, V | $$–$$$

Castle Hill Inn & Resort. On a 40-acre peninsula overlooking Narragansett Bay and the Atlantic, this beautifully renovated, turreted 1874 Victorian inn and adjacent beach houses have everything you could want, including marble showers, fireplaces in each room, and period furnishings. The beach-house and harbor-house rooms are more modern and luxurious. In summer there is a popular Sunday brunch. A full English tea is served each afternoon. There are hiking trails to the Castle Hill Lighthouse and a private beach. Restaurant, in-room data ports, some in-room hot tubs, some kitchenettes, some refrigerators, some in-room VCRs, spa, hiking, beach, bar, laundry service; no smoking. | 590 Ocean Ave., 02840 | 401/849–3800 or 888/466–1355 | fax 401/849–3838 | www.castlehillinn.com | 25 rooms | BP | AE, D, DC, MC, V | $$–$$$$

Hotel Viking. An inn expressly built in 1926 for the guests of mansion owners, the redbrick Viking is elegantly situated at the north end of Bellevue Avenue. The wood paneling and original chandeliers evoke the hotel's sophisticated history. The stately rooms, adorned with reproduction colonial furniture and appointments (draperies and spreads), resemble the grand homes of colonial merchant seamen. Restaurant, indoor pool, hot tub, sauna, bar, meeting rooms, no-smoking rooms. | 1 Bellevue Ave., 02840 | 401/847–3300 or 800/556–7126 | fax 401/848–4864 | www.hotelviking.com | 218 rooms, 4 suites | AE, D, DC, MC, V | $$–$$$$

★ **Ivy Lodge.** The only B&B in the mansion district, this grand (though small by Newport's standards) Victorian has gables and a Gothic turret, as well as 11 fireplaces, large and lovely rooms, a spacious dining room, window seats, and two common rooms. The defining feature is a Gothic-style oak entryway with a three-story turned-baluster staircase and a dangling wrought-iron chandelier. In summer relax in wicker chairs on the wraparound porch. Guests can use the Newport Athletic Club. Cliff Walk is just two blocks away; the beach is 1/2-mi from the inn. Some in-room data ports, some in-room hot tubs, some refrigerators, cable TV, some in-room VCRs, no-smoking rooms. | 12 Clay St., 02840 | 401/849–6865 or 800/834–6865 | fax 401/849–0704 | www.ivylodge.com | 7 rooms, 1 suite | BP | AE, D, MC, V | $$–$$$$

Westerly

Babcock-Smith House. The gambrel-roof, early-Georgian home was built for Westerly's first physician, Dr. Joshua Babcock, in 1734. A 19th-century resident of the house, Orlando Smith, discovered granite on the property; Westerly later developed into one of the country's leading granite centers. | 124 Granite St. (U.S. 1) | 401/596–5704 | $5 | May, June, and Sept., Sun. 2–5; July and Aug., Sun. and Wed. 2–5, or by appointment.

Misquamicut State Beach. Strip motels jostle for attention in Misquamicut, where a giant water slide, a carousel, miniature golf, a game arcade, children's rides, batting cages, and fast-food stands attract visitors to Atlantic Avenue. The mile-long beach is accessible year-round, but the amusements are open only between Memorial Day and Labor Day. | 257 Atlantic Ave. | 401/596–9097 | www.riparks.com | Beach free, parking $14 per car | Memorial Day–Labor Day, daily 9–5.

Water Wizz. Just across from Misquamicut Beach you hear the happy screams from the sliders at Water Wizz, which has a 35-foot giant water slide, and 50-foot speed slides. | 330 Atlantic Ave. | 401/322–0520 | www.visitri.com/waterwizz | $27 | Memorial Day–mid-June, weekends 10–6; mid-June–Labor Day, daily 10–6.

Wilcox Park. Eighteen acres of "Victorian Strolling Gardens" include specimen trees, shrubs, and perennial gardens. A Dwarf Conifer Garden illustrates creative use of small plots. A Garden of the Senses has plants with taste, texture, or fragrance with labels in Braille and raised letters. The lily pond hosts abundant waterfowl, exotic koi, and goldfish and doubles as a skating rink in winter. | 44 Broad St. | 401/596–2877 | Free | Daily dawn–9 PM.

Dining

Prime Time Cafe. American/Casual. The pleasant purple room with big windows over the river that divides Westerly, Rhode Island, from Pawcatuck, Connecticut, is the perfect little spot for a meal in the burger, salad, or sandwich categories. | 1 W. Broad St. | 860/599–3840 | MC, V | ¢–$$

Shelter Harbor Inn. American. In the Westerly community of Shelter Harbor, a farmhouse built in 1700 is now an inn and restaurant serving traditional colonial fare with some updated surprises. The frequently changing menu might include smoked scallops and capellini or pecan-crusted duck breast. Breakfast is good every day, but Sunday brunch is especially popular. There is outdoor dining on two terraces. | 10 Wagner Rd., off U.S. 1 | 401/322–8883 | AE, D, DC, MC, V | $$–$$$$

Weekapaug Inn. Contemporary. The open dining room of this charming inn—replete with linens, silver, flowers, and candlelight—has impressive views of the saltwater tidal pond. Nightly specials might include coffee-crusted filet mignon, or smoked tomato-risotto-stuffed calamari, corn-bread-stuffed quail, baked sea bass with crispy leeks, or dill-marinated grilled salmon. BYOB. Breakfast served. | Spray Rock Rd. | 401/322–0301 | Reservations essential | Jacket required | Closed Sept.–June | No credit cards | $$–$$$$

SOUTH CAROLINA

SEA ISLANDS
THE LOW COUNTRY

Distance: 90 mi   Time: 2 days
Overnight Break: Beaufort

The romantic, saltwater marsh–studded coastal lands of the South Carolina low country, once the domain of rice and cotton planters, set the tone for this drive that passes pristine wetlands framed by palmettos and oaks dripping with Spanish moss. Half of the state's 190-mi ocean shoreline is on these islands, which reach south from Charleston to the Savannah River.

If you're looking for prime beach weather but want to avoid the crowds, go in May or September. Fall and spring are generally lovely and mild—not too chilly or too hot to stroll historic districts or take a canoe ride down gentle rivers. The seafood is fresh and plentiful in these parts, and golf courses have spectacular coastal views.

❶ Start the tour on **Hilton Head Island** (108 mi southwest of Charleston, 164 mi southeast of Columbia, access from I–95, Exit 8 over bridge on U.S. 278). The **Welcome Center and Coastal Discovery Museum** has background information on the island, as well as information about tours. Harbour Town on **Sea Pines,** the oldest and best known of Hilton Head's resort developments, occupies 4,500 thickly wooded acres and has three golf courses, a wide beach, tennis clubs, stables, and shopping plazas. There's quite a bit of outlet shopping on Hilton Head, too.

❷ From Hilton Head, you can take a ferry to nearby **Daufuskie Island** (south of Hilton Head) for a day tour. Though there is now a resort on the island and development continues to encroach, many inhabitants—the descendants of former slaves—live on small farms among remnants of churches, homes, and schools.

❸ The 40-mi route between Hilton Head and Beaufort is one of the most beautiful. In **Beaufort,** which was settled by rich planters, graceful antebellum homes and churches are generally all within walking distance. Tour it by foot or by bike with a map from the chamber of commerce, or take a carriage tour. A few miles away is the **Parris Island U.S. Marine Corps Base,** which welcomes visitors and even gives guided tours. The **Parris Island Museum** exhibits uniforms, photographs, and

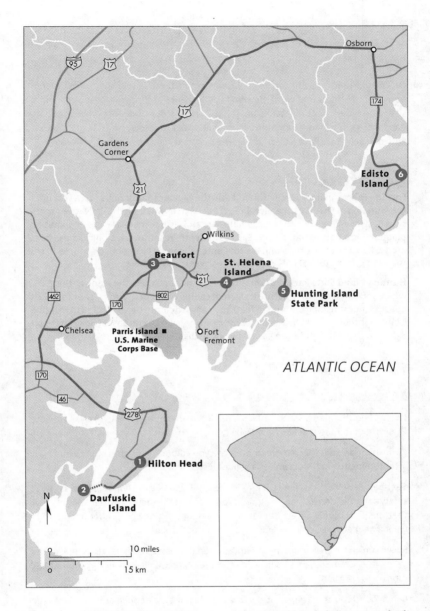

weapons chronicling military history since 1562, when the French Huguenots built a fort here.

④ **St. Helena Island** is the site of the historic **Penn Center,** which served as the first school in the country for freed slaves. Now unofficial headquarters of the Gullah culture, the center is devoted to the preservation of the language, culture, and history of the Sea Islands' Gullah community, which consists of descendants of African slaves brought to the Sea Islands of South Carolina and Georgia.

⑤ From St. Helena Island, head south on U.S. 21 to Hunting Island. **Hunting Island State Park** has a secluded domain of beach, nature trails, camping, and fishing along its

3 mi of public beach—some of it dramatically eroding. The 1,120-foot fishing pier is among the longest on the East Coast. You can climb the 181 steps of the 140-foot Hunting Island Lighthouse (built in 1859 and abandoned in 1933) for sweeping views.

❻ On **Edisto Island,** ancient tomato fields and colonial-era plantations and churches flank country roads that wind through bucolic scenes of simple wood-frame homes sitting on the edge of tidal creeks and salt marshes. Mostly undeveloped, Edisto Beach has modest, one-family rental beach houses and a couple of no-frills restaurants. **Edisto Beach State Park** has cabins by the marsh and campsites by the ocean.

Beaufort

Fort San Felipe. Spaniards built this fort and the village of Santa Elena just a year after the founding of St. Augustine, Florida. Fort San Marcos was added after Native Americans destroyed the town in 1576. Remains are still visible; there are also explanation plaques and a nature trail on-site. Each summer there are archaeological digs; maps are available at the Parris Island Visitor Center. | Behind the depot golf course, Parris Island | 843/228–3650 | Free | Weekdays 9–5, weekends noon–4.

Hunting Island State Park. A dramatically eroding beach sets the scene at this park, where you can swim, walk nature trails, rent cabins, camp, or fish from one of the East Coast's longest fishing piers (1,120 feet). You can also climb the 140-foot 1859 Hunting Island Lighthouse. | 2555 Sea Island Pkwy., Hunting Island, 17 mi east of Beaufort | 843/838–2011 | Park $3, lighthouse 50¢ | Daily 8 AM–dusk.

SOUTH CAROLINA RULES OF THE ROAD

License Requirements: South Carolina's minimum driving age is 16 with a valid driver's license. An international license may be used for 90 days.

Right Turn on Red: Everywhere in the state you can make a right turn at a red light after coming to a full stop, unless a sign is posted forbidding it.

Seat-Belt & Helmet Laws: All persons in the front seat of a moving vehicle must wear safety belts. Children 6 years of age and younger must be secured in a child safety seat that meets National Safety Commission standards. All persons under age 21 must wear a helmet while riding a motorcycle in South Carolina.

Speed Limits: The maximum speed allowed on South Carolina highways is 65 mph unless otherwise noted. Speed limits in residential areas are usually between 35 mph and 45 mph.

Other Regulations: It is against the law to have any type of open alcoholic beverage in moving vehicles. The legal blood-alcohol concentration limit is .10%. At this writing, handheld phone use is legal while driving in South Carolina, but legislation is pending.

For More Information: South Carolina Department of Public Safety | 803/896–9950 or 877/349–7187 | www.scdps.org. South Carolina Department of Transportation | 803/737–2314 | www.dot.state.sc.us.

Marine Corps Recruit Depot. Take a self-guided driving tour through this boot camp, which trains about 20,000 U.S. Marines a year. The grounds include a small historic district, the drill instructor school, a rifle range, the parade field, and the Iwo Jima monument. You can pick up a map of the base at the visitor center, located across from the post office, where all visitors must sign in. | Hwy. 21, then follow signs, Parris Island, 3 mi north of Beaufort | 843/228–3650 | www.mcrdpi.usmc.mil | Visitor center Mon.–Wed. 8:30–4:30, Thurs. 7:30–7, Fri. 7:30–4:30, weekends noon–4.

Parris Island Museum. More than 400 years of military history are chronicled through displays of uniforms, weapons, and photos. | Marine Corps Recruit Depot, Parris Island Bldg. 111 | 843/228–2951 | Free | Sat.–Wed. 10–4:30, Thurs. 10–7, Fri. 8–4:30.

Penn Center. In 1862, Quaker missionaries from the North founded this school for freed slaves; it is now one of the most important African-American historical sites in the United States. In the early 1960s Dr. Martin Luther King Jr. used the center as a training and meeting facility for civil rights workers. Today it preserves the history of the Sea Islands' Gullah community. Many of the campus buildings remain, including a gym, dormitories, and administrative buildings which can be visited on a self-guided tour. The York W. Bailey Museum, formerly the school's industrial building, has displays on the heritage of Sea Islands' blacks. Another building, once the home-economics department, is now a library and archives. | Penn Campus, 16 Penn Circle W, St. Helena Island | 843/838–2432 | www.penncenter.com | $4 | Center daily dawn–dusk, museum Mon.–Sat. 11–4.

Dining

Beaufort Inn. Continental. The mahogany-paneled dining room in this Victorian inn exudes a formal atmosphere, while the wine bar is clubby, with booths and black leather. Try the crispy flounder with yucca chips, or have an appetizer at the bar. You can dine outside on the porch. Sunday brunch. Breakfast served. | 809 Port Republic St. | 843/521–9000 | No lunch | AE, D, MC, V | $$$–$$$$

11th Street Dockside. Seafood. Nearly every table looks out over the water at this classic wharf-side restaurant with a screened porch. Fried oysters, shrimp, fresh fish, a steamed seafood pot, and seafood pasta are the main attractions. | 1699 11th St. W, Port Royal, 5 mi southwest of Beaufort | 843/524–7433 | No lunch | AE, D, DC, MC, V | $$–$$$

Emily's. Continental. One block off the main thoroughfare, this wood-paneled restaurant begins serving tapas at 4:30. If you want to follow up with dinner, your choices might include steak au poivre, Wiener schnitzel, or soft-shell crabs. | 906 Port Republic St. | 843/522–1866 | Closed Sun. No lunch | AE, D, MC, V | $$$

Shrimp Shack. Seafood. Shrimp burgers—deep-fried ground shrimp meat patties—are the specialty at this tiny, ramshackle shack on the way to Hunting Island and across from the marina where boats unload fresh catches. It's open 11 AM to 8:30. | 129 Sea Island Pkwy., St. Helena Island, 9 mi southeast of Beaufort | 843/838–2962 | Closed Sun. | No credit cards | $–$$

Lodging

Beaufort Inn. Gables grace the exterior of this 1930s inn, and antique reproductions and comfortable chairs highlight the rooms, some of which also have fireplaces. Several historic cottages with guest rooms surround the property, including a carriage house with living room and full kitchen. Restaurant, fans, in-room data ports, refrigerators, cable TV, wine bar, business services; no kids under 8 in rooms and some cottages, no smoking. | 809 Port Republic St., 29902 | 843/521–9000 | fax 843/521–9500 | www.beaufortinn.com | 16 rooms, 2 cottages | CP | AE, D, MC, V | $$$–$$$$

Best Western Sea Island Inn. The entrance of this well-maintained chain hotel faces the Beaufort Historic Waterfront on the Intracoastal Waterway. Rooms are basic, and the hotel is in the historic district within walking distance of 18th-century homes, gourmet dining, shops, and art galleries. In-room data ports, cable TV, pool, gym, business services. | 1015 Bay St., 29902 | 843/522–2090 | fax 843/521–4858 | www.bestwestern.com | CP | AE, D, DC, MC, V | $$

Howard Johnson Express Inn. Large trees shade this white stucco building on the edge of a marsh. Rooms overlook the river and get plenty of sunlight. The hotel is 5 mi from beaches and 5 mi from Parris Island. Microwaves, refrigerators, cable TV, pool, fishing, business services, some pets allowed. | 3651 Trask Pkwy. (Hwy. 21), 29902 | 843/524–6020 or 800/406–1411 | fax 843/524–2070 | 63 rooms | CP | AE, D, DC, MC, V | $

★**Rhett House Inn.** Dating back to 1820, this house bordering the historic district and the Intracoastal Waterway has sprawling verandas and white columns harking back to the Old South. Many rooms have gas fireplaces, private balconies, and whirlpool baths. Fresh-cut flowers throughout the inn add a nice touch. Some in-room hot tubs, cable TV, bicycles, business services; no kids under 5. | 1009 Craven St., 29902 | 843/524–9030 or 888/480–9530 | fax 843/524–1310 | www.rhetthouseinn.com | 17 rooms | BP | AE, MC, V | $$$

Edisto Island

ACE Basin National Wildlife Refuge. Named for the rivers that surround it (the Ashepoo, Combahee, and Edisto), this 850,000-acre area is one of the largest, most pristine estuarine ecosystems in North America. More than 100 bird species, sea turtles, otters, and other wildlife live here, some of which are endangered or threatened. | Grove Plantation, Jebossee Island Rd. | 843/889–3084 | Free | Daily dawn–dusk.

Edisto Beach State Park. You can do some excellent shell collecting on the nearly 3 mi of beach at this park; there are also cabins and an ocean-side campsite. To get to the park from Charleston, take Highway 17 South, then Highway 174 East for 28 mi until it ends at the entrance to Edisto Beach. | Hwy. 174 E | 843/869–2756 | Free | Daily 8–6.

Edisto Island Presbyterian Church. Though founded in 1685, the present church dates to 1830. The pink mausoleum of the Legare family at the back of the church's cemetery is said to be haunted by the ghost of Julia Legare, who was inadvertently buried alive there as a child. | 2164 Hwy. 174 | 843/869–2326 | Free | Grounds and cemetery daily 9–5, church open only during services.

Edisto Museum. Artifacts and historical items about the history of Edisto are displayed in this tiny museum. | 2343 Hwy. 174 | 843/869–1954 | $3 | Tues. and Thurs.–Sat. 1–4.

Edisto Water Sports and Tackle. You can sign up for tours of the ACE Basin, inshore and offshore fishing charters, kayaking, parasailing, and shelling cruises. | 3731 Dockside Rd. | 843/869–0663 | Apr.–Nov., daily 7–7; Dec.–Mar., daily 8–5.

Plantation and Island Tours. Native Edistonian Jann Poston gives two-hour van tours of several plantations (most are private), churches, and other points of interest in the area; it's best to reserve two to three days in advance. | Tours leave from the Old Post Office restaurant, 1442 Hwy. 174 | 843/869–1110 | $20 | Tues.–Sat. 10 AM, by reservation.

Dining

Old Post Office. Contemporary. A former post office now houses a simple but elegant dining room where local artwork adorns the walls and old mailboxes decorate the entry. Try the shrimp and grits or the pecan-coated quail with duck-stock gravy. | 1442 Hwy. 174 | 843/869–2339 | Closed Sun., closed Mon. Nov.–Apr. No lunch | MC, V | $$–$$$

Hilton Head Island

Adventure Cruises. You can sign up for 1½- to 2-hour boating excursions, including dolphin-watching, crabbing, dinner cruises, and trips to Daufuskie Island, or charter a fishing trip. | Shelter Cove Marina | 843/785–4558 | $19 | Dolphin cruises weekdays at 11, 2, 5, and 7, Sat. at 11 AM and 7 PM; crabbing excursions Memorial Day–Labor Day, weekdays at 9:30, 11:30, 2, and 4, Sat. at 9 AM; call for times rest of yr.

Audubon–Newhall Preserve. Fifty acres of pristine forest on the south of the island are filled with native plant life, identified and tagged. There are also trails, a self-guided tour, and seasonal plant walks. | Palmetto Bay Rd. | 843/785–5775 | Free | Daily dawn–dusk.

Coastal Discovery Museum. A permanent collection depicts Native American life, and there are changing exhibits as well. Tours of forts, plantations, and Native American sites are given randomly throughout the year. Beach walks vary according to the season, but generally are weekdays during the summer, Tuesday through Thursday the rest of year, and are almost always at low tide. | 100 William Hilton Pkwy. | 843/689–6767 | www.coastaldiscovery.org | Donations accepted | Mon.–Sat. 9–5, Sun. 10–3.

Hilton Head Factory Stores 1 and 2. J. Crew, GAP, Brooks Brothers, Harry and David, and Timberland are some of the more than 80 outlets here. | U.S. 78 | 843/837–4339 | Free | Mon.–Sat. 10–9, Sun. 11–6.

James M. Waddell Jr. Mariculture Research and Development Center. Tour the 24 ponds and research building to see how methods of raising commercial seafood are studied. | Sawmill Creek Rd. | 843/837–3795 | Free | Tours weekdays at 10 AM and by appointment.

Pinckney Island National Wildlife Refuge. Fourteen miles of biking and walking trails lace their way through more than 4,000 acres of salt marsh and small islands ½ mi west of Hilton Head Island. | U.S. 278 | 912/652–4415 | Free | Daily dawn–dusk.

Savannah National Wildlife Refuge. A nature drive winds through this 26,000-acre preserve that was once a community of rice plantations. It's now a sanctuary for migratory birds and other wildlife. | U.S. 17, 8 mi south of Hardeeville | 912/652–4415 | Free | Daily dawn–dusk.

Sea Pines Forest Preserve. On Sea Pines Plantation, this 605-acre public wilderness tract has walking trails, a well-stocked fishing pond, a waterfowl pond, and a 3,400-year-old Native American shell ring, a mound of shellfish remnants formed by age-old Native American "oyster roasts." You can take self-guided or guided tours. | Sea Pines Recreation Department, 175 Greenwood Dr. | 843/842–1449 or 843/363–4530 | $5 | Daily dawn–dusk, except during Heritage Golf Classic in Apr.

Shelter Cove Marina, South Beach Marina, and Skull Creek Marina. All three of these marinas offer kayak nature trips as well as boat rentals and fishing charters. Call for schedules and prices. | Shelter Cove Marina: 1 Shelter Cove La., Palmetto Dunes | 843/842–7001 | South Beach Marina: 233 S. Sea Pines Dr. | 843/671–6699 | Skull Creek Marina: 1 Waterway La. | 843/681–8436.

Dining

Brick Oven Cafe. American/Casual. Velvet drapes, massive chandeliers, and leather booths give a stately feel to this restaurant, which serves pizzas, salads, and pastas until 1 AM. | 25 Park Plaza | 843/686–2233 | No lunch | AE, D, DC, MC, V | $$–$$$

Longhorn Steak. Steak. Bulls' heads, antique pistols, chaps, and spurs hang on the walls; peanut shells cover the floor; and country music plays in the background. Try the Jack Daniels–flavored baked beans and the namesake steaks. Kids' menu. | 841 U.S. 278 | 843/686–4056 | AE, D, DC, MC, V | $–$$$

Old Fort Pub. Southern. Overlooking the marshlands of the Intracoastal Waterway, this casual restaurant serves up such specialties as grilled veal chop with warm Mediterranean salad and pork porterhouse with smoked pear compote. Sunday brunch. | 65 Skull Creek Dr. | 843/681–2386 | AE, D, DC, MC, V | $$–$$$$

Old Oyster Factory. Seafood. Sit on the outdoor deck over the water or inside by the bay windows overlooking Broad Creek. On Tuesday nights in summer the restaurant has excellent views of the town's fireworks. Steamed and raw oysters as well as grilled tilapia are popular dishes. Live music keeps the place hopping late into the night. Kids' menu. | 101 Marshland Rd. | 843/681–6040 | No lunch | AE, D, DC, MC, V | $–$$$

Scott's Fish Market. Seafood. Indoor and outdoor dining are available at this water-front restaurant. Fresh fish is delivered daily; try the pan-seared yellowfin tuna or barbe-cued grouper. Full bar. | Harbourside 1 | 843/785–7575 | Closed Jan., closed Sun. Sept.–May. No lunch | AE, D, DC, MC, V | $$–$$$

THE UPCOUNTRY ALONG THE CHEROKEE FOOTHILLS

ALONG THE CHEROKEE FOOTHILLS SCENIC HIGHWAY

Distance: about 75 mi   Time: 2 days
Overnight Breaks: Clemson, Pendleton

The Carolina Upcountry, renowned for its magnificent scenery and state parks, headlines this drive. Traveling along the Cherokee Foothills Scenic Highway, you travel through peach orchards, tiny mountain towns, and wooded and rocky foothills spiked with waterfalls. The more adventurous can add an extra day to head farther west from Pendleton and raft the Chattooga River.

❶ Begin your tour at the junction of I–85 and Route 11 outside of **Gaffney.** Head west along the **Cherokee Foothills Scenic Highway** (SC 11). Cherokees, and then English and French fur traders, once used this route, which winds through lush forests and along sparkling lakes. The section that travels through Cherokee County is studded with peach orchards; you can see the colorful blossoms each spring and eat the fruit at busy roadside stands in summer.

❷ **Cowpens National Battlefield** is a rustic colonial site where the American militia defeated the British. A walking trail takes visitors through the battlefield; there are also a marked road tour, a visitor center, and a short video presentation.

❸ **Caesar's Head State Park.** On a clear day you can see the sweep of the Blue Ridge Mountains from the elevation of 3,208 feet. The view of **Raven Cliff Falls,** a 420-foot-high cascade, is easily worth the 2-mi hike.

❹ At **Table Rock State Park,** with its landmark rounded dome, has rustic cabins, campsites, lake swimming, canoe and boat rentals, and hiking trails. The Cherokee Foothills Visitor Center is in the park.

❺ **Keowee–Toxaway State Natural Area** has camping, hiking, and picnic areas along Lake Keowee on land that once belonged to the Cherokees. The Cherokee Indian Inter-pretive Center traces the history and culture of the Cherokee Indian Nation.

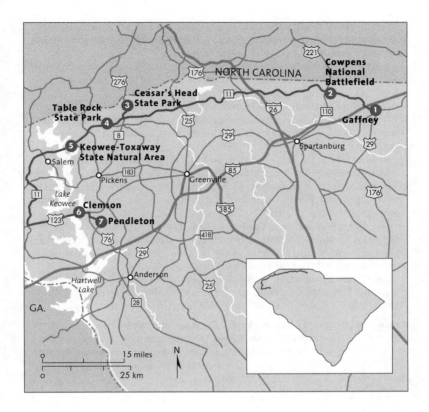

○ 15 miles
○ 25 km
N

6 Continue along Route 11, then take Route 123 East for 12 mi into **Clemson.** The 288-acre **South Carolina Botanical Garden** is filled with blooming plants and trees, heirloom gardens, and nature trails. On-site is the **Fran Hanson Discovery Center,** with exhibits on life in the Upcountry, and the impressive **Bob Campbell Geology Museum.** Also on the Clemson University campus is must-see **Fort Hill,** John C. Calhoun's plantation home. It is now a house museum and National Historic Landmark displaying items that once belonged to Calhoun and his son-in-law, Thomas Clemson. At the **Hendrix Student Center** you can buy the university's famous Clemson blue cheese, plus ice cream and milk shakes.

7 **Pendleton,** the historic district anchored by a charming town square, counts antiques shops and cafés among its more than 40 points of interest. The **Pendleton Visitor Center,** in the 1850 mercantile **Hunter's Store,** has an impressive archive library upstairs. The 1828 **Farmers' Society Hall,** on the town square with a restaurant on the ground floor, is the oldest farmers' hall still in continuous use in the United States.

Clemson

Clemson University. Founded on the estate of Thomas Green Clemson in 1889, the university began as a small agricultural college, and that heritage remains—more than 17,000 acres of farm and woodland surrounding the campus are devoted to research. Student guides conduct walking tours. | 109 Daniel Dr. | 864/656–4789 | www.clemson.edu | Free | University daily; visitor center weekdays 8–4:30, Sat. 9–4:30, Sun. 1–4:30.

Bob Campbell Geology Museum. This museum has interactive exhibits, fossils, minerals and plenty of sparkling gems. | 103 Garden Trail | 864/656–4600 | www.clemson.edu/geomuseum | $3 | Thurs.–Sat. 10–5, Sun. 1–5.

Fort Hill. The antebellum plantation home of John C. Calhoun stands in the center of campus. | Fort Hill St. | 864/656–2475 | Donations accepted | Mon.–Sat. 10–noon and 1–4, Sun. 2–4:30.

Fran Hanson Discovery Center. Natural, historic, and cultural sites in the Upcountry are the focus of exhibits here. You can also get information on the Heritage Corridor, a tourism trail that stretches 250 mi across the state. | 101 Garden Trail | 864/656–4470 | Free | Mon.–Sat. 9–5, Sun. 1–5.

Hanover House. The house museum, built in 1716 by French Huguenots, is on the grounds of the South Carolina Botanical Garden, and is a monument of early French-colonial architecture. It's furnished with 18th- and 19th-century artifacts. | 101 Garden Trail | 864/656–2241 | Donations accepted | Sat. 10–noon and 1–4:30, excluding football home game days; Sun. 2–4:30.

South Carolina Botanical Garden. Azaleas, camellias, hostas, daffodils, and wildflowers are among the flora at this 288-acre garden. Attractions include nature trails and a nature-based sculpture program. | 102 Garden Trail | 864/656–3405 | www.clemson.edu/scbg | Free | Daily 8 AM–dusk.

Tiger Treats. Buy agricultural products made in Clemson, including Clemson blue cheese and blue cheese dressing, ice cream, and other dairy treats at this shop. | Hendrix Student Center | 864/656–3663 | Mon.–Sat. 9–11, Sun. 1–11.

Keowee–Toxaway State Natural Area. A Cherokee Interpretive Center traces the history and culture of the Cherokee Nation. The 1,000-acre park also has camping, a large lakefront cabin, RV sites, and hiking and picnic areas along Lake Keowee. | Rte. 11 | 864/868–2605 | $2 | Park Apr.–Oct., daily 9–9; Nov.–Mar., daily 9–6. Interpretive center daily 11–noon and 4–5 or by appointment.

Stumphouse Tunnel Park. Only a partially sealed tunnel remains of an 1850s project attempting to link Charleston to the Midwest by rail; bring a flashlight so you can walk down the dark, damp 1,300-foot length of the passageway that's open to the public. In one section it continuously "rains" from an opening to the sky above. Scenic hiking is plentiful, especially at the 200-foot Isaqueena Falls. There are nearby picnic areas. | Hwy. 28, Walhalla, 8 mi northwest of Clemson | 864/638–4343 | www.stumphousetunnel.com | Free | Daily 10–5.

Dining

Riviera. Mediterranean. Clemson's best-kept secret is this minimally decorated family-run and -owned restaurant whose Greek and Turkish dishes are prepared by the family matriarch. You can eat outside on a patio. Local musicians perform occasionally. | 391 Old Greenville Hwy. (Hwy. 93) | 864/653–8855 | D, MC, V | $

Tiger Town Tavern. American. A full wooden bar serves cheap beer on tap at this longtime college haunt, which also has club sandwiches, blackened chicken, and great hamburgers. | 368 College Ave. | 864/654–5901 | Closed Sun. | D, MC, V | ¢–$

Lodging

Ramada Inn Clemson. Well established with good management, this four-story chain has rooms surrounding a palm-filled atrium. The hotel has a fun restaurant and offers access to the local Gold's Gym. Weeknights there are complimentary drinks and snacks. Restaurant, in-room data ports, some microwaves, some refrigerators, cable TV with movies, indoor pool, hot tub, bar, business services, meeting rooms, no smoking rooms. | 1310 Tiger Blvd., 29631 | 864/654–7501 | fax 864/654–7301 | ramadaclemson.com | 148 | CP | MC, V | $

Pendleton

Ashtabula. Built in 1825, this two-story clapboard house on 10 acres has been restored and furnished to depict life on an Upcountry farm in the 1850s. | Hwy. 88 | 864/646–3782 or 800/862–1795 | $5 | Apr.–Oct., Sun. 2–6 or by appointment.

Chattooga National Wild and Scenic River. Rapids, waterfalls, and steep cliffs as well as gentle bends and calm pools punctuate this mountain river—made famous in the movie *Deliverance*—that serves as a border between South Carolina and Georgia.
    U.S. Forest Service. Get information about local outfitters that arrange rafting and canoe trips from the local branch of the U.S. Forest Service. | 112 Andrew Pickens Circle, Mountain Rest | 864/638–9568 | www.fs.fed.us/r8/fms | Free | Daily dawn–dusk.

Farmers' Society Hall. Built in 1828 as a courthouse, this columned Greek Revival building is in the center of the village green and is the oldest farmers' hall still in continuous use in the United States. The meeting hall is on the second floor; the ground floor is now a restaurant. | 105 Exchange St. | 864/646–3782 or 800/862–1795 | Free | By appointment only.

Historic Homes. The entire town of Pendleton is on the National Register of Historic Places. You can pick up a self-guided walking tour brochure from the Pendleton Visitor Center, or stroll through town on your own to view the exteriors of these historic homes. | 864/646–3782 or 800/862–1795.

Pendleton District Agricultural Museum. The first boll weevil found in South Carolina and a collection of antique farm tools and equipment commemorate the area's farming history. Also on display is a cotton gin that predates Eli Whitney's. | History La. | 864/646–3782 or 800/862–1795 | www.pendleton-district.org | Free | By appointment only, weekdays 9–4:30.

Pendleton District Historical, Recreational, and Tourism Commission. Extensive genealogy archives and changing exhibits make this more than the typical tourist commission. Inside the historic Hunter's Store, the commission also has information on area attractions and self-guided walking tours, some on cassette tape. | 125 E. Queen St. | 864/646–3782 or 800/862–1795 | www.pendleton-district.org | Free | Commission weekdays 9–4:30. Store Apr.–Oct., Sat. 10–3, Sun. 1–4:30.

Dining

Farmers' Hall Restaurant. Contemporary. Dine on crab cakes, steak salad, fresh trout, or baked chicken stuffed with spinach and feta in this historic property built in 1824 on the town green. Additional sidewalk seating lets you look out onto the town center. | 105 Exchange St. | 864/646–8161 | No dinner Sun.–Tues. | AE, MC, V | $$

Mac's Drive-In. American. Halfway between Clemson and Pendleton, this restaurant is popular with Clemson athletes. You can sit at the counter and enjoy hamburgers, fries, and sweet tea. | 404 Pendleton Rd. | 864/654–2845 | Closed Sun. | No credit cards | ¢

Lodging

Rocky Retreat. If you want to get away from it all, this 150-year-old farmhouse in a quiet spot might be the place. Spend time exploring the nature trail and the 6½ acres of open grassy fields. Guests rock or swing the time away on the big front porch and help themselves to soft drinks and tea in the kitchen. Spacious rooms have lots of windows, gas fireplaces, pine floors, handmade quilts, and eclectic antiques. Hearty breakfasts include eggs and bacon, grits, and homemade breads and jams. Dining room; no room phones, no room TVs, no kids under 10, no smoking. | 1000 Millwee Creek Rd., 29670, 6½ mi south of town | 864/225–3494 | 4 rooms | BP | AE, MC, V | $

Sunrise Farm Bed & Breakfast. Llamas, ponies, goats, sheep, and a potbellied pig roam on 10 acres of green farmland sprinkled with apple and pecan trees, 100-year old magnolias, and crepe myrtles. Four spacious rooms in the 1890 farmhouse, with its 1,000-square-foot porch, have queen beds, quilts, and sunny linens. Each of the two cottages, one a former corncrib, has a kitchen, living room, fireplace, porch, and gas grill. Dining room, grill, picnic area, fans, microwave, refrigerator, in-room VCRs, bicycles, croquet, playground, some pets allowed (fee); no phones in some rooms, no smoking. | 325 Sunrise Dr., Salem 29676, 25 mi north of Pendleton and 2 mi off Hwy. 11 | 864/944–0121 or 888/991–0121 | fax 864/944–6195 | 4 rooms, 2 cottages | BP | MC, V | $–$$

ALONG THE EDGE OF THE GREAT SMOKY MOUNTAINS
FROM JONESBOROUGH TO DAYTON

Distance: 220 mi   Time: 2 days
Overnight Break: Knoxville

Beginning in the starkly beautiful mountain country east of the Cherokee National Forest, this drive takes you to the eastern edge of the Cumberland Plateau and down into Tennessee's Great Valley. It offers you the chance to explore rural East Tennessee and to learn more about the early history and culture of the region. Take this trip in fall, when the leaves turn gorgeous shades of orange and red. This is not a drive to attempt in winter, when the roads can be treacherous.

❶ Laid out in 1780, **Jonesborough** is the oldest incorporated town in Tennessee and was the site of the protracted struggle over the State of Franklin, which would have been the 14th state. Downtown is well preserved; you can get a tour or maps from the **Jonesborough Visitors Center and History Museum,** which has year-round exhibits and special shows and displays that offer a glimpse of the town's everyday life. The **Chester Inn,** near the visitor center, is the oldest frame structure in Jonesborough and the site of the National Storytelling Festival. Jacob Howard printed the nation's first abolitionist newspapers in the **May-Ledbetter House**; it's now a bed-and-breakfast.

❷ Head southwest of Jonesborough on U.S. 11 East for approximately 15 mi to **Davy Crockett Birthplace State Park,** on the Nolichucky River. Crockett was born here in 1786. The spot is marked by a plaque and a reconstructed cabin.

❸ From Davy Crockett State Park, drive south on U.S. 11 East (U.S. 321) for approximately 3 mi to **Tusculum.** Stop at the **Andrew Johnson Library** to see the president's papers and manuscripts, and a collection of Civil War–era newspapers.

❹ Leaving Tusculum, proceed west for approximately 10 mi on U.S. 11 East to **Greeneville,** site of the **Andrew Johnson National Historic Site.** Two homes of the 17th president,

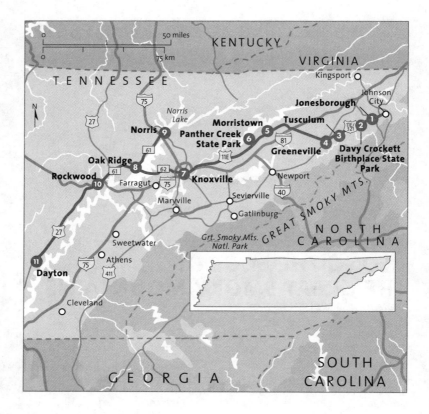

his tailor shop, and his grave site are here. The **Nathaniel Green Museum of Greene County** offers exhibits on Johnson's impeachment and aspects of Greene County history.

⑤ Approximately 20 mi west of Greeneville on U.S. 11 East you'll come to **Morristown,** the boyhood home of Davy Crockett. The **Crockett Tavern and Pioneer Museum** is a reconstruction of the tavern run by Crockett's parents.

⑥ Continue west for about 5 mi on U.S. 11 East to **Panther Creek State Park,** on a portion of Cherokee Reservoir used by the Tennessee Valley Authority for flood-control purposes. The park is ideal for camping and glimpsing deer, waterfowl, and other wildlife.

⑦ **Knoxville** is approximately 40 mi–45 mi west of Panther Creek on U.S. 11 East. This is a good place to spend the night, with a wide variety of dining and hotel options. You might add a day to your tour to see some of the city's attractions. Don't miss the **Blount Museum,** the first frame house west of the Appalachians, or the **Knoxville Museum of Art,** the state's newest and largest art museum.

⑧ Take Route 62 West from Knoxville for approximately 25 mi to **Oak Ridge,** site of the Manhattan Project, the World War II initiative to design and develop nuclear weapons (the first atomic bombs were actually built in Los Alamos, New Mexico). Trivia buffs will want to take note that while scientists tinkered with weaponry in 1940s Oak Ridge, an earnest group called the Oak Ridge Quartet—later known as the country powerhouse Oak Ridge Boys—was just getting its start.

While in Oak Ridge, take in the **American Museum of Science and Energy,** which includes exhibits on the area's atomic history. And consider some walks on the 250 acres and excellent nature trails of the **University of Tennessee Arboretum.**

⑨ Take Rte. 95 (Rte. 61) 15 mi northeast of Oak Ridge to **Norris** to visit the **Museum of Appalachia,** which has re-creations of period cabins, displays of Cherokee baskets, and even old jail cells. While in Norris don't miss the **Lenoir Museum,** which features early Americana, including an 18th-century gristmill next to the museum.

⑩ Take Route 61 South for about 25 mi to U.S. 27 and **Rockwood,** which sits on the southeastern edge of the Cumberland Plateau and offers a terrific view of the Great Valley to the south.

⑪ From Rockwood continue south on U.S. 27 for about 30 mi–35 mi to **Dayton.** Visit the **Rhea County Courthouse,** whose museum has items from the 1925 Scopes Monkey Trial, including the original benches and jury seats.

From Dayton you may wish to continue south on U.S. 27 to Chattanooga, or return to Jonesborough via U.S. 27 North to I–75 East to I–40 North to Route 34 East.

Dayton

Scopes Trial Museum. The museum is inside the Rhea County Courthouse, the site of the famous 1925 Scopes Monkey Trial. Exhibits provide an overview of the trial, in

TENNESSEE RULES OF THE ROAD

License Requirements: You must be 16 years of age to get a driver's license in Tennessee.

Right Turn on Red: Unless otherwise posted, you are permitted to make right turns on red in the state of Tennessee.

Seat-Belt & Helmet Laws: All front-seat adult passengers are required to wear safety belts. Seat belts must be worn by children ages 4–17 in the backseat as well. Children under 1 year or 20 pounds must be in a rear-facing infant seat. Children ages 1 to 3 must be in a forward-facing safety seat. Children ages 4–8 must be in a booster seat. All children under 8 years must travel in the rear of the vehicle, if possible. Motorcyclists must wear helmets.

Speed Limits: The speed limit on rural Tennessee interstates is 70 mph; speed limits on metro-area interstates are regulated by the specific metro area—watch for signs. The speed limit on major highways is 55 mph, unless otherwise indicated on highway signs.

Other Regulations: The blood-alcohol concentration of a driver in Tennessee must not exceed .08%. Passengers in a vehicle cannot possess open containers of alcohol.

For More Information: Tennessee Department of Safety | 615/251–5166 | www.state.tn.us/safety. Tennessee Department of Transportation | 615/741–2848 | www.tdot.state.tn.us.

which lawyers William Jennings Bryan and Clarence Darrow debated whether Dayton public school biology teacher John Scopes had the right to teach Charles Darwin's theory of evolution. The trial no doubt ended more messily than most history students recall, but the case against Scopes was ultimately dismissed. | 1475 Market St. | 423/775–7801 | www.bryan.edu | Free | Weekdays 8–4:30.

Dining

Heartland Grill. American. Two miles south of downtown, this casual eatery offers traditional fare ranging from chops and dinner salads to country-fried steak and chicken potpie. | 9125 Rhea County Hwy. | 423/570–9877 | Closed Mon. | AE, D, MC, V | $–$$

Greeneville

Andrew Johnson National Historic Site. In 1826 the 17th president of the United States (and the first to be impeached) migrated to the town of Greeneville from North Carolina. Here he met and married his wife, Eliza, who taught him to read and write, and opened the tailor shop. He became president following Abraham Lincoln's assassination and led the nation during the troubled years of Reconstruction. The site has two homes, the tailor shop, and Johnson's grave. Stop at the visitor center for information before exploring the grounds. | College and Depot Sts. | 423/638–3551 visitor center, 423/639–3711 site headquarters | Free | Daily 9–5.

Nathaniel Greene Museum. The downtown museum of state history focuses on the accomplishments of such local figures as John Sevier, Samuel Doak, Davy Crockett, and President Andrew Johnson. | 101 W. McKee St. | 423/636–1558 | Free | Tues.–Sat. 10–4.

Dining

Olde Tusculum Eatery. American/Casual. Across from Tusculum College, this full-service cafeteria served as a grocery store in the 1800s. Fresh daily quiches, chicken potpie made with puff pastry, homemade soups, organic salad greens, and sandwiches are among the menu selections. | 905 Erwin Hwy., 5 mi northwest of downtown | 423/638–9210 | Closed weekends. No dinner | D, MC, V | ¢

Jonesborough

Historic District. One of the state's top attractions, downtown Jonesborough has about 40 18th- and 19th-century buildings, most of which are still in use. A walk down the brick sidewalks and along the wrought-iron fences leads you past the Christopher Taylor House (one of the oldest log structures in the state), the May-Ledbetter House (built in 1905 and the first house in town with indoor plumbing, it was also the first abolitionist publishing site), and the Griffith-Lyle House (former home of an early photographer). Tours are available through the Jonesborough Visitors Center. | Main St. and adjacent streets | 423/753–5961 | $1 | Daily dawn–dusk.

Chester Inn. The oldest frame structure in Jonesborough, built in 1797, once hosted Andrew Johnson and Charles Dickens. It is now the site of the National Storytelling Festival. The interior of the house is closed to the public. | 116 W. Main St. | 423/753–5961.

Jonesborough Visitors Center and History Museum. Stop here for a map of the historic district or a guided tour. The museum's permanent exhibits offer a glimpse of life on the early frontier. Behind the visitor center is Duncan's Meadow, site of Andrew Johnson's first duel. | 117 Boone St. | 423/753–1010 or 800/400–4221 | Weekdays 8–5, weekends 10–5.

Dining

Parson's Table. Continental. Rack of lamb and the shellfish medley are big sellers here. The name reflects the building's former life as a 19th-century place of worship. Sunday buffet brunch. Kids' menu. | 102 Woodrow Ave., 37659 | 423/753–8002 | Closed Mon. and Jan. No dinner Sun. | AE, D, MC, V | $$–$$$$

Knoxville

Museum of Black History and Culture. Exhibits at this East Knoxville museum chronicle the history of African-Americans in Knoxville, from slavery to the present. | 1927 Dandridge Ave. | 865/524–8461 | Free | Tues.–Sat. 10–6.

Bleak House (Confederate Memorial Hall). During the siege of Knoxville in 1863, Confederate general James Longstreet used this 15-room home as his headquarters. The period-furnished 1858 house and Mediterranean-style gardens are owned and operated by the local chapter of the United Daughters of the Confederacy. | 3148 Kingston Pike SW | 865/522–7263 | $5 | Tues., Wed., Fri. 1–4.

Governor William Blount Mansion. The first frame house west of the Appalachians, this is one of the most historically significant buildings in this part of the state and is furnished with pieces from the 1790s. Built in 1792 overlooking the Tennessee River, it was the home of William Blount, the first and only governor (1790–96) of the Southwest Territory and a signer of the U.S. Constitution. Unlike the log structures around it, the "mansion" had many glass windows; Indians living in the area at the time called it the "house with many eyes." Guided tours are offered of the restored house. | 200 W. Hill Ave. | 865/525–2375 | www.korrnet.org/blount96 | $5 | Mon.–Sat. 9:30–5.

James White Fort. On a bluff overlooking the Tennessee River, this complex is the site of the first settlement in Knoxville. The restored buildings, dating from 1786, include a loom house, a smokehouse, and a blacksmith's shop. Tours are given by well-versed guides in period clothing. | 205 E. Hill Ave. | 865/525–6514 | $5 | Mar.–mid-Dec., Mon.– Sat. 9:30–4; mid-Dec.–Feb., weekdays 10–4.

Knoxville Museum of Art. The state's largest art museum is an attractive contemporary structure faced in pink Tennessee marble. In addition to its permanent collection of contemporary paintings, sculpture, prints, and mixed media by such artists as Bessie Harvey and Robert Rauschenberg, the museum's four galleries host about 15 exhibits each year. | 1050 World's Fair Park Dr. | 865/525–6101 | www.knoxart.org | $4 | Tues.–Sun. 10–5.

Knoxville Zoo. One of the best zoos in the South covers more than 80 acres of East Knoxville and is home to more than 1,000 animals. Most are housed in natural-habitat environments. The zoo is known for breeding large-cat species and African elephants. The petting zoo and Chimp Ridge are favorite attractions. | 3500 Knoxville Zoo Dr. | 865/637–5331 | www.knoxville-zoo.com | $9.95 | Mid-Oct.–early Apr., daily 10– 4:30; early Apr.–May and early Sept.–mid-Oct., weekdays 9:30–4:30, weekends 9:30– 6; June–early Sept., daily 9:30–6.

Mabry-Hazen House. The 1858 house served as headquarters to both Confederate and Union forces during the Civil War. Today the stately restored building, listed on the National Historic Register, is home to hundreds of antiques and artifacts. Exhibits chronicle the dramatic story of the family that lived here in the Civil War era. | 1711 Dandridge Ave. | 865/522–8661 | $5 | Tues.–Fri. 10–5, Sat. 10–2.

Dining

Charlie Pepper's. Southwestern. Images of jalapeños abound at this West Knoxville restaurant, including such witty touches as stuffed "jackalopes." Consider one of the innovatively prepared steaks, such as the Cajun-style with blue cheese, or try the spinach–Portobello mushroom quesadillas. | 242 Morrell Rd. | 865/291–9453 | AE, D, DC, MC, V | $–$$

Chesapeake's. Seafood. In downtown Knoxville this cavernous restaurant is awash in lobster pots, model ships, stuffed fish, and an aquarium. Selections include Maine lobster and Maryland crab cakes. Two private rooms and an open-air dining area overlooking a garden are available. Kids' menu. | 500 N. Henley St. | 865/673–3433 | AE, D, DC, MC, V | $$–$$$$

Michael's. Continental. In West Knoxville, this dual-purpose facility includes a separate nightclub-lounge with live DJs on the weekends. The restaurant is an intimate spot for casual candlelit dinners, with brass, oak, beveled glass, a fireplace, and an atrium in the lobby. Steak Onassis and peppercorn strip steak are specialties. Kids' menu. Reservations are required on football weekends. | 7049 Kingston Pike | 865/588–2455 | No lunch | AE, D, DC, MC, V | $$–$$$$

Sullivan's Fine Foods. American. In West Knoxville this casual place offers down-home country cooking and blue-plate specials, including meat loaf and pork loin. You can eat on the patio in the shade of a large maple tree. | 7545 N. Shore Dr. | 865/694–9696 | AE, DC, MC, V | $–$$

Lodging

Best Western Cedar Bluff Inn. More than 50 restaurants are within 2 mi of this West Knoxville hotel—some within walking distance. Shopping, movie theaters, and a sports bar are also nearby. In-room data ports, minibars, some refrigerators, cable TV, pool, business services. | 420 N. Peters Rd., 37922 | 865/539–0058 | fax 865/539–4887 | www.bestwestern.com | 97 rooms, 23 suites | CP | AE, D, DC, MC, V | $–$$

Comfort Inn. The standard chain motel with exterior entrances is within walking distance of restaurants. Quietest rooms face courtyard containing the landscaped, outdoor swimming pool. Spacious rooms contain desks and overstuffed armchairs. Cable TV, pool, business services, no-smoking rooms. | 5334 Central Ave. Pike, 37912, 5 mi north of downtown | 865/688–1010 | fax 865/687–8655 | www.comfortinn.com | 100 rooms | CP | AE, D, DC, MC, V | $

Executive Inn. The rooms aren't fancy here, but convenience is key as there are plenty of restaurants and stores within a block or two. Cable TV, pool, no-smoking rooms. | 3400 Chapman Hwy., 37920, 1½ mi north of downtown | 865/577–4451 | www.executive-inn.com | 63 rooms | AE, D, DC, MC, V | ¢

★ **Knoxville Marriott Hotel.** The eight-story atrium lobby adds to the sleek modern feel of this full-service hotel. It's on a hill overlooking the Tennessee River. The combination of scenic views, amenities, and central location makes this an especially good lodging choice. Restaurant, room service, in-room data ports, cable TV, pool, gym, hair salon, bar, playground, business services, airport shuttle, some pets allowed (fee), no-smoking rooms. | 500 Hill Ave. SE, 37915 | 865/637–1234 | fax 865/637–1193 | www.marriott.com | 385 rooms, 20 suites | AE, D, DC, MC, V | $–$$

La Quinta Motor Inn. Less than 2 mi from area attractions, restaurants, and shopping is this West Knoxville base camp. Spacious rooms are complemented by the comfortable, airy breakfast area, where coffee and pastries are set out near a fireplace. In-room data ports, cable TV, pool, laundry facilities, business services, some pets allowed, no-smoking rooms. | 258 Peters Rd. N, 37923 | 865/690–9777 | fax 865/531–8304 | www.laquinta.com | 130 rooms | CP | AE, D, DC, MC, V | $

Morristown

Crockett Tavern and Pioneer Museum. Davy Crockett, born in 1786, grew up in Morristown. This is a reconstruction of the original John Crockett Tavern owned and run by his father; it's now a museum. The original building was burned down after smallpox victims stayed there. | 2002 E. Morningside Dr. | 423/587–9900 | $5 | May–Nov., Tues.–Sat. 10–5.

Panther Creek State Park. On Cherokee Reservoir, the 1,435-acre park has spectacular views. Activities include camping, fishing, boating, swimming, and horseback riding. | 210 Panther Creek Park Rd., off Hwy. 11 E, 3 mi west of Morristown | 423/587–7046 | www.state.tn.us/environment/parks/panther | Free | Daily 6 AM–dark.

Rose Center. The 1892 school building downtown is now a community cultural center. There are a regional art gallery and a historical museum. | 442 W. 2nd North St. | 423/581–4330 | www.rosecenter.org | Free | Weekdays 9–5.

Dining

Angelo's. American. All the woodwork in this restaurant, from the paneling to the tables, dates from the 1940s. Tilapia (a freshwater fish) stuffed with crabmeat and the sirloin and lobster are your best bets. | 3614 W. Andrew Johnson Hwy. | 423/581–4882 | Closed Sun. No lunch | AE, MC, V | $$–$$$

Norris

Lenoir Museum. Learn about dairy farming, woodworking, and the history of nearby Lenoir City at this charming museum. | 221 Norris Freeway | 865/494–9688 | Free | Daily 9–5.

Museum of Appalachia. The 65-acre complex of 30 log cabins displays Cherokee baskets and old jail cells. There's also an Appalachia Hall of Fame. | 2819 Rte. 61, Clinton, 10 mi northeast of Norris | 865/494–0514 | www.korrnet.org/accc/musapp.html | $10 | Daily 8–5.

Norris Dam State Park. Two miles north of downtown Norris, this park is home to the first hydroelectric dam, built in 1936 by the Tennessee Valley Authority. | 125 Village Green Circle | 865/494–0720 | www.state.tn.us/environment/parks/parks/NorrisDam/ | Free | Daily 8 AM–10 PM.

Dining

Golden Girls. Southern. The Golden sisters were cooking long before those interloping "Golden Girls" appeared on TV. Catfish and tenderloin are among the more popular dishes. The restaurant is in a modern log cabin dominated by University of Tennessee mementos. Breakfast served. | 2211 Rte. 61, Clinton, 9 mi northeast of Norris | 865/457–3302 | AE, D, DC, MC, V | ¢–$$

Oak Ridge

American Museum of Science and Energy. Originally named the American Museum of Atomic Energy when it was founded in 1949, the museum eventually changed its name and broadened its mission. Today it's the largest museum of its kind, offering hands-on exhibits about various forms of energy. | 300 S. Tulane Ave. | 865/576–3200 | www.amse.org | $3 | Daily 9–5.

Secret City Scenic Excursion Train. The World War II–era diesel covers 13 mi of track and runs through the Manhattan Project's K25 complex. The rides take place during select weekends; runs are most frequent in October when leaves are at their peak. |

Rte. 58, in front of the East Tennessee Technology Park | 865/241–2140 | $12 | Apr.–Dec., select weekends, Sat. 10–4, Sun. noon–4.

University of Tennessee Arboretum. The 250-acre research facility, 1 mi south of downtown, has 1,500 species of plants and trees. You can walk along short trails through various plant habitats. | 901 Kerr Hollow Rd. | 865/483–3571 | www.korrnet.org/utas | Free | Weekdays 8–5.

Dining

Burchfield's. American. Modern paintings, halogen lighting, and an atrium give this spot a fresh, contemporary look. Favorite dishes include penne with ham, bacon, and red potato, or the Jack Daniels sirloin. Breakfast served. | 215 S. Illinois Ave. | 865/481–2468 | AE, D, DC, MC, V | $$

Magnolia Tree Restaurant. Eclectic. Moussaka and lasagna are the crowd-pleasers here. Stained glass and Tiffany lamps splash the room with color. | 1938 Oak Ridge Tpke. | 865/482–5853 | Closed Sun. | AE, D, MC, V | $

Tusculum

Andrew Johnson Library. The 17th president's papers and manuscripts, as well as Civil War–era newspapers, are housed here in an 1841 building on the campus of Tusculum College. | 60 Shiloh Rd. | 423/636–7348 | www.tusculum.edu | Free | Weekdays 9–5.

Davy Crockett Birthplace State Park. The birthplace of the legendary frontiersman (and congressman) has been preserved by the Tennessee Department of Environment and Conservation. The park consists of 105 partially wooded acres of land along the Nolichucky River, with a museum and a replica of the log cabin in which Crockett was born. Camping, fishing, and picnicking are available. | 1245 Davy Crockett Park Rd., Limestone, 10 mi east of Tusculum | 423/257–2167 or 423/257–2168 | www.state.tn.us/environment/parks/davyshp/index.html | $3 | Daily 8–dusk.

LAKE CHAMPLAIN ISLANDS
FROM MILTON TO THE MISSISQUOI NATIONAL WILDLIFE REFUGE

Distance: 60 mi   Time: 1–2 days
Overnight Break: North Hero

Florida has its keys, and Vermont has the Lake Champlain Islands—a bucolic archipelago running south from the Canadian border to just north of Burlington, in the broadest part of the lake. Although the islands mostly consist of gently rolling terrain, their situation affords spectacular views of both Vermont's Green Mountains to the east, and the Adirondacks of New York State to the west. This is a year-round tour—winter brings a stark beauty to the lake, with bays and inlets sheathed in ice and dotted with ice-fishing shacks. Summertime in all of Vermont is short and glorious, with oppressive heat a rarity and evenings often cool enough for a light sweater. The scenery is perhaps at its prettiest between late spring and mid-autumn: given the climate-moderating influence of the lake, foliage season comes a bit later and lasts a little longer in this part of Vermont.

❶ Begin the drive just south of **Milton** (8 mi north of Burlington, I–89, Exit 17 onto U.S. 2 W). Just before you reach the U.S. 2 causeway (4 mi from I–89) over the eastern portion of Lake Champlain, a right-hand turnoff leads to **Sand Bar State Park** (U.S. 2), which has one of Vermont's finest swimming beaches. The drop-off is so gentle that it seems almost as if you could wade across to the islands; the lake and mountain views are sublime. There are picnic facilities, a nearby boat launch, and Windsurfer rentals in summer.

❷ **South Hero** (2 mi west of causeway on U.S. 2) is the southernmost of the Lake Champlain Islands. According to legend, this island and its companion, North Hero, were named for Ethan Allen and his brother Ira, two heroes of Vermont's early struggle for independence. At South Hero village, turn left onto South Street to reach two of the islands' remaining apple orchards, **Hackett's** and **Allenholm Farm.** This was once prime apple country, although development has taken its toll.

❸ At **Grand Isle** (2 mi north on U.S. 2, then 2 mi west on Rte. 314), the ferry to Plattsburgh, New York (Rte. 314), is the only Lake Champlain boat crossing operating year-

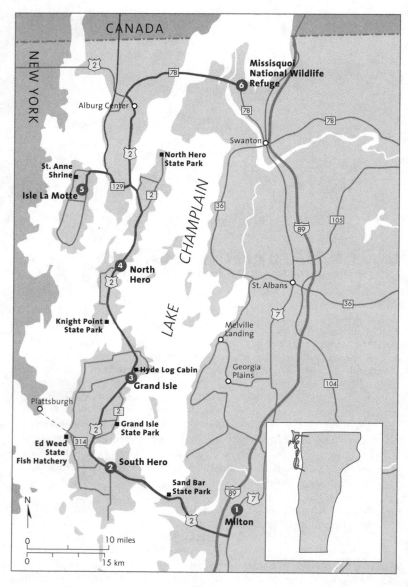

round. Just opposite the ferry dock is the **Ed Weed State Fish Hatchery,** which has exhibits on Lake Champlain's fish species and offers a look at a state-of-the-art trout-hatching operation. East of U.S. 2 (4 mi north of South Hero) is **Grand Isle State Park** (U.S. 2), with tent sites, lean-tos, and swimming (registered campers only). Also on U.S. 2 in Grand Isle is the **Hyde Log Cabin,** believed to be the oldest log cabin in the United States. The 1783 structure was built by one of the islands' earliest settlers, and displays artifacts of pioneer life.

❹ **North Hero** (4 mi north on U.S. 2) is a separate island, with a town of the same name, lying across a causeway—in summer, the drawbridge can be open to allow tall-masted sailboats to pass through. **Knight Point State Park** (U.S. 2) is on the left, just past the causeway. The day-use park has a swimming beach and rowboat rentals. Up ahead, the village of North Hero clusters around the handsome 1824 **Grande Isle County Court House,** built of local marble. The little town faces City Bay (there's nothing remotely like a city in sight), where you can rent a canoe or kayak to enjoy the calm lake waters and magnificent views of the northernmost Green Mountains. To the north, beyond a narrow isthmus across which Indians once portaged their canoes, bear east off U.S. 2 to reach **North Hero State Park,** with attractive campsites and beaches on the island's northern tip.

❺ Isle La Motte (follow U.S. 2 across the bridge leading to the Alburg peninsula—connected by land only to the Canadian mainland—then west onto Rte. 129 and across another bridge; 9 mi total from North Hero) is the smallest of the Champlain Islands. Near the island's northern tip is the **St. Anne's Shrine** (off W. Shore Rd.), run by the Edmundite fathers to mark the spot where the first Catholic Mass in Vermont was celebrated in 1666. On Isle La Motte several of the world's few black marble quarries turned out stone that was used in the U.S. Capitol and in New York City's Radio City Music Hall. At a now-unused quarry on the island's southwest shore and in other outcroppings on Isle La Motte are remnants of the world's oldest **fossil reef,** formed some 400 million years ago when this entire area was submerged beneath warm ocean waters.

❻ The **Missisquoi National Wildlife Refuge** (return over the Isle La Motte Causeway to Alburg, then east on Rte. 129, north on U.S. 2, and east on Rte. 78 and the causeway

VERMONT RULES OF THE ROAD

License Requirements: The legal driving age in Vermont is 16.

Right Turn on Red: You can make right turns on red, after coming to a full stop, unless signs indicate otherwise.

Seat-Belt & Helmet Laws: Vermont law requires all vehicle occupants to be secured with seat belts; children under the age of five must be secured in a federally approved child safety seat. Motorcycle operators and passengers are required to wear helmets.

Speed Limits: The limit on Vermont highways is 50 mph, except as posted otherwise in settled areas; on interstate highways, a 65-mph speed limit is observed unless posted otherwise.

Other Regulations: While operating a vehicle in Vermont, your blood-alcohol concentration must be below .08%. It is illegal in Vermont for any passengers in a vehicle to possess an open container of alcohol.

For More Information: Vermont Agency of Transportation | 802/828–2014 | www.aot.state.vt.us/default.asp. Vermont State Police | 800/429–7623 road conditions | www.dps.state.vt.us/vtsp.

leading to the Vermont mainland; 15 mi total from Isle La Motte) encompasses a 6,300-acre tract of marshland and forest at the mouth of the Missisquoi River, where nearly 300 species of birds have been recorded, and where the canoeing and fishing are superb. From the refuge, drive 10 mi east on Route 78 to pick up I–89 at Exit 21 in Swanton for the return to Burlington (27 mi south).

North Hero

Ed Weed State Fish Hatchery. At this state-of-the-art hatchery, trout are raised to stock size and exhibits tell about fish species native to Vermont. | 14 Bell Hill Rd., 10 mi south of North Hero | 802/372–3171 | www.vtfishandwildlife.com | Free | Daily 7:30–4.

North Hero State Park. This gorgeous lakeside park has campsites, swimming, and Green Mountains views. | 3803 Lakeview Dr., 6 mi north of North Hero | 802/372–8727 | www.vtstateparks.com/htm/northhero.cfm | $2.50 | Mid-May–Labor Day, daily 10 AM–sunset.

★ **Royal Lipizzan Stallions.** Three generations of the Herrmann family perform maneuvers on expertly trained white stallions. | Lipizzan Park, U.S. 2, 1½ mi past the drawbridge that crosses Lake Champlain | 802/372–5683 | www.champlainislands.com | $8–$15 | Performances mid-July–late Aug., Thurs. and Fri. at 6, weekends at 2:30.

St. Anne's Shrine. On the site of Vermont's oldest settlement is this Roman Catholic shrine. There's a striking statue of Samuel de Champlain, as well as a chapel, picnic area, and beach. | 92 St. Anne's Rd., Isle La Motte, 11 mi northwest of North Hero | 802/928–3362 | Free | Mid-May–mid-Oct., daily.

Dining

Margo's Pastry and Café. Café. An assortment of pastries is served at Margo's, along with light fare like soups, salads, quiches, pastas, focaccia, and wraps. You can dine in the café, take it home, or eat outside with views of the lake and a nearby farm. | 200 U.S. 2, Grand Isle, 10 mi south of North Hero | 802/372–6112 | Closed Nov.–Apr. No dinner | No credit cards | ¢–$

North Hero House. Contemporary. On a scenic island in Lake Champlain, the inn (1891) was originally a stopover for steamship travelers. Antiques and collectibles fill the spacious colonial dining room. Contemporary American cuisine is distinguished by many fresh, creatively presented ingredients—try farm-raised trout stuffed with crab and served with a leek-Chablis sauce and Israeli couscous. Lunch is served on the pier. Sunday brunch. No smoking. | U.S. 2 | 802/372–4732 or 888/525–3644 | No lunch | AE, MC, V | $$–$$$$

★ **Shore Acres Restaurant.** Contemporary. Wherever you sit in the dining room, you can gaze out on lovely Lake Champlain and the Green Mountains. The regionally inspired cuisine includes such dishes as spice-crusted chicken with a chipotle–bacon–sour cream sauce. | 237 Shore Acres Dr. | 802/372–8722 | Closed Jan.–Apr. and weekdays mid-Oct.–Dec. | MC, V | $$–$$$

Lodging

North Hero House. You can see the Green Mountains from the hotel's superb lakeside location. Rooms are airy and light, and most have private balconies overlooking the water. The beach has dockage and canoe rentals. The main house was built at the beginning of the 19th century. Restaurant, some in-room hot tubs, cable TV, beach, boating, bar. | U.S. 2, center of town | 802/372–4732 or 888/525–3664 | fax 802/372–3218 | www.northherohouse.com | 22 rooms, 4 suites | BP | AE, MC, V | $$–$$$

Ruthcliffe Lodge. All of the simply furnished rooms are lakeside at this remote lodge on the smallest of the Lake Champlain Islands. Dine in the lodge or on a patio. Restaurant, picnic area, dock, boating, fishing, bicycles; no a/c, no room phones, no TV in some rooms, no smoking. | 1002 Old Quarry Rd., Isle La Motte, 13 mi northwest of North Hero | 802/928–3200 or 800/769–8162 | fax 802/928–3200 | www.ruthcliffe.com | 6 rooms | Closed Nov.–Apr. | BP | AE, D, MC, V | $$

★ **Shore Acres Inn and Restaurant.** At this lakeside motor inn, lawns sweep down to Lake Champlain, and you can contemplate the views from sparkling white Adirondack chairs. The bright and airy rooms contain custom Vermont-made furnishings. The restaurant serves commendable contemporary American fare. Restaurant, some refrigerators, cable TV, 9-hole golf course, 2 tennis courts, lake, dock, fishing, croquet, bar, some pets allowed. | 237 Shore Acres Dr. | 802/372–8722 | www.shoreacres.com | 23 rooms | Closed mid-Oct.–mid-Apr. | D, MC, V | $$–$$$

Thomas Mott Homestead Bed & Breakfast. Small and inviting, this vintage farmhouse-turned-inn, built in 1838 in the Shaker style, draws guests from as far as Europe. There are lake views on three sides of the house and regular quilting demonstrations on weekends; complimentary Ben and Jerry's ice cream is always on hand. Boating, bicycles, cross-country skiing; no a/c, no children under 12, no smoking. | 63 Blue Rock Rd., Alburg, 13 mi north of North Hero | 802/796–4402 or 800/348–0843 | www.thomas-mott-bb.com | 5 rooms | BP | MC, V | $–$$

MIDDLEBURY & THE LOWER CHAMPLAIN VALLEY
FROM SHELBURNE TO LARABEES POINT

Distance: 71 mi   Time: 2 days
Overnight Break: Middlebury

Although just about every Vermont town once had its dairy farms, most of the state's milk production is now centered on the rich bottomlands of the Champlain Valley. South of Burlington, the land that hugs the big lake offers a different type of Vermont scenery—broad and expansive, with the Green Mountains as a distant backdrop. The unofficial capital of this land of milk and apples is a college town right out of central casting.

❶ **Shelburne** (7 mi south of Burlington on U.S. 7) is a suburban community with a countrified air and two prime attractions. The **Shelburne Museum** is a 45-acre New England village. Seven artifacts-filled historic houses (1773–1840) have been moved here from northern New England and New York. On a side road leading to Shelburne Point is **Shelburne Farms,** the core of the estate developed by Dr. William Seward Webb, father of Shelburne Museum donor Electra Havemeyer Webb. The Webb heirs have established a model demonstration farm and cheese-making operation.

❷ The approach to **Charlotte** (5 mi south on U.S. 7, 2 mi east on local Rte. F5 from Charlotte if taking ferry) is characterized by magnificent views of Lake Champlain and the Adirondacks on the opposite shore. The tiny village serves as the eastern terminus for the **ferry to Essex, New York** (Ferry Rd.).

❸ At **Ferrisburgh** (5 mi south on U.S. 7), 19th-century writer Rowland Robinson's farmstead **Rokeby** (U.S. 7) recalls the days when Robinson, like many Vermonters, sheltered runaway slaves heading north to Canada.

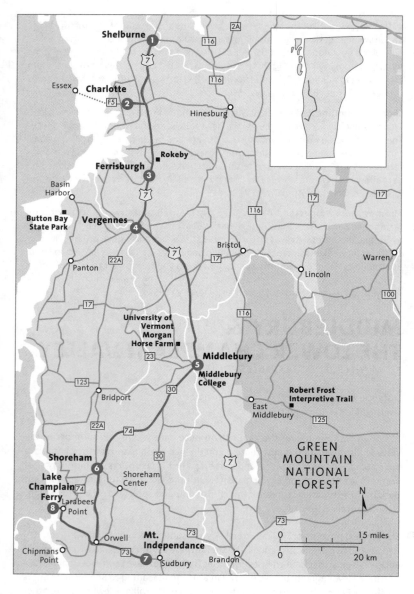

④ **Vergennes** (3 mi south on U.S. 7, then 1 mi west on Rte. 22A) is a vest-pocket community of Victorian homes and public buildings. In this unlikeliest of naval ports a fleet was constructed on the banks of Otter Creek to assault the British in the 1814 Battle of Plattsburgh. This story and much of the rest of Lake Champlain's history is recounted at the nearby **Lake Champlain Maritime Museum** (7 mi east on Basin Harbor Rd., Ferrisburgh). Just south of the museum, off a road that follows the lake shore, stop at **Button Bay State Park** to look for the tiny, perforated pebbles that gave the bay its name.

⑤ **Middlebury** (16 mi south of Vergennes turnoff on U.S. 7) is the home of **Middlebury College.** Founded in 1800, the school is highly regarded for its liberal arts programs.

Middlebury's compact downtown surrounds the falls of Otter Creek; within a short walk are the **Vermont State Craft Center** at Frog Hollow; the **Sheldon Museum** of local 19th-century Americana; the **Vermont Folklife Center,** devoted to regional folklore and the everyday life of times past; and the gracious old **Middlebury Inn.** The 136-foot tower of the 1809 **Congregational Church** is perhaps Vermont's finest; on the college campus, just west of downtown, look for the 1816 **Painter Hall** and the college's Museum of Art. Two side trips from Middlebury are particularly worthwhile. Head 11 mi east on Route 125 to reach the **Robert Frost Interpretive Trail,** an easy path through woods and meadows, marked with quotations from works influenced by the poet's long residence in nearby Ripton. Drive 3 mi north of Middlebury via Route 23 and a side road to visit the **University of Vermont Morgan Horse Farm,** which showcases Vermont's state animal, the sturdily graceful Morgan.

6 Along the way to **Shoreham** (12 mi southwest of Middlebury via Rte. 30 and Rte. 74), you will head deep into the dairy country of the lower Champlain Valley. This is also one of Vermont's prime apple-producing regions; several farms run pick-your-own operations in early fall.

7 At Orwell (6 mi south of Shoreham on Rte. 22A), head west 6 mi via Route 73 and 73A to reach **Mt. Independence** (Rte. 73A), where interpretive displays and self-guided paths explain how this narrow portion of Lake Champlain was secured during the Revolutionary War.

8 At Larabees Point (6 mi north of Orwell via Rte. 73), **Lake Champlain ferry,** the oldest continually operating ferry on Lake Champlain, takes passengers to Ticonderoga, New York, site of the now-restored fortress that was captured by Ethan Allen in 1775.

Charlotte

Mt. Philo State Park. Easy trails up 980-foot Mt. Philo lead to terrific Lake Champlain views. There is also a campsite with hot showers and facilities. | 5425 Mt. Philo Rd. | 802/425–2390 | www.vtstateparks.com/htm/philo.cfm | $2.50 | Mid-May–mid-Oct., daily 10 AM–dusk.

Vermont Wildflower Farm. Stroll through 6 acres of wildflowers and woodlands at this farm, or buy seed mixes for any U.S. growing conditions. | U.S. 7 | 802/951–5812 | www.americanmeadows.com | $3 | May–late Oct., daily 10–5.

Middlebury

Congregational Church. Completed in 1809, the church has a 136-foot spire considered by many to be the most graceful and elegant in Vermont. | Main St. at U.S. 7 | 802/388–7634 | Free | Services Sun. 10 AM.

Henry Sheldon Museum of Vermont History. The 1829 marble merchant's house is the oldest community museum in the country. The period rooms contain Vermont-made textiles, furniture, toys, clothes, kitchen tools, and paintings. | 1 Park St. | 802/388–2117 | www.henrysheldonmuseum.org | $5 | Mon.–Sat. 10–5.

Historic Middlebury Village Walking Tour. A self-guided walk around the center of this lively, compact college town allows you to explore local architectural and historical highlights. You can pick up a map from the Addison Chamber of Commerce. | 2 Court St. | 802/388–7951.

Middlebury College. Smack in the middle of town and founded in 1800, this esteemed institution was conceived as a more godly alternative to the worldly

University of Vermont. The early-19th-century stone buildings contrast provocatively with the postmodern architecture of the Center for the Arts and the sports center. Music, theater, and dance performances take place throughout the year at the Wright Memorial Theatre and Center for the Arts. | Old Chapel Rd. | 802/443–5000 | www.middlebury.edu.

★ **Middlebury College Museum of Art.** Rodin sculptures, along with the work of the respected 19th-century Vermont sculptor Hiram Powers, are highlights of this collection. | Rte. 30 | 802/443–3168 | www.middlebury.edu/~museum | Free | Tues.–Fri. 10–5, weekends noon–5.

Robert Frost Interpretive Trail. This 1-mi pathway through woods and meadows is marked with quotations from Frost poems. There are two picnic areas, one across the street and one on Route 125, ¼ mi east of the trailhead. | Rte. 125, Ripton, 10 mi east of Middlebury | 802/388–4362 | Free | Daily dawn–dusk.

UVM Morgan Horse Farm. The university's farm, just outside town, raises Morgans and gives you a close-up look at specimens of Vermont's state animal—all of whom are descended from a single stallion, Figure, who lived 200 years ago. | 74 Battell Dr., Weybridge, 3 mi northwest of Middlebury | 802/388–2011 | www.uvm.edu/morgan | $4 | May–Oct., daily 9–4.

Vermont Folklife Center. The center has photographs, audiotapes, manuscripts, folk art, and other artifacts of Vermont life past and present. In 1801 this was the home of Gamaliel Painter, founder of Middlebury College. | 3 Court St. | 802/388–4964 | www.vermontfolklifecenter.org | Free | Tues.–Sat. 11–4; oral history archive weekdays 10–4.

Vermont State Craft Center at Frog Hollow. More than a crafts store, the center overlooking Otter Creek mounts changing exhibitions and displays exquisite work in wood, glass, metal, clay, and fiber by more than 250 Vermont artisans. It also sponsors classes taught by some of those artists. Burlington and Manchester also have centers. | 1 Mill St. | 802/388–3177 or 888/388–3177 | www.froghollow.org | Free | Mon–Thurs. 9:30–5:30, Sat. 9:30–6, Sun. 11–5.

Dining

Baba's Market & Deli. Middle Eastern. Authentic Lebanese dishes are the specialty in this cheerful, informal market and café near the college. Among the standouts are kibbe, stuffed grape leaves, moussaka, and pizza prepared in a wood-fired oven. | 54 College St. | 802/388–6408 | MC, V | ¢–$

Dog Team Tavern. American/Casual. Four miles north of Middlebury, this tavern is famous for hand-hooked rugs and local crafts, sticky buns, and generous portions of hearty fare. You won't go wrong with a New York sirloin steak or broiled scallops. Kids' menu. No smoking. | Dog Team Rd. | 802/388–7651 | No lunch | AE, D, DC, MC, V | $–$$

Fire & Ice. American. A 55-item salad bar (with peel-and-eat shrimp), prime rib, steak, lobster, and a house specialty—homemade mashed potatoes—are all choices at this family-friendly spot. Although large, the space is divided into several rooms, each with a different theme, and has numerous intimate nooks and crannies. | 26 Seymour St. | 802/388–7166 or 800/367–7166 | No lunch Mon. | AE, D, DC, MC, V | $$–$$$

Waybury Inn. Contemporary. Dependable hospitality, good food, and a convenient location keep visitors returning to this landmark country inn. The cuisine is a combination of traditional New England favorites and modern variations. Try grilled salmon with citrus oil and fruit salsa, or the horseradish-and-cumin-rubbed filet mignon. Lighter fare is available at the inn's pub. Sunday brunch. | Rte. 125, East Middlebury, 5 mi southeast of Middlebury | 802/388–4015 or 800/348–1810 | No lunch | AE, D, MC, V | $$–$$$$

Lodging

Blue Spruce Motel. This reasonably priced compound comprises a main motel building and a handful of white clapboard cottages set on a green meadow surrounded by evergreens and oaks. Rooms are well maintained, with knotty-pine walls and braided rugs. Kitchenettes, cable TV. | 2428 U.S. 7, 3 mi south of town | 802/388–4091 or 800/640–7671 | fax 802/388–3003 | 16 rooms, 6 cottages | AE, D, DC, MC, V | $

Middlebury Inn. Since 1827, gracious New England–style hospitality has been the hallmark of this three-story brick Georgian inn. The property also encompasses a contemporary motel with Early American–style furnishings and the Victorian-era Porter House Mansion. Rooms, and especially bathrooms, could stand some updating, but this inn has a great location: it faces the village green and is an easy stroll from shops, dining, and the university. Restaurant, cable TV, some pets allowed, no-smoking rooms. | 14 Courthouse Sq., 05753 | 802/388–4961 or 800/842–4666 | fax 802/388–4563 | www.middleburyinn.com | 75 rooms | CP | AE, D, MC, V | $$–$$$$

Sugarhouse Motel. When it's warm enough, this motel allows you to build a campfire on the front lawn and cook your dinner. On the crest of a hill, it affords beautiful views of the sunrise and sunset across the mountains. Rooms have modern, utilitarian furnishings. Refrigerators, cable TV, some pets allowed (fee); no smoking. | U.S. 7 | 802/388–2770 or 800/784–2746 | fax 802/388–8616 | 12 rooms | MC, V | $

★ **Swift House Inn.** The Georgian home of a 19th-century governor contains white-panel wainscoting, mahogany, and marble fireplaces. The rooms—in three buildings—are furnished with period reproductions such as canopy beds, curtains with swags, and claw-foot tubs. Most rooms have Oriental rugs, and nine have fireplaces; some have double whirlpool tubs. Some in-room hot tubs, cable TV, sauna, steam room, pub, meeting room, no-smoking rooms. | 25 Stewart La., 05753 | 802/388–9925 | fax 802/388–9927 | www.swifthouseinn.com | 21 rooms, 1 suite | CP | AE, D, DC, MC, V | $$–$$$$

Shelburne

Shelburne Farms. A Victorian millionaire's estate dating from 1887, the sight is home to cavernous restored barns, a sumptuous inn and restaurant, a working farm, and its own celebrated brand of cheddar. | 1611 Harbor Rd., at Bay Rd. | 802/985–8686 or 802/985–8442 | www.shelburnefarms.org | $6 | Mid-May–mid-Oct., daily 9–5.

★ **Shelburne Museum.** Hailed as New England's Smithsonian, this is Vermont's premier collection of Americana, folk art, and period buildings. Also on the property is the lake steamer *Ticonderoga*. | 6000 Shelburne Rd. | 802/985–3346 | www.shelburnemuseum.org | $17.50 | May–Oct., daily 10–5.

Vermont Teddy Bear Company. North America's largest teddy bear manufacturer allows you to watch the assembly of these little creatures. You can purchase bears and have them shipped anywhere in the world. | 6655 Shelburne Rd. | 802/985–3001 | www.vermontteddybear.com | $2 | Mon.–Sat. 9:30–5, Sun. 10:30–4.

Dining

Café Shelburne. French. A classy bistro serving sophisticated country French fare, this café is among the most romantic eateries in central Vermont. Asparagus and endive salad, rabbit salad over green string beans, and roast lamb are the standouts. | 5573 U.S. 7 | 802/985–3939 | Closed Sun. and Mon. No lunch | AE, MC, V | $$–$$$

Chef Leu's House. Chinese. This well-regarded Chinese restaurant specializes in Szechuan and Mandarin cuisine and also serves a few Vietnamese dishes. Try the peppery orange beef with water chestnuts. | 2545 Shelburne Rd. (U.S. 7) | 802/985–5258 | AE, D, DC, MC, V | $–$$

★ **Inn at Shelburne Farms.** Contemporary. A country inn with relaxed surroundings, this restaurant serves stellar creative New England fare, such as pan-braised rabbit with asparagus risotto and prosciutto; and pancetta-wrapped pan-seared sturgeon with roast potatoes, black kale, and red wine sauce. No smoking. | 1611 Harbor Rd., at Bay Rd. | 802/985–8498 | Closed mid-Oct.–mid-May. No lunch | AE, MC, V | $$–$$$$

Vergennes

Button Bay State Park. Camp and swim on Lake Champlain, and look for the little stone "buttons" that give the bay its name. | Button Bay Rd. just south of Basin Harbor, 6 mi south of Vergennes | 802/475–2377 | $2.50 | Mid-May–mid-Oct., daily 10–dusk.

Chimney Point State Historic Site. The days of French exploration of the Champlain Valley, along with Native American artifacts, are the focus of exhibits in a restored 1700s tavern. | 7305 Rte. 125, at Rte. 17, Addison, 6 mi south of Vergennes | 802/759–2412 | www.historicvermont.org | $2.50 | Late May–mid-Oct., Wed.–Sun. 9:30–5:30.

Kennedy Bros. Factory Marketplace. The focus is on woodenware and furnishings at this 43,000-square-foot outlet, but there are plenty more antiques and crafts for sale. | 11 Main St. | 802/877–2975 | www.kennedy-brothers.com | Daily 9:30–5:30.

★ **Lake Champlain Maritime Museum.** Come discover why Lake Champlain is considered the most historic body of water in North America. Climb aboard a 54-foot replica of Benedict Arnold's gunboat, *Philadelphia II*, rigged, armed, and afloat in the museum's North Harbor. Visit the fully interactive Revolutionary War exhibit, and watch craftsmen continue traditional maritime skills of boatbuilding and blacksmithing. | 4472 Basin Harbor Rd. | 802/475–2022 | www.lcmm.org | $5 | May–mid-Oct., daily 10–5.

Rokeby Museum. Nineteenth-century Vermont author Rowland Robinson wrote his dialect-humor stories in this house. | U.S. 7, Ferrisburgh, 3 mi north of Vergennes | 802/877–3406 | www.rokeby.org | $6 | Guided tours mid-May–mid.-Oct., Thurs.–Sun. 11, 12:30, and 2.

PIEDMONT &
TIDEWATER REGIONS
NORTHERN VIRGINIA TO RICHMOND & HAMPTON ROADS

Distance: 202 mi   Time: 4–5 days
Overnight Breaks: Fredericksburg, Richmond, Williamsburg

Cities rich in history are the stars of this southeasterly drive. From Alexandria in the Washington, D.C., metropolitan area, you travel through Piedmont to Fredericksburg and Richmond, then head through flat coastal plains to Williamsburg and the great port city of Norfolk.

❶ Spend the morning on a walking tour of **Old Town Alexandria,** the seaport town that George Washington and Robert E. Lee called home. The neighborhood of 18th- and 19th-century homes covers about 20 blocks and easily can be seen on foot. At the **Boyhood Home of Robert E. Lee,** you can see how the future Civil War general lived and studied during his formative years. For a taste of Alexandria's early political and social life visit **Gadsby's Tavern Museum,** a once-popular gathering place, now a venue for celebrations honoring George Washington. The venerable **Christ Church,** completed in 1773, has changed little from when George Washington and Robert E. Lee served as its vestrymen. Early medical equipment and herbal remedies common in the 18th century are on display at the **Stabler-Leadbeater Apothecary Museum,** whose customers included George and Martha Washington and James Monroe. Tour the **Carlyle House,** built by Scottish merchant John Carlyle, and discover why this 1753 dwelling was considered the most splendid of its day. Then watch artistry in progress at the **Torpedo Arts Factory,** a former munitions factory that now accommodates the studios of about 160 professional artists and craftspeople.

❷ In the afternoon head south 8 mi from Old Town to **Mount Vernon,** probably the best-known country house in the nation. George Washington's farmhouse has been restored to appear as it did when the president lived here in the late 1700s. The grounds contain restored outbuildings, gardens, two museums, and the tombs of Washington and his wife, Martha.

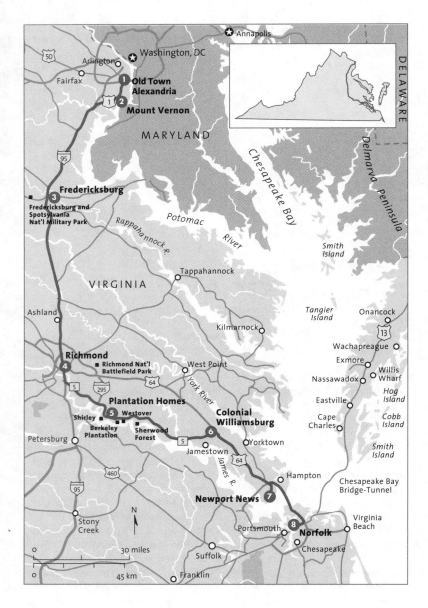

3 About an hour south of Alexandria, 48 mi on I–95, is **Fredericksburg,** another city steeped in history. At the **Fredericksburg and Spotsylvania National Military Park** you can retrace four Civil War battles that were fought in and around the city, talk to park historians, and see exhibits depicting the bloody conflict. In Fredericksburg's historic district, tour the elaborately decorated rooms of the colonial mansion **Kenmore,** built by Fielding Lewis for his wife, Betty, the only sister of George Washington. The home of Washington's brother, Charles, has become the **Rising Sun Tavern,** where today costumed guides interpret 18th-century tavern life. Many of Mary Washington's (George's mother) personal items are displayed at **Mary Washington House.** The future fifth president of the United States practiced law for a time in Fredericksburg, and the **James Monroe Museum and Memorial Library** contains many of his possessions and furnishings.

④ From Fredericksburg get back onto I–95 and continue 58 mi south to **Richmond,** the capital of Virginia. Most of Richmond's attractions lie north of the James River, which bisects the city. The **Virginia State Capitol,** designed by Thomas Jefferson in 1785, is downtown. Among the sculptures of Virginia-born U.S. presidents here is a famous life-size statue of George Washington. The **Museum and White House of the Confederacy** was the official residence of Jefferson Davis, president of the Confederacy; adjacent to it is a newer building that contains a vast collection of Civil War artifacts. East of downtown, in the Church Hill Historic District, is **St. John's Episcopal Church,** where Patrick Henry delivered his memorable "Give me liberty or give me death!" speech in 1775. At the **Richmond National Battlefield Park,** a movie describes the three campaigns fought on the site, and maps outline self-guided tours of the battlefields. If art is more to your liking, visit the **Virginia Museum of Fine Arts,** one of the largest in the South. Its diverse collections range from ancient to contemporary art. Of Richmond's many house museums, probably the most unique is **Agecroft Hall,** a 15th-century English manor that was reassembled here in the 1920s. The house, surrounded by formal gardens, contains Tudor and early-Stuart art and furniture. The graceful **Hollywood Cemetery** is home to the graves of James Monroe, John Tyler, Jefferson Davis, and some 18,000 Confederate soldiers. It also contains beautiful Victorian tombs and sculptures.

⑤ Between Richmond and Williamsburg lies Charles City County, one of the earliest "incorporated" settlements in America. Here you find four historical **plantation homes,** each architecturally significant and packed with family heirlooms. If you take the scenic (and slower) 57-mi route to Williamsburg via John Tyler Memorial Highway (Rte. 5) instead of the rather monotonous 51-mi route on I–64, you can stop off and visit one or all of these estates. Built in 1723, **Shirley** is the oldest plantation in Virginia. It has remained in the same family, the Carters, for 10 generations. Benjamin Harrison, a signer of the Declaration of Independence, and his son, William Henry Harrison, the country's 9th president, were both born at the **Berkeley Plantation.** Virginians say that the first Thanksgiving was celebrated not in Massachusetts but here. **Westover** was home to Col. William Byrd II, a member of the colonial legislature. At 300 feet, **Sherwood Forest** is considered the longest frame house in the country. Built in 1720, it then became the retirement home of John Tyler, the 10th U.S. president.

⑥ **Colonial Williamsburg,** 51 mi east of Richmond, is a colossal living history museum. Covering 173 acres, it is a re-creation of the city that served as Virginia's capital from 1699 until 1780. After your trip back to colonial America, take a walk around the College of William and Mary, the country's second-oldest university. The college's Christopher Wren Building, which dates from 1695, is the oldest academic building in America still in use.

⑦ If time permits, continue east from Williamsburg toward the enormous port of Hampton Roads. In **Newport News** visit the **Mariners' Museum,** whose galleries contain rare maritime artifacts, miniature ships and full-size vessels, navigational instruments, and other fascinating objects of maritime history.

⑧ Take the Hampton Roads Bridge-Tunnel to **Norfolk** and tour the world's largest naval installation, the **Norfolk Naval Base and Norfolk Naval Air Station,** home to about 115 ships of the Atlantic and Mediterranean fleets. If you are traveling during the warmer months, take in the **Norfolk Botanical Gardens,** which has some of the largest collections of azaleas, camellias, rhododendrons, and roses on the East Coast. The **Chrysler Museum** has treasures from ancient Greece, Rome, and the Orient, and also has works by Pablo Picasso and Andy Warhol. Round off your visit by boarding one of the harbor tour boats. **Carrie B. Harbor Tours** runs excursions on a replica of a double-decker 19th-century Mississippi riverboat; the trip takes you past navy ships and submarines, shipyards, and other local points of interest.

To return to Alexandria, take the Hampton Roads Bridge-Tunnel north to Hampton and pick up I–64 West. Continue on I–64 to Richmond. At Richmond, get on I–95 North, which will take you back to Alexandria.

Alexandria

Boyhood Home of Robert E. Lee. Lee lived in this 1795 home from 1812 to 1816 and from 1821 to 1825. It is a fine example of a 19th-century town house with federal architecture. The house was sold in 2000 to private owners who have made it their home. It's no longer open to visitors, but some of the home's furnishings are displayed at the Lyceum. | 607 Oronoco St., Old Town Alexandria.

Carlyle House. The grandest of Alexandria's older houses, Carlyle House was patterned after a Scottish country manor house. The structure was completed in 1753 by Scottish merchant John Carlyle. This was General Braddock's headquarters and the place where he met with five royal governors in 1755 to plan the strategy and funding of the early campaigns of the French and Indian War. | 121 N. Fairfax St., Old Town Alexan-

VIRGINIA RULES OF THE ROAD

License Requirements: To drive in Virginia you must be at least 16 years old and have a valid driver's license.

Right Turn on Red: In most places, drivers can make a right turn on a red light *after* coming to a full stop. The practice is prohibited in some metropolitan areas, however; watch for signs at intersections with traffic lights.

Seat-Belt & Helmet Laws: Seat belts are required for drivers, front-seat passengers, and children 15 and under. Child safety restraints are required for children 5 and under. Helmets are required for motorcyclists.

Speed Limit: The maximum speed limit on most of Virginia's interstates is 65 mph. In heavily traveled corridors, however, the speed limit is 55 mph. Check speed-limit signs carefully.

Other Regulations: The legal blood-alcohol concentration in Virginia is below .08%.

For More Information: Virginia Department of Transportation | 804/786–2801 | virginiadot.org. Virginia State Police | 804/378–3477, cell phone users dial #77 in an emergency | www.vsp.state.va.us.

dria | 703/549–2997 | www.carlylehouse.org | $4 | Tues.–Sat. 10–5, Sun. noon–5, guided tour every ½ hr.

Christ Church. Both Washington and Lee were pewholders in this Episcopal church. (Washington paid £36 and 10 shillings—a lot of money in those days—for Pew 60.) Built in 1773, Christ Church is a good example of Georgian church architecture. It has a fine Palladian window, an interior balcony, and an English wrought-brass-and-crystal chandelier. Docents give tours during visiting hours. | 118 N. Washington St., Old Town Alexandria | 703/549–1450 | www.historicchristchurch.org | Free | Mon.–Sat. 9–4, Sun. 2–4.

Gadsby's Tavern Museum. This museum is housed in the old City Tavern and Hotel, which was a center of political and social life in the late 18th century. George Washington went to birthday celebrations in the ballroom here. A tour takes you through the taproom, dining room, assembly room, ballroom, and communal bedrooms. Friday-evening tours visit the same rooms but are led by a costumed guide using a candlelit lantern. | 134 N. Royal St., Old Town Alexandria | 703/838–4242 | oha.ci.alexandria.va. us/gadsby | $4, lantern tour $5 | Oct.–Mar., Tues.–Sat. 11–4, Sun. 1–4, last tour at 3:15; Apr.–Sept., Tues.–Sat. 10–5, Sun. 1–5, last tour at 4:15; tours 15 mins before and after the hr. Lantern tour Mar.–Nov., Fri. 7–9:30.

★ **Mount Vernon.** The mansion and surrounding lands had been in the Washington family for nearly 90 years by the time George inherited it in 1761. Before taking over command of the Continental Army, Washington was a yeoman farmer managing the 8,000-acre plantation. He oversaw the transformation of the main house from an ordinary farm dwelling into what was, for the time, a grand mansion. You can stroll nearly 170 of the estate's 500 acres, visiting gardens, workshops, the kitchen, the carriage house, the greenhouse, the slave quarters, and—down the hill toward the boat landing—the tomb of George and Martha Washington. There's also a pioneer farmer site: a 4-acre hands-on exhibit with a reconstruction of George Washington's 16-sided treading barn as its centerpiece. As you tour the mansion, guides are stationed throughout the house to describe the furnishings and answer questions. Don't miss the view from the riverside porch out back, overlooking an expanse of lawn that slopes down to the Potomac. A tour of house and grounds takes about two hours. Private evening candle-light tours of the mansion with staff dressed in 18th-century costumes can be arranged. | Southern end of George Washington Pkwy., Mount Vernon, 8 mi south of Alexandria | 703/780–2000, 703/799–8606 evening tours | www.mountvernon.org | $9, $11 combination ticket with gristmill | Mar., Sept., and Oct., daily 9–5; Apr.–Aug., daily 8–5; Nov.–Feb., daily 9–4.

George Washington's Gristmill. After many years of research, this gristmill opened in 2002 on the site of his original mill and distillery. During the guided tours, led by historic interpreters, you'll meet an 18th-century miller and watch the water-powered wheel grind grain into flour just as it did 200 years ago. Tickets can be purchased either at the gristmill itself or at Mount Vernon's main gate. | Rte. 235 between Mount Vernon and U.S. 1, 3 mi west of Mount Vernon | 703/780–2000 | $4, $11 combination ticket with Mount Vernon | Apr.–Oct., daily 10–5.

Mount Vernon Trail. You can walk, jog, or bike the 18½-mi Mount Vernon Trail, which follows the banks of the Potomac River from the south end of George Washington Parkway to Theodore Roosevelt Island, an 88-acre island with a memorial dedicated to the 26th U.S. president. A free map indicating sights along the trail is available at the Ramsay House Visitor Center at 221 King St. | 703/289–2500 National Parks Service | www.nps.gov/gwmp/mvt.html | Free | Daily dawn–dusk.

Stabler-Leadbeater Apothecary. Once patronized by George Washington and the Lee family, Alexandria's Stabler-Leadbeater Apothecary is the second-oldest apothecary in the country (the oldest is reputedly in Bethlehem, Pennsylvania). Some believe that it was here, on October 17, 1859, that Lt. Col. Robert E. Lee received orders to lead Marines sent from the Washington Barracks to help suppress John Brown's insurrection at Harper's Ferry (then part of Virginia). The shop now houses a small museum of 18th- and 19th-century apothecary memorabilia, including one of the finest collections of apothecary bottles in the country (some 800 bottles in all). | 105–107 S. Fairfax St., Old Town Alexandria | 703/836–3713 | www.apothecarymuseum.org | $2.50 | Mon.–Sat. 10–4, Sun. 1–5.

Torpedo Factory Art Center. Torpedoes were manufactured here by the U.S. Navy during World War I and World War II. Now the building houses the studios and workshops of about 160 artists and artisans and has become one of Alexandria's most popular attractions. You can view the workshops of printmakers, jewelry makers, sculptors, painters, and potters, and most of the art and crafts are for sale. | 105 N. Union St., Old Town Alexandria | 703/838–4565 | www.torpedofactory.org | Free | Daily 10–5.

Dining

Blue Point Grill. Seafood. The raw bar, with its array of lobster, jumbo shrimp, oysters, and other seafood, is especially popular at this small and cozy spot. The kitchen is also known for cedar-plank salmon with garlic mashed potatoes. There is open-air dining on the sidewalk and on the covered redbrick patio, shaded by shrubs and cooled by circulating fans. Sunday brunch. No smoking. | 600 Franklin St. | 703/739–0404 | AE, MC, V | $$–$$$

Gadsby's Tavern. American. Strolling minstrels provide the entertainment in this 18th-century tavern-restaurant in the building where George Washington entertained the Marquis de Lafayette. Appropriately enough, the table service is in full costume and character. Specialties include game pie, venison, rabbit, and George Washington's "Favorite Duck." In summer, fresh crabs are served in the outdoor courtyard, which also has a bar. There are weekly and daily specials, and Friday-night beer tastings. Reservations are essential on Friday and Saturday. Kids' menu. Sunday brunch. No smoking. | 138 N. Royal St. | 703/548–1288 | AE, DC, MC, V | $$–$$$$

Red Hot and Blue. American. Late Republican politico and moonlighting blues musician Lee Atwater founded this barbecue joint. The original Arlington location of what is now a chain was frequented by the political "in-crowd" in its heyday. Both political and blues-related photos share wall space, and blues music from the 1950s and '60s plays softly in the background. Specialties are authentic Memphis pit-barbecue and hickory-smoked ribs. Kids' menu. | 6482 Landsdown Centre | 703/550–6465 | AE, D, MC, V | $$–$$$

Union Street Public House. American. With a bar that's as busy as a Metro station at lunch hour, Union Street Public House (originally a sea captain's home—circa 1870) is a social hub for locals as well as such out-of-town notables as Katie Couric, Sam Donaldson, and G. Gordon Liddy. Sandwiches are good, as are selections from the grill and raw bar. Family-style service. Kids' menu. Sunday brunch. No smoking. | 121 S. Union St. | 703/548–1785 | AE, DC, MC, V | $–$$

Lodging

Best Western Pentagon. In the shadow of the world's largest office building, this hotel has free shuttle service to three nearby Metro stops and the attractions around them. Three two-story buildings have outside entrances and conventional motel rooms. The tower section has a restaurant and meeting rooms on the ground floor, and many of its guest rooms have nice views. Restaurant, room service, in-room data ports, in-room safes, cable TV, pool, gym, bar, laundry service, business services, airport shuttle, free parking, no-smoking rooms. | 2480 S. Glebe Rd., 22206 | 703/979–4400 or 800/426–6886 | fax 703/685–0051 | www.bestwestern.com | 206 rooms | AE, D, DC, MC, V | $–$$

Embassy Suites Old Town Alexandria. Adjacent to Alexandria's landmark George Washington Masonic Temple sits this modern all-suites hotel. There is a playroom for children. A free shuttle is available to transport you to the scenic Alexandria riverfront, which has shops and restaurants. A cooked-to-order breakfast is complimentary, as is the cocktail reception every evening. Restaurant, in-room data ports, refrigerators, cable TV, indoor pool, gym, hot tub, sauna, laundry service, business services, meeting rooms, parking (fee), no-smoking rooms. | 1900 Diagonal Rd., 22314 | 703/684–5900 or 800/362–2779 | fax 703/684–1403 | www.embassysuites.com | 268 suites | BP | AE, D, DC, MC, V | $$$$

★**Morrison House.** The architecture, parquet floors, crystal chandeliers, decorative fireplaces, and furnishings of Morrison House are so faithful to the federal period (1790–1820) that it's often mistaken for a renovation rather than a structure built from scratch in 1985. The hotel blends early-American charm with modern conveniences. Some rooms have fireplaces, and all have four-poster beds. The popular and refreshing Elysium Restaurant serves American contemporary cuisine. The hotel is in the heart of Old Town Alexandria, seven blocks from the train and Metro stations. 2 restaurants, dining room, room service, in-room data ports, cable TV, in-room VCRs, bar, piano bar, parking (fee), no-smoking rooms. | 116 S. Alfred St., 22314 | 703/838–8000 or 800/367–0800 | fax 703/684–6283 | www.morrisonhouse.com | 42 rooms, 3 suites | AE, DC, MC, V | $$$$

Fredericksburg

Fredericksburg and Spotsylvania National Military Park. The 9,000-acre park actually includes four battlefields and three historic buildings, all accessible for a single admission price. At the Fredericksburg and Chancellorsville visitor centers you can learn about the area's role in the Civil War by watching a 22-minute video at Fredericksburg and a 12-minute slide show at Spotsylvania, and by viewing displays of soldiers' art and battlefield relics. In season, park rangers lead walking tours. The centers' tour cassettes ($4.95 rental, $7.50 purchase) and maps show how to reach hiking trails at the Wilderness, Chancellorsville (where General Stonewall Jackson was mistakenly shot by his own troops), and Spotsylvania Court House battlefields (all within 15 mi of Fredericksburg).

Just outside the Fredericksburg battlefield park visitor center is Sunken Road, where from December 11 to 13, 1862, General Robert E. Lee led his troops to a bloody but resounding victory over Union forces attacking across the Rappahannock (total casualties reached 18,000). Much of the stone wall that protected Lee's sharpshooters is now a re-creation, but 100 yards from the visitor center, part of the original wall overlooks the statue *The Angel of Marye's Heights,* by Felix de Weldon. This memorial honors Sergeant Richard Kirkland, a South Carolinian who risked his life to bring water to wounded foes; he later died at the Battle of Chickamauga. | Fredericksburg Battlefield-park visitor center, Lafayette Blvd. and Sunken Rd. | 540/373–6122 | Chancellorsville Battlefield visitor center, Rte. 3 W | 540/786–2880 | $4 (includes all 4 battlefields) | Visitor centers daily 9–5, driving and walking tours daily dawn–dusk.

George Washington's Ferry Farm. Washington's boyhood home, once the site of a ferry crossing, is just across the Rappahannock River from downtown Fredericksburg. Ferry Farm, which once consisted of 600 acres, became a major artillery base and river-crossing site for Union forces during the Battle of Fredericksburg. | 268 Kings Hwy. (Rte. 3 E), at Ferry Rd. | 540/370–0732 | www.kenmore.org | $3 | Mid-Feb.–late May and early Sept.–Dec., daily 11–4; late May–early Sept., daily 10–5.

James Monroe Museum and Memorial Library. This tiny one-story building—on the site where Monroe, who became the fifth president of the United States, practiced law from 1787 to 1789—contains many of Monroe's possessions, collected and preserved by his family. They include a mahogany dispatch box used during the negotiation of the 1803 Louisiana Purchase (Monroe was minister to France under Thomas Jefferson) and the desk on which Monroe signed the doctrine named for him. | 908 Charles St. | 540/654–2110 | $4 | Mar.–Nov., daily 9–5; Dec.–Feb., daily 10–4.

Kenmore. Named Kenmore by a later owner, this house was built in 1775 on a 1,300-acre plantation owned by Colonel Fielding Lewis, a patriot, merchant, and brother-in-law of George Washington. Lewis sacrificed much of his fortune to operate a gun factory that supplied the American forces during the Revolutionary War. As a result, his debts forced his widow to sell the home after his death. Kenmore's plain exterior belies its lavish interior. The plaster ceiling moldings are outstanding and even more ornate than those at Mount Vernon. | 1201 Washington Ave. | 540/373–3381 | www.kenmore.org | $6 | Mar.–Dec., Mon.–Sat. 10–5, Sun. noon–5; Jan. and Feb., weekdays by reservation only, Sat. noon–4.

Mary Washington House. George purchased a three-room cottage for his mother in 1772 for £225, renovated it, and more than doubled its size with additions. She spent the last 17 years of her life here, tending the garden where her original boxwoods still flourish today, and where many a bride and groom now exchange their vows. The home has been a museum since 1930. Inside, displays include Mrs. Washington's "best dressing glass," a silver-over-tin mirror in a Chippendale frame; her teapot; Washington family dinnerware; and period furniture. | 1200 Charles St. | 540/373–1569 | $5 | Apr.–Nov., Mon.–Sat. 9–5, Sun. 11–5; Dec.–Mar., Mon.–Sat. 10–4, Sun. noon–4.

National Cemetery. The National Cemetery is the final resting place of 15,000 Union dead, most of whom were never identified. | Lafayette Blvd. and Sunken Rd. | 540/373–6122 | Daily sunrise–sunset.

Rising Sun Tavern. In 1760 George Washington's brother Charles built as his home what later became the Rising Sun Tavern, an Historic District watering hole for such patriots as the Lee brothers (the only siblings to sign the Declaration of Independence); Patrick Henry, the five-term governor of Virginia who said, "Give me liberty or give me death"; and future presidents Washington and Jefferson. A "wench" in period costume leads a tour without stepping out of character. From her you hear how travelers slept and what they ate and drank at this busy institution. In the taproom you're served spiced tea. | 1304 Caroline St. | 540/371–1494 | $5 | Apr.–Nov., Mon.–Sat. 9–5, Sun. 11–5; Dec.–Mar., Mon.–Sat. 10–4, Sun. noon–4.

Dining

Bistro 309. Mediterranean. The windowed facade and vaulted ceiling beckon you into a colorful dining room with touches of copper, an old pine bar, and changing local art. Changing menus employ fresh fish, wild game, and vegetables of the season, with daily specials displayed on a chalkboard. Quail, rainbow trout, and lamb are specialties. | 309 William St. | 540/371–9999 | AE, MC, V | $$–$$$$

Claiborne's. American. On the walls of this swank eatery in the 1910 Fredericksburg train station are historic train photographs. The restaurant—decorated in a dark green-and-navy color scheme with mahogany-and-brass bars—specializes in low-country Southern cuisine. Accompanying the steaks, chops, and seafood are ample vegetable side dishes served family style. | 200 Lafayette Blvd. | 540/371–7080 | www.claibornesrestaurant.com | No lunch Mon.–Sat., no dinner Sun. | AE, DC, MC, V | $$–$$$$

La Petite Auberge. French. Inside a pre-Revolutionary brick general store, this white-tablecloth restaurant actually has three dining rooms, as well as a small bar. Specialties such as house-cut beef, French onion soup, and seafood are all served with a Continental accent. A prix-fixe ($14) three-course dinner is served from 5:30 to 7 Monday through Thursday. | 311 William St. | 540/371–2727 | Closed Sun. | AE, D, MC, V | $$–$$$$

Smythe's Cottage & Tavern. American. Taking a step into this cozy little building of several small dining rooms—once a blacksmith's house—is like taking a step back in time. The surroundings are colonial; the lunch and dinner menus, classic Virginia: seafood pie, quail, stuffed flounder. | 303 Fauquier St. | 540/373–1645 | Closed Tues. | MC, V | $$–$$$$

Lodging

Fredericksburg Colonial Inn. This 1920s motel with moss-green siding and forest-green awnings conceals a center staircase popular for weddings. Rooms are furnished with authentic antiques and appointments from the Civil War period, and the lobby has an old-time upright piano. Breakfast includes beverages, cereal, and coffee cake. Refrigerators; no smoking. | 1707 Princess Anne St., 22401 | 540/371–5666 | 30 rooms | CP | AE, MC, V | $

Kenmore Inn. The front porch seems to beckon you up to the door of this house, a few blocks from the visitor center downtown. Inside, antique furniture abounds. Four guest rooms have working fireplaces. On weekends, you can head to the English pub for live music. Restaurant, pub; no room TVs. | 1200 Princess Anne St., 22401 | 540/371–7622 | fax 540/371–5480 | www.kenmoreinn.com | 9 rooms | CP | AE, D, DC, MC, V | $$–$$$

Richard Johnston Inn. This elegant B&B was constructed in the late 1700s and served as the home of Richard Johnston, mayor of Fredericksburg from March 1809 to March 1810. Guest rooms are decorated with period antiques and reproductions. The aroma of freshly baked breads and muffins entices you to breakfast in the large federal-style dining room set with fine china, silver, and linens. The inn is across from the visitor center and two blocks from the train station. Free parking; no room phones, no TV in some rooms, no smoking. | 711 Caroline St., 22401 | 540/899–7606 | www.bbonline.com | 6 rooms, 2 suites | BP | AE, MC, V | $–$$$

Newport News

U.S. Army Transportation Museum. The only facility in the country devoted entirely to the history of military transportation, this museum has nearly 100 vehicles, including experimental craft, on display. You can see the Flying Crane—the army's largest helicopter—plus dioramas and the world's only captive "flying saucer." | Fort Eustis Bldg. 300 (Besson Hall) | 757/878–1182 | Free | Tues.–Sun. 9–4:30.

The Mariners' Museum. A world history of seagoing vessels and the people who sailed them is the focus of this museum in 550-acre Mariners' Museum park. Items from the RMS *Titanic* are among the exhibits. Some of the scale-model ships on view are so tiny that you must look at them through magnifying glasses; more than 50 full-size craft are also on display, including a Native American bark canoe, a gondola, a coast guard cutter, and a Chinese sampan. In one gallery you can watch a boat being constructed; another gallery is devoted to the figureheads from the bows of sailing ships. You can also see nautical gear, a collection of scrimshaw, and photographs and paintings that recount naval history and the story of private-sector seafaring. The museum is the repository for the USS *Monitor.* Guided tours are given throughout the day. The grounds include a 5-mi walking trail, a picnic area, and a lake where you can fish. | 101 Museum Dr. | 757/596–2222 or 800/581–7245 | fax 757/591–7320 | www.mariner.org | $7 | Daily 10–5.

Virginia War Museum. The museum traces military history from 1775 to Desert Storm; its collection of more than 60,000 artifacts includes a 10-by-10-foot section of the Berlin Wall, a Civil War blockade-runner's uniform, weapons, wartime posters, and photographs. Exhibits on African-Americans and women in the military also are featured. A Vietnam War memorial is on the Huntington Park grounds. | 9285 Warwick Blvd. | 757/247–8523 | www.warmuseum.org | $5 | Mon.–Sat. 9–5, Sun. 1–5.

Dining

Al Fresco. Italian. Distressed, hand-painted walls and a mural of an Italian backyard overlook the water here. *Pollo française* (chicken breast in lemon–white wine sauce), calamari fra diavolo, *vitello alla pizzaiola* (veal with a tomato-wine sauce), and other classics are served. | 11710 Jefferson Ave. | 757/873–0644 | Closed Sun. | AE, D, MC, V | $–$$

Das Waldcafe. German. Outside, Das Waldcafe is a German-style building with *Fachwerk* beams on the facade. Inside, it's a friendly, homey eatery with fresh flowers on each table. *Gulasch* (diced beef with mushrooms), Wiener schnitzel (breaded veal steak), and *Jäger* schnitzel (veal steak with mushroom sauce) are popular. | 12529 Warwick Blvd. | 757/930–1781 | Closed Mon. No lunch Sat. | AE, DC, MC, V | $$

Herman's Harbor House. Seafood. A wonderful collection of turn-of-the-20th-century nautical photos adorns this waterfront restaurant. Check out the working sailboat models before tucking into crab cakes, fried oysters, or soft-shell crab. Steak is also available, and there's outdoor dining on a deck overlooking the water. Kids' menu. Sunday brunch. | 663 Deep Creek Rd. | 757/930–1000 | No lunch Sun.–Mon.; Sept.–May, no lunch Sat. | AE, D, MC, V | $–$$

Norfolk

Carrie B. Harbor Tours. Tour Norfolk's naval shipyards and operating base, plus historic Fort Norfolk, on a reproduction of a Mississippi-style paddle wheeler with an open-air top deck. Tours range from 1½ to 2½ hours. | Waterside Marina | 757/393–4735 | $14 | Apr.–Oct. daily; call for departure times.

Chrysler Museum of Art. One of America's major art museums, the Chrysler has a diverse collection of more than 30,000 objects. You can find works by Rubens, Gainsborough, Renoir, Picasso, Monet, and Pollock, as well as art from African, Egyptian, pre-Columbian, and Asian cultures. Decorative arts include English porcelain and the Tiffany glass collection is renowned. Work by both 19th-century pioneers and contemporary artists hang in the photography gallery, and there are regularly scheduled lectures, films, and concerts. | 245 W. Olney Rd. | 757/664–6200 | www.chrysler.org | Donations accepted | Tues.–Sat. 10–5, Sun. 1–5.

Douglas MacArthur Memorial. General Douglas MacArthur is buried here; he designated Norfolk as the site for a monument to himself because it was his mother's birthplace. The mausoleum is in the rotunda of the old City Hall; 11 adjoining galleries house mementos of MacArthur's career, including his signature corncob pipe. A 25-minute biographical film is screened continuously. | MacArthur Sq. | 757/441–2965 | fax 757/441–5389 | www.whro.org | Free | Mon.–Sat. 10–5, Sun. 11–5.

Hermitage Foundation Museum. The largest privately owned collection of Asian art in the United States is inside this English Tudor–style house, built by the Sloanes, a textile-tycoon family at the turn of the 20th century. Ivory and jade carvings, ancient bronzes, and a 1,400-year-old marble Buddha from China are a few of the prize objects on display. There are also a decorative arts collection with Tiffany glass, Persian rugs, and furniture from the Middle East, India, Europe, and America. You can picnic on the surrounding 12 acres, which border the Lafayette River. | 7637 N. Shore Rd. | 757/423–2052 | $5 | Mon.–Sat. 10–5, Sun. 1–5.

Norfolk Botanical Garden. Azaleas, rhododendrons, and camellias fill this 155-acre garden. Its landscaped Japanese garden is planted with trees native to that country; a fragrance garden for the blind includes identification labels in Braille. The Tropical Pavilion has more than 100 varieties of exotic plants. Throughout are marble statues of famous artists, carved in the late 19th century by Moses Ezekiel. From mid-March to October, boats and trams carry visitors along routes to view seasonal plants and flowers, including 4,000 varieties of roses on 3½ acres. Year-round, you can stroll 12 mi of paths.

There's also a café. | 6700 Azalea Garden Rd. | 757/441–5830 | www.nbgs.org | $6 | Apr. 14–Oct. 15, daily 9–7; Oct. 16–Apr. 13, daily 9–5.

Norfolk Naval Base and Norfolk Naval Air Station. On the northern edge of the city, the naval base has about 115 ships of the Atlantic and Mediterranean fleets. Among them is the USS *Theodore Roosevelt,* a nuclear-powered aircraft carrier with a crew of 6,300, said to be one of the largest warships in the world. You can drive into the base during the day as long as you avoid the restricted areas indicated by signs. Guided 45-minute bus tours operate year-round, departing from the Tidewater Regional Transit kiosk at Waterside Festival Hall (on the waterfront) and from the Naval Base tour office (north of Gate 5 at 9079 Hampton Blvd.). Designated ships are open to visitors Saturday and Sunday afternoons; on national holidays you can see aircraft carriers. | 9079 Hampton Blvd., at I–564 | 757/444–7955 or 757/444–1577 | fax 757/445–0438 | www.navstanorva.navy.mil | $7.50 | Daily 8–4; tour schedule varies, call ahead.

Dining

Doumar's. American. Travel back to the 1950s at this re-created drive-in with car-hop service and seating inside. On display is the original ice-cream-cone–making machine used by Abe Doumar, who invented the cone in 1904. Homemade ice cream (with hand-rolled cones), limeade, sandwiches, and pork barbecue are specialties. Breakfast served. | 1919 Monticello Ave. | 757/627–4163 | Closed Sun. | No credit cards | ¢–$$$

Freemason Abbey. Contemporary. Built as a church in 1873, the restaurant retains the original high ceilings, woodwork, wood tresses, and bell tower. There's also stained glass in the bar. Lobster draws the crowds; other items include prime rib and seafood. Kids' menu. Sunday brunch. | 209 W. Freemason St. | 757/622–3966 | AE, D, DC, MC, V | $$–$$$$

Ship's Cabin. Seafood. Gaze over the Chesapeake bay front from the outside deck. Inside, the restaurant looks like a ship, with pictures of the sea, a rowboat caught in the rafters, and wooden fish hanging from the ceiling. In winter, warm up by one of the fireplaces. Try the grilled tuna with bacon and balsamic reduction or the grilled salmon with lemon vinaigrette. Pasta, steak, and chicken are also available. Kids' menu. | 4110 E. Ocean View Ave. | 757/362–4659 | No lunch | AE, D, DC, MC, V | $$

Todd Jurich's Bistro! Continental. The seasonal menu emphasizes fresh regional flavors—seafood from the Eastern Shore and Outer Banks and locally grown, organic produce—often with an Asian influence. The signature dish is seared native yellowfin tuna with wasabi mashed potatoes. Also popular is steak with garlic mashed potatoes. Check the chalkboard for daily specials, which might include coconut tiger prawns or a variety of crab preparations. | 210 W. York St. | 757/622–3210 | www.toddjurichsbistro.com | Reservations essential | No lunch weekends | AE, D, DC, MC, V | $$–$$$$

Richmond

Agecroft Hall. Built in the 15th century in Lancashire, England, Agecroft Hall was transported to its present location, overlooking the James River, in 1926. Set amid 23 acres of gardens and woodlands, this half-timbered country manor house contains an extensive collection of Tudor and early-Stuart art and furniture (1485–1660) and a few priceless collector's items. The tours begin with a 10-minute slide show about the hall's original English location and the process of shipping it to the United States. | 4305 Sulgrave Rd. | 804/353–4241 | www.agecrofthall.com | $7 | Tues.–Sat. 10–4, Sun. 12:30–5.

Black History Museum and Cultural Center of Virginia. The lives and accomplishments of black Virginians, from Jamestown to the present day, are told through visual, oral, and written records. The history of the Jackson Ward, considered the first community of black professionals, is highlighted. | 00 Clay St. | 804/780–9093 | www.blackhistorymuseum.org | $4 | Tues.–Sat. 10–5, Sun. 11–5.

Hollywood Cemetery. U.S. presidents John Tyler and James Monroe; Confederate president Jefferson Davis; Generals Fitzhugh Lee, J.E.B. Stuart, and George E. Pickett; and oceanographer Matthew Fontaine Maury, "Pathfinder of the Seas," rest in this parklike hilltop cemetery at Albemarle Street. A granite pyramid built of stones quarried from the James River below marks the final resting place of 18,000 Confederate soldiers. Dedicated in 1849, the cemetery's monuments, ironwork, and statuary provide numerous examples of 19th-century funeral art and its symbols. | 412 S. Cherry St. | 804/648–8501 | Free | Mid-May–mid-Oct., daily 8–6; mid-Oct.–mid-May, daily 8–5.

Museum of the Confederacy. The museum has one of the country's largest collections of Civil War artifacts, paintings, and documents, including the sword Robert E. Lee wore to the surrender at Appomattox. You can park free in the adjacent Medical College of Virginia visitor-patient parking deck; the museum will validate tickets. | 1201 E. Clay St. | 804/649–1861 | www.moc.org | $7, $10 combination ticket with White House and Museum | Mon.–Sat. 10–5, Sun. noon–5.

Richmond National Battlefield Park (Civil War Visitor Center). As the capital of the Confederacy, Richmond came under attack from Union troops seven times during the Civil War. This park preserves the sites of two battles that came closest to the Union army's goal of taking over the city—General George McClellan's Peninsula Campaign (1862) and General Ulysses S. Grant's Overland Campaign (1864). The park's 10 units also include the sites of the Seven Days' Battle (June 26–July 1, 1862), Cold Harbor (June 1–3, 1864), and other engagements in the vicinity of Richmond, as well as fortifications used by both sides during the siege of the city. | 470 Tredegar St. | 804/226–1981 | www.nps.gov/rich/home.htm | Free | Daily dawn–dusk.

Chimborazo Civil War Medical Museum. In June 2002, the renovated Chimborazo Visitor's Center was reborn as the Chimborazo Civil War Medical Museum. The museum contains exhibits on medical equipment and hospital life, including information on the men and women who staffed Chimborazo hospital. This building is also the Headquarters for Richmond National Battlefield Park and the Maggie L. Walker National Historic Site. | Eastern end of Broad St. | 804/226–1981 | www.nps.gov | Free | Daily 9–5.

St. John's Episcopal Church. Virginia's second Revolutionary convention met here in 1775. Richmond's oldest place of worship, its original frame building was erected in 1741. Edgar Allan Poe's mother and many famous early Virginians are buried in its cemetery. | 2401 E. Broad St. | 804/648–5015 | $3 | Mon.–Sat. 10–4, Sun. 1–4; closed some weekends for private functions.

State Capitol. Thomas Jefferson designed the State Capitol in 1785, modeling it on a Roman temple, the Maison Carrée, in Nîmes, France. The central portion was completed in 1792; the wings were added in 1906. The Virginia General Assembly, the oldest legislative body in the Western Hemisphere, still meets here. A wealth of sculpture is contained within: busts of Virginia's eight presidents and a famous life-size statue of George Washington by Jean-Antoine Houdon, the only work for which Washington posed. In the old Hall of the House of Delegates, Robert E. Lee accepted the command of the Confederate forces in Virginia; a bronze statue marks the spot where he stood. Guided tours operate continuously throughout the day and delve into the building's history and architectural highlights. | 9th and Broad Sts. | 804/698–1788 | legis.state.va.us | Free | Apr.–Nov., daily 9–5; Dec.–Mar., Mon.–Sat. 9–5, Sun. 1–5.

Virginia Museum of Fine Arts. Five jeweled Fabergé eggs are stellar attractions here. The encyclopedic collection ranges from ancient to contemporary art, from paintings by Goya, Renoir, and van Gogh to art nouveau furniture, African masks, Roman statuary, and British sporting art. Free tours are given. | 2800 Grove Ave. | 804/340–1400 | www.vmfa.state.va.us | $5 suggested donation | Tues., Wed., and Fri.–Sun. 11–5, Thurs. 11–8; tours Tues.–Sun. at 2:30.

White House of the Confederacy Museum. Preservationists have carefully recreated the interior of this mansion as it was during the Civil War, when Jefferson Davis lived here. You can tour 11 period rooms with many original furnishings. Constructed in 1818 of brick, the house is stuccoed to give the appearance of a stone mansion. There are occasional dinners with a Civil War theme. | 1203 E. Clay St. | 804/649–1861 | www.moc.org | $7, $10 combination ticket with Museum of the Confederacy | Mon.–Sat. 10–5, Sun. noon–5.

Dining

Byram's Lobster House. Seafood. Along with live lobster and other seafood, steak, pasta, and lamb chops are served here. There's a full bar, where you can grab a meal if the room is crowded. Local artwork is on display. Early-bird dinners weekdays. | 3215 W. Broad St. | 804/355–9193 | AE, D, DC, MC, V | $$–$$$$

Half Way House. Contemporary. American food is served in an intimate room with low ceilings, brick walls, and fireplaces. The bill of fare includes filet mignon with fried shrimp and chocolate-almond-coconut cheesecake. | 10301 Jefferson Davis Hwy. (Rte. 1) | 804/275–1760 | No lunch weekends | AE, D, DC, MC, V | $$$–$$$$

Hard Shell. Seafood. The downtown–Shockoe Slip spot has a full raw bar. Try the house pasta (mixed seafood tossed with penne), seafood quesadilla, and vegetable strudel. There's an outdoor patio courtyard. Sunday brunch. | 1411 E. Cary St. | 804/643–2333 | Closed Sun. No lunch Sat. | AE, D, DC, MC, V | $$$–$$$$

Lemaire. Southern. Eight small dining rooms, punctuated by marble, heavy drapes, and rich colors, serve regional Southern cooking with European classical and American contemporary influences. The nightly four-course tasting menu comes with wine. Specialties are crab cakes, duck breast, and loin of lamb. Breakfast served. | Main St. between Adams and Franklin Sts. | 804/788–8000 | AE, D, DC, MC, V | $$$$

Tobacco Company. American. The three floors of this restaurant are in a renovated 19th-century tobacco company building. The first floor is a lounge with a bar, couches, a fireplace, and exposed brick walls. The second floor is formal; the third floor is more casual with Greenwich wicker furniture. There is also an open-air garden atrium. The menu includes prime rib, and there's a dessert buffet. Band Monday–Saturday. Sunday brunch. | 1201 E. Cary St. | 804/782–9431 | No lunch Sun. | AE, D, DC, MC, V | $$–$$$$

Lodging

Holiday Inn Richmond Central. You're paying for location when you book a room at this two-building complex: it's in the center of town. Some rooms have balconies, and there is a courtyard in the back. Restaurant, picnic area, in-room data ports, cable TV, pool, laundry service, some pets allowed, free parking, no-smoking rooms. | 3207 North Blvd., 23230 | 804/359–9441 or 800/465–4329 | fax 804/359–3207 | 184 rooms | AE, D, DC, MC, V | $

Inn of Virginia. At the west end of Richmond, near the Shops at Willow Lawn, the inn is just a short walk from downtown. Built in 1950, the three-floor stucco building has a lobby with antique reproductions, and spare and tidy rooms. Restaurant, in-room data ports, cable TV, pool, lounge, laundry facilities, free parking, no-smoking rooms. | 5215 W. Broad St., 23230 | 804/288–4011 or 800/289–9814 | fax 804/288–2163 | www.innsofvirginia.com | 141 rooms | AE, D, DC, MC, V | $

Radisson Historic District Hotel. When the State's General Assembly is in session, legislators make this former Holiday Inn their home. The restaurant looks out onto Franklin

Street, and the rooftop pool has a 16-story view. Restaurant, in-room data ports, cable TV, pool, gym, lounge, no-smoking rooms, free parking. | 301 W. Franklin St., 23220 | 804/ 644–9871 | fax 804/344–4380 | 230 rooms | AE, D, DC, MC, V | $–$$

William Catlin House. Built in 1845, this two-story inn is in the Church Hill Historic District, 1 mi east of downtown. Small, private and intimate, the inn only has five rooms. Four rooms feature queen beds; one net-canopy bed, one regular canopy bed, and a few four-poster beds. One room features double beds. Street parking is available and a complimentary breakfast is included. No smoking. | 2304 E. Broad St., 23223 | 804/ 780–3746 | 5 rooms, 3 with bath | BP | D, MC, V | $$

Williamsburg

Busch Gardens Williamsburg. The 360-acre theme park has more than 35 rides as well as nine re-creations of European and French Canadian hamlets. In addition to roller coasters, the park has bumper cars and water adventures. Shows and rides are included in the admission price. | 1 Busch Pl., off I–64 E, Exit 243A | 757/253–3350 or 800/ 343–7943 | www.buschgardens.com | $47 | Call for hrs.

Colonial Williamsburg. Williamsburg was the capital of Virginia from 1699 until 1780, when it was succeeded by Richmond. Restoration of the town to its 18th-century appearance began in 1926 through the efforts of William A. R. Goodwin, rector of Bruton Parish Church, and John D. Rockefeller Jr., who financed the massive undertaking. The work of archaeologists and historians of the Colonial Williamsburg Foundation continue, and the 173-acre restored area is operated as a living-history museum. There are 88 original 18th-century buildings and another 40 that have been reconstructed on their original sites. Period authenticity governs the grounds, which include 90 acres of gardens. Costumed interpreters lead house tours and demonstrate historic trades. The restored area can only be toured on foot; all vehicular traffic is prohibited to preserve the colonial atmosphere. Colonial Williamsburg offers one-year, two-day, single-day, and specific attraction admission tickets. Arrangements for visitors with disabilities can be made in advance. | Junction Rtes. 5 and 31 (Jamestown Rd.) | 757/220–7644, 757/220–7645, or 800/447–8679 | fax 757/ 220–7702 | www.colonialwilliamsburg.org | $39 | Daily 9–5.

Abby Aldrich Rockefeller Folk Art Center. American folk art, from toys and weather vanes to sculptures, dollhouses, and paintings are showcased here.

Bruton Parish Church. This 1715 church has served continuously as a place of worship; many local eminences, including one royal governor, are interred in the graveyard. | 757/229–2891 | www.brutonparish.org.

Capitol. Exhibition buildings are all over Colonial Williamsburg. Anchoring the eastern end of Duke of Gloucester Street is the Capitol, the center of Virginia's political power from 1699 to 1781; it was here that the pre-Revolutionary House of Burgesses challenged the royally appointed council. A tour explains the development of American democracy from its English parliamentary roots. The building is a reproduction with dark-wood wainscoting, pewter chandeliers, and towering ceilings.

Carter's Grove. Carter Burwell built this mansion on a bluff above the James River in 1755, on land purchased by his grandfather, Robert "King" Carter, one of Virginia's wealthiest landowners. Remodeled in 1919, the house retains its original wood paneling and elaborate carvings, and is furnished in Colonial Revival style. The settlement around Carter's Grove was reconstructed after extensive archaeological investigation and includes 18th-century slaves' quarters. On the grounds you can see exhibits in the Winthrop Rockefeller Archeology Museum, including displays about Wolstenholme Towne, a settlement destroyed by Indians in 1622 that is believed to have been the first planned town in British America. Carter's Grove is closed for renovations until 2005. | 8797 Pocahontas Trail | 757/229–1000 | Mid-Mar.–Dec., Tues.–Sun. 9–5.

Colonial Williamsburg Visitor Center. Purchase tickets for Colonial Williamsburg and pick up a *Visitor's Companion* guide, which lists regular events and special programs, and includes a map of the historic area. The center also shows a 35-minute introductory movie, "Williamsburg—The Story of a Patriot." Information about dining and lodging is available (there's a reservation service). Shuttle buses to the historic area run continuously throughout the day. There's also a bookstore. | 102 Information Center Dr. | 757/220–7645 or 800/246–2099 | www.colonialwilliamsburg.org | Free | Daily 9–5.

Courthouse. Built in 1770, the courthouse was used by municipal and county courts until 1932; the exterior has been restored to its original appearance. Stocks, once used to punish misdemeanors, are located outside the building.

DeWitt Wallace Decorative Arts Gallery. English and American furniture, textiles, prints, and ceramics at this gallery span the 17th to the early 19th centuries. Among the 8,000 pieces in this museum's collection is a full-length portrait of George Washington by Charles Willson Peale.

Governor's Palace. The reconstructed palace, originally built in 1720, was home to seven royal governors and Virginia's first two state governors, Patrick Henry and Thomas Jefferson. It is furnished as it was just before the Revolution, with some authentic period pieces; 800 guns and swords arrayed on the walls and ceilings of several rooms herald the power of the Crown.

Magazine. A 1715 octagonal brick warehouse once stored arms and ammunition; it was used for this purpose by the British, then by the Continental Army, and later by the Confederates during the Civil War. Today, 18th-century firearms are on display within the arsenal.

Public Hospital. A reconstruction of a 1773 insane asylum, the hospital provides a look at the treatment of the mentally ill in the 18th and 19th centuries.

Water Country USA. The amusement park has more than 30 water rides and attractions, live entertainment, shops, and restaurants. The Nitro Racer is a speed slide with a 382-foot drop. The biggest attraction is a 4,500-square-foot heated pool. | Rte. 199 | 757/253–3350 or 800/343–7946 | www.watercountryusa.com | $35 | May 15–May 31 and early Sept., daily 10–6; June–Aug., daily 10–8.

Dining

Aberdeen Barn. Steak. Antiques and casual candlelight dining create a serene look and feel in this rustic wood restaurant. House specialties are prime rib, fresh tuna, and filet mignon. Kids' menu. | 1601 Richmond Rd. | 757/229–6661 | www.aberdeen-barn.com | Closed 1st 2 wks in Jan. No lunch | AE, D, MC, V | $$–$$$$

King's Arms Tavern. American. Costumed servers wait tables while colonial balladeers entertain guests. The restaurant is part of the Colonial Williamsburg Foundation. Dine or have a drink in the garden. The menu has regional American dishes, including peanut soup, game pie, and filet mignon. Kids' menu. | Duke of Gloucester St. | 757/220–7010 | Reservations essential | Closed mid-Jan.–Mar.; closed Tues. May, Sept., Nov., and Dec. | AE, D, DC, MC, V | $$–$$$$

The Trellis. Contemporary. Simplicity and elegance merge in this 800-square-foot space. The interior is done with yellow and green fabrics, walls of handblown glass, and muted golden surfaces. The garden room is a favorite dining section. The soups are particularly savory, and the game, pasta, and seafood choices are safe bets. The Trellis is best known for its chocolate desserts. | 403 Duke of Gloucester St. | 757/229–8610 | www.thetrellis.com | AE, DC, MC, V | $$–$$$

Whaling Company. Seafood. Boats and fishing nets suspended from the rafters underscore that seafood rules here. Standouts are fresh tuna and salmon. Kids' menu. Early-bird dinners Sunday–Friday. | 494 McLaws Circle | 757/229–0275 | No lunch | AE, D, DC, MC, V | $$–$$$$

Lodging

Colonial Houses. Some of the 27 buildings that comprise this property date from the 1800s. There are some rooms with fireplaces and/or private courtyards. You can use the recreational facilities at Williamsburg Lodge and Inn, a few blocks away in the historic district. In-room data ports, cable TV, children's programs (ages 4–12), business services; no smoking. | 302 E. Francis St., 23185 | 757/229–1000 or 800/447–8679 | fax 757/565–8444 | 76 rooms | AE, D, DC, MC, V | $$$–$$$$

Courtyard by Marriott. In a landscaped business park, this property underwent a full renovation in 2003. Most rooms have a patio or balcony. The hotel is near Busch Gardens, the College of William and Mary, and Colonial Williamsburg. Restaurant, in-room data ports, some refrigerators, cable TV, indoor-outdoor pool, gym, hot tub, bar, laundry facilities, business services, no-smoking rooms. | Busch Corporate Center, 470 McLaws Circle, 23185 | 757/221–0700 | fax 757/221–0741 | www.marriott.com | 151 rooms | AE, D, DC, MC, V | $$–$$$

★ **Liberty Rose.** Tree swings, a cozy parlor with a fireplace, and tables for two are among the romantic touches at this antiques-filled B&B. One room has a carved ball-and-claw poster bed, while another has a cherry French canopy bed. Lace-draped windows and silk and jacquard fabrics abound. The inn is a terrific way to experience gentile Southern traditions. In-room VCRs; no kids under 12, no smoking. | 1022 Jamestown Rd., 23185 | 757/253–1260 or 800/545–1825 | www.libertyrose.com | 4 rooms | BP | AE, MC, V | ¢

Williamsburg Sampler. Built in 1976 to represent an 18th-century plantation home, this B&B is ½ mi from the historic district and across from William and Mary College. Rooms have British regency furniture from the 1900s. Picnic area, cable TV, business services; no smoking. | 922 Jamestown Rd., 23185 | 757/253–0398 or 800/722–1169 | fax 757/253–2669 | www.williamsburgsampler.com | 2 rooms, 2 suites | BP | MC, V | $$–$$$$

WESTERN VIRGINIA

CHARLOTTESVILLE, SHENANDOAH VALLEY & THE BLUE RIDGE PARKWAY

Distance: 175 mi;   Time: 4–5 days
Overnight Breaks: Blue Ridge Parkway, Charlottesville, Lexington, Roanoke, Staunton

Some of Virginia's most scenic reaches are highlighted on this drive, which reveals terrific vistas of mountains, valleys, and rolling farmlands. The tour begins in Charlottesville, the most prominent city in the Blue Ridge foothills, and heads west through national park lands to Staunton. From there, you follow the Shenandoah Valley south through Lexington, then pick up the famed Blue Ridge Parkway into Roanoke.

❶ In the foothills of the Blue Ridge Mountains, **Charlottesville** is home to two of Thomas Jefferson's greatest architectural achievements. The third president's mountaintop home, **Monticello,** contains his inventions and personal effects, which reflect quite a diverse set of interests. The grounds include a 1,000-foot-long vegetable garden, vineyards, and orchards that replicate the ones Jefferson cultivated. The **University of Virginia,** founded and designed by Jefferson, has classically inspired pavilions that flank the Rotunda, a half-scale replica of Rome's Pantheon. James Monroe's estate, **Ash Lawn-Highland,** still a working plantation, displays a large collection of the fifth president's possessions. Stay overnight in Charlottesville. Vineyards speckle the countryside, some like Jefferson, Barboursville, and Horton produce award-winning wines.

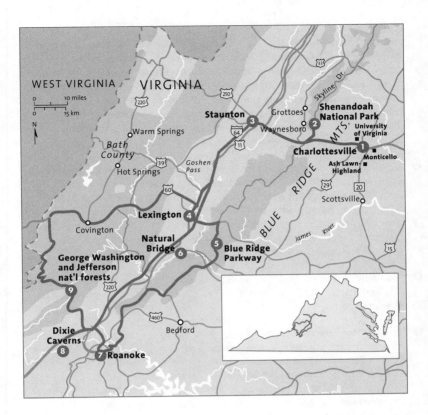

② From Charlottesville, drive 28 mi west on I–64 to **Shenandoah National Park.** This breathtaking park encompasses some of the highest and most scenic portions of the Blue Ridge Mountains. Its roughly 196,500 acres offer hiking, horseback riding, and fishing—and plenty of opportunities to see wildlife close-up. The Appalachian Trail runs the length of the park. Continue west on I–64, crossing into the Shenandoah Valley.

③ **Staunton,** 11 mi from Shenandoah National Park, is one of the oldest cities west of the Blue Ridge. At the **Museum of American Frontier Culture,** an outdoor living history museum, learn how America's Appalachian frontier was settled. It includes four authentically reassembled, 18th-century homesteads from Ireland, England, Germany, and western Virginia. The **Woodrow Wilson Birthplace and Museum** looks as it did in 1856, when the 28th U.S. president was born here. Make time to see a show at the acclaimed **Blackfriars Playhouse** and enjoy modern interactive renditions of Shakespeare's works. There are plenty of historic inns and B&B's in the heart of town. Many are charming, historic Victorians that line the streets. If you have time, stop at the visitor center and pick up a detailed walking tour map with descriptions of each historic property.

④ Continuing south, either on I–81 or the less-trafficked U.S. 11, proceed 55 mi to **Lexington,** a genteel well-preserved town where two Confederate heroes had homes and were laid to rest. **Washington and Lee University,** founded in 1749, is named for the two men intertwined with its past—George Washington and Robert E. Lee. Next door to the university are the imposing neo-Gothic buildings of the **Virginia Military Institute,** founded in 1839. The institute's **George C. Marshall Museum** preserves the memory of the VMI alumnus who served as general and secretary of state, and earned a Nobel peace prize. The **Stonewall Jackson House,** the only home the Civil War general ever owned, offers a glimpse of his private life. For a change of pace, visit the **Virginia Horse Center,** one of the top equine facilities in the United States. Events at this year-round arena range from miniature-horse shows and pony club shows to rodeos and auctions. For such a tiny town, the cuisine is adventurous with some vegetarian, and even vegan, options.

⑤ Just outside of Lexington, head south on the **Blue Ridge Parkway,** a destination unto itself. Governed by the National Park Service, this scenic roadway follows the crest of the mountains into North Carolina's Great Smoky Mountains. Free of commercial intrusions, it has magnificent views of valley, forests, and mountain ranges. Remember to forget time when traveling along this winding road between Charlottesville and Roanoke. The road is meant to be enjoyed. Stop at the scenic overlooks and drive slowly.

⑥ If you want to prolong the drive a bit more, take another detour to **Natural Bridge,** a 215-foot-high, 90-foot-long limestone arch. You can also tour caverns and a wax museum here.

⑦ The Blue Ridge Parkway leads to **Roanoke,** 54 mi from Lexington, a railroad town and center for the arts in western Virginia. It's also a good jumping-off point for side trips. A restored downtown square hosts a regular farmer's market and is the home of a warehouse called **Center in the Square.** The complex houses a theater, a regional history museum, a science museum, and an art museum. The **Virginia Museum of Transportation** has dozens of vintage steam, electric, and diesel locomotives, as well as antique autos, buses, and carriages. Snow leopards and other exotic animals can been seen at the **Mill Mountain Zoological Park,** home to a variety of mammals, birds, and reptiles. Spend the night in Roanoke. For a great view of the city, head to **Mill Mountain Star.**

⑧ At the **Dixie Caverns,** 7 mi from Roanoke in nearby Salem, tour guides take you up the mountain (instead of down) to see a netherworld of mineral formations.

⑨ About 10 mi west of Roanoke, the **George Washington and Jefferson national forests** have trout streams, picnic areas, swimming, horseback riding, and miles of hiking trails. You can spend an afternoon or days in this wilderness, thanks to dozens of developed campgrounds. The main recreation season is April through November.

To return to Charlottesville: take I–81 North from Roanoke to Staunton. At Staunton, get on I–64 East to Charlottesville.

Blue Ridge Parkway

Chateau Morrisette Winery. Travel to the vineyards of southern France without leaving Virginia. This country winery, surrounded by the Rock Castle Gorge Wilderness area, produces a dozen different wines on signature Black Dog, Our Dog Blue, and Sweet Mountain Laurel labels. Take a tour or eat at the upscale, contemporary American restaurant. | Winery Rd., Meadows of Dan | 540/593–2865 | www.thedogs.com | $2 | Mon.–Thurs. 10–5, Fri. and Sat. 10–6, Sun. 11–5.

Humpback Rock Visitor Center. Near the Rockfish Gap entrance to the Blue Ridge Parkway, the center has free maps, picnic tables, and updates on ranger programs. A short trail leads you to a reconstructed pioneer mountain farm, with a cabin, springhouse, chicken coop, and barn. | MM 5.8, Blue Ridge Pkwy. | 540/943–4716 | www.blueridgeparkway.org | Free | May–Oct., daily 9–5.

James River Visitor Center. At this wayside visitor center is a footbridge across the James River and a trail leading to the Kanawha Canal Lock exhibit. Before railroads became the favored mode of transport, engineers built locks to move freight along the river. The restored lock was part of a 200-mi canal system running from Richmond across the Blue Ridge to Buchanan. | MM 63, Blue Ridge Pkwy. | 434/299–5496 | www.blueridgeparkway.org | Free | May–Oct., daily 9–5.

Mabry Mill. Probably the most visited (and most photographed) site along the Blue Ridge Parkway, Mabry Mill consists of a sawmill and a restored water-powered gristmill that produces cornmeal and buckwheat flour for sale. Regular demonstrations showcase blacksmithing and other trades. | MM 176.1, Blue Ridge Pkwy., 24120 | 276/952–2947 | Free | May–Aug., daily 8–7; Sept. and Oct., daily 8–6.

Peaks of Otter Recreation Area. The name "Peaks of Otter" refers to two promontories, Sharp Top and Flat Top. A visitor center has exhibits on forest ecology and regional history. A walking trail takes you to the top of Sharp Top Mountain (elevation 4,004 feet), where a panoramic, 360-degree view awaits. A 23-acre lake is nearby. | MM 86, Blue Ridge Pkwy., 24523 | 540/586–4357 | www.blueridgeparkway.org | Free | Apr.–Nov., daily 9–5.

Rocky Knob Visitor Center. In a converted gasoline station, this center overlooks the Rock Castle Gorge, which is accessible by an 11-mi trail. A variety of activities, from naturalist programs and campfire talks to guided hikes, are available at the center. | MM 169, Blue Ridge Pkwy., 24091 | 540/745–9660 | www.blueridgeparkway.org | Free | May–Oct., daily 9–5.

Dining

Blue Ridge Pig. Barbecue. It's well worth the effort to drive 10 minutes off the parkway for this barbecue joint. There isn't much to this small restaurant decorated with pigs of all shapes and sizes and chaotically wallpapered with hundreds of business cards. Smoke billows out of a small smokehouse behind the eatery, sending a lofting layer of burning hickory into the air. Choose from smoked beef, pork, chicken or ham. The pork in the barbecue pork sandwich is smoked for 18 hours and topped with sweet barbecue sauce, a family recipe. | Off Reeds Gap exit from Blue Ridge Parkway, between MM 13 and MM 14 on Blue Ridge Pkwy.; turn left at the pig statue | 434/361–1170 | No credit cards | ¢

Chateau Morrisette Restaurant. Continental. The winery's three dining rooms are in an elegant stone and gabled building, which was once a private residence. Framed playbills and the vineyard's own wine labels cover the walls. Large bay windows look out at the Buffalo Mountain and the Blue Ridge Parkway. The menu changes with the seasons, and centers on fresh ingredients. Try the Chocolate Oblivion Cake. Reservations are essential for dinner. Open-air dining on patio. Kids' menu. Beer and wine only. No smoking. | Winery Rd., Meadows of Dan, off Black Ridge Rd. from Blue Ridge Parkway at MM 171 | 540/593–2865 | No dinner Sun.–Thurs., no lunch Mon.–Tues. | AE, MC, V | $$–$$$$

Otter Creek. American. Built in the 1950s, this rustic restaurant on the Blue Ridge Parkway is a short drive from the James River. There's outdoor dining on picnic tables by Otter Creek. Choose from three types of pancakes: buckwheat, cornmeal, or buttermilk. Kids' menu. Lunch counter and gift shop. Breakfast served. No alcohol. No smoking. | MM 60.8, Blue Ridge Pkwy. | 434/299–5862 | Closed Thanksgiving–mid-Apr. | MC, V | ¢–$$

Peaks of Otter. American. Floor-to-ceiling windows permit a view of the glorious colors of Sharp Top Mountain and Abbott Lake. Vaulted ceilings, exposed beams, and custom-built wooden tables complete the appealing interior. Under the same roof is a cocktail lounge and a coffee shop. There are a Friday-night seafood buffet, a Sunday country brunch, and an extensive selection of Virginia wines. The baked salmon is a favorite dish. Salad bar. Kids' menu. Breakfast served. No smoking. | MM 86, Blue Ridge Pkwy. | 434/586–9263 | MC, V | ¢–$$

Lodging

Doe Run Lodge. The lodge has condominium-style suites on a quiet mountainside. The suites have mountain views, rustic exteriors, and modern interiors that vary in style. Children under 15 can stay for free. Weekly rates are available. Restaurant, kitchenettes, in-room VCRs, tennis court, pool, sauna, bar, business services. | MM 189, Blue Ridge Pkwy., Fancy Gap 24328 | 276/398–2212 or 800/325–6189 | fax 276/398–2833 | www.doerunlodge.com | 47 suites | AE, MC, V | $$–$$$$

Peaks of Otter Lodge. Surrounded by coniferous trees, this mountain getaway is on a 24-acre lot by a lake. Rooms are simple and comfortable. The only significant difference between rooms is those on the 1st floor have porches while those on the 2nd floor have balconies overlooking the lake. Be prepared to share your yard with unpaying guests—deer abound on the property. Restaurant, bar, business services; no room TVs, no room phones. | MM 86, Blue Ridge Pkwy., Bedford 24523 | 540/586–1081, 800/542–5927 in VA | fax 540/586–4420 | www.peaksofotter.com | 63 rooms | MC, V | $

Charlottesville

Ash Lawn-Highland. James Monroe chose this farmhouse residence in part because it was just a few miles from Monticello, the home of his friend Thomas Jefferson. Part of the house was destroyed in 1840, and the main section of the building dates from the 1870s. The 550-acre property is still a working plantation, and sheep and peacocks roam the grounds. The house is crowded with the fifth U.S. president's possessions, including gifts from notable persons and souvenirs from his time as envoy to France, and a full set of presidential china adorned with bald eagles. The outdoor Ash Lawn–Highland Summer Festival, one of the country's top-ranked summer opera companies, draws music aficionados July and August. | 1000 James Monroe Pkwy. | 434/293–9539 | www.ashlawnhighland.org | $9 | Mar.–Oct., daily 9–6; Nov.–Feb., daily 10–5.

Barboursville Vineyards. Between Charlottesville and Orange, this was the first vineyard in the state to grow only vinifera grapes (vinifera are of European origin; other vineyards were using American hybrids at the time) and one of its top award winners. During the first three weekends of August, "Shakespeare at the Ruins" presents outdoor performances of the Bard's classics in this impressive setting behind the vineyard. | 17655 Winery Rd., near intersection of Rtes. 20 and 23, Barboursville, 20 mi northeast of Charlottesville | 540/832–3824 | www.barboursvillewine.com | Tours free, tastings $3, theater performances $14 | Tastings Mon.–Sat. 10–5, Sun. 11–5, tours weekends 10–4.

Horton Cellars Winery. Taste one of 30 wines at this beautiful Tudor-style winery just beyond Barboursville Vineyard. Over 30 varieties of wines are made on-site, including viognier, cabernet franc, norton (a grape native to Virginia), and a vintage port. Monthly festivals include an annual pig roast, barrel tastings, and a Mardi Gras and Gumbo celebration. | 6399 Spotswood Trail, 20 mi northeast of Charlottesville | 540/832–7440 | fax 540/832–7187 | www.hvwine.com | Free tours and tasting | Daily 10–5.

Jefferson Vineyards. The winery, which offers free tours and tastings, is on the same land that Thomas Jefferson gave to Italian winemaker Filippo Mazzei in 1773 to establish a European-style vineyard. Mazzei is said to have found the soil and climate of Virginia better than Italy's, and the modern-day operation has consistently produced excellent wines. The winery is a 10-minute drive from Charlottesville. If you're traveling in fall, call for information on the annual Harvest Feast. | 1399 Thomas Jefferson Pkwy., 3 mi south of Charlotteville | 434/977–3042 | www.jeffersonvineyards.com | Free, $1 tasting fee | Daily 11–5.

★**Monticello.** Thomas Jefferson, third president of the United States and author of the Declaration of Independence, constructed this mountaintop home over a 40-year period, between 1769 and 1809. It is considered a Revolutionary structure, typical of no single architectural style. Throughout the house are Jefferson's inventions, including a seven-day clock and a "polygraph," a two-pen contraption that allowed him to make a copy of his correspondence as he wrote it. The Thomas Jefferson Center for Historic Plants, on the grounds, includes gardens, exhibits, and a sales area. He and members of his family are buried in a nearby graveyard. | Rte. 53 (Thomas Jefferson Parkway) | 434/984–9822, 434/984–9800 for recorded info, 434/984–9844 for tickets | www.monticello.org | $13 | Mar.–Oct., daily 8–5; Nov.–Feb., daily 9–4:30.

Monticello Visitors Center. Check out the center before visiting the estate, since much of the history of Jefferson's home is not explained on the house tour. The free 35-minute film delves into Jefferson's political career. | College Dr., off Rte. 20 S Exit on I-64 | 434/977–1783 | www.monticello.org/visit/vc_tours.html | Free | Mar.–Oct., daily 9–5:30; Nov.–Feb., daily 9–5.

★**University of Virginia.** One of the nation's most notable public universities was founded and designed by a 76-year-old Thomas Jefferson, who called himself its "father" in his own epitaph. A poll of experts at the time of the U.S. bicentennial designated this complex "the proudest achievement of American architecture in the past 200 years." Edgar Allan Poe's room—where he spent one year as a student until debts forced him to leave—is preserved on the West Range at No. 13. Tours begin indoors in the Rotunda, whose entrance is on the Lawn side, lower level. | The Rotunda, University Ave. | 434/924–3239 | www.virginia.edu | Free | Rotunda and visitors center daily 9–4:45; 30-min to 1-hr historic tours daily at 10, 11, 2, 3, and 4.

University of Virginia Art Museum. Bayly Art Museum. One block north of the Rotunda, this museum exhibits art from around the world from ancient times to the present day. | Thomas H. Bayly Building, 155 Rugby Rd. | 434/924–3592 | www.virginia.edu/artmuseum | Free | Tues.–Sun. 1–5.

Visitor Center. Maps and other brochures about the university can be picked up at the visitor center, about ½ mi from campus. | 2304 Ivy Rd. (U.S. 250) | 434/924–7166 | www.virginia.edu | Daily 9–4:45.

Dining

C.&O. French. French country cooking meets the flavors of the American Southwest and Pacific Rim at this elegant restaurant. Choose from four dining areas. Two are bistrostyle, informal, and cozy, with rustic barn-wood paneling. Another is more upscale and has windows that allow views of the C&O train as it rolls by. The final dining room is a comfortable covered patio with a brick floor and a soothing fountain. Dishes might include fried green tomatoes with lump crab, scallop ceviche, and cilantro oil, or filet mignon Wellington. | 515 E. Water St. | 434/971–7044 | No lunch | AE, MC, V | $$–$$$$

Continental Divide. Southwestern. A neon sign in the window of this local favorite says "Get in here," and you might miss the small storefront restaurant if it didn't. Quesadillas, burritos, spicy pork tacos, and enchiladas crowd the menu. Margaritas are potent. Cactus plants decorate the front window, and the booths have funky lights. It can get crowded and convivial, but customers like it that way. The most popular offering is a Santa Fe enchilada topped with chipotle sauce. | 811 W. Main St. | 434/984–0143 | Reservations not accepted | No lunch | MC, V | $

feast! American/Casual. In the bustling West Main Street Market, this urban wine-and-cheese shop is packed with well-heeled goodies from fancy imported hams and olives to local spreads and wines. The well-priced sandwiches pack most of the delicacies in the store into every bite. | 416 W. Main St. | 434/244–7800 | www.feastvirginia.com | Closed Sun. | AE, MC, V | ¢

Hamilton's at First and Main. Contemporary. A local favorite, this Downtown Mall eatery has a warm terra-cotta interior and an eclectic cuisine. Try the pan-roasted halibut on Cuban black-bean cake with a citrus salsa, or the farfalle tossed with shrimp, country ham, sweet peppers, shiitake mushrooms, and asparagus. In warm weather, the outdoor patio doubles as a great perch to people-watch. | 101 W. Main St. | 434/295–6649 | Closed Sun. | MC, V | $–$$

Mas. Spanish. This upscale tapas bar is often filled with patrons nibbling on the small Spanish appetizers until 1 AM. The creative menu is packed with dishes like spicy, bittersweet chocolate mousse; smoked suckling pig; and a multitude of small extras like a roasted-artichoke-and-goat-cheese spread, which can be paired with freshly baked flat bread, sourdough baguette, or ciabatta. The affordable wine list has over 45 Spanish wines available by the glass. | 501 Monticello Rd. | 434/979–0990 | No lunch | MC, V, AE | $–$$$

Lodging

Best Western Cavalier Inn. This hotel's best feature is its location, directly across the street from the grounds of the University of Virginia and one block from the university's sports arena. Restaurant, cable TV, pool, lounge, Internet, meeting rooms, airport shuttle, some pets allowed. | 105 Emmet St., 22905 | 434/296–8111 | fax 434/290–3523 | www.bestwestern.com | 118 rooms | CP | AE, D, DC, MC, V | $

Boar's Head Inn. A modern luxury resort, this Old English–style inn is part of a 53-acre property. Hospitality reigns, and the amenities include four-poster beds and Italian linens. Hot-air ballooning is among the many available activities, and kids 14 and up can participate in sports programs. Restaurant, dining room, in-room data ports, some refrigerators, cable TV, driving range, putting green, tennis court, 3 pools, exercise equipment, bicycles, bar, business services, airport shuttle. | 200 Ednam Dr. (U.S. 250), 22903 | 434/296–2181 or 800/476–1988 | fax 434/972–6019 | www.boarsheadinn.com | 173 rooms, 11 suites | AE, D, DC, MC, V | $$$–$$$$

English Inn. A model treatment of the bed-and-breakfast theme on a large but comfortable scale, the English Inn has a three-story atrium lobby with cascading plants. The suites have a sitting room, wet bar, king-size bed, and reproduction antiques; other rooms have modern furnishings. Cable TV, indoor pool, gym, sauna. | 2000 Morton Dr., 22901 | 434/971–9900 or 800/786–5400 | fax 434/977–8008 | www.wytestone.com | 67 rooms, 21 suites | BP | AE, DC, MC, V | $

Omni Charlottesville. This attractive member of the luxury chain looms over one end of the Downtown Mall. The triangular rooms at the point of the wedge-shape building get light from two sides. Blond wood and maroon fabrics, in a mixture of modern and colonial styles, decorate the rooms, and potted plants soften the bright seven-story atrium lobby. Restaurant, cable TV with movies and video games, 2 pools (1 indoor), gym, hot tub, sauna, bar, Internet. | 235 W. Main St., 22902 | 434/971–5500 or 800/843–6664 | fax 434/979–4456 | www.omnihotels.com | 204 rooms, 7 suites | AE, DC, MC, V | $$

★ **Silver Thatch Inn.** Contemporary. Four-poster beds and period antiques are just part of the charm of this 1780 white-clapboard colonial farmhouse. The friendly hosts help their guests arrange outdoor activities at nearby locations. The popular restaurant serves contemporary cuisine and has a very fine wine cellar; reservations are required. The chef's grilled beef tenderloin is renowned. Restaurant, pool; no room phones, no room TVs, no kids under 14, no smoking. | 3001 Hollymead Dr., 22911, 8 mi north of town | 434/978–4686 or 800/261–0720 | fax 434/973–6156 | www.silverthatch.com | 7 rooms | BP | AE, DC, MC, V | $$–$$$

200 South Street Inn. Two houses, one of them a former brothel, have been combined and restored to create this old-fashioned inn in the historic district, one block from the Downtown Mall. Furnishings throughout are English and Belgian antiques. Several rooms come with a canopy bed, sitting room, fireplace, and whirlpool. Cable TV, Internet; no smoking. | 200 South St., 22901 | 434/979–0200 or 800/964–7008 | fax 434/979–4403 | www.southstreetinn.com | 17 rooms, 3 suites | BP | AE, MC, V | $$

Lexington

George C. Marshall Museum. Exhibits preserve the memory of the World War II army chief of staff, tracing his career from when he was aide-de-camp to John "Black Jack" Pershing in World War I to when, as secretary of state, he devised the Marshall Plan, a strategy for reviving postwar Western Europe. Marshall's Nobel peace prize is on display. An electronically narrated map tells the story of World War II. | Virginia Military Institute campus, Letcher Ave. | 540/463–7103 | $3 | Daily 9–5.

Natural Bridge of Virginia. This impressive limestone arch (which supports Rte. 11) has been gradually carved out by Cedar Creek, which rushes through, 215 feet below. Surveying the structure for Lord Halifax, George Washington carved his own initials in the stone; Thomas Jefferson bought it from King George III. Also on the property are dizzying caverns that descend 34 stories, a wax museum, and an 18th-century village constructed by the Monacan Indian Nation. | I–81 S, Exit 180, or I–81 N, Exit 175, 20 mi south of Lexington | 540/291–2121 or 800/533–1410 | www.naturalbridgeva.com | Bridge $10, all attractions $17 | Mar.–Nov., daily 8 AM–dark.

Stonewall Jackson House. Confederate General Jackson's private life is on display at the house he lived in for two years while teaching physics and military tactics to the cadets, before leaving for his command in the Civil War. He is revealed as a dedicated Presbyterian devoted to physical fitness, careful with money, musically inclined, and fond of gardening. This is the only house he ever owned; it is furnished now with period pieces and some of his belongings. | 8 East Washington St. | No phone | www.stonewalljackson.org | $5 | Mon.–Sat. 9–5, Sun. 1–5.

Theater at Lime Kiln. The Kiln's solid rock walls create a dramatic backdrop for musicals, concerts, and performances as varied as Russian clowns and Vietnamese puppeteers. Original musicals are staged Tuesday through Saturday, and contemporary music concerts are given on Sunday throughout the summer. | Lime Kiln Rd. | 540/463–7088 | www.theateratlimekiln.com | Plays $13–$19, concerts $20 | May–Sept.; call or check Web site for performance information.

Virginia Horse Center. This venue stages competitions—show jumping, hunter trials, multibreed shows—several days a week. An indoor arena permits year-round operation. Most events are free. | 487 Maury River Rd. (Rte. 39) | 540/463–2194 | www.horsecenter.org | Free | Call or check Web site for show information.

Virginia Military Institute. The nation's oldest state-supported military college, VMI was founded in 1839. With an enrollment of about 1,300 cadets, the institute has admitted women since 1997. | Letcher Ave. | 540/464–7306 visitors center | www.vmi.edu | Free | Visitors center daily 9–5.

Virginia Military Institute Museum. This museum displays 15,000 artifacts, including Stonewall Jackson's stuffed and mounted horse, Little Sorrel, and the general's coat, pierced by the bullet that killed him at Chancellorsville. | VMI, Jackson Memorial Hall, lower level | 540/464–7232 | www4.vmi.edu/museum | Donations accepted | Daily 9–5.

Washington and Lee University. Founded in 1749, W&L, as alums and students fondly call it, is named in gratitude for a large financial gift from the nation's first president and for the Confederate general who served as its president for five years following the Civil War. Today, with 2,000 students, the university occupies a campus of white-column, redbrick buildings around a central colonnade. | Jefferson St. (Rte. 11) | 540/458–8400 | www2.wlu.edu | Free | Campus tours Apr.–Oct., weekdays 10–4, Sat. 9:45–noon; Jan.–Mar., weekdays 10 and noon, Sat. 11; Nov. and Dec., call ahead.

Lee Chapel and Museum. Many relics of Robert E. Lee's family are on display here, including Edward Valentine's statue of the recumbent general. It's easy to sense the affection and reverence that Lee inspired. | Washington and Lee University | 540/458–8768 | leechapel.wlu.edu | Free | Apr.–Oct., Mon.–Sat. 9–5, Sun. 1–5; Nov.–Mar., Mon.–Sat. 9–4, Sun. 1–4.

Dining

Blue Heron Cafe. Vegetarian. Everything about this casual spot is a breath of fresh air—from the brightly colored whimsical art, to the arrangements of freshly cut flowers, to the creative, ever-changing organic menu. Dishes are vegetarian, utilizing the freshest local ingredients. Laurie's grilled tofu sandwich and a tofu-and-rice burger are standard lunch fare. The dinner menu changes weekly, but you might see corn-and-herb polenta with beer-basted eggplant layered with Gorgonzola cheese. There's live music Thursday night, during which appetizers and drinks are served, but no dinner. | 4 E. Washington St. | 540/463–2800 | Closed Sun. No dinner Mon.–Thurs. | No credit cards | $–$$

The Palms. American. Once a Victorian ice-cream parlor, this full-service restaurant in an 1890 building has indoor and outdoor dining. Wood booths line the walls of the plant-filled room; the pressed-metal ceiling is original. Specialties on the American menu include broccoli-cheese soup, charbroiled meats, and teriyaki chicken. | 101 W. Nelson St. | 540/463–7911 | Reservations not accepted | D, MC, V | ¢–$

Southern Inn Restaurant. Continental. "Never trust a skinny cook," reads a large sign in the window of this country-style restaurant on the busy side of Main Street that caters to a mixed university crowd. You can find country favorites like meat loaf with mashed red potatoes and mushroom gravy, as well as Thai tofu patties. The restaurant is loyal to Virginia wines, with almost 20 producers on the menu, including the delectable Barboursville Phelio, a dessert wine. | 37 S. Main St., 24450 | 540/463–3612 | AE, D, MC, V | $–$$$$

Wilson-Walker House. American. This stately 1820 Greek Revival house is ideal for eating elegant regional cuisine. Seafood dishes are a specialty—try the pan-seared, potato-encrusted trout. The restaurant is particularly affordable during the $5 chef's-special luncheon. | 30 N. Main St. | 540/463–3020 | Reservations essential | Closed Sun. and Mon. | AE, MC, V | $$–$$$$

Lodging

Inn at Lexington. The downtown location of this classy inn is unbeatable. Just ½ block from the Stonewall Jackson Cemetery, this massive, 9,000-square-foot colonial was built in 1922 as a fraternity house for Washington and Lee. The rooms are large, each with a sitting area and eclectic decor. Each of the four rooms is different, ranging from Key West to Dutch themes. Cable TV, in-room VCRs, Internet, library; no room phones. | 408 S. Main St., 24450 | 540/463–4715 or 866/288–4715 | fax 540/463–4888 | www.theinnatlexington.com | 4 rooms | BP | AE, MC, V | $$–$$$

Maple Hall. For a taste of Southern history, spend a night at this 1850 country inn, a former plantation house on 56 acres. All rooms have period antiques and modern amenities; most have gas log fireplaces. Dinner is served in three ground-floor rooms and on a glassed-in patio; the main dining room has a large decorative fireplace. Restaurant, tennis court, pool, fishing, hiking, meeting rooms, no-smoking rooms. | Rte. 11, 24450, 6 mi north of town | 540/463–6693 or 877/463–2044 | fax 540/

463–7262 | www.lexingtonhistoricinns.com/maplehall.htm | 17 rooms, 4 suites | BP | D, MC, V | $$–$$$

Natural Bridge Hotel. Within walking distance of the spectacular rock arch of the same name (there's also a shuttle bus), the colonial-style brick hotel has a beautiful location as well as numerous recreational facilities. Long porches with rocking chairs allow leisurely appreciation of the Blue Ridge Mountains. Rooms are done in a colonial Virginia style. Restaurant, snack bar, some microwaves, cable TV with movies and video games, miniature golf, 2 tennis courts, pool, hiking, bar, meeting rooms. | Rte. 11, Box 57, Natural Bridge 24578, 15 mi north of Lexington | 540/291–2121 or 800/533–1410 | fax 540/291–1896 | www.naturalbridgeva.com | 180 rooms | AE, D, DC, MC, V | $

Stoneridge Bed & Breakfast. This circa-1829 Greek Revival house is on 32 quiet acres of forest. The large rooms are tastefully furnished with antiques and reproductions. A former plantation house, the property is packed with antiquated buildings like an old corncrib for harvesting the crop, and a springhouse that provided fresh water. The four-course breakfast is packed with goodies like homemade banana bread, and omelets made with Virginia ham and Vermont cheddar. Hiking, library, some pets allowed (fee); no room TVs, no kids under 8, no smoking. | 246 Stoneridge La., 24450, 5 mi south of Lexington | 540/463–4090 | fax 540/463–6078 | www.webfeat-inc.com/stoneridge | 4 rooms, 1 suite | BP | AE, D, MC, V | $–$$

Roanoke

George Washington and Jefferson National Forests. Encompassing some 1.8 million acres, this forest land stretches from Winchester to Big Stone Gap, and covers the Blue Ridge, Massanutten, Shenandoah, and Allegheny mountain ranges. Fishing, riding, hunting, and skiing are available in these woods. The Appalachian Trail can be accessed near Route 311 in Salem and via U.S. 220 in Troutville. | Headquarters at 5162 Valleypointe Pkwy., 24019 | 540/265–5100 | www.southernregion.fs.fed.us/gwj | Free | Daily 24 hrs.

Market Square. The heart of Roanoke is Market Square, with Virginia's oldest continuous farmer's market, a multiethnic food court inside the restored City Market Building, and several restaurants, shops, and bars. | Bounded by Campell Ave., Salem Ave., Church St., and Jefferson St.

Center in the Square. This restored warehouse contains the Mill Mountain Theatre and three museums, devoted to art, science, and history. The science museum has a planetarium and MegaDome theater. | 1 Market Sq. SE | 540/342–5700 | www. centerinthesquare.org | Science museum $6, with planetarium $8, with MegaDome $9; history museum $2; art museum free | Tues.–Sat. 10–5; history museum also Sun. 1–5.

Mill Mountain Star. The 100-foot-tall star—lighted in patriotic red, white, and blue at night—stands in Mill Mountain Park, 1,000 feet above the Roanoke Valley. From either of the park's two overlooks, Roanoke, the "Star City of the South," looks like a scale model of a city. From the overlooks you can also see wave after wave of Appalachian ridgelines. | Follow Walnut St. south 2 mi from downtown Roanoke; or take spur road off the Blue Ridge Pkwy. at MM 120.3.

Mill Mountain Zoo. Sharing the mountaintop with the star is one of only two nationally accredited zoos in Virginia. Though Asian animals, like a rare Siberian tiger, snow leopards, and red pandas, are the marquee attractions in this cozy zoo, many find the prairie dog exhibit the most entertaining. | Mill Mountain Park; follow Walnut St. south 2 mi from downtown Roanoke; or take spur road of the Blue Ridge Pkwy. at MM 120.3 | 540/343–3241 | www.mmzoo.org | $6 | Daily 10–5; gate closes at 4:30.

Virginia Museum of Transportation. The largest collection of diesel and steam locomotives in the country is found in this downtown museum. Roanoke got its start as a railroad town and was once the headquarters of the Norfolk & Western railroad.

Many of the dozens of original train cars and engines were built in town. | 303 Norfolk Ave. | 540/342–5670 | www.vmt.org | $7.40 | Wed.–Sat. 10–5, Sun. noon–5.

Dining

★ **Carlos Brazilian International Cuisine.** Brazilian. Watch the auburn sun set behind the mountain-rimmed western horizon from this restaurant's hilltop location. Toast the day with a glass of wine as you savor French, Italian, Spanish, and Brazilian dishes. Try the *porco reacheado* (pork tenderloin stuffed with spinach and feta cheese) or the *moqueca mineira* (shrimp, clams, and whitefish in a spicy sauce with coconut milk, lime, and cilantro). | 4167 Electric Rd. | 540/345–7661 | Closed Sun. | AE, MC, V | $$–$$$

The Homeplace. Southern. This early-20th-century farm home in the valley hamlet of Catawba welcomes grimy Appalachian Trail hikers, sharply dressed Sunday church-goers, and Beltway weekenders with equal warmth, serving an all-you-can-eat, all-you-can-grab selection of home-cooked country fare. Fried chicken, mashed potatoes, green beans, pinto beans, and hot biscuits are served to each table for $11 a person; add a dollar for a second meat selection. | 7 mi west of Salem on Rte. 311 N Catawba, I–81, Exit 141, 15 mi northwest of Roanoke | 540/384–7252 | Reservations not accepted | No lunch Thurs.–Sat., no dinner Sun. | MC, V | $

Lodging

Bernard's Landing. A resort on Smith Mountain Lake, Bernard's rents one- to three-bedroom condominiums with water views and two- to five-bedroom town houses (all waterfront) for periods of up to two weeks. The units are separately owned, so their furnishings vary widely; all have private decks. Restaurant, kitchens, microwaves, cable TV, 6 tennis courts, 2 pools, gym, sauna, boating, fishing, racquetball, playground, Internet, meeting rooms. | 775 Ashmeade Rd., Moneta 24121, 23 mi southeast of Roanoke | 540/721–8870 or 800/572–2048 | fax 540/721–8383 | www.bernardslanding.com | 67 units | AE, D, MC, V | $$–$$$$

Hotel Roanoke and Conference Center. This elegant Tudor Revival building, listed on the National Register of Historic Places, was built in 1882 by the Norfolk & Western Railroad. The richly paneled lobby has Florentine marble floors and ceiling frescos. The formal restaurant serves regional Southern cuisine. The Market Square Bridge, a glassed-in walkway, goes from the hotel across railroad tracks to downtown attractions. 2 restaurants, cable TV with movies and video games, pool, gym, bar, Internet, convention center, meeting rooms, airport shuttle. | 110 Shenandoah Ave., 24016 | 540/985–5900 | fax 540/345–2890 | www.hotelroanoke.com | 313 rooms, 19 suites | AE, D, DC, MC, V | $$$

Patrick Henry. Three blocks from Center in the Square, this grand historic hotel has huge rooms furnished with antiques. Admire the 30-foot ceilings, ornate chandeliers, and carvings on the ceilings of the lobby. Restaurant, room service, kitchenettes, refrigerators, cable TV, hair salon, bar, laundry facilities, business services, airport shuttle, no-smoking rooms. | 617 S. Jefferson St., 24011 | 540/345–8811 | fax 540/342–9908 | www.patrickhenryroanoke.com | 117 rooms | CP | AE, D, DC, MC, V | $–$$

Shenandoah National Park

Shenandoah National Park. One of the most popular parks in the national park system, Shenandoah has many varied species of animal and plant life, trout streams, and hundreds of miles of hiking trails. Developed campgrounds are available on a first-come, first-served basis, except for Big Meadows, which requires reservations from mid-May through November. Most have coin showers, laundry facilities, a dump station, and a camp store. In addition to Big Meadows (MM 51.3), the park's campsites are at Mathews Arm (MM 22.1), Lewis Mountain (MM 57.5), Loft Mountain (MM 79.5), and Dundo Group Campground (MM 83.7). All campgrounds have a 14-day limit and allow pets. Backcountry camping requires a permit, available free of charge at the park headquarters, entrance stations, and visitor centers.

Seven picnic areas are scattered throughout the park: Dickey Ridge (MM 4.6), Elkwallow (MM 24.1), Pinnacles (MM 36.7), Big Meadows (MM 51.3), Lewis Mountain (MM 57.5), South River (MM 62.9), and Loft Mountain (MM 79.5). | 3655 U.S. 211 E, Luray | 540/999–3500 | www.nps.gov/shen | Pedestrians $5, cars $10 | Daily 24 hrs.

Dickey Ridge Visitor Center. Near the Front Royal entrance to Skyline Drive, the center distributes maps and dispenses up-to-date information about wildlife, trail conditions, and ranger programs. | Skyline Dr., MM 4.6 | 540/635–3566 | Free | Mar.–Oct., daily 9–5.

Guided trail rides. Wranglers lead you out of the park's Skyland Stables several times daily from May to October and on weekends in November. The route follows White Oak Canyon trail, which passes several waterfalls; you can choose a 1-hour or 2½-hour ride. Book 24 hours in advance. Additional horse trails are available if you bring own horse. | Skyland Lodge, MM 41.7, near Luray | 540/999–2211 | $25–$35 | May.–Oct., daily; Nov., weekends. Times vary; call ahead.

Hiking. Some 100 mi of the Appalachian Trail run through the park, along with 500 mi of other footpaths of varying length and difficulty; some lead to waterfalls, canyons, old-growth forests, and rocky outcrops with sweeping views of the Piedmont and the Shenandoah Valley. Maps are available at visitor centers and entrances. Many trails are accessible from Skyline Drive.

Interpretive programs. In summer and fall, rangers lead hikes, field seminars, evening programs around the campfire, and trips to Rapidan Camp, with special offerings for kids. Schedules are posted on park bulletin boards and at visitor centers. | 540/999–3283 Byrd Visitor's Center.

★ **Skyline Drive.** The scenic highway winds 105 mi through Shenandoah National Park and connects with the Blue Ridge Parkway near Waynesboro. Seasonal activities, supervised by rangers, are outlined in the *Shenandoah Overlook,* a free newspaper you can pick upon entering the park. Skyline Drive runs the length of the park and can be entered at four points: at Front Royal, off U.S. 340; at Thornton Gap, between Luray and Sperryville, off U.S. 211; at Swift Run Gap, between Stanardsville and Elkton, off U.S. 33; and at Rockfish Gap, between Charlottesville and Waynesboro, off U.S. 250 (I–64). The speed limit is 35 mph.

White Oak Canyon and Dark Hollow Falls. There are six waterfalls at White Oak Canyon, 4 mi from Skyline Drive, at MM 51.5. At a height of 77 feet, Dark Hollow Falls is a mile from Big Meadows Lodge, next to the Harry F. Byrd Visitor's Center, at MM 50.5. Dark Hollow is an easier hike from Skyline Drive, while White Oak Canyon Falls is a hike that is very rocky and steep in parts. Dark Hollow can be very crowded. | Skyline Dr. at MM 50.5 and MM 51.5 | 540/999–3283 Byrd Visitor's Center | Free | Daily 24 hrs.

Dining

Skyland Lodge. American. Comfort food reigns at this lodge eatery that serves popular country favorites like chicken potpie and pork chops with mashed potatoes. Fish, chicken, and pasta dishes are staples. If you can, grab a seat at the massive, panoramic window. The views of the valley are one-of-a-kind. | Skyland Lodge, MM 41.7, near Luray | 540/999–2211 | Closed Dec.–Feb. | AE, D, MC, V | $–$$

Staunton

Blackfriars Playhouse. Experience Shakespeare's plays the way the Elizabethans did at a near-duplicate of the Globe Theatre that has rapidly gained worldwide acclaim for its attention to detail. Like those in 17th-century London, most seating consists of benches (modern seat backs and cushions are available) with some stools right on stage. The interactive shows encourage audience participation by leaving the lights on for the entire performance. | 10 S. Market St. | 540/885–5588 | www.shenandoahshakespeare.com | $10–$26.

★ **Museum of American Frontier Culture.** The outdoor museum re-creates agrarian life in early America with American, Scots-Irish, German, and English farmsteads. Master craftsmen were brought from Ulster, Northern Ireland, to thatch the roofs on farm buildings transported from County Tyrone. Livestock has been back-bred and ancient seeds germinated in order to create an accurate portrayal. More than 70 festivals, workshops, and programs are held annually, from sheepshearing at Easter to cornhusking in fall. | 1250 Richmond Rd. | 540/332–7850 | www.frontiermuseum.org | $8 | Dec.–mid-Mar., daily 10–4; mid-Mar.–Nov., daily 9–5.

Woodrow Wilson Birthplace and Museum. The 150-year-old Greek Revival house has been restored to its appearance during Wilson's childhood, with some original furnishings. The 28th U.S. president was born here in 1856, son of the Reverend Joseph R. Wilson, a Presbyterian minister, and his wife, Jesse Woodrow. Some items from Wilson's political career are displayed, including his presidential limousine, a 1919 Pierce-Arrow sedan. | 24 N. Coalter St. | 540/885–0897 or 888/496–6376 | www.woodrowwilson.org | $7 | Mar.–Nov., daily 9–5; Dec.–Feb., daily 10–4.

Dining

L'Italia. Italian. In a downtown brick building, this quiet restaurant displays local artwork. Try the homemade pasta, veal saltimbocca, or broiled salmon, and choose from among 15 to 20 desserts. The tartuffo and tiramisu come straight from Italy. | 23 E. Beverly St. | 540/885–0102 | Closed Mon. | AE, D, DC, MC, V | $–$$$

Mill Street Grill. American. The first restaurant as you come into Staunton on U.S. 11, the Mill Street Grill is in the basement of a turn-of-the-20th-century mill. Walls are original stone and wood, and there are flour bags, stained-glass windows, and other mill relics on display. The baby back ribs and filet mignon with port wine sauce are popular. Try the raspberry brûlée cheesecake. | 1 Mill St. | 540/886–0656 | No lunch Mon.– Sat. | AE, D, DC, MC, V | $$–$$$

Mrs. Rowe's Restaurant. American. A homey restaurant with plenty of booths, Rowe's has been operated by the same family since 1947 and enjoys a rock-solid reputation for inexpensive and delicious Southern meals. The fried chicken—skillet-cooked to order—is a standout. A local breakfast favorite is oven-hot biscuits topped with gravy (your choice of sausage, tenderloin, or creamy chipped beef). For dessert, try the mince pie in fall or the rhubarb cobbler or lemon meringue in summer. | I–81, Exit 222 | 540/886–1833 | D, MC, V | ¢–$$

Wright's Dairy Rite. American/Casual. This old hangout of the Statler Brothers still offers curbside service; orders are brought to your car. Try the homemade onion rings or a thick milk shake, available in nine different flavors. You can even order that 1950s staple, a malted. | 346 Greenville Ave. | 540/886–0435 | www.m-c-b.com/wrights | Mon.– Thurs. and Sun. 9 AM–10 PM, Fri. and Sat. 9 AM–11 PM | ¢

Lodging

Belle Grae Inn. The sitting room and music room of this restored 1870 Victorian house have been converted into formal dining rooms, with brass wall sconces, Oriental rugs, and candles at the tables. The cuisine, which changes weekly, is Continental cuisine with a regional flair. Accommodations are furnished with antique rocking chairs and canopied or brass beds; a complimentary snifter of brandy awaits in each room. Restaurant, some microwaves, Internet; no smoking. | 515 W. Frederick St., 24401 | 540/ 886–5151 or 888/541–5151 | fax 540/886–6641 | www.bellegrae.com | 8 rooms, 7 suites, 2 cottages | MAP | AE, D, MC, V | $–$$$$

Frederick House. Historic houses and restored town houses dating from 1810 make up this inn in the center of the historic district. All rooms are decorated with antiques, and some have fireplaces and private decks. A pub and a restaurant are adjacent. Cable TV, meeting rooms; no smoking. | 28 N. New St., 24401 | 540/885–4220 or 800/334–5575 | fax 540/885–5180 | www.frederickhouse.com | 12 rooms, 11 suites | AE, D, DC, MC, V | $–$$$

Sampson Eagon Inn. Across the street from Woodrow Wilson's birthplace in the Gospel Hill section of town, this restored Greek Revival (circa 1840) has a lot of period charm. In the spacious guest rooms are antique canopy beds, cozy sitting areas, and modern amenities. Don't miss the Kahlúa Belgian waffles for breakfast. Cable TV with movies; no kids under 12, no smoking. | 238 E. Beverley St., 24401 | 540/886–8200 or 800/597–9722 | www.eagoninn.com | 5 rooms | BP | AE, MC, V | $$

WEST VIRGINIA

RIVER CITIES HISTORICAL TOUR ALONG ROUTE 2
LIFE ALONG THE MIGHTY OHIO

Distance: 193 mi   Time: 2 days
Overnight Breaks: Parkersburg, Wheeling.

Meander south on Route 2 from Wheeling to Charleston on this mobile history lesson: several battles of the Revolutionary, French and Indian, and Civil wars were fought in the river cities. Oil barons and other industrialists also left behind an architectural legacy of stately homes and extensive gardens. Early October is an ideal time to visit.

❶ The tour begins in **Wheeling.** A frontier town that witnessed the last battle of the American Revolution, Wheeling was a Union stronghold during the Civil War, served twice as state capital, and later boomed along with America's industrial growth. Industrialist Earl W. Oglebay bequeathed the city's 1,500-acre **Oglebay Resort Park,** with gardens, greenhouses, and fountains; today it also includes a children's zoo, miniature golf course, and restaurants. During the 19th century Wheeling was famous for manufacturing glass and china, and the **Oglebay Institute Glass Museum** showcases glassware produced from 1817 to 1939.

❷ Nine miles south in **Moundsville,** view the region's distant past at **Grave Creek Mound State Park.** Built more than 2,000 years ago by Adena Indians, this ceremonial burial mound is the largest of several mounds that dot the Ohio and Kanawha valleys. On the grounds, the **Delf Norona Museum and Culture Center** displays artifacts from the Adena period (about 1000 BC to AD 1).

❸ Continue south on Route 2 for approximately 32 mi to Milepost 51 and the small town of **Sistersville.** With the discovery of oil on a nearby farm in 1889, this quiet community had a 26-year boom. Oil rigs sprouted on the hillsides, and oil barons built handsome mansions along **Wells Street.** Pick up a map at the Wells Inn for the self-guided walking tour, and stroll through the former business district to see an impressive variety of architectural styles.

❹ Following the Ohio River south along Route 2, drive approximately 45 mi to **Parkersburg.** The city's location at the confluence of the Ohio and the Little Kanawha rivers was instrumental to the economic growth of the area, described at the **Oil, Gas and Industrial Historical Museum,** a turn-of-the-20th-century building with displays of rigs, pumps, tools, and other industrial artifacts.

A few miles downriver, and reached by stern-wheel paddleboat, **Blennerhassett Island Historical State Park** is the site of the palatial home and grounds of Harman Blennerhassett, who allegedly conspired with Aaron Burr in 1805 to join the western part of the United States with Spanish territory to form a new empire. Tour the 7,000-square-foot mansion, picnic in the extensive gardens, or take a horse-drawn wagon ride around the island, which is open May through November.

❺ From Parkersburg, Route 2 joins I–77 for approximately 30 mi. Exit the interstate at Ravenswood (Exit 146) and follow the signs for Route 2. Continue about 30 mi more to **Point Pleasant.** The Ohio and Kanawha rivers meet at an 84-foot-high granite shaft at **Tu-Endi-Wei,** formally Point Pleasant Battle Monument State Park, which commemorates the first battle of the Revolutionary War, fought here on October 10, 1774. Each year, during the first full weekend in October (Friday–Sunday), the **Battle Days** showcases military reenactments, an ox roast, period demonstrations, and the Colonial Ball.

❻ Leaving Point Pleasant, Route 2 once again snakes along the Ohio River, continuing south for about 43 mi to the city of **Huntington.** Founded in 1871 by Collis P. Huntington, president of the Chesapeake and Ohio (C&O) Railroad, the city has always been closely linked to the railroads. The refurbished warehouses and boxcars of **Heritage Village** house an array of shops and restaurants; a statue of Huntington stands nearby. The brick streets of the **9th Street West Historic District** are lined with stately early-20th-century houses and cast-iron fences. Just southeast of the district is the **Huntington Museum of Art,** the largest museum in West Virginia, displaying collections of Ohio Valley glass, firearms, 19th- and 20th-century artwork, and exhibits for children. There is an observatory and marked nature trails on the 52-acre grounds.

Huntington

Blenko Glass Visitor Center and Factory Outlet. See glassblowers at work from an observation booth; some of them may have worked on high-profile projects like the National Cathedral and reproduction glass for Colonial Williamsburg. The adjacent Blenko Historical Museum contains glassware, glassmaking equipment, military uniforms, and historic documents. | Fairground Rd., Milton, 25 mi east of Huntington off I–64 at Exit 28, then 2 mi off U.S. 60 | 304/743–9081 or 877/425–3656 | www.blenkoglass.com | Free | Mon.–Sat. 8–4, Sun. noon–4.

Camden Park. The state's only amusement park, Camden Park opened in 1903. The Big Dipper and the Little Dipper (the children's version of the Big Dipper) are two of the best and oldest wooden roller coasters in America. The 26 acres include rides, picnic areas, and stern-wheeler riverboat cruises on the Ohio River. Big-name entertainment performs on many holidays. | U.S. 60 E | 304/429–4321 | www.camdenpark.com | $18 | Late Apr.–early June and mid-Aug.–Sept., hrs vary, call ahead. Mid-June–early Aug., Tues.–Thurs. and Sun. 11–7:30, Fri and Sat. 11–10. Oct., weekends 5–10 PM.

East Lynn Lake and Wildlife Management Area. The 1,005-acre lake is ideal for boating, fishing, and swimming, while hunting is permitted on the adjacent 24,821 acres of public land. | Rte. 37, East Lynn, 35 mi south of Huntington | 304/849–2355 | Free | Daily dawn–dusk.

Heritage Station. A former railway yard is home to shops and restaurants in restored warehouses and boxcars. A statue of city founder Collis P. Huntington stands nearby. | 11th St. and Veterans Memorial Blvd. | 304/696–5954 | Free | Daily 11–5.

Huntington Museum of Art. A large collection of firearms, silver, glass, Islamic prayer rugs, and 19th- and 20th-century American and European paintings and prints fills this museum, on 54 acres. Art classes and workshops are available to all ages. An extensive collection of rare orchids bloom in the arboretum. | 2033 McCoy Rd. | 304/529–2701 | Free, $3 for selected exhibits | Tues. 10–9, Wed.–Sat. 10–5, Sun. noon–5.

Dining

Calamidy Cafe. Southwestern. Across the street from the Marshall University campus, this large restaurant caters to the college crowd, with long hours, a wide selection of beer, and a diverse menu. Choose from quesedillas; a Santa Fe chicken sandwich dripping with cheese; and dishes such as the Black Goddess Earth Pasta, cracked chili-pepper penne topped with black beans and chicken, and smothered in white cheddar cheese. | 1555 3rd Ave. | 304/525–4171 | AE, D, DC, MC, V | ¢–$$

Celtic Rose Tea Room. Tea. Celtic music greets you as you sip one of a large variety of teas. High tea comes complete with a full selection of scones and finger sandwiches. | 2739 Main St., Hurricane, 20 mi east of Huntington | 304/562–4139 | Closed Sun. and Mon. No dinner | No credit cards | ¢

Rebels and Redcoats Tavern. Continental. Locals often gather after work at this popular pub with a colonial-era feel. Try the chateaubriand for two or the chicken divan. You have to walk through a bowling alley to get here. | 412 W. 7th Ave. | 304/523–8829 | AE, D, DC, MC, V | $–$$$

Rocco's Ristorante. Italian. Be prepared to wait in long lines to occupy one of the candlelit tables that crowd every corner of this small, romantic hideout. Sample a variety of Italian specialties while soft music plays in the background. Specialties include crab-stuffed beef fillet, lobster ravioli, and Sicilian sea bass. | 252 Main St., Ceredo, 10 mi west of Huntington | 304/453–3000 | Closed Mon. No lunch | AE, D, DC, MC, V | $–$$$

Parkersburg

Blennerhassett Island Historical State Park. In 1800 Harman Blennerhassett built a mansion on an island in the Ohio River, where he allegedly plotted with Aaron Burr to establish

WEST VIRGINIA RULES OF THE ROAD

License Requirements: You must be at least 16 years old and have a valid license to drive in West Virginia.

Right Turn on Red: Right turns are permitted at red lights after coming to a complete stop.

Seat-Belt & Helmet Laws: Seat belts are required for all front-seat occupants and backseat passengers under 18; child restraints are required for kids under 2. Helmets are mandatory for both motorcycle drivers and passengers.

Speed Limits: The speed limit on interstate highways is 70 mph and 55 mph on most major state routes. Be sure to check locally posted signs.

Other Regulations: It is illegal to use a handheld mobile phone while driving in nonemergency situations. The legal blood-alcohol concentration for drivers in West Virginia is below .10%.

For More Information: West Virginia Department of Transportation in Parkersburg | 304/420–4595 | www.wvdot.com. West Virginia State Police | 304/746–2100 | www.wvstatepolice.com.

an empire in the American Southwest. After both men were arrested, Blennerhassett fled the island, never to return. The mansion burned down in 1811, but has been reconstructed. You can reach the island via a stern-wheeler shuttle from Point Park in downtown Parkersburg. On the island, take a narrated wagon ride or a guided tour of the mansion. | 137 Juliana St. | 304/420–4800 | Boat to island $7, mansion tour $3, wagon tour $4.50 | May–early Sept., Tues.–Sun. 10–5:30; early Sept.–Nov., Thurs.–Sun. 11–4:30.

Blennerhassett Museum. On the mainland, this museum is a great stop before sailing off to the island. Besides giving a history of the family and the island, the exhibits offer a hefty helping of regional history by displaying artifacts like antique cars and riverboats. The museum has three floors of archaeological and historical displays. | 137 Juliana St. | 304/420–4800 or 800/225–5982 | $2 | Tours May–Oct., Tues.–Sat. 9–5:30, Sun. noon–5:30; Nov.–Apr., Sat. 11–5, Sun. 1–5, or by appointment.

Fenton Art Glass. The largest manufacturer of handmade glass in America, this studio opened its doors in 1898. Tours are available. | 700 Elizabeth St., Williamstown, 10 mi north of Parkersburg | 304/375–6122 | www.fentonartglass.com | Free | Weekdays 8:30–4:30; Closed July 1–14.

Mountwood Park. Near Parkersburg, the 2,600-acre park has camping, hiking, picnic areas, game parks, swimming, fishing, playgrounds, and a large lake. Mountain biking is by far the most popular sport at the park because of the many trails. A hiking trail at the back of the park leads to the restored ruins of Volcano, a once prospering oil and gas town that burned to the ground in the late 1800s. A large mansion, a train station, and a theater are among the restorations. | Rte. 2, Waverly, 14 mi east of Parkersburg | 304/679–3611 | www.mountwoodpark.com | Free | Daily dawn–dusk.

North Bend State Park. This 1,405-acre park has a playground, tennis courts, miniature golf, and swimming. The park has been customized for the blind, with specially equipped bicycles and braille signs on many of the trails. | Rte. 1, Cairo, 21 mi east of Parkersburg | 304/643–2931 or 800/225–5982 | www.wvparks.com/northbend | Free, pool $3 | Daily 8 AM–10 PM.

★ **North Bend Rail Trail.** A 72-mi trail covers the former path of railway track between Parkersburg and Clarksburg. The remote path takes you over 36 bridges and through 13 railway tunnels. Soon after leaving Parkersburg you stumble upon the small town of Cairo (pronounced *kay*-roh by locals) that has small shops like Made in West Virginia as well as a camping lodge and bike rentals. The trail is great for walking or biking. The 8-mi leg of the well-marked trail from Cairo (MM 25.1) to Ellenboro (MM 33.6) is scenic, perfect for a leisurely afternoon bike ride. | From Parkersburg take Rte. 50 E to Rte. 31 S; trail runs through center of town.

Oil & Gas Museum. Engines, oil drills, tanks, documents, and photographs illustrate the history of the oil and gas industry in this region. The homes of many who prospered thanks to the industry are on display as well. | 119 3rd St. | 304/485–5446 | www. little-mountain.com/oilandgasmuseum | $2 | Weekdays 10–5, weekends noon–5.

Parkersburg Art Center. This cultural center has touring exhibitions, shows of local and regional artists, and an interactive art gallery for kids. | 227 Market St. | 304/485–3859 | $2 | Tues.–Sat. 10–5, Sun. 1–4.

Dining

Columbo's. Italian. In the center of Parkersburg, this trattoria serves all the standards, including lasagna, pizza, pasta, and veal parmigiana, but the prime rib is the most popular item. The walls are lined with photos of patrons and pictures of Parkersburg. | 1236 7th St. | 304/428–5472 | Closed Mon. No lunch | AE, D, DC, MC, V | $

Da Vinci's. Italian. This locally owned restaurant is full of surprises. The best-seller is pizza but it's a German pizza, topped with horseradish, corned beef, sauerkraut, and provolone cheese. Sandwiches, seafood, and steak dishes are also available. All of the desserts are homemade. A local favorite is the graham-cracker cream pie. | 215 Highland Ave., Williamstown, 10 mi north of Parkersburg | 304/375–3633 | Closed Mon. | AE, D, DC, MC, V | ¢–$$

Third Street Deli. American/Casual. A New York–style deli, Third Street has sandwiches, salads, and desserts, plus homemade soups. A local favorite is Aztec chowder spiced with a splash of cayenne pepper. Black-and-white tiled floors, linen tablecloths, and local artwork punctuate the interior; a heated patio allows outdoor dining year-round. | 430 3rd St. | 304/422–0003 | Closed Sun. No dinner | AE, D, DC, MC, V | ¢–$

Lodging

Blennerhassett Hotel. Circa 1889, this Richardsonian Romanesque historic hotel in the middle of town has a rustic style. There are antique furnishings on all five floors. If one is available, try a round turret room on a corner of the hotel. Restaurant, room service, in-room data ports, cable TV, bar, Internet, business services, airport shuttle. | 320 Market St., at 4th St., 26101 | 304/422–3131 or 800–262–2536 | fax 304/485–0267 | www.theblennerhassett.com | 92 rooms, 17 suites | AE, D, DC, MC, V | $$

Historic Harnett House B and B. This four-story circa 1885 Victorian mansion was built by local wealthy lumber Barron William Butterworth Caswell and constructed with the highest grade 300- to 400-year-old wood. The woodwork is striking, from the solid walnut grand staircase to the cherry door frames to the gleaming oak hardwood floors. Five rooms of the 34-room mansion are guest rooms, each with 12-foot ceilings and fireplaces. Meander through the grand entrance hall, formal parlor, great room, billiard room, and servants' hallway. Make time to explore the neighborhood; the house sits in the middle of historic Julia-Ann Square with 109 other historic homes. Cable TV, hot tub, Internet. | 1024 Juliana St., 26101 | 304/483–1029 | www.harnetthouse.com | 5 rooms | BP | No credit cards | $

North Bend Lodge. The view of the Appalachian Mountains is spectacular from this lodge on the Hughes River. The scenery includes a bridge overlooking a valley and a river. Activities abound for nature lovers, including fishing and canoeing in a 305-acre lake and hiking with their full-time naturalist. All rooms have solid oak furniture hand made in West Virginia; the cabins are on secluded hilltops. Restaurant, picnic area, cable TV, 2 tennis courts, pool, mountain bikes, hiking, children's programs (ages 3–16), business services. | Rte. 1, Cairo 26337, 4 mi outside of town, 25 mi east of Parkersburg | 304/643–2931 or 800/225–5982 | fax 304/643–2970 | 29 rooms, 8 cabins | AE, MC, V, D | $

Point Pleasant

Tu-Endi-Wei. Formerly the Point Pleasant Battle Monument State Park, Tu-Endi-Wei is the new name of this monument marking the site of the battle that took place on October 10, 1774, pitting 1,100 frontiersmen under the command of Andrew Lewis against Chief Cornstalk's 1,000 warriors. The battle broke the power of the Native Americans in the Ohio Valley; it was the crowning event in what has come to be known as Lord Dunmore's War. | 1 Main St. | 304/675–0869 | www.wvparks.com/pointpleasant | Free | Mon.–Sat. 10–4:30, Sun. 1–4:30.

Mansion House. Built in the late 18th century as a public inn, this house contains local colonial furniture and relics from the battle of Point Pleasant. | 1 Main St. | 304/675–0869 | Free | May–Oct., Mon.–Sat. 10–4:30, Sun. 1–4:30.

West Virginia State Farm Museum. Among the 50-acre museum's 19th-century pioneer artifacts are log cabins built in the early 1800s, a replica of an old Lutheran church, a one-room schoolhouse, a chapel, and a barn. The site hosts many local festivals like the annual Christmas Lights Drive which has over 2 million lights on display.

ily events take place the first weekend of every month. There are picnic
ground Rd. (Rte. 1) off 62 N | 304/675–5737 | Free | Tours Apr.–Nov., Tues.–
Sa.   in. 1–5.

Dining

Melinda's Restaurant. American. You won't find anything deep-fried on the menu, but you will find such comfort foods as macaroni and cheese, meat loaf, mashed potatoes, and homemade coconut-cream pie. Kitchen paraphernalia and old photos accent the dining room. Breakfast served. | 509 Main St. | 304/675–7201 | No credit cards | ¢–$

Wheeling

Artisan Center. River City Ale Works and Restaurant, the Children's Museum of the Ohio Valley, and Industrial Heritage exhibits are a few of the attractions in this restored historic industrial building. The Industrial Heritage Museum has interesting displays recounting the boom days of the industrial period from the 1880s to 1915 when the city was home to 400 working factories and 70,000 residents (now home to fewer than 50,000). Working artisans give demonstrations and sell crafts. | 1400 Main St., Heritage Sq. | 304/232–1810 | Free | Mon.–Thurs. 10–7, Fri. and Sat. 10–8.

Grave Creek Mound Historic Site. The prehistoric burial mound here was built in 250–150 BC by the Adena Indians and is the largest in the world—69 feet high and 295 feet in diameter. Next to the mound and also part of the site is the Delf Norona Museum and Cultural Center. | 801 Jefferson Ave., Moundsville, 12 mi south of Wheeling | 304/843–4128 | www.wvculture.org | $3 | Mon.–Sat. 10–4:30, Sun. 1–5.

Oglebay Resort Park. Gardens, greenhouses, restaurants, and golf courses fill this 1,500-acre municipal park. Popular events at Oglebay include a fireworks display the first weekend of October and the Festival of Lights—a 6-mi stretch of light displays—from early November through late January. | Rte. 88 N | 304/243–4000 or 800/624–6988 | www.oglebay-resort.com | $12 | Daily dawn–dusk.

Good Zoo and Benedum Planetarium. More than 250 North American animal species inhabit this 30-acre zoo with a children's farm, a deer contact area, a natural science theater, and a planetarium. An 1863 train tours a mile of the grounds. Wildlife classes on flowers, plants, and animals are available throughout the year. | 304/243–4030 | www.oglebay-resort.com | $5.95 | Weekdays 11–5, weekends 10–6.

Oglebay Institute Glass Museum. The world's largest collection of Wheeling glassware—produced from 1817 to 1939—is on display here. Don't miss the Sweeney punch bowl, a 225-pound, 4-foot, 10-inch bowl, the largest example of cut lead crystal in the world. | 304/242–7272 | www.oionline.com | $5, combo ticket with Mansion Museum $8 | Weekdays 10–4, Sat. 9–5, Sun. noon–5.

Oglebay Institute Mansion Museum. Items from early Ohio Valley life fill this museum; most were donated by locals. Thirteen period rooms depict the era from 1800 to 1926. The Regina music box is found in the Victorian parlor, a room focusing on Wheeling life from 1837 to 1901. Permanent exhibits include the Wymer's general store in the Wheeling history room, where the proprietor of the collection visits the museum three times a week to discuss the items on display. The Sinclair pharmacy exhibit displays many items once found in a working store in town. | 304/242–7272 | www.oionline.com | $5, $8 combo ticket with Glass Museum | Feb.–Oct., weekdays 9:30–5, Sat. 9–5, Sun. noon–5; Nov. and Dec., daily 9:30–9.

West Virginia Independence Hall–Custom House. West Virginia is the only state formed during the Civil War and it happened in this very house. Built in 1859 as the Wheeling Custom House, the building housed the Loyalists' government for the restored state of Virginia and the conventions that declared West Virginia's independence from the Commonwealth. Guided and self-guided tours are available; reservations are required for guided tours. An interactive map teaches children the history of the state. | 1528 Market St. | 304/238–1300 | $3 | Mar.–Dec., daily 10–4; Jan. and Feb., Mon.–Sat. 10–4.

West Virginia State Penitentiary. Former prison guards lead tours of West Virginia's first territorial prison, built in 1898. Tours include the Alamo Cell Block, where the most dangerous inmates were incarcerated. On Halloween, people flock to the huge Victorian structure for the spooky narrated flashlight tour. | 818 Jefferson Ave. | 304/845–6529 | www.wvpentours.com | $8 | Tours Apr.–Dec., Tues.–Sun. 10–4; Jan.–Mar. tours by appointment only.

Wheeling Suspension Bridge. Opened in 1849, this 1,010-foot suspension bridge, the longest in the world, was the first bridge to cross the Ohio River. It collapsed in 1854, was rebuilt in 1860, and restored again in 1990. In 1999 it was painted red, white, and blue, its original colors. | 10th St. at Main St. | 304/233–7709.

Dining

Coleman's Fish Market. Continental. This stand is a mainstay of the circa 1850 Centre Market. Protocol is to stand in a long line and, in turn, yell your order to the front. The popular fish sandwich is many pieces of fried fish piled high on white bread; it's wrapped in wax paper and served with a side of hot sauce. Don't miss the turtle soup. The stand closes at 5:30 PM daily. | 22nd and Market Sts. | 304/232–8510 | No dinner | No credit cards | ¢–$

Uncle Pete's. American. Views of the Ohio River and its massive valley from the outdoor deck and bar are a great complement to huge, overstuffed deli sandwiches. Pete puts cut rib eye in the Philly steak subs. Wings, soups, and salads are also available. | 1800 N. Main | 304/234–6701 | AE, D, DC, MC, V | $–$$

Wilson Lodge. Continental. Dine at the Glassworks Grill or the more formal Ihlenfeld Dining Room in this lodge at Oglebay Park. Staples at the Grill include the 2nd Street Bourbon, a char-grilled New York strip steak with bourbon butter served on garlic toast, while at the Dining Room it's beef topped with lump blue crab. There are beautiful views of the rolling countryside from both dining areas. | Rte. 88 N | 304/243–4000 or 800/624–6988 | AE, D, DC, MC, V | $–$$$

Lodging

Wilson Lodge at Oglebay. Choose from a room in the expansive lodge or a cottage. Some of the four-bedroom cottages are rustic, with wood floors and log-cabin–style walls, while others are contemporary, with basic, traditional furnishings. The rooms in the lodge are simple but spacious. Activities abound at this sprawling resort. There are a plethora of kid-friendly activities and services like the zoo and the nature center. 2 restaurants, ice-cream parlor, picnic area, snack bar, in-room data ports, some microwaves, some refrigerators, cable TV, driving range, four 10-hole golf courses, miniature golf, putting green, 2 tennis courts, pro shop, 2 pools (1 indoor), lake, health club, hot tub, massage, sauna, fishing, billiards, hiking, volleyball, bar, video game room, shops, baby-sitting, children's programs (ages 3–12), playground, laundry service, business services, some pets allowed, no-smoking rooms, no-smoking floors. | Rte. 88 N, 26003 | 304/243–4000 or 800/624–6988 | fax 304/243–4070 | 212 rooms, 49 cottages | AE, D, DC, MC, V | $$$

WISCONSIN

LAKE MICHIGAN CIRCLE TOUR
FROM KENOSHA TO GREEN BAY

Distance: 180 mi   Time: 2–3 days
Overnight Breaks: Fish Creek, Sturgeon Bay

Driving northward along the Lake Michigan shoreline, especially during spring or fall, the views are breathtaking. Door County is particularly beautiful; cherry and apple blossoms abound in spring, and the fall colors are spectacular. A fair number of sights and businesses are closed in winter, especially those farther north; but the area's natural beauty—especially after a snowfall—more than makes up for a missed restaurant or museum.

❶ **Sheboygan** is nationally known for its sausage and is a great place for bratwurst. **Kohler-Andrae State Park** has a mile-long beach good for camping, swimming, sunning, and beachcombing, as well as acres of sand dunes and four hiking trails.

❷ **Two Rivers,** home of the ice-cream sundae, offers a re-created Great Lakes commercial fishing village and lots of lakeshore access. Step aboard a 1936 wooden fishing tug at **Rogers Street Fishing Village and Museum.** Or bike the **Mariners Trail** along Lake Michigan to **Point Beach State Forest** and its 5½ mi of white-sand beach.

❸ **Sturgeon Bay** has one of the largest shipbuilding ports on the Great Lakes, in addition to a downtown historic district and a residential historic district. Watch a ship being built at **Door County Maritime Museum,** or try for smallmouth bass in fertile Sturgeon Bay.

❹ The small coastal village of **Ellison Bay** is the perfect jumping-off point for a biking tour of Door County's countryside or a stroll along the rocky shoreline at **Newport State Park.** Look out from **Death's Door Bluff** and imagine the days when shipwrecks off this tempestuous coast happened as often as twice a week.

❺ In **Fish Creek** you find a village of historic inns, shops, restaurants, and artists' galleries. **Peninsula Players** is the oldest professional resident summer theater

company in the country. Near town is the southern entrance to **Peninsula State Park** where you can camp, golf, hike, cross-country ski, as well as ride snowmobiles or bicycles.

❻ There's plenty to do in the big city of **Green Bay,** especially if you're a football fan, railroad buff, or nature lover. The **Green Bay Packer Hall of Fame,** newly remodeled and now at Lambeau Field, honors the greats of the green and gold, and offers tours of Lambeau Field. The **National Railroad Museum** has more than 70 railroad cars and locomotives, and is one of the largest rail museums in America. **Bay Beach Wildlife Sanctuary** offers sundry exhibits and dioramas on Wisconsin wildlife.

To return to the start of your tour, take I–43 to **Milwaukee,** then pick up I–94 to **Kenosha.**

Ellison Bay

Death's Door Bluff. This bluff is at the very tip of the Door County peninsula. The narrow passage, only 6 mi wide, connects Lake Michigan and Green Bay. It has turbulent currents year-round and numerous ships sank here many years ago. | 800/527–3529 | Free | Daily.

Door County Maritime Museum. Commercial fishing, shipwrecks, and navigation are the focus of this seasonal museum 5 mi north of Ellison Bay. You can see models, marine engines, photos, a 1917 Berylume pleasure craft, and a 1930s fishing tug. | 12724 Rte. 42, Gills Rock | 920/743–5958 | www.dcmm.org | $4; special rates for children | Memorial Day–Labor Day, daily 10–4.

Door County scenic bicycle route. Small green signs mark the scenic bicycle route along the back roads of Door County.

   Door County Chamber of Commerce. Get maps of the scenic bicycle route and other visitor information from the chamber of commerce. | 920/743–4456 or 800/527–3529 | www.doorcountyvacations.com.

Newport State Park. At this 2,370-acre wild area with 11 mi of Lake Michigan shoreline, northeast of town, you can hike, swim, fish, mountain bike, camp, cross-country ski, and snowshoe. | 475 Rte. NP | 920/854–2500 | www.dcty.com/newport/ | $7 | Daily.

Dining

Shoreline Restaurant. Continental. You can watch the sun set over Green Bay from this restaurant in the Shoreline Resort. Thick burgers, salads, and soups are served at

WISCONSIN RULES OF THE ROAD

License Requirements: To drive in Wisconsin, you must be at least 16 years old and have a valid driver's license.

Right Turn on Red: In most of Wisconsin you can make a right turn at a red light *after* coming to a full stop. At some intersections, "no turn on red light" signs are posted.

Seat-Belt & Helmet Laws: Drivers and passengers must wear seat belts at all times. Children under age 4 must use a federally approved child safety seat. Motorcyclists under 18 are required to wear helmets; adults are not required to do so.

Speed Limits: Speed limits in Wisconsin vary widely. On expressways they range from 50 mph to 65 mph, and on highways from 40 mph to 55 mph. In residential areas, posted speed limits range from 25 mph to 40 mph. In areas where there are schools, signs are often posted indicating speed limits of 15 mph to 20 mph when children are present. Be sure to check signs carefully.

Other Regulations: Drivers' blood-alcohol concentration must not exceed .10%. Passengers in a vehicle cannot possess open containers of alcohol.

For More Information: Wisconsin Department of Transportation | 414/266–1000 | www.dot.state.wi.us. Wisconsin State Police | 608/266–3218.

lunch. Nightly specials like crab-stuffed pasta shells are the stars of the menu. | 12747 Rte. 42, Gills Rock | 920/854–2950 | D, MC, V | Closed Nov.–Apr. | $–$$

T Ashwell. Contemporary. A beach-stone fireplace dominates the dining room and a piano player entertains at the wine bar of this sophisticated spot. Dishes on the frequently changing menu have included sautéed duck layered with foie gras and a cherry and cranberry reduction. You can also choose to dine on the heated porch. | 11976 Mink River Rd., Ellison Bay | 920/854–4306 | AE, D, DC, MC, V | Closed Tues. No lunch | $$–$$$

Viking Grill. American. The whitefish boils served daily from mid-May to October at tables in a garden out back are the big draw for this casual downtown restaurant. Otherwise, sandwiches and fried fish are the favorites throughout the year. | 12029 Rte. 42, Ellison Bay | 920/854–2998 | AE, D, MC, V | Breakfast also available, Fish boils only from mid-May to Oct. | $–$$

Fish Creek

Bike Rentals. To explore bike trails in Newport and Peninsula State Parks, rent wheels with the following outfitters.

Edge Of Park Bike & Moped Rental. | Park Entrance Rd. | 920/868–3344.

Nor Door Sport & Cyclery. | 4007 Hwy. 42 | 920/868–2275 | www.nordoorsports.com.

Peninsula Players. America's oldest professional resident summer theater presents drama, comedy, and musical productions from late June through mid-October. They perform in a covered garden theater on the shores of Green Bay south of Fish Creek. | Peninsula Players Rd., Fish Creek | 920/868–3287 | www.peninsulaplayers.com | $22.50–$28.50 | June–mid-Oct.

Peninsula State Park. This 3,762-acre peninsula, with more than 6 mi of shoreline on Green Bay waters, has an 18-hole championship golf course, hiking, bicycle trails, camping, groomed ski trails, snowmobiling, sledding, swimming, boat rentals, a boat ramp, an observation tower, and fishing. You can see the 125-year-old Eagle Bluff lighthouse. Trail maps and other information are available at the park headquarters. | 9462 Shore Rd., Fish Creek | 920/868–3258 | www.wiparks.net | $7 | Daily 6 AM–11 PM.

American Folklore Theatre. Original musicals and plays are presented June–August in the 750-seat theater in Peninsula State Park. | 920/854–6117 | www.folkloretheatre.com.

Dining

Bayside Tavern. American/Casual. By day, this spot serves such basic pub fare as burgers and soups; by night it's a hopping club showcasing local bands of all kinds. Friday night there's a perch fry. | 4160 Main St. | 920/868–3441 | AE, MC, V | ¢–$

C and C Supper Club. Continental. This downtown restaurant with two large dining rooms, a fireplace, and linen tablecloths is known for baby-back ribs and broiled local whitefish served with veggies and potatoes. There's a Monday-night taco special and brunch on weekends from Memorial Day to Labor Day. | Spruce and Main Sts., Fish Creek | 920/868–3412 or 920/854–4417 | AE, D, DC, MC, V | No lunch; closed weekdays Nov.–Apr. | $$

White Gull Inn. Contemporary. The antiques-filled dining room at this downtown inn built in 1896 is elegant yet cozy. You can order the Door County fish boil or sample the raspberry chicken almondine, which is almond-crusted chicken breast drizzled with raspberry sauce. | 4225 Main St., Fish Creek | 920/868–3517 | fax 920/868–2367 | AE, D, DC, MC, V | Closed Sun. Nov.–Apr. | $$–$$$

Lodging

Cedar Court Inn. One of Door County's oldest resorts, this charmer has several porches, landscaped grounds, and a white picket fence. Inside, it looks like an elegant farm home. The bright motel rooms are decorated with flowers and floral wreaths or framed posters of Fish Creek. Picnic area, some kitchenettes, some microwaves, refrigerators, some in-room hot tubs, cable TV, some in-room VCRs, pool, business services; no smoking. | 9429 Cedar St., 54212 | 920/868–3361 | fax 920/868–2541 | www.cedarcourt.com | 14 rooms, 9 cottages | MC, V | $–$$$

Thorp House Inn, Cottages, and Beach House. A turn-of-the-20th-century Victorian home with a library and many antiques is the center of this complex, which overlooks the harbor from atop a hill. The house and its cottages are listed on the National Register of Historic Places. Mountain bikes and a tandem bike are available for guest use. The lavishly decorated rooms have Victorian furnishings. The cottages are more rustic, with exposed wood. Picnic area, some kitchenettes, some microwaves, some in-room hot tubs, cable TV, in-room VCRs; no a/c in some rooms, no kids, no smoking. | 4135 Bluff Rd., 54212 | 920/868–2444 | fax 920/868–9833 | www.thorphouseinn.com | 6 rooms, 3 suites, 6 cottages | No credit cards | CP | $–$$$

White Gull Inn. Inside this 1896 village inn, antiques-filled rooms are accented by Victorian wallpaper and pencil-poster canopy beds. Cottages have fireplaces, porches, and painted iron beds or sleigh beds. Restaurant, cable TV, business services, airport shuttle; no kids. | 4225 Main St., 54212 | 920/868–3517 or 800/624–1987 | fax 920/868–2367 | www.whitegullinn.com | 13 rooms, 4 cottages | AE, D, DC, MC, V | $$–$$$$

Green Bay

Bay Beach Amusement Park. Twenty-five-cent rides at this circa 1910 amusement park thrill parents. The merry-go-round, Ferris wheel, and Tilt-a-Whirl will thrill kids. | 1313 Bay Beach Rd. | 920/391–3671 | Free | June–mid-Aug., daily 10–9; May and Sept., weekends 10–6.

Bay Beach Wildlife Sanctuary. Native Wisconsin birds and mammals inhabit replicas of their natural habitats on this 700-acre preserve. There's a waterfowl refuge, child-friendly exhibit building, old duck hunting shack, and walking trails. | 1660 E. Shore Dr. | 920/391–3671 | Free | Apr. 15–Sept. 15, daily 8–8; Sept. 16–Apr. 14, daily 8–5.

★ **Green Bay Packer Hall of Fame.** Clock the speed of your punts and passes in the interactive area of the 18,000-square-foot hall of fame in the Titletown Atrium at Lambeau Field. Super Bowl trophies, displays recounting famous games, and Packer memorabilia await. Restaurants and the Packer Pro Shop are also on the premises. | 1255 Lombardi Ave. | 920/496–5700 | Hall of Fame tours $9, stadium tours $10 | Hall of Fame tours daily 9–6, stadium tours daily 9–4. No tours on home-game days.

Heritage Hill State Park. A 48-acre complex of furnished historic buildings, the park is grouped into four areas: Belgian Farm (1905), the Growing Community (1871), Fort Howard (1836), and La Baye (1762). Costumed interpreters are stationed in each historic building. | 2640 S. Webster Ave. | 920/448–5150 | www.heritagehillgb.org | $7 | Memorial Day–Labor Day, Tues.–Sat. 10–4:30, Sun. noon–4:30.

National Railroad Museum. More than 70 railroad cars and locomotives are on display at one of the largest rail museums in America. Exhibits include General Dwight D. Eisenhower's World War II staff car and a Union Pacific Big Boy—the world's largest steam locomotive. The reception center has a library and multimedia presentation. You can take 20-minute train rides along a 1¼-mi track on the grounds. | 2285

S. Broadway | 920/437–7623 | $7 | Mon.–Sat. 9–5, Sun. 11–5; train rides May–Sept., daily at 10, 11:30, 1, 2:30, and 4.

Neville Public Museum. Changing history, art, and science exhibits fill two floors of galleries. A permanent exhibit, "On the Edge of the Inland Sea," takes you through 12,000 years of history in northeast Wisconsin, from the Ice Age to the present. | 210 Museum Pl. | 920/448–4460 | Donations accepted | Tues.–Sat. 10–4, Sun. noon–4.

Oneida Bingo and Casino. This elegant Native American gaming facility has a spacious 850-seat Bingo Hall with a smoke-free area, 60 blackjack tables, and more than 2,500 reel slot and video machines. Table limits range from $3 to $200. There are several restaurants and snack bars, but no alcohol is allowed or served. Free valet, parking, and shuttle bus service from the airport is offered. | Hwy. 172, just off U.S. 43 and U.S. 41, across from Austin Straubel International Airport | 800/238–4263, 920/497–8118 bingo, 920/494–4500 casino | www.oneidabingoandcasino.net | Daily 24 hrs.

Dining

Bistro John Paul. French. This romantic candlelit bistro has generously spaced tables. Beef tournedos and mushroom-crusted halibut are good bets on this four-course menu full of artfully prepared dishes. | 1244 Main St. | 920/432–2897 | www.bistrojohnpaul.com | Closed Sun. and Mon. No lunch | AE, D, DC, MC, V | $$–$$$$

Kroll's. American. Across from Lambeau Field, this Green Bay institution serves up juicy burgers, perch dinners, and, following local custom, chili on spaghetti noodles. | 1990 S. Ridge Rd. | 920/497–1111 | MC, V | $–$$

Titletown Brewing Company. American/Casual. Expect microbrews, burgers, and ribs served up in a remodeled 1898 Chicago & Northwestern railroad depot with 18-foot ceilings, original fireplaces, and a view of the Fox River. | 200 Dousman St. | 920/437–2337 | AE, DC, MC, V | $–$$

Union Hotel. American. Hand-cut steaks and the freshest in fish and vegetables are hallmarks of this brick turn-of-the-20th-century hotel and restaurant, which has been in the same family since 1913. | 200 N. Broadway | 920/336–6131 | No lunch weekends | AE, D, MC, V | $$–$$$$

Sheboygan

Fishing. Trout and salmon are yours to hook and net in the waters off Sheboygan. Catch your "big one" on a mini, half-day, or full-day fishing or cruising charter or set your own boat afloat from a launch at the Eighth Street Bridge or the major launch area at the lakefront. The Sheboygan River is also popular for fly fishing, particularly in fall and spring. The Sheboygan County Convention and Visitors Bureau publishes a Fishing Facts brochure each year (Essentials, Visitor Information).

Dead Reckoning Charters. Any size group is welcome on Captain John Zabel's 35-foot Egg Harbor Sportfisherman. Docked on the riverfront boardwalk, this charter furnishes all equipment so you can catch Lake Michigan trout or salmon. | N6414 Woodland Rd., Sheboygan | 920/467–1111.

Dumper Dan's Sportfishing Charters. Groups of one to six people can climb aboard one of Dumper Dan's three 28-foot Baha Cruiser sportfishing boats. You can troll Lake Michigan for trout and salmon aboard Sheboygan's only multi-boat charter fishing fleet. | 4022 N. 51st St., Sheboygan | 920/457–2940.

Sorry Charlie Sport Fishing Service. Captain Randy Even guarantees the charter trips aboard his 31-foot Uniflite will be successful. The trip is free if he can't steer you to some of Lake Michigan's salmon or trout. | 4226 S. 13th St., Sheboygan | 920/452–9964 | www.u-charters.com.

John Michael Kohler Arts Center. A former family mansion, built in the Italian Villa style, is at the center of this light-filled complex that plays a key role in the rejuvenated downtown scene. A visual- and performing-arts complex devoted to contemporary American art, it also encompasses a turn-of-the-20th-century carriage house and a historic library. Plays and musical events are staged here along with an annual outdoor festival. | 608 New York Ave. (Rte. 23), Sheboygan | 920/458–6144 | Free | Mon., Wed., and Fri. 10–5, Tues. and Thurs. 10–8, weekends 10–4.

Kohler-Andrae State Park. Just south of town is this 1,000-acre park on a mile-long stretch of Lake Michigan beach backdropped by sand dunes. You can fish, beachcomb, swim, camp, and hike 3½ mi of all-purpose woods/dune trails. The Sanderling Nature Center has nature exhibits and interpretive programs. The park is east of I–43, off Exit 120. | 1520 Old Park Rd., Sheboygan | 920/451–4080 | www.dnr.state.wi.us | $7 | Daily.

Sheboygan County Historical Museum. Exhibits in this museum complex on the western edge of town showcase Sheboygan County history. You can visit the 1852 Judge David Taylor home, an 1864 log house, an 1867 cheese factory, and an 1890s barn. Exhibits include Indian history, ice harvesting, local sports, early agriculture, and maritime trades. | 3110 Erie Ave., Sheboygan | 920/458–1103 | $3 | Apr.–Oct., Tues.–Sat. 10–5, Sun. 1–5.

Waelderhaus. The daughter of the Kohler Company founder built this house in 1931 in memory of her father. This "house in the woods" is a replica of the 1850 Kohler home in Vorarlberg, Austria. Its intricate carvings, woodcuts, and iron and pewter work were designed and executed by Austrian sculptor-architect Kaspar Albrecht. The house sits on a high bluff, 3 mi west of Sheboygan, overlooking the Sheboygan River. | W. Riverside Dr., Kohler | 920/452–4079 | Free | Daily tours at 2, 3, and 4.

The Wreck of the Lottie Cooper. This white oak schooner built in 1876 was recovered and reassembled in 1992, and subsequently placed in Deland Park, near Lake Michigan in downtown Sheboygan. You can walk through its hold and see the craftsmanship in the 89-foot center section, which is all that remains of the three-masted schooner that capsized in gale force winds in the Sheboygan harbor in 1894. Both guided and self-guided tours are available. | 882 Broughton Dr., Sheboygan | 920/458–2974 | Daily.

Dining

Il Ritrovo. Italian. Wood-fired pizza is the specialty at this more casual younger sibling to Trattoria Stefano across the street. You can sit at small tables or one of the family-size booths, which are designed for an old-fashioned Italian family with Mama, Papa, and eight more sitting down for the meal. A market selling Italian foods and specialty items and a wine bar are in the next room. | 515 S. 8th St. | 920/803–7516 | AE, DC, MC, V | Closed Sun. | $

The Immigrant. Continental. Each of the six small dining rooms at this upscale restaurant inside the American Club, 5 mi west of Sheboygan, are named and decorated in honor of a different European country. Whether you are seated in the English, the French, or the German room, you can dine on such dishes as rack of lamb, braised rabbit leg, and seared yellowfin tuna. | American Club, 444 Highland Dr., Kohler | 920/457–8000 | Jacket required | AE, D, DC, MC, V | Closed Sun. No lunch | $$$$

Jumes. American/Casual. This neon pink downtown diner has an old-style neon sign outside that still says "air-conditioned." This family restaurant has been open since 1928 serving breakfast all day, burgers, shakes, and daily specials. | 504 N. 8th St. | 920/452–4914 | AE, DC, MC, V | ¢–$

Sturgeon Bay

Door County Maritime Museum. You can watch ships being built, explore an engine room, study ship models, and learn about Door County lighthouses in this 20,000-square-foot museum on the water's edge. | 120 N. Madison Ave. | 920/743–5958 | www.dcmm.or | $6.50 | Memorial Day–Labor Day, daily 9–6; Labor Day–Memorial Day, daily 10–5.

The Farm. This living museum 4 mi north of the city has a petting zoo with farm animals such as goats, cows, and horses, as well as nature trails and log cabins with farm tools and antiques on display. | 4285 Rte. 57 N | 920/743–6666 | $7 | Memorial Day–Labor Day, daily 9–5.

Fishing. People are so devoted to fishing in Door County that they do it in any season. The Lake Michigan waters around Sturgeon Bay are rich with smallmouth bass, particularly off the ship canal.

Fishing hot line. For guidance on what is biting and where and on what call the county's fishing hot line. | 920/743–7046.

Whitefish Dunes State Park. This 865-acre park has more visitors than any other day use park in the state. There's more than a mile of sandy beach, the highest sand dune in Wisconsin, and trails for hiking, biking, and skiing. Bordering Whitefish Dunes on three sides is **Cave Point County Park** (920/743–4456), where Lake Michigan has carved caves out of dolomite rocks. | 3275 Clark Lake Rd. (Rte. WD) | 920/823–2400 | www.wiparks.net.

William S. Fairfield Art Museum. The gallery's permanent collection houses maquettes, drawings, and sculptures by Henry Moore; abstract paintings by Kandinsky; and sculpted works by Alberto Giacometti. The museum is housed in 1907 building in the center of the city's historic downtown. | 242 Michigan Ave. | 920/746–0001 | fax 920/746–0000 | www.fairfieldartmuseum.com | $5 | Mon. and Thurs.–Sat. 10–5, Sun. 11–3.

Dining

Bluefront Cafe. American. Healthy breakfasts and lunches are served in this former retail space a couple of blocks from downtown. Organic pancakes, homemade granola, and quiche are available at breakfast. Lunch is wraps, salads, and quesadillas. | 306 S. 3rd Ave. | 920/743–9218 | MC, V | Closed Mon. No dinner | ¢–$

Dal Santo's Restaurant. Italian. The lighting may be dim but the food is good in this former train station. The most popular dishes are pasta in spicy sauces, but meat and fish dinners are served as well. Try the fried ravioli appetizer. | 341½ N. 3rd St. | 920/743–6100 | AE, D, MC, V | No lunch | ¢–$$

Sage. Contemporary. When no one is on hand to play the grand piano in the center of this stylish restaurant, jazz music is usually played. Come relax at the sofa beside the wine bar at the front of this storefront in downtown Sturgeon Bay before settling in for dinner. Fish, steak, or chops get a fancy treatment with rubs or glazes, from mango to whole grain Dijon mustard. | 136 N. 3rd Ave. | 920/746–1100 | MC, V | No lunch | $$–$$$$

Lodging

Barbican Olde English Guest House. You can choose from three restored late-19th-century houses, all filled with antiques, in the historic waterfront district, one block from the bay or downtown. Two of the homes were owned by L. M. Washburn, a local lumber baron, in the 1870s. The third was built for his daughter as a wedding gift in 1904. Gardens are landscaped with arbors, a fishpond, and a bridge, with wicker furniture on the porches, hanging flower baskets, and some private terraces. Each suite is individually decorated with floral accents and thickly decorated wall coverings. Microwaves, room service, cable TV, in-room hot tubs, in-room VCRs; no room phones. | 132 N. 2nd Ave., Sturgeon Bay 54235 | 920/743–4854 | www.barbicanbandb.com | 18 suites in 3 buildings | MC, V | CP | $$–$$$

Inn at Cedar Crossing. This antiques-filled late-19th-century brick inn is on a historic downtown street. The common areas are elegant and cozy. The restaurant serves regional fare in a Victorian era setting. Rooms are enriched with antique pine furnishings and boldly patterned fabrics and wallpapers. Restaurant, some in-room hot tubs, cable TV, in-room VCRs, business services, airport shuttle; no smoking. | 336 Louisiana St., Sturgeon Bay 54235 | 920/743–4200 | fax 920/743–4422 | www.innatcedarcrossing.com | 9 rooms | AE, D, MC, V | CP | $–$$$

Snug Harbor Inn. A dock at your doorstep and 300 feet of parklike shorefront await you at this inn, a mile from downtown. Some of the motel rooms have waterviews. Modern cottages and luxury suites, adjoining the motel, all face the water. Cable TV, grills, some in-room hot tubs, some pets allowed. | 1627 Memorial Dr., Sturgeon Bay 54235 | 920/743–2337 or 800/231–5767 | www.snugharbor.com | 5 rooms, 6 suites, 4 cottages | MC, V | $–$$$

Two Rivers

Hamilton Wood Type & Printing Museum. Historic printing presses and cut-wood type, in various languages and patterns, are on display in the world's only museum devoted to the preservation and study of this unique craft. | 1619 Jefferson St. | 920/794–6272 | www.woodtype.org | Free | Daily 1–5.

Historic Washington House. This brick-faced 1850 hotel is reportedly the place where, in 1881, chocolate sauce and ice cream first met. The dish, once reserved for the Lord's day, was later called a sundae, after a 10-year-old's supposed plea to "pretend it's Sunday." | 1662 Jefferson St. | 920/793–2490 | May–Oct., daily 9–9; Nov.–Apr., daily 9–5.

Mariners Trail. This paved 12-mi trail begins in downtown Manitowoc at the 8th Street bridge (5 mi south of Two Rivers via Rte. 42) and runs to Point Beach State Forest (5 mi north via County Hwy. O). There are lake vistas, shops, and facilities along the way.

    Fitness Store. For rentals and information contact this bicycle shop. | 1611 Washington St. | 920/794–2245.

Point Beach State Forest. Marsh, hardwoods and conifer forest, dunes, and 5½ mi of white-sand beach all exist on these 2,900 acres. Possible activities include a bracing Lake Michigan swim, tour of 1894 Rawley Point Lighthouse, and spring and fall bird-watching. | 9400 County Hwy. O | 920/794–7480.

Rogers Street Fishing Village & Museum. This restored commercial fishing village on the banks of the East Twin River houses an 1883 lighthouse, photographs, drawings, a shanty, and artifacts from the *Rouse Simmons* ship, which sank in 1912 off Two Rivers. Step aboard a 1936 fishing tug or hear a 5,000-pound Kahlenberg diesel engine being started. | 2102 Jackson St. | 920/793–5905 | www.rogersstreet.com | $2 | May–Oct., daily 10–4; also by appointment.

Dining

Kurtz's Pub & Deli. German. Somewhere between a Wisconsin tavern and a German beer hall, this local institution has been serving cold brew, hot pretzels, and savory Reubens since 1904. Old Octoberfest posters, dozens of tap beers, and rich desserts round out the experience. | 1410 Washington St. | 920/793–1222 | Closed Sun. | DC, MC, V | $–$$

GREAT RIVER ROAD ALONG ROUTE 35
FROM CASSVILLE TO HUDSON

Distance: 300 mi   Time: 2 days
Overnight Break: La Crosse

Wisconsin's portion of the Great River Road is the focus of this drive, which takes you along the state's western border, past bluffs and river towns along the Mississippi. The river here is part of the 360-mi-long Upper Mississippi National Wildlife Refuge and hosts impressive fall and spring bird migrations. Just follow the white-and-green "Wisconsin's Great River Road" signs. By mid-May, attractions are open and the hills are lush green. Summer by the river is warm and languid. The richness of fall colors is matched only by the array of waterfowl on the river. Donning skis or snowshoes is a good way to explore this bluff country in winter, though some attractions are closed.

❶ Quiet **Cassville** (from Rte. 35 follow Rte. 133 W into town), which once made a bid to become Wisconsin's territorial capital, is a great spot to relax and enjoy the river. **Riverside Park** is the departure point for the Cassville car ferry, a neat way to experience the Mississippi or to get over to Iowa. About 5 mi north is **Stonefield State Historic Site,** where you can stroll through the town square in a re-created 1890s rural village. Across the road is the home of Wisconsin's first governor, Nelson Dewey; the grounds include five original buildings and authentic furnishings.

❷ **Prairie du Chien** is a rustic town that packs appeal for nature lovers and history buffs. The main attraction is **Villa Louis,** a Victorian country estate built by the family of fur trader Hercules Dousman. The villa is on the banks of the Mississippi River. **Wyalusing State Park** (follow Rte. 18 [Rte. 35] S and turn right onto County Hwy. C) has an outstanding view of the Wisconsin and Mississippi rivers confluence, as well as hiking and canoeing.

❸ **La Crosse** (take I–90 E off Rte. 35) has a great deal of small-town charm for a large city. Activities might include a brewery tour or a leisurely boat ride. Get details on what's happening at the Wisconsin Travel Information Center in La Crosse on I–90 East, about a mile east of the Mississippi River. For a panoramic view of the city, river, and surrounding countryside, go to **Grandad Bluff**—a park at the end of Main Street that sits 590 feet above the river. At **Riverside Park** you can board the paddle-wheel steamer *Julia Belle Swain,* for a brunch, lunch, dinner, or overnight cruise. If you have the time and the inclination, end the day by taking the Wildlife Drive at **Trempealeau National Wildlife Refuge,** 22 mi to the north.

❹ **Hudson** was named for its physical resemblance to the Hudson River valley in New York. Consider visits to the 1855 Victorian-style **Octagon House,** or **Phipps Center for the Arts.** Trout and smallmouth bass sulk in the cool waters of **Willow River State Park.** To return to the start of your tour, follow the same route back along Route 35.

Cassville

Riverside Park. Near the center of town, this park is the departure point for the Cassville car ferry, which crosses the Mississippi River to Iowa. | Between Crawford and

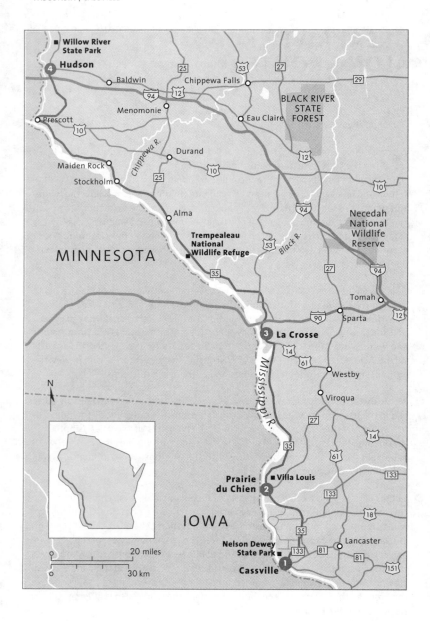

Front Sts. | 608/725–5855 | 1-way ferry $10 per car, $1 on foot | Park: daily dawn–dusk. Ferry: late May–early Sept., Wed.–Sun. 9–9; May and early Sept.–Oct., Fri.–Sun. 9–9; no service during high water.

Stonefield State Historic Site. A mile north of Cassville, this re-created 1890s rural village is the State Historical Society's museum of agricultural history and village life. You can stroll through the town square or visit with costumed merchants and tradesmen in period shops. Historic farm implements are displayed in the museum. | County VV | 608/725–5210 | $8 | Late May–early Sept., daily 10–4; early Sept.–mid-Oct., weekends 10–4.

Dining

Vogt's Town Pump. American. Housed in a onetime hardware store, this downtown Cassville favorite serves Saturday-night prime rib, meat-and-potatoes dinners, and sandwiches. Breakfast served. | 118 E. Amelia St. | 608/725–5175 | No dinner Sun. | D, MC, V | $–$$

Hudson

Marcus Sears Bell Farmstead. This 1884 farmhouse is the centerpiece of the New Richmond Heritage Center. The farmstead includes a barn with granary, a general store, a blacksmith shop, and a one-room schoolhouse. | 1100 Heritage Dr., New Richmond, 18 mi northeast of Hudson | 715/246–3276 or 888/320–3276 | www.pressenter. com/~nrpsinc | $5 | Late May–early Sept., weekdays 10–4, Sat. 7:30–2, Sun. noon–4; early Sept.–late May, weekdays 10–4.

New Richmond Golf Club. Opened in 1923, this 18-hole course is as challenging as it is beautiful. A dress code is enforced (no tank tops) and spikes are not allowed. | 1226 180th Ave., New Richmond, 15 mi northeast of Hudson | 715/246–6724 | Weekdays $17 for 9 holes, $29 for 18 holes; weekends $19 for 9 holes, $34 for 18 holes | Mid-Apr.–mid-Oct., daily dawn–dusk.

Octagon House. Built in 1855, this house is rich in local history and Americana. Furnishings include a grand piano famous for its two accidental dunkings in the St. Croix River while it was being transported. | 1004 3rd St. | 715/386–2654 | $5 | May–Oct., Tues.–Sat. 11–4, Sun. 2–4:30.

Phipps Center for the Arts. Professional theatrical productions and cultural exhibits are year-round attractions here. Tours are available. | 109 Locust St. | 715/386–2305 | Free | Mon.–Sat. 9–4:30, Sun. noon–4:30; tours by appointment.

Willow River State Park. Rent a canoe on Little Falls Lake, catch trout in the Willow River with the help of Kinni Creek Outfitters, or hike through a restored prairie. | 1034 Rte. A, Somerset, 10 mi northwest of Hudson | 715/386–5931, 877/504–9705 Kinni Creek Outfitters | www.dnr.state.wi.us | $10 | Daily 6 AM–11 PM.

Dining

Riverside. American. Enjoy a rib-eye steak with vegetables, potato, and salad either inside or on the patio at this spot that is, as the name suggests, right on the St. Croix River. A few menu items exceed $25. | 1st St. | 715/386–5504 | AE, D, MC, V | $–$$$$

San Pedro Cafe. Caribbean. High ceilings, bright colors, and the smell of wood smoke evoke a cheery island feel. Pizza, meat, and seafood are cooked over oak- and fruit-wood embers. End your meal with a tropical drink or smoothie. Breakfast served. | 426 2nd St. | 715/386–4003 | MC, V | $–$$

Winzer Stube. German. Dark-wood timbers and German murals set the mood, and Marie Schmidt's recipes deliver the tastes of her native Trier. Creamy pâté, piquant red cabbage, paper-thin rouladen, and cinnamon-cream strudel are just a few standouts. The prix-fixe menu, offered Monday, Wednesday, and Thursday, is an excellent value. | 516 2nd St. | 715/381–5092 | Closed Tues. | AE, D, MC, V | $$

La Crosse

Children's Museum of La Crosse. Climb 28-foot Mt. LeKid, step inside a giant mouth, or control river flow on a Mississippi River diorama. | 207 5th Ave. S | 608/784–2652 | $4 | Tues.–Sat. 10–5, Sun. noon–5.

Grandad Bluff. At 590 foot above the Mississippi River, this city park provides great views of the city and surrounding states. | Main St. | 608/789–7533 | Daily 24 hrs.

Riverside Park. Watch boat traffic on the Mississippi from this park, where you can also catch the *Julia Belle Swain*, a paddle-wheel steamer. | State St. | 608/783–6403 | Daily 24 hrs.

Riverside Museum. Inside the La Crosse Convention and Visitors Bureau, which is located on the north end of Riverside Park, this museum has archaeological and local history displays concentrating on the river's importance to the development of the area. | 410 Veterans Memorial Dr. | 877/568–3522 | Free | Memorial Day–Labor Day, daily 10–5.

The *Julia Belle Swain* is a floating palace with all the amenities of old-time river-boats. There are weekend brunch, lunch, and dinner cruises, as well as one- and two-day cruises to Prairie du Chien or Winona, Minnesota. Motor-coach service back to La Crosse is provided for one-day cruises. All cruises include live music. Book two weeks in advance for overnights, two days in advance for meals. | 227 Main St. | 608/784–4882 or 800/815–1005 | www.juliabelle.com | June–Oct., daily; call or check Web site for schedules.

Trempealeau National Wildlife Refuge. More than 100 bird species congregate in this 6,220-acre refuge during spring and fall migrations. Take the 4-mi Wildlife Drive (via bike or car) in morning or evening to see a variety of upland and wetland denizens. | Hwy. 35 (Hwy. 54), Centreville, 30 mi north of La Crosse; turn left at the refuge sign 3¼ mi west of Centreville | 608/539–2311 | Free | Daily dawn–dusk.

Dining

Buzzard Billy's Flying Carp Café. Cajun/Creole. There's usually jazz or blues wailing from the speakers at this family spot. Try the eggplant *pirogues* (scooped-out and stuffed with seafood) and order a piece of Cajun-blackened fish—walleye, catfish, and white-fish may be among your choices. | 222 Pearl St. | 608/796–2277 | AE, D, DC, MC, V | $–$$

Elite Mediterranean Cafe. Mediterranean. A gourmet storefront grocery and bubbling marble fountain set the stage for a memorable dining experience, complete with ivy growing from the latticework. A broad range of European and North African food and wine is served. The falafel, hummus, tabouleh, and shish kebabs are outstanding. | 512 Main St. | 608/784–9115 | Closed Sun. | AE, D, DC, MC, V | $–$$

Fayze's. American. Brick walls adorned with La Crosse memorabilia set a casual tone at this restaurant-bakery famous for sandwiches served on soft white Lebanese rolls known as *talame* rolls. Breakfast served. | 135 S. 4th St. | 608/784–9548 | D, DC, MC, V | $

Freighthouse. American. On the National Register of Historic Places, this late-19th-century former train station is casual and offers such specialties as fresh seafood, prime rib, and steak. The Chicago, Milwaukee, and St. Paul railroad cars are still on view outside the restaurant. Drinks and appetizers are served on the deck overlooking the Missis-sippi River. | 107 Vine St. | 608/784–6211 | Reservations not accepted | No lunch | AE, D, DC, MC, V | $$

Lodging

Chateau La Crosse. A wealth of Victorian details lies hidden behind the Gothic exterior of this 1854 castle, which is listed on the National Register of Historic Places. Afghan onyx tiles enclose the fireplace in the library and the master bedroom has hand-painted murals and gold-leaf edging. A champagne breakfast is served in private parlors. Restau-rant, in-room data ports, cable TV, business services. | 410 Cass St., 54601 | 800/442–7969 or 608/796–1090 | fax 608/796–0700 | www.visitor-guide.com/chateaulacrosse | 4 rooms | BP | AE, D, DC, MC, V | $$–$$$$

Days Inn. Most rooms in this French Island motel have wonderful views of the Mississippi River. It's 4 mi from downtown. Restaurant, cable TV, pool, hot tub, bar, business services. | 101 Sky Harbor Dr. 54603 | 608/783–1000 | fax 608/783–2948 | 148 rooms | AE, D, DC, MC, V | $

Radisson. Many rooms in this eight-story hotel have views of the Mississippi River. The large lobby has marble floors; paintings depict the riverfront during the 1900s. Hotel staff is notably friendly and helpful. Restaurant, cable TV, pool, gym, hot tub, bar, business services, airport shuttle, some pets allowed. | 200 Harborview Plaza, 54601 | 608/784–6680 or 800/333–3333 | fax 608/784–6694 | www.radisson.com | 170 rooms | CP | AE, D, DC, MC, V | $$–$$$

Prairie du Chien

Effigy Mounds National Monument. This 1,481-acre monument 5 mi down the Iowa side of the river from Prairie du Chien (Hwy. 18 W to Hwy. 76 S) contains 191 known prehistoric mounds of various shapes built by the Woodland Indians. There are numerous scenic hiking trails in the area. | 151 Hwy. 76, Marquette, IA, 5 mi northwest of Prairie du Chien | 563/873–3491 | www.nps.gov/efmo | $3 | Daily 8–4:30.

Prairie du Chien Museum at Fort Crawford. Medical history from the 1800s to the present is the focus at this museum. Relics of 19th-century medicine in Wisconsin include displays of Native American herbal remedies, an old-fashioned drugstore, a dentist's office, and a doctor's office. | 717 S. Beaumont Rd., south end of town at Rte. 35 and U.S. 18 | 608/326–6960 | $4 | May–Oct., daily 10–5.

Villa Louis. The family of fur trader Hercules Dousman built this Victorian estate on the west side of town. Its collection of china, glass, artwork, books, and silver was used by the Dousman family from 1843 to 1913. Exhibits in the former carriage house depict Prairie du Chien's early history. Exhibits in the old Astor Fur Warehouse, on the villa grounds, explore the early fur trade. | 521 Villa Louis Rd., off U.S. 18 | 608/326–2721 | $8.50 | May–Oct., daily 9–5.

Wyalusing State Park. Point Lookout, inside this 2,700-acre park, overlooks the impressive confluence of the Mississippi and Wisconsin rivers. Possible activities at the park include canoe rental, hiking, and cross-country skiing. | 1308 State Park La. | 608/996–2261 | www.dnr.state.wi.us/org/land/parks/ | $10 nonresidents, $5 residents | Daily 6 AM–11 PM.

Index